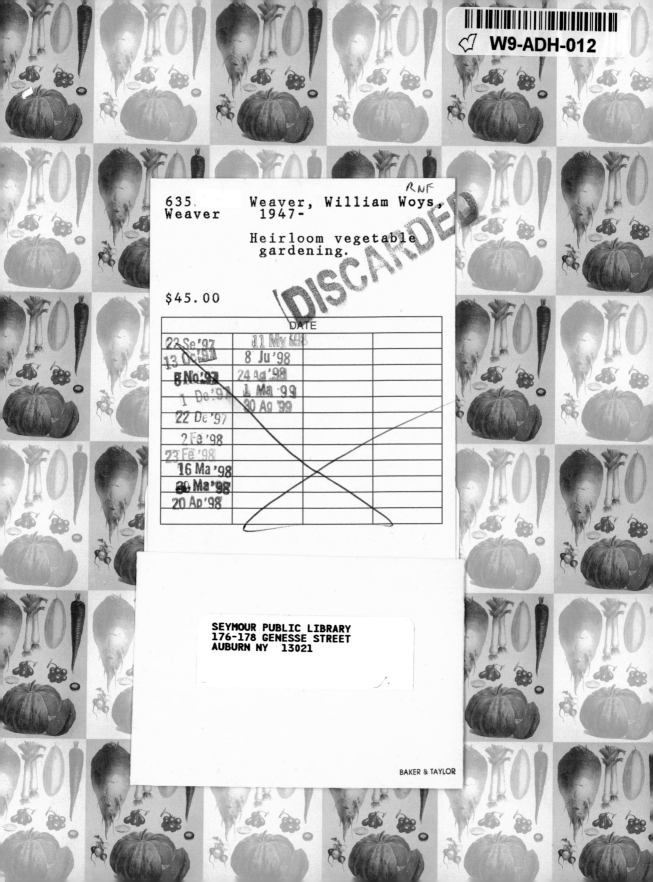

❦ Also by William Woys Weaver ❧

Heirloom Vegetable Gardening

Heirloom Vegetable Gardening

A Master Gardener's Guide to Planting, Growing, Seed Saving, and Cultural History

❧❦❧

William Woys Weaver

Photography by L. Wilbur Zimmerman
Drawings by Signe Sundberg-Hall

Henry Holt and Company
New York

Henry Holt and Company, Inc.
Publishers since 1866
115 West 18th Street
New York, New York 10011

Henry Holt® is a registered
trademark of Henry Holt and Company, Inc.

Published in Canada by Fitzhenry & Whiteside Ltd.,
195 Allstate Parkway, Markham, Ontario L3R 4T8.

Library of Congress Cataloging-in-Publication Data
Weaver, William Woys.
Heirloom vegetable gardening: a master gardener's guide to
planting, growing, seed saving, and cultural history/
William Woys Weaver; photography by L. Wilbur Zimmerman;
drawings by Signe Sundberg-Hall. — 1st ed.
p.   cm.
Includes bibliographical references (p.   ) and index.
1. Vegetables—Heirloom varieties.   2. Vegetable gardening.
I. Title.
SB324.73.W43   1997   96-26588
635'.0973—dc20   CIP

ISBN 0-8050-4025-0

Henry Holt books are available for special promotions
and premiums. For details contact: Director, Special Markets.

First Edition—1997

Designed by Betty Lew

Printed in the United States of America
All first editions are printed on acid-free paper. ∞

1 3 5 7 9 10 8 6 4 2

To

Klaus and Ingrid Stopp,

Mainz, Germany,

for the gracious gift of the **Album Vilmorin**.

It turned my garden into a book.

CONTENTS

FOREWORD

I often argue that the kitchen garden is the essential American garden. The whole world of important economic plants is grown here; it's the earth's melting pot of immigrant vegetables. When Thomas Jefferson used the term *garden,* he was reserving it not for his flower beds or ornamental grove but for his thousand-foot-long vegetable garden here at Monticello. The geographic origins of the vegetables grown at Monticello attest to the reach of Jefferson's gardening sensibility: from the Mandan corn and Arikara bean collected from Dakota Indian tribes by the Jefferson-sponsored Lewis and Clark expedition, to the broccolis and cauliflowers sent by Jefferson's Italian friend and fellow brother of the spade, Philip Mazzei, to giant twenty-four-inch cucumbers sent from Ohio by its governor, Thomas Worthington. Jefferson said that "the greatest service which can be rendered any country is to add a useful plant to its culture," and he cultivated over 250 varieties of eighty-nine species of vegetables. Thomas Jefferson's Monticello kitchen garden was an Ellis Island for immigrant crops; it's the fertile expression of the New World horticultural and culinary imagination.

Today, foreign visitors are fascinated by the diversity found in this restored garden. Our hot, humid summers and our cool spring and autumn seasons enable us to imitate microclimates the world over. Northern Europeans are both envious of and curious about our ability to grow such equatorian crops as sweet potatoes, okra, field peas, and sesame, and to so easily abound in the luxury of our sun-loving tomatoes, eggplants, peppers, squashes, and beans. The scope of this Monticello vegetable garden reflects the boundless scale of the New World, stretching seemingly limitlessly to the horizon.

The Monticello garden is not only a testament to the complex intellect and soaring imagination of Thomas Jefferson but a garden laboratory, a living museum of nineteenth-century vegetable varieties. Although only a hopeless romantic would disparage the progress in plant breeding that has resulted not only in miraculous disease and insect resistance but, in many cases, in tastier vegetables, recently many writers have discussed the need to broaden the genetic base of our agricultural and horticultural crops to prevent a recurrrence of a disaster on the order of the Irish potato famine or the Southern corn blight of the early 1970s. A broad spectrum of diverse varieties provides insurance against a virus-induced plague on the high-strung hybrids that so dominate world agribusiness. It seems ironic that while federal legislation protects endangered wild plant and animal species, and there is a justified public outcry over the forthcoming demise of a snail darter or lousewort, the loss of thousands of horticultural varieties, useful plants seemingly dear to the pragmatic American sensibility, is quietly ignored. The efforts of organizations such as the Seed Savers Exchange are to be applauded.

The plight of today's historical seed savers is that, unlike fruit trees, which often live for hundreds of years, most vegetables are annuals, and their seed has a restricted viability. When Jefferson wrote that "I am curious to select only one or two of the best species or variety of every vegetable," he was describing the scientific process so essential to his experimental garden. The proliferation of varieties enabled him to selectively eliminate inferior types, so he could declare that the Arikara bean "is one of the most excellent that we have had. I have found one kind only

HÖCHSTEIN DEL.   SEARS Sc.

superior to them, but being very sensibly so, I shall abandon the Ricaras [Arikara]." Just as Jefferson would discard a bean variety not to his taste, so have many other vegetable varieties been lost over the last 150 years, overlooked often because of a lack of productivity or resistance to disease or, more recently, an inability to adapt to mechanized methods of culture, harvesting, or transportation. Other older varieties are the lost parents of our modern hybrids, and their genetic character lies buried within the superbred varieties of today's seed catalogs.

The issue is further complicated by the lack of documentation as to the character of early vegetable varieties. While Bernard M'Mahon, author of *The American Gardener's Calendar* (1806), Jefferson, and other writers and gardeners provide names, there were no varietal descriptions of vegetables in the United States until the publication of Fearing Burr's *The Field and Garden Vegetables of America* in 1863. One of the pitfalls of attempting to describe and locate Jefferson's vegetable varieties, and one of the central issues facing seed savers today, lies in the use of personal nomenclature. For example, Jefferson often listed varieties according to the person from whom he received the seed ("Leitch's pea"), its place of origin ("Tuscan bean"), or a physical characteristic such as color ("yellow carrot") or season of harvest ("forward pea"). But there is no local literature that describes Leitch's pea, and should someone give us what they called Leitch's pea, there is no way to verify that theirs is the same as Jefferson's. We have names but no identity.

That's why *Heirloom Vegetable Gardening* is so important. This book is an encyclopedia, a dictionary to our lost vegetable heritage—defining the vocabulary of our vegetable past, providing a guide to an untranslated language. A common complaint against Seed Savers Exchange is the lack of scholarly documentation about the thousands of heirloom vegetable varieties found in their collection. There are names, thousands of them; colorful and evocative, echoing the rich traditions of American rural life. But they are names with no identity, no description: intangible vegetable ghosts that haunt us; without faces, without substance. What exactly is a Wild Goose or a cutshort bean; a Hackensack melon or a Brandywine tomato? Now, finally, we know.

Heirloom Vegetable Gardening is a lot of book. It is a history of the vegetable and a horticultural guide to the culture of nearly 700 varieties (250 of which are profiled in detail), as well as a cookbook for the curious; its scope reflects the remarkable range of Will Weaver—chef, gardener, and historian; a scholar and novelist who knows how to keep the sparrows away from the Black Tuscan Palm Tree kale. *Heirloom Vegetable Gardening* will stand as a landmark work, a mountainous reference to which forthcoming studies will aim.

Peter J. Hatch
Director of Gardens and Grounds
Monticello

INTRODUCTION

It never occurred to me that I would be writing a garden book when I first began to write about food more than twenty years ago. Yet as I now ask myself which came first, cooking or gardening, the answer is obvious. Even as a child, I had my own little garden plot, miniature tools, and the persistent temperament required of a grown-up gardener. I must have inherited this inclination, for both of my grandfathers tinkered with plants. In fact, my grandfather Weaver was more than a hobbyist, he was a collector and breeder of all kinds of rare and exotic things. Most of all, he taught me to be curious.

I can still recall his garden in West Chester, Pennsylvania, overflowing with delightful scents, curious and fantastic flowers, and many good things to eat. Happily, I have managed to preserve a number of treasures from his garden, his strawberry rhubarb from an old cousin in Lancaster County, his miniature deep blue iris, a yellow tomato from my great-grandfather Hickman, and much more. These are heirloom plants, the living hand-me-downs from generation to generation. And that is the subject of this book.

Actually, I inherited these plants only in a manner of speaking. My grandfather died in 1956, and it was some ten years later, with the help of my grandmother, that I began to salvage what I could from his collection. Many of the hardier plants had simply become naturalized; others had disappeared altogether. Many jars of seeds, long stored in a dark corner of the cellar, proved to be bug-eaten or dead. But the happiest discovery, and one with direct bearing on the pepper section of this book, was a large collection of baby food jars stowed away in the very bottom of my grandmother's deep freezer. Freezing prolongs the viability of most seeds, and in those jars were some of my grandfather's rarest peppers. I later learned that they had been given to him by Horace Pippin, a local artist who struck up a friendship with him in the 1930s.

Their mutual interest was not art but bees, for my grandfather also kept hives. Pippin had a bad arm, a war injury I believe, and he often visited my grandfather to get his arm stung. My grandfather did not like wasting good honeybees that way, but since this was an old-time remedy for rheumatic pains, he obliged Horace as a favor. In return, Pippin brought my grandfather a great many seeds that came to him through his connections with West Chester's old and well-established black community. Among these were the cayennes Ole Pepperpot (page 262) and Buist's yellow cayenne (page 256), two hot peppers used during the nineteenth century by the Augustins, a famous black catering family in Philadelphia. I will never forget the first time I tried to germinate Ole Pepperpot. Only six seeds sprang back to life after nearly a month of fretful waiting. From those six I now have stocks aplenty, but the pepper came that close to extinction.

Many of my grandfather's seeds also came from Mennonite relatives in Lancaster County, particularly through the truly vast web of Weavers he drew together through his work on our family history. This genealogical work brought him into contact with old Lancaster County gardeners like the late Frank Weaver, who at the turn of this century operated greenhouses along the Lincoln Highway a few miles east of Lancaster borough. Years later, it was my own reconnection with Frank's daughter, Frances Weaver Ament, that again opened up old seed-saving channels in the family. Frances saved seeds, and from her I have since reacquired some of my grandfather's lost stock, as well as many things that he never dreamed of growing but certainly would have enjoyed.

Now that I look back on it, I think it is fair to say that I grew up immersed in a love for plants, and that it was a special kind of total immersion that resulted by virtue of who I am. My grandmother Weaver (née Hickman) is descended from old Pennsylvania Quaker families, many of whom were directly involved in horticulture. Through her I can claim as an ancestor Joseph Pennock, who developed the Pennock apple, as well as Joshua Pierce, whose early nineteenth-century arboretum near Kennett Square, Pennsylvania, became the nucleus of what is now the world-famous Longwood Gardens. But the Quaker connection does not stop there.

Susan Darlington Hannum, my grandmother's grandmother, was the niece of Dr. William Darlington, a Chester County botanist of nineteenth-century fame, and provided him with a great deal of information about plant life along Pocopson Creek, where the family owned farms. I still have the pamphlet on the Darlington family history that Susan received as a gift from William Darlington at a family reunion in 1853. But what I value most is my copy of Dr. Darlington's rare *Flora Cestrica*, which he published at West Chester in 1837. Now outdated as a scientific work, it brims with chatty observations and personal commentaries that I find as fresh and readable today as when they were written more than 150 years ago.

The Darlington family connection shifts the focus of this discussion out into the lush Chester County countryside, to the banks of the Brandywine River, where my grandmother grew up. The Brandywine and its famous landscapes have been immortalized in paintings by the Wyeths. But those of a botanical bent head up the river's west branch toward Northbrook, the site of an old Indian town where my grandfather found the Lenape cutshort bean and where the Marshalls for many years operated a sawmill. This is a countryside rich in its historical associations with the native Lenape people, from whom we have inherited a number of vegetable varieties.

I became reschooled in these local associations when I assumed the position of clerk of the Marlborough Friends Meeting near Unionville, Pennsylvania, within walking distance of Northbrook. In fact, the Marshalls had been members of that meeting for many years. One of the regular attenders was an aged cousin of mine who had become something of a living legend. This was Mary Larkin Thomas (1886–1982), an old-time Quaker who spoke the Plain Language, practiced homeopathy, and taught me how to save seeds. Both Mary's grandmother, Quaker minister Rachel Cook Hallowell, and Mary's mother had been well known locally as herb doctors. They were experts in botanical medicines and had extensive gardens from which they drew their remedies. Since Mary had actually met her great-grandmother, who was born in the 1700s, I felt that through her I had indeed stumbled upon an original source. Furthermore, Mary had a photographic memory and definite opinions.

Mary had grown up in New Garden, near Kennett Square, Pennsylvania. Her house stood directly across the road from Dr. Ezra Michener's. A friend of Philadelphia seedsman Robert Buist (1805–1880), Michener was a well-known horticulturist, author of the *Retrospect of Early Quakerism* (1860) and *A Manual of Weeds* (1872). Many plants from his garden found their way into the Thomas's, including The Pearl tuberose introduced by Peter Henderson in 1867–68 and a stand of comfrey that Mary's mother considered one of her most important medical herbs.

Mary continued her mother's training in simples through a small garden in West Chester. It was Cousin Mary who finally persuaded me to move permanently into the realm of plants. She was adamant: this was a Quaker thing, a fitting activity for a pacifist, and a moral requirement for a nurturing temperament. This nonviolent approach to nature, or rather a kinship with it on a spiritual level, was not just Mary's philosophy; it was pervasive among the Pennsylvania peace sects, whether Quaker or Amish, and it sets the philosophical framework for this book. Certainly, it touches upon some of the basic reasons for writing it.

As I came to know Mary, we began trading seeds and plants. In fact, by that stage in her life she was looking for someone to take on the responsibility of maintaining many of the flowers, vegetables, and herbs that her family had grown, in some cases since the early nineteenth century. Mary's collection was not large, but it was choice. From her I acquired her great-grandmother's intensely fragrant spearmint, blue dogbane, a giant rose cleome from the 1870s, a rare pink lily of the valley, and quite a few unusual vegetables. These included the true Catawissa onion (page 232), which we—she and I during a field trip—gathered from an abandoned farm near Catawissa, Pennsylvania. Mary also gave me a curious bean called Blue Shackamaxon (page 54), which her mother obtained during a 1906 trip to the site of Pennsbury Manor, William Penn's seventeenth-century estate on the Delaware River.

Then there were the peppers and rare ornamentals her mother inherited from Dr. George Thomas (1808–1887), a cousin and well-known botanical collector in the 1800s who owned a fine garden at Whitford, Pennsylvania. Dr. Thomas not only preserved M'Mahon's Texas bird pepper (page 264), a descendant of seed sent to Philadelphia by Thomas Jefferson, but also raised martynias (page 189), rare Japanese plants, and a large number of hothouse exotics, including the stock from which my China orange and caper bush are descended. I am not certain which part of the caper plant I like best: the edible buds, the exquisite flowers, or the seedpods. I pickle the pods with my *cornichon vert* Petit de Paris (page 156). Dr. Thomas's wife used West India burr gherkins (page 159).

Now that I look at the list of heirloom plants that came to me via Cousin Mary, I can honestly say that the collection is one of a kind, and doubly valuable for some of the old Thomas family papers that came with it, including a unique 1839 catalog of plants offered for sale by yet another cousin, David Thomas, a nurseryman at East Aurora, New York. I have felt privileged to share some of the Thomas heirlooms with Monticello and with Seed Savers Exchange in Decorah, Iowa. I am certain, as I establish seed purity for more and more of my heirlooms, I will gradually add them to the Heritage Farm collections maintained by the exchange. Since I am a life member and a listed seed source in the yearbook, this is a process that will continue for many years. Membership in Seed Savers Exchange is by far the easiest way to begin collecting heirloom plants. There are also broader ramifications, which I deal with in the second chapter of this book, for heirloom vegetables are not only nostalgia in edible form but the genetic basis for our future. Thus there are important scientific reasons for preserving them.

Mary Larkin Thomas would agree; and in an odd, serendipitous way, she has revisited this book through the eyes of my photographer, Dr. L. Wilbur Zimmerman. Mary Larkin, Wilbur's late wife, hailed from the same clan of Quakers as my cousin. Wilbur is clerk of Haverford Friends Meeting, to which I now belong, as well as a former president of the Pennsylvania Horticultural Society. The society's annual flower show is now world-famous and has grown in its new quarters to ten acres of extraordinary beauty. Thus, I find myself again in the guiding hands of Friends, and this has given added depth to my undertaking. Best of all, Wilbur is also an epicure who appreciates the labels on the wine corks scattered in my garden. I toss them there like coins into a fountain, each one a wish for a friend.

The basis of good cookery is the kitchen garden, for without it the chef is nothing. The hoe is merely a tool of the kitchen. Yet how many cooks are trained to know that moment when the ice bean (page 59) has reached perfection, or when the Musselburgh leek (page 227) is most succulent? These are not plastic-wrapped vegetables of the supermarket, long ago suffocated in the stale air of transport trucks. These are the fruits of flavor brought to high intensity by freshness and the blush of natural perfection. This connectedness of soil and hearth has not been lost on me. I thank my grandfather for being so thoroughly Pennsylvania Dutch that he taught me to value the garden soil under my nails as a mark of humility and a fatherly concern for the land.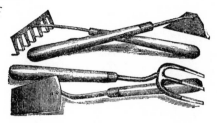

It was out of this concern that I felt called upon to commit this story of American heirloom vegetables to print. Much of this book had been floating in my head for several years, because *Hortus Third* falls embarrassingly short of its mission, leaving the heirloom vegetable to little more than a footnote. Many are not mentioned at all. A blind eye is the weapon of neglect. How can we possibly neglect the vast richness of our culinary heritage when it is this very food that defines who we are? There must be a source gardeners can turn to for guidance, if only a mere outline of what is available. What we need is a *Hortus Third* on vegetables, but the task of documenting such a food patrimony is daunting. In any case, the challenge of research is one that I enjoy; thus curiosity about the histories of the many vegetables I grow led me to research, for I am deeply interested in their historical context as well as their edibility. Above all, this book has evolved into a study of the heirloom vegetable as material culture, not as a decorative element in garden design. This is a family album of what America has eaten.

Many of the vegetables in this book have fascinating stories. Why these vegetables came about is as much a telescopic view into the economic history of the past as it is a study in broader aspects of social history. Rare-ripes, pickled martinoes, goober peas, crock nubbins, leek bulbs—as a food historian I could list pages of old foods that were once part of our everyday diet. This immense culinary diversity has been one of the strengths of our culture, and it is the basis for further culinary development.

Of course, there are also pressing scientific reasons for preserving heirloom vegetables, and I take this up in chapter 2. Genetic diversity is nature's way of maintaining life as we know it. The genetic diversity that may be lost through the extinction of kitchen garden vegetables is an issue that spills over into the political arena, for it touches directly on mankind's ability to feed itself. The harsh lessons of the potato famine of the 1840s seem sadly forgotten. One of the objects of the heirloom seed movement is to prevent such a calamity from ever happening again.

It is my intention to tell the story of the heirloom vegetable by guiding my readers through my garden. I have come to know the vegetables mentioned in this book by growing them. I know what they look like, how they feel, how they taste. I want this to be a type of lesson book on how to cultivate and appreciate these plants. The cultural advice and botanical descriptions are written in simple, nontechnical terms because this is, foremost, a book for beginners. It is a starting point, and I have tried to be honest about some of the difficulties in raising for seed such biennials as cabbage or beets. By trial and error, I have discovered many shortcuts that I hope will put my reader far ahead of me when I first took up my hoe.

William Woys Weaver
Roughwood
Devon, Pennsylvania

Chapter 1

The Kitchen Garden in America

❧⬥❧

In the Greek of Homer, the word for leek, *práson*, was also the root word for a garden bed: *prasia*. Such a linguistic connectedness between the kitchen vegetable and its place of cultivation does not exist in English. When the Anglo-Saxons invaded Britain, they found an indigenous Celtic culture focused on cattle breeding and husbandry, which they too adopted. Thus, we have inherited a linguistic and cultural perspective of the garden much different from that of the Mediterranean peoples.

This is not to say that we were never a nation of gardeners; but as a country that became heavily industrialized in the nineteenth century, much of America lost its daily contact with the land. Today we must consider the old metaphor of the leek against the international symbols of American cookery: the hamburger and French fries.

Since the coming of industrialization, we have gazed nostalgically toward the Mediterranean for guidance, for a return to the birthplace of "real food," for a recovery of color, taste, and aroma. This mythology was created more than a hundred years ago by writers like Janet Ross, whose *Leaves from Our Tuscan Kitchen; or, How to Cook Vegetables* (1899) offered consolation through escape. It is a genre of writing that has sold steadily ever since; the world of the émigré epicure is a world exactly as he wants it. The Mediterranean happens to be one of the last agricultural fringes of Europe. It is false history to imagine that other parts of the Continent in preindustrial times did not also enjoy similar pleasures of peasant simplicity or directness of connection between garden and hearth. Yet the Mediterranean has the advantage, at least in European terms, of preempting the rest by virtue of the civilizations it produced in the past. This obvious historical fact must serve as a constant reminder to the American horticulturist that we did not start at ground zero in the recent past, whether we define that as 1492, 1776, or the date on great-grandfather's immigration papers. Our gardening and culinary histories began elsewhere and are a continuation of something basic and human with deep roots in classical antiquity. This is the long view of history that characterizes my work as a writer, food historian, and gardener.

I have always held the belief that American cookery will not evolve its underlying character beneath the artificial lights of a professional kitchen. It is a more holistic process that involves sunshine as a major ingredient. It begins in the kitchen garden, where the cook moves among ingredients still attached to the soil. It was like that one time in America, even if only an idea acted out in its most elaborate forms by the well-to-do like Thomas Jefferson or William Hamilton of Philadelphia.

Let us not forget that Amelia Simmons, author of the first American cookbook in 1796, also wrote about the vegetables in her kitchen garden and remains even today highly quotable on this subject. Henrietta Davidis, the most popular German cookbook writer in the nineteenth century and a proponent of middle-class fare, also wrote books about kitchen gardens and vegetables. Her most famous cookbook was published in German at Milwaukee in 1879 and served as a household bible for a large segment of the Midwest in the late nineteenth century.

It is not necessary to smell the sea from beneath the bending limbs of an olive tree to experience the rejuvenating sensuality of a landscape dotted with garden plots and flowers. We have our own Peaceable Kingdoms in America, if only we would go outside to behold them and learn their simple pleasures. Our gardens are full of plants with stories, many of which I will relate in the following pages. They bring into the kitchen pedigrees as perennially fresh as the plants themselves, and knowing them, understanding their past, is not just part of savoring the added dimension these heirlooms lend to our daily experience; it is also a means of acquiring a certain kind of knowledge that made the "particular customer" of yesteryear. The market gardeners at the turn of this century lamented the decline of this selective and well-informed consumer because with this decline in care for ingredients came a decline in cookery. The rest is history.

⮜ THE CLASSICAL ROOTS ⮞

We know from botanical and archaeological books surviving from the Roman world that there were recognized varieties of many common garden vegetables: carrots, turnips, leeks, cabbages, and cucumbers, to name a few. We also know that gardening techniques were highly developed, certainly in the gardens of the wealthy. Onions, for example, were cultivated in special beds called *cepinae*, and the gardeners who maintained them were known as *ceparii*. This type of specialization provides clues about the refinement of cookery and philosophical connectedness between the ancient Roman kitchen garden and hearth, but it tells us little about the vegetables themselves, what they looked like or how they tasted.

American archaeologist Wilhelmina Jashemski has tried to address some of these issues by actually digging into ancient garden soil. Her *Gardens of Pompeii* (1979) is widely cited for its treatment of Roman ornamental gardens, landscaping, and even vineyard layouts. In many cases, she was able to connect botanical subjects in fresco paintings with actual plant remains preserved in the ground, or with similar plants extant today. I was delighted to discover that my pale pink oleander matches one in a fresco at the House of the Fruit Orchard in Pompeii. So I will always imagine that it was the goddess Flora who scattered my oleander petals across the lawn, and that lurking behind my lemons is a turtledove cooing softly to Pan. But search as we will for clues in ancient frescos, there is next to nothing about Roman vegetables or the Roman version of the *jardin potager,* the place where the modern French grow their culinary ingredients. I suppose, to the Roman mind, such subject matter would have been equated with painting views of a kitchen sink.

Yet there are ways to discover ancient vegetables from other perspectives. For example, we can create inventories of the plants that we know were cultivated in classical antiquity and ascertain whether there are surviving examples today—there is even a small circle of heirloom gardeners who specialize in such ancient foodstuffs. Those garden vegetables, with their richly documented histories, are the true undisputed heirlooms of antiquity. Most of the world's cultures can claim such heirloom plants, whether from the New World or the Old.

From the Roman world we know that the leaves of horsetooth amaranth (page 321), the *bliton* of the ancient Greeks, were cooked like spinach and used as stuffings or in pesto. The ancient Gauls used the arrow-shaped leaves of Good King Henry (page 324) to fatten chickens for special feasts, as well as rabbits and young geese. A perennial herb related to lamb's-quarters and quinoa, it was incorporated into the green sauces served with these meats. Marshmallow was considered a delicacy, its young flower buds cooked as a potherb (very similar in texture to okra) and its boiled roots stir-fried with onions and drawn butter. I grow these ancient vegetables, and I have prepared them according to antique recipes. But the results were never completely satisfactory, because I have no way of knowing what cultural tricks Roman gardeners employed to make the vegetables more palatable. All we have to work with are plant survivors that have reverted more or less to a wild condition.

When plants are preserved by man, generation to generation, seed to seed, the gardener intervenes in nature, for we are maintaining them in an artificial state desirable only to us, as in the huge variety of tomatoes and the many forms of beets. This is not a natural condition; it is natural for plants to undergo constant adaptation and genetic change. That is how they ensure their own survival. Therefore, even as I may admire a Pompeian fresco with a pink oleander like one in my garden, I must hasten to remind myself that the two are similar but not the same. This is a basic rule in understanding the nature of all heirloom vegetables. Genetic change is inevitable.

We know that many common vegetables have undergone gradual genetic alteration, because there is pictorial evidence to prove it. It is evidenced not in stylized fresco paintings but rather in a manuscript medical book surviving from the Roman era. The *Codex Vindobonensis Medicus Graecus* of Dioskorides, written in A.D. 60, was copied at Constantinople between A.D. 500 and 511 and illustrated with hand-colored pictures. The original manuscript survives in the Austrian National Library at Vienna, and many of the plants depicted in it include such familiar vegetables as radishes, cowpeas, and fava beans. In several cases, these are the oldest known "scientific" pictures of certain vegetables, and for this reason I will refer to the codex of Dioskorides from time to time in the course of this book.

The German botanist Udelgard Körber-Grohne has analyzed the vegetable illustrations in the codex of Dioskorides in her *Nutzpflanzen in Deutschland* (1988) and set this material in the context of plant archaeology. Since she also raises heirloom vegetables from the ancient world in her garden at Stuttgart, her firsthand knowledge of plant behavior sets her work apart from others in the field. Körber-Grohne's research is useful because it creates a continental European framework for the origins of the American kitchen garden and many of the Old World vegetables associated with it.

The fava bean illustrated in the codex of Dioskorides presents an intriguing case study, because it is the fava bean of Roman cookery, not the fava we eat today. The two are distinctly different varieties. The plant shown in the codex has a stout, stumpy stem, unlike modern favas. Archaeology has confirmed that this was a characteristic of the plant in ancient times. Since the plants were gathered after harvesting the beans and used as straw in barns, quite a few archaeological sites have produced intact carbonized specimens. Even more interesting, from the standpoint of cookery, the pods depicted in the codex are not like the pods of the modern broad bean.

The pod of the Roman fava (*Vicia faba* var. *minor*) was diminutive, resembling the common horse bean (*Vicia faba* var. *equina*) of today, or the medieval fava bean called Martoc (page 96), which has been preserved by seed savers in England. Carbonized favas from Roman sites prove that the seeds were small, like peas; some were even the size of lentils. This may be one reason why Roman cooks chose to puree the beans in many of their recipes, for the large broad beans that were once popular in colonial America did not appear until the ninth century A.D. Plant historians have pinpointed Spain as the origin for this new variety. The Agua Dulce broad bean (page 95) may be considered a classical heirloom of this type.

It would appear that in spite of the lack of supporting written records, considerable innovation in gardening was taking place in Europe during the so-called Carolingian Renaissance of the ninth century A.D. especially in Moorish Spain. While the Roman kitchen garden has remained something of an enigma in archaeological terms, the ninth century has yielded several important elements connecting classical antiquity with the present. Indeed, as it turns out, the Roman kitchen garden survived into the Middle Ages in a unique fashion. The raised bed system that I use in my Pennsylvania garden may be traced directly to the *jardin potager* of imperial villas.

The oldest surviving garden plans relative to kitchen gardens are those of the medical herb gardens of the cloisters of St. Gall in Switzerland and Reichenau in Germany. Both of the plans for the cloister *herbularius*, as the herb gardens were designated, date from the 800s. The St. Gall garden, outlined on an original parchment plan of the cloister dating from 816, was for many years accepted by scholars as the ultimate source for the idea of creating a quadrant *Innenhof* or *atreolum* and dividing it up into garden beds. This plan or garden type was copied by cloisters and monasteries all over Europe.

The garden at Reichenau was described by Walahfrid Strabo in his *Hortulus*, a series of poems written between 842 and 849. The garden described by Walahfrid was divided like the St. Gall plan into sixteen beds, each devoted to one plant. This division also tallied with the old Roman method of creating specialized beds for each vegetable. In a scholarly analysis of Walahfrid's work, both its literary and botanical implications, Hans-Dieter Stoffler (1978) brought archaeology into play. After considerable exploration of the actual site of Reichenau, archaeologists determined that the layout was influenced by a former imperial villa.

Reichenau is situated on an island in Lake Constance and was established within the walls of an abandoned site that evidently had not suffered the ravages of vandalism like many buildings of its size on the mainland. Thus the monks appropriated surviving structures and continued some of their functional uses for several hundred years before endeavoring to build anew. This pattern was repeated elsewhere in Europe; indeed, whole villages sprang up within the confines of some *villa rustica* sites, a subject explored by John Percival in his study of the Roman villa in Europe north of Italy (1976). The implication of the Reichenau discoveries, however, is significant, for they point to garden plans predating St. Gall, and at Reichenau in particular, superimposed over a preexisting Roman garden. Thus Reichenau becomes the Roman link, and through the European cloister gardens built along this design, the Roman kitchen garden becomes the model garden for all of Europe.

From the Middle Ages down to the nineteenth century, the kitchen garden laid out in quadrants with raised beds and pathways between was promoted as the most efficient means of feeding the household. By the Renaissance it was widely used in urban settings, as old city views confirm. And during the Enlightenment, it was held up as the most rational approach to self-sufficiency, a survival kit for farming classes then becoming more and more literate. During the eighteenth century the Pennsylvania Germans brought this form of intensive gardening to North America, where it was often copied and much discussed in agricultural and horticultural journals. It is continued to this day by many Old Order Mennonites, whom the Pennsylvania Germans consider the very best of all their kitchen gardeners. J. H. Ditrich's *Baiersches Natur- und Kunst-Gartenbuch für Gärtner* (1803), written for educated peasants, argued that such enclosed gardens offered better protection from destructive animals and from the infiltration of weeds, that the soil could be brought to a greater degree of productivity (he used night soil from chamber pots), and that vegetables could be planted more densely. Ditrich's arguments are still as true today as when Walahfrid Strabo composed poems about his cloister garden in the 800s.

It is thus no coincidence of history that the Pennsylvania Dutch farmer gained a national reputation in this country for his fine produce. The English horticultural journal the *Gardener's Journal* (1832, 74) remarked that in America "it is chiefly among the Dutch and German settlers that vegetables are cultivated; and the overplus beyond their family wants is occasionally offered for sale." It was to these farmers that many Americans were forced to appeal for kitchen supplies, since there were no organized markets in many parts of the country until much later in the century.

Raised bed gardens have recently received renewed attention under the name "lazy bed" gardens, but the concept is the same. For a small area, a plan laid out in William N. White's *Gardening for the South* (1868, 15) is quite workable. The woodcut provides a sketch of his general plan, with walkways four and a half feet in width. The central walk should be five or six feet wide, conveniently broad enough to allow a cart or large wheelbarrow to pass through without damage. I failed to account for this crucial measurement in my own garden plan and now must work from small wheelbarrows.

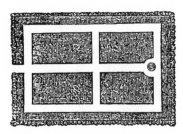

William White's plan for a kitchen garden (1868).

White surrounded his kitchen garden with a boxwood hedge to conceal it. He was quite set on the idea of hedges, even hedges of Osage orange, holly, and pyracantha, all of which require constant trimming. They also provide excellent cover for rabbits and groundhogs. I prefer a close latticework fence because rabbits and groundhogs cannot climb through it, and deer will not jump over it. A fence is also more practical because it can be used to support runner beans, gourds, or other climbing vegetables intermixed with flowering vines. Gooseberries and currants or other perennials can be raised around the outside perimeter of the fence, or the space can be devoted to annuals if a decorative appearance is desired. In any case, box is slow growing, and it is many years before the hedge will achieve the right look. The overall design of a kitchen garden should economize on work and maximize growing space, both vertical and horizontal. White's book was originally published before the Civil War, and while he never mentioned slaves, it is obvious from his text that the intensive labor implied by many of his suggestions was not based on a workforce paid by wages.

The shortcomings of White's garden design illustrate why it is not always practical to reconstruct garden plans from the past. Certainly such old plans should not be viewed as necessary blueprints for the future; but as grid systems for managing ground, they are extremely efficient. It is important to remember that the Roman villa occupied the best land, which was flat, a fact that allowed for the evolution of this garden concept. On sloping or hilly ground other solutions, such as planting beds to follow the contours of the land, may be needed. This system is quite feasible for small-scale farming. Yet if I were to lay out a vegetable garden on a large, flat piece of ground, starting from scratch, I believe I would follow, in general terms at least, the classic quadrant plan as published in 1847 in Robert Buist's *Family Kitchen Gardener*. This is an adaptation that takes into account American gardening practices and our climate. I have reproduced Buist's plan with its explanatory key because it allows for great flexibility in plant choices from region to region. The central area, with its fruit trees pruned low, makes a delightful (and prac-

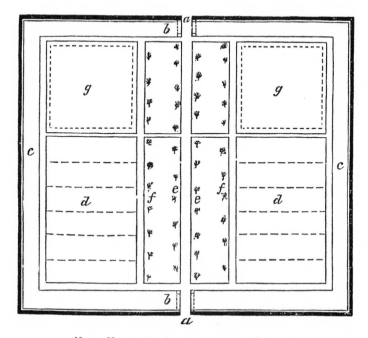

Robert Buist's plan for a kitchen garden (1847).

tical) place for summer meals, and the shade of the trees can be put to good use for such shade-loving herbs as chervil, woodruff, sweet violets, lady's bedstraw, betony, and many others. Thus, the kitchen garden assumes the added distinction of *herbularius,* and transforms itself into a visual and spiritual Garden of Eden.

⋑ PARADISE REGAINED ⋐

It is always a pleasure to peruse the travels of the German physician Leonhard Rauwolf during nine months of 1575 and relive some of the wonder and excitement of his botanical discoveries in North Africa and Syria (see Dannenfeldt 1968). His was no pleasant excursion, fraught as it was with extraordinary dangers that forced him to resort to disguises, bribery, and the smuggling of plant specimens. His perseverance against great odds is a constant reminder of the enormous burst of scientific curiosity during the Renaissance that sent men like Rauwolf into distant places for the sake of plants.

I was amused to read that at Aleppo in Syria he found celery, which he called *Eppich,* an archaic term we still use in Pennsylvania Dutch. He also observed white and yellow carrots (true orange carrots had not yet been developed), arugula, cauliflowers, and kohlrabies, all familiar vegetables in the cloister gardens in Europe. But he also observed two varieties of beans, New World beans. One of these was probably the white runner bean that old European botanical works refer to as the Arab bean (page 78), a bean still cultivated in Near Eastern kitchen gardens where the Turks once ruled.

The commercial pressure for spices, the accidental discovery of the New World, the quest for colonial empires, all of these large events in history exposed the kitchen garden to a new array of culinary influences, and this change has accelerated. The American kitchen garden appeared on the scene toward the end of the age of discovery, if we choose to pinpoint its "birth" in the seventeenth century, with the establishment of English colonies along the Atlantic coast. The garden was brought to our shores as a European transplant: in form a direct descendant of the *hortus* of the Middle Ages, in spirit an immigrant with considerable intellectual baggage. As a child of Europe, the kitchen garden quickly evolved a personality of its own. The mental framework was not a recreation of a lifestyle imitating ancient Rome—ostensibly as the Renaissance villas of Italy were intended to do—but more in keeping with the Protestant philosophies of the early settlers, a physical materialization of the New Jerusalem, an Eden restored.

The sixteenth and seventeenth centuries witnessed the rise of plant collecting as a scientific endeavor as well as an expression of status and wealth. The purely scientific gardens, like those at Padua (founded 1545), Leyden (founded 1587), and Oxford (founded 1621), were assembled to take advantage of the medical possibilities offered by exotica gathered in from Asia, Africa, and the New World. According to John Prest in his history of botanic gardens (1988), these collections would not have assumed the form they did were it not for the discovery of the Americas. This set into motion a new set of imperatives; the existence of the New World, its diverse peoples, and its vast array of hitherto unknown plants challenged the authority of the Bible and overthrew the credibility of the classics that had defined science to that point. Science was therefore obliged to seek God through the observation of things, as man was obliged to do before the Scriptures existed, so that a greater truth could be discerned through patient seeking.

This was quite a revolution in European thinking, and on the basis of this new perspective, the botanical gardens of Europe were constructed. The kitchen garden, though not as noble in its intentions as a proving ground for such philosophies, nevertheless assumed this pseudo-religious character, as Walter Punch has pointed out in his history of American horticulture, *Keeping Eden* (1992). The essence of these plant collections, whether medical or culinary, was that they were brought together as a representation of Paradise on earth. Thus it was no coincidence that John Parkinson's great English herbal of 1629 was called *Paradise in Sole*, or that Saluste du Bartas's *Oeuvres* (1611) depicted God on the title page waving down from the sky at Adam and Eve. Indeed, the whole idea of returning to a prescriptural innocence was lifted to its culinary apotheosis in *Adam's Luxury, and Eve's Cookery*, a 1744 English cookbook employing only produce from an earthly Eden.

The underlying presumption in this cookbook was that Adam and Eve did not kill the animals that shared the garden with them; therefore they ate no flesh. They were personified as pacifists, nonviolent in their relationship to nature and to all other living things. This primeval simplicity appealed to such pacifist sects as the Quakers in England and the Mennonites in Germany, Holland, and Switzerland. As a result, both religious groups promoted botanical activities as consistent with their beliefs. Not surprising, several important figures in seventeenth- and eighteenth-century botany came from these sects: Agnes Block (1629–1704) in Holland, John Bartram (1699–1777) in America, and William Curtis (1746–1799) in England.

Agnes Block was a Dutch Mennonite who owned the estate of Vijverhof at Loenen on the River Vecht, near Amsterdam. She possessed one of the finest botanical gardens in Holland, commissioned famous artists to render drawings of her exotic plants and flowers, and was the first person in Europe to succeed in growing hothouse pineapples. She corresponded extensively with other European plant collectors and botanists, even with royalty, for there were many monarchs casting jealous eyes on her beautiful gardens.

Agnes Block is not known to have directly influenced seed exchanges in colonial America, but in 1709 other Dutch Mennonites in Amsterdam provided assistance (with money from her estate) for the first groups of Mennonites to settle in Pennsylvania. Throughout the eighteenth century members of Agnes Block's congregation continued to send household goods, plant stock, and seeds to their coreligionists in America. This channel of communication provided an important source of European kitchen vegetables reaching the Middle Colonies through Philadelphia. Christian Lehman of Germantown was one of the agents in the 1760s for Dutch bulbs and nursery plants. This Dutch connection bypassed the usual London business networks and remains to this day one of the most fascinating, yet largely unexplored, chapters in American gardening.

Agnes Block provided a role model for many Mennonites in this country who became involved in horticulture. Perhaps the most influential was Jacob B. Garber (1800–1886) of Lancaster County, Pennsylvania. His extensive correspondence can be found in many horticultural journals of the nineteenth century. He was deeply involved with Reuben Weaver (yes, a relative of mine) in the promotion of grape culture, especially the Martha, and introduced a number of vegetables, among them Chinese *woh sun*, now commonly known as Celtuce (page 179). His hothouse, built in 1837 near Columbia, Pennsylvania, was one of the first of its kind to be heated by steam boilers. Many new varieties of garden plants emanated from that greenhouse, including the Martin's carrot pepper (page 261) of this book.

John Bartram was a self-taught botanist who established an international reputation for his important plant discoveries in North America. He maintained a nursery near Philadelphia; the

RESIDENCE OF JOHN BARTRAM,
BUILT WITH HIS OWN HANDS, A.D. 1730.
Sturdy and strong it still stands on the eve of its 200th anniversary.

John Bartram's house is now maintained as a museum.

original site and the house he built himself are now preserved as a museum. Bartram specialized in ornamentals, which he shipped to England as plant stock for landscaping schemes on large country estates. In return he imported many plants to the colonies, and some of the earliest and most reliable references to colonial American garden vegetables can be found in his letters, which were published in book form in 1992 (Berkeley and Berkeley).

William Curtis was an English Quaker who was apprenticed at the age of fourteen as an apothecary. He gradually developed broader interests in plants and natural history. In 1778 he opened his own botanical garden in London. After several moves of location and the generous backing of patrons, he eventually possessed a collection of more than six thousand species. These formed the core of his teaching collection and the subject of a career in public lecturing. More important, in 1787 he founded *Curtis's Botanical Magazine,* which is still published by the Royal Botanic Gardens at Kew. This is considered one of the premier journals of the botanical world, and I have consulted it often to reconstruct some of the vegetable profiles in this book.

It is easy to become absorbed in the exquisite color plates that fill the early volumes of *Curtis's Botanical Magazine.* The asparagus pea (page 48), which I steam and dress in salads, is there. Its red flowers are edible and make a cheerful garnish for early summer recipes. Other volumes have my frangipani, my blue passionflower, my scarlet four-o'clock, the *Cobea scandens* that I train over an arch each summer, lemon verbena (my tree is twenty-four years old), mignonette, bladder hibiscus, and a host of other flowers that I interplant between my vegetables to attract butterflies and other pollinators. So too is Cupani's sweet pea, introduced into England in 1699. Happily the plate in Curtis matches the specimens in my garden. It is not difficult to imagine vermilion mounds of scented Cupani's draping over the garden fences at Pennsbury, the great estate laid out by Pennsylvania's first governor, William Penn. Penn was an agriculturist with a bent toward pomology, but he also had an interest in gardening. He appears to have been one of the first to create a botanical garden in this country, if only a small one for his own pleasure and use.

⋙ THE ANGLO-DUTCH GARDEN ⋘

Penn's country house was built in the Dutch style, not surprisingly since his mother was Dutch and Penn had traveled through the Low Countries on a religious concern in 1677. By that time Holland had become the leading center of gardening innovation, both in garden design and in the improvement of plant varieties—not just tulips, for which the Dutch are still famous, but a vast array of fruits and vegetables for the kitchen garden as well. Period Dutch still lifes overflow with this produce. Some of the oldest varieties of currants in my garden bear such names as Witte Hollunder and Witte Parel, both of which date from late seventeenth-century Holland.

The berries of Witte Parel are transparent, resembling fish eggs, the only "caviar" served in my little Hesperides.

The botanical connections between England and Holland—and ultimately America—were sealed in the seventeenth century when William of Orange became king of England. William of Orange built extensive gardens both in Holland and in England during his reign, with the result that the Dutch penchant for gardening was taken up by the English with even greater zeal. Scholars have generally overlooked this chapter in gardening history, yet in terms of heirloom vegetables, it is especially important, particularly since the Dutch associated the garden and the kitchen so closely.

The most famous Dutch cookbook of the period, *De Verstandige Kock* (available in translation as *The Sensible Cook*; Rose 1989), originally appeared in 1667 as part of a garden book by Pieter van Aengelen. In 1668 it was combined with a more famous garden work by Jan van der Groen, chief gardener to William of Orange. Van der Groen's treatise was translated into French and German and expressed the most current ideas about life in the country. One activity in this aristocratic, philosophical seclusion was pottering about in the vegetable beds, seeking ways to perfect spring peas, or perhaps the ideal leek. The cookbook and gardening collection (there were several other treatises included) was given the collective name *Het Vermakelijck Landtleven* (*The Pleasurable Country Life*), and went through numerous editions. A copy of the 1683 edition belonged to the Van Cortlandt family in the Hudson River valley; thus the ideas expressed in this important work are known to have reached America.

This idealization of the gentleman gardener was further developed in England and in the American colonies. English works on this type of gardening abound. William Penn's library at Pennsbury was cataloged in 1687 and included such influential period works as Leonard Meager's *English Gardener* (1682), Sir Hugh Plat's *Garden of Eden* (1675), Nicolas de Bonnefons's *French Gardener* (1669), and John Evelyn's *Kalendarium Hortense* (1676). Evelyn's nephew lived in Bucks County not far from Pennsbury. Yet it was probably William Penn's own *Some Fruits of Solitude* (1693) that connected all of this most directly with an American audience. This delightful collection of aphorisms was widely circulated among American and English Quakers and provided a model for country living among Philadelphia's colonial gentry.

The most famous of these was undoubtedly William Hamilton, whose extraordinary landscaped estate Woodlands near Bartram's nursery rivaled "what may be seen in England," to quote Thomas Jefferson. In fact, if we explore the history of American heirloom vegetables, we quickly discover that it was the well-to-do gentleman farmer or wealthy merchant at his country retreat who tinkered with vegetables and flowers and brought forth some of our earliest American varieties. Furthermore, most of the early garden books were written for just such individuals. In England, the name of Thomas Andrew Knight (1759–1838) of Downton Castle, Herefordshire, stands out for the number of heirloom vegetables that still bear his name. In America, Thomas Jefferson's gardens at Monticello survive as a lasting monument to this type of enlightened gardening, but Jefferson was not alone.

Educated, well-financed plant collectors could be found in most of the East Coast cities during the colonial period, and as these individuals organized themselves into agricultural and horticultural societies in the late eighteenth and early nineteenth centuries, innovation predominated in three areas of the country: eastern Massachusetts, focusing on Boston; southeastern Pennsylvania, focusing on Philadelphia; and in the region surrounding Charleston, South Carolina. The list of names of the important figures involved in vegetable improvement is impressive and long. Many of these gardeners are mentioned specifically in the plant profile section of this book. Their productions varied from new varieties of squash and potatoes to improved forms of lettuce, cabbage, and watermelons.

It is easy to see that these three regional centers of innovation also represented three distinctly different climate zones and regional cookeries. Consider the rich assortment of highly regional ingredients represented in the "soup bunches" that were once common in the markets of our coastal cities. Reflecting the culinary styles of each region, these elaborate forms of bouquet garni were mostly made and sold by black women. The most famous for its elaborateness was the Charleston Soup Bunch shown from an old woodcut. It contains celery leaves, a crescent of sweet potato pumpkin, onions, very small turnips and carrots, and sprigs of sweet herbs. In short, it represents all the necessities for creating a well-flavored soup stock, the *jardin potager* gathered together in one symbolic bouquet.

Charleston soup bunch with slices of pumpkin and baby vegetables.

The inherent American character of our soup bunches, be they from Boston or Savannah, serves as telling evidence that our kitchen gardens could not depend on Europe either for seed or for garden manuals. Our climate and soils required American varieties. Thus English garden books like Thomas Mawe's *Every Man His Own Gardener* (1779), still a useful reference on heirloom vegetables, were soon replaced by such American works as Bernard M'Mahon's *American Gardener's Calendar* (1806) and, later in the nineteenth century, by works devoted to specific regions of the country. England lies so far north of us that tomato culture is almost impossible without the aid of hothouses or protective cloches. Where would an American vegetable garden be without its rows of Brandywine tomatoes (page 340), its limas beans, sweet corn, and squash?

European garden books simply could not account for the diverse mixture of European, New World, and African plants that gave the American kitchen garden its unique personality. Furthermore, the English kitchen garden that provided a model for Americans in colonial times itself fell victim to the grand landscaping schemes developed in Britain during the late eighteenth and early nineteenth centuries, particularly the rage for parklike settings. Great country houses were set stark naked like Grecian temples in the center of meadows populated with sheep and cattle. The bucolic idealism of landscape architects like Capability Brown works in engravings, but the panoramic views from the house are devoid of vegetable gardens; not even the cold frames of lettuce or the plump marrows swaying from their vines are in sight, for everything has been hidden away behind trees. I am thoroughly convinced that the decline of English cookery was in part brought about by a fear of peasant life, by this retreat into chilly sanctuaries set far away from the humanizing influences of the *jardin potager.* Happily, in America, our retreat was imitated on a smaller scale. In fact, for some of us it never happened, especially not among the Pennsylvania Dutch.

❦ NOT FAR FROM PARADISE ❧

When I drive over the mountains from Oley, a farming valley famous in Pennsylvania for its scenic architecture, I pass by a grove of wild chestnut trees, some old stone fencing, a Mennonite church, and a house with a green tile roof vaguely reminiscent of a counterpart in Palestine, finally arriving at a tavern where five roads meet. Opposite the tavern stands a cannon and a flagpole surrounded by canna lilies. This is New Jerusalem. It nestles in the heart of a Pennsylvania Dutch countryside not often visited by tourists. Yet the view from New Jerusalem is surprising, for directly ahead lies the East Penn Valley and a broad band of kitchen gardens that would feed the envy of any European farmer.

The Pennsylvania Dutch have maintained a proximity to the soil that is anchored to it not only by occupation but by religious attitudes. Perhaps it has something to do with their unique cultural history, perhaps it has something to do with their sense of clan and place. For the Pennsylvania Dutch, the *jardin potager* is real. They work barefooted in it. They sit there during summer picnics. They discuss it endlessly at dinner. It is a religious experience.

The tenacity with which these people have clung to their kitchen gardens is perhaps best illustrated by the number of American heirloom vegetables that use the term "German" or "Amish" in their names. The Pennsylvania Dutch—all of the various religious groups, not just the Amish—are great seed savers and remain so to this day. As one gardener said to me, "Gude Sume, Gude Gaarde"—"good seeds, good gardens."

The Pennsylvania Dutch have always been fascinated with garden and plant symbols. *The Picture-Bible of Ludwig Denig* (Yoder 1990) explores a 1780s pictorial narrative of the New Testament by a Pennsylvania Dutch apothecary whose interest in pietistic religious ideas went much further than simply reading books. His manuscript Bible, now considered one of the great products of eighteenth-century American folk art, is populated with symbolic flowers and garden scenes based on such devotional works as Johann Arndt's *Wahres Christenthum* (True Christianity) and his *Paradies-Gärtlein* (Little Garden of Paradise). Arndt reconstructed medieval mysticism along Protestant lines and was one of the most popular of all the religious writers among the Pennsylvania Dutch. Benjamin Franklin even printed an edition of *Wahres Christenthum* in 1751.

The Pennsylvania Dutch fascination with gardens and flowers as metaphors of life stems from their pietistic interest in the concept of the enclosed garden (*hortus inclusus*), a theme in Christian art for centuries. It originated in a love song in the Song of Solomon that the rabbis later spiritualized as an allegory about God and Israel. Catholic mystics saw the enclosed garden as a symbol of the Virgin Mary, Protestants saw in it the virtues of Christ. For pacifist sects like the Mennonites, this became both a physical Eden beyond the kitchen door and a spiritual condition, each individual being a garden of God, and therefore called upon to flower and bloom. To the outside world, these ideas may present a heady approach to gardening, but Pennsylvania Dutch hymns, poetry, and sermons are riddled with these images. Thus, the Dutch are in contact with this symbolism every day.

For those Pennsylvania Dutch who originally came from Switzerland, especially the Amish and the various Mennonite groups, the kitchen garden carried additional intellectual baggage. It had developed, even in the seventeenth century, into a concept not readily equivalent to its Anglo-American counterparts. Perhaps because of the peculiarities of geography (limited land) and widely varying microclimates, the Swiss brought the kitchen garden into a high level of cultivation. One of the most famous Swiss examples in America was the "Garden of Eden," an estate developed by Zürich-born Dr. Henry Schnebly at Hagerstown, Maryland. Albert Hauser has documented the history of this kind of Swiss garden in his *Bauern Gärten der Schweiz* (1976), the term *Bauerngarten* referring here to a type of rural kitchen garden, enclosed, divided into quadrants, and usually featuring raised beds. These are gardens that are worked by hand, like my own, with hoe cultivation as opposed to plow.

The earliest Swiss work dealing with this type of garden and written for the general public was Daniel Rhagor's *Pflantz-Gart* (1639). In it are described many of the practices brought to America by the Swiss immigrants. The theme in this and other similar Swiss works was *Bourgeoisierung*, a transformation of elite cultural ideas into something solidly middle class. Because this idea of a middle-class kitchen garden could be tied to a peculiarly middle-class type of cookery, such as that advocated by Henrietta Davidis and referred to in German as *bürgerliche Kochkunst*, it became deeply ingrained in German-speaking culture as a thing apart from aristocratic and secular ideals. Protestantism anointed the kitchen garden with a working-class worth, with religious boundaries and a moral vision that made it impervious in many ways to the decadence of shifting styles and tastes. It became an end to the good life rather than a means. Its religious focus was one fundamental reason why the Pennsylvania Dutch remained insulated from the "English" practices of the gentlemen farmers elsewhere in the country, and why these two worlds existed side by side but did not always communicate.

The histories of the Pennsylvania Dutch and of the mainstream American kitchen gardens parted ways long ago. Yet ultimately, each in its own way yielded to a major shift in gardening that occurred during the Civil War. This was the development of professional market gardening. Most of the vegetables we now preserve as heirlooms originated in the fever of experimentation that occurred to transform earthly Eden into profit.

⊷ GARDENING FOR GOLD ⊶

Early nineteenth-century garden books do not discuss money. Certainly those in the vein of Thomas Fessenden's *New American Gardener* (1828) skirted commercialism as rather arcane to the higher matters of horticulture. The English type of horticultural writing that epitomized literary productions of the period, the large folio encyclopedias compiled as parlor books, dominated the "gothik" sitting rooms of that age. The tone of the *Transactions of the Royal Horticultural Society* (1812–48) certainly reflected this: rich in diverting intellectual exercises, perhaps somewhat dotty in an abundant obsession with sea kales and cauliflowers, yet thoroughly comfortable, good reading for port and leather chairs.

The American classic compiled in this manner—but not the only American book of its sort—was Fearing Burr's *Field and Garden Vegetables of America* (1865; original edition 1863). This thick, leather-bound tome covered a huge array of vegetables on a variety-by-variety basis. Burr was inspired by *The Book of the Garden* (1853–55) by Scottish horticulturist Charles McIntosh, but it was William White's manual on gardening in the South that struck a chord that something larger and more nationwide should be undertaken. Burr's work is now treated as a bible among collectors of heirloom seeds, yet the book has many shortcomings. In an effort to appear up-to-date, Burr included a large number of French vegetable varieties lifted from the Vilmorin-Andrieux *Description des plantes potagères* (1856). A majority of these were completely unknown in this country at the time Burr's book appeared. He also knew little about popular local American varieties outside of Massachusetts—the Jenny Lind and Anne Arundel muskmelons were not mentioned, for example—and he did not recognize many well-known African-American vegetables, among them cowpeas and the old goober pea (*Voandzeia subterranea*) grown extensively by slaves before the 1850s. The most glaring deficiency, however, is that the book was not kept current, thus failing to discuss American vegetable varieties introduced after the Civil War, which was most of them.

More significantly, Burr concentrated only on those vegetables that he considered fit for commercial farm gardening, omitting entirely many worthy vegetables well suited to small kitchen gardens. On this point in particular the author made many incorrect judgment calls. His remark about The Student parsnip that appeared in the *American Horticultural Annual* (1867, 135) is classic: "I should judge that it will never be known in the markets, and will soon be dropped from seedsmen's catalogues." The Student is probably one of the most important parsnip varieties to be developed in the nineteenth century.

Burr's lack of vision can be forgiven, for every generation has its blind pundits, but most irritatingly Burr knew many of the leading horticulturists personally or through correspondence, yet provided little in the way of documented histories of the vegetables he discussed. This was information readily available at the time, and which we would be eager to know today. Admittedly, Victorians were not interested in heirloom vegetables. Their theme was improvement, not preservation, and genetic diversity was not an issue.

To get at the core of things, where frankness and controversy raged round and round, where the devastating truth about certain dealings and the frauds of many new varieties came baldly out, it is necessary to turn to more popular sorts of literature, such as Thomas Fessenden's *New England Farmer,* John Loudon's *Gardener's Magazine,* or *Le Bon Jardinier* of the Vilmorin seed house. Internationally, the Vilmorins were without a doubt the most famous seedsmen in the world, and they fixed a keenly skeptical Gallic eye on all of the latest horticultural developments.

The Vilmorin firm was established at Paris in 1775 by Pierre Philippe André Levêque de Vilmorin (1746–1804) and continues to this day. The Vilmorins are especially important to the evolution of the American kitchen garden; not only did they supply American firms with seed, but the U.S. Patent Office for many years in the nineteenth century distributed new Vilmorin vegetable varieties to farmers in several parts of the country so that they could be field tested under American conditions. Seeds from these trials found their way into rural seed networks and have joined ranks with many American heirloom vegetables.

Perhaps as important, the Vilmorins issued a series of large hand-colored lithographs of vegetables between 1850 and 1884, one plate a year, under the collective title *Album Vilmorin: Le Jardin potager.* This famous print collection is one of the most remarkable productions of the nineteenth century and serves as visual documentation for many heirloom vegetables today. The artists commissioned to create this series (all women, incidentally) also produced the sketches and drawings that were incorporated into the revised edition of the Vilmorin-Andrieux garden book, published in 1885 as *Le Jardin potager.* This was translated into English that same year and became one of the most widely used garden books of its kind.

Seed companies and magazines raided this book for pictures; there are few American seed catalogs or garden books that do not have illustrations lifted directly or discreetly redrawn from *Le Jardin potager*. But alas, *Le Jardin potager* has flaws, for it is both Francophile and entirely Eurocentric. The plants are not arranged according to any scientific method; indeed, the botanical attributions are quite unreliable, sometimes containing fabulous fictions. There are also a number of curious agendas buried in the text—for example, a garbled account of how the white Belgian carrot (page 126) was developed by a member of the Vilmorin clan. Furthermore, while the vegetables discussed may thrive in France, this is not to say that they are adapted to America, as I can well attest. But for all its clumsiness, the book remains a standard reference for popular European vegetable varieties, and there are seed savers today whose collecting goals are focused only on this Vilmorin list.

Regardless, Fearing Burr and the Vilmorins, as important as they were, did nothing to change the nature of the American kitchen garden as fundamentally as Peter Henderson.

Henderson (1822–1890) was born in Scotland, trained as a gardener, and came to the United States in 1843. After working for the seedsmen George Thorburn (1773–1863) in New York and Robert Buist (1805–1880) in Philadelphia, he established his own company in Jersey City in 1847. His book *Gardening for Profit* appeared in 1865 and quickly became one of the most popular American garden books of the nineteenth century. Henderson is credited with teaching American gardeners how to grow fruit and vegetables on a large commercial scale. In this way, he revolutionized kitchen gardening and turned it into market-oriented farming.

Peter Henderson

His timing was perfect; with the industrialization then taking place, large numbers of Americans were moving from farms into the cities. This created a class of consumers who did not possess their own gardens and thus were dependent on urban markets for food. The truck gardener found a commercial niche, and many small farmers moved into this line of work during the latter part of the nineteenth century because it was reliable and because they were not placing themselves in direct competition with the large mechanized farms that were moving into commodity crops like wheat and corn.

Garden literature from this period reflects the heavy emphasis placed on profitability, especially size, as though an enormous strawberry should somehow outmatch its smaller, more flavorful competitors in salability. The myth of size is an American weakness, and we have made a culture of it. The gardener who could deliver the largest and earliest produce to market reaped the highest rewards regardless of quality. Across the entire range of kitchen vegetables, *early* and *mammoth* became buzzwords for profit. Many heirloom vegetables developed in this period carry these terms in their names. In reality, in spite of the claims of seedsmen, a good number of these vegetables were not even new varieties but simply selections of existing varieties given new labels. Sorting out vegetable histories can be exasperating for this reason, especially since seed catalogs cannot be trusted.

Old seed catalogs play an important role in the heirloom seed movement. Some of the richest catalogs for heirloom vegetables are those of seedsman James J. H. Gregory of Marblehead, Massachusetts. His *Annual Catalogue of Choice Garden and Flower Seeds* ranks among the classics of this type—and many people enjoy collecting them. For one thing, the illustrations in historical catalogs like these provide a nostalgic reminder of olden times. B. K. Bliss & Sons' *Illustrated Potato Catalogue* from the 1870s is still a useful guide to period potato varieties, and the woodcuts are a rare visual treat. Yet many of the drawings in seed catalogs were in fact exaggerated to make the vegetables appear larger or more succulent than they really were. I have culled illustrations of Red Wethersfield onions (page 220) from several period seed catalogs, and not one onion resembled any other. Which depicts the true variety? The old and respected seed firm of Landreth & Sons in Philadelphia turned to photography in 1889 for this very reason. But cameras often miss features apparent to the human eye, so perhaps there will always be compromises.

Seed catalogs play a role in heirloom gardening similar to cookbooks in cookery. They form an ephemeral literature that, in the nineteenth century at least, served more as a reflection of what had already happened than as a beacon of invention. "New" in cookery usually means reinvented, and the same can be said for many vegetables. Low's Champion (page 62), a New England bean "introduced" in the 1880s, was actually a reintroduction of an earlier native American bean that had fallen out of fashion. Similar examples are legion.

On hindsight, the golden age of truck farming peaked between 1880 and 1940. Some of the most influential garden books from this period were Tuisco Greiner's *How to Make the Garden Pay* (1890), distributed to customers of the William Henry Maule seed company, and William Rawson's *Success in Market Gardening* (1892), a self-published work by a market gardener and seedsman in Boston who made a fortune in produce. Rawson was also the business successor to B. K. Bliss & Sons of New York, and through that acquisition became one of the country's leading suppliers of seed potatoes.

Aside from garden books, there were also many culinary crossovers, cookbooks issued by seed companies to help promote seed sales and to encourage repeat customers. The old Quaker firm of W. Atlee Burpee & Company commissioned Sarah Tyson Rorer of the Philadelphia Cooking School to write a manual on vegetable cookery. Her *How to Cook Vegetables* appeared in 1891 and was distributed as a bonus to Burpee's customers. A seed purchase of $3 entitled them to a paperback copy; a $5 seed purchase was rewarded with the oilcloth edition, ready for use on the kitchen table.

In this same vein, the U.S. Department of Agriculture published Maria Parloa's *Preparation of Vegetables for the Table* (1906) as much as a boon to farmwives as a guide to eating cheaply. Parloa's guide was published as a Farmers' Bulletin, but it was also distributed bound up with other bulletins on cookery and canning, baking, and meat preserving under the collective title *Uncle Sam's Cook Book.* Parloa's was only one of many governmental publications issued at the turn of this century with an intent to educate the consumer on ways to judge and use American produce.

Peter Henderson once lamented that it was the demise of the "particular customer" that eventually changed the way market gardeners did business. Boston and Philadelphia had been bastions of the type of consumers who demanded to know the background of their produce, how it was cultivated, and the comparative taste of different varieties, and tolerated no compromises in freshness and quality. This gave rise to hundreds of vegetables that sold themselves by virtue of having passed through this critical gauntlet: Boston lettuce, Philadelphia Market tomato, and much more. The New York market was different. As long as the produce *looked* good, it was possible to sell it. Henderson's greatest fear was that this standard would prevail nationwide once vast quantities of produce began moving across the country rather than coming from nearby farms. He was to be proved correct.

It was not just the demise of the educated customer that contributed to this change. A shift to industrialized farming after World War II, which flooded the marketplace with inexpensive produce, brought about the demise of truck farming. However, the most fundamental alteration to the picture arrived in the form of hybrid vegetables—plants that do not produce true seed, therefore obliging the gardener to purchase new seed every year—in the 1940s. The heirloom seed movement developed in part as a reaction to this situation, and the broader implications will be explored in the following chapter.

Certainly, some concerned individuals understood what was happening, and in their own pioneering way, they helped set the stage for what has developed today into a full-fledged worldwide movement to save traditional food resources. Eleanour Sinclair Rhode in England was one of these. Her nursery at Cranham Lodge near Reigate in Surrey became a seed-saving emporium and a point of dissemination of many truly rare old vegetable varieties. The Blue Coco bean, the Carlin pea, Hubbard squash, the Red Fig tomato, the pea bean, Black Spanish radish—her seed lists read like the index of this book. Furthermore, Mrs. Rhode was a prolific writer who produced numerous works on herbs and gardening now considered standards in the field. Her *Uncommon Vegetables*, first published in 1943, is the only book I know of that comes close to mine in its treatment of specific heirloom varieties, although Mrs. Rhode's is only ninety-four pages in length.

Eleanour Rhode's books were also published in this country, and she had an avid following here as a result, among them Rosetta Clarkson, editor of the *Herb Journal.* Mrs. Rhode was keenly aware of the connectedness between kitchen garden and cookery, and she imbued all of her books with a love of food. In particular, she entertained great respect for Edward Ashdown Bunyard, a connoisseur of fruits and vegetables and son of the famous Victorian pomologist George Bunyard. George Bunyard is remembered in the name of an English lettuce called Bunyard's Matchless, otherwise known in the United States as Deer Tongue. However, it was the son who wrote books, among them *The Anatomy of Dessert* (1934) and *The Epicure's Companion* (1937), and they are still delightful to read and still vastly informative on the uses and qualities of what are now heirloom fruits and vegetables.

Edward Bunyard's influence, like Mrs. Rhode's, was transatlantic, for many Americans in gardening circles appreciated their books immensely, my grandfather among them. I also think it would be fair to say that Mrs. Rhode's seed packets were once hot black market items for American gardeners who visited her nursery between the world wars. Many gardens in the vicinity of Boston, Philadelphia, Chicago, Detroit, and Richmond, Virginia, still bloom with herbs and cuttings smuggled into this country on the persons of well-connected ladies with winning manners and what is known as a customs smile. All gardeners are felons at heart.

Unfortunately, this was a small and urbane group, and their efforts did not curtail the decline of traditional vegetables in this country. The passionate energy for saving culinary heirlooms erupted in the 1970s, a child of grassroots America, not of the horticultural societies or garden clubs. These organizations remain focused on the decorative arts side of gardening, landscape design and ornamentals, although this is now beginning to change. Hybrids did indeed bring an end to an era. When we glance back over the past century at the name Bloomsdale, we are forced to consider the fate of the Landreth seed farm near Bristol, Pennsylvania, which produced the vegetables bearing that name. Not far from there was Fordhook Farm, the old Burpee experimental grounds in Bucks County. Perhaps there is no more fitting reminder of the grand demise of American seedsmanship than to note that Fordhook Farm, one of the greatest seed farms in this part of the country and the birthplace of hundreds of heirloom vegetable varieties, is now a bed-and-breakfast.

Chapter 2

The Heirloom Vegetable Today

There have always been seed savers of one sort or another in this country. One of the most well known in recent times was John Withee in Massachusetts, who during the 1970s established the Wanigan Associates Collection, assembled from some four hundred collectors, of old-fashioned bean varieties. Withee was inspired by a passion for beans and by a fear that many of his old-time favorites would disappear. His collection of more than 1,100 bean varieties is now housed at Heritage Farm in Decorah, Iowa, and maintained by Seed Savers Exchange.

Unfortunately, individuals with Withee's foresight and energy have been the exception rather than the rule. The conscious effort to organize this type of conservation gardening into a unified purpose outside government-funded projects has occurred only within the past twenty years, although there have been pioneering efforts that date back a century. The most famous of these is the Vavilov Institute, established in 1895 at Saint Petersburg, Russia. It is named after one of its most famous plant geneticists, Nikolai I. Vavilov (1887–1943).

Vavilov was interested in the preservation of genetic diversity, and his work with heirloom plants in this area has greatly influenced the thinking of all groups involved in the heirloom seed movement. Vavilov focused on the genetic diversity of agricultural crops and their wild relatives. Seeds were gathered and stored in scientifically controlled environments called gene banks. This was augmented by botanical gardens that maintained nonconsumable plants.

Genetic diversity is the slight genetic variation that appears in "open-pollinated" plants, those pollinated by natural means such as insects, rain, dew, or wind. Genetic diversity may express itself in varying shades of green in the leaf coloring of a certain cabbage variety, or in the shape of different tomatoes on the same plant. Sometimes it expresses itself in unseen traits, such as resistance to virus or, in corn, with higher starch content in the dry seed. Genetic diversity is what ensures the survival of a species when it is subjected to stress, such as disease or adverse environmental conditions, allowing it to adapt to changing climates.

Vavilov's example was replicated by governments in most parts of the world because gene banks were directly tied to matters of state. Rare or important species—for example, crops crucial to a national economy—could be preserved in gene banks and used as a basis for continued improvement. The U.S. Department of Agriculture supports several gene banks with this mission in mind. The basic method for preserving seed to ensure its long-term viability is to freeze it. In its simplest terms, a gene bank is a deep freeze that holds plant life in limbo until it can be studied or grown out again to refresh the seed. Unfortunately, because gene banks are usually government funded and linked to scientific research, they are not readily accessible to the gardeners who may want to obtain rare seeds and grow them. Gene banks do not see their mission in a commercial light. Seed sales not only would place them in direct competition with seed companies but could easily become an added bureaucratic burden, sidetracking them from important research. Shortage of government funding, however, is changing this attitude.

The Institut für Pflanzengenetik und Kulturpflanzenforschung, a state-sponsored gene bank at Gatersleben in the former East Germany, is now forming working agreements with such private seed-saving organizations as Seed Savers Exchange in Decorah, Iowa, and Arche Noah in Schiltern, Austria. Many heirloom vegetables, such as the Riesentraube tomato (page 350), now in circulation among members of these two organizations can be traced to Gatersleben. Of course, a number of American seed savers are also accessing USDA collections in this country, and this is greatly expanding our heirloom vegetable lists. The Puhwem and Sehsapsing (both page 146) corn came from seed obtained directly from the USDA.

◄§ GENETIC DIVERSITY AND ϗ► ENVIRONMENTAL ACTIVISM

Genetic diversity is one of the cornerstones of the heirloom seed movement. Just as it expresses itself through a broad spectrum of concerns, so there are several types of gardeners drawn to it, from those with complex philosophical readings on the meanings of the earth and mankind's role here to outspoken critics of agribusiness and government.

Alan M. Kapuler's former Peace Seeds, now part of a collaboration with Seeds of Change under the name of Deep Diversity, produces heirloom-seed catalogs based on the theories of botanist Rolf Dahlgren, whereby all plant life is organized into major kinship structures and "coevolutionary layouts" resembling genealogical fan charts. Plants are selected for molecular properties, biodiversity, and their role in providing amino acids essential to building proteins. Diet and nutrition are therefore embedded in such holistic approaches, a reordering of philosophical priorities oftentimes at odds with the old Judeo-Christian worldview.

The usefulness of the heirloom vegetable in fulfilling certain spiritual sensibilities finds its expression across the board among American seed savers, from the followers of Rudolf Steiner, whose biodynamic agriculture is essentially a theory of nutrition based on soil-building techniques, to born-again Christians who come to Jesus in their gardens. Without taking a position on any of these views (other than what I have already stated in my introduction), I think it is essential to point out that it is this very diversity of purpose that gives the seed-saving movement its continuing energy; as with plants, diverse ideas fertilize one another. What we cannot afford is a monocultural perspective. It was monocultural thinking that caused the potato famine. We study its agony in history books, but have we learned its lesson?

Most of the varieties of potatoes being raised in Europe and North America up to the 1840s were genetic clones of a handful of potatoes brought out of South America during the seventeenth and eighteenth centuries. A clone is a plant (or animal) that is genetically identical to its parent. We make clones of potatoes because we cut up the tuber and raise new plants from these pieces, rather than from seed. We do the same when we take grafts from fruit trees. Clones of this kind are not really heirlooms; they are living history, genetically pure replicas of their ancestors.

The problem with the clone potato population in the 1840s lies in the fact that since the potatoes were so closely related, they all carried the same genetic strengths and weaknesses. The disease that struck the European potato fields, decimating the crop almost overnight, originated in Mexico. Mexican potatoes, over years of exposure to the disease, had produced strains of plant more resistant to it. The South American potatoes had not. Thus in a very short period of time the potatoes were wiped out due to their narrow genetic base, and millions of people starved.

Today, the hybrid vegetables that are being promoted over the old heirloom varieties contain the genetic weaknesses of monocultural cultivation. While it is true that geneticists can carefully breed hybrids to be resistant to certain known diseases, that Huge Unknown—the newly mutated virus—may undo their handiwork overnight. This has become especially frightening to some gardeners, and there is a strong grassroots movement to grow heirloom vegetables as a hedge against massive crop failures in the future. Part of this movement are a number of small seed companies (listed on page 391) that cater to the heirloom market and are continuously reintroducing exciting old varieties from their trial gardens. Seeds Blüm was even generous enough to send me seed samples of some vegetables a year or so in advance of their release to the public. That sort of cooperation, and a sincere willingness to help, is a common bond among seed savers. Support for the small seed companies is one way to help keep food production in the hands of the consumer.

The great fear among European gardeners was that the European Parliament would pass certain legislation brought up as draft law in 1988. This was the Legal Protection of Biotechnological Inventions act, which stated that plants, animals, and human genes would be patentable, and that farmers would not be able to save seed from their crops and freely reuse this seed for crops the next year. Patented crops and livestock would require annual royalties—as high as 80 percent of the original seed cost—from any offspring. The public outcry against this was enormous, and in the spring of 1995 the law was voted down, but the political situation in Europe is still unsettled, and it is against the law to sell seed for plants that are not on national seed registers. This includes a vast number of heirlooms not presently sold by commercial seed houses. Not even the Henry Doubleday Research Association in England, a nonprofit foundation, can sell seed from its collections to help underwrite its stated mandate.

With a similar specter of legislated extinctions hovering over us, American activism against the "patenting of life," as it is called in Europe, has assumed large-scale proportions. Even the Christian right has gotten involved, since the environment is viewed as God's work, and there are clear scriptural mandates to respect and maintain it. However, the most direct counterattack has come from brilliant plant breeders like Tom Wagner in California, who created a large number of tomato varieties the old way and released them through his tiny Tater Mater Seed Company. His cross between two heirloom tomatoes, Yellow Fig (page 349) and Evergreen (page 337), resulted in Green Grape, one of the most popular small tomatoes today. Another of the Wagner creations is Green Zebra. With Alice Waters promoting his tomatoes at Chez Panisse, her restaurant in Berkeley, and produce farmers taking up the cause, this type of genetic guerrilla warfare can quickly undermine the profitability of such patented bioengineered vegetables as the Flavr Savr™ tomato, which has been marketed under the brand name MacGregor's, the true Dorian Gray of the tomato kingdom.

Sustainable agriculture has been another venue of resistance to agribusiness, with small-scale farmers providing local markets with an array of specialty produce unavailable through long-distance shipping. Biointensive minifarming is one new name for it. It focuses less on standard farming techniques than on new ways to coax large harvests from small areas of ground.

The Common Ground Garden and Mini-Farm at Willits, California, has been taking the lead in promoting small-scale agriculture, not to mention its heirloom seed offerings through the Bountiful Gardens catalog. Through its publications, workshops, and interns from Third World countries, much attention is focused on intensive farming techniques useful to anyone involved with kitchen gardening: compost crops, double digging, hexagonal plant spacing, manual tools, and such traditional ethnic growing methods as lazy bed gardening, from Ireland. Lazy beds are built up above ground level, and the soil is deeply worked, with yields similar to those of the raised gardens of the Pennsylvania Dutch.

❧ ETHNOBOTANY AND THE AMISH VEGETABLE ❧

In an article about the Landreth & Sons seed company, which appeared in the *Pennsylvania Farm Journal* (1853, 136), a description of the firm's "Bloomdale" trial farm near Philadelphia provided a fascinating glimpse into the state of horticulture in this country in the years preceding the Civil War. In 1853 Landreth devoted fifty acres to peas, an impressive figure but not altogether surprising given the Victorian love for peas of all sorts. More startling, Landreth reported sending four tons of vegetable seeds to India, and similarly large quantities to California, New Mexico, South America, and the West Indies. Today, seed collectors are traveling through India, South America, and the West Indies in search of "native" varieties. In fact, many of these heirloom vegetables may have started in seed packets from somewhere else more than a century ago.

Simple purity of life close to the land, whether of the peasant in Thailand, the Hopi Indian in New Mexico, or the Amish farmer in Iowa, has enormous appeal to Americans alienated by the complexities of modern urbanized living. This yearning for rustic simplicity is evident everywhere in our attitudes to rural life in general, and in the way we present food in restaurants and magazines, not to mention in mass media advertising. The "natural" foods of the tropical rain forest, the "purity" of crops tilled by the American Indian, the sacred character of the Amish commitment to the land, these are recurring themes of an intensely appealing kind and express themselves everywhere in the seed-saving movement.

Indeed, one of the earliest uses of the term *heirloom* in connection with seed saving came from an American Indian context. An article on "Indian Vegetables" in *Meehan's Monthly* (October 1892, 156) noted that a reader of the magazine in Tennessee living near a community of Cherokees had obtained a snap bean from a chief named Silver Jack and that the bean was being maintained as an "heirloom." Unfortunately, Silver Jack's snap bean was not described in enough detail to connect it to a variety known today, unless by some coincidence it happens to be the

Jack's snap of Seed Savers Exchange. Otherwise, it may be extinct or preserved under another name.

It is easy to overromanticize the American Indian role in seed preservation, even though evidence may seem quite compelling. The forced removal of peoples from their historical lands, the collapse of one group into the other, the predominance today of the largely nomadic Great Plains cultures as an overarching symbol of the American Indian, all have taken their toll on the original diversity of native American foods and foodways. Yet there are some bright spots.

Quaker relations among the Iroquois between 1795 and 1875 have recently been explored by Professor Carol Karlsen of the University of Michigan. Implicit with the cultural impact of Quaker attempts to bring education and progressive farming methods to the Iroquois was the distribution of seed. It is difficult to know whether the Scotia, or Genuine Cornfield Bean (page 68) of the 1820s was a commercial introduction to the Iroquois or a native variety improved by American seedsmen. Likewise, the Delaware Indian Turtle Bean is also the *Fisherbuhn* of the Pennsylvania Dutch, and the Dutch Caseknife (page 56) of Europe, a very old European variety, incidentally.

In their *Description of a Journey and Visit to the Pawnee Indians* (1914; the trip occurred in the spring of 1851), Moravian missionaries Gottlieb Oehler and David Smith took pains to describe the Pawnee way of life. Yet they did not make detailed reports on Pawnee ethnobotany, the plants used by the Pawnee as food and medicine. They do not even provide confirming evidence that the very beautiful brown-speckled Pawnee bush bean (page 52) now so popular among seed savers is actually an original Pawnee variety. The bean's botanical traits—compact bush, uniform pods, lack of runners—all point to the intervention of sophisticated plant breeding. When this bean is grown side by side with a number of old European bush varieties, there are startling similarities that suggest it probably was introduced (or reintroduced) to the Upper Midwest by German settlers in the 1850s or 1860s. Only where Native Americans have lived in relative isolation from white contact can we be more certain of the plant origins.

Gary Nabhan's award-winning research among the desert peoples of the Southwest is often cited as a model for the collection and documentation of native plant species. Nabhan is a true ethnobotanist fully committed to carrying the seed exchange back to the peoples of origin, especially in the Sonora Desert, where he engages in research. Most important to growers of heirloom plants, Nabhan was one of the founders of Native Seeds/SEARCH in Tucson, Arizona. This organization publishes seed catalogs for plants from the Sonora region and is directly involved in helping native peoples reclaim their traditional food cultures.

In the same way that Indian earth-connectedness has fascinated modern American gardeners, "Amish" has been absorbed into the vocabulary of seed saving. Varietal names such as Amish paste tomato or Amish Walking Onion (page 232) for the tree onion indicate not so much an Amish-bred vegetable as an approved seed source for the plant, for the word *Amish* implies a relationship to the land, a source unspoiled by pollution, chemical fertilizers, and unethical farming practices. Very few Amish have been involved in commercial plant breeding. I can only think offhand of Isaac N. Glick of Lancaster, who was not only in business at the turn of this century but also made significant contributions by developing or promoting a number of new vegetable varieties. Glick introduced his Eighteenth Century beet, a long, dark red beet with bright green leaves, in 1906. He also offered many heirlooms still popular today, such as Stow-ell's Evergreen corn (page 147), Early Snowball cauliflower, Icicle Radish (page 305), Hacken-sack melon (page 200), Golden Ball turnip (page 358), and Champion of England pea (page 243). The Glicks are still in business, and to them I owe a special debt of gratitude for my greenhouse.

However, the Amish are great seed savers, and many old vegetable varieties have been pre-served in their gardens. Since these vegetables often come down without their original names, they acquire backyard designations that can seem confusing to anyone trying to sort out plant histories. A classic example of this is the well-known Brandywine Tomato (page 340), which was developed not by an Amish farmer, as legend would have it, but by the Johnson & Stokes seed company of Philadelphia. The real Amish vegetables come from seed collectors like Rebecca Longenecker of Elizabethtown, Pennsylvania. She has supplied me with a wonderful selection of seeds garnered from her Amish neighbors, including the Hersh Sugar Pea, an unnamed soy bean, and the Gross Nanny Green Pole Bean (page 64). The pole bean is the same as von Martens's *Halbrothe Kugelbohne* (1869, 76); the dwarf form is called the Beautiful Bean in the *Beans of New York* (Hedrick 1931, 76), and the *Zuiker Boon* from the Cape of Good Hope. In England it is popularly known as the Pea Bean and is still sold by some seed houses. It appears to be a very old cross between the White Marrow pea (page 243) and the Red Cranberry pole bean (page 65). In the United States, small marrow beans were often called pea beans.

The Landis Valley Museum near Lancaster, Pennsylvania, has undertaken a massive project to collect and document the ethnobotany of the Pennsylvania Germans and their North Amer-ican diaspora. Many of the discoveries of the Heirloom Seed Project are now available through an annual seed catalog that includes a fascinating array of heirloom plants. Landis Valley has been responsible for introducing several rare Pennsylvania Dutch heirloom vegetables into seed-saving networks, including the Red Brandywine Tomato and the Amish Nuttle Bean (page 53). The museum's primary focus, however, is the periodization of its plant collections—that is, placing the vegetables and fruits in their correct historical settings. Landis Valley is an open-air museum, a collection of houses replicating a farm village, and as such it is only one of a large number of historic sites in this country that view heirloom vegetables as living antiques.

⬥§ THE HISTORICAL GARDENER §⬥

The Skansen movement in Sweden during the 1890s gave birth to the concept of the open-air museum re-creating peasant life as a metaphor of cultural identity. Entire villages were reconstructed, with historic buildings dismantled and reassembled to establish a mood and setting reminiscent of the formative years of the nation's persona. Not surprisingly, at the heart of these buildings were kitchens, dark, smoky rooms where ladies in archaic garb prepared dishes on an open hearth symbolic of the cultural struggle between life on the land in former times and the enticements of today's well-stocked supermarket.

Skansen is now a term in many languages for an open-air museum. This concept has translated itself into historical sites in the United States, from towns like Mystic, Connecticut, and Colonial Williamsburg in Virginia to Pleasant Hill of the Shakers in Kentucky and restored Spanish missions in the Southwest. In each case there is a historical interest in the kitchens, in the foods prepared, and in the gardens that supplied the households with produce. The promotion of women's studies and the study of various functions of women in traditional farming societies have greatly added recent momentum in heirloom gardening as a study in period vegetables.

The National Colonial Farm at Accokeek, Maryland, began raising colonial farm crops of the Chesapeake region more than twenty years ago. Old Sturbridge Village at Sturbridge, Massachusetts, began collecting New England heirloom vegetables, including varieties disseminated by the Shakers, well before the U.S. Bicentennial. The Bicentennial caused many American gardeners to reassess their historic roots, encouraging a renewed interest not only in early American life but also in the various ethnic communities that cultivated distinctive kitchen gardens in the nineteenth century. As a result, heirloom gardening in this country has become far more complex than in England, for example, because of the large number of overlapping cultural histories that make up our national character.

As a case in point, I could offer Hans Buschbauer's *Amerikanisches Garten-Buch* (1892), published as a guide to the German-American kitchen garden in the Upper Midwest. When one reads through this book, it becomes obvious that the author has accommodated his garden ideas to North American conditions. He recommends just as many well-known commercial American vegetable varieties from the 1880s and 1890s as older, more traditional ones. Indeed, telltale woodcuts from the Vilmorin *Le Jardin potager* (1885) creep into his text, and there are certainly touches of up-to-dateness in his discussions of Defiance lettuce (very much talked about at the time) and crosnes (*Stachys affinis*), a root vegetable from Asia that had only been introduced to American gardeners in 1889. Thus the ethnic sketch of Buschbauer's kitchen garden became a very mixed bag of vegetables indeed.

Recently the Monticello Foundation has taken an interest in Thomas Jefferson's mountaintop vegetable garden, a terraced affair with a spectacular view toward the southeast. Jefferson's gardening interests are well documented, and the names of the varieties of vegetables he grew can be located in early garden sources. To bring this aspect of Jefferson's daily life into better focus for visitors to his house, an extensive plant collecting program has been undertaken. It supports itself financially in part through the sale of plants and seeds with Jeffersonian associations. Under the direction of Peter Hatch, it has been highly successful.

Because of the nature of seed saving and the genetic shifts that occur in plants propagated this way, it is difficult to find vegetables dating from Jefferson's period (pre-1826) that exactly match those that he grew at Monticello. In fact, documented vegetable varieties predating 1800 are even rarer and may not number more than a few hundred. This is not many, considering that there are today several thousand tomato varieties, and this does not even begin to touch the numbers of such vegetables as fava beans, peas, or radishes. In any case, within the last ten years Monticello has become a leading force in the preservation and dissemination of early American plant varieties, especially with an eye toward their documentation and their role in Jefferson's garden schemes.

❧ SEED SAVERS EXCHANGE ☙

The heirloom seed movement in this country has now coalesced into a unified effort for all the reasons I have just discussed: concern about the environment; a new interest in food history; and a sense of loss over disappearing plant varieties, perhaps with terrifying implications for the future. A small group of gardeners sharing these concerns organized in 1975 under the oversight of Kent Whealy, then of Princeton, Missouri. Thus Seed Savers Exchange was born.

Seed Savers Exchange is now the largest grassroots organization of its kind in the United States. It has relocated to Heritage Farm at Decorah, Iowa, established extensive seed collections, and is presently involved in gathering threatened plant varieties in the former Soviet Union, indeed in all parts of the world. The exchange has undertaken an active publication program, and many books such as Suzanne Ashworth's *Seed to Seed* (1991) may be considered among the most useful of their kind, whether for raising heirloom vegetables or simply for gardening pleasure.

Some members of Seed Savers Exchange also maintain large seed collections of their own, such as special collections of corn, sweet potatoes, or squash. SSE member Carolyn Male's collection of tomato varieties in Latham, New York, is famous internationally. Other members have built seed collections around a specific region or time period, as in my case, the Delaware Valley before 1850. These satellite collections contribute samples to the seed collection at Heritage Farm and in many cases help maintain the seed purity of certain endangered varieties. Nearly all of the satellite collections offer their seeds only through the annual SSE seed listing; thus, membership in the organization becomes a membership in a vast worldwide network of interlinked seed savers. With a little patience it is possible to locate almost any known heirloom vegetable, provided that it is not extinct. Every vegetable profiled in this book is available through Seed Savers Exchange or through the specialized seed firms listed on page 391.

Seed savers in other countries, in particular Arche Noah at Schloss Schiltern in Austria, have modeled their seed organizations after Seed Savers Exchange. Arche Noah has been concentrating on heirloom vegetables from German-speaking Europe as well as from the former Iron Curtain countries of Eastern Europe. Under the old Communist governments, considerable money was devoted to preserving traditional foods at open-air museums and gene banks, but now the money is gone, and with no funding in sight, Eastern Europe is losing large amounts of rare genetic material every year. The task that Arche Noah has cut out for itself is enormous; the name that this organization has chosen for itself could not be more appropriate.

Some seed organizations have evolved quite independent of Seed Savers Exchange but now cooperate closely with it. The most famous of these is the Heritage Seed Programme at the Ryton Organic Gardens, Ryton-on-Dunsmore, near Coventry, England. This seed collection, first organized in 1958 by horticulturist Lawrence Hills, was named in honor of Henry Doubleday, a nineteenth-century English Quaker. The Henry Doubleday Research Association (HDRA) is the parent organization that oversees the various projects at Ryton. Like Heritage Farm in Decorah, Iowa, Ryton Organic Gardens are open to the public. More than 18,000 members of the seed program at HDRA receive a selection of free heirloom seeds every year as part of their membership privileges. I have added a number of unusual plants to my collection in this manner.

Lacking in all of these efforts, however, is one essential element. While much time and effort has gone into preserving seed of heirloom vegetables, no one has undertaken extensively to identify and document their histories. Oral history and folkloric tales are sometimes useful in piecing together the underlying reasons for why a given heirloom vegetable was saved, the Cherokee

Trail of Tears bean (page 71) being a prime example. We would understand more clearly the relationship such heirlooms had to one another—black pole beans arranged into related botanical groups, in the case of the Cherokee bean—and why these variant forms were developed if we had access to some type of plant genealogy. Surprising things come to light when we explore in depth plant histories such as that of Stowell's Evergreen corn (page 147) and why it got that name. The plant profiles in the following chapter are intended to fill this need.

Chapter 3

A Grower's Guide
to Selected Heirloom Vegetables

❧❦❧

Raising heirloom vegetables is as much a gardening challenge as it is a world of discovery. It was certainly a surprise to me, when first glancing through the plates of the *Album Vilmorin*, that I could count over forty-five vegetables still available today under the same varietal names. And if the plates are indeed true to the original vegetables, then our heirlooms also look like their nineteenth-century ancestors. Among these are the Purple Vienna Kohlrabi (page 112), the large yellow tomato (page 346) from my grandfather's collection, the Blue Coco Bean (page 541), the Ruffled Pimento Pepper (page 266), even the Early Rose Potato (page 274), and the Jersey Shallot (page 223), an old kitchen standby for well over 150 years. In fact, I have tried to include as many vegetables as possible from the *Album Vilmorin* because it is such a remarkably accurate source of historical documentation.

Other types of heirloom vegetables included among my profiles range from backyard mongrels like the Shenandoah Tomato (page 351) to such historically significant vegetables as the White Belgian Carrot (page 126), a commercial variety that emerged from an important horticultural experiment. There are also a number of species vegetables like Malabar Spinach (page 328), which lack varietal names since they have not undergone extensive commercial breeding. Several of the native American vegetables, like Besler's Cherry Pepper (page 253), developed distinctive characteristics presumably during pre-Columbian times.

The names of heirloom vegetables can be confusing, since seedsmen often renamed vegetables to make them appear "new" in their catalogs or garden books. An old woodcut for the Early Scarlet Horn Carrot (page 124) appeared in the 1904 edition of Peter Henderson's *Gardening for*

Profit (1865) under the guise of the "Half-Long Red Stump Rooted Carrot," as though this were a distinctly different variety. It is small wonder that gardeners created their own vocabularies for vegetables when so many bewildering inconsistencies cropped up in respected books. Some vegetables simply sloughed off their slick commercial names in the process of grassroots gardening. I am constantly reminded of the bush bean that came to me one year under the dubious name "Farting Triumph." The puzzle was not solved until I discovered a French seed catalog with a bean called Triomphe de Farcy, nothing to do incidentally with the implications in the Americanized name. Some gardeners just forgot original names and assigned something new and convenient to take care of the omission, as in the case of Dr. Neal's Tomato (page 342). These homemade aliases greatly complicate the work of garden and food historians, especially since the same vegetable may have as many as twenty names. The examples that I have provided in the sections on lettuces and potatoes will hopefully clear the air and not mislead some seed collectors into imagining that these old aliases represent long-lost varieties.

Mongrels occurred when crosses, sports, or mutations resulted from standard varieties. A large number of heirloom vegetables have evolved in this way, like the Quaker Pie Pumpkin (page 290) and Martin's Carrot Pepper (page 261). In the case of the pumpkin, it was discovered in a private garden, then sold to a commercial seed house and distributed nationally. In the case of the pepper, the variety was only circulated among Old Order Mennonites in Pennsylvania and Ohio.

Every region of the country has its vigilant seed savers on the lookout for old or unique vegetable varieties. Illinois seed saver Merlyn Niedens discovered the Pitman Valley Plum Tomato, a Pennsylvania Dutch variety that is now distributed through Southern Exposure Seed Exchange. My friend Charles Loper has inundated me with exotic seeds brought back from the islands of Greece, the Egyptian Market in Istanbul, and the coast of Turkey, including a rare and beautiful dwarf hollyhock found growing among the ruins of Ephesus. Most of us who save seeds rely on friends who scour the countryside a little closer to home. Al Lotti, a gardener in Allentown, Pennsylvania, has provided me with innumerable treasures gleaned from farm stands in the East Penn Valley, including the *Maxatawny Hinkelhatz* pepper (page 260); a reddish bronze groundcherry naturalized in Northampton, Pennsylvania; and an old Moravian garlic, not to mention the wonderful Italian heirloom vegetables that have been preserved in his own family. Generous friends like Al are the backbone of the seed-saving movement and one of its great pleasures. In fact, anyone can discover an heirloom, given a little patience and good luck. Do not forget that it was a casual hiker who discovered the 150-million-year-old Wollemi Pine in Australia, the world's oldest heirloom plant. Not everyone is destined to make such a spectacular find, yet it is often surprising what can be collected from an abandoned field or along the boundaries of old gardens. Seed saving and plant collecting are not expensive pastimes, and this is why they have become so popular as a class project in schools and why they are expanding so rapidly at the grass-roots level.

⤜§ SEED PURITY §⤛

It is possible to enjoy heirloom vegetables, as many gardeners do, simply by planting them from year to year and replenishing seed each winter from Seed Savers Exchange or from specialty seed houses. A great many gardeners approach heirlooms as a hobby, and there is nothing wrong with this. Indeed, as a seed grower, I am far more willing to reduce my seed stocks by sharing them with hobbyists than to let the seed age in storage and eventually go to waste. As far as I am concerned, anyone who has an interest in growing plants from seed is a potential convert to seed saving, and my seeds are the best propaganda, since they speak for themselves.

Ideally, seed growers like myself, particularly those of us who supply the offerings in Seed Savers Exchange, hope that gardeners will find a few heirlooms that do well for them and start maintaining their own seeds. Gardeners cannot rely on a few growers to produce the bulk of the heirlooms in circulation, which unfortunately is the present situation with many of the cabbages and other biennials. This defeats the purpose of keeping food production in the hands of the consumer, and it drastically lowers the odds that a particular variety will survive over time. If there is one motivating factor behind my book, it is that I firmly believe heirloom vegetables will never be safe from extinction unless we use them. They must be part of our daily lives.

This increases the commitment of the gardener because it requires a knowledge of seed-saving techniques. Seed Savers Exchange has greatly simplified this task for the beginner with its publication by seed saver Suzanne Ashworth, *Seed to Seed* (1991). This excellent guide is available directly from Seed Savers Exchange or through most bookstores and has been recently translated into German. I have included similar seed-saving advice for all the vegetables profiled in this book. Some of this advice is derived from wise old garden books from the eighteenth and nineteenth centuries; all of it has been tested in my garden repeatedly. In some instances, what I have learned from direct experience may go beyond what is presently available in many gardening publications. Much of my historical research is definitely new.

I am particularly interested in providing information that will help gardeners determine whether or not their plants are growing true. A plant grows true when it conforms to the genetic program bred into it, which of course relates to seed purity. Here is a typical example from the nineteenth century of what happens when seed purity is compromised.

In 1866–67, several American seedsmen began promoting the Rat-Tailed Radish (page 303) as a novelty in one of those ongoing cycles of "new" (but not really) offerings intended to keep customers streaming back to their seed catalogs. Most of the garden journals at the time dismissed the radish as "worthless." Correspondence in the *American Agriculturist* for August 1868 raised interesting objections to the radish that revealed the root of the problem: bad seed-saving techniques.

A gardener in Jeffersonville, Indiana, complained to the editors that the first year (1867) the Rat-Tailed Radish was planted, it produced the long, purple-brown seedpods that are its most significant feature. On planting the seed the second year (1868), the pods were green and entirely unlike rat tails. The conclusion was that the plant had crossed in 1867 with other radishes in the garden—a correct assumption. Implicit in this was the fact that the Indiana gardener was also saving seed from other radishes and had allowed them to bloom at the same time as the rat-tailed radish. Furthermore, the gardener remarked that the seeds were taken from one plant (only one "specimen" had been raised). This runs contrary to sound seed-saving practice. Radishes cross with radishes regardless of whether they produce fancy edible roots or crunchy pods for pickles. They are all the same species; and saving seed from one plant alone only increases the likelihood that the worst traits will be perpetuated. In short, the rat-tailed radish did not receive a fair trial.

This brings me again to the subject of genetics, since impure seeds lead to genetic degradation of plant varieties. Genetics are indeed complicated, and if the truth were known, we understand far less than we imagine, even though scientifically it is possible to understand a great deal. Yet understanding certain basics about plant genetics greatly advances the gardener's ability to save seeds intelligently and to correct unwanted crossings. In fact, as Luther Burbank demonstrated long ago, it is possible to engage in back-breeding to retrieve characteristics that lie buried deep within the genetic code of each plant. I have been able to "restore" many of my grandfather's old peppers by resorting to such breeding practices.

The best guidebook to plant genetics for the layman is Carol Deppe's *Breed Your Own Vegetable Varieties* (1993). Even if gardeners have no intention of creating their own "designer vegetables" (as I call them), the explanation of the processes of hybridization is basic information of enduring usefulness to anyone who plans to garden seriously. Combine this with *Rodale's Successful Organic Gardening* (1993) or John Jeavon's *How to Grow More Vegetables* (1995), and all the tools are in place for bountiful harvests for many years to come.

❧ CHOICES FOR SMALL GARDENS ❧

Old American garden books, like those of Bernard M'Mahon and Thomas Fessenden, followed the English format of dividing material by seasons. This approach was useful on the one hand and vexing on the other. For example, a discussion of cucumbers might begin with cold framing young plants in April, yet only in a subsequent chapter—much further in the book—did we ascertain when and how to transplant them into the garden. This arrangement of material, with its progression of important steps hanging at the end like a German verb, led to unnecessary confusion and to an overkill of cross-referencing. Later American garden books collapsed everything together, arranging all that gardeners needed to know about cucumbers under that vegetable. This is the format I have chosen for my vegetable profiles, including their histories, culinary tips, and seed-saving hints.

In England, where the climate is more or less uniform across the country, the old style of garden book worked remarkably well as a type of national planting calendar. In the United States, the climate is so radically different in various parts of the country that we must proceed according to our own local conditions; thus our garden books can only aim for generalities unless they are written for a specific region like the Pacific Northwest or New England. Lost in this Americanization process has been the crucial feature of seasonality, a sense of keeping pace with natural cycles. For today's alternative gardener, especially those interested in heirloom vegetables or in macrobiotic dietary habits, seasonality is critical. Thus, one of my foremost objectives in selecting vegetables for this book was to choosing those that would recapture this sense of seasonality and in fact push back the seasons, shortening the length of downtime for the garden between December and March. It is very surprising what can be accomplished without the aid of cold frames, or with a little salt hay and foresight. Another consideration has been garden size.

The implication of the French term *jardin potager* is that this is a garden from which one gathers ingredients for soups or stews, as opposed to an open field with large-scale crops. Historically, the American kitchen garden has encompassed a somewhat broader range of vegetables than its European counterparts, mainly because we prefer to grow corn and squash, even though these are usually treated as field crops. Corn and many types of large squash were grown in small fields away from the house, so that there were essentially two types of household gardens supplying the kitchen. Old wills often mention these corn or potato patches, especially in regions of the country where such small fields provided subsistence crops for the farmer and his family.

The corn patch, if this is an appropriate name for the auxiliary kitchen garden, was a cultural add-on to the purely European *jardin potager* because it was a remade version of the old native American cornfield. Pole beans could be trained up the corn; pumpkins and groundcherries were allowed to run rampant over the ground. Some gardeners of heirloom vegetables still enjoy gardening according to this ancient system, since it allows for low maintenance and a number of crops can be raised on the same plot of ground simultaneously. Space, unfortunately, is a problem for most gardeners. I suspect that eight out of ten of my readers live in suburbia on small lots. Therefore, my initial reaction is always to leave out the corn and large squash because they require too much room, and seed-saving techniques for both of these vegetables can be tricky.

The same may be argued against potatoes, soybeans, chickpeas, fava beans, lentils, and a host of other foods that were originally raised as field crops. Today, many gardeners who enjoy heirloom vegetables sometimes plant a row or two of these field crops just for the pleasure of growing and harvesting them themselves. This is particularly true of corn, since Americans (unlike other cultures) like to eat it on the cob, and corn must be picked fresh for the best results. Actually, sweet corn tastes best when it is raw; cooking it destroys some of the flavor.

Out of deference to the corn and pumpkin lovers, I have included a number of heirloom varieties that I have found to work well in small spaces. Not surprising, four of my corn selections are pure Native American varieties. My choices have been influenced by growing conditions in southeastern Pennsylvania, for corn is highly sensitive to climate. Some varieties do better in the South, others in the North. The corns I have chosen more or less strike a middle ground. Otherwise, I have omitted field crops altogether, choosing to concentrate on those vegetables that do indeed belong to the classic *jardin potager.*

All the vegetables in this book are arranged into categories for convenient reference in more or less alphabetical order. Any system of organization has inherent problems unless arranged scientifically by order, genus, and species. Yet this book is written for the average gardener, and I think it would seem strange to most people to lump melons, cucumbers, and squash together, even though they are all cucurbits, but of different species. I am aware of the imperfections of this system and have tried to explain the various botanical relationships as simply as possible without using technical language. I have relied on *Hortus Third* in spite of its many imperfections. The most glaring deficiency is that it is strongly Anglophile and focuses heavily on flowers. It amazed me to discover that while essentially two paragraphs were devoted to beets, several pages were devoted to begonias. Some American vegetables are not even in it, nor are some of the most important vegetable breeders of the nineteenth century, unless they also happened to have promoted flowers. To use Victor Hugo's apt metaphor, *Hortus Third* is like a lettuce blasted to immense size by a thunderbolt. But it is still lettuce.

It will become evident in the course of reading this book that there is a confusing lack of uniformity in scientific nomenclature and in horticultural names applied to garden vegetables. In reading garden literature, it is often difficult to know which variety is being discussed because there is no worldwide cataloging system that establishes a standard. It is my hope that someday there will be a global numbering system for plants and vegetables similar to the ISBN numbers for books. This would enable gardeners everywhere to know precisely which plant was under discussion regardless of its name in any given language; Latin nomenclature, used since the Renaissance, is miserably inadequate and not as precise as many laymen assume. Until a better system is devised, I would prefer to use the Seed Savers Exchange accession numbers; these at least provide a code that leads directly to a specific variety. Unfortunately, even the Seed Savers system is plagued with duplications that must be weeded out. Thus, for the present, we are without a truly accurate reference tool, a problem also inherent in the U.S. Department of Agriculture seed collections. I have referred to USDA or to Seed Savers accession numbers only where a specific strain is being discussed.

Nomenclature aside, I am most keenly interested in documenting old vegetable varieties, since they are a form of material culture and thus reflect our social history. I am not happy with the state of our knowledge about many of the heirlooms we grow, and I have tried to correct this by adding material from my own research where I thought it reliable. Unfortunately, there are many holes in history, and it is going to take a team of researchers several years of ransacking old agricultural records to uncover the full stories on many varieties. I apologize for errors. I have had to rely on old materials that were themselves riddled with flawed historical information. Sometimes I simply had to make a judgment call, because dates of introduction can be highly subjective. Was a plant introduced when someone brought it from France and raised it quietly for many years, or when it was turned into commercial seed and made known to the public? Generally it is only the latter date that we know, as in the case of the Musselburgh Leek.

Such historical material is the core of this book because it provides us with a point of reference. Often there are early descriptions that are useful in determining whether the heirloom we are preserving is actually growing true to type. My material on the heirloom peas should be useful in this respect. Such documentation also provides a link between the many related varieties, giving us an understanding of how one gave rise to the next. This is vital for creating genetic histories. It also provides a glimpse into the factors that motivated plant breeders: why, for example, the Garnet Chile Potato was used to create Early Rose, which in turn gave rise to Early Ohio. Many heirlooms lose their shrinelike purity when we come to realize that in the first place they were created solely for profit.

I have added recipes to many of my discussions, with the intent not of expanding this into a cookbook but of reaching into the past to illustrate how some of the vegetables were used. The recipes are meant to be read as documentary evidence, but I think many of them contain enough information that some experimental cooks will have no trouble approximating them should they so desire. I would hasten to point out that the style of recipe writing in the past was much different from that of today. In traditional societies where individuals began to learn old ways at an early age, there was less of a need to commit many things to print, and recipes in particular reflect this. Most of them were written more as structural outlines than as blueprints for a specific dish. I mention this only to point out that the recipes should be read both for what they include and for what they presumed was common knowledge at the time. Naturally, recipes assume that one must be able to read, but it is not necessary to be literate in order to be a good cook—or a good gardener, for that matter. Amelia Simmons, whom I cite often in this book, was "author" of

American Cookery in 1796. Actually she dictated the book from memory, because she could not read or write. In her own way, she lived very well because she was a woman who understood food, that special breed of cook who took up cookery in the vegetable garden.

Artichokes and Cardoons

"It is good for man to eat thistles, and to remember that he is an ass. But the artichoke is the best of thistles, and the man who enjoys it has the satisfaction of feeling that he is an ass of taste." *Kettner's Book of the Table* (1877, 42) could not have put it more succinctly, for the artichoke is indeed a noble weed, an epicure's morsel, and alas, a nutritional empty box. Yet the greatest agony of the artichoke is not its thorniness—which it has in abundance—but that it inflicts upon the palate the desire to eat many, and not one is a match for wine. There is no more effective way to assassinate a great wine than to serve it with artichokes. While the Jerusalem artichoke may slide down the gullet on a silken Vaucluse and later take its revenge in the gut, the artichoke takes its revenge in the mouth, for its chemistry deadens the palate, turning great wines to must. I cannot claim that artichokes are easy to grow, not in most parts of the United States at least, and I cannot say that they are particularly productive, for one good bud per plant is about all one can expect. Yet we grow them. We pamper them. And they reward us now and then with a meal.

Fearing Burr listed fourteen varieties of artichokes and thirteen varieties of cardoons in his *Field and Garden Vegetables of America* (1865, 139–43). It was a good thing he could read French; he pinched that list from the 1856 edition of the Vilmorin *Description des plantes potagères.* A glance through Shaker seed lists of the period will reveal few references to artichokes, a more honest gauge of what middle America was actually growing as opposed to a wish list of horticultural exotics. John Russell, owner of the New England Farmer Seed Store in Boston, listed only the Green Globe in 1828, but this was without question a superior variety. Alexander Watson, in his *American Home Garden* (1859, 114–15) was a little more practical than Fearing Burr, for he listed only two varieties, a purple artichoke and a green one. These were the heirlooms that Americans knew; indeed, the green one had been cultivated here since the late 1600s, but only in the gardens of the gentry.

Globe Artichoke
Cynara scolymus
Of all the heirloom varieties, the globe artichoke is by far the easiest to cultivate and the one variety that appears most often in our old garden books. In an article entitled "Tried Varieties of Vegetables" in the *American Garden* (1889, 10:57), it was the globe artichoke that was recommended most highly for its consistency. For this reason I put it above the others, and as I grow it myself, I

can verify that it will submit to far more abuse than more tender sorts, particularly the purple Sicilian, a showstopping purple-headed variety that I also cultivate. Admittedly, the showy purple Sicilian is also a challenge and would not be possible without the benefit of a greenhouse.

Robert Buist's *Family Kitchen Gardener* (1847, 19–20) explained the differences between the two historical varieties, the globe artichoke and the green artichoke. The first had a purplish tint to its head, which was round or ball-like. The scales (bracts) of this variety turned in at the top. It was preferred both for its more abundant edible parts and for its flavor. Today, it is no longer one distinct variety but represents a whole group of subvarieties that have been developed from it. For example, the strain that I grow is known in France as Grande Beurre. The green artichoke, known in the seventeenth and eighteenth centuries as the French artichoke, possessed open scales and was far more prolific in producing buds. It was also hardier and thus better adapted to cultivation in cold climates. It was this latter variety, with a "perfumed taste," that was raised by William Penn at Pennsbury in the late 1600s and by other colonial American gentry.

The green globe artichoke, often available in seed shops today, is a nineteenth-century cross of the two earlier types, the object being to combine the benefits of both. I do not think that the hardiness is any more improved over the old green variety, but then, I am not raising artichokes in a climate that they particularly like; as Robert Buist has pointed out, north of Virginia artichokes require a good deal of protection if they are left in the open ground over the winter. If the root freezes, the plant dies. I have mulched my plants heavily, only to lose them in January. I now resort to raising them in pots, which are moved to my greenhouse once the weather turns cold. However, it is also possible to dig up the roots after frost and store them over the winter like dahlia tubers. This technique might work for gardeners in New England.

Green Globe Artichoke

Artichoke seed should be started indoors in the early spring and the seedlings transplanted to pots, then moved to the garden after all threat of frost has passed. The plants should be set out on hills four feet apart with one or two plants per hill. The artichoke produces huge silvery gray leaves that are quite striking as garden ornaments in their own right, but they cannot be crowded. Artichokes need good air circulation during humid weather, otherwise they will develop mildews, molds, and other fungus diseases.

Do not expect an artichoke crop the first year, for it is usually the second-year plants that begin to produce. They will yield crops for five to seven years, but regardless, new beds should be started every year. When the plants send up flower heads, only one or two buds should be left on the stem in order to increase their size. These are harvested right before the flower head opens to bloom. Artichokes that bloom will produce seed, but the seed is not usually true. Not only do artichoke varieties cross with one another, artichokes also cross with cardoons. It is therefore common practice to propagate the plants from suckers, choosing the best that appear over the course of the growing season.

The center of artichoke culture in the United States is now California, and many heirloom varieties from France and Italy are being grown there. In the mild climate of that region, artichokes will go to seed and become an invasive weed extremely difficult to eradicate. In areas of the country where it is impossible to raise artichokes, I suggest using the green, unopened flower heads of the sunflower. Sunflower buds can be cooked like artichokes, and they have a delightful nutty flavor. Furthermore, they can be used in the following recipe instead of artichoke hearts.

Regarding the other ingredients, the Victorian penchant for butter can be scaled back to a few tablespoons (I suggest 4) and replaced with olive oil. Instead of the truffles and morels, a few chopped fresh figs and some minced fennel may appeal to palates terrified of costly ingredients. Beyond that, I need only mention that the recipe comes from an admirable source: George Augustus Sala's *Thorough Good Cook* (1895, 37).

Artichoke Pie

❦

Boil twelve artichokes, break off the chokes and leaves and take the bottoms clear from the stalks; line the dish with puff-paste, and lay on this four ounces of fresh butter. Place a row of artichokes; strew over them pepper, salt, and beaten mace; then another layer of artichokes; strew on more spice and a quarter of a pound of butter cut in small pieces. Boil half an ounce of truffles and morels, chopped small, in a quarter of a pint of water, and pour into the pie, with a gill of white wine. Cover your pie and bake.

Cardoon
Cynara cardunculus

The cardoon is a much hardier plant than the artichoke and makes an extraordinary ornament in the garden even when it is not being grown for culinary purposes. The leaves of the plant are not easy to miss, for they grow anywhere from four to six feet tall. In the early nineteenth century, the French raised cardoons in large quantities in Provence, at Tours, and in the region around Montpelier. The French Quakers, who were Philadelphia's link to Montpelier, brought the cultivation of the cardoon to this country early in the 1790s. Many varieties were grown in the city to serve this influential community with names like Bouvier, Girard, and Grellet. Some of the varieties grown were the common, the Spanish, the red, and the prickly variety known as Cardon de Tours. All of these old varieties were used in soups, in stews, and even in salads. Outside of Philadelphia, cardoons were generally raised only by Francophiles like Thomas Jefferson, or by kitchen gardeners farther south in Charleston, Atlanta, and particularly in Louisiana. Of the old varieties, I recommend the Spanish and the *cardon de Tours.* The Tours variety is very small and therefore does well in small gardens, not to mention that it is several light years ahead of its competitors when it comes to taste. The Spanish cardoon, or *cardo común,* grown in this country since the eighteenth century, is much less thorny. The wild card is the red-stemmed *cardon à côtes rouges,* which in visual effect is probably the most striking on a dish.

Cardon de Tours

The cardoon was not a creature of English cookery, as Andrew Mathews pointed out in his discussion of the vegetable (1828, 46–47); thus it would hardly follow that colonials could spread an enthusiasm for it into far-flung places. Mathews was convinced that it was not cultivated among the English because it required "skill in cooking." He evidently knew nothing of good English cooks or of the Bible Christians, a vegetarian sect that emigrated from Manchester and established its headquarters in Philadelphia in 1816. Allowing no form of animal protein and no animal manures, this sect became a strong force in the cultivation of unusual vegetables and one of the organizing forces behind the American Vegetarian Society. In defense of the John Bull cook, I think frankly that the skill is in the growing, for unlike artichokes, cardoons may be treated as annuals, and where the winter is mild, they can provide a good crop from November through February. The trick is to tie each plant up into a bundle with string, then scatter salt hay over them, and finally earth up the ground so that the hay forms an envelope that blanches the cardoons for at least one month. Then they are ready to harvest.

Philadelphia seedsman Bernard M'Mahon described how to grow the plants in his *American Gardener's Calendar* (1806, 197):

> The stalks of the leaves being thick, fleshy, and crisp, are the eatable parts, being first blanched by landing them up like celery, to two or three feet high, to render them

white, tender, and of an agreeable flavor, which otherwise would be rank and bitter: they are in perfection in autumn and winter.

Sow the seeds towards the latter end of this month [March], or beginning of next, broadcast in a bed of rich earth, and cover them about three quarters of an inch deep, when the plants are three inches high thin them to four or five inches distance, that they may not be drawn up weak; keep them free from weeds, and towards the latter end of May or beginning of June, they will be fit to plant where they are intended to remain for perfection.

I find that they are best thinned and planted in a ditch in sandy soil 8 to 10 inches apart. The plants can then be hilled up in the fall and harvested about a month later. Cold weather will halt their growth; therefore as long as the plants can be kept from freezing, the blanched hearts will remain fit for the table. A thick layer of salt hay thrown over the hills in November usually preserves them into January in my garden. I prefer the shoots poached and served cold as a salad. But beware: the chemistry of cardoons is no different from that of the artichoke. A fine dish of cardoons will not make a fine wine dazzle. Better to serve beer.

The culture of the cardoon is the same as for the artichoke, except that the method of planting is different. Cardoons will cross with artichokes, and therefore must be isolated or caged if the seed is to be used for propagation. The flower resembles a common thistle and therefore can be gathered when the seed is dry and ready to "blow" (float off in the wind). However, the dry flower heads, picked immature and dried in the shade, can be used to curdle milk. This is a valuable alternative for making cheese without rennet, a point of special interest to vegetarians. In fact, several traditional cheeses from the Montpelier region were made exclusively with cardoon flowers rather than with rennet, and this was thought to have had an important influence on their flavor.

Asparagus

The ancient Greeks cultivated asparagus, but this was the species *Asparagus acutifolius*, not the one that we raise today. The Romans evidently were the first to take *Asparagus officinalis* (our culinary asparagus) in from the wild and develop it into cultivated forms. Asparagus was one of their most favored vegetables, valued as much for its culinary merits as for its medical properties. The ancient Roman belief that asparagus strengthens the sexual organs persists even to this day. I am tempted to attribute this more to the shape of the vegetable than to its chemical action, which results in odoriferous urine, hardly romantic.

Judging from illustrations in old herbals, the asparagus of the past was rather gawkish, tall and narrow, very similar in appearance to wild asparagus. The fat-stemmed types with which we are more familiar evolved in the eighteenth century. Yet for all the claims about their relative merits, there were only two basic types: green and white, based on the color of the spears. Joseph Cooper's Pale Green Asparagus, so famous in colonial America, was a white-stemmed variety. The old dark green varieties were often tinged with red or violet on the bud end. It is out of these that the modern purple-stemmed varieties have been developed.

Raising heirloom asparagus is almost as tricky as raising heirloom potatoes because the old varieties are often highly susceptible to diseases as well as to root-boring insects. Some of the turn-of-the-century American varieties like Barr's Mammoth and Palmetto are still extant, the latter an especially flavorful green-stemmed variety cultivated in the South. Unfortunately, they are difficult to come by, whereas the most

Barr's Mammoth Asparagus

popular of the nineteenth-century American varieties, Conover's Colossal, is readily available in seed from Bountiful Gardens in Willits, California. Since seed is the cheapest and safest way to propagate disease-free plants, I heartily recommend Conover's Colossal for beginners, but with certain qualifications.

Raising asparagus seed requires patience; three to four years must pass before the plants are mature enough to produce harvests. To begin cutting them any sooner would only destroy them. Furthermore, with seed, there is no telling which produce male or female plants until they grow and bloom. The universal rule with asparagus is to cultivate the males because they are more productive and last longer. Therefore, when growing from seed, always overplant in anticipation of roguing out the females and replacing them with males. This brutishness in the asparagus bed is unfortunately a fact of life because properly maintained, the males will produce for at least twenty years. Do not count on the females to last half as long.

I grow Conover's Colossal as my heirloom asparagus. As a backup against crop failure, I also cultivate Jersey King, a disease-resistant variety developed by Rutgers University, as well as Purple Passion (also marketed as Passionate Purple), a striking new variety that has such a high sugar content that it can be eaten raw. This last variety is really a "half-heirloom," since the parent that gave it its unique color was an heirloom asparagus discovered in an abandoned garden in a remote valley of southern Switzerland. In any case, these three varieties come on at slightly different times and provide a delightful variation of color at table. Because of the diseases that can strike asparagus unexpectedly, I do not think it wise to grow only one variety; a mix is far more prudent, although they should be grown at a considerable distance from one another.

Conover's Colossal Asparagus
Asparagus officinalis

J. M. Thorburn & Company of New York introduced this variety in 1868. Yet it was not until Peter Henderson wrote an extensive article about this new asparagus in the January 1870 issue of the *American Agriculturist* that growers were finally convinced of its merits. The perennial problem was that mammoth varieties of asparagus appeared from time to time only in the end to cause disappointment, and very few people in the 1860s were willing to believe that the vegetable could be improved. Peter Henderson admitted his own skepticism until he saw the asparagus firsthand, and his glowing testimonial doubtless gave Conover's Colossal the boost it needed. Soon thereafter, it became one of the most popular American asparagus varieties of the nineteenth century.

Distinctive for its fat, one-and-a-half-inch-thick stumpy stems, as shown in the old woodcut, this variety was developed by S. B. Conover, a produce commission merchant in New York's old West Washington Market. This is the same S. B. Conover who introduced the Early Mohawk potato, a cross between Peach Blow and Buckeye.

Conover's Colossal Asparagus

Conover created his new asparagus from an unnamed European variety introduced in 1863. He selected seeds over a period of years with an eye for size, and his asparagus evolved into a unique variety. His experiments were undertaken in the fields of Abraham Van Siclen of Jamaica, Queens. At the time, Van Siclen was well known for his vegetables, especially for his Oyster Bay Asparagus, a variety then popular with New Yorkers.

Peter Henderson went out to Jamaica to inspect Van Siclen's asparagus side by side with Conover's and judged Conover's superior not only for its stem size but also because each root produced anywhere from fifteen to forty sprouts. That kind of productivity would impress any market gardener for its profitability. Yet while Conover had a talent for breeding new varieties, Van Siclen, his partner in this deal, was the true key to success because he developed a method for raising asparagus that has been recommended ever since. It is a guaranteed way to ensure that asparagus beds will last a lifetime. For this reason it is worth repeating here, but with two provisos.

First, the fresh country air in Jamaica, New York, of the 1860s was salty from the ocean and from Long Island Sound. A salty mist pervaded the fields on many early mornings. Salt acts as a fertilizer on asparagus when applied in small quantities. Therefore, inland asparagus beds should be dressed once a year with a light scattering of fine rock salt to compensate for this deficiency.

Second, Van Siclen's subsoil was very sandy, and this drainage helps prevent root rot and other problems that often develop in asparagus crowns. Wild asparagus prefers to grow on stony but well-drained ground. Add coarse sand with a large percentage of small round pebbles to the soil where the asparagus bed is to be laid out. This will create a soil texture that asparagus prefers, and the pebbles will help retain cool ground temperatures in the summer, a feature that helps discourage wilt.

Van Siclen's method was designed for field culture but can be adapted to small gardens. It is the intensive soil preparation that is important. He dug rows 6 feet apart and spaced his plants 4 feet from one another. (In a small garden this spacing may be cut in half.) The ground was tilled to a depth of 1 foot and then cut into furrows 1 foot deep. These were filled 3 inches deep with well-rotted manure, then covered with a thin layer of topsoil. The plants were set on top of this with the crowns some 7 to 8 inches below the surface. They were then covered with 3 inches of soil. Once they began to grow, the plants were covered again to bring the soil level to the surface. Planted deep like this, the asparagus only requires fertilization once a year. This initial care in laying out an asparagus bed will ensure an abundant crop in the years to come, but the plants must not be cut the first or second season, since this weakens them. In heavy soils, where there is a great deal of clay, the crowns should not be planted as deep, even if sand is added.

When growing asparagus from seed, the procedure is slightly different. Prepare the soil the same way, but fill the furrows so that they are level with the ground. Plant the seed directly on this prepared earth as soon as the soil is dry enough to work in the spring, then pat it down to press the seed into the soil surface. Seedlings must be kept weeded thoroughly, since they are weak until well established. When they are about 10 inches tall, thin them to 12 inches apart. In the fall, cut the dead foliage off at the ground, but not before it has been killed by frost. Cover the young crowns with about 3 inches of rotted manure or mulch. Salt hay is excellent as a winter protection the first year.

Harvesting asparagus is a matter of taste and personal judgment, but of course, my recommendation is to harvest it young. A few experiments with a sharp paring knife will quickly demonstrate to the beginner when this stage has arrived. Cut neatly and cut deep. If the base of the spear feels gritty as one cuts, this is a sure sign that the stem has gotten tough and pithy. Ripe stems should cut like butter. It helps to use a sharp knife with a sickle-shaped blade. Special asparagus knifes can be found in some garden supply shops.

There are many ways to prepare asparagus, but overcooking it is by far the worst. The following historical recipe is taken from William Verrall's *Complete System of Cookery* (1759). Verrall was chef of the White Hart in Lewes, England, an inn patronized by Benjamin Franklin, who much admired Verrall's cooking. The chef's recipe reveals some interesting points about the differences between English and French modes of preparation. By "grass" he meant sparrow grass, a vernacular term for asparagus, and by *jus* or "gravy," he meant clear stock, such as chicken stock or beef stock.

Des asperges au jus clair

❦

For this, trim and scrape your grass neat and clean, set them over the fire in but little cold water and salt: the reason of this is, the French prefer crispness and yellow in asparagus and French beans, to what we are always in so much care to make green and tender; but they eat it (as they do many other vegetables) for a hot sallet; boil your grass but a little time, and serve them to table with nothing but gravy and the juice of oranges or lemons.

ASPARAGUS PEA
Psophocarpus tetragonolobus / Tetragonolobus purpureus

A legume that is neither asparagus-like nor a pea, this cheerful garden vegetable may be considered esoteric by some but is an epicurean treat to the initiated. It is so easy to grow that I wonder I do not see it in more gardens, for it will tolerate the same sort of arid, worn-out ground preferred by nasturtiums. As far as I am concerned, there is always a spot for it in my garden, if for no other reason than its profusion of bright red flowers, which the Victorians found quite pleasing. James Vick of Rochester promoted it in his seed catalog (1872, 62) as an ornamental mixed with sweet peas.

The origin of this plant, also known as the winged lotus (it is not a lotus either!), appears to be northwest Africa, but during classical antiquity it was dispersed throughout the Mediterranean. Unfortunately, the archaeological record has not yielded much on the early history of the plant or its uses, but it is mentioned in many Renaissance herbals. Philip Miller, in 1734, was one of the first garden writers to mention that the pods were edible. Bernard M'Mahon of Philadelphia sold seed in the early 1800s under the name Winged Pea, the name by which it was known in colonial America. The old Philadelphia gentry used to serve it as a garnish on fricasseed frog's legs.

The flavor of the cooked pods is highly aromatic and not akin to asparagus as its name would imply, but the pods must be harvested very young, perhaps no more than three-quarters of an inch long, otherwise they become tough and stringy. The pods retain their color when cooked and are best blanched or steamed for about 15 minutes, then added to other dishes for visual interest and texture. They can be mixed with peas, added to stir-fries, or combined with rice and whole-grain dishes.

Seeds can be started indoors in April and the seedlings thinned to small pots. They may be transplanted to the garden in May or after all threat of frost has passed. The plant is annual and comes to crop very quickly in the course of two-and-a-half months. Thus if planted in mid-

May, it will begin blooming in June and peak by July 4. Three successive plantings one month apart will ensure a crop all summer.

The plants spread laterally and close to the ground. They should be planted about 1 foot apart. Since they are low and spreading, they can be planted in front of taller vegetables or even along the top of a wall so that they drape over it. The flowers are self-pollinating and will not cross with any of the other vegetables in this book. To gather seed, let the plants produce pods and die. Gather the dry pods and take out the seed. Store in airtight containers away from direct light. Seed will remain viable for at least three years.

Beans, Lima Beans, and Runner Beans

There is probably no vegetable that evokes more loyalty from its collectors than the humble bean. The array of colors, shapes, and sizes is breathtaking, and to say that the choices for collectors is numerous would be mere understatement. Seed Savers Exchange has over 4,000 varieties in its collection, and that is not all of them. This huge diversity is the result of the very nature of the bean itself, its constant transformation from generation to generation, which results in new combinations of color and a vast array of other genetic features.

The bean in early America was not so numerous, for as we move back in time, we discover that the functional uses of the bean took priority over many characteristics we look for today. With certain pole beans, for example, it was the ease of drying the pods and their storability over the winter that took priority over tenderness when fresh. For Native Americans, who tended to categorize beans quite differently from Europeans, it was usefulness as a source of bean flour or adaptability in dumplings and hearth breads that received emphasis.

Of course, for the Native American, the bean was associated with religious ritual, and its colors held sacred meaning. It is tempting to imagine that the orange-and-maroon lima bean discussed on pages 75–76, a bean similar to one buried in the graves of the ancient peoples of Peru, moved up the continent through Mexico and into the land of the Hopi. It is equally tempting to suggest that this distant food of the Incas came to the Hopi with similar religious trappings. But in the case of beans, nature is constantly assembling and reassembling her creation in such a way that similar things often emerge in several places at the same time. Their relationship is not always direct.

The discovery of the New World bean and its many forms revolutionized world agriculture, yet for several centuries the scientific approach to this body of plants has been chaotic at best. At the very outset, Europeans began calling them *fasiolius,* the name previously used for cowpeas by the Greeks and Romans. This led to heated debates about the origin of the bean and whether or not it was from the Old World or the New. As long as Europeans thought American Indians were the Lost Tribes of Israel—an idea that survived into the nineteenth century—it was logical to conclude that their foodstuffs also originated in the Middle East.

The oldest depiction of the common garden bean in a European work is thought to be a 1543 woodcut of a bush bean in the German herbal of Leonhart Fuchs. Later in the same century, in 1553, another German herbalist by the name of Georg Oelinger made a watercolor of a red pole bean that is probably related to the variety known today as *frijoles rojos*, or Montezuma Red. While this is a bush variety, it can also appear as a pole bean. One of the important lessons in understanding beans and their evolution is to discard the myth that pole beans and bush beans represent different species. Botanically speaking, the two are only extreme forms of the same thing. For every red pole bean there is—or can be—a corresponding bush form, not to mention a number of intermediate types. All of the common garden beans, regardless of shape, color, or size, belong to the same species and therefore will readily cross with one another when conditions are right. Scientists have designated the genus into which our garden beans are now grouped as *Phaseolus*, the species being *vulgaris*. Lima and runner beans represent separate species and are therefore treated separately in sketches following this one.

There have been various attempts since the eighteenth century to organize beans scientifically and provide them with logical nomenclature. It has not worked. Horticulturists still rely on rather unscientific ways to define beans. A pole bean is obviously one that climbs, but it can also be a "snap" bean (eaten as a green pod), a "shelly" bean (the green seeds are cooked like fresh peas), or a "dry" bean, its dry seeds soaked and prepared in recipes like Boston baked beans—a recipe, incidentally, originally prepared by the English with field peas or with horse beans (page 95). Beans are also further categorized by pod type. Wax beans are any sort with pods that ripen yellow. This yellowness has been tinkered with by breeders to create a whole group of beans that are so tender they can be eaten raw.

Beans eaten in pod form are also called string beans because years ago it was necessary to remove the tough string that acts like a zipper where the two halves of the pod come together. Strings are tough, and chewing does not break them down in the mouth. Many beans today lack strings, which have been selectively bred out of the plants. There is probably no name that stands out more significantly in the history and development of American stringless beans than that of Calvin N. Keeney (1849–1930).

Keeney established a seed company at LeRoy, New York, as an outgrowth of his interest in snap beans. By examining beans in the field, he was able to identify plants with stringless traits. Through careful selection and breeding, he became the leading producer of high-quality stringless beans, beginning with Keeney's Stringless Refugee Wax in 1884. Keeney also developed many varieties that were sold by other seed companies, the best known being Burpee's Stringless Green Pod, introduced in 1894. According to Robert F. Becker (1994, 8–9), former professor of horticultural sciences at Cornell University, most of the stringless bean varieties that we know today owe their origin to Keeney's work. Therefore, when I acquire an old bean variety said to have been cultivated by the Indians for centuries, one of the first things I test it for is whether or not the pods have strings. If it is a stringless variety, then it came from the Keeney tribe, to be sure. Native Americans prior to contact with Europeans did not eat snap beans the way we do. They boiled the pods at the shelly stage and pulled the beans between their teeth, discarding the pods. To them strings were not an issue.

Another native American trait in old bean varieties is the runner that appears on bush beans. There is an extremely attractive bush bean called the Pawnee bush bean that has white seed with brown speckles. The bushes are neat (no runners), the pods hang straight down in uniform clusters, and the pods themselves are identical in size and shape to several Bush Beans developed in Central Europe during the nineteenth century. This is not an old Indian bean. White man has tinkered with it. A true bush bean of pre-Columbian type will send out a runner, perhaps as long as 3 feet. This weedy appearance also involves a tangle by summer's end, but that is the way old bush types grew. Most likely, Indian women trained them around the base of sunflowers or some other convenient large-stemmed crop so that the runner had something to wrap around. I use small bamboo sticks. Dead brambles or tree branches can be used if authenticity is demanded.

The great bean book of the nineteenth century is Georg von Martens's *Die Gartenbohnen* (second edition, 1869). It contains thirteen plates of beans in color so that it is possible to take an unknown bean and, as if on a Ouija board, push it around until it matches up with the right picture. This method is not fail-safe, but it works as a starter. The hitch comes in the descriptions; some beans may have identical seeds, yet the flowers can be a different color, the leaves and vines of a different size, indeed, the pod color could be quite another thing. My White Ice Bunch Bean and my Ice Bean share similar names and have identical seed, but the varieties are distinct, for the Ice Bean develops a purple-blue pod, while the other is a wax bean.

Dr. von Martens was the original bean counter, and I visualize him up at all hours of the night studying his beans under a reading glass. He attempted to organize the beans scientifically by shape, which is not a good idea because there are a great many beans with intermediate shapes. But since von Martens's system was used by subsequent authors, his classifications appear everywhere. He used the term "zebra bean" for the pinto types with a large stripe down the sides; he used the term *Eckbohne* for cutshorts, pea-sized beans with a rhomboid shape. He had "egg" beans and "date" beans and "pellet" beans, and a host of other categories that probably lend more confusion to the discussion than order. Nonetheless, his scholarship was meticulous and his categories colorful, and once the reader is able to get past his idiosyncratic science, his bean descriptions are still without equal. Even the venerable *Beans of New York* (Hedrick, 1931), a bean bible with many flaws, relied heavily on von Martens for much of its underlying research. With a better grasp of German, the authors of that work might have avoided some of their faulty conclusions.

Today beans are organized scientifically according to how the seeds germinate and whether the two seed halves push above the surface or remain below it. Taxonomists are still at work on a major reordering of all the Leguminosae, the family to which beans belong, but this will not change the basic day-to-day reality of kitchen gardening, which brings me to my selection of beans for this book.

There are so many beans to choose from that no matter which ones I pick, there will always be omissions in someone's mind. If I were to use my own historical kitchen garden as a criterion, then John Russell's 1828 seed catalog would be a perfect guide to the heirlooms appropriate to my house. His offerings for bush beans included Early Yellow Cranberry, Early Mohawk, Early Yellow Six Weeks (a wax bean), and Early China. His pole beans included White Cranberry, Red Cranberry, Saba Lima (a speckled sort), and White Dutch Caseknife. Several of these beans have ultimately found their way onto my list.

But this is a book for committed beginners, and over the years, experience with certain varieties recommends them both for small gardens and for easily cultivation. Mary Ann Fox of The Bean Patch Heirloom Seeds in Shelbyville, Indiana, has provided me with valuable advice. She raises hundreds of beans in large quantities for the market, and her sensibilities are different from mine (I tend rather toward the exotic). Mary Ann is also a member of Seed Savers Exchange, so her beans are drawn from that large seed pool of heirlooms. Most important, however, she likes beans for the way they cook. She particularly likes beans such as Magpie (also known as Superlative), Pawnee bush, and the red speckled Hungarian bean called Piros-Feher because these beans keep their color patterns after they are cooked (most beans do not). Some of her favorites are on my list, but not exclusively. She likes Black Valentine, but it is the Red Valentine that tells the story.

Magpie or Superlative Bean

Ease of cultivation, of course, is another point. I seem to prefer pole varieties because they are vertical and thus take up less space. They can be trained to grow on corn or sunflowers, and when grown in such a combination, they also help fix nutrients in the soil as well as certain fungus growths on the roots of corn that protect the corn from disease. I start all of my beans in the greenhouse so that the plants are a good foot tall before they are planted. June 3 is the historical Bean Day of the Pennsylvania Dutch, the time when the first bean crop was traditionally put in the ground. This date also happens to be perfect for the climate where I live. The best plan is to learn what seasonal cycles are typical for the locality in which one gardens, using state or county climate maps, not the oversimplified USDA maps published for the whole continent.

For bush beans, logic dictates that they be spaced a foot apart. I waste no seed to rot, cutworms, or crows since I start the beans in pots, and spacing is much easier when the actual plants are visible rather than imagined. It does not set the plants back to be transplanted in this way as long as the root ball is ample and not disturbed in the process. In any event, by forcing my beans, I have a three-week lead on most gardeners in my area, and I can also plant more varieties in succession over the course of the summer.

Beans are self-pollinating but will be crossed by bees that force their way into unopened blossoms—bean flowers shed pollen before they open. Cross-pollination is dependent on a range of factors; thus, in one garden it may occur often, in another not at all. If flowers desirable to bees are planted near beans, bees will go there first. I always have many flowers near my beans in order to reduce the probability of crossing. As double insurance against possible crosses, never plant two bean varieties of the same seed color in proximity. If a red bean crosses with a white one, the cross will be visible in the seed, not so with two black beans. Best of all, keep different bean varieties at least twenty feet apart. Beans for seed purposes should be dried on the plants and selected from plants displaying the best characteristics of that variety. I choose the most perfect-looking seeds as well, a technique also used by the Indians. Seed beans properly stored will remain viable for four to five years.

Amish Nuttle Bean
Phaseolus vulgaris

This is an old cutshort variety with two divergent histories. On the one hand, it was preserved among the Amish farmers of southeastern Pennsylvania under the name *Gnuddelbuhn*, which translates as a bean resembling a dropping (the literal translation of *Gnuddel* is "turd"). If it is this shape that provided the origin of the folk name, then indeed the bean does have the general appearance of rabbit droppings. Such is Amish humor. The Amish use the dry bean for rich stewy soups and similar dishes traditionally served at their Sunday gatherings; thus the beans fills an important culinary niche in their culture. But the bean also has an alternate history that is not connected with the Amish.

As early as 1802 Bernard M'Mahon of Philadelphia was selling this bean as the Corn Hill Bean. Other seedsmen are known to have listed it as the Corn Hill Pole Bean and Cornfield Pole Bean, sometimes even as the Red Cutshort, although it does not resemble the true red cutshort (SSE BN 1095) of the South. One of the distributors of this bean in the Upper

Amish Nuttle Bean

South was the seed firm of J. Bolgiano & Sons of Baltimore, which offered it for sale during the 1840s. The names connecting the bean with corn culture came from the Seneca and other Iroquois peoples. The Seneca of Oklahoma referred to it as the Corn Hill Bean, and it was so listed in F. W. Waugh's study *Iroquois Food and Food Preparation* (1916, 225). Seneca informants considered it one of their oldest bean varieties.

True to its old name, the bean is ideal for corn hills, especially for the shorter varieties of corn that are about 5 to 6 feet tall. It is also a late-season bean, requiring 90 days to ripen on the vine—early September for Pennsylvania. The flower is white and the pods bumpy and short, which is typical of cutshorts. The pods range in length from 3 to 4 inches, with 4 to 5 seeds per pod—very prolific by any measure. The dry bean is drab purple-gray, marked with garnet speckles. The helium is reddish brown.

Blue Coco Bean
Phaseolus vulgaris

Also known in this country as Purple Pod and Blue Podded Pole, the Blue Coco bean is one of the oldest of the purple-podded pole bean varieties still under cultivation. It was known in France as early as 1775, and throughout the latter part of the eighteenth century it proved quite popular with American gardeners. By itself it is quite distinctive, and was shown attractively displayed in the *Album Vilmorin* (1870, 21). But when grown side by side with other purple-podded varieties, it is easily confused with them because many of the differences are slight. In any case, the other varieties are thought to have evolved out of Blue Coco. Therefore is it unwise to grow Blue Coco in the same garden with other purple-podded beans, since crossing may go undetected. In particular, do not grow it in the vicinity of the Lucas Bean, which it closely resembles.

Blue Coco has the advantage of hardiness and productive vines a good 8 to 9 feet in length. It is short season (about 60 days), more resistant to bean beetles than green-podded varieties, and survives dry weather better than many pole beans. It is also ornamental due to its rose-pink flowers, leaves tinged with purple, and of course its long purple-blue pods. The beans are harvested young as snap beans; their color disappears during cooking. The mature pods are thick and rather flat, and normally measure from 6 to 8 inches long. The ripe seed is chocolate colored, although the brown will vary due to soil and latitude. The dry bean can also be used in cookery. It has a rich, meaty texture.

Blue Shackamaxon Bean
Phaseolus vulgaris

This old variety of pole bean was preserved among the Quaker farmers of southeastern Pennsylvania and South Jersey. It is said to be a Lenape bean dating from before 1800. Seeds were preserved by Samuel Miller, a seedsman of Mechanicsville (Bucks County), Pennsylvania. During a 1906 boat trip up the Delaware River to the site of Pennsbury Manor organized by the Friends Historical Association, several individuals received samples of Miller's seed from Mahlon Moon, a local history buff who believed that the beans had been cultivated at the manor for many years. My seed descends from Moon's distribution. The name Shackamaxon refers to a place along the Delaware River in the present-day Kensington section of Philadelphia. The bean was never grown commercially and therefore never appeared in general literature on American bean varieties.

The blue bean of von Martens (1869, 27) shared some physical characteristics with Blue Shackamaxon, but no history was provided. It is possible that his bean was an Old World cultivated strain of its New World counterpart. The oldest strains of Blue Shackamaxon (color plate 7) were grown by Pennsylvania farmers more as curiosities than as table vegetables. For this reason, the bean never underwent concerted breeding improvements.

The vines reach 6 to 7 feet with rose-pink flowers. It is easy to visualize this bean twining up the towering stalks of Puhwem Corn (page 146), the garnet-red bean pods a striking contrast to the reddish silks of the corn. The Blue Shackamaxon shelly bean is bright navy blue, the mature cutshort is blue-black. When the pods dry, they turn a purple-blue color similar to that of Blue Pod Capucijner peas (page 241).

Oral history relates that Blue Shackamaxon was cooked in "black mush," a type of early American polenta made with blue or black cornmeal. Among the Lenape peoples, the bean probably had a ceremonial purpose, since its color closely resembles the clamshell beads used by the Lenape for wampum.

The dry bean can be used in any recipe calling for Mexican-style black beans. The shelly bean is a natural match for blue corn succotash made with Sehsapsing (page 146) or some similar blue corn.

Brown Lazy Wife Bean
Phaseolus vulgaris

Not a true Lazy Wife, this pole bean is the *P. vulgaris badius S.* of von Martens (1869, 29). It was known in southern Germany and among the Pennsylvania Dutch as the *Linsenbohne*, or lentil bean, since it resembles a brown lentil in shape and color. In fact, the color is normally described as chestnut. It was used as a soup bean throughout the poorer agricultural regions of Germany, Switzerland, and northern Italy. In this country, it was commonly grown in the hill regions of western Pennsylvania, Maryland, West Virginia, and Ohio, the region from which it may originate.

The true origin of the bean is unknown, but it is believed to have been taken from Pennsylvania to Switzerland about 1705 by David Bondeli, a land agent who helped organize the 1710 Swiss Mennonite emigration to America. From Switzerland, the bean spread throughout the alpine regions of Europe. In colonial Pennsylvania the bean was sometimes used in conjunction with chinquapin flour to make dumplings, flat hearth beads, and soups. It was also combined with lentils and was one of the beans used in the vegetarian dishes of Ephrata Cloister during the early part of the eighteenth century.

The flower of the bean opens pale yellow, then fades to white. The vines are about 8 feet long and produce curved pods 3 to 4 inches in length. The dry bean ripens in 80 to 90 days. The vines will tolerate some shade and therefore can be grown on corn. Today, the bean is raised as a snap bean, but it is best as a dry bean, for it has a rich, lentil-like flavor.

Beurre de Rocquencourt Bean
Phaseolus vulgaris

There are not many bush beans that can be described as elegant, but this French heirloom bean certainly qualifies. It was developed out of the old black-seeded Algerian Butter Bean, once so popular in early nineteenth century France. When the plant is full of golden yellow pods, it is truly an ornament to the kitchen garden. It forms a compact bush about 1½ feet tall laden with 6-inch-long narrow beans. Each pod produces 7 black seeds. The pods ripen in 55 to 60 days but may be harvested much younger. A mature plant, with the leaves stripped away to expose the beans, is shown in color plate 3.

Caseknife Bean
Phaseolus vulgaris

Developed in Italy during the seventeenth century, this bean is one of the oldest documented pole beans cultivated in American kitchen gardens. Its name refers to the broad, slightly curving table knives once in use in the late seventeenth and early eighteenth centuries. It has a similar commercial name, *Schwertbohne*, in Germany, literally meaning "sword bean." Yet the bean also went by a number of vernacular names, the most common in this country being the Clapboard Bean. It appeared under this name in Amelia Simmons's *American Cookery* (1796, 14).

The oldest strain of caseknife is white-seeded, although many subvarieties were developed in the nineteenth century. One of the leading French varieties was the Soissons, introduced into this country in 1841, according to the *Magazine of Horticulture* (Hovey 1841, 134–39). There is also an old brown-seeded variety still in circulation in this country. However, the white-seeded sort is the one cultivated by Thomas Jefferson and the subject of this discussion. It was considered the best of its type by most early American horticulturists.

The vines are robust growers, reaching 8 to 9 feet, one of the characteristics of the old, original strain. The flower is white fading to yellow, yielding long, flat pods 8 to 9 inches in length with white kidney-shaped seeds. The pods make excellent snap beans when harvested about 5 inches long and a quarter-inch wide, although historically, 6½ inches was considered the proper stage, especially for drying the beans or for shredding them for pickles. At 5 inches, the pods have a rich flavor similar to butternuts and do not require stringing. The dry beans, useful in winter cookery, mature in about 75 to 80 days, the snap beans in about 60.

Historically, there were a number of dwarf or bush versions of this bean, particularly in Germany and Italy. One of the German varieties cultivated today is *Pfälzer Juni* (Palatine June), a bean that is forced, then planted outside and brought to market in mid-June with little bundles of summer savory. Another Palatine bean, and probably the closest surviving variety to the original caseknife beans of the 1600s, is the *Pelzer Schwertebuhne* (Palatine Caseknife Pole Bean) preserved by the Wendel family of Weilerbach in the Rheinland-Pfalz. I offer the Wendel heirloom through Seed Savers Exchange under its old Palatine name.

White Dutch
Caseknife Bean

Egg Bean or All-In-One Bean
Phaseolus vulgaris

In the German Rhineland there are several variant forms of this bush bean with egg-shaped seeds, most of which are mentioned by C. A. Fingerhuth in his 1835 study of the agricultural botany of the lower Rhine. The pale-yellow-seeded variety was known in France as the *haricot de Sainte Hélène*, but most of the others were simply called Canada Beans (*haricots du Canada*). The light brown variety, which is the subject of this sketch, is known in this country by several aliases, including Dutch Caseknife and Fisher Bean. It is not a true caseknife type, but it is the same as the *Eierbohn* of von Martens (1869, 63) or more commonly, the *Einbohn*, or All-in-One Bean.

The origin of this bean is presumed to be eastern North America, for it was known in its original form at least to a number of Algonquian peoples. It is thought to have been related to the Turtle Bean of the Unami-speaking Delawares, but if so, the bean has undergone considerable improvement since its transplantation to Europe, since it no longer exhibits many of the "wild" qualities of true aboriginal beans.

The Egg Bean is a variety of bush bean about 15 inches tall and quite prolific. It was cultivated among the Pennsylvania Dutch and is now offered by the Landis Valley Heirloom Seed Project as the Fisher Bean, after the family that preserved it. The flower opens yellow, then turns pink. The green seeds are used as a shelly bean when very young, but on the whole, this variety is cultivated mostly as a dry bean for soups and winter dishes. The dry bean ripens in 90 to 100 days and is tan in color, with a maroon circle around the eye. It has an excellent meaty flavor and holds its shape well when baked. In fact all of the beans of this type were great favorites with the French for cassoulets and similar preparations.

The following recipe for an Anglo-Canadian version of the ubiquitous baked bean is taken from *The Home Cook Book*, published in Toronto in 1887.

Canadian Baked Beans
❦

Boil the beans, until they begin to crack, with a pound or two of fat salt pork; put the beans in the baking-pan; score the pork across the top, and settle in the middle; add two tablespoons of sugar or molasses, and bake in a moderate oven for two hours; they should be very moist when first put into the oven, or they will grow too dry in baking. Do not forget the sweetening if you want Yankee baked beans.

Hickman Snap Bean
Phaseolus vulgaris

The name of this popular pole bean refers to the Hickman family of Draper Valley, Virginia, from whom the beans were first obtained by seed savers. The history of the bean is otherwise obscure, although it is known that the Hickmans came down from Pennsylvania in the 1730s, so the bean may have originated somewhere else. But since the bean shares traits with the Old Virginia Brown Cornfield Bean, which is said to be of Cherokee origin, it is probably an amalgam of several varieties. It is certainly one of the few heirloom beans that produces many types of beans at once, a true sign of a recent cross.

The bean is circulated among seed savers as a snap bean, for which purpose it is excellent. However, this is one of the finest dry beans of all the heirlooms now in circulation and much overlooked for this quality. The beans themselves probably contribute an interesting balance of flavors because they are a curious mix of colors and variant shapes. The colors include dark slate gray, chocolate brown, honey tan, black, and a gray white, but not all in the same pod. There are also several pod types, the largest measuring 7½ inches long with 9 beans per pod, another measuring 6½ inches long and quite narrow. Others fall between these extremes. The dry bean may be harvested in 90 days.

Some gardeners have reported that after they have grown this bean for several years, it degenerates into two bean types, one with slate gray seeds, the other with taffy brown seeds. I have also observed this, but it has not in any way compromised the quality of the dry bean when cooked. The secret to its excellent flavor, which resembles country smoked bacon when properly prepared, is sea salt used liberally.

Ice Bean or Crystal White Wax Bean
Phaseolus vulgaris

Nineteenth-century German authority on beans Georg von Martens claimed that while Dutch plant breeders had hybridized the Ice Bean, turning it into one of the most intensely bred of all bush beans, it was the English who first developed it as a forcing bean for hothouses. The French, who once used the bean extensively as a garnish in high-style food presentations, lumped it together with similar sorts under the generic name *haricot princesse*. Italian horticulturist Achille Bruni reported that several forms of this bean existed in southern Italy long before 1845; thus we are dealing with a bean of considerable horticultural interest and a convoluted genealogy.

The bean is not well known today, at least among American gardeners, probably because we were never much for cultivating beans in greenhouses. Since the bean was created for forcing, it does not always thrive in the open ground. Its pods are tough if raised outdoors in arid climates, or when they not harvested at exactly the right moment. Yet the harvests are epicurean if properly attended to, and the dainty little beans a blueblood's feast when gently poached in white wine and brought to the table in picturesque bundles tied with chives. They are visual treats because the pods are miniature, with a cool, silvery green color that looks misted or frosted—hence the bean's name. The pods retain this coloration after cooking, especially if they are steamed.

The bushes are small, with the pods close to the ground. In a greenhouse, they would be low for easier picking. However, in spite of its highly inbred character, the variety retains some very old traits, among them runners often 3 feet in length. To keep the pods off the ground, it is advisable to support each plant with a small bamboo stake. Let the runners tangle themselves around that rather than one another. Allow 45 to 60 days from planting to harvest, but plant in succession for a continuous crop until frost. The pods are 3 to 3½ inches long and at their best for harvesting for only a day. The plants must be checked every morning. Once the tenderness has left the pods, the beans can be picked for shelly beans. Nineteenth-century seedsman James Vick of Rochester, New York, recommended the Ice Bean exclusively as a shelly bean, and I do agree with him that it makes a delicious faux *petit pois* with a rich, nutty flavor. However, the dry bean is also quite useful, for it is small and white and can be cooked like barley. When the pods ripen on this variety, they begin to turn purple, a true mark that this is the correct strain of ice bean.

There are many other beans circulating under this name. One of them, the White Ice Bunch Bean, is not synonymous. Its pods ripen yellow, but otherwise the bean may be used like the Ice Bean of this sketch. In the Midwest, a bean circulated among the Germans in the nineteenth century with the name *Speckbohne*, has recently come into circulation among

Ice Bean or Crystal White Wax Bean

seed savers from a source in Klemme, Iowa. This bean is indistinguishable from the true Ice Bean.

The small beans of the Ice Bean were also used to make an excellent soup like the one given below from Lettice Bryan's *Kentucky Housewife* (1839, 21). What she actually proposes in her recipe is a soup made with bean-and-rice dumplings. By "liquor," she means soup stock.

Dried Bean Soup
🐦

Take the small white beans, which are nicest for this purpose, hull them, and parboil them in clear water till they begin to swell. Then rinse them in clean water, and boil them very tender, with a piece of salt pork; then take out the pork and beans; mash the beans to a pulp, and season it lightly with pepper; mix with it an equal portion of boiled rice, which has also been mashed fine; make it into small balls or cakes; put over the yolk of egg, slightly beaten, dust them with flour, and spread them out on a cloth to dry a little. Having seasoned the liquor with salt and pepper to your taste, put in a large lump of butter, rolled in flour, boil it up, stir in half a pint of sweet cream, and then put in the cakes or balls. Serve it up immediately, or they will dissolve, and make the soup too thick. This is a plain, inexpensive soup, but a very good one.

Indiana Wild Goose Bean
Phaseolus vulgaris

A bean of unknown origin but with extraordinary culinary merits, Indiana Wild Goose deserves better recognition. It is a vigorous pole bean with 8-foot vines and good resistance to drought. The flower is yellow fading to white, producing large, flat pods 5 to 6 inches long and ¾ inch wide. There are normally 6 beans per pod. When the beans reach the shelly stage, the pods acquire a handsome rose-pink blush. The dry seed may be harvested in 100 days. At first, the ripe bean is flesh colored, then it turns to khaki. The vines are highly productive, and the bean has a rich, nutty flavor. Best of all, the bean seems to do well in most parts of the country, for I have received good reports from members of Seed Savers Exchange in Washington State, California, Georgia, Ohio, and New Hampshire.

Lazy Wife (Hoffer's Lazy Wife) Bean
Phaseolus vulgaris

The Lazy Wife of America kitchen gardens is not the original German bean of the same name once popular throughout southwest Germany, Alsace, and Switzerland. That bean, known as the "True Lazy Wife of Swabia," is a scarlet red, pellet-shaped

Indiana Wild Goose Bean

bean identified by Georg von Martens (1869, 72) as *P. sphaericus purpureus* M. He had this to say about it: "In Stuttgart, I found these beans for sale not only from all the commercial garden suppliers as Purple Cardinal Pole Beans, Stringless Cardinal Beans, and Early Imperial Snap Beans, but also they were called by common gardeners Lazy Wife Beans (*Faule-Weiber-Bohnen*) because one need not string them before cooking." It was this stringless feature that earned the bean its colorful name. The Swabian bean and the Pennsylvania Dutch bean share only one similarity: they are both *Kugelbohnen*, a type of bean Germans likened to grapeshot owing to its shape and size. Otherwise, the bean we call Lazy Wife, and which the Pennsylvania Dutch call *Faule Fraa Buhne*, is an altogether different variety. For one thing, the bean is white.

The *Faule Fraa* of Pennsylvania was introduced into this country in the latter part of the eighteenth century under its standard German name *Sophie-Bohnen* (Sophia Bean), the *Phaseolus sphaericus albus* of von Martens and the White Cranberry discussed in the *Gardener's Chronicle* (1842, 236). Actually, these last two beans are slightly different, but they were generally treated as the same variety and often allowed to mix. The Philadelphia seed firm of William Henry Maule asserted in the 1890s that the bean originated in Bucks County, Pennsylvania. Maule's bean may have been a Bucks County selection, but the bean had been sold to local farmers as early as 1802 by Bernard M'Mahon under the name Round White Running. It was also known as the San Domingo bean. It would appear that Maule simply rediscovered a common old German variety and created a new name for it.

The bean is a vigorous climber and can withstand some shade, which makes it ideal for growing on corn. The vines are 4½ to 5 feet tall, with abundant foliage. The flowers are white, the pods glossy green, about 5½ to 6 inches long. There are normally 5 to 7 seeds per pod. The pod is flat, slightly curved, and when the seeds are fully formed, bulged and bumpy. The beans are ivory white.

The pods are considered excellent for snap beans, but as a shelly bean, this variety is unequaled by any other. The dry bean is an excellent soup bean. The Pennsylvania Dutch normally puree it when cooking it in soups.

Light Brown Zebra Bean
Phaseolus vulgaris

The "zebra" bean is a pinto bean recognized by Georg von Martens as a distinctive bean type notable for the dark zebra stripes running lengthwise down the sides of the beans. Some zebra beans familiar to Americans include Oregon Giant and its Swiss counterpart *Weinländerin* (Maid of the Wine Country), Scotia, and Tennessee Wonder. The origin of this group of beans, which includes a wide range of shapes and colors, is probably Mexico or the American Southwest. However, the beans were dispersed at such an early date that is now difficult to sort out their tangled history. One of the most colorful to my mind is the zebra bean called Rio Zape, a violet

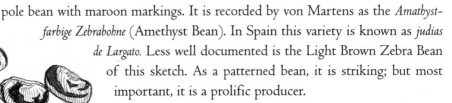

Light Brown Zebra Bean

pole bean with maroon markings. It is recorded by von Martens as the *Amathyst-farbige Zebrabohne* (Amethyst Bean). In Spain this variety is known as *judias de Largato.* Less well documented is the Light Brown Zebra Bean of this sketch. As a patterned bean, it is striking; but most important, it is a prolific producer.

The bean is widely known among American seed savers by a variety of thoroughly incorrect and misleading names. It is often called Refugee Bean, which it is not. It has come to me as Thousand-for-One Bean, which, again, it is not. It has even been called an old Pennsylvania Dutch bean, even though the Pennsylvania Dutch do not have a name for it. But von Martens knew it, calling it *Phaseolus zebra spadiceus* S., and it is one of the best bush beans of its kind.

Italian botanist Gaetano Savi, who gave this bean its Latin name in 1822, described its color as *nocciola* (hazel), which I find poetic. The bean certainly deserves a better name than the one it has. In any case, it is a vigorous bush variety about 14 inches tall, producing rose-pink flowers. The pods yield 5 to 6 seeds each; they are shown in the drawing with their distinctive zebra markings. The plants are extremely sensitive to weather conditions and will slow down or speed up their ripening to accommodate it. They are a good 60-day bean when all things are equal. I have harvested the beans in the early fall, leaving the bushes completely stripped of pods, only to have the plants revive during a warm spell and produce a second crop before frost. Perhaps it should be called the "fail-safe bean," because for a beginning gardener, it is one heirloom that repays the effort ten times over.

The dry bean is the part used, and it can be incorporated into any recipe where Mexican pinto beans are called for. It also makes a delicious bean paste. And since a strain of this bean was discovered in Ethiopia in the early 1840s, it can also be used in East African recipes with perfect authenticity.

Low's Champion Bean
Phaseolus vulgaris

This popular New England bush bean was introduced in 1884 by the Aaron Low Seed Company of Boston. The *American Garden* (1889, 57) suggested that the bean was an entirely new variety created, as Low himself claimed, by crossing a wax bean with a "green bean." Later field tests revealed that it was merely an old strain of the Dwarf Cranberry Bean under a new name. Its popularity, however, is still widespread, and for bean flavor, it has few peers both as a shelly bean and as a snap bean.

Low's Champion Bean

The plants grow about 12 to 15 inches tall, remaining very compact, and bear pods that hang down straight to touch the ground. The flowers are pale pink, yielding long, flat stringless pods about 4½ to 6 inches long. There are normally 4 to 5 seeds per pod, oval in shape, and very dark red when ripe. The beans ripen in 70 days and are therefore considered one of the best for short-season areas, hence the immense popularity of this variety in New England.

Mostoller Wild Goose Bean
Phaseolus vulgaris

The history of this bean, as related by one of the Mostoller family, appeared in the *Somerset Democrat* (Somerset, Pennsylvania) for December 9, 1925. It is one of those bean varieties that has become a metaphor for the heirloom seed movement; its story is well known and was reprinted in the 1984 *Fall Harvest Edition* (1984, 148–50) of Seed Savers Exchange. The family's story about the bean connects it to Civil War veteran John W. Mostoller, who shot a wild goose with beans in its craw. The beans were planted in 1866 and then preserved by the family as an heirloom vegetable ever since. There is a possibility that this tale is indeed true, yet it is important to keep in mind that seed found in the craw of a goose is one of the most recurring themes in American horticultural literature, and is often folkloric.

The problem with the genealogy of the Mostoller Wild Goose bean is that while the legend is winning, the goose must have flown a long distance; there is a family of beans from northern Italy, the Porcelain Bean among them, to which our goose bean belongs. Furthermore, it is not a bean recognized by von Martens, which would suggest that the variety and all of its Italian relatives developed *after* 1870. This includes the Snowcap Bean, which is identical to the Mostoller bean, except for slightly different coloring—purples instead of browns.

No matter. The bean is excellent baked and is delicious in soups. The huge vines seem to thrive when allowed to clamber up giant sunflowers. Otherwise, it is a pole bean that would easily choke out corn. It should be raised for best results in teepees or on very tall stakes. This is because the vines can attain a height of 10 to 12 feet (6 to 10 feet, the normal description, is too conservative). The flower is white, producing pods of about 5 inches long and containing 4 to 5 seeds per pod, sometimes 6. The seed is very large, white on the underside and heavily speckled with brown and maroon over an orange patch around the eye. If nothing else, the bean is striking for its ornamental quality, which it loses once cooked.

Pea Bean or Frost Bean
Phaseolus vulgaris

The English make quite a fuss over pea beans. Jeremy Cherfas, former head of genetic resources at the Ryton Organic Gardens in England, wrote a short piece on pea beans for the garden's newsletter in 1994 because there has been a resurgence of interest in this family of heirloom beans. It is evident that Americans and British gardeners use the term "pea bean" quite differently, even though we are both discussing beans with seed of the same general shape. In America, the term is applied to white, pea-like Marrowfat Beans, such as the Boston Navy Bean.

Our white pea beans originated with the Iroquoian peoples of New York State, and there are now well over a hundred distinct varietal forms, as well as many synonyms. All of the white pea beans are bush types. The pea bean of this sketch, however, is the two-color pole variety of England, known in this country as the Frost Bean, or Fall Bean. In *Beans of New York* (Hedrick 1931, 72) the bush form is called the Beautiful Bean, and is only present in the book as an illustration, for there is no discussion of it in the text.

Amelia Simmons called this bean the Frost Bean in her *American Cookery* (1796, 15), noting that she felt it was only fit for shelling. As a shelly bean, it is indeed fine; as a dry bean even better. This bean first came to me not as the Frost Bean but as the Gross Nanny Green Pole Bean (*Der Grossnanni ihr griene Schtangebuhne*) preserved by the Miller family near Elizabethtown, Pennsylvania. The Millers use it as a snap bean, but it is excellent as a baked bean or boiled for bean salads.

The seed is white, with a large irregular splash of maroon around the eye. Georg von Martens (1869, 76) identified this pole bean as the *Halbrothe Kugelbohne* (Half-Red Grapeshot Bean). The Miller bean blooms with a yellow flower fading to white; von Martens's example had rose flowers. Evidently, there are two variant forms of this bean in terms of flower color; otherwise, the plants are the same. In Germany the young pods were eaten green in salads. In South Africa the same bean was known as the *Zuiker Boon* and served with sour-cream dressings. James J. H. Gregory introduced the bicolored pea bean in his 1875 catalog. It was considered quite new at that time. In England, however, it became one of the most popular of all dry pole beans, valued in particular for its meaty flavor and its reliability in northern latitudes with cool weather. In the American South, it is called the Fall Bean for this reason.

One year I planted a crop on July 1, and by September 1 it was producing heavily. For me, it has become a good late-season bean, since I can plant as late as August 1 for green beans in October and dry beans in November. I believe that the ability of this bean to produce so late in the season when evening temperatures are cool or even chilly is one reason it has earned the colloquial name Frost Bean.

The vines range from 8 to 9 feet in length, producing pods about 4 to 5 inches long. The bean is not tolerant of drought. If conditions are dry, the beans will become shriveled or sunken instead of plump.

Red Cranberry Pole Bean
Phaseolus vulgaris

Amelia Simmons called it the "Cranbury" bean in her *American Cookery* (1796, 15), describing it as "rich, but not universally approved" when compared against the Caseknife Bean and the Windsor Broad Bean (see fava beans, page 92). This curt observation reveals a great deal about subtle class distinctions in colonial America, for both the Caseknife and Windsor Bean were considered genteel, whereas the Cranberry Bean was not. Garnet-red like the old horse bean and field pea of Elizabethan England, the Cranberry Bean fulfilled its role in America, or in the New England part of it, as a boon to the yeoman farmer. As such, it was and still remains one of the oldest varieties of bean cultivated since colonial times. It was certainly known before 1670, and it may be the red bean planted by the Indians of Maine noted in Lescarbot's 1612 account of New France.

The name of the bean is thoroughly appropriate, since a basket of the dry beans can easily fool a casual onlooker into believing the beans are fresh cranberries. This association with the cranberry, however, is not a colonial American invention, for the name was borrowed from native Americans. Furthermore, the red color also gave rise to another name, the Tory Bean, thus uniting the bean with political history. There are many beans sold as cranberry beans, but only one strain is the true one. Aside from Seed Savers Exchange and USDA, it is preserved for the public to see firsthand at Old Sturbridge Village in Massachusetts, where seed can also be purchased. Where would the New England kitchen be without its Cranberry Beans?

German bean specialist Georg von Martens (1869, 76) categorized the true Cranberry Bean as a *Kugelbohne* or

Mottled Cranberry Bean

grapeshot bean, like the Lazy Wife. In fact, the White Cranberry Bean was crossed with the red sort to create the speckled varieties now known as horticultural beans. Before the horticulturals underwent hybridizing in England during the early part of the nineteenth century, the red-and-white crosses were simply known as mottled cranberry beans. A few strains of this early sort still survive. When the white cranberry was recrossed with the original horticultural strain, it yielded a variety known as Concord. And so it goes; an entire book could be devoted to the cranberry bean and its vast family tree.

Georg von Martens was also aware of this huge progeny and the many labels under which the true Red Cranberry was known in Europe. It is the *Phaseolus sphaericus haematocarpus* Savi of his bean book, the so-called *Purpurhülsige Kugelbohne* of Germany. In South Africa, it was known as the Ducat Bean, or Cape Bean, elsewhere as the Lark Egg Snap Bean and St. Michael's Bean (it ripens by St. Michael's Day). None of these names fit so neatly as the Cranberry Bean, and to tell the truth, in all its simplicity, the bean is strikingly beautiful.

Its vines are slow to start, but as the season progresses, they begin to grow rapidly. The flowers are pink, producing straight 5-inch pods with rounded ends, flat at first, but then growing swollen and bumpy as the seeds develop. Historically, the bean was harvested as a shelly bean or as a dry bean, normally with 7 to 8 seeds per pod.

The Arlington Red Cranberry (SSE BN 533), introduced in 1885 by R. & J. Farquhar of Boston, is not accepted as a distinct variety but as a stringless selection of red cranberry with a slightly different-shaped pod.

Red Cutshort Bean
Phaseolus vulgaris

This excellent bean has been ignored in horticultural literature; nonetheless it has existed in the South for many years. *Beans of New York* (Hedrick 1931) incorrectly assigns the name red cutshort to the Cornhill Bean, now known as the Amish Nuttle Bean. The two could never be confused, not even by children. The true Red Cutshort is nearly the same red color as the Red Cranberry Pole Bean, although a shade brighter. Its pod is similar to the Amish Nuttle Bean, vines the same length, and it also requires the same long growing season. As with all cutshorts, the seed is small—a feature I happen to like—and the pod production prolific.

The bean can be used like a red mung bean in cookery, but Southerners have preferred to use it with rice and dried okra dishes, especially in the Deep South. Culturally, it served the southern farmer in the same manner as the Red Cranberry Bean in New England. Among the native peoples of the South, the bean was used for flour and cooked in combination with cornbreads or dumplings.

The vines are about 8 to 10 feet long, producing 5-inch pods with 6 to 8 small red seeds in 75 days. If the beans are harvested young as a snap bean—for which they are popular—the vines will produce all summer until frost. The vines can tolerate some shade and therefore can be cultivated on corn hills.

Red Cutshort Bean

Contrary to reports in the *Beans of New York*, Georg von Martens was quite familiar with cutshort beans, which he called *Eckbohnen* (beans with "square corners"). Regarding the red cutshort of this sketch, which von Martens called *Phaseolus gonospermus purpureus* Martens or *Purpurrothe Eckbohne*, he recognized several subvarieties. It closely resembled a French variety sold in the 1860s by the Paris seed firm of Beaurieux under the name *haricot rouge de Chartres.* Not surprisingly, when von Martens tried to grow cutshorts, they would not come to crop for him any better than lima beans. Germany is simply too far north.

As an alternate experiment, in 1858 von Martens acquired a red cutshort bean from Russia sold by the seed firm of Rampon in Lyon under the name *haricot de Russie,* as well as another red cutshort from the Russian city of Aigur on the Amur River along the Manchurian border. This latter variety, which had evolved under northern conditions, brought forth a small crop of beans. But the experiment convinced von Martens that cutshorts are not only long-season beans, they do far better in southern latitudes where the night air is warm. I would take von Martens's conclusions to heart. This is not a bean for Minnesota or Idaho.

Red Valentine Bean
Phaseolus vulgaris

In 1889 the *American Garden* (1889, 57) remarked on the introduction of the Extra Early Red Speckled Valentine, calling it a "capital round bean." Ever since valentine beans have come on the market in this country, they have been valued for their long, pencil-shaped round pods, the snap bean par excellence. And not surprisingly, since years earlier, the *American Agriculturist* (1870, 123) put the Early Red Valentine at the top of the list for American kitchen gardens. Over the years, the number of valentine types and subvarieties has proliferated to such a degree that the history of this bean has gotten lost in a tangle of commercial claims.

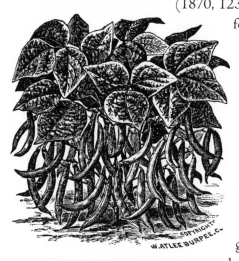

Red Valentine Bean

Fortunately, Georg von Martens was able to sort out its history when the individuals involved in the development of this variety were still living. In his bean book, he styled the bean *Phaseolus oblongus turcicus,* Savi, since Gaetano Savi had actually been the first botanist to catalog it. In German, the name was given as *Türkische Dattelbohne* (Turkish date-shaped bean) owing to the widespread presumption that it had been introduced into Europe from Turkey. Actually, Prince von Neuwied was the first to observe the bean among the Indians living along the Missouri River in 1815–17, and he noted its name in their language: *ohmenik pusaehne* (as written phonetically in German).

The bean was taken to Europe—by whom it is not determined, but certainly Prince von Neuwied would be a logical candidate—where it acquired the name Thousand-for-One Bean at the hands of Dutch plant breeders. In England, the bean was called the Refugee Bean or Purple-Speckled Valentine. In Germany, it was called Thousand-for-One, Little Princess, and Salad Snap Bean. It made its appearance in this country about 1837 at David Landreth's seed farm near Bristol, Pennsylvania. From there, it was launched as a new bean, never mind the Missouri Indians. In any case, there is only one original Refugee Bean, original Thousand-for-One Bean, original Valentine Bean—and it is this one.

The bean produces a bush about 15 inches tall and, typical of the old sorts, throws out a runner some 2 feet in length. The flower is a rich rose pink; the 5½-to-6½-inch pods, long and narrow, are ideal for snap beans, the primary use of this variety. True to its name, the oblong seed is heavily speckled in deep wine red arranged in a zebralike pattern, with a flesh pink ground.

Pod profile of the Red Valentine Bean

Scotia or Genuine Cornfield Bean
Phaseolus vulgaris

This old bean acquired its common names late in the nineteenth century, for it cannot be found in most horticultural works until its commercialization in the 1890s. Georg von Martens called it the *phaseolus zebra carneus* Martens, although it was only one of ten similar zebra beans listed by Savi in 1822. In the Veneto of northern Italy, the bean was known as *fasioi tavarini.* In fact, it could be found in most parts of Europe. Von Martens considered it one of the most beautiful of all the zebra beans and also the most common.

It seems strange that our records would be so silent on this bean when it is thought to have been indigenous. This assumption is doubtful, even though the bean was recorded among the Iroquois at the turn of this century as a bread-and-soup bean. In several Iroquois dialects the bean is even referred to as a "wampum bean," one of the gift foods used for settling contracts and marriage dowries in Iroquois society. Just the same, the bean does not appear to have been among the Iroquois until after contact with whites, for the true source of the bean is Mexico. Thus, instead of calling this a cornfield bean, it would be more authentic to refer to the Scotia bean as *frijoles de milpa,* the name by which it was known when it entered Louisiana with Spanish occupation in the eighteenth century.

Scotia Bean

The obscure origin of the bean has always been outweighed by its productivity, for the bean is doubtless one of the best yielders of its type. The vines grow 14 to 15 feet long and produce

6-inch pods with 8 to 9 beans per pod. The beans are buff or flesh colored with brown zebra markings, although not as pronounced as on most other zebra types. This is a 90-day bean and a heavy cropper that grows well on corn. It can be harvested as a snap bean, but is best as a shelly bean or as a dry bean.

Sulphur Bean
Phaseolus vulgaris

The name of this bush bean is in fact a catchall term for a number of similar beans that spring from a common source. Because they have crossed and recrossed over the years, very few of them now fit neatly into old horticultural descriptions. Fearing Burr recognized two varieties, the Golden Cranberry and the Canada Yellow. They are considered synonyms by *Beans of New York* (Hedrick 1931), but Canada Yellow comes closest to matching the Sulphur Bean of Seeds Blüm, the most authentic strain I have thus far encountered on the market today.

Georg von Martens referred to this bean as the Yellow Egg Bean, and it was known earlier to Italian botanist Gaetano Savi. The French referred to one of their yellow hybrids created from a yellow-and-white cross as the *haricot petit Nanquin* (Little Nankeen). This name referred to the resulting color, not to a place of origin. This hybrid, which was not yet stable when it was introduced in 1839, came to be known as China Yellow. The Sulphur Bean should not be confused with the bean called Early China, also known as China Red Eye. This last bean was well known in New England and was often mentioned by Thomas Fessenden in his agricultural works, including *The Complete Farmer* (1839, 154).

The Sulphur Bean is a bush variety about 16 inches tall that produces pink flowers. The pods are about 5 inches long and contain a dry seed ripening in about 95 days to a soft sulphur yellow. Around the eye of the bean is a small pink-brown ring. The ring around the eye of Golden Cranberry is green; otherwise the two beans are similar. Either one may be sold as the Sulphur Bean. I have even seen the two mixed in the same seed packets. The true Sulphur Bean, however, is the object of epicures, for it is famous as a stewing bean that cooks down to a creamy texture. It is extremely popular in the South as an ingredient in bean gravies, and when pureed, it makes an excellent base for soup.

Turtle Bean or Turtle Soup Bean
Phaseolus vulgaris

Prior to the war with Mexico (1846–48), the Turtle Bean was largely uncultivated in the United States except by a small circle of seedsmen and plant collectors. The only exception to this was Louisiana and other parts of the Gulf Coast where early contact with Mexico occurred. In those areas, the bean was also an important ingredient in the diet of slaves, hence its vernacular name *pois à negres* in the French-speaking Caribbean. Along the hot Gulf Coast of Mexico, where the bean originated, it is known as *frijoles de Tampico* or simply as *frijoles negros*. Its counterpart from the cool Mexican highlands, also a black bush bean, is the Veracruzano that was introduced into the United States by soldiers returning from the Mexican War.

Georg von Martens (1869, 27) noted that several German seed houses had tried unsuccessfully during the 1840s to introduce the bean into that country as an alternative to the failed potato crop, but concluded that "for us it was too black and too small," not to mention that the growing season in much of Germany was too short for it. Round, black, and ugly, this was a bean that Europeans could not cook with milk or cream. Indeed, anything cooked with it turned a dark inky color. Yet as von Martens pointed out, the Turtle Bean was well known under many different names in many parts of the world because it had been widely disseminated by the Spanish during the 1600s. He recorded identical samples from Louisiana, Algeria, Brazil, Portugal, and Chile, and noted that Mexican settlers had introduced the bean into Texas well before 1815. From there it spread into many of the Indian tribes residing in the lower Great Plains.

Under the heading of "Valuable New Vegetables," the *Horticulturist* (1848, 464) launched a campaign to introduce the bean to American gardeners under the enticing name of Turtle Soup Bean. The New York seed firm of Grant M. Thorburn & Company was most active in commercializing it, but other seedsmen also followed suit. Furthermore, the U.S. Patent Office distributed seed to farmers in several parts of the country. It is interesting that the bean was not initially sold on its old merits as a dry bean, for resistance to

Black Turtle Bean

black-colored food was very strong in that period. Rather, it was marketed as a snap or string bean, since the pods remained tender for a long time. Very few beans at the time could compete with it on that point.

History does not record the name of the creative cook who transformed these beans into ersatz turtle soup, but anyone with a little pepper wine (page 267) on hand can easily see how it happened. In any case, the sherry transformed a mundane gray broth into an acceptable gentleman's dish, whether or not it resembled real turtle. One of the earliest recipes for turtle bean soup was published in the *Horticulturist*, and the knowledge that it came from the hand of Alexander Jackson Downing (or more likely his wife) doubtless added to its glamour. But it was Henry Ward Beecher's recipe that became the most famous and indeed the most popular with period cookbook authors. This was the same Henry Ward Beecher whose articles on gardening in the *Western Farmer and Gardener* were collected and republished in 1859 as the best-seller *Plain and Pleasant Talk about Fruits, Flowers and Farming*.

Jane Croly published his recipe in her *Jennie June's American Cookery Book* (1874, 327). It needs little clarification other than a footnote to explain that a "bean digester" is a type of Victorian stewpan with a tight-fitting lid. It functioned along the same principle as a pressure cooker. Of course, being a minister, Beecher abjured the sherry.

Henry Ward Beecher's Favorite Turtle Bean Soup

🐛

Soak one and a half pints of turtle beans in cold water overnight. In the morning drain off the water, wash the beans in fresh water, and put into the soup digester with four quarts of good beef stock from which all the fat has been removed. Set it where it will boil steadily but slowly till dinner, or five hours at least—six is better. Two hours before dinner put in half a can of tomatoes or eight fresh ones and a large coffee cup of tomato catsup. One onion, a carrot, and a few of the outside stalks of celery, cut into the soup with the tomatoes, improves it for most people. Strain through a fine colander or coarse sieve, rubbing through enough of the beans to thicken the soup, and send to table hot.

Because this is a midseason bean, requiring about 100 days from planting to harvest, the turtle bean will produce good crops in most parts of the United States. The original strain is a semirunner, producing a bush with a sprawling vine about a yard long. I recommend growing the bean on deer netting, trellising, or on 3-foot stakes so that the bean pods will not rest on the ground. This will prevent crop loss in the event of wet weather.

Cornell University recently developed the Midnight Black Turtle Soup Bean, introduced commercially by Johnny's Select Seeds of Albion, Maine. This is an improved upright strain that does not sprawl. Market gardeners may prefer this for harvesting convenience, and I cannot detect any difference in flavor. But Midnight Black should not be confused with the original heirloom variety.

Trail of Tears Bean
Phaseolus vulgaris

Historical documentation of this bean is thus far lacking, but recent oral history is rich. The seed came to Seed Saver's Exchange in 1985 from Dr. John Wyche, a dentist of Cherokee descent who lived in Hugo, Oklahoma. Dr. Wyche also owned the Cole Brothers Circus, which supplied him with elephant manure for his extensive vegetable gardens. He was fascinated with Cherokee foodways, and from his Cherokee connections obtained the bean now known as Trail of Tears (SSE BN-1485).

According to Cherokee tradition, the bean was carried from North Carolina to Oklahoma during the forced march of the Cherokee Nation during the winter of 1838–39. Several thousand Cherokees died en route; thus the bean has become a potent symbol of their struggle for survival and identity. Because of this association, the Trail of Tears Bean is doubtless one of the most haunting of all the vegetables in the garden.

The beans produce vines with rich olive-green leaves with brown veins. The plants reach about 8 feet tall and must be well supported—they will grow well on tall corn. The 6-inch pods ripen to a maroon brown that dries into horizontal bands of black and tan. The seed is jet black, oblong, and very shiny. The young pods are used as snap beans, but the original use of the bean among Native Americans was for flour. It was also cooked in combination with blue and black corns. The Indians often added ash of certain herbs to their stews instead of salt. This alkaline action released the vitamin B in the corn and turned black beans blue. A little baking soda will cause a similar reaction.

Lima Beans

Lima beans are among the oldest documented New World vegetables, traceable back to at least 5,000 B.C. in Peru. According to reports from Spaniards who first occupied Peru, lima beans were only eaten by the Incas and other Indian elite. The rest of society consumed common beans. Small-seeded varieties of the lima were also known in Mexico during pre-Columbian times, yet there is not much evidence that lima beans had spread northward to American Indians beyond the Southwest until introduced by European settlers. Mottled forms are known to have grown in Florida around old Indian sites, but may have been introduced through early contact with the Spanish. The Spanish and Portuguese were largely responsible for disseminating the lima bean to other parts of the world. Our English word for it, which refers to the Peruvian capital of Lima, more or less confirms the South American origin of the seed first studied by European botanists. Some of the old German herbals called it *Mondbohne* or "moon bean" in reference to the quarter-moon shape of the seed pod. The moon still figures in the species name *lunatus*, "moon-shaped."

Once, while visiting friends in Germany, I was invited to prepare an American dinner. I wanted lima beans, but they were nowhere to be found. Then, quite by accident, I discovered them, but the package was labeled in Chinese. In Germany, lima beans are exotics found only at American military bases or in Chinese grocery stores. This is an odd twist for a vegetable as American as apple pie, but the truth is, the lima bean has not found favor in European cookery. Due to Europe's northern latitude, limas do not often produce flowers in regions north of the Alps. The heavy European soils that bring forth cabbages in abundance will yield to the fava bean but not to the lima.

However, Georg von Martens recognized the importance of the lima outside of Europe, and in the second edition of his classic book on beans (1869), he added a section on limas that is both brief and curious, for it is based mostly on the study of the seed. Remember, this was a botanist who could only grow limas in flowerpots, and his conclusions were tempered by this somewhat awkward mode of inquiry. The image of von Martens hovering over his seedlings is certain to make an American gardener smile, considering that the Carolina Lima can erupt into a vine well over 16 feet long. It was this huge vine size that discouraged many people from raising limas in the first place. Yet *Meehan's Monthly* (1892, 12) recommended limas for this very reason, noting that for market gardeners, the bean was always profitable because the difficulty of getting poles meant that it was not as widely grown in home gardens as it could be.

Henderson's Bush Lima, introduced in 1889, eventually changed this. As *The American Garden* (1889, 124) pointed out, "for many years we have worked hard, and doubtless many others did, to secure a new type of an inimitable lima bean which would not need the costly and unsightly poles, but without success, when suddenly from the Virginia mountains it is heard that plain farmers have had such a thing for years and said nothing about it." Like many heirloom vegetables today, the bush lima rose from obscurity after years of cultivation in one locality. The only complaint against Henderson's introduction was the smallness of the bean.

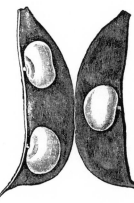

Henderson's Bush Lima

Limas are categorized into horticultural types, and one determining characteristic is the seed. The small-seeded limas are often referred to as sieva limas. They are annuals and are classified by botanists as *Phaseolus lunatus* var. *lunonnus*. The large-seeded limas are perennials and sometimes classified as *Phaseolus lunatus* var. *limenanus* or *Phaseolus limensis* var. *limenanus*. The obvious inadequacy of this taxonomy reflects the very unsettled nature of science in its attempt to organize beans in a logical manner. It becomes a nightmare when these limas are crossed and recrossed to produce new varieties. All types of limas will cross readily, even though limas are self-pollinating. Because they contain rich nectar, lima bean flowers are very attractive to bees. Therefore, two varieties of lima bean should not be grown in proximity unless they are caged or bagged, rather inconvenient for the large vining types in any case.

Seed saving is not complicated. Lima bean seeds are harvested from pods dried on the vine. Many of the truly old varieties like Carolina Lima have small pods that actually pop open when touched or when jostled by the wind. This is a characteristic of the truly old, primitive limas as well as of the wild ancestors of the limas we cultivate today. The dry seed pods are also woody and sharply pointed; thus, it is better to wear gloves when harvesting dry seed. Seed of most limas remains viable for three years.

For culinary purposes, limas can be harvested young and eaten fresh or ripened and dried for winter use. Dried young limas were popular in the past, and the technique for drying them is quite similar to that used by the French for *flageolets verts.* The *Pennsylvania Farm Journal* (1853, 197) recommended drying the beans in an airy loft: "Pull and shell the beans a little younger than they are usually gathered for use in the summer season. Spread them thinly upon the floor of a garret or an airy loft, and occasionally turn them until they are dry. Soak them twelve hours before cooking, in warm water, and when cooked they will be as tender, plump, and good as at any season of the year." My great-grandmother dried her limas that way, having first spread the attic floor with newspapers. Lima beans dried green reconstitute themselves and are far more tender than the beans ripened on the vine. Most of the old varieties listed on the following pages are excellent when dried this way.

There are hundreds of heirloom limas available to gardeners today, some varieties very similar to one another, some so unusual that they are only grown as curiosities—I think the Brazilian black-seeded limas fall into this last category. For the sake of variety, I have included several with unusual colors, but still useful as culinary beans. My favorite is Dr. Martin's, and I still maintain plants descended from seed my grandfather bought from Dr. Martin when he was selling the limas for 25 cents apiece.

Carolina Lima Bean
Phaseolus lunatus var. *lunonnus*

This 80-day variety is known to date from pre-Columbian times. It was depicted by Matthias de l'Obel in 1591 and is thought to be the "bushel bean" known in the Carolinas as early as 1700.

There are claims that this bean is indigenous, but more likely it was introduced from Jamaica. Thomas Jefferson grew this variety at Monticello in 1794, and visitors can see the beans rambling over their tall poles even to this day. The popularity of the Carolina Lima in the South gave rise to a great many synonyms, among them Carolina Sewee, Saba, Sivy, and West Indian. This bean has the advantage of being one of the earliest of all the limas, and for a dry bean it is prolific, best suited for drying green. As a shelly bean it is not as desirable, although it was used as such in colonial times.

The vines are vigorous, reaching 10 to 12 feet in length, in good ground even as long as 16 feet. Each vine produces many small pods about 3 inches long, as shown in the drawing. The pods normally contain 3 chalky white seeds, very small and flat.

Carolina Lima or White Saba Bean

Dr. Martin's Lima Bean
Phaseolus limensis var. *limenanus*

The precise date of introduction of this famous heirloom lima (SSE BN-47) is not known because Dr. Martin grew it for some time before he began selling seed. My grandfather placed it somewhere about 1935, and most people who first grew this variety believe this date to be accurate. The bean was developed by Dr. Harold E. Martin (1888–1959), a Philadelphia dentist who owned a farm on Street Road near West Chester, Pennsylvania. My great-grandfather Weaver was also a dentist, and through that connection my family got to know Dr. Martin and his bean trials.

Dr. Martin's hobby was growing vegetables, but he was also well known as an activist for preserving farmland. Today he is remembered for his lima bean, which is probably one of the largest-seeded varieties grown. It is also one of the finest limas for the quality of its shelly bean, very sweet, with none of the unpleasant starchiness common to many other limas. But Dr. Martin's beans need room.

The vines reach 16 to 20 feet and bear huge, flat pods yielding 2 to 3 seeds each. The young leaves of the vines are distinctive, blotched with dark and light green somewhat like the pattern on a watermelon rind—an indication that the seed is growing true. The seed itself often measures 1½ to 2 inches in diameter, sometimes larger, and is pale green when ripe rather than white. It is important when saving seed to renew it every other year, because the viability drops quickly in this variety. Also, be certain to save seed from only the largest beans.

Seed savers Merlyn and Mary Ann Niedens, whose seeds are well known in Seed Savers Exchange, developed a variety called Illinois Giant by crossing Dr. Martin's with a speckled variety called Christmas. Their variety has the large seed of Dr. Martin's bean and the drought resistance of the other. For gardeners who have trouble with Dr. Martin's where summers are excessively hot, perhaps Illinois Giant would be worth a trial.

I have also experimented with Dr. Martin's, crossing it with Willow Leaf, which is known for its heat resistance. The resulting vines look promising, first because they are dwarfed and therefore easy to trellis, and second because they are twice as productive as Dr. Martin's, yet retain the large-size bean. Experiments like this are half the fun in growing heirlooms, a bit like a painter's palette for creating new culinary treats.

Hopi Lima Bean
Phaseolus lunatus var. *lunonnus*

This is not a true garden variety in the sense of Dr. Martin's or the Carolina Lima; rather, it is a strain of lima preserved among the Hopi peoples, which exhibits characteristics of crossing. The bean is used primarily as a dry bean among the Hopi, who also sometimes grind it for flour. Pure seed is small, the same size as the Carolina Lima, orange in color, with maroon-red markings.

Hopi Orange Lima Bean

Nicholas Joseph de Jacquin (1727–1817) obtained samples of a lima bean similar to this sort from the island of Bourbon in the Indian Ocean during the eighteenth century. However, there is reason to believe that it originated in South America, the product of a cross between a solid maroon red sort and a plain orange-seeded variety, for it comes very close in appearance to an orange sort with dark markings found in pre-Columbian graves in Peru.

The age of the Hopi lima is not known, but if it existed for any length of time in the Southwest, it was most certainly plain orange in its original form, because it is not completely fixed as a variety. Even today, it produces both plain and speckled seed. Georg von Martens (1869, 96) discussed the plain orange sort that was introduced from Brazil into West Africa during the 1600s. I obtained plain orange seed from Cameroon in 1993 and found it to be identical to Hopi lima in most ways, colored markings aside. When crossed with the Red Lima (page 77), it yields seed with the distinctive maroon-red markings.

Visually, the seed of Hopi lima is quite attractive, and since the vines are short, 6 to 8 feet long, and very productive, this is an easy variety to grow, producing crops in about 75 to 80 days. Since it is a desert variety, or at least a tropical one, it is resistant to heat and drought. For seed-saving purposes select only the seed with the finest markings; otherwise the variety will deteriorate into a plain orange-seeded sort and a purple-red one.

King of the Garden Lima Bean
Phaseolus limensis var. *limenanus*

This old standby was developed by Frank S. Platt of New Haven, Connecticut, in 1883, but not made known commercially until 1885, when an article describing it appeared in the *Farm Journal* (1885, 27). The original picture from that article is shown. The advantage of this variety is that it was developed in lower New England and is therefore better suited to northern gardens than many of the old varieties like Carolina Lima, or even more recent ones like Dr. Martin's.

King of the Garden Lima

The vines range in length from 6 to 9 feet and are productive over a long period of time. The pods measure 5 to 8 inches in length and contain 5 to 6 seeds per pod. Vines come to crop in about 90 days. The seeds are large, usually dull white tinged with green when dry, and covered with small wrinkles. The shelly bean is said to taste like honey, but I think it tastes more like fenugreek. As a flavor combination, this bean goes well with curries.

Red Lima Bean
Phaseolus lunatus var. *lunonnus*

This heirloom variety was introduced commercially in 1990 by Southern Exposure Seed Exchange under the name Worcester Indian Red Pole Lima. It is said to be of Native American origin, but it conforms in many ways to the old red limas known since colonial times in several parts of North and South America. In fact, Georg von Martens obtained samples of this lima from Indonesia in 1868. Von Jacquin recorded it even earlier in 1770. In this country, the red limas were never considered of commercial importance and thus were grown more as a poverty food than as a preferred sort.

The shelly bean is uninteresting and tough, but the dry bean, which is deep maroon red, is both handsome and excellent cooked with red corn or ground for flour, two uses for which it was valued by the American Indians. In the South slaves cooked this bean with brown goober peas (page 166) and mixed the bean paste with with red sweet potatoes (page 332) to make *fufu* dumplings. The bean was noted in *Country Gentleman* (1864, 47), but no mention was made about its hardiness. In fact, it is one of the hardiest of all the limas discussed here. It normally yields 2 seeds per pod and produces consistently over the summer. The seeds and pods are the same size as the Hopi Lima and burst open when dry in the fall.

Speckled Lima Bean
Phaseolus lunatus var. *lunonnus*

There are a number of speckled or mottled heirloom limas, very similar in shape of seed and coloration, but widely different in pod and vine type. The best known of these is the Florida Butter or Speckled Pole Lima, an old variety of unknown origin but thought to descend from the speckled sorts once cultivated by the Indians in that section of the country. The author of *Beans of New York* (Hedrick 1931, 87) speculated that this variety evolved out of a speckled sieva-type bean, and this is quite possibly so. Boston seedsman John Russell listed a Speckled Saba Lima in his 1828 seed catalog, certainly one of the earliest references to this type. Massachusetts seedsman James J. H. Gregory listed a speckled lima bean in his 1864 catalog, and this like Russell's appears to be the same as the Mottled Sieva described by Fearing Burr. The true Speckled Lima or Mottled Sieva is identical to the Carolina Lima except for the mottled coloring on the seed. It is as old as the white-seeded Carolinas and may have been more widespread at one time. Early accounts refer to it growing up trees and virtually weighing them down with an abundance of pods.

There is also a dwarf mottled variety worth mentioning. It is called Simmons Red Streak Lima or John Harmon Lima, a Pennsylvania Dutch variety taken to West Virginia, where it was preserved. The vines are about 4 feet long, with most of the pods toward the bottom. The leaves of the plant are crinkled and waxy on the top, the flower color white. Like the speckled lima, this is a white bean splashed with maroon as though dipped in color. For gardeners concerned about space, this dwarf variety is excellent, and the shelly bean is not too bad either, although it must be picked very young.

Willow Leaf Lima Bean
Phaseolus lunatus var. *lunonnus*
This 100-day variety is believed to have been introduced in 1891 as a sport of the Carolina Lima by W. Atlee Burpee of Philadelphia, although Thomas Mawe mentioned a willow leaf sort in *Every Man His Own Gardener* (1779, 482). The name of this variety is derived from its leaf, which is shown in the drawing. I am not convinced that it resembles a willow leaf; to me it looks more like bamboo. It is because of this decorative leaf, however, that the bean is often grown as an ornamental. Otherwise, it resembles Carolina Lima, and like that variety, it is drought resistant and thrives in long, hot summers. It also requires large poles for support, since the vines reach anywhere from 8 to 10 feet or more (mine grew to 22 feet the first year!). The leaves and pods are a dark glossy green. The pods are 3 inches long and contain 3 smooth white seeds.

Willow Leaf Lima

Runner Beans

Runner beans belong to the species *coccineus* and therefore will not cross with common garden beans or with lima beans. The Spaniards were the first to see runner beans in the New World and the first to introduce them into Europe. The French name for runner bean, *haricots d'Espagne*, recognizes this path of introduction. However, in old German herbals, runner beans are often called *Arabische Bohnen* (Arab beans), since the first specimens came into German botanical collections by way of Turkey. Runner beans take their name from the fact that they are vigorous climbers, and unlike most beans, wrap themselves counter-clockwise around poles or stakes.

Runner beans are known to have been introduced into England in 1633 by John Tradescant, gardener to Charles I. Tradescant knew four sorts, a red-flowering variety, a bicolor (red and white), a white-flowering sort, and a black-seeded one. These early introductions have been equated with the varieties now known as Scarlet Runner, Painted Lady, White Dutch, and Black Coat respectively. Black Coat was mentioned specifically by German botanist Michael Titus in his *Catalogues Plantarum* (1654), so there is no doubt about the age of this variety. Its flowers are a distinctive orange-red.

The commonest culinary runner bean on the Continent was the white, in England the scarlet sorts. In this country the scarlet runner bean was normally raised as an ornamental, while the white sorts were used in cookery. For American gardeners lima beans supplanted the runner bean as a kitchen garden vegetable except in areas where limas were difficult to grow. Runner beans of all sorts are generally used as shelly beans, and when cooked in this manner, they resemble fresh limas. The pods toughen as they mature, but if harvested young, they can be used like snap beans. In fact, the *Gardener's Magazine* (1830, 177) recommended shredding them and salting them down to make a type of sauerkraut. The old Pennsylvania Dutch method was to "whittle" the beans diagonally into long shreds called *Schnipple,* hence the Pennsylvania Dutch name for the bean kraut: *Schnippelbuhne.* The Germans did this with the white varieties and called the pickle *Sauerbohnen.* Whatever, it is much milder than sauerkraut and can even be served with fish.

Georg von Martens (1869, 82) devoted considerable space to the white runner bean because of its importance in European kitchen gardens. He collected samples from many regions and recorded their local names: *haricot de Sainte Magdaleine* in Algeria, *judias blancas* in Spain, *fagiolo da brodo* in Naples, and *fasolone* in Apulia, to name just a few. Sorting out the many existing varieties can be daunting, but for the heirloom gardener, the four sorts known to John Tradescant can be cultivated with certain reassurance that they were known in this country at least by the eighteenth century. Of course, it is presumed that runner beans were raised here in the seventeenth century, although documentation is lacking. It is true, however, that their culinary merits were not noticed in England until the 1750s, which would account for the lag of interest on this side of the Atlantic.

Nineteenth-century American cookbook author Eliza Leslie often mentioned the scarlet runner bean as a worthwhile vegetable, from which we may assume that it was probably not completely familiar to all her readers. She took care to explain how to cook the pods in her *Directions for Cookery* (1851, 197). Or should I say, overcook them?

Scarlet Beans

🐛

It is not generally known that the pod of the scarlet bean, if green and young, is extremely nice when cut into three or four pieces and boiled. They will require near two hours, and must be drained well, and mixed as before mentioned with butter and pepper. If gathered at the proper time when the seed is just perceptible, they are superior to any of the common beans.

Runner beans are not difficult to grow, but they do have certain peculiarities that can be considered advantageous on the one hand and inconvenient on the other. The beans are native to the highlands of Central America and therefore are not only day-length sensitive but, more important, prefer cool weather. If they are planted soon enough in the spring, the vines will begin flowering before the onset of summer, thus assuring a crop of seed. Long periods of hot weather cause the flowers to drop and not set pods; in many parts of the United States, flowering ceases in July and August. In areas of the country where summer evenings are cool, runner beans will bloom profusely throughout the season, just as they do in England.

In their native habitat, runner beans are perennial. They develop a thick tuberous root that can be lifted in the fall and stored like a dahlia. This feature was well understood by gardeners even in the 1600s, but literature on the technique is more recent. English horticulturist John Cuthill published an essay, "On Taking up the Roots of the Scarlet Runner in the Autumn," in the *Gardener's Magazine* (1834, 315), and his advice is still useful today. Lifting the roots, as shown in the drawing, has two advantages. Vines from tubers produce more abundant crops of beans than those raised annually from seed.

Root of the White Dutch Runner Bean

Furthermore, the tubers can be started in pots early in the spring, either in a cold frame or in a greenhouse, and thus the plants will have a head start when they are set out and flowering many weeks in advance of newly started vines. These points are particularly important where runner beans are being raised as a food crop.

For seed saving, keep in mind that runner beans have large flowers attractive to bees. Of all the beans in the garden, runner beans are mostly likely to cross if planted in proximity. I would recommend growing only one variety at a time, or at most two varieties widely separated and of entirely different seed color. Planting flowers nearby that are attractive to bees will help reduce the likelihood of crosses if there are other runner beans in the neighborhood. Seeds are gathered from the dry pods in the fall. Their viability is about three years.

White Dutch Runner Bean

Purple Hyacinth Bean
Dolichos lablab

I have included this under runner beans because it is treated like a runner bean when cultivated as a food crop. However, this bean is a different genus and species from all the other beans in this book and therefore will not cross with them. But it will cross with other *lablab* species. Unlike the runner bean, which is a New World plant, the hyacinth bean hails from tropical Asia and thrives on heat.

Visitors to Monticello are usually astounded by the grand display made by this bean when it is allowed to run over arbors the way Thomas Jefferson preferred to cultivate it. The purple flowers and seed pods are ornamental from any standpoint, and the dark purple leaves only add to its striking character. I have yet to learn why it is the Venetians call these beans *moneghine*, which means "little nuns" and seems ill-suited to the showiness of the plant. But perhaps it has to do with the seed, which is black and white. The young purple seed pods are edible and commonly consumed in Asia. In America, however, the bean is grown mostly as an ornamental.

Matthias de l'Obel illustrated a white variety of hyacinth bean in his *Plantarum seu Stirpium* (1591) under the name *Phaseolus brasilianus*, mistakenly interpreted as a runner bean even though the seed is clearly a *Dolichos*. Bernard M'Mahon sold the Purple Hyacinth Bean as early as 1802, but the plants were raised in the United States mostly by wealthy plant collectors like William Hamilton of Philadelphia and the scientifically curious like Thomas Jefferson. It is a telling comment on the popularity of the bean that it did not appear until 1824 in *Edward's Botanical Register* (#830), and then only with a note that it was mostly raised from imported seed. This bean will not produce flowers in England unless raised in a greenhouse. I have found that of all the varieties of hyacinth bean now available, only the purple one of this sketch does best in my part of the country. The white-flowering, green-podded variety available from some seed houses does not bloom in Pennsylvania, and I do not recommend it to gardeners outside California or the subtropical parts of the country. Its growing season is simply too long.

Hyacinth beans may be cultivated like runner beans because they too require trellising or a fence to grow on. Hyacinth beans are also perennial, but short-lived. Therefore, they cannot be dug up and overwintered in the same manner. Saving seed is the best method of propagation. The secret is to start the plants early in large flowerpots, get them well on their way, then set them out when the weather is warm enough to plant tomatoes. Seeds are saved from the dry pods in the fall. Seed viability appears to be about three years.

Warning: The dry seeds of the Hyacinth Bean contains cyanogenic glucosides in toxic amounts. Asians treat the beans to remove the toxins, but for safety's sake, I would recommend *not* eating the dry beans unless you are perfectly familiar with the cooking process. Be absolutely certain that the seeds do not fall into the hands of small children who might swallow them. The toxins work much more powerfully on children than on adults.

Beets and Chards

Hortus Third recognizes two categories of beet: the Cicla group, which includes leaf beets and chards; and the Crassa group, or root beets. It does not acknowledge the fact that *Mangold* is often used incorrectly by English and American seedsmen for a type of large-rooted fodder beet. In German, where this term first appeared in medieval herbals, *Mangold* is used exclusively for chard. Its etymological origin is unknown, but may stem from Gaulish. The Germans, as well as many other Europeans, do not adhere to *Hortus Third,* and as far as beets are concerned, they recognize four cultivated forms, not two. I mention this because many of the heirloom beets that survive today originated in Germany; thus it is important to understand how they fit into the European frame of reference.

The four cultivated forms recognized by the Germans are chards (*Beta vulgaris* var. *cicla*), common garden (*Beta vulgaris* var. *esculenta*), turnip beets (*Beta vulgaris* var. *rapa*), and sugar beets (*Beta vulgaris* var. *altissima*). These divisions are purely horticultural but deeply ingrained in European thinking due to the high level of importance that the beet has played in continental culture since classical antiquity, far more than in England or America. Regardless of the manner in which beets are divided by horticulturists, they are all variant forms of the same thing and thus will readily cross.

Chards are characterized by their large stems and leaves, just the opposite of what beet growers want in root beets. The leaf is the part eaten, both raw and cooked, while the root is minimal, at least during the first year. Second-year chards can develop roots of immense size, but they are woody and inedible. By stripping the leaves of second-year plants on a regular basis, it is sometimes possible to prolong the harvest into the late summer and thus produce flowers at a later time than other beets. This technique can be used to advantage by seed savers where there is more than one variety of beet being grown at the same time. It also strengthens slow-bolting characteristics in the plant.

The common garden beet used for culinary purposes has been perfected over the centuries to achieve a smooth rounded shape and small leaves. Small leaves mean that more plants can be crowded together in a limited space, a feature important to kitchen gardeners. The Chioggia or Bassano-type beet may be considered a standard for this class. Yellow table beets have been known since at least 1583 and may very well date from the Middle Ages. Many gardeners prefer them to red, since the color does not run.

The turnip beet is not much different except for its large leaves and exceptionally large root, which is usually coarse in texture even after prolonged cooking in a pressure cooker. This type of beet is generally treated as a fodder crop for livestock, and of all the beets, it is the one most threatened by extinction due to shifts in agricultural technology. Some gardeners of late have taken a fancy to these fodder heirlooms, such as the Pennsylvania Dutch variety called Deacon Dan's. The difficulty with these beets is that they are the field pumpkins of the beet world and require large open fields with deeply tilled soil. Some of them can weigh as much as 15 pounds, but they need good, sandy soil to develop such a large size.

The fodder beet first appeared in Germany's Lower Rhineland about 1561, where the soil is ideal for their cultivation. They became widespread as a farm crop during the following century under the general name *Mangelwurtzel*, from *Mangold* plus *Wurtzel*. The dialect corruption of *Mangold* into *Mangel* has been commonly misinterpreted as "scarcity," when in fact *Mangelwurtzel* simply means "root beet."

Sugar beets were developed in Upper Silesia (now in Poland) during the 1740s. By 1786 they had become an important commercial crop as an alternative source of sugar, an investment in progressive agriculture heavily financed by the king of Prussia. Sugar beets were intended to compete with cane sugar, not to serve as a table vegetable. In fact, the sweetness was considered repulsive to many cooks in the eighteenth and nineteenth centuries. Today, some gardeners in this country enjoy raising sugar beets precisely for their sweetness. The American love affair with all things sugary has even crept into our taste for root vegetables.

The beet itself is not sweet, at least in its wild state. It is native to the coastal areas of much of western Europe and the Mediterranean, inhabiting ground only a few hundred yards from the high tide mark. Beets were first gathered from the wild as a forage crop, mostly for the spring greens, then later brought under cultivation. It is known from archaeological evidence that they were grown in Northern Europe as early as 2000 B.C. by the Celts, long before the Romans entered the region.

The ancient Greeks and Romans knew both red and white varieties of table beet, as well as a Sicilian beet called *sicula*. This last variety has been identified as chard, and linguistic evidence suggests that it was disseminated throughout the Mediterranean by the Phoenicians. Chard did not originate in Switzerland, as many Americans now imagine, but the green variety known as "Swiss" chard does very much resemble the old *sicula* of Sicily and probably descends from it. The most common use for chard leaves in ancient Greece and Rome was as a wrapping for baked eel. Fish can be prepared in this same manner.

Roman military sites in several parts of Europe north of the Alps have yielded quantities of beet seeds, although it is not possible to determine from the seed whether they were for table beets or for chard. The earliest written record referring to beets in the Middle Ages survives from the A.D. 812 garden inventory of a royal estate at Treola (the present-day Triel-sur-Seine near Versailles) in France. Again, there is some ambiguity, since the term *beta* was used, and this was a word applied both to table beets and to chard.

The implication of this rather complex history is that the beet arrived on our shores in myriad highly developed forms during the colonial period. Because it was a root vegetable easily stored over the winter, many colonists considered it an essential winter food, especially during the infamous period known as the Six Weeks Want. This was a phase in the agricultural calendar running from the end of January through the middle of March when most stored vegetables were used up but planting had not yet begun. During this time, the sprouts from beets in cold storage were especially valued. Today we are not so pressed by these seasonal times of stress, but it is important to keep in mind that with a little planning, the kitchen gardener can maintain a well-supplied cellar and not rely so heavily on store-bought food. Boston seedsman John B. Russell listed the three most popular varieties of beet in his 1828 catalog: Early Blood Turnip, Orange Turnip Rooted, and the Green Beet for stews and soups. The last variety was not a true root beet but a type of spinach beet resembling chard. All three beets are also mentioned in the eighteenth century.

Beets are biennial and must be dug up in the fall anyway, since they will not overwinter where the ground freezes hard. The best beets should be selected for seed and stored in cool, damp sand until the following spring. They can be planted close together so that when they bolt, good cross-fertilization will occur. Beets in flower can stand as high as 5 or 6 feet; thus it is a good plan to stake them well to keep the seed from touching the ground. When the plants begin to die, the seed clusters can be collected and further dried on sheets of paper. When the seed clusters are thoroughly dry and brittle, they can be gently rolled to break them open. This will release the seed, usually 3 to 5 per cluster. Beet seed will remain viable for about six years.

But remember, all beets and chards will cross; thus it is best where small gardens are concerned to increase seed for only one variety a year, unless the plants can be brought to flower at very different times. Three beets and three chards can be maintained on a six-year cycle. For seed saving purposes, reserve at least eight to twelve plants for each variety. What are the best heirloom varieties to grow today? I have tried quite a few. The *American Agriculturist* (April 1870, 123) recommended the Bassano, the Early Blood Turnip Beet, and the newly introduced Egyptian Beet for kitchen gardens. These three heirlooms form a triumvirate of the best sorts for heirloom beginners. I have added a few others to round out a selection of colors and flavors.

Bassano or Chioggia Beet
Beta vulgaris var. *crassa*

I first encountered this Italian heirloom in an open market in Castelfranco many years ago. Several country women were selling it under the quaint name *barbabietola di Chioggia, barbabietola* referring to its diminutive size. Chioggia is a romantic fishing town on the Adriatic coast south of Venice. It is a place to which Venetians flee to escape tourists and relish real Venetian home cooking. For this reason, Chioggia has long been a symbol of authentic Venetian culture, and its name has gradually crept into the horticultural vocabulary of Italian gardeners as a stamp of culinary correctness. I mention this only to point out that the salt marshes of Chioggia did not produce this beet; in fact it was originally called the *barbabietola di Bassano* after the Venetian hill town famous for its grappa. The original Bassano beet was flatter on the bottom than the present-day Chioggia, and the skin was a duller red where it touched the soil, but otherwise they are the same beet.

Le Bon Jardinier (1841) described the introduction of the Bassano beet into France from Italy, where it was already well known in most of the northern parts of the country. Charles Hovey's notice of the beet in his *Magazine for Horticulture* (1843, 99) brought it to the attention of American gardeners. However, it was not until the late 1840s that the Bassano was cultivated to any extent in the United States, and at that, mostly as a specialty beet for urban buyers. There seems to have been some initial resistance to it due to the fact that it was not a true red, which was preferred for pickles.

The root of the Bassano is flattened like a turnip. The skin is bright crimson red, and when sliced, the interior reveals white flesh veined with rose rings, as shown in color plate 12. The mature beets measure 2 to 2½ inches in diameter and are very delicate when cooked. The baby beets are also quite delightful. They are so tender that they may be eaten raw or, if somewhat larger, after the merest blush of steaming.

Bastian's Extra Early Red Turnip Beet
Beta vulgaris var. *crassa*

In Italy the Bassano beets came to market in June because they could be planted in the late winter and develop during the cool moist weather that characterizes northern Italy that time of year. Here, we must plant them in the early spring or in the late summer, depending on when we want them to crop. The market gardener with the earliest beet was always ahead of his competitors, and Bastian's Extra Early Red was developed to capture that advantage. This large, olive-shaped red beet was introduced in 1871 by seedsman Henry Dreer of Philadelphia. It proved quite popular, although *The American Garden* (1889, 57) noted that in spite of its dark red color, the beet tended to blanch to a yellowish shade when boiled, thus losing its fine appearance. Cooking it, however, does not diminish the flavor. Bastian's beet was further improved and released in its present form in 1886, according to a notice in the *Farm Journal* (1886, 29).

Bastian's Extra Early Red Beet

Crosby's Improved Egyptian Beet
Beta vulgaris var. *crassa*

This is a beet that has undergone several major alterations to better acclimatize it to American growing conditions. Its parent was the Egyptian Beet first introduced commercially in Germany, then introduced into this country in 1869 by B. K. Bliss & Sons of New York. The Germans claimed that the variety could be traced to Egypt and replicated features of an ancient Egyptian beet. This assertion cannot be supported by archaeology.

New York seedsman Peter Henderson trialed the Egyptian Beet in 1869 and 1870. Based on those field tests, he recommended the beet to the readers of the *American Horticultural Annual* (1871, 119). Since seed was extremely scarce and expensive, it was several years before the beet came into general use in the United States. However, market gardeners were intrigued by its earliness (50–60 days) and its excellent, rich flavor. But there were problems with its gross, uneven shape, which resulted in waste when submitted to the cook's paring knife. This valid complaint was not taken lightly, for within ten years an improved strain appeared that has now become a standard among beet growers. Enter Crosby's Egyptian Beet in 1880.

This new strain was perfected by Boston market gardener Josiah Crosby and introduced by James J. H. Gregory of Marblehead, Massachusetts. The beet underwent further alteration and was introduced as Crosby's Improved Egyptian Beet by W. W. Rawson & Company of Boston in 1888. Rawson was successor to B. K. Bliss of New York and the author of *Success in Market Gardening.* Thus, having been perfected by many hands, the beet received a glowing endorsement in the *American Garden* (1889, 321). Ever since then this beet has been a perennial favorite with American kitchen gardeners and more or less replaced the old Blood Turnip Beet. It has also been used by European beet breeders to create many additional subvarieties, and it is not rare to see *Crosby's piatta rosso-nera d'Egitto* or *Crosby's betterave rouge noir d'Egypte* in European seed catalogs even to this day.

Crosby's Improved Egyptian Beet

The beet is characterized by smooth skin of a reddish slate color, bloodred flesh, and a small size that guarantees tenderness. It is extremely early, ready for harvest in June or July. Harvesting is easy because most of the root forms above the ground, thus requiring no digging. But the beet must be brought into storage before the first frost, because it cannot bear hard freezing. This is also true of the original Egyptian Beet, as well as the Egyptian Flat Beet, a late variety with a top-shaped root similar in form to the Milan turnip (page 359). These last two heirloom varieties are available from the German seed house of Carl Wilhelm Garvens of Sarstedt, but are not readily available in this country. It is my intention to offer the Egyptian Flat Beet through Seed Savers Exchange within the next two years because this type of flat beet, shaped like a Lady Apple, was never popular outside of Germany and may soon become extinct. Fortunately, Will Bonsall of the Scatterseed Project (which supplies seed through Seed Savers Exchange) has been maintaining the beet for a few years, so hopefully as more gardeners grow it, its benefits will become better known. It is difficult to understand why this beet has not been more popular; it is not only remarkable for its shape and color but also easy to slice with little or no waste.

For beet soups or any recipe where a truly bloodred color is wanted, this beet will supply that need. For pickling eggs the Pennsylvania Dutch way it is excellent, and for staining aprons inevitable. I keep on hand a much-battered "beet" apron to avoid purple splatters on my best ones. Also, it is a good idea to wear rubber gloves when cooking with large quantities of red beet, since the beet juice will stain the fingers and turn the fingernails brown.

Early Blood Turnip Beet
Beta vulgaris var. *crassa*

With this beet we enter the eighteenth century, for the Early Blood Turnip is one of the oldest surviving varieties from that period. Furthermore, it was also one of the most popular with early American gardeners, because it did well in a wide variety of climates. A handsome picture of it appeared in the *Album Vilmorin* (1855, 6). The root is round, about 4 to 4½ inches in diameter, and when ideally formed, it has the shape of an inverted onion dome, the sort seen on Russian churches. The skin is violet-red, the flesh red with paler red rings. The leaves are almost black and have provided chard breeders with a source of color for many varieties of rhubarb chard. The beet can be planted early for summer harvest or late for a fall harvest, and is best when pulled before fully grown.

Early Blood Turnip Beet

Its name is due to the fact that when cooked, the beet exudes a thick juice, similar in consistency to blood. This rich texture was particularly well liked by colonial cooks, especially the Pennsylvania Dutch. Christopher Sauer's herbal, in the installment for 1774, dealt with the blood beet as prepared among the Germans in Pennsylvania and Maryland: cooked in red wine and honey, pickled by baking gently in crocks of vinegar, and served as salads with oil and vinegar.

A related variety called Bull's Blood is equally red and as rich. It has purple-red leaves, but is only good as a spring beet harvested young. If allowed to mature too much, it becomes woody. Old Sturbridge Village has undertaken to maintain the Early Blood Turnip Beet, but seed is also available from a number of small seed firms. Seed for Bull's Blood is scarce.

There is also a yellow form of the blood beet generally known as Yellow Turnip-Rooted or Orange Turnip-Rooted. It is sold today under the name Golden Beet, shown in color plate 13. Its leaves are yellow-green, with yellow ribs and veins. The flesh is dense and sweet. I prefer it to many red beets, even though its brilliant color fades to a dull yellow when cooked. It is excellent pickled with strips of lemon rind, fresh bay leaves, and garlic. Vinegar seems to restore some of the intense color and enhance the sweet flavor of the beet.

Red Castelnaudary Beet (*Betterave Rouge de Castelnaudary*)
Beta vulgaris var. *crassa*

The Castelnaudary is an old French beet about 12 inches long that is more or less carrot-shaped. Fearing Burr mentioned both the red and the yellow varieties in his *Field and Garden Vegetables of America* (1865, 14–15 and 17–18), although at the time they were completely unknown in this country, except among a few connoisseurs. Burr wrote a highly descriptive piece promoting the beet in the *American Horticultural Annual* (1867, 133), and the following year James J. H. Gregory listed the beet in his 1868 seed catalog. This is considered its official date of introduction on this side of the Atlantic.

This beet has always been rare in the United States, even though seed is still readily available among seed savers. Its merits, aside from the unusual shape, are its fine, delicate flavor and its usefulness in winter salads. The carrot shape allows for quicker cooking and easier slicing, and it can be pared like a carrot before cooking. Its major drawback, if it can be called that, is that the beet requires deeply tilled soil to develop a good shape. It seems to thrive best in loose, sandy soil and therefore should be cultivated like a carrot.

The following recipe was intended for the yellow Castelnaudary beet. It is taken from *A Handbook of Foreign Cookery* (1845, 123–24).

Red Castelnaudary Beet

Betterave jaune de Castelnaudary

🐦

Boil it in water. It is eaten as a salad or as a fricassée; if the latter, when boiled cut it in slices; put it into a saucepan with butter, chopped parsley, chives, a pinch of flour, a little vinegar, salt and pepper: let it boil a quarter of an hour. It may also be eaten with a white sauce.

Red Crapaudine Beet (*betterave Crapaudine*)
Beta vulgaris var. *crassa*

The Crapaudine beet is known to date from at least the seventeenth century and may be much older. A "black" swollen-rooted variety of chard was known as early as 320 B.C. in Greece and may in fact be the ancient progenitor of this distinctive black-skinned beet, according to food historian Andrew Dalby (1996, 83). In any case, it was raised in this country during the eighteenth and nineteenth centuries by wealthy individuals who could afford to import seed from France at their own expense. Beyond that, the beet was not generally available from American seedsmen until James J. H. Gregory began offering it in his seed catalogs during the late 1860s. Gregory noted in his 1868 catalog that the "French esteem this as best of all for table use," which was entirely true. Its flavor is unmatched.

However, the outer skin of the beet is remarkable, since it resembles tree bark and is about as easy to remove. While epicures in the dining room extolled its exquisite taste and its proverbial Frenchness, American cooks railed against the Crapaudine with ax in hand. If the barky skin can be said to have a benefit, it is clearly in the protection it affords the beet while in the ground. I left a row of Crapaudines in the garden over the winter one year, and they were not only undamaged by a hard freeze but actually sent out leaves under deep snow. I would therefore recommend the beet for its hardiness. On clay soil it tends to be tough, but on sandy ground the beet grows more round in shape and less dense. And, happily, the skin seems to slip off easier after prolonged cooking.

The leaves of this beet are also quite distinctive, being a dark metallic purple, "mulberry color," as it was called in the 1600s. They make perfectly stunning salad greens, but they are much subject to leaf miners during hot, dry weather. I suggest keeping the plants well watered so that they are not weakened. Insecticidal soap applied regularly to the leaves will eliminate the leaf miners.

Chards and Spinach Beets

Here we have problems with terminology; as Eleanour Sinclair Rhode noted in her *Uncommon Vegetables* (1946, 55), chards are the blanched stalks of young globe artichoke leaves. These are prepared in cookery, like cardoons. This should not be surprising, since *chard* is a corruption of the French word for cardoon. So it is in England, but in this country, chards are the leaves of a certain type of beet that British gardeners refer to as the Silver Beet or Sea Kale Beet. Americans have long since forgotten that "Swiss chard" originally meant Swiss cardoon, one of those curious euphemisms like "Jerusalem artichoke" (page 167) that has little to do with botanical reality.

The Silver Beet or Sea Kale Beet (the chard of America) is mentioned by John Parkinson in his *Paradisus* (1629). This is a variety of chard with a thick white stem. As I have already mentioned, this type of beet has been known since classical antiquity, and its ancient name, *cicla,* is of Punic (Phoenician) origin. In old garden books it is often referred to as a "white beet," which can be confusing since there was a white-rooted variety of common table beet. Ottavio Targioni-Tozzetti (1825, 34) referred to chard in his Italian botanical dictionary as *beta cicla* or *bietola bianca* (white beet); this ambiguity was not limited to English alone. Furthermore, the French added their own layer of confusion by referring to chard, especially the red and yellow varieties, as Chilean beet (*poirée à carde du Chile*).

Richard Bradley, in his *Country Housewife and Lady's Director* (1732, 2:110), called chards beet chards, which appears to be the usage that came to America. Under the beet chard, Bradly supplied a recipe for a pie consisting of one-third part chopped chard, one-third part chopped spinach (orach may be substituted), and one-third part chopped French (round-leafed) sorrel. This was made sweet with sugar very much like the old Pennsylvania Dutch sorrel pies of the last century. Many cooks in this country (and in France) still throw away the chard leaves, using only the stems. This is because most chards, especially the red varieties, turn black after they are cooked, one reason, I think, why the Pennsylvania Dutch used dark brown sugar in their chard-and-sorrel pies.

This discoloration can be avoided altogether by resorting to a little kitchen secret called a blanching stock (*blanc*). For a typical recipe serving four to six persons, the chard should be blanched in 3 quarts of well-salted water into which about 4 tablespoons of flour has been sifted. This is whisked smooth to remove all lumps and then gradually brought to a boil. Once it is boiling, the heat is reduced, and lemon juice or vinegar is added. Then add the chard and cook uncovered only long enough to tenderize it (10 to 15 minutes). Drain immediately and use in casseroles, in microwave recipes, or with mixed vegetables. Due to a chemical reaction it undergoes in the starchy water, the chard will retain its color and not blacken after cooking.

All chards and spinach beets are biennial. For seed-saving purposes, they must be lifted and moved into winter protection in regions where the ground freezes. They are too tender to overwinter in the open garden. I pot mine up and put them in my greenhouse. A cool greenhouse is best; otherwise the chards will bolt before they can be moved out of doors the following spring. For seed saving, always plan on a minimum of eight plants; twelve is preferable for genetic diversity. But even eight plants will yield so much seed that it will be difficult to use all of it up, so share it with friends.

Spinach beets differ from chards in that they are hardy and can be overwintered under salt hay in most areas of the country where winter temperatures do not consistently push below 0° F. Spinach beets will produce heavily until a hard frost and then revive quickly the following spring. They will cross with beets and chards; thus precautions must be taken if they are to be raised for seed in the same garden.

Sea Kale Beet or Swiss Chard
Beta vulgaris var. *cicla*

This was grown in America in the eighteenth century and was the most common sort of chard found in our gardens. It is characterized by very white stems, often 1½ inches broad, and short, spreading leaves resembling spinach in color. Of all the chards, this is the hardiest, although it cannot be overwintered like spinach. Some American seedsmen referred to this as Green Chard or Green Sea Kale Beet to distinguish it from the Silvery Sea Kale Beet, a broad-stemmed variety grown in England but seldom seen in the United States.

Chilean Beet
Beta vulgaris var. *cicla*

Developed in the 1830s, this variety of chard was definitely known to American gardeners by 1848, although it was often grown more as an ornamental than as a vegetable. This is the case in France even today. There are three distinct varieties or subvarieties, the red, the yellow, and the crinkled-leaf. American seedsmen usually refer to the red variety as rhubarb chard. The yellow type is generally called golden chard, the name that appeared with it when it was first introduced. The yellow is by far the rarest in this country, although Seeds Blüm offers a fine strain with very rich coloration.

Since all of the colored chards were created by breeding them with beets that had exceptionally striking leaves, there are all grades of color and intensities available. There are coppery leaves with pink veins, rust purples with metallic splashes, vibrant reds, and pumpkin oranges with olive-green leaves. Some of these are shown in color plate 14. The crinkled-leaf chard, called White Curled Swiss Chard by Vilmorin (1885, 280), was introduced into England in 1828 as a "new" French variety. It appeared shortly thereafter in this country, although it remained a specialty vegetable until later in the century. A selection called Lucullus was introduced in the 1890s and is still popular today. The leaves of this type of chard are characterized by curling and crimping, much like a savoy cabbage. This adds nothing to the flavor. There are colored versions of this, both in red and in yellow.

Spinach Beet or Perpetual Spinach Leaf Beet
Beta vulgaris var. *cicla*

The *American Horticultural Annual* (1869, 128) remarked that this was "not altogether a new variety" and that it "deserves to be better known." I repeat these words because they are as true now as they were in 1869. The beet was well known in England in the eighteenth century and was consistently listed by our seedsmen from 1800 onward, yet no amount of recommendation seems to have increased its popularity. Its hardiness in our climate certainly has its benefits. On the other hand, if the plants are not kept well watered or clear of leaf miners, they can present a discouraging appearance. Leaf miners on beets are one thing, but when they riddle luxuriant greens with so many tunnels that the leaves look like ferns, it is no wonder our gardeners give up. Leaf miners have their season, and if the spinach beets are planted early enough in the spring, they will be large enough in June to withstand the attack. Insecticidal soap will kill the miners, and removing infested leaves only encourages the plants to produce more.

Eleanor Sinclair Rhode noted in *Vegetable Cultivation and Cookery* (1944, 65) that the outer leaves must be picked on a regular basis anyway; otherwise they grow large and coarse and draw off flavor from the young ones. A 20-foot row will repay itself handsomely with a constant supply of greens from May through November. They can be eaten raw or cooked like spinach, which they resemble in taste. The stems have an earthy quality that I do not find objectionable. It can be modified with a little lemon juice or zest of orange. In raw salads, nuts are more compatible with the flavor, as are mushrooms.

Broad Beans (Fava Beans)

The popularity of the fava bean has undergone a peculiar evolution in America. In the colonial period it was an extremely common feature of our kitchen gardens and remained so into the 1840s, yet it gradually fell out of fashion, only to be replaced by the lima bean. More than anything, the development of the bush lima and its preference for our hot summers sealed the fate of the fava bean. But the decline also reflected a larger shift in American tastes from English cookery to a cookery more suited to our lifestyle and national preferences.

Amelia Simmons discusses two popular varieties of fava beans in her *American Cookery* (1796, 14–15), the Windsor bean and the horse bean, two very opposite types of favas. The first was most certainly associated in this country with genteel cookery of an Anglocentric kind—recipes for the bean can be found for example in *The Virginia House-Wife*, while the latter was almost exclusively a working-class vegetable. The horse bean has been rehabilitated recently and is now being sold as a dry bean under the name "baby favas."

Philadelphia seedsman Bernard M'Mahon offered fourteen varieties of fava beans in 1806, which may be read as an attempt to cater to a strong demand among the wealthy who depended upon him for seed. His Broad Spanish may be equated with the Agua Dulce I have chosen to include in this book. Of all the favas, it does the best for me. However, many of the old varieties, whether from M'Mahon's catalogs or those listed by Fearing Burr in 1865, are not easily available today, and this hampers me greatly in recommending heirloom varieties for my readers. My overall favorite is Early Mazagan, one of the most popular varieties in the colonial period because it came into season before the plants were destroyed by our summer heat. Unfortunately, it cannot be had except from a few growers in England; therefore I must omit it but with heavy heart.

The oldest depiction of a fava bean appeared in the great codex of Dioskorides prepared at Constantinople between A.D. 500 and 511. Signe Sundberg-Hall, the artist who has prepared all of the drawings in this book, has redrawn the plant from the *Codex* to show it in a more lifelike form. It appears to be one of the *equina* type of favas, with two, at most three, seeds per pod. When the ancient Greeks and Romans mentioned beans in their writings, they meant favas, for that was the only sort of bean known to them at the time. There is a recipe in the Roman cookbook by Apicius (Flower and Rosenbaum 1974, 138–39) for *fabaciae virides et Baianae* (green fava beans and beans from Baia), which proposes several ways of cooking and serving them.

Fava beans have been under cultivation for such a long time—many thousands of years—that the wild ancestor is now extinct. There are some undomesticated beans closely related to the wild ancestor, but they are not the favas from which our present culinary varieties evolved. The culinary varieties are divided into three types: *Vicia faba* var. *minor*, small, rounded-seeded varieties resembling lentils and often referred to as "field beans"; *Vicia faba* var. *equina*, midsize and rather oblong beans often resembling peas; and *Vicia faba* var. *maior*, the large, flat-seeded varieties presently used in cookery. All of these varieties will cross with one another, thus giving rise to hundreds, perhaps thousands, of intermediate forms. It is clear from classical authors that favas were used in both the green and dry state, but only archaeology has con-

The fava bean of
Dioskorides, 512 A.D.

firmed that the *minor* and *equina* varieties were known in antiquity. The large-podded (*megalosperma*) varieties like Windsor Long Pod and Agua Dulce originated in the Iberian Peninsula and cannot be documented prior to A.D. 800. Anyone experimenting with Roman recipes from *Apicius* must be careful to use *equina* or *minor* type favas for the proper visual effect and flavor.

Historically, the *equina* favas were raised in the Celtic regions of Britain and northwest France and used as a dry bean in winter cookery. In fact, there is not much historical evidence suggesting that any of the fava beans were originally harvested green in regions north of the Alps, unless consumed as a luxury food. Rather, dry favas were more commonly used to make flour for hearth breads or broken up into grits for porridges.

All of the favas discussed in the following pages are cultivated the same way. Seed should be planted as early as possible in the spring, preferably at the same time as peas or potatoes. Or, start the seedlings indoors in pots and transplant them to the garden as soon as the weather is mild. Young fava plants will withstand hard frosts, and some varieties are hardy to 12° F. In many places they can be overwintered by simply covering the plants with straw. The tops may die back, but the roots will sprout again in the spring. Since favas thrive in cool, damp weather—one reason why they do so well in England—it is far better to plant them early rather than later. Hot weather not only causes the flowers to drop, but also heralds black aphids, which attack favas ruthlessly. Henry Ward Beecher (1859, 223) confirmed years ago in his treatise on gardening that all varieties of favas, "in our hot dry summers, are very difficult to raise."

The black aphids will sap the plants of their strength, and if allowed to go unchecked, will severely damage the crop. They can be controlled with insecticidal soap applied liberally at regular intervals. Sifted wood ashes also work, especially if applied before a gentle rain. The alkaloids in the ashes will kill soft-bodied insects without damaging the plants. But black aphids are not the only problem. Slugs present a far greater threat to favas in the early spring than frost. With little to eat, they are attracted to the young bean plants and will strip them to the ground in the course of a night. They will even climb mature plants to eat the flowers. Diatomaceous earth must be scattered copiously around the base of the plants; otherwise destruction will surely ensue. For more on diatomaceous earth, refer to my discussion of slugs under Parà Cress (page 330).

Once the plants begin setting pods, crop the tops (the greens are edible raw or cooked) so that the strength is directed into seed development. The young pods may be harvested like string beans, or when more mature, the shelly beans may be harvested and cooked like limas. The outer skin is always removed from the beans before serving. It was common in early American cookbooks to serve the beans mashed to a puree consistency. To serve them in the skins was considered rustic and vulgar.

After the beans are harvested, the plants may be thrown into a heap and dried in the sun. They will turn black and brittle. This straw makes excellent mulch for the garden. For seed-saving purposes, however, set aside at least ten plants and let them run to seed. When the plants begin to die (the pods also turn black), the pods can be harvested and dried in an airy room away from the direct sun. When the pods are brittle and the seeds fall out easily, pick out only the most perfect and best-colored seeds and pack them into airtight containers. Use the culls for cookery. Favas raised as dry beans are also prepared this way.

Fava beans are self-pollinating, but bees will cause considerable crossing, especially bumble bees, which are particularly attracted to the flowers. Since favas bloom so early in the season, they are even more prone to crossing than many other common vegetables. The suggested isolation distance is a mile, which means that varieties planted any closer must be caged to preserve seed purity. Essentially, it is safer to grow one variety at a time. The seed is good for five years; therefore, by rotating annually, it is possible to maintain several varieties.

Agua Dulce Bean
Vicia faba var. *maior*

This is the Agua Dulce Long-Podded of Vilmorin (1885, 25), a variety that originated in Spain as a selection of *haba de Sevilla*, also called *haba de Tarragona*. It is a *megalosperma* type that traces through *haba de Sevilla* to the late Middle Ages. It was introduced commercially in the middle of the nineteenth century and was illustrated in the *Album Vilmorin* (22, 1871), but was not grown in the United States until quite recently. However, the *haba de Sevilla* was raised in Mexico since the period of Spanish settlement, and therefore, Agua Dulce has many close relatives in the numerous old Mexican varieties that evolved in the Southwest. Many of those varieties are still available from Native Seeds/SEARCH.

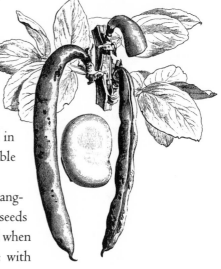

The plant is about 3½ feet tall, with huge, broad pods ranging in length from 6 to 7 inches. There are usually 4 or 5 seeds per pod. The dry seed is flat and rather honey-colored, and when boiled and worked to a paste, makes a natural marriage with pureed chickpeas. Individually, the plants are not highly productive, but a large plot of perhaps two hundred plants would sup-

Agua Dulce Broad Bean

ply a household amply. This variety always outproduces the others in my garden, all things equal. I can only assume that this has something to do with the fact that I am on the same latitude as Spain and that the sunlight in my garden reminds it of home.

Horse Bean or English Bean
Vicia faba var. *equina*

Amelia Simmons explained in her cookbook why this bean was worthy of the kitchen garden (1796, 15): "*English Bean*, what *they* denominate the *Horse Bean*, is mealy when young, is profitable, easily cultivated, and may be grown on worn out grounds; as they may be raised by boys, I cannot but recommend the more extensive cultivation of them." All of which is true, but since one plant only produces 8 or 12 seeds, this is a bean that is best raised in a small field. Since the plants do not branch and grow about 32 inches tall, they can be planted close together. The pods are 2¼ inches long and contain 3 small round, brown seeds. I grow this fava mostly as a dry bean to grind for flour. But since it is an heirloom variety readily available and resembles the sort of beans raised in Roman times, I take a certain degree of pleasure in using it to create fanciful dishes of an antique sort. The shelly bean is mealy, as Amelia Simmons pointed out, and therefore excellent for bean dips. Most important, the old varieties of favas like this one are extremely rich in basic proteins, carbohydrates, and vitamins. For this reason, vegetarian cookery has taken a new look at the fava bean and its culinary possibilities.

When planted in early April, the plants come to pod in early June but quickly succumb to the heat. As an experiment to see whether a fall crop would be more productive, I planted seed at the end of July. By early December the plants had achieved their normal height, but no flowers were in sight. Freezing weather did not damage the plants as much as bitter cold wind. Even if my weather had been mild, it would have taken the beans six months to come to pod in the fall, rather than three in the spring. This can only mean that most favas are indeed day-length sensitive, and shorter days will prolong the necessary growing season. For gardeners in areas of the country where winters are mild, this calculation should be taken into account. I might add, however, that the White Windsor (page 97) will succeed as a fall crop in my region if forced in a greenhouse then planted outside in early September.

Martoc Bean
Vicia faba var. *maior*

To the casual eye, this fava appears identical to the horse bean. If I accidentally mix the seeds, I cannot tell one from the other. However, there are differences, and these are most evident on the living plants, as botanists would point out. This issue was altogether immaterial to the medieval farmers who raised this bean, for this a true medieval variety, and the reason was simple. Botanists have discovered in the Near East and Morocco, where medieval field patterns still persist in many areas, that the farmers grew all their fava varieties together in very small plots. Due to crossing, each field developed its own peculiar mix of varieties, and this resulted in its own "signature" fava. Beans were identified not by commercially uniform varieties but by their field or place of origin. This is quite evident in the reference in Apicius mentioned earlier, where the author recognized a certain type of fava bean from the town of Baia. The Martoc is an English example of this process.

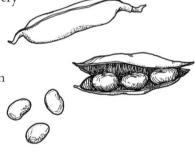

Martoc Broad Bean

The Martoc fava is presumed to be one of England's oldest strains, and perhaps the oldest pure strain of its type from anywhere in Europe. It was salvaged from oblivion by the Henry Doubleday Research Association, having been preserved for many years in the garden of an English bishop. It exhibits all of the characteristics of an old-style fava (2 seeds per pod), and I am convinced that it may be an *equina* x *maior* of certifiably ancient origin. Since the dry beans are rather flat, there is consensus that this variety is a *maior*, but a very primitive one. When I set the beans beside my Dutch Gray

Peas (page 244), there is an obvious similarity in color and shape, even to the same black "eye" at the helium (the belly button of the bean). This curious coincidence throws some light on the taste preferences of medieval cooks and may suggest a reason why seventeenth-century New Englanders took so quickly to the Cranberry Bean (page 65). It looked like something they knew already.

Since the Martoc was cooked as a dry bean like the old gray peas, it made a murky brown porridge that today would have few takers unless heavy into ale. Yet for nuttiness and texture it is unsurpassed, and it offers a range of culinary possibilities, especially when cooked with whole grains like spelt, mixed with oats, or even broken into bits and used like nuts in stuffings or puddings.

The dry bean must be blanched before cooking. The beans are placed in boiling water for 10 to 15 minutes, then drained. The outer skin of each bean must then be removed (a job for servants in the old days), and the beans simmered in water or meat stock for about 30 minutes, or until tender.

Windsor Broad Bean
Vicia faba var. *maior*

It is redundant to grow the Windsor Broad Bean and the Agua Dulce in the same garden because they are so similar in appearance that they could be confused easily. However, in northerly regions of the United States where the summers are cool and short, Windsor Long Pod is definitely the strain of Windsor bean recommended. For the heirloom enthusiast, the Windsor Broad Bean (synonymous with White Windsor) is the bean of the old American gentry, and for an eighteenth-century dish of broad beans American style, this is the bean of scripture.

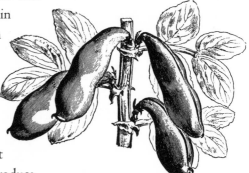

Windsor Broad Bean

For this is a white-seeded fava bean with huge, erect pods, as shown in color plate 16. True Windsors produce only 2 beans per pod, like 2 morels to an apple tree. Windsor Long Pod produces 4 to 6 beans, not quite so rare and wasteful, and demanding fewer servants in the scullery. There was a definite social division between those who grew Windsors and those who grew Windsors of a lesser sort.

The *Transactions of the Horticultural Society of London* for 1833 undertook a lengthy excursus on all the fava bean varieties then under cultivation in England. Naturally, the Windsor surfaced ahead of the pack. Yet it is important to remember that it is of Spanish origin and entered England from Portugal in the 1300s. Its oldest name was Small Spanish, which places it on more equal footing with Martoc. Only through careful selection did it achieve its present form, and in fact, the "New Long Pod" was not announced until 1837, when London seedsmen Field & Childs exposed it to commerce.

Not satisfied that the last word was the last, the *Gardener's Magazine* (1836, 259–60) published a trial of the known varieties of Windsor bean, listing all of the common synonyms, as well as the basic specifications. The dry seed should be "of white colour" and very large. Well, they are greenish white and, like Dr. Martin's lima (page 75), lose their natural ability to germinate after three years. In commerce, however, the truly green Windsors were called Tokers (now called Green Windsors) and the small seeds sifted out of the seed stock were sold as Mumfords, practices that have given rise to the false impression that these were distinct varieties. There are probably several hundred popular names for various types and conditions of Windsor beans, but the truth is, they are all the same bean. The true Windsor is a noble fava with a flavor very close to a butternut. I can well appreciate why Thomas Jefferson grew it.

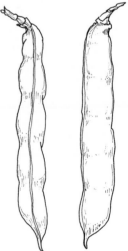

Windsor Long Pod Broad Bean

Susannah Carter's *Frugal Housewife* (1792, 44–45) contains the following recipe for boiling broad beans:

To Boil Broad Beans

❦

Beans require a good deal of water, and it is best not to shell them till just before they are ready to go into the pot. When the water boils, put them in with some pick'd parsley, and some salt; make them boil up quick, and when you see them begin to fall, they are enough. Strain them off. Garnish the dish with boiled parsley, and send plain butter in a cup, or boat.

Cabbages

I doubt that the average grocery store shopper is aware that kohlrabies, broccoli, cauliflower, brussels sprouts, kale, and heading cabbages are all variations of the same plant. Since these vegetables often come to season at different times and are often displayed in separate areas of our markets, it is only natural not to think of them in this unified fashion. Yet the gardener must confront this reality, for when it comes to saving seed, this kinship is crucial.

Many of the vegetables in this book have distinguished genealogies, but none are more complicated than those of the brassicas, owing to the crossing of various forms and the ease with which these plants can be altered through selective cultivation. They are also extremely rich in many of the basic nutrients required by humans; thus their place in the historical kitchen garden was established long, long ago. Unfortunately, since they are biennial, all of the brassicas present special difficulties for the gardener who wants to preserve heirloom varieties. At the outset, I must confess that this problem presented me with many knotty choices, for while there are hundreds of heirloom varieties to choose from, not many of them are as simple to grow as lettuce.

While glancing through the 1867 seed catalog of the Baltimore seedsmen E. Whitman & Sons, I noticed that they pragmatically advised such old standby varieties of cabbage as Early Wakefield, Early York, Ox Heart (a French variety), and Winnigstädt. I have decided to follow this same course at the expense of the more exotic heirlooms that are now surfacing among seed savers. The same may be said of the kales and cauliflowers, and all the other brassicas listed in this section. However, I have tried to build into my selections a certain degree of variety; enough, I believe, that after a few seasons the beginning gardener will know which types are most practical for the garden and which are not. Need I remind my readers that with cabbages, soil is everything, and fertility is all the rest? Good cabbage land must be well manured.

I should point out that all the members of the genus *Brassica* and the species *oleracea* trace their genetic origin to northwestern Europe, specifically to the coastal region extending from western France to Holland and including the southern coast of England. This family of vegetables was first cultivated by the ancient Celts, who also gave us our basic cabbage vocabulary. The Celts had several words for cabbages, which in itself implies a high level of cultivation. The Celtic word *kol* became *Kohl* in German; *kal* became *kale* in English. The Celtic term *bresic* became *brassica* in Latin, and *kap*, a term for heading cabbages, became *Kappes* in German and *cabbage* in English.

The Romans knew cabbages well and cultivated a great many varieties. They differentiated three basic types: a crinkled or curly-leafed type equivalent to curly-leafed kale; a smooth-leafed sort similar to open-headed cabbages like Green Glaze (page 109); and wild cabbage with small round leaves gathered as a colewort or collard. The Romans also grew cauliflower, which they called *cyma*, and tall cabbages with large stems like the *couve tronchuda* or Portugal Cabbage (page 107). Descriptions of the old varieties survive in Roman agricultural literature, but without the aid of pictures (which do not survive), it is not possible to form a definite impression about their specific appearance or how they might be related to one another. This is important when discussing heirloom cabbages, because many of them may be much older than documentation suggests. In any case, to me some of the most interesting cabbages from a culinary standpoint are also historically some of the oldest. If I had my choice, I would recommend the English variety known as Vanack. It is an old Sussex and Hampshire cabbage that was preserved in the gardens of the countess of Bridgewater at Ashbridge, Hertfordshire, and in the gardens of the earl of Egremont at Petworth since the middle of the eighteenth century. But alas, seed is not generally available, and so it is with many of the most fascinating cabbages.

The most commonly grown heirloom members of the cabbage family may be divided into eight cultivated forms, classified in the following manner, according to *Hortus Third*:

1. Cabbages that form heads: *Brassica oleracea* var. *capitata* L. American truck farmers usually divide this into the Wakefield group, cabbages with pointed heads, and the Copenhagen group, cabbages that form heads in the shape of round balls. Actually, there is also a third group which includes the drumheads, cabbages with broad, flat heads. One of the best known of the early American varieties in this last group was Large Bergen, also called Great American.

2. Savoy cabbages, characterized by blistered or puckered leaves: *Brassica oleracea* var. *bullata*. Savoys come in a variety of head shapes, from very loose, leafy heads resembling kale to monstrous drumheads. For flavor, I think the best savoys are the smallest varieties. Savoys are also extremely hardy, more so than many of the other heading cabbages.

3. Italian broccoli, asparagus broccoli, sprouting broccoli, and all forms of broccoli that do not form solid heads: *Brassica oleracea* var. *italica* Plenck. These are easy to grow, but sensitive to drought and cold weather.

4. Portugal cabbages or *couve tronchuda*, cabbages with thick stems used like celery: *Brassica oleracea* var. *tronchuda*. There are many subvarieties. In the St. Gall cloister garden (A.D. 820) in Switzerland, a bed was set aside for cabbages (*caulas*) of a sort similar to the *tronchuda* group.

5. Kohlrabi: *Brassica oleracea* var. *gongylodes* L.

6. Broccoli and cauliflowers: *Brassica oleracea* var. *botrytis* L.

7. Brussels sprouts: *Brassica oleracea* var. *gemmifera*. This group is the most recent historically, for it did not appear until 1785.

8. Cow cabbages, tree kales, collards, and rosette-headed kales: *Brassica oleracea* var. *acephala*. Most of the oldest forms of cabbage belong to this group.

When purchasing seeds, be certain that the packages are clearly marked according to botanical group. There are kales and cabbages from Asia which do not belong to the *oleracea* species. It is important to know this when growing out plants for seed-saving purposes, and it is even better to check a reliable reference if there is any question. I have purchased seed from seed companies only to discover that the contents were not properly identified; there is no excuse for this.

Most of the heirloom varieties presently available date from the nineteenth century, one of the exceptions being Early York, an English variety introduced from Flanders in the early eighteenth century. A strain called Large York was once grown extensively around Philadelphia; its equivalent among the Pennsylvania Dutch was Large Early Schweinfurt, a Palatine variety introduced in the eighteenth century, but not available commercially in this country until almost a hundred years later. Even Chinese cabbages have been known in the West for a much greater length of time than many gardeners would suppose. The *chou chinoise* (*pe-tsai*), a member of the genus *Brassica*, but of the species *rapa*, and several Chinese mustards were introduced into Europe in 1836. According to an article in *Le Bon Jardinier* (1839), the seed was brought from China by missionaries. Otherwise, a large portion of the surviving heirlooms are improved strains rather than facsimiles of the original introductions. The difficulty of overwintering cabbages of all sorts for seed-saving purposes has greatly limited the availability of many varieties among seed savers. More reliable is the seed from the small seed houses listed at the back of this book, since several of them specialize in heirloom cabbages. They are able to grow many different varieties under contract, whereas the home gardener must rely on one or two varieties brought to flower at different times—hand pollination is simply out of the question. Serious seed savers might want to refer to J. M. Lupton's *Cabbage and Cauliflower for Profit*, first published in 1894, as a useful guide to raising heirloom American cabbages. His article "Development of the Cabbage" in the *American Garden* (1890, 289–91) is particularly useful for understanding how cabbages were evaluated in the nineteenth century and why some varieties were preserved while others were not.

Seed saving is compounded by the fact that cabbages are out-pollinating, which means that pollen must be transferred from one plant to another rather than from flower to flower on the same plant. Therefore, many more plants are required to produce seed with a good genetic balance. Ten plants are an advisable minimum. There are several ways to deal with this.

First, whole plants can be dug up, potted, and stored over the winter in a cool shed, cool enough to keep them dormant but not so cold that they freeze. Or, if there is sufficient corn in the garden, save the stalks and bury the cabbages as shown in the old woodcut. The corn stalks form an insulated barrier,

Method of storing cabbages under corn.

especially effective if the cabbages are laid in a shallow pit. Throw sod over the corn or a tarp so that raccoons cannot dig into the hill. In the spring, replant the cabbages and let them bloom for seed.

Second, there is another method that also saves a great deal of space. When harvesting the cabbages, trim them off as close to the head as possible, leaving the stem undamaged. Mark the stems of the plants that produced crops most true to type. Dig up those stems with their roots and store them in damp sand in a Styrofoam ice chest. Put the chest in a cool shed or garage where the stems will not freeze. Planted in the spring, the stems will develop sprouts and flowers. Seed can be saved from these flowers.

Lastly, cabbages can be propagated by cuttings, which eliminates the necessity of saving seed. Select the stems of the best plants and slice them into quarters from top to bottom, making certain that each piece has roots. Dip the roots in hormonal rooting compound and plant in sand in flower pots or in a cold frame. In the spring the cuttings can be planted like seedling cabbages. This process can be continued from year to year, thus perpetuating and increasing the cabbages with the best traits. This technique is especially useful where several varieties are being grown together and there is a definite need to avoid crosses. Cuttings can also be taken from woody stems by slicing across right above the leaf nodes, but this method is tricky and requires experience. Normally, roots will develop at the nodes where sprouts would form. However, if the stems are too green and soft, the cuttings may rot before they take root.

I have used all of these techniques successfully for everything except kohlrabi. I have not attempted it with kohlrabi due to the nature of its root, and frankly, it is much easier to order fresh seed so that I can concentrate on the cabbages that are rare or difficult to obtain. At some point, every gardener must decide which vegetables to perpetuate through seed-saving techniques and which to obtain from seedsmen. It is far better to grow one or two of the *oleraceas* well than to drown enthusiasm in a baptism of crop failures or strange-looking culinary mules.

Other brassicas treated in this book include rocket (page 313), two cresses (pages 313 and 317), and radishes (page 295). In general, the seed viability for the cabbages, kales, cauliflowers, and brussels sprouts listed in the following pages is four to five years. However, I would suggest not saving seed beyond three years. Old seed sometimes produces deformed plants, and weak plants are particularly vulnerable to insects and disease. Formerly, it was common practice among gardeners to plant two-year-old seed, as the *Gardener's Magazine* (1828, 246) pointed out: "All the brassica seeds are apt to run when newly saved and early sown." There seems to be some logic to this.

Black Tuscan Palm Tree Kale
Brassica oleracea var. *acephala*

I first stumbled upon this variety of *cavolo di Palma* in Ottavio Targioni-Tozzetti's *Dizzionario Botanico Italiano* (1825, 45–46), curiously wondering to myself whether it could be more impressive than Jersey Cow Cabbage, for surely it does not grow as tall. Later, when I saw the kale in the gardens of the Villa Barbero at Maser high in the hills of the Veneto, I realized immediately that I could not be without it. The Black Tuscan Palm Tree Kale is truly one of the most beautiful kales to grace any kitchen garden. In fact, many gardeners plant it simply for its ornamental merits. There is probably no more spectacular combination than to see this gray-black kale interplanted with vivid green Silesia lettuce (color plate 18), although the Venetian lettuce called *cappuccio ubriacona frastagliata* ("drunken woman frizzy-headed") will do its own to create a carnival effect—and ever so Italian.

The Black Tuscan Palm Tree Kale dates from the eighteenth century and figures in a number of old Tuscan recipes. Prepared like chard, it has an affinity for olive oil and shallots, and goes very well with grilled Chioggia sea pumpkin. It is best when chopped, because the old leaves can be stringy; in fact concentrate on the very young leaves at the top, for they are the most tender. The same may be said for its German counterpart, *Lerchenzungen Grünkohl* (lark's-tongue kale), a frizzy dark green kale with long, narrow leaves similar in shape to the Tuscan variety. It is also medium in height, and therefore the two can be planted together for a stunning visual effect. The German variety is completely winter hardy in Pennsylvania; in fact frost improves the flavor. The Tuscan kale, unfortunately, is extremely tender and will not overwinter in areas where the ground freezes. Even heavy frosts seem to damage it. Plants must be dug up and stored in a cool shed over the winter; I simply move the ones designated for seed saving into my greenhouse.

Since the Tuscan kale grows 2 to 3 feet tall, even higher where the ground is particularly rich, it should be spaced about 3 feet apart in order to develop a good "palm tree" shape. It can also be planted as a single specimen. The slate gray, crinkled leaves are long and narrow, often 24 inches long, and gently drooping; thus the plants require elbow room. The German sort is somewhat shorter and therefore looks better when planted in front of the Tuscan kale. Cabbage worms do not seem to bother either variety, but caterpillars of other butterfly species do. More of a problem are finches and sparrows, which sit on the plants and peck out holes in the leaves. They can leave a handsome bed of kales looking sad and shredded in a matter of days. Bird netting is the only method I have found to deal with this.

Borecole or Dwarf German Kale
Brassica oleracea var. *acephala*

A vegetable with a long history in the United States, Dwarf German Kale first arrived here with Pennsylvania Dutch settlers in the early eighteenth century. However, one of the first historical references thus far uncovered appeared in the correspondence between London plant collector Peter Collinson and John Bartram, the Philadelphia botanist and nurseryman. In March 1735 Collinson sent Bartram seeds for "Winter Green Cole" and "Brown Cole," the latter a strain also known as Deep Purple Kale. Collinson's seed had come to him directly from Germany, where the varieties were known as *Grünkohl* and *Braunkohl* respectively. The extremely winter-hardy green variety was generally planted in September in order to overwinter and provide greens or sprouts in early spring. A century and a half later American horticulturist Charles Parnell wrote an article on "Sprouts, or Dwarf German Greens" for the September 1885 issue of *Vick's Illustrated Monthly Magazine.* In it he described the extensive truck farm industry in the vicinity of New York City devoted entirely to this vegetable.

Whether or not the plant we know today is genetically identical to its eighteenth-century ancestor may be difficult to prove, but visually it is identical to the kales depicted in paintings and woodcuts of that period. The plant is short, about 2 feet tall, with bluish green, frilly leaves. As a garden vegetable, it is one of the most reliable and easy to grow of all the brassicas in this book. A detail of its leaves is shown in color plate 19. For culinary purposes the greens may be treated like spinach, but unless chopped or shredded, they are really too coarse to be served raw in salads. They are perfectly suited to the type of Pennsylvania Dutch casserole salads called *Schales,* which are heated slightly to tenderize the ingredients. Also raised by the Pennsylvania Dutch was a related kale called *Mosbacher Grünkohl,* resembling a cross between curly green kale and *couve tronchuda* or Portugal cabbage (page 107). It is 2 to 2½ feet tall with large, broad, yellow-green leaves. It tastes like broccoli.

For an early harvest, seeds may be planted 4 to 6 weeks before the last frost, about the same time for planting onion sets and potatoes. Otherwise, seeds may be started indoors in flats, the seedlings hardened off and planted in the garden once the ground has dried out after spring thaw. Fall crops are planted 6 to 8 weeks before the first frost, or even later if plants are intended to overwinter for spring greens and seeds. This kale is so hardy that it does not require winter protection. I have continued to harvest it from right under the snow.

For seed-saving purposes it is important to remember that the flowers are not self-fertile; thus more than one plant is needed to produce seed. I would advise planting 10 plants close together for seed purposes. This will ensure a good level of pollination as well as genetic diversity in the seed. The kale can also be propagated by root cuttings.

The following recipe, translated from Anna May's *Die Kleine New Yorker Köchin* (1859, 22), outlines how the kale was prepared in a skillet.

Braunen Kohl zu Kochen (To Cook Kale)

❦

Remove all the leaves so that only the heart with its tiny leaves remain for cooking. Then boil the greens until slightly tender, drain in a colander, and press out the excess liquid. Put a nice piece of butter and a little lard in a skillet, add the kale, and sauté over a high heat. Add salt and chopped onion, and when thoroughly cooked, add a few spoonfuls of bouillon and some sugar. Cover and let this sweat for a few minutes. Also, one can add a few small potatoes cooked in their skins, quartered and browned in a skillet with butter and sugar.

Brussels Sprouts (Red)
Brassica oleracea var. *gemmifera*

Brussels sprouts developed as a mutation of Flanders Kale (*chou caulet de Flandre*) about 1785; thus this group of cabbages represents the most recent accession to the species. For a long time it was considered the ultimate luxury cabbage for one simple reason: it is extremely difficult to grow. The French prefer large sprouts, the Belgians small ones. The smaller sorts are easier to grow, but I would not recommend Brussels sprouts at all were it not for the fact that some gardeners have extremely good luck with them. Most important, they do not take up much room. This is a vegetable that is mostly vertical, and therefore it can be grown among rows of lettuces, carrots, and other low vegetables. Furthermore, a few good plants will yield an abundant crop, as many as 100 to a plant. Therefore, it is important to think of Brussels sprouts in terms of interplanting; they are slow growing and, if planted in a solid patch, will only tie up that portion of the garden for the entire season.

Brussel Sprouts

Another problem is that there are really no pre-1900 heirloom brussels sprout varieties readily available to seed savers. The red variety that I grow was created by crossing an old green variety with Flanders Kale, which happens to be a purple-red. The sprouts are perfectly beautiful miniatures of red cabbages. I made the decision that if I was going to trouble myself with the miseries of coddling Brussels sprouts to perfection, then I wanted something I could not find in a supermarket. That has been my guiding principle, even though I have never had more failures in the garden than with Brussels sprouts.

Raising Brussels sprouts is a study in humility, for they demand much and give little in return unless they are perfect. My failures with Brussels sprouts have only prompted me to keep at it until I got it right. Half the success in gardening is to remain open-minded and turn mistakes into lessons. Leave Brussels sprouts off the list unless you have a serious interest in mastering them. Otherwise, stick to kale.

Brussels sprouts need a very long, mild growing season, and therefore they do much better in parts of the South than in other sections of the country. If seed is sown in northern areas in May for planting in June, there is a chance of a decent harvest by November. In the South, plants can be set out in July, with harvests in December. The sprouts come to crop very quickly and do not linger in their sprout state for very long. If neglected, they will burst, bud out into small shoots, or rot.

To encourage the formation of sprouts, it is necessary to pull off some of the leaves below each sprout so that the energy of the plant is directed into the buds. Cropping the top or head will help with some varieties, but this is itself a culinary delicacy and should not be destroyed, particularly if the plants are being saved for seed. Harvest the largest buds first so that the smaller ones will benefit. Cut the sprouts from the stem neatly, leaving as much of the spur as possible. This precaution will result in a second crop of sprouts. Always keep the plants well watered, but do not fertilize them heavily. If the ground is too rich, the plants will develop large leaves at the expense of the buds. The most common insect pest to attack the sprouts are gray aphids. They are ugly, and they will disfigure the plants quickly. Insecticidal soap will kill them on contact; wood ashes dusted over the plants before a light rain will also work.

Cannonball Cabbage
Brassica oleracea var. *capitata*

Because of its diminutive size, this is my favorite heirloom cabbage for small gardens. One of my friends described it as resembling a mammoth Brussels sprout, and I think that is a pretty fair assessment of its appearance. It was introduced in 1868 by James J. H. Gregory of Marblehead, Massachusetts, and was most likely a strain of Copenhagen. Gregory himself described it as having a head "about as round and hard as a cannonball." The entire cabbage, including outer leaves, grows no larger than 12 inches across, but it is extremely dense and perfect for shredding into coleslaw or sauerkraut. It is usually described as maturing with Winnigstädt, which means that it should be treated as a fall cabbage.

Cannonball Cabbage

I would suggest planting the seedlings in August; if they are planted in the spring, disaster will ensue. The small heads are so tight that they cannot take a great deal of hot weather and high humidity. They will crack and, if the day is particularly hot, actually burst open. I protected the cabbages with sun screens, and even that did not help. However, Cannonball would probably do very well in areas where the summers are cool. It is such a fine little cabbage, very neatly formed, and deliciously tender when cooked, that it is well worth a trial. Just be certain to keep it well watered.

1. Asparagus pea (page 48) edible flowers and ripe pods.

2. The purple-podded Blue Coco Bean (page 54) and White Caseknife Bean (page 56). The Caseknife Bean is shown in both the shelly and ripe-pod stages.

3. Buerre de Rocquencourt wax bean (page 56), bottom right, and the Ice Bean (page 59), top left.

4. Wild Pigeon Bean, Mostoller Wild Goose Bean (page 63), and the Sulphur Bean (page 69).

5. *Red Cranberry Pole Bean (page 65).*

7. *Blue Shackamaxon Bean (page 54).*

6. *Scotia or Genuine Cornfield Bean (page 68) growing with Sehsapsing corn (page 146).*

8. *From left to right: Pawnee Bush Bean (page 52), Rio Zape Bean (page 61), and Munsi Wolf Bean or Speckled Minisink, a rare Lenape pole bean from the region of the Delaware Water Gap.*

9. *Shown here as dry beans, from left to right: Speckled Saba or Bushel Bean (page 77), Dr. Martin's Lima Bean (page 75), and Carolina Lima (page 74).*

10. From left to right: white Dutch Runner Bean (page 79), Painted Lady Runner Bean (page 79), and Black Coat Runner Bean (79).

13. Golden Beet (page 88).

11. Purple Hyacinth Bean (page 81) showing the brilliantly colored pods.

14. Various types of chard or sea kale beet, including the white stemmed Swiss chard (page 91), the red Chilean Beet (page 91), and Golden Chard (page 91).

12. Bassano or Chioggia Beet (page 84).

15. Hardy Spinach Beet (page 91) photographed in December.

16. Windsor Broad Bean (page 97). The green seeds are harvested as shelly beans at this stage.

17. Detail of the flower of the Agua Dulce Broad Bean (page 95).

18. Black Tuscan Palm Tree Kale (page 102) with Silesia lettuce (page 186).

19. Detail of Dwarf German Kale (page 103). This variety remains green all winter.

20. Couve Tronchuda or Portugal Cabbage (page 107). The cooked stems taste have a similar to broccoli.

21. Early Jersey Wakefield Cabbage (page 108) is most tender when harvested very young, as shown here.

22. *An assortment of cabbages: Red Drumhead (page 116), the small round-headed Cannonball (page 106), and the pointed Winnigstädt cabbage (page 119).*

23. *Green Glaze Collards (page 109) are resistant to cabbage worms.*

24. *January King (page 110) is a savoy cabbage that changes color as it grows.*

27. *Parisian Rondo or Golden Ball carrot (page 122), a nine-teenth-century variety developed for cold frames.*

25. *Jersey Cow Cabbage (page 112), shown here as a first-year plant about seven feet tall.*

28. *Sea Kale (page 119) has powdery gray leaves.*

26. *Purple Vienna kohlrabi (page 112). The skins may be dried and used for winter soup stocks.*

29. *White Belgian Carrot (page 126) and Long Red Surrey Carrot (page 123).*

30. *Red Celery (page 134) retains its distinct flavor and firm texture even after cooking.*

31. *Soup Celery or smallage (page 135) may be cultivated like parsley.*

32. *Chayote (page 136) requires at least two plants for proper fertilization. The vines produce abundantly all summer.*

33. Ha-Go-Wa or Seneca Hominy Corn (page 144) is noted for its large round kernels.

35. Sehsapsing or Oklahoma Delaware Blue Corn (page 146) is a dark blue-black corn when mature, but it can also be harvested as a sweet corn when young, as shown here.

36. Cornichon vert "Petit de Paris" (page 156) is best harvested when very small.

34. Puhwem or Oklahoma Delaware White Corn (page 146), shown here with young red silks.

Couve Tronchuda or **Portugal Cabbage**
Brassica oleracea var. *tronchuda*

Some cabbages are difficult to grow, while kales come up like weeds. Portugal cabbage is just plain fun. It is always rewarding because it is showy, there are many varieties to choose from, and the taste is similar to delicate broccoli. I have grown it every year since I have had a garden. I consider it the centerpiece and plan everything else around it. My enthusiasm for it began as a type of ardent curiosity, an archaeological look at a "relic" vegetable. For this family of cabbages is closely related to the Jersey Cow Cabbage and *chou de la Sarthe.* Therefore, it is a type closely akin to the sorts raised in Western Europe during classical antiquity. It would not look strange on the dining tables of Roman Spain. I thought it would be like cow cabbage when I first planted it, but I was wrong. It has a charm all its own.

I was surprised to learn in the preface to Robert Buist's *Family Kitchen Gardener* (1847, v) that this cabbage had been introduced here in the 1820s as a fodder crop, only to be reintroduced again in the late 1840s under its Portuguese name as a new delicacy for daring gourmands. It was originally introduced into England in 1821 from the neighborhood of Braganza in Portugal, only to fail in the English winter, or so the *Gardener's Magazine* (1827, 434–35) claimed. Actually the date of introduction is incorrect, and there must have been other factors at work in that failure because as I write this, my Braganza is standing in nearly a foot of snow, untouched by a recent brush with 12°F weather. In any case, much of the seed brought into England at that time was sent via the wine merchants, the same Madeira trade that channeled so many Portuguese and Spanish vegetables into Boston and Philadelphia in the

Couve Tronchuda Cabbage

nineteenth century. It was through a similar network that Stephen Switzer first acquired seed in 1728 under the name *Coves Murcianus,* noting that many English gentlemen had eaten it in Portugal. Unfortunately, he did not report in his *Compendious Method* (1731, 19) how his experiments with the cabbage fared.

The 1820s reintroduction consisted of two varieties, a tall one about 2 feet in height called Braganza and a "dwarf" sort called Murciana, growing about 18 inches in height. This latter variety was the same trialed by Switzer nearly a century earlier. All of the varieties of *couve tronchuda* are characterized by large, spreading, ribbed leaves, as shown in color plate 20. The cabbages form no heads; rather it is the rib part of the leaf and the heart or top of the stem that are eaten. The Portuguese term *tronchuda* means "having a great stalk," which indeed it does, although the bottom part is tough and woody. The different varieties are distinguished from one another by their leaf color, shape, habit of growth, and texture when cooked. The Manteiga is buttery, while the Pencuda Espanhola forms a loose head.

Both the Braganza and Murciana varieties were introduced into the United States in 1847 by Boston seedsman Joseph Breck. The *Horticulturalist* (April 1848, 464) published an article on this "new" vegetable, including suggestions on how it should be cooked. If *couve tronchuda* remained out of the mainstream kitchen garden in this country, at least it had adherents in the Portuguese communities of New England. In his Cape Cod cookbook *Vittles for the Captain* (1941, 14), N. M. Halper observed that the Portuguese who settled in the sea towns along the Massachusetts coast were avid cultivators of *couve tronchuda* and that it was found "in every Provincetown garden." Halper published a recipe for kale soup using this vegetable, plus several other Portuguese-style dishes. I find that the hearts and young tender leaves are excellent when steamed (10 to 12 minutes). The large, old outer leaves are tough but may be used for preparing an excellent soup stock.

Seed should be started in late May for a fall crop or in August for an overwintering crop. The spring greens are the best. The plant thrives in cool, showery weather and can be grown as a winter cabbage in mild parts of the country. A temporary cold snap does not injure it as much as repeated freezing and thawing. If grown in the open, it should be protected from dry winter winds. Since many of the varieties are tender, it is probably better to dig them up for winter storage rather than risk loss. Only by trial and error is it possible to determine which will do best in a particular microclimate.

Early Jersey Wakefield Cabbage
Brassica oleracea var. *capitata*

Early Wakefield, an English cabbage from Yorkshire, was preceded by Large Wakefield, a cauliflower introduced in this country in 1843. American gardeners were naturally confused by these two very similar names. Worse, when Early Wakefield was planted, it degenerated into about twelve subvarieties, few of which had qualities suited to our needs and climate. The much-heralded English import became a curse.

However, a German truck gardener in northern New Jersey perfected an early, uniform strain from Wakefield plants, and Peter Henderson eventually obtained rights to it. This became the Early Jersey Wakefield that he made famous in later editions of his *Gardening for Profit* (1865). Seed was released commercially in 1868. This is a cabbage born of seedsmen's hyperbole, only

Early Wakefield Cabbage

to prove itself over time to be much better than its creators could have imagined. Today it is one of the classic American heirloom varieties. Originally raised almost exclusively in Bergen and

Hudson counties, New Jersey, the cabbage and its center of cultivation eventually shifted to Long Island.

Although it was developed as a field cabbage for commercial culture, Early Jersey Wakefield is particularly well suited for small gardens due to its size. And because it is hardy, it may be raised successfully in USDA zones 5 and 6, but it is not recommended for the South unless planted as in the fall as a winter cabbage. Better for southern gardeners to plant Charleston Wakefield, a variety developed by Henderson in 1892 specifically for the South. In Pennsylvania, large healthy plants often overwinter without protection; Early Jersey Wakefield thrives best, however, when cultivated over the winter in cold frames.

Early Jersey Wakefield Cabbage

The head of the cabbage is heart- or cone-shaped, forming a well-rounded point surrounded by copious pale green leaves. The leaves are sometimes tinged with pink on their "sunny" side. The harvested heads generally weigh 2 to 3 pounds. The young greens make excellent collard; in fact, I prefer cooking the cabbage before it forms complete heads, as shown in color plate 21. Charleston Wakefield grows somewhat larger, with more widely spreading leaves, usually a dark green in color. Harvested heads may weigh 4 to 6 pounds.

Green Glaze Collards
Brassica oleracea var. *acephala*

When we think of collards in this country, we immediately associate them with the South. Many varieties of collards were developed there, and names like Georgia and North Carolina Blue Stem were once quite popular at the turn of this century. Yet the collard was not originally unique to one region of the country, nor was it a specialized type of cabbage. The term is a dialect corruption of *colewort*, which in the seventeenth century was applied to small kales or to cabbages in their leafy state before they began forming heads. Coleworts were usually the thinnings pulled from the garden to make room for the stronger plants. In the 1702 cookbook of Gulielma Penn (1966, 16), there is a recipe for a beef "pudding" that is made by stuffing a colewort leaf with chopped beef, then boiling it.

By the latter part of the eighteenth century, distinct colewort varieties evolved in this country through accidental crossing between kales and cabbages. Most of these varieties never earned commercial names because they were highly localized in distribution and generally viewed as a poverty food. One of the oldest to survive, however, is the Green Glaze collard, a colewort that evolved out of the Green Glaze cabbage introduced in 1820 by David Landreth of Philadelphia. This collard is distinguished by its color, which is bright lemony green, and the waxy surface of its leaf (color plate 23). This waxy surface forms a natural protection against cabbage worms because they cannot chew through it. As a result, this is also one of the few cabbages that is generally insect free, although the harlequin cabbage bug (a red-and-black beetle) will attack it in the fall.

The mature plants grow about 1½ feet tall and form loose, leafy heads much like lettuce. The plants are tender in regions where winters are severe and therefore must be overwintered for seed-saving purposes. In the North this means digging up the plants and storing them in a root cellar, or potting them up and maintaining them in a cold frame or cool greenhouse. They may be replanted in March in order to have them bloom in April or early May. The spring plants will also produce a good crop of small sprouts.

Collards are best gathered when young or in the fall after nipped by frost. The following recipe is taken from Mrs. E. R. Tennent's *House-Keeping in the Sunny South* (1885, 89).

Jowl and Greens

🍏

Put one and a half pounds of meat, or half a good-sized jowl in three quarts of water. When it begins to boil skim carefully; in two hours add the greens, a pinch of soda, and a table-spoonful of salt. When done skin the jowl, remove to a dish, pile the greens around it, and garnish with slices of hard boiled eggs.

January King Cabbage
Brassica oleracea var. bullata

The *American Horticultural Annual* (1869, 134) remarked that "no family garden is complete without its patch of Savoys for the table." And yet savoy cabbages were never grown in the United States as extensively as in Europe, perhaps because their tenderness precludes their culture in many parts of the country. Nevertheless, I stand by my opinion that they are the best sort of heading cabbage, and with few close competitors. The Pennsylvania Dutch always considered the savoy cabbage the very finest sort for sauerkraut, and to serve savoy in any form was always a compliment to guests.

On the other hand, the field of heirloom savoys is not crowded even though many of the names are today quite unfamiliar. Amelia Simmons (1796, 14)—bless her good taste—listed two varieties that were more or less perennial favorites with those Americans who grew them. One was the green savoy, "with the richest crinkles . . . it will last thro' the winter." The other was yellow savoy, "next in rank, but will not last long; all Cabbages will mix, and participate of other species, like Indian Corn." The old word was *cavort*, and indeed, Amelia Simmons was one of the first writers in this country to understand the sex life of cabbages. "This is new, but a fact," she wrote, and I salute her for this frank observation.

The Peale family of Philadelphia included savoy cabbages in many of their paintings, I am convinced out of respect for their status among cooks, for they chose to depict prize-taking specimens. Bernard M'Mahon's 1815 seed catalog listed only two savoys, the yellow and green varieties advocated by Amelia Simmons. These two varieties remained more or less the American standards until the Civil War.

By the 1890s, American seedsmen were listing as many as seven varieties developed here, one of the finest being Marvin's Savoy, introduced in 1891. Unfortunately, most of the old varieties are now difficult to locate; a large portion of them are extinct. Personally, I prefer a late Victorian variety from England called January King, which is considered a semi-savoy, the secret I think to its hardiness.

Keep in mind, however, that January King is both a distinct variety and the group of cabbages that have been developed out of it. Thus there is January King, and there are January King types. It is important when buying seed to understand this difference, happily a distinction that is almost exclusive to England and not something one is likely to run across in American seed catalogs. The cabbage that I grow is the original variety, and seed for it is available from a number of English and American firms. It is one of my most successful cabbages, a result perhaps of my peculiar soil conditions and microclimate. Furthermore, I plant it on the cool side of my garden, where it is shaded at midday, and this tricks it into thinking it is home in foggy England.

The heads of January King are small and dense, weighing more than a pound. They keep well under refrigeration, as long as two months. The small size of the plants makes this variety excellently suited for the kitchen garden. The leaf coloration is terrific and seems to change daily. The overall color is blue-green, but there are dapples of true turquoise, blushes of purple on the outer leaves, and streaks of violet on some of the leaf stems. Sometimes I think it is too beautiful to harvest, it should just sit there and preen in the sun.

I plant seed in December in my greenhouse. The cabbage thrives in cool greenhouses and makes a good collard. In March I move the best plants to the garden, thus providing myself with a harvest in June. For fall harvests, seed is planted in May. In England the plants are overwintered in the open for harvests in February. Frost (not a hard freeze) mellows the flavor. For seed-saving purposes, seed must be planted in May so that the plants may be vernalized in November, then taken into storage for the winter. In spite of his name, January King is not king of January weather in this country. He needs protection.

Kohlrabi (Purple and White Vienna)
Brassica oleracea **var.** *gongylodes*

There are only two kohlrabies that I would recommend for the small garden, the Purple Vienna and the White Vienna. Both of these were considered "breakthrough" varieties, since they were so superior to the sorts that had been grown up to the time of their introduction. They were illustrated in color in the *Album Vilmorin,* the purple variety in 1863 and the white one in 1869, which only added to their acclaim. In 1773 Benjamin Franklin sent John Bartram seeds for a coarse variety of "Cabbage Turnip," recommending it as a fodder crop for cattle. There are several old large-rooted varieties that would serve this purpose, but the two Vienna sorts, dating from the 1840s, are small and delicate. When young, they can even be eaten raw.

White Vienna Kohlrabi

There is no difference between the two except in color. The purple one is shown in color plate 26, at its peak of perfection for harvesting. The culture is the same as that for cabbage, except that kohlrabies can be planted much closer together, about 8 inches apart. I interplant them with leeks, so that as the kohlrabies finish in June, the leeks grow and fill the space. Kohlrabies are best planted early, as soon as the threat of frost has passed. They mature quickly and will turn woody in hot weather. They can be planted again in mid-August for a fall harvest, but should be gathered before a hard freeze. Freezing will split them.

Kohlrabies are normally peeled before they are cooked. They can be used like turnips, except that the flavor is much more delicate. But why waste the peelings? The Pennsylvania Dutch spread them on paper and dry them. Once dry, they can be stored in airtight jars and used during the winter to make soup. Certainly! Pour boiling water over the dried peelings and let them reconstitute. Simmer until the stock is completely flavored by the kohlrabi peels (about 25 minutes), then strain and discard the peels. This makes an excellent base stock for vegetarian soups.

Jersey Cow Cabbage or Walking Stick Cabbage
Brassica oleracea **var.** *acephala*

Perhaps my partiality for this unusual cabbage stems from the fact that it is the first cabbage I ever grew. Back in the early 1970s, I obtained seed from J. Stevens Cox of St. Peter Port on the island of Guernsey in response to a little pamphlet he sent me outlining the history of the cabbage. I was naive enough at the time to imagine that I was one of the first to grow it in this country. In fact, it has been grown here off and on since the 1840s. Yet I will say that growing the cabbage made me keenly aware for the first time that there was truly such a thing as an heirloom vegetable outside my own world of Pennsylvania. In one hand I had a packet of seeds, in the other a monograph providing its pedigree. My expectations of the cabbage were not disappointed either, for purely by luck, I planted it in the spring prior to one of the mildest winters on record. It overwintered in the ground, and by the time it blossomed the following June, I had a forest of cabbages nearly 16 feet tall. The neighbors were impressed.

One of the earliest American references to this cabbage surfaced in 1841, when seed was sent from France to a Mr. Page, then postmaster of Philadelphia. He shared seed with several interested gardeners who agreed to trial it. It overwintered and flowered, but only grew 2 feet tall, much to their disappointment. I suspect that Page's seed was misidentified. It was probably the Sarthe Cow Cabbage (*chou fourrager de la Sarthe*), a related variety that is much shorter in height.

Parker and Cox (1970) outlined the general history of the cabbage in their monograph. The cabbage was introduced into England in 1827 when the comte de Puysage sent seed from La Vendée, and the seed was divided among six horticulturists, who then trialed it. In their original habitat the cabbages grow from 12 to 20 feet tall owing to the mildness of the climate. Elsewhere, they generally grow only half that size. The cabbage was initially introduced with the idea of promoting it as a fodder crop because as the plant grows, the bottom leaves are pulled off and fed to cows. Sixty plants were considered sufficient fodder for one cow over the course of three or four years. By pulling off the lower leaves, the plant is encouraged to grow upward, which is how it is made to attain such heights. James J. H. Gregory of Marblehead, Massachusetts, advertised seed for the cabbage in the *American Agriculturist* (February 1868, 73) specifi-

Jersey Cow Cabbage from an 1836 woodcut.

cally as a fodder crop for cattle. Victorian gardeners did not consider it dignified food for humans, but prior to that age of overwrought sensibilities, humans did indeed eat it.

The young leaves are quite tender and can be cooked like collards. In the spring, the stalks send off side shoots that are particularly tender. On the islands of Jersey and Guernsey, farmers make a stew with it called *soup à choux* or *soupe à la graisse,* which is composed of the cabbage, a piece of slab bacon, and potatoes. Parsnips or turnips sometimes take the place of the potatoes. The cow cabbage makes a good stewing cabbage, and the heart or small leaf head at the top is by far the most delicate part.

It is known today that this type of cabbage is quite ancient, similar in many ways to the cabbages grown by the Celtic peoples residing on both shores of the English Channel. Furthermore, this coastal region lies at the center of the genetic home of all the cabbages of the *oleracea* species. The farmers on the Channel Islands even used the long, woody stalks as purlins in the roofs of their cottages. Around these they tied their thatch, a practice dating from Roman times and confirmed by archaeology. The ancient Gauls and Britons also baked hearth breads by wrapping them in the large leaves. Jersey Cow Cabbage is excellent for this application; I have experimented with it many times.

Only on rare occasions have I had the cabbage overwinter in the open. Our winters are usually too severe for this. Gardeners wishing to overwinter it for seed purposes will succeed if the plants are dug up in the early fall—select six to eight of the best—and potted. They can be overwintered in a cool shed. As long as the stems do not freeze and are kept alive, the plants will push new growth in the spring. It is not necessary to worry about leaves that may drop off over the winter; rather, it is better that the plants be held in a dormant state. Once replanted in the spring, the stems will revive. It is normal for this cabbage to attain its maximum height the second year and then flower in the third. This may mean that some gardeners will want to raise it exclusively in tubs rather than dig it up two years running. The seed pods are attractive to birds and may need protection under netting in order to properly dry on the plants. Do not throw away the stems when the plants die. They are tough and, when seasoned and dried, make excellent walking sticks. Craftsmen on the Channel Islands still turn out walking sticks for the tourists. If this sounds like too much work, then at least use the stems for bean poles; they are much sturdier than most bamboos.

Purple Cape Cauliflower
Brassica oleracea var. *botrytis*

With so many farmers raising first-rate cauliflower only a few miles away from where I live, I thought I had no incentive to grow it. However, the unusual varieties show up only rarely at market, and the heirlooms not at all. If I want something different, I must grow it myself and out of this necessity (or perverse desire) I have undertaken to raise a number of cauliflowers. Long ago, the *American Garden* (1889, 58) remarked that "cauliflower is not an easy success." As much as I would like to see heirloom varieties preserved, I cannot see much future for the old varieties of cauliflower. The plant is too demanding of labor. It thrives in wet, heavy soil and needs constant watering during hot weather. In order to obtain beautiful heads, the plants must be tied up as shown in the old woodcut. This requires a commitment to hand labor that is not profitable unless carried out on a large scale. In the nineteenth century, Suffolk County on Long Island was well known as the "Cauliflower County," and from there the very best cauliflowers grown in this country originated. Today, the low price of California cauliflower on the open market is largely due to the fact that it has come to us soaked in chemicals that have allowed the producers to shortcut the old cultural methods. Cauliflower was a vegetable created by hands. It was a vegetable luxury, like a fine piece of furniture, or a hand-woven cloak.

A number of heirloom cauliflowers are still extant, but not too many of them are generally available. I think that Purple Cape, developed in South Africa in the eighteenth century, or perhaps even earlier, is one of those old varieties that may be counted on to yield crops with exquisite flavor. The variety first surfaced in 1808, when it was introduced into England from South Africa by Marmaduke Dawnay, who first cultivated it in Surrey. Seeds procured in Italy produced the same variety; so there is an argument as to where it originally evolved. George Lindley men-

Old method of packing cauliflower for market.

tioned it in his 1831 garden book, and in 1843 it is listed among the new cauliflowers recently introduced into this country in Charles Hovey's *Magazine of Horticulture* (9:98). Do not forget that it was competing at the time with Metcalf's New Pink, Large Wakefield, and Hyatt's Cream. None of these have survived the test of time with grace. We will leave off discussion of Green Cape and Early Purple, since these varieties surfaced like bubbles on the lake of good eating, only to disappear before chefs had an adequate time to record their glories.

I prefer to recommend Purple Cape because it is hardier than the rest, and I am not embarrassed by its unusual shade. Soil usually determines the final color, but white it is not. I would call it a greenish bronze-purple, shifting to rose, most of which fades when cooked. It does not cook a clear white, hardly a problem when mixed with other ingredients, but this lack of bleached whiteness was viewed years ago as a mark against it, since everything had to look good in béchamel. For the aficionados of white-white cauliflower, allow me to suggest Boston Market, a strain of the French variety called Half Early Paris (*chou-fleur demi-dur de Paris*). It may seem amusing today, but in the 1840s many American gardeners had no idea what a cauliflower was, let alone how to grow one. Robert Buist was obliged to describe it in his *Family Kitchen Gardener* (1858, 44) as having "a white head, very similar to a basin rounded full of the curd which is commonly called Cottage Cheese."

Cauliflowers were grown by wealthy Americans during the early nineteenth century, and to them we owe its cultivation in this country. Gregory Lee, gardener to C. J. Wolbert, Esquire, of Frankford (now part of Philadelphia) wrote an article on his technique for raising cauliflowers that appeared in the *New Genesee Farmer* (1840, 9). Essentially, Lee planted seed broadcast in September, moved the best seedlings to a cold frame in October, and the following April planted them in the garden. By the end of May he began harvesting cauliflowers twice the size of those grown for fall harvesting. His technique works. It works brilliantly in my climate, but it is also labor intensive, and I am not convinced that it is economical. Perhaps that was the point entirely, for in old cookbooks, those whole heads of poached cauliflower brought to table with much fanfare were implicit metaphors of luxury. Most of the foods we eat today have lost this kind of symbolism.

Red Drumhead or Roter Trummel Cabbage
Brassica oleracea var. *capitata*

Red cabbages were harvested in the fall and used for pickling. At one time they were as much a part of the American Christmas as cranberries. Today, they are available most of the year and the varieties offered have been bred for other uses, primarily for shredding in salads. One of the oldest of the red cabbages raised here was Red Dutch, which is still available. It dates from the eighteenth century; in fact, it may even date from the late seventeenth century, since cabbages very much like it have been identified in Dutch still life paintings from the 1600s. I find it rather coarse unless used in pickling; it is perfect when reconstructing eighteenth-century recipes, and it is one of those hardy sorts of cabbage that manage to produce year after year. However, I prefer Red Drumhead.

I grow it because it does exceptionally well in the region around Philadelphia, and I happen to like the sight of the purple-red plants in the garden. They change the shade and intensity of their colors as the sun moves through the sky, sometime rose, sometimes blushed with deep blue. Added to their physical beauty is one very practical consideration: cabbage worms do not bother red cabbages as much as the green sorts. The worms that do appear are easy to spot because their camouflage is their cabbage-green color, which fails them entirely on Red Drumhead. This variety was introduced from Germany in the early 1860s from the seed firm of Frederick Wilhelm Wendel of Erfurt. In many areas of the country, it replaced Red Dutch owing to its better adaptation to hot weather. If planted too early, however, it may bolt, especially during a hot spell. For an October harvest, I would suggest the end of April or the middle of May for setting out the seedlings. Every year I plant at a different time because nothing of late has been "normal." Instinct, I guess, is the best rule.

Red Drumhead forms a large, round, flat head. It was bred to be dense and easy to grate in the old-style cabbage graters, the sort with a wooden box that slid back and forth over the blade. The shape of the cabbage fit into these graters better and with less waste than with small round heads. I have rarely bought seed that has produced many heads true to type, and while this might be discouraging to the perfectionist, it can be easily remedied by saving seed from only those plants that produce good heads. Save the stumps to produce the seed. Or better, take graftings from those root stumps and use them exclusively for the next crop. This will increase pure seed dramatically.

Sea Kale
Crambe maritima

One of the earliest writings on the cultivation of sea kale appeared in the form of a paper read by John Maher before the London Horticultural Society in 1805. It was eventually published in the Society's *Transactions* (1812, 13–20) and was rather detailed in its discussion of the plant and its treatment as a vegetable. However, by that time seed for sea kale was already being sold in the United States, and a number of well-to-do Americans were raising it. Although it is a hardy perennial, the technique for transforming it into edible shoots in the early spring requires considerable labor. As *Meehan's Monthly* (July 1892, 109) pointed out many decades later, the "trouble of blanching is why it is so seldom seen on American tables." From a commercial standpoint, it is not profitable in this country, and for this reason it was generally raised only in households that employed gardeners. In short, it was a culinary status symbol and remains so, albeit a very attractive one.

The plant is native to the coast of England and Ireland, and until the eighteenth century, it was foraged from the wild rather than cultivated in gardens. The kale grows along beaches just beyond the high-tide line. During the winter it is often buried under drifting sand, and in this manner the new spring shoots are blanched. Because these pale white shoots came into season long before asparagus and other garden vegetables, usually in February and March, they were considered a great delicacy. English grocers found that they could realize a handsome profit by selling them, providing an economic motivation to bring the plant under cultivation and increase production.

By the 1760s sea kale was being raised in the neighborhood of Dublin, and by the late eighteenth century market gardeners around London began growing it for sale. Several methods evolved regarding its culture, the "Bath method" considered one of the best and least expensive. Kale raised at Bath was thought to be the best in England. Gardeners discovered that by growing the kale on ground sloping gently toward the sun, the plants grew more vigorously. The soil was double dug and mixed with plenty of rotted manure. Plants were buried under leaves in wooden frames at least two feet deep. This ensured that the plants were covered deeply enough to keep the shoots from reaching the light. The alternate method was to bury the plants under pottery cloches. This

Sea Kale at harvesting stage.

was considered uneconomical for commercial purposes, but many private gardeners preferred it. Thomas Jefferson used this method at Monticello, ordering specially made cloches from a potter in Richmond. Reproductions of these cloches can be purchased from the garden center at Monticello.

The most important point in raising sea kale is that the ground must be well drained where it is planted. It will not grow where water stands on it for any length of time, in spite of its maritime origins. I raise my sea kale in a bed raised up over a two-foot layer of sand, where it imagines that it is growing on a beach and is quite content. I feed it occasionally with fish emulsion and scatter sea salt around it in the spring. I think the salt improves the flavor of the buds, but this is not something everyone can taste. To me the flavor is most pronounced when the kale is accompanied by a very crisp white wine.

Plants are generally started from seed and should be transplanted to the site where they are to grow, spacing them about 24 inches apart. The kale looks a bit like rhubarb except that the leaves are pale gray. A light covering of straw in the winter is sufficient protection in northerly regions of the country. Some gardeners raise it only for ornament in landscaping. For culinary purposes, however, the plants must be covered in the fall. Large plastic flowerpots will work just as well as pottery cloches, but they should be well anchored with a brick or stone on each one to keep them from blowing over in a winter wind. Furthermore, the new shoots are strong and might tip the pots over.

The Bath method of dressing sea kale was also supposed to be the best. The shoots were poached 20 minutes, then served in bundles on toast with white sauce. An American recipe from *Mrs. Parker's Complete Housekeeper* (1890, 227) handled it a little differently.

Sea Kale
❦

Pick and soak in cold water. Drain and shake. Put in very little boiling water; when tender take up, put in a sauce-pan with butter, cream, salt and pepper. Let simmer. Dish up, pour over melted butter and lay poached eggs on top.

I forego the cream and butter and poach it with stewing oysters and bits of smoked sturgeon. A few shreds of chervil root (page 372) and the zest of bitter orange; this makes me happy.

Incidentally, sea kale has a near relative in *Crambe cordifolia*, often called giant baby's breath. It blooms in June and July on imposing 8-to-10-foot stems. Sea kale likewise has an impressive flower, which is highly fragrant and can be used as an accent in landscaping.

Winnigstädt or Winnigstedt Cabbage
Brassica oleracea var. *capitata*

The particulars about the introduction of this cabbage into the United States are thus far not well documented, although it appears as early as 1864 in American seed catalogs. It is known, however that this variety or a cabbage very similar to it was imported in the eighteenth century under the general rubric of Brunswick cabbage. Winnigstedt, the town after which this variety is named, is situated in the German state of Braunschweig, and many immigrants came to this country from that area of Germany following the American Revolution. The cabbage was raised for many years among the Pennsylvania Dutch before it was noticed commercially by our seedsmen. The Germans in this country planted it in June and raised it almost exclusively as a fall cabbage for sauerkraut. Unfortunately, it was not well adapted to some sections of the United States where Germans settled; thus Philadelphia seedsman David Landreth bred it with American varieties to develop a more acclimated strain.

Landreth also bred Winnigstädt to create a similar Pennsylvania German variety called *Früher Kegel,* a name usually translated as Early Cone, or Early Cone-Shaped. Unfortunately for Landreth, the name created an inadvertent pun, since *Kegel* is also Pennsylvania Dutch slang for an illegitimate baby. Not too many seedsmen would want to call a promising new cabbage "early bastard"; I am sure the old German farmers had fun with that one. Tall, narrow, wrapped into a point, it resembled Early Sugar Loaf, a variety resembling romaine lettuce with ashy blue leaves mentioned by Boston seedsman John Russell in 1828 and by English garden book author George Lindley in 1831.

Winnigstädt Cabbage

Winnigstädt is a large, glossy dark green cabbage resembling Jersey Wakefield, but is better suited to field culture than to kitchen gardens. It grows best in loose sandy soils. Yet for family use ten or fifteen plants will certainly suffice for making a batch of kraut, since the heads are large and very dense. Like Early Jersey Wakefield, the head of this variety is pointed, usually ending in a small twist. The outer leaves of the plants may spread anywhere from 3 to 4 feet across, and therefore require a good deal of space. If the cabbage has a weakness, I would list at the top its attractiveness to cabbage worms. They get down inside the head, where they go undetected and eat it out from the center. For this reason, it is important to monitor this cabbage more than any of the others listed in this book.

The flavor of the raw cabbage is almost sweet, thus it makes very good coleslaw and raw salads. Of course, next to savoy, it is one of the finest cabbages for sauerkraut and any sort of cabbage

Filderkraut, an old pointed variety.

pickles. I place it on a par with the *Quintal d'Alsace,* an Alsatian fall cabbage introduced to this country in 1868. Quintal is also good for sauerkraut. Both varieties are excellent with braised duck and recipes using white wine.

Carrots

The carrot is another vegetable that we have inherited from classical antiquity. The codex of Dioskorides from Constantinople (A.D. 500–511) shows an orange carrot, somewhat branching in the root, with small, dense leaves. The Romans called carrots by two names, *carota* and *pastinaca,* which has thoroughly confused some classical scholars, since *pastinaca* also meant parsnip as well as wild carrot, or what we call Queen Anne's Lace. The Romans seem to have lumped things together according to how they were used or by certain visual similarities, and this is further complicated by the fact that both wild and cultivated carrots were used in cookery and medicine. If the carrot in the codex is indeed orange, then the implication is clear that Roman kitchen gardens contained carrot varieties that later became extinct. Some botanists argue that the codex depicts a yellow carrot, for which there is certain continuity into the Middle Ages. Having seen the original codex in Vienna myself, I would stand by orange, for it certainly looks as orange as any carrots I grow. This excursion into carrot colors is not altogether arcane; in order to create orange carrots, we must also have violet ones, and violet carrots were not local by any stretch of the Roman imagination.

While the white carrot is native to Europe, the genetic origin of both yellow and violet carrots is believed to be Afghanistan. Both the yellow and violet carrots were mentioned by Arabic writers and moved westward through Iran into Syria, and then into Spain by the 1100s. This could very well have been a reintroduction of something the Romans had known already, but documentation is lacking for such an assumption, and archaeology cannot differentiate between the seed of cultivated and wild carrots. What is known for certain is that by the early 1300s, the violet carrot was being raised in Italy, where it was first mentioned as an ingredient in a compote. It was stewed with honey and served as a dessert.

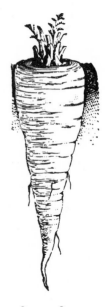

By the 1600s three types of kitchen-garden carrots had evolved: the white brought in from the wild, the yellow tracing its origins to Afghanistan, and the violet variety just discussed. The white carrot survived into the nineteenth century, as did the yellow, which had been raised in Flanders since the 1500s as the Lemon Carrot (*carotte jaune longue*). This was also the first carrot variety introduced into England. The deep orange, carotene-rich vegetable now associated with the word *carrot* evolved in Holland during the late 1600s, when it first appeared in Dutch paintings of the period. The Common Early Horn is mentioned in Dutch sources as early as 1740, as well as a long scarlet type. Both were sent to America by Dutch Mennonites and were therefore cultivated in Pennsylvania many years before they were intro-

Flanders Carrot

duced into other parts of colonial America. Out of these two Dutch orange-colored carrots most of the later culinary carrots evolved, including the early American variety called Long Orange.

Today there are many delightful heirloom carrots to choose from. No kitchen garden is complete without carrots, yet carrots are extremely site sensitive. The reason there are so many varieties is that seedsmen must have carrots to fit a wide range of situations, soil and climate being only two considerations. The W. Atlee Burpee seed catalog for 1912 published a useful illustra-

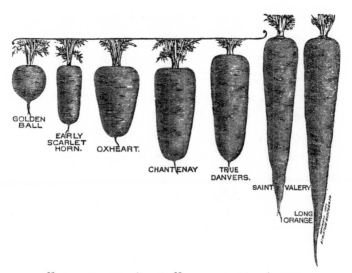

GOLDEN
BALL

EARLY
SCARLET
HORN.

OXHEART.

CHANTENAY

TRUE
DANVERS.

SAINT VALERY

LONG
ORANGE

Best carrot varieties from the Burpee seed catalog of 1912.

tion (above) of what are now considered the leading heirloom varieties of carrots. Burpee still offers many of these old-time favorites of the kitchen garden, although several have undergone considerable improvement since 1912. All of these carrots are orange and therefore, from the botanist's standpoint, variant forms of the same thing. Which indeed they are; they will all easily cross with one another and degenerate into the orange sister of Queen Anne's Lace. The shapes, however, are important, because they are designed to accommodate particular soil types.

Starting from the right, Golden Ball can be grown on fairly heavy ground. It is a strain of Early Frame, a type of carrot that grows quickly and was used historically as a garnish for roasts and fanciful food presentations. It was bred in the early nineteenth century as a variety for cold-frame culture and will overwinter well given proper protection. If planted too late in the spring, it will split as hot weather advances. Otherwise, it is very crisp and delicate, better for salads or raw dishes than in cooked ones. It has been reintroduced as a strain called Parisian Rondo, which the impressionable hover over as something new and exotic.

The Oxheart or Guérande is a French variety from Nantes developed in the 1870s. It is almost 6 inches long, grows quickly, and may weigh as much as a pound when fully mature. It is used primarily in cookery as a stewing carrot, for which it is well suited, for one carrot does a pot. In my garden it often develops into ugly shapes and sometimes splits in cold weather. It cannot be overwintered where the ground freezes.

The Chantenay is said (incorrectly) to have been developed in 1829, although there is no mention of it in French or English sources until fifty years later. It is a deep red-orange and does well in heavy soils, one reason for its popularity in the United States. It is also called Red-Cored

Chantenay owing to the brilliant scarlet color of its core. It is only slightly longer than Oxheart, growing to about 6 or 7½ inches, depending on soil. There is a wide range of variant forms huckstered under the name of Chantenay, but the original needs no improvement.

The True Danvers is an American variety developed in Connecticut in the latter part of the nineteenth century as a crop to interplant with onions. Since carrots and onions are compatible in the field, the Connecticut onion farmers used True Danvers to increase the productivity of their land. The carrot is hardy and does well in heavy New England soils, thus remaining popular with American gardeners in short-season areas of the country.

The Saint Valery is sometimes considered an intermediate type as expressed by Vilmorin (1885, 167), but it is so variable today that there is little reason to treat it as a separate variety. It is for practical purposes synonymous with the English variety called Long Red Surrey, shown in color plate 29. Some would even equate these with James's Scarlet Intermediate, a carrot of definite eighteenth-century origin and worthy of cultivation. Grown side by side, these three carrots often appear identical. After they are cooked, there is no telling them apart. Perhaps it would be better to call them distinctive strains rather than separate varieties, bad seed aside.

The Long Orange is an American variety from the early nineteenth century. It is one of those narrow, spindle-shaped carrots that can only be grown successfully as a table crop in loose, sandy soil. Seed was sold nationwide by the Shakers, but the carrot was mostly used as a fodder crop for livestock, and therefore its shape, color, and other salient features were never considered as important as its keeping qualities. This was the carrot fed to cattle to make the milk yellow for butter production, one reason why whole milk years ago was so rich in beta-carotene.

Carrots are biennial and therefore must be overwintered for seed-saving purposes. Seed should be planted where the carrots are to grow and thinned to allow for proper development according to the size and shape of the root. It is always better to give carrots room—a good 6 inches between plants—so that they will develop more perfectly. Thinnings can be used in soups and salads.

The object of many carrot breeders has been to reduce the size of the tops so that more carrots can be planted closer together. Yet if the carrot root is not shaded by its leaves and is exposed to the sun above the surface of the ground, the skin will likely turn green or brown and the top part of the carrot will be bitter. If the roots should be exposed, mound up the soil to cover the shoulders, or use sand. The best fertilizer for carrots is old coffee grounds. It appalls me to see restaurants dump their coffee grounds in the garbage when they could be recycled to good advantage in carrot beds.

For seed-saving purposes, select the most picture-perfect carrots in the fall—at least six specimens, better ten. Prune off the tops, leaving about 1 inch of the stems. Fill a Styrofoam ice chest with damp sand and place the carrots on their sides in layers. Cover well and seal with heavy tape. Label the chest so that its contents are clearly marked and dated, then store the chest in a garage or outbuilding that remains cold over the winter but which will protect the carrots from freezing.

In the early spring, as soon as the ground can be worked, plant the carrots as close together as possible. In the course of the summer, they will bolt and bloom. The plants may grow as tall as 4 feet and therefore require staking. Staking will also keep the seed off the ground, since the plants become top-heavy during rains. Once the tops begin to dry out and the flower heads (called umbles) turn brown, they can be snipped off with scissors and dried indoors. Roll the dry flower heads between the hands over a sieve. Collect the seed, date, and jar it. Carrot seed is good for three years.

Now the question is, What to plant? I have cast my vote for the following three carrots; they not only offer the widest possible choice in terms of color but are also the easiest to grow in a wide variety of soils and, most important, have the most distinctive flavors. One carrot is orange, one is violet, and one is white.

Early Horn Carrot
Daucus carota

Amelia Simmons (1796, 12) recommended sowing carrots among the onions "on true onion ground," and the best carrot for this purpose is one she knew quite well. The Early Horn carrot is an eighteenth-century variety from Holland that has been perennially popular with American gardeners. In fact, it was one of the carrot varieties consistently promoted by the Shakers and listed in their *Gardener's Manual* (1843, 12).

James Seymour, kitchen gardener to the countess of Bridgewater, was also a great promoter of the carrot in England. In an 1841 article on it, he recommended Early Horn over all others for table use due to its size and keeping qualities. Its size is important. Measuring 6 inches long and about 2 inches in diameter, this cylindrically shaped carrot does not taper to a point and can therefore be grown in shallow soils where other carrots will not succeed. Seymour recommended pulling it when it is young and tender, advice as good today as in the 1840s. Its culinary qualities are superb, for it is not given to a tough core, and the bright orange-red skin presents a handsome visual effect in the kitchen. It is also an early-season carrot, designed for culture in hotbeds and cold frames so that it can be brought to table in March and April. For such early cropping, seed must be sown in February.

Early carrots often bolt late in the summer, in which case seed should be saved only from those that bolt last. It is important not to create an early-bolting strain. If there are early carrots that have not bolted and they have a fine shape and color, store them over the winter in damp sand, then plant them the following spring rather than taking seed from fall plants.

Violet or Purple Carrot
Daucus carota

The ancestral home of this carrot is Afghanistan, where it figures largely in the cookery of that country. However, this has been a well-known variety in Europe since the Middle Ages and was used by the Dutch to create the cross with the Lemon Carrot that resulted in the race of orange carrots we know today. Because it turns brown when cooked, the violet carrot has never been a great favorite of chefs, but light cooking retains the color, and it is extremely ornamental in raw salads.

The carrot was mentioned consistently in garden books and seed catalogs in this country down to the latter part of the nineteenth century, then disappeared. The *Album Vilmorin* (1857, 8) depicted it sliced to expose its yellow core, and the Vilmorins listed it in their 1885 garden book. In this country, Southern Exposure Seed Exchange began offering it again in 1991. The carrot is quite unusual: slender, spindle-shaped, growing about 9 inches long, and about 1 inch in diameter at the crown. The smooth skin is a deep purple, almost amethyst color, which also penetrates the flesh to the core. The core is bright yellow; thus, when sliced, it is eye-catching. The flavor is similar to that of a wild carrot, high in terpenoids and low in sugars. It goes well with lamb and beef.

The Vilmorins considered the carrot better suited to warm climates, but unlike most carrots, this one thrives in wet, heavy soil. Most of the violet carrots that I have grown have bolted the first year, coming to flower late in October. This seems to be a characteristic of this variety. But it has a horticultural advantage that goes beyond cookery, since the flowers range from rose pink to lavender and violet. They are far more beautiful than the white flowers of the common wild carrot, and would probably submit to improvement as a cut flower.

The following recipe is well adapted to the use of violet carrots in dessert recipes. It comes from Benjamin Smith Lyman's *Vegetarian Diet and Dishes* (1917, 249).

Angel Locks
🐛

Scrape and wash a pound and a half of fine red carrots; cut them in very fine strips like straws; put them one or two minutes into boiling water; then take them out, and drain them. Into a saucepan put a pound of sugar with a cupful of water; boil ten minutes, and put in the carrot strips and a lemon-zest chopped very fine. When the syrup is well boiled down, squeeze upon the carrots the juice of a lemon. When the syrup is completely boiled down, take it from the fire; spread the strips upon a plate; let them cool; pile them up in the shape of a pyramid, and serve up.

White Belgian Carrot
Daucus carota

The story of the White Belgian Carrot is a fascinating study in what can be done with plants taken from the wild. Under the heading of "Nouveautés" in *Le Bon Jardinier* for 1838, an account was given about Henry Vilmorin and how he found a wild carrot on the coast of Belgium. Over the course of four years, he carefully selected seed to produce a white carrot of large size with a tender, fleshy texture. Vilmorin's object was to show that this selective improvement could be done with any wild plant, and that the Romans had probably developed many distinctive varieties that are now extinct or reverted to their wild form.

An article confirming Vilmorin's experiment appeared in the *Gardener's Magazine* (April 1840, 209–10). It was written by a gardener from the vicinity of Canterbury, England, who reported how Vilmorin had sent him seed in the winter of 1832–33 to trial. He raised the carrot and found that it preferred sandy soil and to his mind was best suited as a field crop for horses. Since then, the English have always viewed the white Belgian as a fodder carrot, even though it is perfectly good for human consumption. In fact, in his *Modern Housewife or Ménagère* (1850, 89), Alexis Soyer specifically called for the white Belgian carrot in his recipe for a purée called *Crécy à la Reine*, which he described as "uncommon and delicate."

White and Yellow Belgian Carrots

The date of this trial is important to keep in mind, since it was not until 1839 that the carrot gained commercial recognition under the name New Green-Topped White, and it was not until 1841 that Charles Hovey introduced the carrot into the United States. In essence, the entire process of creating the new variety and testing it in the field took about ten years. This timetable appears to hold true for most heirloom vegetables, so dates of introduction are also in many ways highly artificial. The most important lesson to come out of Vilmorin's experiment, however, was that wild carrots taken from inland sites rather than from the seaside would not yield to improvement. The clear meaning of this was that wild plants had to be taken away from the environment where they grew in order to successfully transform them into useful vegetables.

This spawned a large number of experiments in Europe that resulted in the improvement of dandelions (page 321), the round-leafed variety of corn salad (page 310), and the parsnip called The Student (page 236), to name just a few. Because it had such a watershed effect on horticulture, Vilmorin's experiment was discussed and rediscussed for many years. Even in 1890, the *American Garden* (11:143) reviewed the event as a turning point in kitchen gardening. Not surprisingly, with all due honors, the carrot was commemorated in the *Album Vilmorin* (1851, 2), shown life-size.

Vilmorin's white carrot was no stranger to America, for David Landreth & Sons carried seed for much of the nineteenth century, and Robert Buist even discussed it in *The Family Kitchen Gardener* (1847, 42), noting that in France it was used for making soups. Vilmorin also brought out a yellow and an orange strain, which were distributed in this country. All three forms are large, often measuring 24 to 28 inches long. The part of the carrot that sticks up above the ground has green skin, but the flesh is not bitter or grassy.

In order to grow carrots of this large size, as shown in color plate 29, the ground must be heavily trenched to about 36 inches in depth and well mixed with sand. Otherwise, the carrot is relatively trouble free and overwinters well under straw. It survived one of the severest winters on record a few years ago without the slightest damage. Because the roots break up the soil so well, this is an ideal vegetable to plant on ground that will be sown with leeks or onions the following season.

Diced and sweated with chopped leeks, olive oil, and a few fresh bay leaves, this carrot makes an excellent starter for soup stock.

Celery

There are three forms of cultivated celery: stem celery (var. *dulce*), root celery or celeriac (var. *rapaceum*), and soup or leaf celery (var. *secalinum*). All three forms belong to the same species and therefore will cross if grown in proximity. Of these three, only the soup celery is known for certain to have been cultivated in ancient times, although there do appear to have been a number of different varieties. Just how much they resembled modern stem celery remains to be seen.

The ancient Greeks referred to celery as *sélinon*, and they differentiated several varieties, including one with crinkled leaves. It was not until about 1870, with the introduction of a French curly-leafed variety from Niort (Vendée), that gardeners could again, after so many centuries, enjoy the benefits of a crinkled ornamental celery. The Greeks used their crinkled-leaf variety as a culinary garnish much in the same way that we use parsley today. It was also used as a component in wreaths for festivals and funerals. In fact, celery enjoyed a cult status.

In 628 B.C. the Greeks established a city in Sicily called Selinunt ("celery city") on the Selinus River, which may be considered the celery capital of the ancient world. Selinunt issued coins ornamented with celery leaves, but not simply for decorative appearance. Celery was used extensively in the cult practices connected with the god Linus (the mythical creator of melody and rhythm), and therefore celery was associated with music. Equally important (or because of its divine associations), celery was also a medical herb. This medical aspect was equally important to the Romans and was continued in herbals during the Middle Ages. In fact, celery was usually grouped with medical herbs rather than with vegetables.

The Romans considered celery as important to their cookery as dill and coriander, and few archaeological sites connected with Roman occupation lack specimens of celery seed. In general, the Romans used the leaf in combination with other green herbs to create pestos. The seeds were ground with asafetida seeds and other herbs to yield spice powders that were used as flavorings much like Indian curry powders. Today, celery seed is mostly harvested from soup celery, the one variety that we grow that most resembles the celery of antiquity.

Medieval herbals normally grouped celery with parsley and lovage, often treating them as variant forms of the same plant. Botanically speaking, all three are umbellifers and therefore part of the same family, but they are entirely different species and will not cross in spite of the similarity of their flowers—a misconception that is still widespread. In the seventeenth century, celery moved from an object of materia medica to a cultivated vegetable. As gardeners learned to propagate thicker-stemmed varieties, celery gradually replaced Alexanders (page 320) in cookery. Both plants were blanched by "banking" or earthing up soil about the base of their stems to remove bitterness. However, blanching reduces nutritional value.

Cultivating celery in this manner successfully requires considerable hand labor and some skill. For this reason, stem celery was not a common garden vegetable in this country until the nineteenth century. Even then, it remained a specialty crop cultivated more by market gardeners and the wealthy than by ordinary folk. Where it was grown, the most common sorts were the white-stemmed varieties that did not require much earthing up to be palatable. Of course, soup celery (also known as smallage) was popular since it was easy to cultivate and overwinter.

Bernard M'Mahon listed five varieties of celery in 1806, including celeriac and the Red-Stalked Solid. This last variety is still available and is really quite an excellent vegetable, although vastly different from what we now are accustomed to. It is discussed below under red celery. Most celery varieties raised in this country during the early nineteenth century came from England, such as Seymour's Superb White, a variety developed near Snaith in Yorkshire and introduced in 1839 (in the United States in 1842), and Bailey's Red Giant, introduced in 1841. Seymour's Superb White was one of the varieties recommended by Fearing Burr (1865, 317), but as the *American Agriculturist* (1868, 102) pointed out, imported seed could not be used for commercially grown celery because in our climate it produced hollow stalks.

With the revolution in market gardening that followed the Civil War, there was enormous pressure among American growers to develop celery varieties adapted to our climate. Between 1875 and 1900 the list of new varieties became huge, and many of these are still available today. The railroads enabled certain localities of the country to specialize in large-scale celery growing. Kalamazoo, Michigan, became one of the most important centers of celery growing. Close behind it in terms of output was Horseheads, New York. Both places had marshland soils in which celery thrived and the kind of cool weather that brings celery to perfection.

Tuisco Greiner, author of *How to Make the Garden Pay*, produced a small manual in 1893 called *Celery for Profit*, distributed by W. Atlee Burpee. Greiner was himself an upstate New York celery grower, and his book is full of interesting facts about varieties from that period. It is still a useful guide on celery cultivation today, especially for kitchen gardeners interested in raising heirloom sorts on a small scale.

Celery seed is easy to grow; it is the next step that always proves tricky. James Seymour, son of the originator of Seymour's Superb White, reported on the merits of nine varieties of celery in the *Gardener's Magazine* (1841, 76–77). From his observations it is evident that all varieties cannot be treated the same, as true now as it was then. Yet there is one procedure that is consistent: celery seedlings should be planted about 1 foot apart, in trenches a good 12 inches deep. The trenches collect rainwater and make irrigating easier during dry spells. Celery is a marsh plant in the wild, and it has never lost its love of water. It is the high moisture content of the stalks that ensures the crispness we like in celery today.

As the plants grow, soil is filled in around them in order to blanch the stems. The downside to this—a common complaint years ago—was that the harvested celery was so full of dirt in the middle of the heads that it could not be cleaned unless pulled apart, not a good feature for market growers. It was this marketing problem that encouraged the development of self-blanching varieties. However, the trench method is fine for kitchen gardeners who are consuming their own produce, and it allows for some practical adaptations not available to large-scale growers. For example, the *Gardener's Magazine* (1830, 554–55) recommended digging celery trenches between every other row of potatoes. This space-saving idea is excellent, and it consolidates the work of trenching and earthing up to one part of the garden (refer to my discussion of earthing up potatoes starting on page 267). Furthermore, the two vegetables are compatible and can be raised in the same types of soil.

Rather than trenching, celery can also be blanched by laying two long planks along each side of the row so that only the leaf tops stick out, or plants can be individually wrapped in tubes of cardboard or heavy paper. The drawback to this is that because the stems are still exposed to the air, they are ready targets for aphids and must be checked vigilantly, since birds and other insect predators cannot get at them.

Knowing when the celery is ready to harvest is a matter of personal experience and cannot be gained from books. Celery should never be planted so early in the spring that it begins to mature during the hottest part of the summer. This will only cause it to toughen, and if the summer heat is truly stressful to the plants, they may very well bolt and go to seed the first year. End of May, early June, this is probably the best time to plant the seedlings, but each area has its own microclimate that will dictate not only planting times but also harvest. Ideally, celery should be planted so that it comes to perfection in the fall. A light frost will not hurt it. Yet if it is left in the ground too long, the stems become pithy and stringy. A certain amount of trial and error is the only advice I can recommend, and for those who have never grown celery, I would certainly steer clear of the fancy, thick-stemmed sorts. Go with red celery and a little soup celery. They are hardy, easy to grow, and will provide clues about how to proceed with other, more finicky varieties.

Formerly, when celery was not available year-round (as it is now), celery had to be dug before frost, the roots trimmed, and all the green tops pruned off. The plants were then packed in dry sand and stored in a cool, dry place. J. W. Russell's "Method of Preserving Celery through the Winter for Family Use," which appeared in the *Magazine of Horticulture* (1840, 94–95), outlined this old method in considerable detail. It serves as a reliable guide for historical sites and offers a good way to store celery plants earmarked for seed. In the spring, the seed celery must be replanted in the ground and allowed to run to flower. In some areas where winters are mild, celery can be overwintered with a covering of straw, but moles may attack it while buried, and this can result in disastrous losses. I have problems with voles, which are even worse.

An alternate method is to dig up the plants and hold them over the winter in a cool greenhouse. I have tried this, and it works as long as the temperature is truly cool, by which I mean upper thirties and lower forties; otherwise the plants will bolt prematurely, and what is worse, if the temperature is too warm, the plants may develop celery leaf blight. This disease can spread to all other Umbelliferae in the greenhouse, including the toughest sorts of parsley. Since there is no organic means to deal with the leaf blight effectively, the results can ruin a year's worth of hard work. The blight does not thrive in cool, shady conditions, so with care it can be avoided. If it should crop up in the garden, it can be deterred by moving the plants to a partially shaded location. Celery does not need full sun, particularly during the hottest part of the day.

Celery for seed saving should be planted out after the threat of frost has passed. At least eight plants should be selected for this purpose, but I would recommend twice that if at all possible. Once the plants flower and turn yellow, check the seed heads. When they turn brown, they may be rubbed onto sheets of paper. Let the seed dry two weeks before storing it in jars. Celery seed should remain viable for eight years.

Celeriac

Apium graveolens var. *rapaceum*

In 1827 the Vilmorins sent seed for a new variety of celeriac to England, where it was distributed to members of the Royal Horticultural Society. We hear nothing of its success or failure, although a year later John B. Russell of Boston listed it in his seed catalog. Try as they might to promote the vegetable, American seedsmen never have excited American gardeners. The Pennsylvania Dutch were probably the only group in the East who raised celery root on a regular basis, and so it remains.

There is a universal ring to nineteenth-century American comments about celery root, echoed by this remark from *Meehan's Monthly* (1892, 28) about the small demand for seed: "This is probably from the fact that most of our vegetable tastes seem to be derived from England than from the continent of Europe, and the vegetable is not freely used in England any more than with us." It was explained this way in *Vick's Illustrated Monthly Magazine* (1880, 112): "Our German population make a great deal of this vegetable, and no doubt, those of us unacquainted with it have yet to learn that it has really valuable qualities. The favorite method of preparation is to cook the root in soup, slice it and eat it with salt, pepper and vinegar."

In David Landreth & Son's German-language seed list (1875, 72), only one variety of celeriac was listed, with the remark that the seed was imported. Seedsmen of that period kept quantities of celeriac seed in stock partly to bulk out their catalog lists, but also for another reason. The lack of seed sales was in this case no loss; if the seed failed to sell, it was sold in bulk to pickling houses. In fact, James Vick of Rochester usually quoted a wholesale and retail price for old seed earmarked specifically for this use.

Actually, celeriac is no more difficult to grow than turnips, but it does require two important things: well-worked soil and ample

Old-style celeriac showing small root and large top.

water. It is planted in rows 18 inches apart, with plants spaced 8 inches apart. The root, which is the part eaten, will form partly in the ground and partly projecting out of it. As the root enlarges, it is wise to earth up soil around it to blanch it and to keep it from drying out. Otherwise, it may develop a tough "hide" and become woody in the interior. The roots may be harvested at any size preferred, yet if allowed to grow too old in the ground, they will certainly toughen. Reserve only the best specimens for seed-saving purposes and overwinter them in sand in the same manner described for beets (page 84). Of course, crop off the tops about 1 inch from the base of the stems.

There are several heirloom varieties, most of them extremely large (often weighing 3 to 4 pounds each). Among these are Giant Prague and Early Erfurt. These are not to my mind well suited to small gardens and not as easy to grow as the Apple-Shaped Celery (*céleri-rave pomme à petite feuille*). This is a more dwarf version of Early Erfurt, with small leaves, purple stems, and a very round, smooth root about the size of an orange. The flavor is excellent, and there is less waste because the root may be pared easily. In spite of the French name by which it is most commonly known, this variety was commercialized by the German seed firm of Frederick Wilhelm Wendel of Erfurt.

The most wonderful celeriac of all, my undying favorite, is the little one with the big name: Tom Thumb Erfurt Turnip Rooted Celery. The German is worse. If the English name is cut out of this page, like a small fortune cookie saying, it can be wrapped around the little celery root—about the same size as a walnut—with some paper left over. This is not a dwarf celeriac, it is a bonsai celeriac. It is perfect in mixed vegetable dishes, just the right size for garnishing, and very quick to cook in a microwave. The Vilmorins dismissed it in their garden book, but cooking styles have greatly changed since the 1880s, and this is one heirloom that has a very up-to-date usefulness. Unfortunately, seed is so scarce that it may be some time before this vegetable is available in this country.

The variety depicted in the old woodcut is the Apple-Shaped Celery. The tops can be used as soup celery and the pared skins dried for winter soup stocks in the same manner as kohlrabi skins (page 112). This is the variety that Pauline Schultz probably had in mind for the celery root salad recipe in her *Deutsch-Amerikanisches Koch-Buch* (1891, 166), translated below.

Apple-Shaped Celeriac

Sellerie-Salat (Celeriac Salad)

🐦

Clean a few medium-sized, smooth white celery roots, cook them in salted water until tender but not soft, cool in cold water, then cut the roots into quarters. Cut these into thin slices, then sprinkle pepper and salt over them and serve with vinegar and olive oil.

Golden Self-Blanching Celery
Apium graveloens var. dulce
There are a number of golden varieties that make good garden celeries, among them Golden Heart, also known as Kalamazoo. This was the celery that earned Kalamazoo, Michigan, the name "Celeryville." Yet for all the strong points and rich golden yellow center of Golden Heart, it is Golden Self-Blanching that pulls ahead every time as decidedly the best for small gardens. It is smaller in size and not as prone to hollow stems.

Introduced in 1886, this celery is characterized by robust growth and dense, stocky stems that recommend it as an excellent storing celery. As the celery matures, the stems change from pale green to yellowish white without the need to bank up soil or resort to other types of covering. It does particularly well on low, damp ground. I plant it in part of the garden that floods during summer rains. It comes to perfection about the middle of October.

A Bunch of GOLDEN SELF-BLANCHING CELERY,—from a Photograph.

Golden Yellow Celery
Apium graveolens var. *dulce*

According to the *Revue horticole*, a market gardener by the name of Chemin developed this variety at Issy, France, in the 1870s out of a variety known as Sandringham or *céleri plein blanc court hâtif*. This was the same as Fearing Burr's Early Dwarf Solid White (1865, 316). Chemin's was one of the first self-blanching celeries to appear commercially and caused what the *Revue horticole* referred to as a "revolution" in celery culture. Long known in Europe as Chemin's Celery or *céleri plein blanc doré*, it went by the name Golden Yellow Celery in the United States.

Golden Self-Blanching Celery

Golden Yellow Celery

This variety is characterized by yellow leaves and stalks, very yellow, almost lemon in color. It attains a height of roughly 2 feet, at which point the leaf extremities turn golden yellow. It will stand out in a field of celery for this one feature. The stems are naturally white, but they can be made even whiter and more tender by banking up with soil. Of all the old French varieties of this type, this is by far the most decorative, the easiest to grow, and the least bothered by aphids.

Pascal Giant or Giant Pascal Celery
Apium graveolens var. *dulce*

Pascal Giant was heralded in the *Revue horticole* as the finest of the large-ribbed varieties to come under cultivation. Introduced in 1890, it was immediately seized upon by commercial growers due to its size and flavor. The celery was developed in France as a selection of Golden Self-

Pascal Giant Celery

Blanching, and therefore blanches even more easily than the parent variety, turning white in a matter of days.

The plant grows 2 feet tall and has light green leaves on huge, 2-inch-thick stems with a nutty, somewhat butternut-like flavor. The woodcut at the bottom of page 133 shows a perfect specimen. In spite of the thickness of the stems, this celery is not stringy, but if it is not kept well watered, the stems will likely become hollow or dry, a drawback with all large-stemmed varieties. This celery should be raised as an early fall crop because it does not store well over the winter.

Red Celery
Apium graveolens var. *dulce*

Red celery has been grown in this country since the eighteenth century but limited to the gardens of the well-to-do, for it was always considered a gentleman's vegetable. Why this was so, I do not know; it is one of the easiest celeries to cultivate, and in Pennsylvania it winters over with no more protection than a thick covering of salt hay. Yet Peter Henderson remarked in *Garden and Field Topics* (1884, 163) that "the red [celery] is as yet but little used in this country, though the flavor is better and the plant altogether hardier than the white." Red celeries are indeed well known among connoisseurs for their rich walnut flavor, but if they are not banked up, or if they are raised under the intense sunlight of the Deep South, this delightful quality can turn to bitterness. Red celeries are creatures of cool, moist weather.

There are several red varieties available among seed savers. My favorite is the plain old sort from the eighteenth century. It is simply called Red Celery, because its originator is as unknown as the circumstances surrounding its development. Color plate 30 shows the celery freshly harvested. Its stems are wine red—deeper or lighter depending on the soil—and the leaves are dark green. The plant reaches a height of about 18 inches, but can be made to grow somewhat taller if banked up with soil. I earth it up only slightly so that the stems turn pink on the bottoms but remain red at the top.

The stems are not thick like commercial celeries of the supermarket, yet the flavor is intense—real food taste—and this particular variety holds its color when cooked. I like the look of this celery in salads, in mixtures of cooked vegetables, and alone as a poached vegetable entrée. It is also excellent in soups because it does not cook soft and the leaves can be used like Italian parsley. Red celery takes celery back to the point in its cultural development where it was still a vegetable with character rather than reduced, as it is today, to a pallid, watery garnish. The following recipe takes advantage of the robust taste of old-time celery. It comes from Mary Brotherton's *Vegetable Cookery* (1833, 46), a vegetarian cookbook issued for the use of the Bible Christians, an English sect that established its headquarters in Philadelphia in 1816. This large and influential group, which would not consume vegetables fertilized with animal manures, not only contributed to the evolution of Philadelphia's "particular customer," but many of its members were instrumental in founding the American Vegetarian Society.

Celery Porridge

❧

Cut some celery and endive small, and stew them well in some vegetable broth; when quite tender, add a little butter browned, and a little flour if requisite; stew them ten minutes longer, and serve it up with fried sippets of bread, or a slice of toast laid at the bottom of the dish.

Soup Celery or *Céleri à Couper*
Apium graveolens var. *secalinum*

The ancient Greeks differentiated between soup celery and wild celery, calling the latter *eleioséli-non* ("swamp" celery). Soup celery is commonly sold in England as "wild" celery, but beware; the term is incorrect and causes much confusion on this side of the Atlantic because we have a native plant by the same name. Our wild celery is *Vallisneria americana*, a North American herb that grows along the coast and produces seed relished by wild ducks. This game, foddered on wild celery, is prized by our connoisseurs for the flavor the seed imparts to the birds when cooked. We do not have a wild form of *Apium graveolens*, except in localities on the West Coast where the species has naturalized.

The wild celery of Europe grows in salt marshes in coastal areas and is weedier in habit than soup celery. It is also smaller, with a much darker leaf. However, the two will cross because they belong to the same species. Soup celery is best described as a wild celery brought under control and transformed into a dignified potherb through long cultivation. Its leaves resemble parsley, although the flavor is intense, akin to celery seed. There is also a definitive salty aftertaste.

The plant, shown in color plate 31, grows in clumps and may reach 2 feet in height. Six or eight plants are usually sufficient for a kitchen garden and will supply greens most of the year if raised in a cold frame. The more soup celery is cut, the better it thrives. The leaves are absolutely essential for soup stock, and historically, served as a key ingredient in soup bunches like the example from Charleston, South Carolina, shown on page 136.

White Plume Celery
Apium graveolens var. *dulce*

According to the *Farm Journal* (1884, 9), this variety was introduced in 1884 by Peter Henderson & Company of New York, a fact confirmed by Henderson's own advertisement in that issue of the magazine. *Vick's Illustrated Monthly Magazine* (1883, 376) announced earlier that Henderson would be releasing the new variety and that it was nothing more than Chemin's celery under a new name. Vick's accusation caused a minor war of nerves between seeds- men, and if the desired result was to anger Peter Henderson, he ignored it. (The Vilmorins did not.)

Henderson's revenge came quietly in his *Garden and Farm Topics* (1884, 167), in which he explained that White Plume was a sport of Golden Half-Dwarf. Regardless of how it happened, the variety was quickly recognized as an important addition to the vegetable garden. It became the leading self-blanching variety among American garden- ers, and a favorite of hotels and restaurants for its highly ornamental character.

Part of the charm of this celery lies in its dwarf habit, almost 12 inches in height, and the compact arrangement of the stems. The stems are white, and the yellowish leaves have a fine, ferny or feath-

White Plume Celery

ery quality quite unlike common celery. The eating quality of the stem is very good, since it is crisp and snaps like an apple. But the celery does not store well, and therefore its crop value declines toward the end of December. In the nineteenth century it was one of the most popular celeries sold at Christmas.

Toward the end of the 1890s, pink varieties came into fashion, and a Pink Plume Celery even- tually appeared on the market. It is now rare, but is probably one of the most ornamental of all the Victorian specialty types.

Chayote (Chocho or Merliton)

Although treated as an exotic by most of our greengrocers, this truly versatile vegetable has a long history in American cookery, especially in the Deep South. Prior to 1900 there were about a dozen recognized varieties, some white, others green, many with sharp spines on the surface of the skin. The plant is a rampant grower, with vines similar in appearance to large tree-climbing gourds. Each vine is highly productive, yielding as many as 100 fruits, which are usually harvested when 6 to 8 inches in length (color plate 32). Where the ground does not freeze in the winter, the plant can be cultivated as a perennial; otherwise the roots may be dug up after the first frost and stored like dahlia tubers. Furthermore, the pear-shaped fruit can be used in innumerable ways in cookery as a substitute for squash, cucumbers, and potatoes. It can also be pickled as a passable substitute for artichoke hearts, makes convincing French fries and delicious gratins and pies, or can be eaten raw in salads. In Lena Richard's *New Orleans Cook Book* (1940, 84) chayotes are stuffed and baked like eggplants. It amazes me that this vegetable is not more popular in this country; it will even store for several months in a refrigerator.

The chayote (*Sechium edule*) is native to Mexico but has been naturalized throughout Central America and the Caribbean under a variety of colorful local names—evidence of its popularity in the folk cookery of these regions. It was raised as *chocho* in Jamaica during the eighteenth century and exported to North American markets along the eastern seaboard. It was also grown along the coast of the United States as far north as Charleston, South Carolina, well into the 1850s, especially by people of African descent. The Civil War completely disrupted its cultivation, and it was not until the 1890s that serious attempts were undertaken to reintroduce it as a truck-farm product under the name Vegetable Pear. However, in Louisiana, where it is known as the merliton, it has been a basic ingredient in local cookery since the 1700s.

The vines require a sturdy fence or trellis for support and can be trained over arbors like grape vines. It is important to tie the stems to the supports at critical places, or the weight of the fruit will pull the entire plant to the ground. Where the plant can be cultivated as a perennial, the root will develop into a yamlike tuber that can be harvested and used in cookery much like a potato due to its high starch content.

To raise the fruit in Pennsylvania, where I treat the plants as annuals, the vines must be started in a hothouse in January (a sunny windowsill will serve as well). Let a ripe chayote stand in a warm place in the kitchen until it begins to sprout, then stick it into potting soil, sprout end up. The fruit will shrivel and grow quickly into a vine that can be planted outdoors when the threat of frost has passed. Since the plant requires twelve hours of sunlight to produce fruit, it is important to get it in early enough so that it is blooming by early June. Most important, two plants are required for cross-fertilization. One vine alone will produce no fruit. Once established, the plants will yield prodigiously over the summer.

Meehan's Monthly (November 1891, 76) remarked that the chayote was troublesome to grow, which I wholeheartedly question. It is not particular about soil and grows like a weed even during droughts. Aside from requiring a long growing season, my vines are remarkably free of pests and are not subject to squash beetles or powdery mildew. For the organic gardener, this is the perfect vegetable: it thrives on neglect.

Corn (Maize)

Corn is doubtless our most studied, our most tinkered with, and, some would claim, our most debased of all New World vegetables. Its history is long and complex, and the literature of corn is immense. Betty Fussell's recent *Story of Corn* (1992) is a good introduction to how corn evolved from a Native American food of deeply sacred character into the sugar-enhanced Coca Cola corns of today. The late Sophie Coe's *America's First Cuisines* (1994) traces this story back to its roots in Mexico and Peru. The American industrialization of corn, the genetic revolution that has produced a whole new generation of corn varieties so unlike the robust corns of the past, has brought about fundamental changes in American agriculture that represent the very antithesis of what genetic diversity and seed saving is about. The irony of it all is that corn, the ancient benefactor of the Indians, a living spiritual dimension of their culture and its symbiotic relationship with the land, has become one of the world's cash crops. Because of this it is now inextricably enmeshed in political corruption and rapacious environmental destruction. There is no vegetable that closes the ranks among seed savers and proponents of sustainable agriculture more effectively than corn.

Unfortunately, corn is not an easy plant to preserve as an heirloom vegetable. It originated as a mutation and cannot survive in the wild. Therefore, its existence is wholly dependent on the intervention of man to ensure that it can pollinate and produce seed. The Indians were keenly aware of this and treated corn with a religious dedication found in no other cultures. Furthermore, their attitude toward corn was colored by a desire not to increase its productivity but to preserve its sacred character, for in their eyes it had human qualities. The purity of seed color and of corn type were paramount, for they had metaphysical meanings in Native American religion. For this reason, the Indian was also one of the most sophisticated savers of seed, able to accomplish through simple observation and without scientific training what whites must learn through years of university education. The American Indians were plant geneticists before the term was invented.

The Indians appear to have categorized their corns by intended use: for flour, for hominy and porridge, for popping, and so forth. Each corn had its adjunct ceremonies and festive recipes. We have inherited some of these corns from native peoples, and we have selectively borrowed some of their dialect names (such as flint) for corn types, but we use them in much different ways. The profundity of the changes that occurred as the cultivation of corn shifted from the Indian to the white man is acutely evident in Porter A. Browne's *Essay on Indian Corn* (1837), which cataloged thirty-five of the most commonly raised varieties at the time. Very few were pure Indian sorts, and only a couple are known today; the rest are probably extinct.

Browne organized his corns by color. Among the yellows he listed King Philip Corn, which is still available. Under white corn, he mentioned Smith's Early White and Mandan, in this case a sweet corn, not the Mandan corn familiar to seed savers today. His list of red corns was the largest, including Guinea Corn, William Cobbett's Corn, Dutton Flint, and a curious Mexican corn "found in a mummy." Per-

King Philip Corn

haps the Mexican corn released in the 1860s by Massachusetts seedsman James J. H. Gregory attempted by virtue of its provocative name to cash in on a similar implied ancient authenticity, like the Anastazi bean of today.

Horticulturists divide corn differently than did either the Indians or the early corn specialists like Browne. All of the cultivated varieties belong to the same species and therefore readily cross with one another. In fact, corn is one of the easiest of all garden vegetables to cross, since it relies on windblown pollen for fertilization, and even the slightest puff of air can carry pollen a great distance. This promiscuity results in many varieties that fall between the five or six recognized types generally accepted by horticulturists. Of the garden varieties, these include popcorn (var. *praecox*), dent corn (var. *indentata*), flint corn (var. *indurata*), soft corn, and sweet corn (var. *rugosa*). If this discussion is shifted to Mexico, everything is turned topsy-turvy by the huge number of corns that evolved there. Their complicated pedigrees were analyzed in Paul Mangelsdorf's *Corn* (1974), one of the breakthrough studies on the origins of this plant.

Popcorn is one of the oldest and hardiest of all the types and can be grown where many other corns do not thrive. It can be planted earlier in the spring than other varieties, but of course it will cross easily with any type of corn planted near it. Since popcorn pops best when the kernels are over a year old, this is a corn that must be allowed to ripen on the stalk, then properly dried indoors before storing in containers free of insects and moisture. Freezing it immediately before it is popped will increase the rate of popping. I have included two old varieties in my selection that not only pop beautifully but have a flavor not found in modern commercial varieties.

Dent corns are characterized by a dent or crease in the kernel, hence the Indian name "she-corn." This type of corn is starchy and is generally used for roasting, corn bread, and hominy. It is a type best acclimated to the South and Southwest, where it seems to have developed the greatest number of varieties. Flint corns are the northern counterpart to this type. The kernels contain a high percentage of opaline, a mineral that gives the corn its gritty or "flinty" texture when ground. Flint corns are normally used for grits and hominy, as are many field corns.

Flour corns or soft corns are characterized by a kernel that is mostly starch when ripe, and therefore lends itself to grinding for flour. All North American Indians involved in agriculture maintained flour corns of one kind or another. Even though they are believed to have had a tropical origin, corns with this genetic feature were among the first to be dispersed by the Indians to all parts of our continent. The Tuscarora corn on my list is one of the classic Eastern corns of this type.

The Indians of North America distinguished between two types of sweet corn, the "green" or unripe corn of most corn types when they are in the so-called "milky" stage, and a corn with heavily wrinkled kernels that is naturally sweet by genotype. The sweet corn of white culture is this latter type. Historically, true sweet corn was a latecomer, reaching what is now the United

States in the 1300s. It originated in Peru, where it is still used to make *chicha*, a fermented drink made in pre-Columbian times. Sweet corn derives its sweetness from a recessive gene, a mutation that has made it defective in converting sugar to starch. This characteristic was utilized by Native Americans for storing slow-ripening late-season varieties as "fresh" corn during part of the winter or for caramelizing the corn while in the husk over hot coals. This slow drying process resulted in a sweet-tasting dry corn that could be eaten as a snack or used in stews and vegetable mixtures.

According to anthropologist Helen Rountree (1990, 52), the Powhatans of Virginia made a corn-and-bean dish called *pausarowmena* that served as a staple dish during the winter. In the late summer, "green" corn or a variety of sweet corn was harvested and roasted in the husk over hot coals until dry and slightly caramelized, very much in taste and texture like the present-day dry sweet corn of the Pennsylvania Dutch. This dry sweet corn was stored in middens and reconstituted as needed with water. It was stewed with two types of beans, a large pole variety and a small bush bean. This combination of dried sweet corn and two distinct types of beans constituted the real "succotash" of the Powhatans and related peoples in the Middle Atlantic region.

All open-pollinated corn must be planted differently from hybrids. For best results, plant the seed in blocks or squares 5 to 6 rows wide. John Brown, a farmer who lived on Lake Winnepesaukee in New Hampshire and who developed the variety known as King Philip Corn, noted in *The Report of the Commissioner of Patents* (1856, 175–76) that farmers in his region were still planting corn "the old way" in rows 4 feet apart in hills 3 feet from one another, four to six plants per hill. This method works well for heirloom varieties and will ensure good pollination with room between the hills for squash. Pole beans may be planted among the clumps of corn and allowed to climb up the stalks.

Among the Indians in the East, corn seed was generally treated in an herbal tea before it was planted. F. W. Waugh described some of these decoctions in *Iroquois Foods and Food Preparation* (1916, 18–20). After soaking in the tea, the corn was left wet in a basket so that it would sprout a little before planting. This treatment was thought to protect the corn, and may in fact have produced an odor to camouflage it from birds and insects. It had the additional benefit of separating viable seed from weak ones and avoiding seed that might otherwise rot in the ground.

For seed-saving purposes, there must be 200 seed-producing ears in the garden. Ripe, dry seed corn is taken from 25 to 50 of the very best ears and mixed together to ensure genetic diversity. Kernels must be hand-sorted for color and all of the best characteristics of the variety. Because it is a mutant, corn propagated from a small gene pool will undergo inbreeding depression quickly and irreversibly, just as humans do when they breed with close kin. This is the reason for the numbers given above. Geneticists have determined that they represent the critical mass in the gene pool for continued diversity and the healthy survival of the corn variety. There is no way to get around this; saving seed for corn requires space because 200 ears of corn translates into at least 100 plants arranged in 25 hills if planted the old way. Furthermore, seed corn must be allowed to ripen on the plants, then allowed to dry thoroughly before being sorted for storage. Sweet corns will remain viable for three years; the others five to ten years, sometimes longer. Animals can be a serious threat to a seed-saving program, so it is always advisable to overplant with a certain margin of loss in mind. However, the gardener need not be helpless before the ravages of raccoons, nature's most expert corn thieves.

Ears of corn can be protected from raccoons and squirrels by wrapping the ears with ¾-inch-wide packing tape, the sort with reinforced webbing of fiberglass or plastic. Circle the ear with the tape above where it is attached to the stalk, then gird the ear about 2 inches below the tip. Allow 24 inches of tape per ear, but do not wrap the tape so tightly that the corn cannot expand properly in the husk. The tape will keep the animals from pulling the ears off the stalks, and since the tape is reinforced, raccoons and squirrels cannot properly chew through it. It also foils crows.

If crows prove to be a special nuisance, the *Farmer's Almanac* for 1864 had this effective advice: "Soak a few quarts of dried corn in whiskey, and scatter it over the fields for the crows. After partaking one such meal and getting pretty thoroughly corned, they will never return to it again." I would use the brand of corn whiskey called Rebel Yell. It seems to fit the remedy and evoke some of the sounds I now associate with the birds at the height of their raucous inebriation. Incidentally, it works.

Black Mexican Corn
Zea mays

Also known as Black Sugar and Slate Sweet, this famous sweet corn was introduced in 1864 by James J. H. Gregory of Marblehead, Massachusetts, under the name Mexican Sweet Corn. It appeared at a time when Gregory was also introducing his Mammoth Chihuahua Tomato and a number of vegetables originating from New Mexico. The seedsman always remained coy about the true origin of his corn, but horticulturists soon ascertained that it was a hybrid created largely from North American varieties.

Sectional detail of Black Mexican Corn

A commentary on the corn in the *American Garden* (1888, 299) revealed that an accidental cross between the Blue Squaw Corn of the Dakotas and a common sweet corn produced a hybrid similar to Black Mexican. This suggested that Gregory had crossed a blue soft (flour) corn with a variety similar to the white sweet corn brought back from General Sullivan's campaign against the Iroquois in 1779. But there are also traces of flint corn in his hybrid, which may point in the direction of the Mexican White Flint Corn distributed to farmers by the United States Patent Office in 1854. A three-way cross is possible. Whatever the case, the origin of Gregory's Black Mexican was more upstate New York than south of the border.

Origin aside, Gregory's corn was an instant hit, at least in New England where short-season sweet corns had been difficult to come by. His corn is also one of the most popular of all heirloom sweet corns raised today. It matures in 75 to 80 days, so home gardeners do not have to wait half the summer for a crop. In addition to this, the plants themselves are small and well adapted to gardens with limited space. The stalks are about 6 feet tall and particularly remarkable for their pale green leaves and silks. The cobs measure 6 to 8 inches and are cylindrical in shape, about 1½ inches in diameter. The cob is white, with eight rows of slate-black kernels.

The corn is normally harvested a few days before it begins to change color from white to purple. At this stage it is eaten as a sweet corn. Once the kernels change to deep blue or black, the sugars change to starch and the kernels become tough. The ripe dry corn can be used for flour corn or for porridge (mush).

Country Gentleman (Shoepeg) Corn
Zea mays

This popular variety of sweet corn was introduced in 1891 by Peter Henderson & Company of New York. It is still grown commercially for canneries and is well suited for freezing. Thus, of all the heirloom corns on my list, this is one that is most likely to be found in supermarkets in the frozen foods or canned goods section. Many of my readers may have eaten it without knowing it.

Country Gentleman, named for the famous nineteenth-century American agricultural magazine, was created as a cross between Ne Plus Ultra, a variety introduced in 1882, and Stowell's Evergreen, yielding a larger ear than either parent yet retaining the "shoepeg"-shaped kernels of Ne Plus Ultra. The stalks of Country Gentleman are 6 to 7 feet tall, with 8-inch ears. The long, narrow white kernels are arranged not in rows but in an irregular, tightly packed zigzag pattern, one of the distinctive characteristics of this variety. The corn ripens in 90 to 100 days with a flavor that is rich, sweet, and milky.

While this corn is widely used in canning and freezing, it is delightful, indeed at its best, when fresh. Its milkiness

Country Gentleman Shoepeg Corn

recommended it to the creamed corn recipes once so popular with Victorian cooks, but it was equally delicious in summer pies. The following recipe appeared in an article called "New Ways

to Serve Corn" in *Table Talk* (1897, 284), a household magazine published in Philadelphia under the editorship of cookbook author Sarah Tyson Rorer. In the recipe, "butter the size of a walnut" means 2 tablespoons.

Corn Custard Pie
🐦

One cupful of grated corn, one half of a cupful of milk, salt and cayenne to taste, butter the size of a walnut, one rounded tablespoonful of cornstarch, yolks of two eggs. Bake with an under crust only, and when done cover with a meringue made from the whites of the two eggs, to which add a pinch of salt and also one of cream of tartar; no sugar. Brown delicately.

Gourd Seed Corn (Texas Strain)
Zea mays

Gourd seed dent corns were cultivated by Native American peoples as a flour corn, and because of their productivity, they are still best suited to this use. There is considerable evidence that both white and yellow varieties were grown in southern Virginia, the Carolinas, and other parts of the Upper South at the time of the first white settlements in that region. In spite of the fact that it is considered a southern corn, gourd seed varieties were also known to the Iroquois, who cultivated them in the mild microclimates along the Finger Lakes and in the Genesee Valley of western New York.

Porter Browne mentioned both the yellow and the white gourd seed corns in his *Essay on Indian Corn,* and noted that there were seven subvarieties of the yellow. There were probably many subvarieties of the white as well, although most of these are now extinct. He described the true yellow type as having 24 rows to a cob, while the white might have as many as 36. There was also a hybrid variety created by crossing Sioux (a yellow flint type) with the Yellow Gourd Seed, thus yielding a cob with 16 rows. Maryland White Gourd Seed, the most popular white variety in the late nineteenth century, also had 16 rows of kernels on its cobs, evidence that it too was

Gourd Seed Corn sometimes called Horse Tooth Corn.

probably the product of an early cross. Many of the old gourd seed varieties were crossed with northern corns so that they could be grown outside the South.

Although it was popular with farmers as a feed grain, particularly for poultry, references to gourd seed corn are spotty. A farmer near Sandusky, Ohio, described in *The Report of the Commissioner of Patents* (1856, 178) how he had been growing gourd seed corn the old way by planting it in hills 4 feet apart, but then raised productivity dramatically by shifting to drill planting. One of the leading promoters of gourd seed corn, especially the Maryland White Gourd Seed, was seedsman George A. Dietz of Chambersburg, Pennsylvania. His advertisements can be found in the *American Agriculturist* throughout the 1870s. Due to their high yields, as much as 255 bushels per acre, gourd seed corns continued to be cultivated until the advent of hybrids. Between 1940 and the present, many of the old varieties became extinct, but because of the corn's resistance to a number of diseases, there has been renewed interest in it recently.

A strain of Maryland White Gourd Seed, now called Texas Gourd Seed, was discovered in Texas and reintroduced commercially by Southern Exposure Seed Exchange in 1987. It had been taken to Texas by German farmers from the Upper South in the late nineteenth century and retains many of the characteristics of the original white variety. This is the gourd seed corn generally grown among seed savers. The plants are about 8 feet tall, with two ears per stalk. The thin, "horse tooth" or gourd seed–shaped kernels are cream colored and arranged in 18 to 22 compact rows. It is the characteristic shape of the kernels that gives this corn its distinctive name. The corn is resistant to drought, does well in clay soils, and ripens in about 120 days. The young, unripe corn can be picked "green" and eaten like sweet corn. However, at this stage of ripeness, I think it is best grated for fritters, puddings, and pies. Of course, it makes excellent flour, equal to any *masa harina* from Mexico, and as a coarse meal, makes excellent cornbread.

Ha-Go-Wa (Seneca Hominy or White Flint) Corn
Zea mays

Like other Iroquoian peoples, the Senecas have preserved a large number of ancient corn varieties, as Arthur Parker in his study on *Iroquois Uses of Maize* (1910, 42) has put it, "with a zeal that has in it a religious and patriotic sentiment." Ha-Go-Wa is one of the varieties that the Senecas connect with their tribal identity, which is not surprising, since this is truly one of the oldest of their documented sorts. There is strong evidence that it was observed by French explorer Jacques Cartier in 1535–36, which certainly points to pre-Columbian origins. Therefore, as an heirloom corn, Seneca Hominy comes with both an ancient pedigree and a rich culinary history.

This corn is hardy and thrives in most sections of the country where summers are short, yet it also does well in the South, especially if it is planted early. Best of all, it is a medium-height corn, about 6 to 8 feet tall—perfect for small gardens—and if planted in early May, comes to tassel in early July. The corn yields two 8-inch cobs low on the stalk, and since its leaves are rather narrow, it does not shade large, leafy varieties of pumpkins or melons growing around it. Watermelons are excellent companion plants, particularly low varieties like Rattlesnake (page 384) or King and Queen (page 382).

The kernels of Ha-Go-Wa are large, round, and white, often arranged irregularly as shown in color plate 33. Typical cobs should have twelve rows of kernels. Off-color kernels, such as yellow or red, which are telltale signs of crossing, should be reserved for cooking rather than for seed.

The Senecas use this corn exclusively for large hominy, small hominy (grits), and cornmeal, usually in the form of mush. The dry corn can be parched in the oven to create a variety of toasty flavors and a finer texture in the meal. The dry kernels can also be pounded to produce cracked corn (samp), an excellent quick meal, especially when cooked with beans. The very young ears or "green" corn can be eaten raw or boiled like sweet corn.

Howling Mob Corn
Zea mays

This variety was developed by C. D. Keller of Toledo, Ohio, and introduced in 1906 by W. Atlee Burpee of Philadelphia. Keller was interested in creating an early sweet corn to compete with the later-season sorts. Ripening in about 80 days, Howling Mob effectively filled this niche for market gardeners for many years. The name alludes to the crowds of eager buyers who are supposed to gather around when the corn appears for sale.

The plant is a vigorous grower, about 4½ to 5 feet tall, with two ears per stalk. The ears measure 7 to 9 inches in length, with 12 to 14 rows of white kernels. The husk is extremely thick and is known to protect the corn from damage by the green corn worms that are normally endemic to early-season varieties. The husks are excellent for wrapping dumplings and corn breads, and for steaming fish and shellfish. Even though this variety is not old, the husks are quite well suited for making woven foot and bed mats of the sort made by native peoples centuries ago.

Howling Mob Sweet Corn

Pennsylvania Butter-Flavored Popcorn
Zea mays

The origin of this corn is not presently known, although it predates 1885. Once popular among the Pennsylvania Dutch, it remained out of the public notice for many years until it was reintroduced commercially in 1988 by Southern Exposure Seed Exchange, a small seed company in

Earlysville, Virginia. The flavor of this popcorn is unique. There are no commercial popcorns quite like it. It tastes buttered without butter, a feature that should appeal to popcorn lovers who want to reduce the fat in their diet.

The stalks of this variety are about 8 feet tall, with two ears per plant. The cobs measure from 4 to 6 inches long, about 1½ inches in diameter at the base, tapering to 1 inch at the top. Each ear contains 26 to 28 rows of white kernels, which ripen in about 120 days. This and White Rice are among the most productive popcorns I have grown.

Puhwem (Oklahoma Delaware White) Corn
Zea mays

This fine old flour corn was preserved by the late Nora Thompson Dean ("Touching Leaves Woman"), one of the former leaders of the Delaware community and well known among American Indians. The stalks of this variety are noteworthy for their height, ranging from 9 to 10 feet, some reaching as much as 15 feet. Each stalk produces two cobs with pinkish red silks about 5 feet from the ground. (Refer to color plate 34.)

Such tall corn would not normally recommend itself to kitchen gardens, but since the plants are extremely sturdy and deep rooted, they are resistant to wind damage. Therefore, the corn makes an excellent support for tall twining pole beans, such as Indiana Wild Goose (page 60) or Lentil Beans (page 55). The shady space beneath the corn can be used for squash, small pumpkins, cucumbers, even small lettuces. Furthermore, Puhwem tassels middle to late August, thus it is a perfect late-season crop when planted with early and midseason varieties. Iowa seed saver Barry Haglan has grown this corn for some time and has found that it comes to crop there even later than in Pennsylvania, generally toward the end of October or early November. Based on this, I would not recommend the corn for areas north of Zone 6.

Among the Delawares, this corn was used primarily for making corn flour, which was combined with cornmeal, bean flour, or pumpkin paste to make ash cakes and dumplings. European settlers used flour corn in combination with other grain flours—such as two parts buckwheat to one part Puhwem for buckwheat cakes—or used it to make American adaptations of sponge cakes, rusks, or pound cakes. Puhwem can be used like rice flour in most baking recipes.

Sehsapsing (Oklahoma Delaware Blue) Corn
Zea mays

Although this corn was found among the Caney River Delawares in Oklahoma and preserved in the corn collection at Iowa State University, there is a reasonable likelihood that it originated in southeastern Pennsylvania, for it fits the description of an old sort known to have been cultivated by the Lenape peoples from pre-Columbian times. Swedish geographer-engineer Peter

Lindström noted during his visit to the Delaware Valley in 1654–56 that the Lenape peoples living in the vicinity of the present Bordentown, New Jersey, raised a black corn and that they had grown it for many years. It is possible that he saw a variety similar to Sehsapsing, which is indeed black when fully mature. The fact that it is also a 90-day corn that thrives in Zones 6 and 7 further supports this. It happens to be one of my favorites because it is ready-made for small gardens.

The diminutive plants grow no taller than 6 feet, often shorter, with one 6-to-7-inch cob per stalk. The cobs are generally 1½ feet off the ground. Yet for its small size, this is not a stingy corn; the plants sometimes send out side shoots at the base, thus forming clumps of as many as 2 to 8 stalks. From a distance, the corn presents a wild, grassy appearance. For people accustomed to seeing endless fields of genetically engineered silage corn, Sehsapsing stands apart as a spirit untamed.

Each 5-to-8-inch cob contains 8 rows of succulent white kernels, which when eaten young are much sweeter and better flavored than most commercial sweet corns sold today. As the kernels mature, they gradually turn blue, then deep purple, until finally, when they are dry and shriveled, they become ashen black. Sehsapsing is therefore a Native American relative of the sweet corn developed in the nineteenth century under the name Black Mexican (page 141).

Sehsapsing has two primary uses. As a "green" corn, it serves as sweet corn and can be used in any recipe where fresh corn is called for. Once it begins to mature, however, the sugars quickly convert to starch. Therefore, it makes an excellent flour corn, very soft but very dark gray. By itself, this color is no more off-putting than that of Hopi blue corn. Mixed with bean paste or with other wholemeal flours, the color blends in.

Like the nubbins (baby ears) of Iroquois white sweet corns, the nubbins of Sehsapsing were also pickled in vinegar by early American cooks. According to Dr. James Mease in a notice in the *Gardener's Magazine* (1830, 483), the ears were considered fit for pickling "when the size of the middle finger."

Stowell's Evergreen Corn
Zea mays

Perhaps one of the most popular of all American heirloom corns today, this old-fashioned sweet corn is still generally available from many seed companies, although there are now several strains. Much touted as a sweet corn, Stowell's Evergreen was not originally developed with a sultry summer picnic in mind. Nor was it given high marks when it was first introduced. The variety originated as a cross between Menomoni Flour Corn and the Iroquois Northern Sugar Corn brought back from the Sullivan expedition in 1779. This hybrid was created and first grown by Nathan Stowell of Burlington, New Jersey, a few years prior to 1849.

The corn became known nationally due to James Jay "Manure" Mapes, editor of the *Working Farmer* and inventor of a popular fertilizer. Mapes is considered the original booster of the corn because he enthusiastically sent out free seed samples to readers of his publication. Public reaction was mixed. The *Pennsylvania Farm Journal* (1853, 40) remarked sourly, "He who expects to find this article of corn as much superior to the common kinds, as the ambrosia of the gods was to the food of mortals, will lay down his cob and pick his teeth in disappointment." In a continuing discussion of the corn on the following pages of the journal, a commentator observed, "The only drawback to be apprehended . . . is the danger of its crying back to the original form from which it was produced—a danger that is common, I believe, to all hybrids, until long cultivation has fixed their peculiarities."

What saved Stowell's Evergreen, even after disastrous trials between 1850 and 1852, was the secret buried in its name, the one strength that Stowell had intentionally bred into it in the first place. The corn could be pulled up in the fall before fully ripe, root and all, and hung upside down in a cool pantry or garret. From these semiwilted plants, fresh corn could be picked well into February, thus prolonging the fresh corn season. This storage concept was borrowed from the Iroquois, who stored their sweet corn in this manner, and this is why the corn was called "evergreen." In the era before canning, this corn filled an important niche in the rural American diet.

Stowell's Evergreen Sweet Corn

Stowell's Evergreen is now raised as a late-season sweet corn. The plants grow 7½ to 8 feet tall and produce ears about 30 inches off the ground. The ears measure 7 to 8 inches long and about 2¼ inches in diameter, although somewhat tapering and rarely filled at the tip. There are 16 rows of white kernels on a white cob. When dry, the kernels are wrinkled and fall easily from the cob.

Tuscarora Corn
Zea mays

The precise origin of this variety of flour corn is not known. However, it is assumed to have moved north with the Tuscarora nation when it joined with the Iroquois in 1722. The Tuscarora, who have given the corn its name, came from the Upper South in what is now North Carolina. Another old name for this corn variety was Turkey Wheat, a name also used in early Virginia accounts for a similar flour corn raised by the Powhatans and other peoples from that region. It is quite possible that Tuscarora is closely related to that ancient corn. Seed savers who have raised it in the South have reported that it does well even in Louisiana. This may support claims of the Tuscarora themselves that their corn first evolved in that part of the country.

Even though Tuscarora is still extensively cultivated by the Iroquois peoples, it has never received much attention by whites. H. N. Langworthy, a farmer living in the vicinity of Rochester, New York, complained in *New Genessee Farmer* (1840, 8–9) that Tuscarora was an excellent corn but little known among American farmers. The reason, he suggested, was that the corn was not "heavy," and therefore not salable to distilleries for whisky or usable as pork feed. Because the corn had little use as a commercial crop, Fearing Burr (1865, 590–91) was not enthusiastic about it.

Its primary use is still as a midseason (120-day) flour corn. The plants are 6 to 8 feet tall and produce 12-inch red cobs with 8 rows of large, marble-white kernels when ripe. The cobs taper in diameter from 2¾ inches at the top to 3 inches at the bottom. The young or "green" corn can be used like sweet corn. The flour from the mature kernels is snowy white and extremely soft. The mature kernels do not shrivel when dry.

Langworthy challenged the editors of the *New Genessee Farmer* to visit his farm, where his wife would prepare a number of dishes made with Tuscarora corn, among them johnny cakes, breads, and pancakes with "fixin's." Mrs. Langworthy's recipes are reproduced below from the *New Genessee Farmer* (1840, 25). Where she called for "salaeratus," read baking powder (the chemical reaction is similar), and where she suggests tartaric acid, read cream of tartar. The Tuscarora cornmeal that she used was ground fine, to a consistency similar to Mexican *masa harina*.

Tuscarora Flour Corn

To Make Light Johnny Cakes, and Indian Pan Cakes

🐛

Take two parts of Tuscarora, or other fine corn meal, and one part of wheat flour; mix up with butter-milk, or good sour milk, slightly warmed, adding a little salt. Mix rather thin for Johnny cakes or bread, and thinner still for pan-cakes. When ready to bake, add a heaping teaspoonful of salaeratus, dissolved in water, and stirred in. It will immediately ferment, and should be baked without delay, taking care to bake thoroughly if thick. If buttermilk or sour milk is not at hand, water may be used, and before adding the salaeratus, add half a teaspoonful of tartaric acid. Or, if preferred, yeast may be used instead of acid, observing to allow it time to ferment and become

*a little sour (a little of the batter left over from the previous day, will answer as well as yeast),
then add the salaeratus as mentioned, just before baking, and the cakes will be very light, sweet,
and wholesome, especially if made from the Tuscarora or flour corn.*

White Rice or Egyptian Popcorn
Zea mays

This popcorn should not be confused with the sweet corn introduced in
1878 as Egyptian or Washington Market. White Rice is a much older variety, although not grown by whites until the 1820s and 1830s. Prior to that
it was grown by a number of Native American peoples, including the Iroquois. The plants are short, about 5 feet tall, bearing ears 4 to 7 inches in
length and some 30 inches off the ground. The kernels are white, large, and
shaped like grains of rice, hence the name. On the ears of corn I have grown,
there are normally 22 rows of kernels, so a great deal of popcorn can be harvested from a small patch. There is a red variety of rice corn, but it pops
white like this one.

White Rice Popcorn

Cowpeas

Cowpeas (*Vigna unguiculata*) are not generally considered among the vegetables fit for the
kitchen garden, yet in recent times the heirloom varieties have taken their place beside okra
and sweet potatoes, and many of the other vegetables that distinguish the American garden
from its European counterparts. Because cowpeas require considerable space, they have always
been treated as field crops. On the other hand, they are no more troublesome in this respect
than sweet potatoes, and the bush varieties can be raised like bush beans. If there is a drawback, it is only that cowpeas cannot be grown in much of the country due to their need for a
long, warm growing season. For this reason their culture is most closely associated with the
South.

In the codex of Dioskorides from Constantinople (A.D. 500–511), a cowpea plant is
shown in full bloom with several pods, some mature, some very small and green. It is identified in the manuscript as *fasiolus*, the term now used for New World beans (*Phaseolus vulgaris*).
Originating in Africa and cultivated in Egypt since about 2500 B.C., cowpeas have evolved
into hundreds of distinct forms. The Romans called them by three names: *phasiolus, dolichos,*
and *smilax*, probably in reference to varietal distinctions now lost. Roman cooks prepared the
young green pods just as we cook string beans today. Most interesting of all, however, the
plant in the codex is a bush variety very compact in habit and nearly identical to the variety

depicted by Camerarius in his 1586 herbal, suggesting a fascinating continuity of more than 1,000 years.

Botanists have determined that the genetic homeland of the cowpea is the Niger River Basin of West Africa. The Bantu peoples in particular have developed the cowpea to a high level of cultivation. It is this West African source that also provided the genetic stock for the cowpeas that came to the New World in connection with the slave trade. This close association with African Americans and the New England perception of the pea as a fodder crop for slaves undoubtedly provided Fearing Burr with grounds for omitting cowpeas entirely from his book on American vegetables.

It was not due to a lack of cowpeas or that the historical record was silent on their early culture in this country, for references to cowpeas abound. Thomas Jefferson raised a French variety of cowpea he referred to in 1774 as black-eyed peas (Betts 1944, 49). They were planted beside the corn patches, where many gardeners plant them even today. Other planters throughout the South also raised cowpeas. Most of the varieties appear to have been introduced from the Caribbean or from Brazil rather than directly from Africa. During the eighteenth century, they were quickly adopted into the diet of poor whites as well, who dubbed them crowder peas, from the Scotch-Irish word *crowdy*, a porridge.

Several varieties are documented from before the Civil War: Mountain Crowder, considered the finest sort; White Crowder, a middling variety; and Gray Crowder, often referred to as the "poor man's pea." Tennessee White crowder and Running Conch are two white heirloom varieties still available today. The Gray Crowder is also being maintained by heirloom collectors. However, the most famous variety from the early half of the nineteenth century was Clay, the cowpea included in the soldiers' mess by the Confederate Army. This variety is still grown in the South, where it is treated with an enthusiasm verging on devotion.

Today, most of the heirloom cowpeas are grown in the South or Southwest, and the choice of colors alone is impressive, certainly as varied as that of beans. There are also many unusual shapes. One that I have raised is the Rice Cowpea, an 80-day pea that produces exquisite

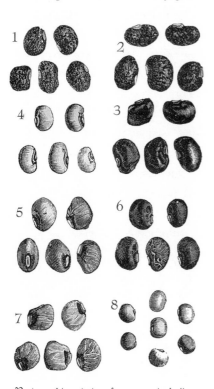

Various old varieties of cowpeas, including Whippoorwill (1), Speckled Java (2), Black Field Cowpea (3), Sugar Crowder (5), Red Ripper (6), and White Crowder (7).

tiny seeds about double the size and shape of a grain of round rice. They cook in 40 minutes without soaking and make wonderful additions to rice or whole grain dishes.

Cowpeas were raised outside the South more as a crop to improve the soil or to serve as mid-summer pasturage, since the plants could not often produce peas in short-season areas. Yet soil improvement is one reason why cowpeas ought to be grown in kitchen gardens, regardless of whether they are raised for food. Cowpeas absorb more nitrogen from the air than clover and draw up large amounts of phosphorus to the surface ("Cow Pea" 1901, 48–49). Grown simply as green manure, the peas will leave the soil enriched for the next crop. On ground where I planted cowpeas one season, I planted Musselburgh leeks (page 227) the following year. I have never had finer leeks than those.

Whippoorwill Cowpea

There is one heirloom cowpea that can be grown in many areas of the United States because it is hardy and produces consistently under adverse conditions. It is Whippoorwill, a variety with short, bushy plants and long pods that comes to crop between 70 and 90 days. The seed is small, brown in color, with speckles. It is often mentioned in seed catalogs of the late nineteenth century, and in my part of Pennsylvania it was used as hay for dairy cattle and as a crop for hog pastures. They ate very well. I have grown Whippoorwill several times and have never been disappointed. Many varieties of cowpeas turn moldy or drop their leaves when cool weather sets in. This variety continues right up to frost, and that is why I recommend it. It can be used in cookery like any common black-eyed variety.

The following cooking advice is taken from Elizabeth Winston Rosser's Virginia cookbook called *Housekeeper's and Mothers' Manual* (1895, 275).

Blackeye or Field Peas

❦

There are many varieties of the field pea, but those commonly known as the blackeye are the most delicate; gather before they are hard, shell, and boil until they are tender with a small piece of bacon, adding one-half an onion, well chopped, to the boiling water; drain and wash well, and make into cakes, and fry a light brown; garnish with bits of fried bacon. Boiled plain is a frequent way of preparing them, or mash well after boiling, with the addition of a little onion. Season with pepper, salt and butter; put in a baking-dish, and bake for one-half hour. Serve in the dish in which it is baked. If used after they are dried, soak in cold water.

Cucumbers

The cucumber is an annual that originated in India, where its wild ancestor *Cucumis hardwickii* Royale may still be found in the subtropical valleys of the Himalayas. This ancient cucumber is bitter, as a protection against animals eating it before it is ripe. This natural bitterness still lingers in many cultivated forms, often in the skin or, in the very long-fruited varieties, in that portion of the cucumber closest to the stem.

Cucumbers were first brought under cultivation in the Indus Valley, but from there their culture spread into China and the Near East by the seventh century B.C. China and Japan developed many of the very long-fruited varieties that served as breeding stock for some of the long cucumbers we know today. The ancient Greeks were the first Europeans to cultivate the cucumber, and Roman authors have left a considerable body of information concerning its cultivation and pickling. The Romans made crock pickles with cucumbers very similar to those prepared today by the Germans and Eastern Europeans. Since cucumber seeds have been excavated from Roman sites in London, it has been assumed that the culture of the cucumber spread throughout western Europe during the Roman Empire. The oldest medieval documentation has come to light in archaeological remains found at Krakow, Poland, dating from A.D. 650 to 950. Unquestionably, such old remains would suggest that the Polish cucumber pickle and its Jewish variants have extremely long pedigrees in central Europe, reaching the Slavs even before Christianity.

In spite of its widespread cultivation in Europe, the cucumber does not grow very well in England because of the country's cool weather and its northern latitude. This has led archaeologists to surmise that the cucumber seeds found in London may have come from imported vegetables, or from the gardens of a well-to-do villa, for Roman aristocrats maintained cold frames and heated buildings that made the cultivation of exotics possible. Yet it was not until the sixteenth century, when English aristocrats began to install cold frames and hothouses, or "stoves," as they are still called, that the culture of the cucumber became widespread in the British Isles. Since then, the English have raised the cultivation of the greenhouse cucumber to an art form, and most of the heirloom varieties that they have preserved to this day were originally developed for forcing.

In colonial America the cucumber did very well. Our hot summers appeal to its subtropical temperament, and many of the soils along our eastern coast are of the loose, sandy kind that cucumbers like. Thus, while the cucumber was for a long time a symbol of the gentleman's kitchen garden in England, in this country it quickly became as common as the watermelon. In fact, the two were sometimes grown together in the same patch. When we look at the lists of cucumbers grown in colonial America, names like Long Green Turkey and Long Roman seem baffling because it is difficult to equate them with many of the heirlooms we know today. The Early Cluster has survived more or less intact, along with the Round Prickly Cucumber, now more commonly known as the West India Burr Gherkin. The burr gherkin belongs to a different species than the true cucumber.

In his *American Home Garden* (1859, 139), Alexander Watson cited Early Cluster, Short Green, Long Green (white spined), Early Frame, Extra Long, and White Turkey as the best varieties for the kitchen garden. The problem with such heirloom cucumbers is that while the varieties were many, the differences were few, and this holds as true today as it did years ago. Most of the American heirloom varieties readily available are commercial strains from the late nineteenth century. Names like Boston Pickling and Telegraph are still familiar to seed savers, but are now rarely seen on the market. The Long Green and Early Cluster of Watson are still available, the former a slicing cucumber, the latter used for pickling.

My personal preference is for cucumbers that are small and unusual. The green monsters of the seed catalogs are generally tasteless, and once sliced, they could pass for any number of shorter varieties. The long ones make sense in restaurant kitchens, where large numbers of cucumbers are consumed on a daily basis, but in the home they often go to waste in the refrigerator before they are completely used. The small ones suit my purposes best. Furthermore, they can double as pickling cucumbers, and vines that produce small fruit are also generally the most prolific.

My selection of heirloom varieties is motivated by this bias, and since cucumbers are a challenge to grow organically, my choices are also based on trial and error, picking out those varieties that have worked best for me without requiring sprays. When I see large, flawless cucumbers in supermarkets, I can appreciate how much high-test chemistry it took to puff them up to such bugless perfection. My cucumbers are drug free. Perhaps my vines would never win prizes at a flower show, but the fruit is good, and I do not have to dip it in wax to make it look better.

Cucumbers have enough problems to begin with. They are subject to wilts, powdery mildew, and a host of predatory insects, all of which work quickly to destroy a crop. There have been seasons when I refused to plant cucumbers simply to spare the garden of these headaches. Of all the maladies, the squash beetles and striped cucumber beetles seem to do the most damage. Insecticidal soap only annoys them, and shouting does no good. They are arrogant and single-minded in their destruction. They usually feed at night but remain active in the early morning when the dew is still on the plants. Dusting the vines with lime will drive them off without hurting the cucumbers, but it is exceedingly hard on human skin. I have found this advice from the *Farmer's Almanac* for 1864 to be quite helpful:

To Preserve Vines from Bugs

❦

The best remedy we have tried is to plant onion seed with the cucumber—and after the plants are up, to sprinkle ashes on every hill just before a fall of rain, which makes a ley and kills the bugs almost instantaneously; the smell of the onion when up will keep the flies off. We have adapted this method for a number of years, not only on our vines, but on vegetables such as beets, parsnips, etc. It promotes their growth and loosens the earth around the roots.

Topsetting onions produce an abundance of bulblet clusters that can be planted whole among the cucumbers. By the time the cucumbers are done, the bulbs will have sprouted into perfect little clumps of "spring" onions that can be harvested for fall salads. The greens can be used like chives. The alkalized dew or rain mentioned in the old bug remedy also neutralizes incipient fungus growths. Overplanting in anticipation of losses and getting the cucumber vines in early are two passive ways to deal with the bug problem. Strong plants always have better natural defenses, so feeding the vines with fish emulsion on a regular basis will help them combat the insects more effectively.

Cucumbers are always healthiest when planted on gentle ridges or hills because the soil around their roots must be well drained. To save space, I train my vines up netting, which also allows me to monitor the insects better. The downside is that I have smaller harvests. The reason for this is that the male and female flowers are on different parts of the plant. The male (staminate) flower is close to the main stem, while the female or fruit-bearing flowers are on the ends of the shoots. On trellised plants, the male and female flowers often end up on opposite parts of the vine, which reduces rates of pollination. When grown on hills, the vines run together, which places the male and female flowers side by side. The bees do the rest. In hothouses the vines must be pollinated by hand unless they are the seedless sort.

Cucumber hills should be 4 to 6 feet apart, with three strong plants to a hill. Ground that has been planted with cowpeas (page 150) the year before will produce higher yields than ground that is fertilized as the cucumbers are growing. Cucumbers thrive best when temperatures are between 70° and 75° F, but usually burn out by mid-August. Successive plantings over a three-week period in June may avoid this, although cucumbers are somewhat day-length sensitive, which means that productivity decreases when there is more than 11 hours of daylight. Years ago, especially among the Pennsylvania Dutch, it was customary to destroy the old cucumber hills in August and plant them with fall and winter lettuces such as Brown Dutch, Landis Winter, or Speckled.

For seed-saving purposes, cucumbers must be left on the vines until they ripen, usually when they turn bright yellow or orange. Set aside the best vines for this purpose and do not use them for harvesting. Once cucumber vines begin to produce fruit with seed, fruit production slows down or stops altogether. Let the ripe fruits hang on the vines about 15 days after they turn yellow, even if they should begin to shrivel. I pick the fruit and let it ripen even further on trays in my kitchen. Then, just about the time the fruit begins to rot, I press out the seed into jars of water and let this stand for several days until the seed mass begins to ferment. If there is any doubt, the odor will give fair warning when this has happened. The bad seed will float to the top with the scum. Skim this off and throw it away. Wash the good seed in a sieve and spread to dry on screens. Properly stored, the seed will remain viable for ten years. Do not save seed from cucumber vines that are producing bitter fruit, for this will only increase the likelihood that bitterness will become even more pronounced in the progeny. Furthermore, save seed from only the most perfect specimens, taken from vines most resistant to insects and disease. Different varieties of cucumber will cross with one another, but not with melons, squash, or burr gherkins.

Boothby's Blond Cucumber
Cucumis sativus

This variety recently surfaced in Livermore, Maine, where it had been preserved by the Boothby family for several generations. It has become quite popular among seed-saving circles and appears to be a strain of a white cucumber called Salad that was introduced in 1920 by Aggeler and Musser of Los Angeles. It is similar to Salad, but more diminutive, at its best when harvested about 3 inches long. Like Salad, it has black spines and turns a bright orange-yellow when ripe. The plants begin bearing in about 55 days, and the young fruit is excellent raw or in pickles. I use the very small, immature fruit (color plate 37) to make white cornichons. They look well when mixed with *petit de Paris.*

Cornichon vert petit de Paris
Cucumis sativus

In response to a demand for a cornichon superior to the West India Burr Gherkin, the French developed an exceedingly small pickling cucumber which was introduced in this country during the late 1870s under the name Small Pickling or Gherkin Cucumber. A woodcut of it appeared in *Vick's Illustrated Monthly Magazine* (1878, 30). As more and more gherkin varieties began to appear on the market, the small pickling cucumber was differentiated from the others by the name Parisian Pickle. Additional aliases can be found in period seed catalogs, but they all refer to the same thing.

For many years French stock was used to breed American gherkins so that it became difficult to find seed for the pure *cornichon vert petit de Paris*. This was especially true when I began growing this cucumber, more than twenty years ago, so I was obliged at the time to locate a seed source in

Lichtenberg, Alsace. Fortunately, seed is now more generally available both through Seed Savers Exchange and from many small seed houses. The American strains are more climate-worthy, but they lack a certain delicacy of shape and crisp snap of the French original, which is shown in the palm of my hand in color plate 36. I suspect that this is the same tiny pickle, lathered with mustard, that one is most likely to find at the center of German *Rollmops*.

The *petit de Paris* is by far the best of all the small heirloom cornichons, black-spined, a vigorous grower, and not too quick to succumb to beetles—possessing a streak of Gallic vituperousness, perhaps. The ripe fruit bloats into a rather large yellow-orange beast resembling the Kirby cucumber in shape. Seed is prolific.

Crystal Apple White Spine Cucumber
Cucumis sativus

My weakness for white cucumbers is now fully exposed. This one is shaped like a large kiwifruit, which should come as no surprise considering it was developed in Australia. It was introduced in

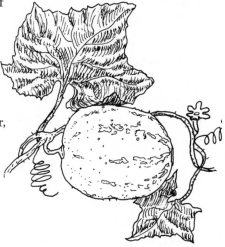

the 1920s by the seed house of Arthur Yates & Company of Sydney, but is ultimately traceable to China. It has been described all too often as a form of the Lemon Cucumber, which it is not, although the two may share a common ancestry. The Lemon Cucumber illustrated in *The Vegetables of New York: The Cucurbits* (1937; color plate facing page 99) is actually the Crystal Apple Black Spine cucumber, which is an inferior sort to both the lemon and white-spined forms. The drawing here, done from life, shows the true Crystal Apple White Spine.

The fruit is pale white, with faint green markings running vertically from the blossom to stem end. The shape is blocky, rather blunt on both ends, and ideal for slicing. The texture is crisp and keeps well after picking. I have had fruits last in the refrigerator for two weeks

Crystal Apple White Spine Cucumber

without noticeable deterioration. As the fruit ripens, the green markings change to yellow, a good sign that it is no longer at its best for picking.

Early Frame Cucumber
Cucumis sativus

Stumpy, blunt-ended, this is one of the earliest maturing of all the heirloom cucumbers in this book. This variety has been grown in this country since the eighteenth century and is without a doubt the most tried and true of all our old cucumber varieties. It can be used for slicing or for pickles, and is best for either purpose when about 6 to 7 inches long. The spines are black, the skin surface somewhat warty, with pale green lines running vertically from the blossom to stem end. It is the classic cucumber of the old-time barrel pickles. The mature fruit for seed-saving purposes is a deep russet.

Jersey Pickling Cucumber
Cucumis sativus

Every gardener should raise a cucumber variety that was developed to take advantage of the local climate. These regional varieties always do better than the more exotic ones, and often come through adverse weather conditions when the others fail. For me, the Jersey Pickling Cucumber fills this niche, and I have had extremely good success with it even though my soil is nothing like that of Burlington County, New Jersey, where this cucumber was developed.

Jersey Pickling Cucumber

David Landreth offered seeds for it in 1875, but evidently the cucumber was in circulation for a number of years among Jersey farmers before it became better known commercially. It is presumed to be an intermediate variety created by crossing Long Green with Short Green, the result resembling Early Cluster in its physical characteristics. The fruit is best suited to dill pickle recipes and should be harvested when 7 to 8 inches long. The spines are black.

Lemon Cucumber
Cucumis sativus

Introduced in the early 1890s as a novelty, this cucumber has many admirable qualities as a slicer for salads. The fruit is round, or should be, and white skinned, with bright yellow streaks. Fruit is harvested when 2½ to 3 inches in diameter. Paring is unnecessary because the skin is thin and lacks all trace of bitterness.

Organic gardeners have recently rediscovered this cucumber because it is more resistant to fungus diseases than many white varieties, and particularly resistant to rust. Furthermore, it remains highly productive until frost and tolerates drought. These features have made it extremely popular in California, but since the vines are especially attractive to squash beetles, I find that I must overplant in order to ensure enough cucumbers during the course of the season.

West India Burr Gherkin
Cucumis anguria

For many years the presumed origin of this curious old vegetable was thought to be Jamaica, but in fact it originated in Africa and was introduced into Jamaica in connection with the slave trade in the seventeenth century. French botanist Charles Naudin (1859, 11) explored its origins: *"Est commune à la Nouvelle-Grenade, où les fruits sont d'une usage vulgaire dans l'alimentation."* Naudin located seed in Algeria for a plant known there as *concombre arada*, which proved to be identical to the burr gherkin, thus exploding the myth. *Curtis's Botanical Magazine* (1870, 5817) published a handsome color plate of the vine, flowers, and fruit—rather belatedly, to tell the truth, because by then half the cookbooks in England and the United States contained recipes for pickling it. The wood engraving below was taken from the 1868 *American Agriculturalist*.

The burr gherkin was introduced into the United States by Minton Collins of Richmond, Virginia, in 1793. His seed came from Jamaica. The popularity of burr gherkins as a pickle spread quickly, for Amelia Simmons mentioned them in her *American Cookery* (1796, 13) and many of our cookbooks before the Civil War contained recipes. The benefits of the gherkin were its weediness, its productivity, and its failure to attract insects; it could be counted on when other cucumbers might fail.

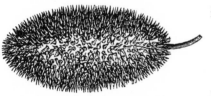

West India Burr Gherkin

The West India Burr Gherkin is not without its pitfalls, for the mature fruit is spiny, bitter, and seedy. Only the small, undeveloped fruit can be used for pickling, best when about 1½ inches long or shorter, at which stage they resemble *petits cornichons*. Two recent introductions from the Amazon, *achocha grande* (*Cyclanthera pendata*) and *achocha pequinta* (*Cyclanthera spinosa*), can be treated like burr gherkins in their immature stage. Their culture is the same as that of cucumbers, except that the plants are vigorous climbers and require substantial trellising. Squash bugs and cucumber beetles ignore them. The odd-looking fruit is covered with rubbery green spines.

Burr gherkins seem to do best when allowed to run over the ground like watermelons. They can be planted among corn or pole beans, and can be planted side by side with melons and other cucumbers. Burr gherkins will only cross with other members of the *anguria* species. For seed-saving purposes, let the fruits ripen on the vine until they turn yellow. Remove the seed and ferment it like other cucumber seed. Fermenting not only separates the good seed from the seed mass but sterilizes the seed.

Eliza Acton published a long, complex recipe for pickling burr gherkins in her *Modern Cookery* (1848, 352–53). Since it reveals a lot about the technology of pickling and how the gherkins were once used, I have appended it below.

To Pickle Gherkins, or Cucumbers
❦

Let the gherkins be gathered on a dry day, before the frost has touched them; take off the blossoms, put them into a stone jar, and pour over them sufficient boiling brine to cover them well. The following day take them out, wipe them singly, lay them into a clean stone jar, with a dozen bay leaves over them, and pour upon them the following pickle, when it is boiling fast: as much vinegar as will more than cover the gherkins by an inch or two, with an ounce and a quarter of salt, a quarter ounce of black peppercorns, an ounce and a half of ginger sliced, or slightly bruised, and two small blades of mace to every quart; put a plate over the jar, and leave it for two days, then drain off the vinegar, and heat it afresh: when it boils, throw in the gherkins, and keep them just on the point of simmering for two or three minutes; pour the whole back into the jar, put the plate again upon it, and let it remain until the pickle is quite cold, when a skin or two separate folds of thick brown paper, must be tied closely over it. The gherkins thus pickled are very crisp, and excellent in flavor, and the color is sufficiently good to satisfy the prudent housekeeper.

By stone jar, Acton meant a salt-glazed stoneware crock. Her method of pickling would not satisfy our sense of hygiene today, but do note that she has altogether omitted alum. Here is a useful tip: fresh bay leaves, grape leaves, or cherry leaves may be used in place of alum to create crisp pickles. I use fresh bay leaves because they give the pickle an excellent flavor, and I am therefore not obliged to answer the question: If alum makes pickles crisp, what does it do to our arteries?

White Cucumber
Cucumis sativus

I grow this heirloom because it is both consistent and yields a larger fruit than Boothby's Blond. It is excellent for slicing. The history of the cucumber, however, is obscure. It was preserved in the Pennsylvania Dutch community, and it first interested me for this reason. Seed is readily available from the Landis Valley Museum and through Seed Savers Exchange. It was thought to be a strain of White German, a cucumber grown in the latter part of the nineteenth century and sold principally by the seed house of James J. H. Gregory of Marblehead, Massachusetts. More likely, it is a form of White Wonder, a similar variety introduced by W. Atlee Burpee in 1893, because this variety shows up consistently in seed catalogs patronized by the Pennsylvania Dutch. In fact, the Lapark Seed & Plant Company of Lapark (Lancaster County), Pennsylvania, sold White Wonder well into the late 1920s. The 1926 catalog, which also carried an illustration, recommended picking the fruit when it was 6 to 8 inches long, rather over the hill for my taste.

Better to pick it when 4½ to 5 inches. At harvesting stage the fruit is ivory white, but as it matures, it develops warts and turns orange. The spines are black.

Eggplants

It must be a peculiarity of our culture that in spite of the great diversity in the world of eggplants, Americans have been slow to expand their taste for this vegetable. At the beginning of the nineteenth century, American seedsmen could list perhaps three eggplant varieties, about the same for tomatoes, only to see the tomato explode into a national cult following the Civil War. A similar taste revolution is presently underway with peppers, but the same cannot be said for the eggplant. Perhaps it is the fate of the eggplant to remain a captive of its weaknesses; its demand for hot summer nights in order to fruit, its attractiveness to the destructive flea beetle, and most important, its defenselessness against fusarium and verticillium wilt. Such a preamble of maladies would be enough to frighten off the most determined of gardeners, yet all things considered, the eggplant is not as difficult to cultivate as many would think.

There has been a recent influx of new and exotic eggplant varieties from Asia and Africa, many of them belonging to the so-called tomato-fruited species (*Solanum integrifolium*), which is hardier, more fruitful, and more resistant to flea beetles. Some of these, like the orange-fruited Turkish Italian, are eaten when green, since most of the members of this species are bitter when ripe. The Hmung Red, introduced from Southeast Asia at the close of the Vietnam War, is extremely bitter, but it is that very characteristic that Asian palates find attractive. The Turkish Italian was reintroduced commercially in 1990; at the turn of this century it had been introduced as an ornamental, its fruits resembling waxy tangerines.

Large Prickly Stemmed Eggplant

In 1575 Leonhard Rauwolf encountered eggplants while collecting botanical specimens at Aleppo and noted that the locals called them by two names: *melongena* and *bedenigian*. He made no mention of colors in his journal, but it is evident that plant collectors in Europe were actively gathering several distinct varieties. The 1613 *Hortus Eystettensis* (1994, color plate 63) showed a magnificent eggplant bush loaded with fruits in various stages of ripeness. The eggplants themselves were about the size of goose eggs, the familiar purple color, and very thorny about the calyx and stem. The drawing on page 161, based on a Philadelphia still life painting from the early 1820s, shows not only the same sharp thorns but also the large type of lobed fruit then considered the best variety to cultivate. Not without reason, this old variety was known as Large Prickly Stemmed Purple and often grew to the size of a soccer ball. Seedy and tough, it has been replaced by smaller, more flavorful varieties.

The eggplants that Rauwolf saw in 1575 originated in India, but many centuries before then they had spread to China and the Near East. It is believed that they were introduced into Spain by the Arabs, and from there into Italy. Eggplants are creatures of the tropics, thriving in hot climates with night temperatures above 50°F, and for this reason they have become thoroughly acculturated into the cuisines of the Mediterranean region. A very old Greek variety in my collection called *Phlaska* is large, purple-black, and more or less teardrop in shape. It is a larger version of the eggplant depicted in the *Hortus Eystettensis* and dates at least from the 1820s. It is the closest thing I grow to the variety known as Large American depicted in the *Album Vilmorin* (1871, 23).

Large American, a variety developed here in the early nineteenth century, was by far the most widely grown during that period. It was also known as American Large Purple, with pear-shaped fruit measuring about 8 inches long and 7 inches in diameter at its thickest point. Plants normally produced two large fruits and a very small third one, so it was necessary to have quite an extensive bed of them if fruit was to be harvested all summer. This and many of the other old varieties mentioned by Fearing Burr (1865, 597–601) have passed into oblivion, or have been so improved that today they hardly resemble their heirloom ancestors. The four varieties that I have chosen for this section have the benefit of still being available while offering a range of shapes and flavors. Under most of these I have mentioned related varieties that are also worthy of cultivation.

The culture of eggplant is very similar to that of peppers, for seed must be started indoors early in the spring, preferably February. After the plants have germinated and are large enough to thin, move the strongest ones into small pots so that they can have a head start before being set out after the threat of frost has passed. Plant these 12 to 14 inches apart in the warmest, sunniest part of the garden. If they are large-fruiting varieties, assume that they will require staking once fruiting begins. If it should appear that they are being attacked by wilt (the plants will look limp, as though they have not been watered), pull up the plants and destroy them, preferably by burning. Do not bring them into contact with other garden plants, particularly tomatoes and potatoes, and never put plants affected by wilt in a compost heap. This will only spread the disease further. Scatter wood ashes thickly over the infected soil. After a few rains have soaked the ashes into the ground, plant the spot with onions or leeks and continue to plant them on that spot for three years. Turn the soil over in the fall to expose it to winter freezing, which helps to sterilize it.

Eggplants are primarily self-pollinating, but varieties within the same species will cross due to bees, which visit the flowers on occasion. For seed-saving purposes, isolate the plants by at least 50 feet. Seeds must be ripened in the fruit, so fruit selected for seed must be left on the plants until it turns yellow or brown and begins to wither. Seed can be squeezed or scraped out of the fruit over a bowl of water. The good seed will sink to the bottom. It then can be washed and drained in a sieve. Spread on paper to dry for at least three weeks, then store in jars like pepper seed. Seed will remain viable for about seven years.

Black Beauty Eggplant
Solanum melongena

This is the most recent of the varieties I have selected, for it was not introduced until 1902. Considered one of the earliest of the large-fruited varieties, coming to crop about 10 to 14 days ahead of the others, it was popular with truck gardeners. It was also the only eggplant listed in *Jung Quality Seeds* (1929, 7), the catalog of the J. W. Jung Seed Company of Randolph, Wisconsin, for the very simple reason that it was the only eggplant that would produce well in gardens in short-season areas of the country. Not only that, its history is rather interesting.

David Landreth's *Land-und Garten-Kalender* (1875, 61), a German-language almanac and seed catalog, listed only three varieties of eggplants that year, all of them purple: Large Round Purple, Large Early Purple, and Black Pekin. According to the *Maryland Farmer* (July 1867, 197), the Black Pekin had been introduced from China in 1866 by Boston seedsman Charles Hovey. It quickly became one of the most popular varieties of the period and was crossed with Large Early Purple to create the variety later introduced as Imperial Black Beauty, otherwise known as Black Beauty. This hybrid combined the jet-black color and smoothness of its Chinese parent and the early bearing qualities of the American strain.

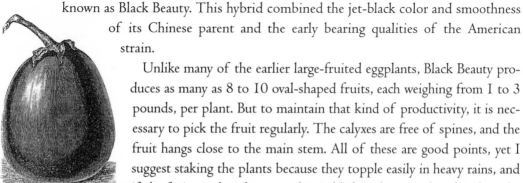

Unlike many of the earlier large-fruited eggplants, Black Beauty produces as many as 8 to 10 oval-shaped fruits, each weighing from 1 to 3 pounds, per plant. But to maintain that kind of productivity, it is necessary to pick the fruit regularly. The calyxes are free of spines, and the fruit hangs close to the main stem. All of these are good points, yet I suggest staking the plants because they topple easily in heavy rains, and if the fruit touches the ground, it is likely to become discolored on the blossom end, perhaps even wormy before it ripens.

Black Beauty Eggplant

Early Long Purple Eggplant
Solanum melongena

This variety is recorded in this country as early as 1855, but little thus far has surfaced concerning its true origin, which is presumed to be Japan. It was popular because of it size, about 9 inches long and about 1½ to 2 inches in diameter. This long, narrow club shape made it better for slicing and frying and not as pithy as some of the larger-fruited sorts. Furthermore, it was extremely hardy and could be raised in most parts of the North and even in southern Canada.

The flowers are large, purple, and quite showy. Unfortunately, the calyxes are thorny, and some of the branches also have occasional thorns. The bushes are rather spreading in habit and sometimes break down during heavy rain, thus I recommend staking. For some reason this variety is less prone to flea beetles than Black Beauty.

This variety has been crossed with a long white variety to produce several handsome strains with purple stripes, among them Antigua, a 90-day variety with 8-inch fruit, and a long, slightly twisting variety I found in Greece called *Tsakonike.* The latter variety is best harvested when 6 inches long and 1¾ inches in diameter. It is extremely fragrant when cooked. All of these long, narrow varieties turn a yellowish brown when ripe for seed-saving purposes.

Early Long Purple Eggplant

A popular way of cooking this type of eggplant was stewing it, then baking it in a casserole dish. The following comes from Mrs. M. E. Porter's *New Southern Cookery Book* (1871, 141).

Stewed Egg Plant
🎄

Purple egg plants are better than the white. Put them whole into a pot with plenty of water; let them simmer till quite tender. Take them out, drain, peel and mash them smooth in a deep dish. Mix them with grated bread-crumbs, powdered sweet marjoram, a large piece of butter, and a few pounded cloves. Grate a layer of breadcrumbs over the top, put in an oven and brown; send to table on the same dish.

Listada de Gandia Eggplant
Solanum melongena

The Listada de Gandia is truly one of the most beautiful eggplants I have grown. It was originally introduced into southern France during the early 1850s as the Striped Guadaloupe. The

Guadaloupe eggplant, an old cross of a purple and a white variety, was illustrated in the *Album Vilmorin* (1870, 21). Fearing Burr mentioned the Guadaloupe eggplant in his *Field and Garden Vegetables of America* (1865, 599), but only in passing, since his information came from the Vilmorin garden book of 1856. Frankly, I have not found many references to it in American seed catalogs of the period, although James Vick did offer it in 1872, "fine fruit and beautiful" at twice the cost of his other eggplants.

This is a hot-weather variety true to its tropical origins, for it thrives when temperatures stay in the high nineties. When last year's (1995's) merciless heat wave was so hot even the flea beetles had trouble moving about, I had a bumper crop. Under normal conditions, this variety requires about 110 to 120 days, but if it is planted early enough, I have never had difficulty with it in Pennsylvania. I would not recommend it, however, for New England or the Upper Midwest. The plants themselves are small, ranging from 12 to 14 inches tall, and the fruit is likewise variable, most about 6 inches long, oval, and not too seedy. It is better to harvest the fruit a little bit young than to wait for the skin to toughen, a sure sign that old age has set in.

Old White Egg Eggplant
Solanum melongena

The earliest type of eggplant to reach England in the 1500s was a white ornamental variety with fruit the size, color, and shape of a chicken egg. As a result, English is the only European language that associates the *melongena* with the appearance of an egg. This quaint old variety is edible when very young (at about 2 inches long), and for this reason I have chosen to include it in my list of recommended heirlooms. It is also quite a conversation piece for children, and anyway, I like to grow it. In color plate 40, I have mixed several specimens with the fruits of the Black Egg variety and a real brown chicken egg, just to give a sense of scale. There is also a Dwarf White Egg, which grows on a smaller plant and has fruit the size of duck's egg, about 1¾ inches long. I raise it every other year so that there is no chance of crossing it with the larger variety.

It is not difficult to find references to the Old White Egg in early American sources, for quite a few people in this country grew the plant as an ornamental. Boston seedsman John Russell was careful to point out in his 1828 seed list that the small white sort was purely decorative, and Roland Green (1829, 26) included it in his book on flower gardening for this very reason. The plant has the added benefit of having its fruits turn bright yellow when ripe, which gives the whole plant an odd Easter-like appearance at the end of summer, especially if grown with one of the purple egg varieties. The most stunning of the nonwhite egg varieties, however, is the Black Egg, which produces perfectly edible 3-inch egg-shaped fruits. The stems of the plant are also black, which adds to its striking appearance. This is an old variety from China that was collected by the USDA in the 1930s along with Manchuria, a green egg-shaped variety, also edible. All of these egg-shaped varieties are prolific producers on compact bushes about 2 feet high. They will also cross with one another, so they should never be grown together for seed-saving purposes, unless of course it is the object to create some curiously marbled varieties. I am working on one right now that is green, purple, and white. It might look pretty interesting on a focaccia.

Goober Peas (Groundnuts)

This long forgotten African-American legume closely related to the fava bean was once an important garden crop among blacks in the South. An annual originating from West Africa but now distributed over most of that continent, *Voandzeia subterranea* is known by a wide variety of names, including Congo goober, groundnut, and bambara. Because it produces a female flower head (called a "peg") that bends down after pollination to touch the ground and thus forms a seed pod beneath the surface of the soil, it is often confused with the peanut (*Arachis hypogaea*). The confusion is further strengthened by the fact that the goober pea can be pounded to a paste resembling peanut butter. The seeds can be eaten green like shelly beans or soaked overnight and prepared in the same manner as dry peas. The pods can be cooked like snap beans, and the leaves are edible as well, usually cooked as a green. The dry bean is also ground for flour, and the seed paste yields an oil widely used as a cooking oil in Africa. It is probably one of the most all-purpose vegetables in the garden.

In her article "Groundnut Stew from Sierra Leone," which appeared in the *Anthropologists' Cookbook* (1977, 91–92), Gay Cohen noted that a visitor to that region of Africa in the 1840s observed that stewed groundnuts and guinea fowl were considered a national dish. Unfortunately, in most of the African cookbooks written for non-African audiences, peanuts are generally substituted for groundnuts in whatever form the recipe may require. The two are not the same.

A discussion of the groundnut and its use in this country unfolded in the *Gardener's Monthly and Horticulturist* (1885, 281–82) in response to questions about the origin of the southern terms *goober* and *pindar*, both of which are African. *Pindar*, a word for the peanut, appears to come from *mpinda*, while *goober* stems from *guba* or *ginguba* (when it is stewed). H. W. Ravenel of Aiken, South Carolina, clarified some of the early history of the goober pea, noting that these old terms were once used exclusively by blacks and that "50 to 60 years ago" (1820–1830) the pea had been extensively cultivated by slaves along the South Carolina coast. There, as in Africa, it was cooked with rice as a dish for special occasions.

The goober pea requires a growing season of about 120 frost-free days, thus it can be cultivated anywhere that peanuts can be grown. In Pennsylvania I start the plants in my greenhouse to give them plenty of time to develop before planting in the ground. This is normally done in

Various types of Goober Peas.

large pots so that the peas are large and branching when they are set out, at the same time as tomatoes. Since the peas are tender and will not thrive in cool spring weather, there is no reason to plant as soon as the threat of frost has passed.

Individual plants should be spaced no less than 3 feet apart to allow for spreading. The male flowers, generally yellow on most varieties, pollinate rather nondescript female flowers on the same plant. Since the pegs form underground, normally with one seed to a pod, it is advisable to work the soil deeply with sand before planting. The addition of calcium helps promote pod development. High summer temperatures, even drought conditions, do not bother the peas as much as long periods of rainy weather, so the ground where they are cultivated must be well drained at all times.

The most common variety is the white-seeded (it has no particular name in this country), which is also the color mentioned in historical sources. It is available from Deep Diversity as well as through Seed Savers Exchange. I also cultivate a red-seeded variety from Botswana. The two will cross and therefore must be grown at least half a mile apart, or during alternate years. Seed viability appears to be the same as for Spanish peanuts, about four years. This is based on personal observation, since viability data does not seem to be readily available.

To save seeds and harvest the crop, allow the plants to turn yellow at the end of the season— or better, let them be nipped by frost. Pull up the bushes whole to cure in a dry, frost-free place out of direct sun for 2 to 3 weeks. Once the pegs are cured and thoroughly dry, the seeds can be removed and stored in airtight jars. The seeds are round and smooth, roughly the size of a chickpea, about ½ inch in diameter.

Crops that are to be used only for consumption can be dried in the open in direct sun in the same manner as peanuts. Sunlight, however, destroys germination rates, so these peas cannot be saved for seed. Seed for flour or for paste like peanut butter is normally dry-roasted before it is ground. The fresh flour and paste should be refrigerated, otherwise they will turn rancid.

Jerusalem Artichokes

Until about thirty years ago, the Jerusalem artichoke was practically a forgotten vegetable. Today there is renewed interest in it, because we now know that it contains free glutamine and is very high in free amino acids, nutritional points of considerable importance. The difficulty has been the knobbiness of the root, which has made it difficult to peel. I, for one, do not feel like throwing half the nutrients away with the flick of a paring knife, so I eat them unpared. However, there are those who want Jerusalem artichokes to resemble potatoes, and to please this faction, breeders have come up with new varieties that are more uniform in shape and size, free of knobs, and therefore easier to peel.

New varieties like Fuseau, Garnet, and Stampede are now appearing under the commercial names of Sunroot or Sunchokes. Dubbing the Chinese artichoke with the French name *crosne* (page 362) did little to increase its popularity, but then, no one has tried to breed the knobs out of *crosnes.* Thus it remains to be seen what this marketing tactic will do for the Jerusalem artichoke. Breeders may have made it somewhat more lovely for magazine photography, but they have not bred out of it its remarkable ability to induce flatulence. This is not a vegetable to be served with beans.

In her *American Cookery* (1796, 13), Amelia Simmons made this perceptive observation about Jerusalem artichokes: "The Jerusalem is best, are cultivated like potatoes, (tho' their stocks grow 7 feet high) and may be preserved like the turnip radish, or pickled—they, like Horse Radish, once in the garden, can scarcely be totally eradicated; plowing or digging them up with that view, seems at times rather to increase and spread them." Words of true wisdom for the gardener who is thinking of planting them. On the other hand, their very invasiveness and productivity are reasons enough for their recommendation, for this is a very low-maintenance vegetable. They only require the right location.

At the time Amelia Simmons was penning her remarks about the Jerusalem artichoke, the vegetable was undergoing a gardening renaissance, for between 1785 and 1825 it was extensively cultivated, and many local varieties evolved. Then it quickly fell out of fashion and was soon neglected by all but the poorest of country gardeners. In Europe, however, it remained a popular exotic. Charles Bailly de Merlieux pointed out in his *Maison rustique du XIXe siècle* (1837, 1:451) that the Jerusalem artichoke was widely cultivated in eastern and southern France, where it was served as a fritter, fried in batter.

In the United States, where the Jerusalem artichoke is native, the tubers were not sold under varietal names until very recently, so the heirlooms that have begun to surface generally take their names from the place where they were found. Many of the American heirloom varieties available through Seed Savers Exchange appear to be duplications or variant forms of the same strain, slight differences arising due to soil or culture. Dave's Shrine is the same as Wolcottonian Red and Judy's Red. However, there are also several distinctive varieties worthy of note. Among these are Jack's Copperclad, a long, pointed tuber that is copper-purple and rose; Mulles Rose, found in Stacyville, Maine; and Waldoboro Gold, an unusual yellow-rooted variety from the Maine

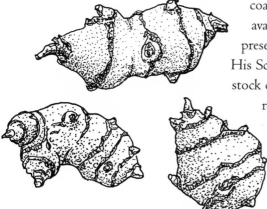

Beaver Valley Purple Jerusalem Artichoke

coast. Many of the rarest Jerusalem artichoke varieties available through Seed Savers Exchange owe their preservation to Will Bonsall of Farmington, Maine. His Scatterseed Project, which distributes seed and plant stock only through Seed Savers Exchange, has earned the respect and gratitude of preservationists on several continents.

Jerusalem artichokes are easy to grow. The tubers are planted in well-worked soil in the spring. Over the summer the bed should be weeded to prevent competition with the young artichoke shoots. As Alexander Forsyth pointed out in his article on the culture of the Jerusalem artichoke in the *Gardener's Magazine* (May 1840, 259), it was determined long ago that to increase the size of the tubers, the plants should be topped at 18 inches in the summer and earthed up with a mixture of rotted manure and mulch. In the fall, after frost has killed the tops, the roots can be harvested as needed. Some gardeners store them in damp sand, others leave the tubers in the ground and cover them with straw over the winter. Either method will preserve them.

Several varieties of artichoke can be grown in the same garden. Only the seed will produce crosses. As long as the plants are propagated by their tubers, plant purity can be maintained. It is a good idea, however, to raise the artichokes in contained beds, otherwise they will increase on their own rapidly and run through hedges, clog lawn mowers, and bully their way into parts of the garden where they are not wanted. No one would call them elegant, yet lest we imagine that this "windy root" (as it was sometimes called in the eighteenth century) had no place in elegant cookery, I append the following recipe from the Philadelphia edition of Francatelli's *French Cookery* (1848, 378). This is how the vegetable once was served in many American hotels.

Jerusalem Artichokes, *à l'Italienne*

❦

Turn the artichokes into any fancy shape, place them in circular order in a deep sauté pan thickly spread with butter; season with mignonette pepper, nutmeg, salt, and lemon juice; moisten with a little [chicken] consommé, put the lid on, set them to simmer very gently over a slow fire for about half an hour—during which time they will, if properly attended to, acquire a deep yellow colour. Roll them up in their glaze, dish up, pour some Italian sauce round them, and serve.

By mignonette pepper, the chef meant a mixture of white and black pepper ground together. His Italian sauce was a tomato sauce. For some reason, cooked in this erudite manner, the artichokes loose their flirtatious ability to elicit gas.

Beaver Valley Purple Jerusalem Artichoke
Helianthus tuberosa

The variety that I grow, which I offer through Seed Savers Exchange under the name Beaver Valley Purple, is the same Jerusalem artichoke illustrated in my *Pennsylvania Dutch Country Cooking* (1993, 107–8). I discovered it by accident while visiting Sarah Morgan, an elderly Pennsylvania Dutch cook well known for her rich chocolate cakes made with sauerkraut and porter beer. As our conversation about food unfolded, it became evident that Sarah was also an accomplished gardener and saver of seeds, particularly old varieties. She took me into the garden and unearthed an *Aerdebbel* (as she called Jerusalem artichokes in Pennsylfaanisch) that grew in many areas of the Beaver Valley where she lived. The plant had been in the garden when she and her husband bought the farm in the 1920s, and even then it was considered an heirloom by old-timers in the neighborhood.

Whatever its true age, Beaver Valley Purple is a distinct variety, its tan root heavily tinged with purple and demarcated with purple-brown bands. Not far from the spot where Sarah dug the artichokes, she also unearthed a purple-black potato known as the Black Mercer. This is a potato from the early nineteenth century, long thought extinct. It has a purple skin with white flesh.

Lettuces

In Greek mythology, the torrid love affair between the goddess Aphrodite and the dazzling youth Adonis ended in a gruesome salad. For after Aphrodite hid Adonis in a bed of lettuce, he was killed there by a wild boar. Adonis's violent death was therefore connected in the ancient Greek mind with lettuce, which assumed the role of religious and cultural metaphor for "food for corpses" and, more broadly speaking, for male impotence (the core of the Adonis theme). For this reason, Athenaeus, the author/compiler of the classical work *The Deipnosophists* (the rambling dinner conversations of several learned epicures), devoted an entire chapter of table discussion to lettuce and its ability to render male lovemaking worthless. For the ancient Greeks, perfumes and spices were equated with virility and seduction. Lettuce was the opposite.

In this light it strikes me as curious that eating lettuce as a component of a voluptuous meal would gain favor at all, yet it did. About the time of the emperor Domitian (A.D. 81–96), it became fashionable among the Roman elite to serve a lettuce salad as an appetizer before the first course, a custom that we practice even to this day. Was the lettuce salad intended to act as an antidote to the passions that subsequent courses of meat might inflame? This may have been one of the medical purposes of the original leafy appetizer. Certainly, by the Roman era, lettuce had already reached Italy with fascinating baggage—cultural, medical, intellectual, and religious. Of all the European garden vegetables, its history is one of the most colorful.

Lettuce was first cultivated by the ancient Egyptians, and since it played a role in their religious rituals, they have left ample records in the form of wall paintings and tomb reliefs as to the nature of the lettuce they grew, some of the oldest images dating from as early as 2680 B.C. This was a variety of lettuce about 30 inches tall, like a giant head of romaine lettuce with pointed leaves. The drawing below is based on a tomb relief in the Egyptian Museum in Berlin. The relief shows lettuce in such clear detail that it is possible to recreate its salient botanical features. To me, the lettuce resembles Lion's Tongue (color plate 42) on a much larger scale. In any case, Egypt perfected the cultivation of the tall or upright lettuces now known as cos or romaine, and this cultural knowledge was passed to the Greeks. The Romans in turn acquired lettuce culture from the Greeks, referring to the new plant as *lactuca* (which means "milk") in reference to the white juice exuded by the stems. The word *lactuca* is now used by botanists to represent the genus to which lettuce belongs

The Roman agriculturist Columella (A.D. 50) mentioned several varieties of lettuce, among them Caecilian (both red and green), Cappadocian, Baetican, and Cyprian. Some of the varieties

Lettuce harvest. From an Egyptian wall carving in the Egyptian Museum, Berlin. Note the raised bed.

Dwarf Cos Lettuce

we know today may descend from these old sorts. Columella and other writers who discussed lettuce were quick to point out the Romans ate lettuce raw only when it was very young; otherwise they cooked it like spinach and served it with an oil and vinegar dressing. The custom of cooking lettuce, or poaching it to be more accurate, was continued in many areas of post-Roman Europe, but in nearly every case, this was done only with the large cos types. Otherwise, the oil and vinegar dressing was poured hot over the lettuce, another serving method practiced by the Romans.

Medieval references to lettuce abound, especially as a medicinal herb. Hildegard of Bingen (1098–1179), the famous practitioner of natural medicine, mentioned lettuce in her medical writings. Likewise, lettuce appeared in many of the earliest published herbals. Joachim Camerarius (1586) was one of the first authors to depict a small cabbaging lettuce of the tennisball type. Furthermore, he mentioned the three basic types of lettuce we know today: heading lettuce, loose-leaf lettuce, and the tall or cos sorts. Tall lettuces were referred to as cos because some of the earliest seed came to Europe from the Greek island of Cos. During the Byzantine period, Cos was a center of lettuce growing. Since this tall lettuce was first grown in papal gardens at Rome, the French called it romaine. In the 1880s market gardeners in the area around San Francisco began calling cos lettuces romaine, and the French name has now spread to the rest of the country. However, in older American garden books all romaine types are referred to as cos, and many old varieties from England, such as Bath Cos, still retain the older terminology.

Between Camerarius and the early eighteenth century, many of the basic heirloom types we know today evolved in France, Italy, and Holland. The Dutch in particular were active in creating many of the old standard varieties, and their influence survives in such varietal names as Brown Dutch and Early Dutch Butterhead. In the early eighteenth-century work called *Adam's Luxury and Eve's Cookery* (1744, 45–47), a number of familiar lettuce varieties were discussed, among them Brown Dutch, Green Capuchin, and Silesia. Brown Dutch is still available through Seed Savers Exchange, and Green Capuchin, with its deep green coarse leaves, is now known as

Tennisball (black seed) and is taken up under the sketch on Salamander (page 185). Silesia has also undergone a name change and is now commonly called White-Seeded Simpson or Early Curled Simpson.

Volume 3 of Willich's *Domestic Encyclopaedia* (1802, 89–90) enumerated many of the most popular lettuces of the day, names that were familiar to most early American gardeners. Among these were Silesia (one of the most popular), Imperial (still available), Royal Black, and Upright White Cos (the common green romaine lettuce of our supermarkets). Willich also pointed out that both Brown Dutch and Green Capuchin were extremely hardy and could be overwintered under straw, a handy piece of advice that I have put to the test several times and quite successfully. As cold-frame varieties, many of these old heirlooms are excellent. Obtaining seed is often another matter.

Lettuce seed is one of the bread-and-butter items of modern seed catalogs. Lettuce is easy to sell because it is easy to grow, and it is perennially popular as a vegetable in even the smallest of garden plots. Lettuce is one of the few vegetables that can be grown just about anywhere, on windowsills and balconies, on roof gardens, in flower pots by the kitchen door. As a result seedsmen have been more unscrupulous with lettuce then with many other vegetables, and this has made it difficult to sort out the histories of some of the most popular heirloom varieties today. In order to keep selling it, seedsmen have changed variety names often. The heirloom lettuce known as Hanson, which is distinct and unmistakable from any other lettuce, has sixteen commercial aliases. The unwitting gardener may buy these from different seedsmen on the presumption that they are distinct varieties, but this is not the case. They are identical, the same seed in different packets.

This practice of creating house aliases for well-known varieties arose in part as a means of deflecting attention from the fact that the seed house was selling a lettuce developed by a competitor. The present attempt to patent hybrids is a commercially motivated response to this sort of bewildering free-market switch-and-run that still takes advantage of the customer. When Salzer's began selling Silesia (aka Early Curled Simpson) as German Butter Lettuce, sales rose. When word got out that this was the same old Simpson lettuce everyone knew, Salzer's changed the name to LaCrosse Market Lettuce. This practice was so common among American seed houses that old seed catalogs can be used only with utmost caution when attempting to document heirloom varieties.

Several times in the past horticulturists have tackled the shifting sands of commercial lettuce terminology and, by growing out all the varieties side by side, were able to determine which were valid varieties and which were not. W. H. Bull of Hampden County, Massachusetts, undertook a useful growout for the *American Garden* in 1890, in particular taking note of the best of the varieties then available. He was thoroughly convinced that Boston Curled, Curled India, Hanson, and

Simpson were too old-fashioned and obsolete. It is a commentary on his Victorian progressiveness that these varieties are not only still with us but far more reliable than many of the highly inbred sorts presently on the market.

The most useful guide to heirloom lettuces, however, is Lester Morse's *Field Notes on Lettuce* (1923), which resulted from field tests at the C. C. Morse & Company seed farm in the Santa Clara Valley, near San Francisco. This company was established in 1877 to raise seed for most of the major American seed companies in the country. The Morse field notes therefore form an unbiased overview of what was grown and how it compared side by side in the field. For heirloom lettuces developed before 1900—my focus in this section of the book—Morse's insights are valuable, and a careful reading will reveal many discrepancies between heirloom varieties of the past and what we are growing today under the same name. Furthermore, Morse noted that of the 1,100 lettuce varieties he could list by name, only 140 were truly distinct, if slight differences were allowed. In truth, the real number of pre-1900 lettuce varieties is probably about 75, the remainder being subvarieties or variant forms. A survey of lettuce varieties in France, Germany, and Holland in 1866 could confirm only 65 sorts after eliminating the synonyms, and even several of those were questionable.

Not only do American lettuces have large numbers of confusing aliases but foreign lettuces seem to change name every time they cross a border. *Cappuccio ubriacona frastagliata* ("drunken woman frizzy-headed"), a pink-red fringed Italian lettuce with a name I thoroughly enjoy, is also known as Rossa di Trento, the name of a popular Italian chicory. In France it has a completely different name. Likewise, the *laitue lorthois* of France is the Trocadero of England and the Big Boston of America. And so it goes. I have tried to provide some of the better-known aliases with all of my selections lest my readers be misled by something they see in a seed catalog.

One of the great difficulties in describing lettuce is that varietal differences are often visual, and it is almost impossible to verbalize subtleties apparent only to the human eye: tones of green, blushes of color, three-dimensional surface textures, details that do not transfer well into line art or color photography. Signe Sundberg-Hall, the artist who has worked closely with me on this book, has made the same observation. The only way to convey many of the features peculiar to lettuce is through the medium of watercolor. It is interesting that in the *Album Vilmorin*, where the artists could wash the lithographs with color, the lettuces reproduced convey a true sense of their appearance in the garden. In any case, most descriptive works on lettuce fall short in one way or another, no matter how detailed the botanical terminology. Quite simply, lettuces are beautiful, Adonislike, the butterflies of the vegetable garden in terms of their fleeting beauty. They are best studied firsthand.

Nevertheless, lettuce growers use certain basic terms to qualify lettuces by type, terms that imply a certain physical appearance of the lettuce at its peak for harvesting. The first of these terms is curled-heading, which means that the edges of the leaves are curled or crumpled and that the lettuce forms a head or ball when mature. Curled-nonheading is the same leaf type, but the head is loose, forming a bunch like Black-Seeded Simpson. Cabbage or butterhead lettuces all have flat leaves, usually thick, with the interior leaves appearing oily. Early Dutch Butterhead, one of my favorite winter lettuces, has leaves that appear dappled with dark brown wax. It is this waxiness that protects the lettuce during cold weather. Cos is the general trade term for all upright or tall lettuces, the varieties we now call romaine. The last type is called cutting lettuce, which is loose, leafy lettuce cut young for salads, what the Italians call *lattuga a cespo da taglio* ("cut and cut again"). Cutting lettuces were introduced into England in 1827 and into this country about 1829. The best-known variety of cutting lettuce introduced at that time was *laitue épinarde*, a name rendered into English as Spanish lettuce. Today, this is known as oak leaf lettuce.

Vaux's Self-Folding Lettuce

Another way to differentiate lettuce is to categorize it by the color of its seed. Most seed is described as either black or white, although in fact there is gray seed and brown seed. Some brown seed is called yellow in old garden books if the brown is a light shade. I would consider the brown-seeded varieties to be a distinct category halfway between the black- and white-seeded sorts, but this is not universally accepted. Each seed color has produced a line of lettuces that is genetically related; sometimes lettuces have the identical appearance but different color seed. This seed color difference is a true marker for deciding which variety is under discussion. Therefore, in all of my sketches of specific lettuce varieties, I also provide the seed color. The eighteenth-century lettuce called Green Capuchin had black seed; it is not Green Capuchin if the seed is white or some other color.

Saving seed from lettuce is extremely easy on the one hand and messy on the other. First, the lettuce must be allowed to bolt or produce flower heads. Seed should only be saved from lettuces most true to type, and which bolt *last.* Saving seed from lettuces that are quick to bolt will only produce a strain that runs to seed quickly, especially during hot weather. The flower heads of most lettuces are about 3 feet tall and made up of tiny clusters of yellow blossoms. Seed is ready to harvest when the plants begin to yellow and the flower heads form "feathers" like dandelions. Strip the plants of their leaves and cut off the flower heads, turning them upside down in brown paper bags. Mark and date the bags, then set them in a dry, airy room away from the direct sun. Let the seed mature about a month before removing it from the seedheads.

To do this, roll the dried flowers between the fingers over a large work bowl. Feathers will fly everywhere (this is the messy part). The seed will drop into the bowl along with feathers and debris, which must be separated. Sift off debris larger than the seeds, then winnow the seed out of doors, blowing gently to lift the light materials away from the seed. If this is done carefully, the seed should separate, and the yield will be large. From eight to ten choice lettuces, I have harvested as much as ½ cup of seed, enough to sow an entire field. Some varieties have tiny seed or low seed yields, but once the seed-saving technique is mastered, there will be no reason to buy lettuce seed again, except to acquire new varieties.

Lettuces do cross. The controversy among horticulturists is just how far to distance the varieties. Some gardeners space their plants 5 feet. This is risky. I would suggest 20 feet. Furthermore, never save seed from volunteers that come up in the garden. Volunteers are an inevitable byproduct of seed saving, and some old varieties like Stoke, an English lettuce dating from pre-1840, are also self-sowing. In either case, do not save seed from plants that come up on their own. Their seed purity is questionable, and since lettuces are notorious for throwing sports and reversions to ancestral types, volunteers are only interesting if they look like a promising new variety worth cultivating as an experiment. Many heirloom varieties came into being in this very manner—Hanson was the product of a cross that occurred in a kitchen garden in Maryland. It is also necessary to remove any wild lettuce that is growing in the vicinity of the garden. Wild lettuce (*Lactuca serriola*) is found throughout the United States and will cross with garden lettuce under certain circumstances. The resulting cross will be tough and bitter. Likewise, Celtuce or Asparagus Lettuce should be isolated from other lettuces because it belongs to the same species, and while it is of Asian origin, there is a possibility it will cross with the leafing sorts. Again, 20 feet is a safe distance. Seed is saved from it in the same manner as other lettuces. All lettuce seed will store for three years under optimal conditions. If seed accumulates, share it with friends. Renew the supply often.

When planting lettuce, it is a huge mistake to follow the instructions on seed packets that advise planting it thickly in a row and then thinning. This is a great way to waste seed and end up with crowded lettuces. Only the cutting lettuces can be planted this way successfully; the others should be started in flats, then thinned into large flats. When the seedlings are large enough to plant in the garden—after the fifth or sixth leaf—space them evenly about 8 inches apart or more, depending on the variety. I space some of the large heading lettuces 14 inches apart. That way, they have plenty of room and will form huge, perfectly shaped heads. Lettuce that is crowded together attracts slugs and may be subject to stem rot at the base. Lettuce needs air circulation like any other plant. Furthermore, the more sunlight that strikes the leaves, the better the color and the higher the concentration of nutrients. The blanched white centers of lettuces like Iceberg contain very little food value.

In 1930 the U.S. Department of Agriculture reissued Farmer's Bulletin 1609, *Lettuce Growing*, and listed the leading varieties of lettuce then under cultivation. Among the commercial varieties grown on a large scale, there were only six: Big Boston, Hanson, Iceberg, May King, New York, and Salamander. All of these are heirlooms—American garden classics in their own way—and I have included lettuces of this type in my profiles.

Bath Cos Lettuce
Lactuca sativa var. *romana*

There are two types of this eighteenth-century English variety, one white-seeded, the other black-seeded. The white-seeded variety is generally called Brown Cos. Its leaves are cool gray-green, deeply toothed, and tinged with red in the edges and veins as well as the stems. The leaves do not wrap tightly into a head except at the very center. The leaves turn pale brown where tinged by the sun, but this variety is normally tied up to blanch it a few

days before harvesting. A well-formed head is about 14 inches in diameter. Plants should be well spaced in the garden to account for this. Normally, this variety is planted in the late summer to be ready for harvest in the fall. It is very hardy and will overwinter in parts of the South.

The black-seeded variant, called Black-Seeded Bath Cos, is smaller and dark reddish brown. It is also raised as a fall lettuce and is known in England as Coolings Leviathan. The leaves of this sort overlap differently from the other, somewhat like a rosebud that is opening partway. It also squatter and slower growing.

Another old cos lettuce from the same period is the Spotted Cos or Aleppo (white-seeded), mentioned as early as the seventeenth century. This is a shorter type of romaine lettuce with large,

Bath Cos Lettuce

floppy leaves of a bright green color. The leaf surface is savoyed (covered with bubbles) and heavily speckled with reddish brown spots. It measures about 16 inches in diameter and is considered the tall form of the French *Laitue Sanguine* (white-seeded).

Big Boston or Trocadero Lettuce
Lactuca sativa

This white-seeded variety was introduced in this country in 1887 from France. It was first sold commercially in 1890 by Peter Henderson & Company of New York, and since Mr. Henderson thought it looked like Boston Market, only much larger, he created the American name Big Boston. Today it is widely circulated under Henderson's name and under its original French name, *Laitue Lorthois*.

The lettuce is a heading type, medium large in size, and globular when well formed. The leaves are a light green color, tinged with brown on the margins of the outer leaves. The leaves are smooth with a bright sheen, very brittle and quite tender, good qualities for salads. The inner part of the head is golden yellow.

Other commercial aliases of this lettuce are Tait's Forcing White, Giant White Forcing, Tait's Pride of the Point (Tait got tired of the first name), Schisler's New Market, Stoke's Standard, and Standard Head Lettuce.

Big Boston Lettuce or Trocadero

Black-Seeded Simpson Lettuce
Lactuca sativa

One of the most famous of all American lettuces, this variety was introduced by Peter Henderson & Company of New York in the 1870s. It is a nonheading type, very crisp and light yellowish green with large leaves. Of all the lettuces listed here, this is the most difficult to keep true when saving seed. Also, in spite of its popularity with kitchen gardeners, it rots easily at the base of the stem and is sensitive to radical weather changes. This is counterbalanced by its quick growth and fine quality at maturity. Bon Ton is a selection of Black-Seeded Simpson, identical in all respects except small size.

Commercial aliases include: First Early (Great Northern Seed Company), Earliest Cutting (Landreth), Carter's Long Stander, and Longstreath's Earliest.

Boston Market Lettuce
Lactuca sativa

This is the same as White-Seeded Tennisball. Refer to my discussion of tennisball lettuces under Loos Tennisball. Many grocers in this country call this variety Boston lettuce as though it is a generic type, a practice that is somewhat misleading. Vilmorin (1885, 307) considered it nearly the same as a Dutch variety called *Seelander Latouw*, a possibility in physical appearance only, for the Dutch sort has black seed, not white.

Brauner Trotzkopf Lettuce
Lactuca sativa

This is a distinct American variety also called Hardhead and Weber's Brown Head. The seed is white. Its exact origin is not presently known, but David Landreth & Sons listed it in the firm's 1875 German-language seed catalog. It is considered a German-American variety, a cabbaging or butterhead type similar in size to Tom Thumb, measuring 6 to 7 inches in diameter. It appears to be a dwarf version of Large Brown Winter lettuce. Large Brown Winter (white seed) was known to Fearing Burr, but not this form of it. Vilmorin (1885, 295) called it Early Cabbage or Dutch Butterhead. The leaves are crimped and dappled with red brown, which darkens to maroon toward the center. The surface of the leaves is shiny, as though waxed. The leaves have greenish white edges and ribs. It is a very handsome lettuce when mixed with Tom Thumb, and because it is a winter variety, it thrives in cold frames. It is also extremely slow to bolt.

Brauner Trotzkopf Lettuce

Brown Dutch Lettuce
Lactuca sativa

The standard variety is black-seeded, nonheading, medium in size, and handsome deep lime green, tinged with bluish green in the center. It is described by the Abbé Rozier (1785, 215) under the name *Laitue brune de Hollande*. The leaves are large and floppy, with ruffled edges tinged with pink or rose, and tend to lie flat against the ground in heads measuring about 12 inches across. The back side of the leaf has small hair-like spines on the rib. Brown Dutch (white-seeded) is identical in appearance but as a documented variety is much older, for it is mentioned by Stephen Switzer (1731, 21) and other early horticultural authors. The white-seeded sort is often called Sugar Lettuce or Swede in old garden books. It was one of the most popular fall and winter lettuces in colonial America. Spotted Brown Dutch (black-seeded) is the same as the old variety known as Palatine, Brown Genoa, and Haarlem. It dates from the seventeenth century.

Brown Dutch Winter Lettuce

Celtuce or Asparagus Lettuce
Lactuca sativa var. *asparagina*

The accepted history of this useful and distinctive Asian variety is that it was introduced into France in the 1880s but did not reach the United States until 1938. W. Atlee Burpee is credited with commercializing it here in 1942. Quite the contrary, Celtuce came to the attention of

American horticulturists in the 1850s and was grown by a small circle of specialists since that time. It was introduced to them by the Mennonite plant collector Jacob B. Garber (1800–1886) of Lancaster County, Pennsylvania. Garber also figured out that it was the stem of the plant that was eaten, not the leaves, even though the leaves make a perfectly respectable salad.

Under the heading "Hoo Sung" (today written as *woh sun*), Garber published an article about his experience with celtuce in the *Florist and Horticultural Journal* (1854, 248). According to Garber's own account, he had raised the vegetable for a number of years from seed originally obtained from a Dr. Kennicott in Illinois. Dr. Kennicott might rightly be called the introducer of Celtuce, because it was he who brought seed from China in the 1840s. But it was Jacob Garber who discovered how to use it: "The stems being very tender, and when from a quarter to half an inch in diameter, and eighteen inches to two feet high, may be cut into lengths and cooked in the same manner as asparagus."

Celtuce is raised like lettuce, but because it is a large, spreading plant, it should be spaced about 16 inches apart. The young leaves may be harvested as greens, but when the plant bolts to produce flowers, it is the stem that is considered the best part. Harvesting the stems, of course, reduces the seed crop, so it is best to set aside several plants for seed purposes. The flowers are yellow like lettuce flowers, and the seed is harvested in the same manner.

There are several distinct varieties of Celtuce, which unfortunately do not have distinguishing names outside of Asia. There are broad-leafed sorts resembling tobacco, speckled varieties, and some types with long, pointed leaves like fingers. Many of these are available through seed-saving networks, but very few American gardeners grow them for their stems. Since Celtuce bears hot weather well, it is often grown as a midseason substitute for salad lettuce.

Curled India Lettuce
Lactuca sativa var. *capitata*

There is a great deal of confusion about this early American lettuce with brown seeds. In garden literature, it is often treated as though it is Curled India Head lettuce, which it is not, since this is an old alias of Iceberg or Marblehead Mammoth. It is not the same as India either, although it is a form of it. From all appearances, it is a cross between India and Beauregard. It has the crispness and heading quality of Iceberg and the sharply toothed leaf margin of Beauregard. White's *Gardening for the South* (1868, 243) described Curled India as light yellow-green and highly curled, which is true. Its leaves are blistered and shiny, as though glazed with ice. It is an excellent summer lettuce and far superior in quality to Iceberg. Its smaller size makes it ideal for kitchen gardens where space may present a problem.

Gotte Jaune d'Or Lettuce
Lactuca sativa

Since this variety is now widely circulated under its French name, I have listed it that way, but it is a well known tennisball type identified in old garden books as White-Seeded Tennisball, Golden Tennisball, and Golden Forcing. As might be ascertained from the name, this lettuce was once popular as a cold-frame sort as well as a hothouse variety. The Abbé Rozier (1785, 216) remarked that it was grown extensively between November and February as a forcing lettuce in the north of France but was completely unknown in the south of that country. Due to its small size, it is extremely easy to grow in flats and for this reason was used like Tom Thumb. The heads measure no more than 8 inches in diameter. Even though this is a tennisball type and technically should form a head about that size, the head of this lettuce is loose, more twisted

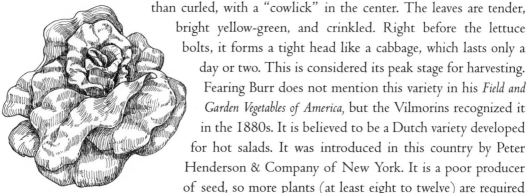

than curled, with a "cowlick" in the center. The leaves are tender, bright yellow-green, and crinkled. Right before the lettuce bolts, it forms a tight head like a cabbage, which lasts only a day or two. This is considered its peak stage for harvesting. Fearing Burr does not mention this variety in his *Field and Garden Vegetables of America,* but the Vilmorins recognized it in the 1880s. It is believed to be a Dutch variety developed for hot salads. It was introduced in this country by Peter Henderson & Company of New York. It is a poor producer of seed, so more plants (at least eight to twelve) are required for seed-saving purposes.

Gotte Jaune d'Or Lettuce

Hanson Lettuce
Lactuca sativa

Remarks about this lettuce in the Vilmorin garden book (1885) clearly indicate that the French were not getting pure seed. Even today lettuces sold under the name of Hanson will vary greatly. This variety was introduced in 1871 by Henry A. Dreer of Philadelphia, and I have chosen to show one of Dreer's original advertisements, since it illustrates Hanson at its best. Any lettuce sold as Hanson that does not form a head as shown is not Hanson. Dreer obtained the lettuce from a Colonel Hanson in Mary-

The HANSON LETTUCE.

The most tender, sweet, and delicious variety grown; free from any bitter or unpleasant taste; heads large and solid, often weighing 3 lbs. **Single pkge 25 cts. 5 pkgs $1.** A LIBERAL DISCOUNT TO DEALERS. ☞ *Send for* **Dreer's Garden Calendar for 1874,** *168 pages, illustrated, with practical directions. Mailed* **FREE** *to all applicants.* **HENRY A. DREER, 714 Chestnut St., Philadelphia, Pa.**

Advertisement for the introduction of Hanson Lettuce.

land, who stated that it had been growing in his family's garden for many years and that his grandfather had imported it from abroad. More likely Hanson is a cross between Curled India and Early Curled Simpson, since it bears characteristics of both. Hanson is white-seeded, light green in color, with curly leaves that are fringed on the edges. As can be seen from the old wood engraving, it is a heading lettuce, extremely crisp and excellent in sandwiches. It withstands the heat well but is often subject to slug damage.

There are several commercial aliases for this variety. The most commonly appearing names are Ewing's Excelsior, Gardener's Favorite, King of the Market, Los Angeles Market, Louisville Market Forcing Lettuce, Ryder's Green Globe, Toronto Gem, Toronto Market, and Nonpareil.

Hubbard's Market Lettuce
Lactuca sativa

This old and popular white-seeded variety was developed in Chatauqua County, New York, by a market gardener whose name was given to the variety when it was released by Chase Brothers of Rochester. It is a cabbaging or butterhead lettuce with dark green crumpled leaves. The edges of the leaves are straight. It is now often sold as White Summer Cabbage, although the original Hubbard strain was darker green and larger in size than the old variety known as White Summer Cabbage. It is an excellent lettuce for summer, especially in the North. In the South, I would recommend it as a fall lettuce. The seed is white.

Hubbard's Market has thirty-five commercial aliases, among them All-Year-Around (white seed), Eichling's Early Market, White-Seeded German, Ullathorne's Memphis Lettuce, Top Notch, Peer of All, and Hollow-Leaved Butter.

Iceberg Lettuce
Lactuca sativa var. *capitata*

There is a code of disdain among foodies in this country for the very old American lettuce variety we now call Iceberg. Its association with the worst sorts of American fast foods has been responsible for this, yet homegrown Iceberg is one of our finest and most reliable summer lettuces. Its early American progenitor was Ice (white-seeded), which began appearing in seed lists in the 1820s. The *Gardener's Magazine* (1827, 436) announced it as a variety "new" to English growers and identified it as a variety of American origin. Unfortunately, the developer

Iceberg Lettuce

of this lettuce is not presently known, nor are the circumstances surrounding its creation. It was sometimes called India Head or Marblehead Mammoth and often confused with Curled India, which is similar and equally old.

Iceberg is a heading variety of a medium green color. The leaves are wavy and fringed, the margins tinged with brown. It forms a compact head that is white inside; it is usually the head, stripped of its outer leaves, that is seen in the markets. There are many selections of Iceberg sold as distinct varieties. Imperial Valley Iceberg, raised in Southern California, and Mountain Iceberg, grown in Colorado, are regional names for New York, not true Iceberg. New York (white-seeded) was introduced in 1886 by Peter Henderson & Company. In France it was known as *chou de Naples blonde,* and in England as Neapolitan. It resembles Iceberg in some ways, although the head is flatter, the color much deeper green, and the leaves only slightly curled along the edges. Batavian Red-Fringed lettuce is true Iceberg, but with considerable red coloring.

Loos Tennisball Lettuce
Lactuca sativa

There are three recognized tennisball varieties: white-seeded, black-seeded, and stone. The white-seeded tennisball is one of the oldest cultivated sorts in this country and is generally known by the name Boston Market. In France, it is sold commercially as Victoria, not to be confused with the German Victoria, which is a different variety and known in this country as North Pole (white-seeded). Boston Market was grown as a forcing lettuce in cold frames and hothouses, and its history is treated in greater detail on page 178.

Black-seeded tennisball is the same as Salamander (page 185). Stone tennisball (black seed) is a distinct English variety similar to Tom Thumb, but darker green, larger, and more savoyed. It is the same as the French Tom Thumb and similar to Stonehead Green (white seed). Loos Tennisball (gray-seeded) is probably a cross of one or more of these types, for it is intermediate between the dwarf character of Tom Thumb and a butterhead. The heads of Loos Tennisball measure about 7 inches in diameter and form loose, soft, fluffy balls. It is an extremely attractive sort introduced about 1853. Since it can be planted close together, it is ideal for small gardens.

The tennisball lettuces that formed small tight heads were often pickled in salt brine in the seventeenth and eighteenth centuries for use during the winter. The following recipe is taken from *Adam's Luxury and Eve's Cookery* (1744, 142–43). The expression "unsalt" meant to soak the vegetables in several changes of fresh water to remove the saltiness. Cos lettuces could also be preserved in this manner.

To Keep Lettuce

❦

Choose the hardest, take off the large Leaves, and blanch them in Water, and drain them. Then stick them with Cloves, and season them with Pepper, Salt, Vinegar, and Bay leaf. Cover them well, and when you would use them, unsalt them and stew them.

Mignonette Lettuce
Lactuca sativa

There are two variations of this lettuce, a green and a bronze (both with dark brown seed). The green is commonly described as the original variety, but this does not tally with early catalog descriptions or with Lester Morse's *Field Notes on Lettuce* (1923). The original introduction was the bronze sort first marketed by Peter Henderson & Company of New York. Prior to introducing it (Henderson also named it), Henderson had distributed seed to a number of horticulturists, so the lettuce appeared almost simultaneously in several catalogs. William Henry Maule of Philadelphia introduced it in 1898, and this is more or less the accepted date of its commercialization. It is now circulated as Mignonette Bronze; the other later subvariety is called Mignonette Green.

Both sorts are curled heading lettuces with highly crumpled leaves. The heads are about 7 inches in diameter, compact, with the outer leaves heavily savoyed. The bronze variety is a brownish color, referred to as "russet-colored" in old catalogs, and tinged with dark green. It is quite distinctive, hardy, and fairly drought resistant. Plants should be spaced 12 inches apart for the best shaped heads. Due to the tightness of the heads, it is often necessary to slit them two or three times so that the seed stalk can form. The green sort is prone to slugs and therefore should not be grown on heavy clay soil.

Oak Leaf Lettuce
Lactuca sativa

Vilmorin listed this lettuce under the name *laitue épinarde* (black-seeded) as early as 1771. The Abbé Rozier (1785, 210) listed two distinct varieties, one with white seed and one with black. Both were well known in France as cutting lettuces, but were not introduced into England until 1827. Cutting lettuces were not popular in the United States until later in the nineteenth century, although some individuals cultivated them from imported seed. Thomas Jefferson raised a cutting variety called Endive-Leaved (*laitue chicorée*).

The oak leaf sort is a pale green color and forms a rosette some 12 to 24 inches across. The leaves are heavily lobed and undulating. This variety is extremely hardy and can be overwintered in cold frames in the North or in the open in the Deep South.

There were two American varieties of the oak leaf sort, one called Philadelphia Oak Leaf (white-seeded), the other Baltimore Oak Leaf. The Philadelphia variety was developed in the 1840s. It was darker green than the French oak leaf and characterized by a lobe resembling a finger on the end of each leaf. The French lettuce called Cocarde has similar lobing. The Baltimore variety was pale green and more of a cabbaging type, with round, lobed leaves.

Red Besson Lettuce
Lactuca sativa

This is one of the most handsome of all the lettuces I grow and a great favorite of visitors to my garden. It is known in France as *Besson rouge* or *Merveille des Quatre Saisons* (black seed—actually a dark black-brown). The lettuce is a cabbaging or butter-head type with heads 12 inches in diameter. The leaves are wine red and savoyed, and they darken as the lettuce matures. The undersides of the leaves are pink, as are the stems. This variety was illustrated in the *Album Vilmorin* (1882, 33) with extraordinary veracity to color, indeed one of the finest lettuce illustrations of the period. This lettuce was not listed in American catalogs until late in the nineteenth century, usually under the name Continuity. For the best-formed heads, plant individual lettuces 14 inches apart.

Red Besson Lettuce

Salamander Lettuce
Lactuca sativa

Salamander was one of the most popular lettuces of the nineteenth century. It was listed by B. K. Bliss & Sons of New York in 1871 under its British name All-Year-Around. Landreth and several other large seed houses also listed it that way, even though it had been grown in this country for many years as Black-Seeded Tennisball, and in the eighteenth century as Green Capuchin. That earlier name was derived from *capucine*, the French term for nasturtium or Indian cress (page 326). Correctly speaking, All-Year-Around, the name by which the lettuce is best known today, was a British strain of Black-Seeded Tennisball that headed two weeks earlier; otherwise it was identical. In the United States, the lettuce was widely cultivated on Long Island for the New York market, even though lettucemen always recommended it as a forcing lettuce rather than a field variety. In the field the green is deeper, and the leaves tend toward bitterness if the weather is unseasonably warm.

Salamander is considered a cabbaging variety, as shown in the woodcut. It has thick, savoyed, deep green leaves. The young leaves sometimes have small spines on the outside edges. White-seeded Salamander is a distinctly different variety, synonymous with Hubbard's Market Lettuce and White Summer Cabbage.

There are over forty-nine commercial aliases for this lettuce, all of which Lester Morse grew side by side in his lettuce trials in California. Some of the better known aliases are Eclipse, Farquhar's Long Standing, Fearnaught, Bridgeman's Large Butterhead, Northrup-King's Market Gardener, Sutton's Matchless, Sherman's Newport Head, Tender and True, and XXX Solid Head.

Silesia or Early Curled Simpson Lettuce
Lactuca sativa

Dating from the seventeenth century, Early Curled Silesia (white-seeded) is one of the oldest cultivated varieties of nonheading lettuce in this country. It forms a tight bunch of light green crumpled leaves about 12 to 14 inches across. It is quick growing and very hardy. It was also known as Curled German Batavian. Today it is generally called White-Seeded Simpson, a name that came into use in the 1850s when the Simpson strain was introduced; it matured earlier than the older sorts. Due to its hardiness, this lettuce was preferred for overwintering. It can be grown in cold frames or simply covered with straw. Hard freezing does not kill it.

Among the Pennsylvania Dutch, this lettuce was normally planted in the old cucumber beds in August and September in order to have a succession of harvests through December. It was often planted together with Brown Dutch, Landis Winter Lettuce, and Speckled Lettuce.

Speckled Lettuce
Lactuca sativa

This type of lettuce has been grown in this country since the eighteenth century. There were three basic sorts, all rather similar in general appearance, but on close examination, their differences were enough to qualify them as distinct varieties. Today, they are mistakenly treated as one, and it is quite possible that seed switches have unwittingly taken place, which only muddles the issue further.

Willich's *Domestic Encyclopaedia* (1802, 3:90) observed that if Brown Dutch and Black-Seeded Tennisball were planted together and allowed to cross, "The future produce of seed will be a new and very excellent kind of this plant, forming extraordinary large heads, the leaves of which are sprinkled with deep red spots, and uncommonly tender." This appears to be the method by which our early American variety was created.

Amelia Simmons mentioned only one lettuce variety in her *American Cookery* (1796, 13–14): "The purple spotted leaf is generally the tenderest, and free from bitter." She was referring to a variety of speckled lettuce referred to in old garden books as Spotted Butter (white seed) or Dutch Speckled Butter, a variety thought to have originated in Holland. It is a cabbaging or butterhead type, light green in color, and tinged with brown. The leaves are speckled with reddish brown, crumpled, and straight edged. It was a favorite hothouse lettuce in Philadelphia during the early nineteenth century, and I can attest to the fact that it thrives in greenhouse conditions. It is even less prone to aphids than many lettuces. This is the same lettuce noted in the *Gardener's Magazine* (1837, 13), which stated that seed from France had been dis-

tributed some years earlier to members of the London Horticultural Society. Judging from historical evidence, this lettuce was much more popular in America than in England and was grown here much earlier. It was known commercially in this country as Philadelphia Dutch Butter, although David Landreth & Sons sold it as Indispensible. Hornberger's Dutch Butter was considered the best selection of this speckled sort.

The speckled lettuce of this sketch is a variety preserved among the Mennonites of Ontario, Canada, and accessioned by Seed Savers Exchange in 1983. That seed originated with Urias Martin of Waterloo, Ontario, but is

Speckled Lettuce

generally thought to have come from Pennsylvania. This is a butterhead cabbaging lettuce with somewhat blistered or savoyed leaves, as shown in the drawing. It fits the description of the commercial variety known as Golden Spotted (white seed), introduced in 1880. The spotting is brownish red, similar to markings on a quail's egg. It is the same variety as Thorburn's Orchid. It is not true *sanguine ameliore,* with which it is often equated.

Sanguine ameliore (white-seeded) is an old French variety often mistaken for the other two. It has a deep reddish brown mottling clustered thickly toward the center of each tongue-shaped leaf. Most significant, the interior of the head is pink; only in this variety is this the case. *Sanguine ameliore* was introduced in this country in 1906 by C. C. Morse & Company of San Francisco under the commercial name Strawberry Cabbage Lettuce.

Tomhannock Lettuce
Lactuca sativa
Introduced by W. Atlee Burpee in 1886, this delightful white-seeded lettuce originated in northern New York State. It is a curled, nonheading type, medium green in color, tinged with red-

Tomhannock Lettuce

dish brown. The leaves are upright and outwardly spreading, and rolled over along the edge, as shown in the old wood engraving on page 187. Although it was considered a good hot-weather lettuce in the North, it was generally grown as a fall salad lettuce, since it is slow to bolt and, because of its hardiness, will not suffer from light frosts. This variety deserves to be better known.

Tom Thumb (Wheeler's) Lettuce
Lactuca sativa

Tom Thumb (black seed) was introduced by the English firm of H. Wheeler & Sons in 1858, although Ipswich seedsman William Thompson was growing *laitue gotte à lente monter* (the French name given to Tom Thumb by Vilmorin) as early as 1850. The French variety called *Tom Pouce,* which is the French counterpart to the English variety, is larger, darker green, and more savoyed than Tom Thumb. It is also the same lettuce as Stone Tennisball. In order to keep all of this straight and not produce confusion (!), the Tom Thumb introduced in 1858 is generally called Wheeler's Tom Thumb. It was introduced into the United States in 1868 by James J. H. Gregory of Marblehead, Massachusetts, but was never popular in this country.

As its name would imply, this is a dwarf lettuce of the cabbaging or butterhead type with dark green leaves that are heavily crumpled. It heads into a fine little ball. It is easy to grow in hothouses and cold frames and does not require a great deal of space, since the heads measure from 3 to 4 inches in diameter. The lettuce makes an excellent garnish for buffet tables, and since it thrives in cold frames, it can keep the kitchen well supplied with lettuces all winter. Its commercial aliases in this country were Landreth's Forcing, Holmes's Forcing, and Early Green Stone (black seed).

White Paris Cos Lettuce
Lactuca sativa var. *romana*

This white-seeded lettuce is generally planted in the early spring so that it heads before the onset of hot weather. It is the most common of all the romaine types grown in this country and probably one of the most attractive as well. It is an eighteenth-century variety, sold in this country as early as 1802 by Bernard M'Mahon of Philadelphia. M'Mahon sold it under the name White Cos; in France it is known as *blonde maraîchère.*

This variety is characterized by tall, narrow, upwardly pointing leaves with heavy white ribs. The leaves are blunt and rounded on the ends, light green in color, with the inner leaves folding around one another. A well-formed head may weigh anywhere from 5 to 6 pounds. This lettuce is a heavy drinker and will never develop its famous crispness unless it is kept well watered. This is also one of the popular lettuces that was used for stewing, especially if the heads were tied up in the garden and blanched before harvest.

The following recipe is taken from Baron Brisse's *366 Menus* (1886, 32). It surprises me that the baron would cook his lettuce for 2 hours; 30 minutes is quite sufficient. But the process is not boiling, rather sweating, with a very small amount of water. This is the reason for the buttered parchment paper, which prevents the lettuces from sticking to the pan.

Laitues au jus (*Stewed Lettuce*)
❦

Clean, blanch, and trim your lettuces, tie them in bunches, putting two or three together, simmer for two hours in a saucepan with stock, a bouquet of herbs, chopped onions, salt, and pepper, line the saucepan with buttered paper. When cooked untie the lettuces and serve with their own sauce, which must be reduced and passed through a tammy.

MARTYNIA (DEVIL'S CLAW)

Named for John Martyn (1699–1768), a professor of botany at Cambridge, this tropical annual is now a common weed in several parts of the United States. Louisiana martynia (*Proboscidea louisianica*) is considered a native of the Gulf Coast states and the species most closely associated with Cajun cookery. All of the plants belonging to the *Martynia* and *Proboscidea* genera were commonly called martinas or martinoes in early American cookbooks. They produce hooked green pods that can be cooked and eaten like okra, or pickled. The flowers, which resemble catalpas, are quite ornamental, and some of the species are fragrant.

Hortus Third (1976, 715 and 912) lists a number of species for both genera, although there is really little difference between them. I take issue with the classifications because I have had several cross. This is most obvious when white-seeded and black-seeded varieties of different "genera" cross and produce pods of mixed seed on the same plant. Since the scientific classifications cannot be trusted, for seed-saving purposes, I suggest growing only one type of martynia during a given season, especially since seed purity can only be ensured with isolations of at least half a mile.

The Louisiana martynia is an annual of easy culture. It was illustrated in 1807 in *Curtis's Botanical Magazine* (26:1056), although seeds were sent to Paris in the early part of the eighteenth century. It was grown in Europe primarily for its flower, yet in England it rarely sets seed unless raised in hothouses. A dark purple–flowering species from Brazil (color plate 46) was introduced via Mexico in the 1840s under the name *Martynia fragrans* and has since naturalized in the Deep South and Southwest. For culinary purposes, I recommend it over the others, since its pods are small and tender, and its flower is a cheerful addition to the kitchen garden. The yellow martynia from Brazil, now classified as *Ibicella lutea,* is presently quite rare in North American gardens. It was illustrated in *Edward's Botanical Register* (11:934) in 1825 and was the preferred martynia of our nineteenth-century cooks. The flower is eye-catching, since it is brilliant yellow with red speckling in the throat, admittedly my favorite of them all.

Martynias are cultivated like okra insofar as they will thrive where okra does best. This means that they prefer hot, humid weather and warm summer nights. The plants vary from low and sprawling to tall, erect, branching bushes. All of them have large fleshy leaves covered with minute sticky hairs. The stems, leaves, and young seed pods exude a liquid with a strong musky smell more overpowering than okra. All of the martynias produce seed pods that are edible when young, but many varieties quickly develop a woody core that renders them useless to cookery. As the pods mature, the woody core enlarges until the green shell falls away to expose a black beaklike pod. When the pod splits open, the seeds are exposed. In hot climates, the seed falls to the ground and new plants are started. In northern parts of the United States, seed must be gathered, dried, and started indoors in the spring in order for the plants to come to crop. In Pennsylvania, however, fallen seed often overwinters in the ground and sprouts the following spring, usually in May once the soil has warmed.

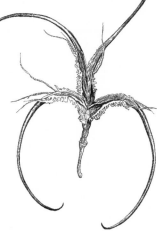

Dried seed pod of Martynia

The dried seed pods are often utilized in dried flower arrangements, for when they are broken open and spread apart, they resemble odd-looking claws with sharp, curving points. The points can inflict serious wounds and therefore should be treated with respect. In the Southwest, the pods are called devil's claws, and several varieties are distributed under this name by Native Seeds/SEARCH. American Indians in the Southwest use black fibers from the pods in basket weaving and gather the seeds as food, since the kernels can be eaten like sunflower seeds.

Martynias have either white or black seeds, and I think it would be prudent to divide them into two groups based on this difference. Furthermore, some types hold their flowers high above the leaves while others hide them among the branches. These physical traits do not determine genera, but from a gardening standpoint they provide clues useful in separating varieties. For the most part, the martynias with flowers held above the plants are also the types with small pods useful in cookery. The others produce large pods better suited to basket weaving.

One of the earliest American recipes for pickling martynia pods appeared in Mrs. Abell's *The Skilful Housewife's Book* (1846, 112), but the following instructions are reproduced from an old Maryland cookbook called *The Queen of the Kitchen* (1870, 200).

Martinas
❦

Put tender martinas in a strong brine for a week, take them out and drain them, and put them in cold vinegar. To 1 gallon of vinegar put 3 pounds brown sugar, ½ cup of allspice, ½ cup of pounded cloves, ½ cup of black pepper, 2 tablespoons of celery seed, 3 pods of red pepper, pound them all together and boil them in the vinegar and pour it over the martinas. Scraped horse-radish is an improvement if added. Keep the jar closely covered and in a dry place.

For the pepper pods, I would suggest the dry pods of Buist's Yellow Cayenne, Goat Horn Pepper, or Ole Pepperpot.

Melons

The Egyptians were among the earliest peoples to cultivate melons, and they have left good documentation in the form of tomb paintings and actual archaeological specimens. What they raised was the so-called chate melon (*Cucumis melo* var. *chate*), a melon with a cucumber-like fruit. During the Roman period, the cultivation of melons spread to nearly all regions of the Roman Empire where climate conditions were favorable. Unfortunately, Roman melon varieties have proved elusive even from written documentation, because without names beside pictures, we have no real idea what they were like. The same is true of medieval sources and botanical works of the Renaissance, for melons were often equated with cucumbers and watermelons and, even later, confused with New World squash.

It is known that the Armenian Cucumber (a true melon) and the cantaloupe were introduced into Italy from Armenia in the 1400s. Green-fleshed melons similar to the Nutmeg Melon appear in Italian, Spanish, and French paintings in the 1500s, but there do not seem to have been distinct commercial varieties as we now know them. Mostly, melons were grouped according to the place where they were grown regardless of similarities or differences, as in the case of the Cavaillon melons in France. Constant crossing probably blurred varietal distinctions much as it did with fava beans (see discussion on page 93), and since melons can deteriorate quickly if seed purity is not properly maintained, there seems to have been an active trade in seed from well-known melon-producing areas on both sides of the Mediterranean. This is certainly evident in the names of the melons first grown in this country, for Philadelphia seedsman Bernard M'Mahon, who listed thirteen melon varieties in 1806, offered seed from Minorca, Malta, Portugal, and North Africa. It is obvious that this seed was traveling across the Atlantic in company with wines, lemons, capers, and other culinary products from those areas.

There is not much written on melon culture in the eighteenth century, although a useful little tract written by Abbé Vilin under the title *Traité de la culture du melon* appeared at Amiens in 1774. It is practical for its insights into melon propagation of that period, the use of hotbeds and cloches, pruning vines for better productivity, and other hands-on considerations. Unfortunately, it is exceedingly rare, and the good abbé's focus was not on the range of melon varieties then available. As a result, he did not include a list, which would have been helpful to horticultural historians today, especially since very few seed catalogs survive from that era. In fact, Vilin had been attacked in print by a satirist in one of those convoluted kitchen garden controversies that only Frenchmen can puff out to the limits of learned indignation. Preoccupation with those polemics imposed itself on his pamphlet, which served as his response.

The only other sources on melons, at least for the old French heirloom varieties still available, is volume 6 of Abbé Rozier's *Cours complet d'agriculture* (1785, 472–89) and M. Jacquin's *Monographie complète du melon* (1832). Rozier discussed many early varieties, their names, and peculiarities of cultivation based primarily on the writings of Descombes. Much of what is now known about the origins of many old French melons was preserved by Descombes, who may be relied upon as much for his facts as for his fantasies. The most scientific work, however, was Jacquin's, which attempted to organize the melons botanically, describe them in minute detail, and most valuable of all, illustrate them in engravings.

Perhaps more apropos to the American situation is John William Lloyd's *Muskmelon Production* (1928), a market gardener's handbook written by a professor at the University of Illinois. Lloyd's emphasis was directed toward melon varieties of commercial importance, particularly melons that ship well, a trait that has little relation to kitchen gardening. His overview of the development of such well-known melons as Netted Gem and Rocky Ford can provide a useful perspective, but the lack of garden varieties is glaring. In the monograph series *The Vegetables of New York: The Cucurbits* (1937), considerable attention was given to melons, but with the honest observation that their early history was

Baltimore Market Melon

murky. Documentation for the early varieties imported into this country exists in the form of seed lists and garden accounts, yet pictorial evidence is often lacking, so we have only guesswork in most cases when it comes to reconstructing what some of those melons were like. One of the exceptions is the Anne Arundel Melon of eighteenth-century Maryland, for which there is ample documentation in the paintings of Philadelphia artist Raphaelle Peale. It is interesting that the authors of the 1937 monograph presumed the Anne Arundel Melon to be an improved strain of Acme or Baltimore Market, introduced in the 1890s. Based on unreliable claims in seed catalogs, that might seem to be the case. More important, it highlights the lack of careful research that went into the work and leaves us wondering today how much of it can be relied upon.

It is evident from eighteenth-century accounts that melons were indeed raised in our kitchen gardens and that they were extremely popular with the Indians. Seed traveled quickly into the backcountry, to such an extent that melons appeared long before white settlers. Even to this day there are melons associated with certain Native American groups, especially in the West, and these melons have been cultivated so long that they have evolved into distinct varieties. Many of these descend from the three most popular muskmelons grown by early American gardeners, the Citron Melon, the Nutmeg Melon, and Murray's Pineapple Melon. All of these historical varieties are still available today.

Unfortunately, melons are so dependent on soil and hot weather for their best qualities that it is often difficult to grow them outside the regions in which they were developed. It is pointless to try and raise melons in potato country, although Montreal Market might offer a solution for gardeners in cool summer regions. I have tried to make some suggestions in this regard with each of the heirlooms I have selected. Personally, by trial and error, I have found that in my garden it is baking hot, sandy soil that has the best effect on melons. Therefore, I have a bed in which I have mixed a large quantity of sand, situated in the sunniest, most exposed part of my garden. Without it my melons fail, or they are so miserable in size and flavor that it is hardly worth the effort to grow them. It is also useful to have a cold frame to get the melon plants well on their way before setting them out in the spring. If the plants are started in pots, so much the better, because their roots will not be disturbed when moved to the garden. I allow six plants to a hill. But getting them into production by mid-June is the secret to success, because most of us have only a 30-to-60-day window in the summer when the nights are sultry hot and therefore most agreeable to melons. For me, the hottest weather normally falls between July 15 and August 15, and this is when my best melons come to fruit. In the South this is extended on both sides, from June 15 to September 15, but the long period of humidity in that part of the country also takes its toll on the melon vines in the form of mildew, rust, and other heat-related maladies. Dry air is best, which is why melons do so well in Colorado, and why Rocky Ford became such a standard variety among American growers.

Productivity of individual vines is increased by pruning. Many gardeners are afraid to do this for fear of killing the vines, but pruning is essential, and when properly attended to, it does more good than fertilizer. When the vines are about 2½ feet long, remove the end buds. This will encourage lateral buds to form, and the vine will soon branch. This does several things for the plant. It does not have to send nutrients so far from the roots, so it is not so heavily taxed by rampant growth. The energy of the plant is thus directed into the branches and the fruits that form on them. Only allow one or two fruits to form on each vine. A few perfect fruits are far better than a bushel basket of tasteless miniatures. In the old days, the little ones pulled from the vines were pickled as "mangoes," but there are mango melons specifically for this purpose. Small, green melons can be used in stir-fries or sliced like cucumbers in salads. I use them for chutney.

For seed saving, a few perfect melons will suffice. They should be chosen for their appearance and trueness to type. Furthermore, the melons that come on earliest ought to be earmarked for seed, since this will encourage the plants to produce earlier and earlier each season. The real catch, of course, is to save seed from the best-tasting fruit, but since seed stock must be allowed to stand 20 days *after* it ripens, it is difficult to know which fruit is the best flavored. To compensate for this, I save properly matured seed from the best and earliest melons, and mix with this seed from the best tasting ones I have eaten. This seems to strike a good balance.

Properly matured melon seed will remain viable for at least ten years. This is good for the gardener because it allows a program of growing different melons over a period of years without worrying about seed loss. Even though melons are arranged into seven botanical groups, it is not crucial to know these because all melons are the same species, and therefore they will readily cross. Growing one variety a year is the best way to ensure seed purity. Also, something else happens. The older seed is better than the new. Many gardeners in the eighteenth and nineteenth centuries preferred ten-year-old melon seed; others preferred four-year-old seed. Old seed was valued over fresh because it produced plants with shorter vines and more intensely flavored fruit. H. L. Barnum, in his *Farmer's Own Book* (1836, 73), remarked that "seed is best after it has been kept two years. It will grow if twenty years old—and it should be carried in the pocket a week or two before planting." I am not certain what the pocket treatment did to the seed, although it has been suggested that the warmth of the body may trigger enzymes that increase rates of germination.

All of the melons that I have selected for this section were chosen from a long list of available varieties. My criteria were ease of culture, culinary interest, and, most important, availability of seed. Hans Buschbauer, in his *Amerikanisches Garten-Buch* (1892, 129), recommended a number of melons to German-American gardeners in the Midwest: Hackensack, Nutmeg, Netted Gem, Early Christiana, Delmonico. These are melons that will do well in most parts of the country, and most of them have found their way into this book for that one practical consideration.

Anne Arundel Melon
Cucumis melo var. *reticulatus*

The authors of *The Vegetables of New York: The Cucurbits* (1937, 62) stated that the Anne Arundel was first introduced commercially by the seed firms of Griffith & Turner of Baltimore and George Tait & Sons of Norfolk, Virginia. In fact, the melon had been grown in Anne Arundel County by a small circle of Maryland farmers for more than 150 years.

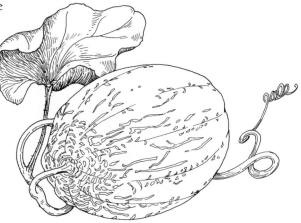

Anne Arundel Melon

Anne Arundel may be a cross between a true smooth-skinned cantaloupe and a nutmeg-shaped muskmelon, for it exhibits some traits of both. Its originator is unknown, although it was cultivated in the 1730s by a certain Dr. Hill, an avid horticulturist living in Londontown, Maryland, not far from Annapolis. To the famous Peale family, which produced so many painters in the eighteenth and early nineteenth centuries, the Anne Arundel melon was viewed as a symbol of their Maryland roots. As such, it appeared in many Peale paintings, especially those by Raphaelle Peale.

The melon is green-fleshed and nutmeg-shaped like the old china melon molds, and when ripe, its skin turns bright yellow. There is some webbing, typical of the true muskmelon, but it varies from fruit to fruit and never completely covers the rind, as can be seen from the examples shown in color plate 48. The purest strain of the old Anne Arundel melon was preserved by the Schramm family of Schramm's Turkey Farm at Pasadena, Maryland. From them I obtained my seed. The melon is now in circulation among members of Seed Savers Exchange.

A similar muskmelon—known as Acme, Baltimore Market, Knight's Early Maryland, and a host of other aliases—was introduced in 1884 by David Landreth & Sons of Philadelphia. It appears to be a form of Anne Arundel recrossed with an oval muskmelon. Fortunately, the Peale paintings of the Anne Arundel are botanically accurate, so we have them as reliable points of reference when comparing the melon with other closely related varieties. In flavor, the Anne Arundel resembles a honeydew (the White Antibes of French seed catalogs). The small unripe melons, about the size of a goose egg, were used in pickles. The ripe fruit was sometimes cut up like apples and baked in pies.

Armenian Cucumber or Snake Melon
Cucumis melo var. *flexuosus*

Of all the melons on this list, this is one of the oldest of the heirlooms, yet one of the most neglected by our gardeners. It was introduced from Armenia into Italy in the 1400s along with

Armenian Cucumber

the true cantaloupe and raised off and on by European horticulturists since then. It never became a market melon in Western Europe and never evolved into a vast array of subvarieties like the muskmelon. It has always been a curiosity, and those who do grow it treat it as a cucumber. In fact, many people think that it is a cucumber and go to great pains to keep it from crossing from other cucumbers in the garden. It will not cross with cucumbers, but it will lend a distinct cucumber taste to any melons it happens to cross with in the vicinity. Fearing Burr (1865, 196–97) treated it as a species separate from melons, listing it under the name Snake or Serpent Cucumber, which doubtless contributed to the confusion about its correct botanical status.

The melon is quite popular in Greece (the source of my seed) and the eastern Mediterranean, where it is usually harvested young when it resembles a small chayote in shape. As the melon matures, it grows in length and proceeds to coil about the ground in the manner of a snake. Individual melons can reach a length of 3 feet, although only 2 or 3 inches in diameter. The outer skin is pale green and covered with small ridges. The flesh is greenish white and resembles cucumber in flavor. It can be treated in cookery like a cucumber.

American gardeners in the past seem to have grown it more for display purposes than eating. The melon often appeared at county and state agricultural fairs to lend interest to harvest displays, or the melons were ornamented in some humorous fashion. Sometimes they appeared among competitions for cucumber pickles, but on the whole, the Armenian cucumber has never played an important role in our cookery. This may change because the melon is prolific and in some ways easier to grow than true cucumbers.

For seed-saving purposes, the melons must be allowed to fully ripen. The skin will turn yellow. As with all melons, this one must be further matured 20 days past peak ripeness to ensure that the seed undergoes a proper aging process. This precaution will increase rates of germination and the seed viability. The seed of this melon will remain viable for five to ten years.

Blenheim Orange Melon
Cucumis melo var. reticulatus

This is an English hothouse variety that has recently reappeared in seed lists of heirloom vegetables. The melon was developed in 1881 at Blenheim Palace in Oxfordshire, England, and took its name from an apple called Blenheim Orange also developed at the same place. The melon was quickly recognized by Vilmorin (1885, 335) as one of the leading English red-fleshed sorts. The melon was offered by a number of seedsmen in this country well into the 1930s. The R. & J. Farquhar Company of Boston carried Blenheim Orange and several other English forcing melons in its 1925 catalog, mostly for the benefit of gardeners with large, well-equipped hothouses. Yet of all the hothouse melons, this variety is probably one of the best for open culture in our kitchen gardens. It responds well to our climate and does not exhibit the weaknesses inherent to many other forcing types.

The rind of the fruit is thick, the flesh deep reddish orange and extremely fragrant. The fruit ripens in about 100 days and is therefore a good melon for cool, short-season regions of the country. The melons weigh about 2 pounds. If the weather is rainy during the height of the summer, this melon will develop the right color, but the fruit will be mealy and more like a pumpkin in taste than a muskmelon. However, it thrives under arid conditions provided it is kept well watered. The fragrance of the fruit is attractive to squirrels, field mice, and raccoons, so the fruit must be covered with wire screen or netting to protect it during the final stages of ripening.

Citron Melon or Green Citron Melon
Cucumis melo var. reticulatus

This melon has at least twenty aliases, proof in itself of the enormous popularity the variety once enjoyed. The *American Journal of Horticulture* (1868, 235) noted that it was an abundant bearer, an important criterion for kitchen gardeners. This melon was also one of the oldest varieties of muskmelon cultivated in this country, and prior to 1880 it was the most widely grown, particularly in the South. Philadelphia seedsman Bernard M'Mahon offered it for sale in 1806, but it appeared even earlier in the garden account books of many well-known Americans, including Thomas Jefferson.

The flesh is yellowish green, the melon shape globular, weighing from 2½ to 3 pounds each. The netting on the skin resembles that on Jenny Lind, a melon developed from it.

Citron Melon

The skin is yellowish brown with green mottling. Of all the heirloom melons, this is not the best for flavor, although it can be quite sweet and aromatic. Its strength lies in its earliness, for it begins producing fruit well in advance of all the other varieties in this book. It therefore stands with Blenheim Orange as a good melon for short-season areas.

Delmonico Melon
Cucumis melo var. *reticulatus*

Named for the famous New York restaurateur Charles Delmonico, this melon was introduced in 1889 by Peter Henderson & Company and first served at Delmonico's when it was located at Fifth Avenue and Twenty-sixth Street on Madison Square. The melon originated in Nebraska and later underwent improved breeding, which gave rise to the Perfected Delmonico. The original variety is smaller than the improved version, weighing from 4 to 5 pounds. The fruit is oval, about 8 inches long and 6 inches in diameter. It is heavily netted on a thick rind with prominent ribs. The flesh is salmon orange. Lately Thomas, in his journalistic history *Delmonico's* (1967), made no mention of the melon, which has far outlived the restaurant of the same name.

Early Christiana Melon
Cucumis melo var. *reticulatus*

According to the *Horticulturist* (1847, 149), this melon was developed by Captain Josiah Lovett of Beverly, Massachusetts, by crossing the green-fleshed Maltese Melon with the Nutmeg Melon. The Malta melon was raised in this country as early as the 1780s as a winter melon because it could be stored well into January or February. In any case, by 1847 Lovett's cross had become known among growers in Massachusetts, but it was not until the 1850s that the melon became generally available outside New England. Since then, it was generally considered one of the finest orange-fleshed melons of its type.

The fruit is globular but slightly flattened on both the stem and blossom ends, thus resembling in shape some of the old varieties of "apple"-shaped tomatoes. The melons usually weight from 2 to 2½ pounds and are ribbed, but not deeply. The netting is mostly found on the ridges rather than in the furrows. The skin is greenish brown, with patches of golden brown. The skin is also quite thin, or rather, tender and easily damaged. For this reason, the fruit does not ship well and is best when allowed to ripen until it is ready to drop from the vine.

Emerald Gem or Netted Gem Melon
Cucumis melo var. *reticulatus*

This melon became one of the most popular American muskmelons of the late nineteenth century. It appeared as a chance seedling in the garden of William G. Voorhees of Benzie County, Michigan. Commercial rights were purchased from him by W. Atlee Burpee, who introduced the melon in 1886. In an article about the melon, the *American Garden* (1889, 124) considered it a "milestone" in melon breeding, for it exemplified the new type of muskmelon then being developed by American seedsmen: good quality of flavor and stability of type. Thus Emerald Gem remains even today one of the finest varieties of muskmelon for the American kitchen garden.

The fruit is relatively small, weighing 2½ to 3 pounds and globular in shape. On perfectly shaped fruit, the ribbing is evenly spaced and the greenish skin heavily laced with fine webbing. The flesh is pale orange, soft, juicy, and very sweet, with a spicy aroma suggesting cardamom and cinnamon. The flesh immediately under the skin is bright green, even when the rest of the melon is ripe.

Emerald Gem Melon

Green Climbing Melon (*Melon Vert à Rames*)
Cucumis melo var. *reticulatus*

These small green melons might be characterized as the French counterpart to our old Citron Melon, except that this is a vigorous climbing sort and quite different in skin texture. The variety was preserved by INRA (the French National Institute of Agronomic Research) and came into seed-saving circles in this country through Seed Savers Exchange. The plants of this melon are cultivated as climbing vines, usually draped over fences, and from a distance the dark green fruit resembles acorn squash. The skin is hard enough that the late-season fruits may be picked before frost and stored as winter melons. They will keep into late December and therefore make ideal additions to the Christmas menu served fresh, in conserves, or pureed and used as fillings in tarts.

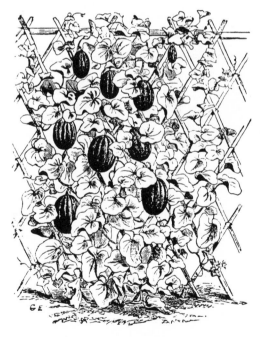

Green Climbing Melon

The fruit is oblong, about 4 inches to 5 inches in length and about 4 inches in diameter. The skin is flecked with pale green. The flesh is also green, very juicy and sweet, especially if the melons are trained over a fence that receives sun most of the day. An extremely handsome illustration of the melon appeared in the *Album Vilmorin* (1875, 26). Since it is an early melon that ripens quickly when raised off the ground, it is ideal for small gardens. This melon in particular is perfect for individual servings due to its diminutive size. I am surprised that is it not seen more often in our better restaurants, because it is the epitome of light cuisine.

Hackensack Melon
Cucumis melo var. *reticulatus*

Hackensack is a variety that evolved in New Jersey about 1870 as a selection of Green Citron, which it closely resembles. It was developed for Jersey farmers as a market melon designed to compete with the Green Citron shipped from the South. It became the most popular green-fleshed melon on the New York market, and in 1882 Peter Henderson & Company introduced the variety on a commercial basis. Up to that point, seed had been in circulation among only a small handful of growers.

The melons weigh from 5 to 6 pounds and are conspicuously ribbed, as can be seen in the woodcut. This same woodcut was pilfered by several seed companies and reused to represent other varieties. The J. W. Jung Seed Company of Randolph, Wisconsin, included it in the firm's 1929 catalog to represent Early Fordhook, a new Burpee variety. Regardless, the woodcut represents a true picture of Hackensack, and it can be seen that the netting is coarse and heavily interlaced, one of the variety's characteristics. The skin turns golden yellow mottled with green when ripe. The flesh is light green with a tinge of yellowish green near the placenta (seed mass). The outer skin is thick and tough, which makes this a good shipping melon.

Hackensack Melon

Jenny Lind Melon
Cucumis melo var. *reticulatus*

The seed catalog of William Henry Maule for 1898 remarked, "It is astonishing that this, the most delicious small melon, is so little known outside the State of New Jersey." Maule was not mistaken in this observation, for Jenny Lind was a melon grown almost exclusively for the Philadelphia and New York markets and not well known outside that region. Fearing Burr did not even mention it in his *Field and Garden Vegetables of America*, and he certainly knew who Jenny Lind was. Today, this melon is one of the most popular among seed savers. It has an unusual shape, its flavor is first rate, and it seems to thrive in many places where other muskmelons prove difficult to grow.

The melon is said to have been developed from the Center Melon, an old Philadelphia variety dating from before 1840 and originating from Armenia. The actual developer of the Jenny Lind melon is not presently known, and the accepted date of its introduction (1846) does not tally with Jenny Lind's famous tour of the United States. The Swedish singer did not arrive in this country until four years later (under contract with Phineas T. Barnum to sing), and her famous debut in Philadelphia did not take place until October 1850. This would suggest that if the melon did indeed exist before 1850, it probably had another name; while she was famous in Europe, Jenny Lind did not achieve superstar status in this country until after she came here.

This is a case where popular mythology has run ahead of historical fact.

Jenny Lind Melon

Miss Lind's melon is often described as turban-shaped. Color plate 49 shows it with its prominent ribbing, somewhat oblate in form. The blossom end bears a "button" or knob, which is considered one of the determining features of this variety. When the melon is ripe, the skin is brownish orange, mottled with green. The flesh is light green, and soft and sweet like the voice of the "Swedish Nightingale" in whose honor it was named.

Mango Melon or Garden Lemon
Cucumis melo var. *chito*

This is both a varietal name and a generic term for a collection of similar melons variously called Orange Melon, Vegetable Orange, Melon Apple, Garden Lemon, and Vine Peach. The *American Garden* (1890, 304) considered all of these to be variant forms of the same thing rather than distinct varieties. Indeed, the only difference between the Garden Lemon and the others is that it ripens with a yellow skin (color plate 50), whereas the others often ripen with an orange skin. In shape, the Garden Lemon is usually oblong or egg-shaped; the others are often round. Pure seed is rare, since all of these are allowed to run together, and it is often the case that the melons have acquired stripes, mottling, or traces of netting by crossing with muskmelons or with the fragrant and completely inedible Queen Anne's Pocket Melon (*Cucumis melo* var. *dudaim*).

Because the mango melons were used in cookery and not eaten raw, their texture was far more important than sweet flavor. They were prepared in preserves like citron watermelons, in sweet pickles, fried like eggplant, or "mangoed" as a condiment for roast meats. They can also be used in stir-fries or sliced and baked in pies like apples. For such applications a firm, crisp flesh is critical. In flavor, all of these variant forms taste a bit like cucumbers lightly brushed with lemon juice.

The melons originated in China and were introduced into this country from there in the 1880s. Samuel Wilson, a seedsman in Mechanicsville (Bucks County), Pennsylvania, offered seed in the *Farm Journal* in February of 1889. He was one of the first to advertise these melons, calling them Vegetable Peach. The Pennsylvania Dutch were particularly fond of mango melons because they worked well in sweet-sour preserves, very similar to the way they were pickled in the Orient. The most popular method of pickling, however, was to mango them, a process that gave the melon its most common name. The following recipe is taken from Mrs. M. E. Peterson's *Preserving, Pickling and Canning* (1869, 28). Any small green melon the size of a goose egg can be used.

Musk Melon Mangoes
🐛

Take small musk melons and cut an oval piece out of one side; take out the seeds with a teaspoon, and fill this space with a stuffing of chopped onions, scraped horse-radish, mustard-seed, cloves, and pepper corns, and sew in the piece with a needle and coarse thread. Put them in a jar, and pour boiling vinegar, with a little salt in it, over them. Do this two or three times, then put in fresh vinegar. Keep in stone jars, or pots tightly covered.

Montreal Market Melon
Cucumis melo var. *reticulatus*

W. Atlee Burpee discovered this melon at the St. Anne's Market in Montreal during a visit there in 1880. In 1881 he offered the seed commercially, and the melon was an instant success. It became the most widely grown muskmelon in New England, Canada, and the Upper Midwest, not only because of its large size but because it yielded the best-flavored melons for short-season gardens.

The fruits resemble Hackensack but are larger, heavier, more uniformly netted, and more uniformly green in the flesh. The melons normally weigh 9 to 10 pounds, with prominent ribs about 2 to 2½ inches apart. The outer skin is green, mottled with greenish yellow. The flavor is aromatic, reminding me of crushed ginger leaves. A little shredded zest of lime greatly enhances the taste.

Montreal Market Melon

37. The Lemon Cucumber (page 158) does not require paring. Beside it, on the right, is a small Boothby's Blond Cucumber (page 156), which can be pickled like a Cornichon vert.

39. Listada de Gandia eggplant (page 164) is valued both for its fine flavor and its striking appearance.

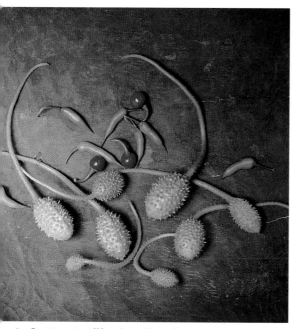

38. Freshly picked West India Burr Gherkins (page 159) were often pickled with small hot red peppers like Besler's Cherry Pepper (page 253).

40. Old White Egg (page 165) and Black Egg eggplant (page 165) are shown with a brown chicken egg to give a sense of scale.

41. Celtuce or Asparagus lettuce (page 179) is raised as a summer lettuce both for its leaves and broccoli-like stems.

43. Loos Tennisball lettuce (page 183) is a typical cabbaging variety.

42. Lion's Tongue lettuce is a semi-cos variety with long pointed leaves.

44. Speckled lettuce (page 186) is one of the most popular heirloom sorts grown today.

45. Tom Thumb lettuce (page 188) is about the size of a large carnation.

46. The young pods of martynia or Devil's Claw (page 189) may be prepared in cookery like okra.

48. The Anne Arundel Melon (page 195) traces back to the 1730s.

49. Jenny Lind Melon (page 200) is often described as turban shaped. The small, unripe melons were formerly stuffed for pickling.

47. Detail of the handsome flower of **Proboscidea louisianica** (page 189).

50. Mango or Garden Lemon Melon (page 201) is a tart-tasting melon that can be used in fruit salads or stir-fries.

51. *Chinese Wolfberry (page 206) is a perennial vine that yields a bounty of red berries that are excellent for drying.*

54. *Stubby (page 215) and Cow Horn okra (page 215) are two heirloom varieties from the nineteenth century. Also shown are two small martynia pods at the stage when they can be cooked like okra.*

52. *The West African Garden Huckleberry (page 207) can be used for making pies and preserves.*

55. *Heirloom shallots, from left to right: Small White shallot (page 223); in the center, Prince de Bretagne (page 223), and White Potato Onion (page 233) harvested green as "rare-ripes"; Besançon Sweet Yellow Shallot (page 223) on the right; and Jersey Shallots (page 223) on the bottom.*

53. *The groundcherry (page 208) is a summer favorite among the Pennsylvania Dutch, who even make soups with the berries.*

56. *Welsh Onions or bunching onions (page 223) overwinter well and may be used as substitutes for leeks.*

57. Tree onion (page 232) or Red Catawissa.

58. Fleener's Topsetting Onion (page 231) produces tiny bulbs that are ideal for pearl onions.

59. The green seeds of garlic chives may be dried and used to flavor cooking oils.

60. Arbogast Sugar Pea (page 240).

61. *Risser Sickle Pea (page 246) is a variety tracing back to the eighteenth century.*

62. *Golden orange Jamaican Scotch Bonnet pepper (page 252) and its more modern relative, the Chocolate Habañero.*

63. *Besler's Cherry Pepper (page 253) dates from the 1500s.*

64. *Buist's Yellow Cayenne Pepper (page 256) and the red Ole Pepperpot pepper (page 262) are two heirloom varieties from my grandfather's collection.*

65. The Fish Pepper (page 258) is an African-American heirloom that began as a mutation in the nineteenth century.

67. The Pennsylvania Dutch Hinkelhatz pepper (page 260) appears in both red and yellow forms.

66. The Goat Horn pepper (page 259) is thought to be the same as the Long Drooping pepper of Philadelphia seedsman Bernard M'Mahon, who offered it for sale as early as 1805.

68. Martin's Carrot Pepper (page 261) ripens from orange to red.

69. Tabasco pepper (page 263) is highly ornamental but requires a long growing season.

70. The Texas bird pepper (page 264) grows wild in southwest Texas and northern Mexico.

72. Delicata squash (page 284). In storage the fruit turns yellow.

71. Several varieties of heirloom potatoes. On the left, Conestoga (page 271). The three large rose-colored potatoes; Bliss's Triumph (page 272). The pale pink potatoes (far right and bottom): Garnet Chile (page 275). The long, narrow potatoes are Austrian Kipfelkrumpl (page 273). The greenish example in the center is intended to show a potato exposed to sunlight; such potatoes are poisonous and should never be eaten.

73. Golden Hubbard squash (page 285) on the right, Symmes Blue Hubbard squash (page 285) sliced in half.

74. Pattypan or cymling squash (page 286) can be used at several stages of ripeness. The young green fruit (center) may be eaten raw. The mature fruit (top and right) can be stored like winter squash.

Murray's Pineapple Melon
Cucumis melo var. *reticulatus*

The pineapple melon presents us with a rather convoluted history. The earliest reference to it thus far has surfaced in the papers of Thomas Jefferson, who planted it in 1794. It was not a foreign variety, but a muskmelon developed or at least perfected on these shores. It was first offered commercially in a seed catalog of Grant Thorburn & Sons of New York in 1824. The originator of the melon has not been identified.

There are two variant forms, a green-fleshed sort known also as the Jersey Citron Melon, and a red-fleshed one. Both of these were exported to Europe where they became well known as the *melon ananas d'Amerique à chair rouge* and *chair vert* of the Vilmorin garden books. The green one was illustrated in color in the *Album Vilmorin* (1854, 5). Both varieties are still available today. The fruit is roughly the size of a large softball, the green-fleshed sort usually about 6 inches in diameter, the red about 4 inches in diameter. The shape is generally round, and because the fruit is small, this melon is ideal for cultivation on a fence or trellis, thus saving a great deal of space.

The red variety has slightly marked ribs, with distinctive green furrows and light netting. The flesh is bright watermelon-red and fragrant, with a seed cavity about the size of a walnut. The green variety has pale green flesh with a yellowish tinge about the seed mass. Its leaves, like the fruit itself, are slightly larger than those of the red. Its skin is also more heavily netted. The vines of both types are heavy producers, each plant yielding as many as 6 to 8 melons.

Because of their size, the melons are perfect for dessert cups, since the small seed cavity can be filled with a scoop of sherbet or a shot glass of Madeira. Nineteenth-century Philadelphia chef and restaurateur James Parkinson once served them filled with champagne "snow" garnished with caviar. The diminutive proportions of the melons provide a highly decorative aspect to any table setting and lend an interesting touch to fruit arrangements. The small, unripe melons are also excellent for pickling or candying. Amelia Simmons (1796, 13) recommended them for melon mangoes.

Prescott *fond blanc* Melon
Cucumis melo var. *cantaloupensis*

This melon is the only true cantaloupe on this list. The American custom of referring to all muskmelons as cantaloupes developed in the 1880s as a marketing term for any melon shipped in crates. This usage has since spread to all parts of the country in an attempt to give the muskmelon a less awkward-sounding name. True cantaloupes are smooth-skinned or warty, require a long growing season, and are not grown to any large extent in the United States, even though their hard skin makes them ideal for shipping. The name cantaloupe, as we use it, is the French spelling of Cantaluppi, a papal estate near Rome where the first of these melons were grown in the 1400s.

The Prescott *fond blanc* belongs to a group of cantaloupes that the French call "rock melons," and there are many variant forms. Bernard M'Mahon of Philadelphia began importing several of the standard varieties as early as 1800. His Large African was the Algerian of Vilmorin, his Black Rock Vilmorin's *melon cantaloup noir des Carmes* (an eighteenth-century variety that originated at Saumus in Narne-et-Lorie) and his Black Portugal and the pear-shaped Mogul cantaloupe were still available in France in the 1880s. Most of these melons, being desert melons to begin with, need a hot, dry climate to come to perfection. They were raised in this country by the wealthy who could afford greenhouses and hotbeds and full-time gardeners to attend them. Fearing Burr (1865, 177) commented on the Prescott *fond blanc* and, of all the melons of this type, considered it the best, although the French consider the Black Rock the easiest to grow. Both are 80-to-85-day melons.

Prescott fond blanc Melon

The white Prescott melon, however, is quite a curiosity and well worth the effort of coddling it to fruit. The melon is flattened on both the top and bottom as though it had been dropped when soft, like a ball of bread dough. Thus the melon is normally about twice as wide as it is tall, weighing from 5 to 9 pounds. It is usually 5 to 6 pounds in my climate, which is similar to that of Burgundy. The ribs are large, uneven, wrinkled, and covered with knobs or warts. The warts are dark and light green on a whitish skin. The flesh is dark salmon-orange, quite a contrast to the rind, thick, juicy, and a delight to eat. For best results, only allow one melon per vine.

The French made ice cream molds imitating the Prescott melon. A variety of ice cream colors and flavors were used to recreate the carnival affect that the melon presents when ripe and freshly cut. I happen to own one of those old molds, dating from the 1870s; because it is life-size, it helped me guess when the melon was ready to pick the first time I grew the Prescott. Cantaloupes do not slip from the vine when ripe. Rapping on them like watermelons seems to be a reliable method; *then* wait two days to pick them. Then wait again. Place the harvested melons on a sunny windowsill until the rinds become pliant when pressed with the thumb. Left to ripen on the ground, these melons will take on an earthy taste rather than build up an intensely sweet flavor. Always serve melon at room temperature. Chilling any type of melon destroys the flavor. It is like putting ice cubes in red wine.

Rocky Ford Melon
Cucumis melo var. *reticulatus*

Rocky Ford is a place in southern Colorado where the arid climate is ideal for melon culture. Once the railroads were built into the state to serve the mining industry, the same trains returning to Chicago and other points East also provided the means for a lucrative trade in Colorado produce, especially melons.

W. Atlee Burpee's Netted Gem muskmelon was planted at Rocky Ford in the 1880s. J. W. Eastwood raised the melon in 1885 and is credited with the creation of the strain of Netted Gem that eventually became Rocky Ford. Other growers in the area also selected promising strains so that the Netted Gem gradually evolved from an oblong melon to a round one with heavy netting. In his book *Muskmelon Production* (1928, 15), John Lloyd provided a photograph showing the old Netted Gem beside its Rocky Ford progeny. Rocky Ford was long considered a synonym for a type of Netted Gem, but under the careful guidance of the Rocky Ford Cantaloupe Seed Breeders Association, the melon finally became fixed as a recognized variety.

The fruit weighs from 1½ to 2 pounds, with dark green skin that turns yellow-bronze when ripe. The flesh is green with a band of golden yellow near the seed cavity. The seed cavity is small and triangular shaped in cross-section. Rocky Ford thrives in areas with climates similar to southern Colorado. In the East the melon tends to deteriorate over a few generations and revert to something resembling Netted Gem.

Turkish Casaba Melon
Cucumis melo var. *inodorus*

The melon takes its name from Casaba (Kassabah) in Anatolia, some thirty miles northeast of Smyrna (Izmir) in Turkey. The original casaba melon could only be raised to perfection in the vicinity of that place. Even in the nineteenth century, when the melon had become well known, casabas were rare in Istanbul and considered a great luxury. The growing season of the melon is so long that in this country it can only be raised on a commercial basis in California and parts of the Southwest.

Nevertheless, there were several attempts to grow the melon in this country, for it is known that the U.S. Patent Office distributed seed for a casaba-type melon in 1850. Henry Dreer of Philadelphia offered a true casaba for sale in his 1867 seed list, and this appears to be the first real attempt to commercialize the melon. The melon that he introduced was sometimes called Winter Pineapple by other seedsmen. Its original Turkish name is not known.

The casaba belongs to a group of melons divided roughly into two types, one with smooth skin, as in the Winter Valencia, and one with wrinkled skin, which is the mark of the casaba. Most of the true casabas ripen with a yellow skin, although the Winter Pineapple of Dreer was light green. The flesh of all of these sorts is snowy white and extremely sweet.

I grow a variety of casaba called *Hasan Bey*, but it is not an heirloom variety as far as I can determine. It was found in the Egyptian Market in Istanbul and differs from the typical casaba in that its skin is black-green when ripe. It stores well like a winter melon, but in Pennsylvania it must be started in a hotbed in order to bear fruit. I place black plastic picnic plates (the sort that come out at Halloween) under the melons as they mature. This greatly reduces insect and worm damage from underneath, a problem with all melons, and warms the ground around each melon so that it imagines it is in Turkey.

Winter Valencia Melon
Cucumis melo var. inodorus

Related to the so-called honeydew (the White Antibes of the French), this old-fashioned winter melon was listed by American seedsmen as early as the 1830s. Fearing Burr (1865, 180) called it the Green Valencia, and it was discussed in some detail by Charles McIntosh in his *Book of the Garden* (1853–55).

In 1805 Thomas Jefferson raised a similar melon called the Malta Melon or Green-Fleshed Malta Winter Melon, the *melon de Malte d'hiver à chair verte* of Vilmorin (1885, 330). The Malta melon and its various subvarieties were also discussed in some detail by the Abbé Rozier (1785, 476), who noted that they were cultivated primarily in Italy, Provence, and Languedoc. In this country, the melon was planted about July 15 so that it would ripen late, for harvesting right before frost. The melons were then placed in storage to mellow and used through the months of December, January, and February. Properly harvested, these melons increase in flavor and sweetness during storage and are a welcome delicacy when compared with the green and grassy-tasting fruits shipped to most parts of the country during the winter.

The Winter Valencia is cultivated in the same manner as the Malta Melon. It has dark green, wrinkled skin with creamy white flesh. Like the Malta Melon, the seeds are not loose but embedded in the flesh, like those of a cucumber. The meat of the melon can be preserved in sugar like the citron watermelon, or cooked to a purée consistency and turned into a species of green marmalade. It can also be sliced and baked in pies or shredded and baked in custards with dried figs and chopped fennel.

Miscellaneous Nightshades

Chinese Wolfberry or Chinese Boxthorn
Lycium barbarum

Formerly treated as two separate species, *Lycium chinense* and *Lycium halimifolium*, but now recognized as one, this woody vine with narrow deciduous leaves is an attractive plant for the kitchen garden fence. The leaves are edible and can be dried for tea, but it is the fruit I find most interesting. Reddish orange, it hangs in clusters resembling barberries (color plate 51). The flavor reminds me of a cross between a sun-dried tomato and a dried cranberry. The dried fruit is excellent in rice, bean, and lentil dishes, and can be used in pickles. The dried berries are popular in Asian cookery and can usually be found in Asian markets. I propagated seed from a few dried berries found in a Vietnamese market in Philadelphia, although seed is available from several of the firms listed in the back of this book.

In areas of the country that are USDA Zone 8 and warmer, the plant has naturalized and become common on waste ground. In warm climate areas it also tends to sucker more under the ground and thus can become quite invasive. In the South it is known as Matrimony Vine and was first introduced in the area of Charleston during the middle of the eighteenth century. It is a very close relative of the Carolina wolfberry used by native Americans. In the South the plant grows into a large rambling bush that needs support, but in the North it usually dies back to the ground each winter. In Pennsylvania, it requires a protection of mulch over the winter.

Garden Huckleberry
Solanum melanocerasum

The botanical origin of this vegetable is obscure, but it is believed to be a form of the common nightshade that evolved into a distinct species under long cultivation in West African gardens. Because it was raised mostly by blacks in North America, it was not given much notice in early garden literature, other than to lump it together with the wild nightshade, to which it is closely related. It is believed to have come to North America sometime in the late seventeenth century in connection with the slave trade and is now naturalized in parts of the South as well as sections of Kansas and Nebraska. Volga Germans who emigrated from Russia and settled on the Great Plains during the latter part of the nineteenth century incorporated the Garden Huckleberry into their cookery, and many of their descendants still raise it today.

The plants are large and spreading and from a distance vaguely resemble pokeberry bushes. They attain a height of 3 to 4 feet and are resistant to drought. Seed is started indoors like tomatoes, then thinned to pots and hardied off. They can be planted as soon as the threat of frost has passed. One of the old botanical names for this berry was *Solanum intrusum,* an appropriate name, since it will reseed profusely anywhere it is planted. Birds, however, avoid the fruit.

The black berries (color plate 52) measure about ½ to ¾ of an inch in diameter and are edible when ripe, although bitter. They are cooked as a vegetable, but most commonly they are prepared in pies and preserves, since sugar greatly improves the taste. It is a taste that one either likes or dislikes. The rotting fruit has a carrion odor that West Africans find appealing and which is present in the dried berries. There I draw the line.

The Garden Huckleberry should not be confused with the Sunberry or Wonderberry (*Solanum burbankii*) introduced by Luther Burbank, ostensibly as a cross between *Solanum guineese* Lam. and

Solanum villosum Dunal. That cross has been questioned, but many seed houses incorrectly equate the Garden Huckleberry with it. The true Garden Huckleberry is also well established in other parts of our hemisphere. The following description from *The Tropical Cook Book* (1920, 75–76), published by the Ladies' Club of Herradura in Havana, explains how it is prepared in Cuba:

> The plant of the garden huckleberry grows very large here, and, with some cultivation, the berries attain a great size. To get the best flavor they must not be picked until they are very ripe, by which time they will have lost the bright, shiny appearance they have at first. The "mora," the Cuban name for the wild huckleberry, is to be found in almost any field which has been cultivated at any time. The flavor is similar to that of the huckleberry and is preferred by many people. The berries are very small, but by fertilizing and cultivating, the plants will produce more and larger berries. Both kinds of berries are used a great deal for sauce, and dulces of all kinds, being worthless raw.

The *mora* referred to here is the common nightshade (*Solanum nigrum*), with which the garden species is usually confused. The ladies' club also published a number of recipes for Garden Huckleberry, one of which was commonly served at Frohock's Cafeteria on O'Reilly Street in Havana. It contains all the necessary chemistry for transforming the berries into a decent confection.

Garden Huckleberry Preserves

❦

Put in the stew pan, cover with cold water and allow it to come to the boiling point. Add a half teaspoonful of baking soda, allow this to boil up, turn off the water and add fresh water. Boil until tender, put through a colander, add a half pound of sugar to a pound of fruit, and enough cornstarch to thicken it. Allow this to boil thoroughly, stirring constantly.

Groundcherry
Physalis ssp.
Toward the end of July and continuing right up to the first killing frost, produce stands all over the Pennsylvania Dutch country offer for sale small berries that come from the garden in little tan husks or "lanterns." Transformed into jellies, jams, pies, indeed, into a host of dishes, these are the so-called groundcherries or *Juddekaersche*, one of the culinary symbols of Pennsylvania Dutch cookery.

Closely related to the tomato, groundcherries belong to a large genus of plants known as *Physalis,* and there are many common names for the prolific members of this tribe. This has led to inevitable ambiguities in the scientific classifications of *Physalis* species and subspecies, confounding plant and food historians alike. Craig C. Dremann's tract *Ground Cherries, Husk Tomatoes, and Tomatillos* (1985) attempts to tackle this issue from the standpoint of a seedsman with long experience growing them. I am of the opinion, shared by many, that the *Physalis* genus is in serious need of reorganization; those of us who grow these plants on a regular basis know that the published botany does not tally with what goes on in the field. Therefore, I shall be rather coy with my nomenclature.

In spite of this, the rich, confusing vocabulary associated with this genus is also proof in itself that a garden plant with so many common designations has obviously been under cultivation for a very long time on the popular level. The late American botanist Oliver Perry Medsger, writing in the 1930s, confirmed this with his observation that groundcherries have been in cultivation in the eastern United States for at least 150 years. The *Farm Journal and Progressive Farmer* (May 1857, 141) lashed out at the idea that groundcherries were an innovation in any way new to country cooks. The following tirade expresses a common nineteenth-century attitude about the groundcherry outside areas of Pennsylvania Dutch influence.

The "Ground Cherry"

🐛

We see that the venders of this worthless thing are still at their old tricks, and with so much craftiness that they deceive the very elect. Our good friend of the Maine Farmer has listened to the humbug tale, and is so far deceived as to "recommend a general trial of it." Now, Doctor, we have had some experience with this plant—have destroyed thousands in a year as mere pests. Instead of the fruit being, as the pedler represented, "valuable for pies, puddings, and preserves, and making a good wine to boot," it is not fit to be used for any such purpose, and is not, where even the most ordinary fruits or berries can be had. The whole scheme of selling this "ground cherry" is a cheat.

Thus spake the *Boston Cultivator* in all its New England blueness, a swipe of arrogance that can be well appreciated by Suzanne Ashworth, who is the groundcherry conservator for Seed Savers Exchange. The Pennsylvania Dutch simply laugh. Through the process of natural hybridizing or intentional selective breeding, a number of strains of groundcherries peculiar to the region have evolved. Seeds from these cultivars have moved to all parts of the United States, indeed, anywhere the Pennsylvania Dutch have settled. For these reasons—and to the chagrin of New Englanders—the groundcherry and its near cousin the husk tomato or tomatillo constitute one of the ethnic symbols of the culture.

Regardless of disagreements over nomenclature or their culinary worth, all botanists and experienced cooks agree that as with tomatoes, the herbaceous parts of groundcherries—the root, stems, leaves, and flowers—are toxic to humans. I am putting this up front because most unripe groundcherries are also toxic to humans to one degree or another and thus should never be given to anyone in the green state. I have seen them served underripe in some very famous restaurants in New York and can only comment that in folk medicine such fruit was considered a powerful emetic, with emphasis on powerful. But, of course, that is New York.

The safe culinary rule with all groundcherries is to harvest them ripe, and that means when the husks fall off the plants. Next, eat them well cooked, such as in catsups, sauces, soups, or pies. The ripe fruit can be eaten raw, but it is better to try one berry first to see whether a reaction occurs. Persons with known allergies to tomatoes should never eat groundcherries or tomatillos. Do not even try them. Most people can enjoy groundcherries without any problems, but for the small minority who do have a sensitivity, the precaution is better than the convalescence.

One of the earliest references to groundcherries surfaced in the journal of Aédée Feuillée (1682–1773), who was sent by the king of France on a botanical expedition to Peru and Chile from 1709 to 1711. The intrepid explorer not only found red currant tomatoes (page 348) washed up on a beach, he discovered that the locals made a spread for butter and toast: "one makes of it a preserve with an agreeable and refreshing taste, which is given to the sick to restore their appetite" (1713–25, 3:5). This jam was made with the fruit of what is now called *Physalis peruviana*, a tropical perennial otherwise known as Cape Gooseberry or Poha. *Curtis's Botanical Magazine* (27:1068) published a scholarly vignette about the berry in 1807, observing that it had already established itself in the Cape of Good Hope, the East Indies, and New South Wales in Australia. The *American Garden* (1888, 282) complained that the Cape Gooseberry was being offered as something new and valuable when it had been known to Americans for more than a hundred years and was "no better" than a dozen native species found in most parts of the United States. The problem with the Poha is that it is truly tropical at heart and is not likely to come to fruit in many parts of the United States. I have grown it for many years and have rarely gotten more than perfect specimens of the leaves. To obtain fruit, I must overwinter it in tubs.

The true groundcherries of early American kitchen gardens are annuals much better adapted to our untropical growing seasons, since they come to fruit in 65 to 75 days. Historically, there were three types of groundcherries and two types of tomatillos cultivated in my part of the country, not overlooking the fact that several of them were native to the Southwest and thus also a part of the regional cuisine there. Of the groundcherries, there were yellow-, orange-, and bronze-fruited varieties. Of the tomatillos, the most common had green-yellow or purple fruit. The groundcherries have fuzzy leaves, and for this reason they are often described botanically as *Physalis pubescens.* The tomatillos, or husk tomatoes, have smooth leaves and a different stem structure, as well as a different flower on close examination. They are described botanically as *Physalis ixocarpa.* There are many other differences between these plants, but the important point for the gardener unfamiliar with them is that the groundcherries I describe here will all cross with one another; thus they are all the same species, whatever we choose to call it. The tomatillos will also cross, but not with the groundcherries. Thus it is better to grow one groundcherry and one tomatillo each season than to battle with the unknown, for their genetics and methods of reproduction are poorly understood. Since the seed will keep for at least five years, it is possible to alternate varieties from year to year and in this manner preserve their distinctive culinary features.

Regardless of whether they were groundcherries or tomatillas, the oldest colloquial name for both plants in colonial America was wintercherry. This term is recorded by Henry Muhlenberg and Benedict Schipper in their 1812 Pennsylvania German dictionary. It was equated with the Pennsylvania High German word *Judenkirsche,* a term more correctly applied to the Jerusalem cherry (*Solanum pseudocapsicum*), but in the popular mind the two were the same thing. Thus *Juddekaersche* became the common Pennsylvania Dutch name for all members of the *Physalis* genus. The term *wintercherry,* although totally fallen out of use, reveals an interesting sidelight on the way groundcherries were harvested in the eighteenth century.

In the fall, right before frost, entire groundcherry plants were pulled up, the roots shaken dry, then hung upside down indoors in a dry, airy room. Preserved in this manner, the berries would keep in their husks for several months. Thus they could be harvested as needed all winter. This simple preservation technique is still practiced by Indians in temperate parts of Mexico and was probably known to the Indians who once resided in the eastern woodlands, for there were groundcherries native to that part of the country. Unfortunately, since none of the *Physalis* genus was of economic importance to colonial commerce, its various members were mostly ignored until the nineteenth century, when botanists began to catalog regional plants in earnest.

The yellow or common groundcherry is variously designated as *Physalis pruinosa* or *Physalis pubescens.* This is the groundcherry most familiar to gardeners and the one most readily available from seed houses. The plants grow as sprawling bushes some 2 feet tall, with branches spreading as much as 3 or 4 feet over the ground. The leaves are gray-green and covered with down. The fruit hangs from the stems in husks and is ripe when the husks drop to the ground. The most common named variety is Cossack Pineapple, which has lemon-yellow fruit and a distinct pineapple flavor. Groundcherries of this description were known in the eighteenth century. English gardener Thomas Mawe (1779, 486) noted that in Britain they could only be cultivated in greenhouses.

I also raise another yellow-fruited cultivar which I call New Hanover. Physically, it resembles Cossack Pineapple, but the flavor of the fruit is distinctive, somewhat like that of a yellow tomato. During a vegetable tasting held by the American Institute of Wine and Food in my garden several years ago, this groundcherry was preferred over all the others. New Hanover was preserved by the late Katie Hoffman Slonaker (1903–1983) on her farm at New Hanover, Pennsylvania. The plants in Katie's garden were short, compact bushes that did not sprawl, but when moved to my garden, they began growing like the others. This suggests to me that soil may affect groundcherries more fundamentally than previously thought.

The orange groundcherry is another variant form. It has fruit that is orange or apricot colored, and tastes distinctly of tangerines. This cultivar is distributed among seed savers under the name Aunt Molly (*Aent Moll* in Pennsylvania Dutch) and appears to be a variant form of Goldie, a variety sold by the Walter Schell seed company of Harrisburg, Pennsylvania, in the 1920s. Botanist William Darlington described the orange groundcherry in 1837 and called it *Physalis pennsylvanica* with a question mark. He presumed it to be native and noted that it was more sought after and better eating than the others. It is not native, for it was introduced from the Caribbean like the other groundcherries of its species, but it was probably introduced quite early in the seventeenth century.

I raise another variety of groundcherry, which in Pennsylvania Dutch is known as the *Lecha Juddakaersche* or Lehigh County groundcherry. It is thought to have been introduced by the Moravians, brought back from South America by some of their missionaries in the early nineteenth century. The fruit ripens orange-bronze or brown. It is naturalized throughout the northern parts of Lehigh County, Pennsylvania, and in neighboring Northampton County. It is also the rarest of the three forms of groundcherry that I offer through Seed Savers Exchange.

The husk tomato or tomatillo was introduced from Mexico in the 1840s and is simply known among the Pennsylvania Dutch as the large groundcherry or *Lutzert-Tomatt* (lantern tomato). These colloquial names were borrowed by English-speaking Americans, especially in the Midwest. All of the members of this species produce fruit that expands in the surrounding husk and eventually breaks through it. The flavor of the fruit is most similar to that of a tomato, and it can be used in either its green or ripe state because the chemistry of the *ixocarpa* is different from that of the groundcherry. There are many varieties and subvarieties of tomatillos, but only two fall into the category of heirlooms for most of the United States outside of the Southwest.

The large green husk tomato is now available in several forms, the most common being the variety called Toma Verde, but the old one is a cultivar that grows into a small sprawling bush no more than 2½ feet tall. The leaves are small and the fruit is smaller than most of the Mexican tomatillos commonly available in markets. It comes to fruit late in the season, late October and early November, and is therefore difficult to grow in areas where frost comes earlier. Frost does not damage the fruit in the husks, but it does cause all the fruit to drop. The ripe fruit is green-white, sometimes heavily tinged with yellow, and sweet. Seeds are distributed by the Landis Valley Museum under the name Huberschmidt groundcherry. It appears to be a variant form of the jamberry or sweet tomatillo of southern California.

The purple husk tomato grows into a very tall, sprawling bush with branches spreading as much as 6 feet. The fruit is purple-black when fully exposed to the sun, but if shaded, the coloring will appear in patches. This variety is sold by several seed companies under the name Purple de Milpa, but was originally introduced in the 1840s from Mexico. Several correspondents with the editor of the *American Agriculturist* (1858, 340) reported having it in their gardens from as diverse areas of the country as Hempstead, Long Island, central New Jersey, and Wisconsin. It has now become naturalized in several parts of the southeastern United States. Because it requires a long growing season in order to bear fruit, it cannot be grown successfully in areas colder than USDA Zone 6. However, the plants are rampant growers and are not overly sensitive to cool weather, or even to an occasional light frost. Because they take up a great deal of room, this variety of tomatillo was often planted among the tepees of pole beans or in the fields among the corn and pumpkins.

Seed saving techniques for groundcherries and husk tomatoes are the same as those for tomatoes. Refer to the fermentation process on pages 339–40.

OKRA
Abelmoschus esculentus

Okra is part of a larger migration of tropical plants that came to the New World in association with the slave trade. Thus it shares a common passport with such vegetables as the garden huckleberry (pages 207–08), the watermelon, and the true goober pea (*Voandzeia subterranea*). Today okra is one of the symbols of southern cookery in this country, and also one of my favorite vegetables. I grow several varieties, and every year I try to add a few more to my collection. The many variant forms that exist in this species never cease to amaze me, whether in the shape of their pods or in the showiness of their flowers.

Okra is a first cousin to the hibiscus and cotton. Its culture in this country dates to the early eighteenth century, perhaps even earlier, for it was brought into the North American colonies from the West Indies. Its old name among gardeners and botanists was ketmia, since they treated it as a form of hibiscus. Two early areas of cultivation centered on New Orleans and Charleston. By the latter part of the eighteenth century, okra began appearing in gardens in the Middle States, especially in the region around Philadelphia, which at one time had a large Creole population. Okra was depicted in a number of still life paintings by members of the

Philadelphia Peale family during the 1820s, so it is possible to form an impression of what those old varieties were like.

For one thing, their pods were thorny around the base. This thorniness, like that in old eggplant varieties, has been bred out over the past hundred years. Furthermore, the pods have undergone a gradual transformation in shape. The pods of the older sorts were long, narrow, and pointed, so pointed that the tips could inflict a nasty wound, especially once the pods had dried. They were also heavily ribbed, which caused them to toughen quickly. For these reasons, plant breeders have aimed for smaller, smoother pods that remain tender longer. These differences are quite noticeable when heirloom and modern okra varieties can be compared side by side.

Charles Parnell, writing about okra in *Vick's Illustrated Monthly Magazine* (May 1888, 144) remarked perceptively that in spite

Old style okra.

of the claims of seedsmen, there were only two truly distinct varieties: the dwarf green, smooth-podded, 3 to 4 feet tall; and the long green, 5 to 6 feet tall, with long ribbed pods.

Most of the okras that existed in the nineteenth century were only passing backyard variants of these two basic types, for okra adapts itself quickly to its environment, especially outside the tropics. Thus, dwarf types grow taller, tall varieties grow shorter, and many variations can appear on a plant-to-plant basis in the same garden. Any seed-saving activity must always keep this in mind, with a clear focus on plants that are true to type.

Buist's Dwarf, a variety introduced before the Civil War, was originally 2 feet tall and designed for small gardens. It quickly adapted itself within a few generations of release, reverting in some ways to its more primitive ancestors. The only dwarf heirloom variety readily available today that closely resembles the okras depicted in old still-life paintings is the Early Dwarf Green, which produces long pods, as shown in the drawing. The plants range in height from 2½ to 3 feet and produce abundantly throughout the season.

The tall or giant okra of Fearing Burr (1865, 606) is most similar to the heirloom variety now known as

Dwarf Green Okra

Cow Horn, which may grow as tall as 7 or 8 feet and produce 12- to 14-inch pods. It comes to crop in about 90 days and cuts an impressive figure in the garden no matter where it is planted. The pods, which are now widely used in dry flower arrangements, are best for culinary use when 5½ to 6 inches long.

A variety known as Stubby (color plate 54), and one of my favorites, is both short, about 3½ feet tall, and stumpy podded. It is best harvested for culinary purposes when 2½ inches long. If allowed to mature much beyond that, the pods become tough and stringy. This variety is also the most day-length sensitive and will virtually shut down by early September, dropping flowers and leaves as though touched by frost.

Stubby Okra

Finally, there is a trilogy of late nineteenth-century okras that I call the "three velvets." Green Velvet, Red Velvet, and White Velvet. White Velvet was first introduced by Peter Henderson and Company of New York. It was mentioned in *How to Make the Garden Pay* (1890, 220) as something quite different from the old standards. In pod, perhaps; but none of the velvets grow into the sort of bushes depicted in period seed catalogs. The woodcut of White Velvet is a compliment to an artist's ability to create vegetables beyond nature. The heirlooms we grow today under these names have shifted away from their original, dwarf forms. Both the red and green sorts may grow as tall as 6 feet. They are also sensitive to cool weather. Of the three, Red Velvet is the most distinctive. It has a rose-colored flower and a red pod that retains its color after cooking. All of the velvets are characterized by soft, downy, thornless pods.

White Velvet Okra

Growing heirloom okra is not complicated, and all of the varieties just mentioned can be treated the same way. Furthermore, aside from an occasional Japanese beetle, okras are fairly free of pests and diseases. But since okra is a tropical plant and cannot tolerate much cold, it is essential to start the seedlings indoors early in the spring and have them well established in individual pots before moving them to the garden. It was the old rule of thumb that okra could be planted once the corn was four inches tall. Okra likes warm ground, the richer the better, so it is best to wait until the ground is ready for beans. Planted too early, young okra plants may rot at the stems, especially if the weather turns unseasonably cool and rainy. Small seedlings are also highly vulnerable to birds, so it is better to plant okras after the seedlings have developed a number of leaves.

Dwarf varieties are usually planted about 2 feet apart, the larger sorts 3 feet. I plant them all about 2 feet apart and have not noticed any difference in pod size or productivity. Okra plants produce large fanlike leaves, but not many of them, so the plants can be crowded a little more than other types of tall-growing vegetables. The tall sorts will also require staking because they tend to be weak at the roots. Planted a little closer together, they seem to hold one another up better during high winds.

When to harvest the pods is a perennial question. An honest answer is that it comes with trial and error. Take a paring knife into the garden and test a few pods by slicing them in half. If the blade cuts through like soft butter, the pod is ready to cook. If there is resistance, as though cutting through a green apple, the pod is too mature. Blind people harvest the best okra because they can tell which pods are ready by gently pinching them. Finally, okra is a generous plant. Constant harvesting only encourages it to produce more.

For seed-saving purposes, I suggest setting aside a few specimen plants, all true to type, and let them run to seed. This will avoid worry about seed at the end of the summer when there are so many other chores to be done. Okra seed is ready to harvest when the pods have begun to turn brown and split along the ribs. Remove the seed—it is gray-black—and let it dry thoroughly indoors before storing. Keep in mind that while okra is self-pollinating, its attractive flowers are frequently visited by bees and other insects that can cause crossing. Different varieties must be isolated by one mile or allowed to flower and produce seed for only a limited period of time. Once one variety has produced a sufficient number of pods (10 is a good number), flower production can be halted by nipping them off before another variety comes to blossom. By staggering the times of flowering on my seed stock, I have managed to preserve seed purity without difficulty. This technique can be used with many other types of vegetables and is especially recommended where gardens are small.

Okra was eaten the year around in the past. During the summer it was prepared fresh, often stewed with tomatoes, dipped in batter and fried like a fritter, or added to gumbos. For winter use the young pods were pickled or sliced and dried like fruit. Dried okra was reconstituted by soaking it a few hours in boiling water, the same technique we use with beans. The unripe seeds were mixed into rice dishes or cooked alone like peas. When ripe, they were roasted and ground to make a type of ersatz coffee that was once popular among blacks in the South. When mixed with peanuts roasted and ground the same way, the beverage resembles chocolate.

Under the heading "Okra and the Science of Soups," the *Horticulturalist* (1847, 118–21) published a recipe for a *potage* from New Orleans. It appears to be authentic, since it calls for filé, the ground, dried leaf buds of sassafras. Gumbo filé was as much a thickening agent as it was an exquisite flavoring, particularly well suited to crab or shellfish.

Gumbo Soup

🍎

Take a [guinea] fowl of good size, cut it up, season it with salt and pepper, and dredge it with flour. Take the soup kettle, and put in it a tablespoon of butter, one of lard, and one of onions chopped fine. Next fry the fowl till well browned, and add four quarts of cold water. The pot should now, being well covered, be allowed to simmer for a couple of hours. Then put in twenty or thirty oysters, a handful of chopped okra or gumbo, and a very little thyme, and let it simmer for a half an hour longer. Just before serving it up, add about half a tablespoonful of feelee powder. This soup is usually eaten with the addition of a little cayenne pepper, and is delicious.

It might be noted that the term *dredge* in this recipe means to dip or roll around in flour so that it completely coats the pieces of meat. A few crushed pods of the *piment bec d'oiseau noir* (page 254) in the place of cayenne would give this heirloom recipe one final brushstroke of authenticity.

Onions (Alliums)

Onions, garlics, leeks, and shallots are all members of the genus *Allium*. They have recently become more respectable in the medical world because it has been discovered that they contain quercetin, a natural substance that suppresses some types of cell mutations that lead to cancer. This might explain why the ancients considered onions and red wine, which also contains quercetin, so important to good health. Along with viticulture, the many varieties of alliums that we cultivate in kitchen gardens trace their origin to the Old World. Their history in America has been one long, gradual adaptation to our soils and climate, for in spite of their hardiness, there are no vegetables more sensitive to these conditions than the alliums.

My collection is concentrated primarily in garlics, shallots, and topsetting onions, secondarily in leeks. Many of my rarest alliums came into my collection due to the generosity of John Swenson, a member of Seed Savers Exchange. John participated in an important botanical expedition into Central Asia about ten years ago in search of rare alliums, with rich results. I have a long list of plants that were gathered during that expedition, including *Allium farctum*, discovered in Afghanistan in 1972, *Allium altaicum* from Mongolia, and giant Siberian chives (*Allium ledebourianum*), not to mention a huge collection of rare garlics and shallots.

Louis Van Deven, another Seed Savers Exchange onion collector, and author of a little booklet called *Onions and Garlic Forever* (1992), has also provided me with plant stock and much advice. He has been especially helpful in assembling a choice collection of such native American alliums as ramps (*Allium tricoccum*), topsetting meadow garlic (*Allium canadense*), and the unusual Douglas onion (*Allium douglasii*) from the Wallowa Mountains of Oregon. But there are many others. Louis is special. He has opinions. His letters roll into dissertations full of salty observations on forty-five years of gardening experience. He has given my collection a personal dimension that I suppose is only evident to me: when I am out among my garlics, it is almost as though he is standing nearby, lecturing.

Eighteenth-century American kitchen gardeners did not have the luxury of friends in Seed Savers Exchange. They had to rely heavily on imported seed because seed saved from plants grown here degenerated quickly. And since onions imported from Spain and Portugal could be purchased cheaply—at least in the seaport cities—there was no pressing economic reason to develop our own varieties until after the Revolution. But then it happened quickly.

The Wells Brothers of Wethersfield, Connecticut, began raising onions on a commercial basis in 1788. The mucky lowlands of Connecticut's sunken coastline were perfect for onion culture. Soon many port towns on Long Island Sound became involved in shipping onions up and down the Atlantic coast, as well as exporting them to the West Indies. Southport, Connecticut, became America's onion emporium, and even today, long after the demise of the onion farms in that area, old buildings connected with the onion trade still stand along Southport's waterfront.

The Connecticut onionmen raised their crops in onion beds on the same principle as the *cepinae* of the ancient Romans. The beds were heavily fertilized, but crops were never rotated. The *American Agriculturist* (1868, 357) reported that the Wells Brothers had been raising onions in the same fields for 80 years. This is what makes good onion ground. The lesson here, which applied to all the alliums, is to create permanent onion beds in part of the kitchen garden. Over time, the ground will mellow out and produce excellent yields. The common fear about this non-rotation method is that it will encourage onion maggots, which attack the bulbs. This problem can be dealt with by making a strong tea of burdock leaves and applying it when it is at room temperature around the base of the plants.

Many of the heirloom onions grown in America today, varieties like Yellow Danvers, Red Wethersfield, and Southport White Globe, were developed by the onion farmers themselves through careful selection. The globe onion came to us from England, but under Yankee guidance, it evolved into a thoroughly American variety. There were also seedsmen connected with the onion growers, who took the Connecticut varieties and perfected them for commerce. Among these was the firm of Comstock, Ferre of Wethersfield, which made Connecticut onion seed well known even in the 1840s. The Shakers also acquired many of these onions and further promoted them through their seed lists. The Large Red of their 1843 seed catalog was the same onion later known as Red Wethersfield.

Unfortunately, New England onions cannot be grown in warmer parts of the country, so seed trade with Europe continued in an ongoing effort to fine-tune onion varieties to the widely diverse soil and climate conditions that exist in this country. The *Farmer's Encyclopaedia* (1844, 859) listed fourteen varieties of onions, among them Portugal, Globe, Lisbon, James's Keeping Onion, Silver Skinned, and Strasburg. All of these were imported varieties.

James's Keeping Onion is an eighteenth-century English variety from Surrey that is still available, one of the few named onion varieties from that century for which this holds true. It may grow successfully in parts of the country above 39° north latitude. The Portugal, Lisbon, and Silver Skinned onions were planted in my part of the country, not surprisingly, since we are on the same latitude as Spain and Portugal. In fact, the Silver Skinned was also known as Philadelphia White and was once used extensively in pickling. Strasburg was also called Yellow Dutch and was a preferred variety among the Pennsylvania Dutch.

B. K. Bliss & Sons of New York advertised in their 1873 seed catalog five onions that they considered the best for American kitchen gardens. Having grown all of these five at one time or another, I think that this selection has a certain timelessness about it, for it will appeal to many levels of gardening experience. I have used the Bliss list for my choice of onions, although personally, I prefer small onions, shallots, leeks, and garlics because they do not occupy as much space as the larger varieties. Furthermore, there is a catch-22.

Heirloom onions are mostly available as seed, not as onion sets. Therefore, the seed must be planted in flats in May or June, then thinned and planted in the garden by mid-August or early September. These seedlings will then make sets that can be dug up, dried, and saved until spring, or overwintered in the ground and thinned the following year. When transplanting the onion seedlings, it is advisable to trim the tops back a few inches to encourage root growth. This will also result in better onions sooner. The clippings can be used like chives in salads and soups— why waste them? However, seedlings cannot be planted in the spring with the expectation of harvesting onions the first year unless the onions are small-bulbed varieties to begin with. More likely, seedlings planted in the spring will go dormant over the summer unless watered profusely. I mention this only to warn the reader that growing fine onions is not as easy as staking up a tomato vine. There have been times when I have been down on my knees with a grapefruit spoon planting onion seedlings one by one, each the size of a blade of grass, wondering to myself all the while why I had not stuck to shallots.

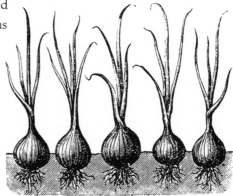

Onion sets properly thinned.

Some small seed houses have begun offering sets for many heirloom onions. More would do so if they received encouragement from customers. Where sets are available, I would urge my readers to avail themselves of this service, or pool resources with several gardening neighbors and convince a small grower to grow sets for them. However, if the sets are homegrown, the Pennsylvania Dutch had the following advice for overwintering them. (I have translated this from *Der Hoch-Deutsche Germantaun Calender* for 1838.)

To Grow Very Large Onions

❦

Store the onions all winter long near a warm stove, and plant them as usual in the spring. The onions will grow so large that each one will weigh more than a pound.

I thought I would mention this because it works, although I am not sure why.

When growing any onions for seed, select only the finest specimens, replant them in a corner of the onion bed, and let them come to flower. When the tops begin to yellow, the seed can be collected. Onion seed is black and looks like leek seed and the seed of garlic chives, and this should be warning enough to label it carefully. Furthermore, all varieties of onions (*Allium cepa*) will cross with each other, with most topsetting onions (*Allium cepa* var. *proliferum*), and with some Welsh onions (*Allium fistulosum*). For seed purity, they must be isolated by at least a mile.

Since the original dates of introduction and the names of the originators are not presently known for Bliss's select five onions, I will simply list them and provide descriptive material that seems pertinent. In truly hot regions of the country where these onions cannot be raised, I would suggest Giant Rocca, a mild Italian onion introduced from England in 1872 by Rochester, New York, seedsman James Vick; or Burpee's Prizetaker, a yellow-skinned, white-fleshed onion introduced in 1888.

Wethersfield Large Red Onion
Allium cepa var. *cepa*

The bulb of this onion, originally known as Large Red, grows 6 to 8 inches in diameter. It is oblate in shape, slightly flat on top and bottom. The skin is purple-red, the flesh purple-white, and stronger flavored than most yellow onions. It was used extensively in pickling red cabbage in the nineteenth century. It is a good storage onion.

Wethersfield Large Red Onion

Thomas DeVoe noted in his *Market Assistant* (1866, 339) that prior to the 1830s red onions were "principally sold, fastened on a wisp of straw about the size of a man's thumb, which were called a 'string' or 'rope of onions.'" Garlics are often tied up and sold this way today.

White Globe Onion
Allium cepa var. *cepa*

Also known as Southport White Globe, this onion is perfectly round in shape, with a smooth white skin. This variety is always recommended over all other white onions for American kitchen gardens in old garden books because it can be grown in many parts of the country, including the Upper South. Unfortunately, it is not a good keeper, but it makes delicious soup. The following recipe, a study in simplicity, is taken from the Norwich, Connecticut, cookbook of Mrs. Elizabeth F. Ellet, *The New Cyclopaedia of Domestic Economy* (1873, 183).

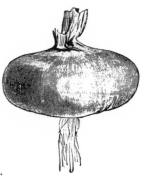

White Portugal Onion

Onion Soup
🍂

Onions, peeled, pared, and cut into pieces, then shred into a pan and fried in either oil or butter, without any broth, but simply having boiling water poured over them, and some toasted bread, seasoned merely with pepper and salt, are considered very refreshing when thus made into a soup, and much used by ladies throughout Europe after the fatigues of a ball.

White Portugal Onion
Allium cepa var. *cepa*

Also known as Philadelphia White and Philadelphia Silver Skin, this variety was introduced from Portugal in the 1780s. The shape of the bulb (above) is oblate, flat on top and bottom. It is a medium-sized onion that can be raised from seed planted in the spring. It normally produces a number of small (undersized) bulbs that are excellent for pickling or for use as pearl onions.

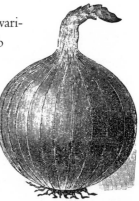

Yellow Danvers Onion
Allium cepa var. *cepa*

This onion is known under many aliases, including Danvers Yellow, Round Yellow Danvers, and Yellow Globe Danvers. It is a highly pro-

Yellow Globe Danvers Onion

ductive, round, yellow-fleshed strain developed out of the old common yellow onion introduced from England in the eighteenth century. Bulbs are normally about 3 inches in diameter and about 2¾ inches tall. Seed can be planted in the spring for a September harvest. The skin is a distinctive brownish yellow. In spite of its many merits, it does not store well.

Yellow Globe Onion
Allium cepa var. *cepa*

Also known as Southport Yellow Globe, this onion is not as uniform in productivity as the preceding, but it is better acclimated to warmer parts of the country. It resembles White Globe except for its color. The skin is reddish yellow. The onion is an excellent keeper.

Southport Yellow Globe Onion

Shallots
Allium cepa var. *aggregatum*

I have so many shallots that I hardly know where to begin digging when it comes time to harvest them. Entire beds are devoted to shallots alone. There are different colors, different shapes, different intensities of flavor. I am not certain what the biblical shallots were like, but they were evidently well appreciated and disseminated over a large part of the Mediterranean world during Roman times. They are referred to specifically in the A.D. 820 cloister plan of St. Gall in Switzerland, and we know from their name that even then they were presumed to come from Ashkelon, a city in what is now Israel.

Colonial Americans called them "scallions" or "scullions," and so did my grandmother, who preferred the young greens to the minced bulbs. I think it was this once-common preference for the tops that caused many people to confuse scallions with bunching onions, and to disdain the bulbs as a type of garlic. Robert Buist (1847, 119) observed, "Though it has been two hundred years in cultivation, very little of the article is used in this country, unless by the French." Shallots were something found in the kitchen gardens of the well-to-do. The poor treated them like garlic, and kept the bulbs like olive oil, for home remedies.

The oldest American variety of shallot for which there is any definite proof that it is indeed an heirloom is a nameless white-skinned shallot presently in circulation among seed savers. It is often called white heirloom shallot or small white shallot simply as a matter of convenience. In some ways, it fits the descriptions of the Italian Shallot or Cape Shallot introduced in 1837, although it could very well be an English strain developed from it. It is found in many old kitchen gardens across the South. The bulbs now being circulated among seed savers originated in a garden in Newport, North Carolina. They are generally about 2 inches in diameter.

We are on firmer ground with the Jersey Shallot, which was first noted in *Le Bon Jardinier* in 1840 under the name *éschalote de Jersey*. It had been raised in Scotland for some years prior to that under the name Russian Shallot. Scottish gardeners often dubbed foreign and unusual vegetables as "Russian," which has sometimes led food historians astray, since it had nothing to do with a Russian connection. Philadelphia gardeners used "Spanish" in this same context. Thus, the Russian shallots of Scotland and the Spanish shallots of Philadelphia came from the island of Jersey, also famous for its cow cabbages (page 112). American gardeners were introduced to this variety in the 1840s under the name false shallot, since it was presumed to be a species of onion that resembled a shallot. The problem with this logic was that shallots *are* onions; botanically they are the same species.

The *Album Vilmorin* (24:1873) depicted it as a variety synonymous with *éschalote d'Alençon*. More properly, this is the large Russian strain of the Jerseys, and frankly, one could argue that is not even a strain, just large bulbs separated out from the small. Vilmorin (1885, 523) also stated that the Russian shallots of England belonged to a different variety of shallot, fully contradicting the firm's own seed lists of forty years earlier. The Jersey shallot grown from seed will often produce very large bulbs like the so-called Russian strain, weighing as much as 6 ounces or more. These can then be selected out for size. There is no mystery. I have done this many times. The Alençon is just the French name for the big ones.

Two later French varieties that are now very popular among onion collectors are the Besançon sweet yellow shallot and the Prince de Bretagne, the latter one of the leading heirloom varieties of Brittany. It is also the reddest. All four of these heirlooms are highly recommended for heirloom kitchen gardens. They are shown in color plate 55.

Shallots are cultivated like onion sets. They should be planted about 6 to 8 inches apart after the first frost in the fall. They will overwinter in the ground without protection and emerge the following spring. Like garlic, shallots produce much larger and much healthier bulbs if they are vernalized by this cold-weather treatment. In the summer, after the tops turn yellow, the bulbs may be dug and stored in a cool dry place. If the Jersey shallots appear to be sending up flowers, cut them off so that all the strength of the plant may be concentrated in the bulbs. If Jersey shallots bloom, they will cross with the same alliums listed for common onions on page 217.

Welsh Onions or Bunching Onions
Allium fistulosum

This species is subdivided into many varieties and often referred to in commercial seed catalogs as Japanese bunching onion. Some of the most popular varieties today are indeed of Japanese origin, among them Ishikura. However, the heirloom variety that was introduced into England in the 1500s as poultry feed originated in Siberia, and when mature has a stem much like a leek, yet the leaves are hollow like onions. It is shown in color plate 56. This is the historical variety of early American kitchen gardens and the one depicted in *Curtis's Botanical Magazine* (1809, 1230).

This variety was called Welsh onion because when the seed was sent to England in 1562, it came from a Swiss botanist who referred to it as *Welsch,* which means foreign. Another layer of confusion was added to this because the Welsh onion became the poor man's leek, and leeks, of course, have been long associated with Wales. The plant is extremely hardy and may be treated as a perennial. The large two- or three-year-old plants can be culled for the kitchen, while the small onions that form along the sides can be replanted to start more clumps. Furthermore, the onion flowers profusely, and the seed is easy to cultivate simply by scratching the ground in the bed and scattering the seed broadcast.

In *The American Home Garden* (1859, 160), Alexander Watson devoted a lengthy discussion to the Welsh onion and recommended it for private gardens. Since the white variety is much easier to cultivate than leeks, I quite agree with his conclusions. Fearing Burr (1865, 138) listed two varieties, the white Welsh onion (the variety of this discussion) and the red Welsh onion. Burr's information was taken from the Vilmorin garden book of 1856. I doubt he ever saw the plants, because he noted (incorrectly) that they were not found in gardens in this country. What he meant was that they were not a commercial product readily salable in markets at that time. This is confirmed by Thomas DeVoe's *Market Assistant* (1866), which made no reference to them whatever.

As a working man's substitute for leeks, the Welsh onion was cultivated in this country since the early eighteenth century, perhaps even as early as the 1680s. It was a source of spring greens, but it was not raised, as it is today, primarily for its small delicate green onions, so important to French and Asian cooking. Furthermore, confusion arises in old garden books when it is not clear what is meant by a "bunching" onion, for many onions called Welsh onion or *ciboule* actually belonged to other species. I have in my collection a fine bunching onion of medieval Polish origin, but it is *Allium ursinum,* a cultivated form of bear garlic. Even the topsets of tree onions can be planted whole to form perfect bunches of delicate onions for the fall.

After the Civil War, when market gardening assumed commercial importance and when Victorian cookbooks began to reform America's rustic eating habits in a large way, delicate spring onions became a necessary ingredient in urban middle-class cookery. Market gardeners found that they could force small sets of Southport White Globe and White Lisbon onions to produce bunching onions quite as delicate as the French varieties. White Lisbon yields bunching onions in 50 days, a highly profitable turnaround. A good portion of the spring onions sold in American markets today are White Lisbon. The Southport onion was developed even further into a special bunching strain called Southport White Bunching, although its use is now declining.

Leeks
Allium ampeloprasum

The oldest evidence of the cultivation of leeks comes from Egypt in the form of actual plants buried in grave sites as part of the votive meal for the afterlife. I have seen these dried, shriveled-up Egyptian hors d'oeuvres at the University of Pennsylvania Museum, and that they dated from between 1550 and 1320 B.C. was the least interesting thing about them, impressive as it was. It was the shape of the leaves. I would never have guessed that they were leeks. The leaves of the ancient varieties were consistently long and narrow, more like rocombole garlics in appearance. Some of the remains have since been identified as *Allium kurrat,* which is similar to leek. I am now inspired to grow it; if I ever want to host a pharaonic feast, or a Roman meal in the Alexandrian mode, or stowaway snacks for my mummy case, I will most certainly need this vital ingredient.

The Romans also raised leeks, although somewhat different in physical characteristics. The *porrum capitatum* of Roman gardens was actually depicted in full color in the codex of Dioskorides dating from A.D. 500 to 511. It is not thick in the stem like the leeks we know today, and it has a bulb similar to its wild relatives; though the leaves are large and broad, and there is no doubt about its leekness, I wonder whether it did not have the lingering aroma of ramps. It just looks as though it ought to taste very strongly of something. Working people in colonial America did not object to strong onion tastes. The rank wild garlic that infests lawns in my part of the country was introduced in the late 1600s to flavor milk and cheese, although the odor carries for a good city block. Leeks, by comparison, are bland.

The true leek of early America appears to have been a gentleman's food. In glancing over Bernard M'Mahon's 1815 seed catalog, with its huge selections of turnips, cabbages, peas, and radishes, there are only two varieties of leek, the Common Leek and the Broad-Leaved Leek. This says a great deal about its culinary role in the cookery of the period. Yet the situation did improve rapidly, at least in the cities.

Thomas DeVoe reported in the *Market Assistant* (1866, 335) that leeks were sold in the markets tied up in bundles with bunches of parsley for use in soups. He added: "The leeks, when properly blanched, are boiled, and served with toasted bread and white sauce, and eaten as asparagus." This is exactly how my great-grandmother prepared them. But she only made the dish on special occasions (using culls) because she sold her best leeks for a high profit in Philadelphia. She raised Musselburgh leeks, and so do I.

There is other anecdotal evidence about the popularity of leeks in this country, although much of it points in the direction of the South. Perhaps the climate, with its mild winters, encouraged the cultivation of leeks more than in the North. A letter to the editor of *Vick's Illustrated Monthly Magazine* (1881, 256) complained about the lack of good vegetables in Columbia,

Missouri: "I have only resided here about two or three years, having lived in Louisiana, where the Leek-bed was considered a treasure, as they came on so much earlier than other vegetables in the spring." A leek bed is indeed a treasure, and I am certainly a glutton to have four, but since I eat leeks almost every day, it is a "just sufficiency," to quote an old Quaker phrase, and a healthy sufficiency at that. One more thing: Leeks in the markets are expensive and often not worth the crates they are shipped in. Keeping a leek bed is plain common-sense economics. When it is properly maintained, it will provide a constant supply all year long.

Leeks are propagated from seed. They are started in flats in the late winter and, when they are large enough to have three or four leaves, moved to their permanent location. They can be planted early because light frosts will not injure them. Space the seedlings about 12 inches apart, 16 to 18 if they are to be interplanted with kohlrabies, radishes, or other small root vegetables. Leeks are also highly compatible with turnips, and the onion smell will keep many insects away. Different varieties of leeks can be planted in succession over a two-month period so that they come to crop at different times. Leeks left in the ground over the winter normally produce an epicurean delight the second season. This is known as the "leek bulb," small bulbs that form about the base of leeks that are ready to bloom. Some of the bulbs can grow quite large, perhaps an inch in diameter, and make a perfect substitute for shallots. The longer the leeks are in the ground, the larger the leek bulbs become, and they can be further increased by breaking off the flower spikes.

As I write this, with deep snow on the ground, Musselburgh, the Lyon Prizetaker, Saint Victor, and Monstreux de Carentan are standing in the garden. I recommend three of these as heirlooms. The fourth, Saint Victor, is a recent selection of an old French variety called Bleu de Solaise, which is well worth growing if seed can be had. I am not certain that Saint Victor is in any way superior to the others for culinary purposes, but on the other hand, it outshines the rest in looks, for its leaves are tinged with violet and blue and add a cheerful decorative touch to the kitchen garden. Never forget, the eye eats first.

The Lyon Prizetaker Leek
Allium ampeloprasum

This is an English variety with long, thick stems that began appearing in American seed lists about 1886. It matures in 135 days.

Monstreux de Carentan Leek
Allium ampeloprasum

The ancestor of this leek was the Gros-Court from Rouen, which produced immense fat stems, often 13 inches in diameter. Its size was not equaled by its tenderness, so it was used by the Vilmorins in the 1820s to breed large size into other varieties. The *monstreux de Carentan* is one of those descendants. It is characterized by short stems, about 6 to 8 inches in height, with a thick base often 3 inches in diameter or larger. I have grown some as large as 5 inches in diameter, due I think to a spell of cool, wet weather. Because this variety is sensitive to drought and heat, it is not commercially grown in some parts of the country. For example, I would certainly not recommend it for southwest Texas unless well irrigated. It was introduced into the United States in the 1880s under the name giant Italian leek, which has caused some confusion about its origin. The Vilmorins depicted it in the *Album Vilmorin* (1883, 34) just about the time it was becoming well known in Europe.

Monstreux de Carentan Leek

Musselburgh Leek
Allium ampeloprasum

I could claim a certain sentimental prejudice regarding the subject of the Musselburgh leek, owing to my great-grandmother's penchant for growing it. And when I make her leek pie with

Musselburgh Leek

figs and fennel root, this sentimentality can verge on pure rejoicing. Yet the Musselburgh stands quite on its own, with a little Scottish independence thrown in; it is the tough reliability of this one that makes it past a long list of leeks with much fancier names. I use tough in the sense of durable, for I have never pulled a tough Musselburgh in all my years of gardening.

This delicious leek appears to have evolved out of an older French leek known as Gros-Court, a huge sort, very fat at the base, cultivated by a certain market gardener by the name of Duvillers near Paris. This leek merchant found the strain on a farm in the vicinity of Rouen, and for a number of years made a good profit off his discovery. The ever-vigilant Vilmorins obtained seed and in the 1820s used Gros-Court to create several commercial varieties now well known for their large size. One of these they sold to English market gardeners, who cultivated it under the name London Flag. Under this English name, it became one of the most widely cultivated leeks in the United States well into the 1870s.

Vilmorin seed for a sister strain traveled to Edinburgh, where Scottish seedsmen developed it into a variety of their own, shorter than London Flag and a paler shade of green. But it adapted well to the northerly climate, and this has been one of its perennial graces. Introduced in 1834, the leek was named for Musselburgh, a coastal town on the Firth of Forth where many market gardens were once situated. Today, the town has been swallowed up as a suburb of Edinburgh.

For all the merits of London Flag, it was eventually surpassed in this country by the leek from Scotland. W. W. Rawson noted in his *Success in Market Gardening* (1892, 145) that Musselburgh was by then the principal market variety. I cannot argue with him on that point, nor with my great-grandmother's judgment. This is one leek that will do very well in most parts of the country. It should be treated as a biennial.

Garlics
Allium sativum

The early American attitude toward garlic may be summed up by Amelia Simmons's one-line discussion of the subject in *American Cookery* (1796, 12): "Tho' used by the French, [they] are better adapted to the uses of medicine than cookery." The discussion of American heirloom garlics is about as long. Simply put, among Anglo-Americans garlic was not well liked. Other ethnic groups used it—the Spanish in the Southwest, the Pennsylvania Dutch, the French in Louisiana—but the Yankee kitchen rarely smelled of garlic unless it was to fumigate for disease. I find this historical disdain contradictory, considering the old Anglo-American love of "rareripes," green bulblets of potato onions that were eaten raw with vinegar. This delicacy was just as pungent as garlic, and a lot harder on the digestion. Nineteenth-century cookbook author Eliza Leslie remarked in one of her books on behavior that garlic was unbecoming because it alluded to certain unpleasant body odors. In an age when people did not bathe with regularity, this may have been the root of

Potato Onion

the old American dislike for garlic. Now that we do not stink so much, we like to eat it. Of all the alliums grown today, American gardeners are the craziest for garlic, proven medical benefits aside. What many gardeners do not realize is that the elephant garlic, which has gained in popularity recently, is not a garlic at all but rather a type of leek that forms bulbs. It does not have the medical constituents of true garlic. What constitutes a garlic then? There are essentially two types.

All garlics belong to the genus *Allium* and the species *sativum;* thus if they produce flowers, they will cross. Crosses will occur in the topsets that form from the flowers, not in the bulbs already underground. I mention this because during gardening workshops, many people are confused about how members of the onion family cross. The species is further divided out into two groups called "softneck" (var. *sativum*) and "hardneck" or rocombole (var. *ophioscorodon*). The soft-neck garlics are called braidable varieties because their tops are soft-stemmed and dry into a grass that can be tied together with other garlics to form them into long chains. Garlics are often sold this way in markets, although it is a waste of money if they are a variety that does not store well. The softneck varieties are propagated from bulbs reserved after harvest. All garlics should be planted in the late fall for best bulb development the following year.

The hardneck varieties form topsets on stems that rise up like snakes. The seedhead is covered with a membrane resembling a hood. Before they open, the flowers unroll like the long beaks of cranes; once open, they look like cobras. I trust these descriptions because they were given to me by children who often visit my garden in groups, and children have good imaginations. These hardneck or rocombole varieties are the ones depicted in medieval herbals. They are extremely hardy and may be treated as perennials. However, they thrive better in rich soil, and do better north of 37° latitude. This type of garlic is propagated from its tiny topsets. They are planted in the ground like onion sets and allowed to grow for two years. After that, the bulbs may be dug and harvested. The small ones are returned the ground and replanted along with a few new topsets. In this manner, the garlic is maintained for many years.

My burden now is to recommend some heirloom varieties that are easy to grow yet have some historical connection with our culture. We have been flooded recently with heirloom garlics from other parts of the world, and many of these are truly culinary surprises. I think, however, that I will choose three red heirlooms, since white-skinned garlics are common in supermarkets. All three of these are available from the seed houses listed at the back of this book. These firms also offer many of the Asian varieties that I have tried, so it would be worth the effort to obtain their catalogs. I think, at last check, that I have fifty-three different sorts of garlics, but many of them are so rare that they can only be obtained through Seed Savers Exchange. Lastly, my three choices store well, which is a very important consideration. The fancy white-skinned garlics are not always good keepers, as many cooks already know.

German Red Garlic (Rocombole)
Allium sativum, var. *ophioscorodon*

This is a medieval garlic strain that was brought here by German immigrants in the eighteenth century. It is a vigorous grower, often reaching 5 to 6 feet in height. The leaves are deep green and arranged opposite each other, as shown in the drawing on page 230. There are usually 10 to 15 cloves in a cluster. The flavor is robust. The Pennsylvania Dutch use the leaves of fall and spring sprouts in cabbage salads.

I will be offering through Seed Savers Exchange in 1997 or 1998 the Maxatawny Garlic, an extremely rare variety of German rocombole garlic that was brought to Pennsylvania by the Moravians in the 1740s. It originated in Silesia in what is now western Poland and was preserved by the Helfferich family for homeopathic medicines. The bulbs are bronze in color.

Inchelium Red Garlic
Allium sativum var. *sativum*

One of the most productive of all the heirloom garlics, this softneck variety is also an artichoke type. This means that its bulbs cluster in layers like artichoke petals. The variety was discovered on the Coleville Indian Reserva-

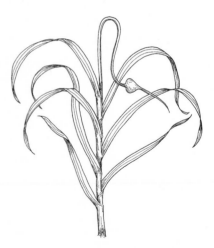

German Red Garlic, a medieval variety.

tion at Inchelium, Washington. It has consistently won high marks (often taking first place) in garlic tastings. From a culinary standpoint, it is probably one of the best of the American heirloom reds.

Spanish Roja Garlic (Rocombole)
Allium sativum var. *ophioscorodon*

Introduced in the latter part of the nineteenth century, this red rocombole type has been consistently popular with kitchen gardeners. The bulbs are about 1½ to 2½ inches in diameter with 6 to 12 cloves per bulb. It is popular with many cooks because it is easy to peel. It also has a very fragrant taste, much more intense than that of many white garlics. However, it cannot be grown in areas that do not have cold winters.

Tree Onions and Potato Onions

Although the potato onion is a form of shallot, while the tree onion represents a more distinct varietal group, both have been hybridized with each other to produce many intermediate forms. The two are sometimes confused and both have been called Egyptian onions at various times in the past. Because it is a shallot, the potato onion may have a Mediterranean origin, yet there is no evidence that it came from Egypt. On the other hand, it was the potato onion that was first called Egyptian by English seedsmen, not the topsetting onions. There is nothing Egyptian about the tree onion, and I sincerely hope that American gardeners stop using that name altogether. It was invented in England most likely as a marketing gimmick.

Tree Onion or Topsetting Onion
Allium cepa var. *proliferum*

Cultivated topsetting onions appeared in American and English gardens in the late eighteenth century more or less out of nowhere. It is a very curious piece of horticultural history that such a distinctive vegetable would have gone unnoticed until the 1790s and that it would burst upon the kitchen gardens of England without a shred of documentation, yet as a thing foreign and exotic. This is an onion that is not easily missed. It produces a stem about as thick as a human thumb at its base, which can be eaten like a shallot, at least in the mature plants. Many plants produce no bulblike roots at all, but resemble large bunching onions. When the plant blooms, it sends up a hollow flower stalk that produces clusters of small onions called bulbils. In some varieties, the bulbils attain a large size and can be harvested as pearl onions. Many varieties produce bulbils that are much smaller, and some are not worth gathering for culinary purposes. The pri-

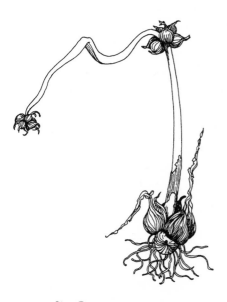

Tree Onion with rareripes.

mary usefulness of this class of onion lies in its early production of greens in the spring—it is one of the first green plants to break through the snow—and in the bulbils, which can be used in pickling or in general cookery like shallots.

The earliest reports of this onion thus far place specimens in Edinburgh in the early 1790s and in the nursery of a Mr. Driver near London in 1796. Botanists at the time quickly dismissed any Egyptian connection because it was "well known" long before the British fleet blockaded Napoleon in Egypt, the confrontation that led to the folkloric discovery of the onion (I have visions of its roots clinging to the Rosetta stone as it was lifted from the sand). The botanical explanation was that it originated in Canada and therefore was a form of *Allium canadense.* This would make the French Canadians extremely happy, if only it were true. Yet in this scientific vein, Sydenham Edwards referred to the onion as the Canada tree onion in his 1807 garden book, and when such things go into print, they often become semiofficial.

Curtis's Botanical Magazine (1812, 1469) approved of the Canadian origin and illustrated a handsome specimen not quite like any I have seen: the flesh of the bulbil was white, but there was a purplish tinge to the skin similar to the colors found in the leaves of the Saint Victor leek. It was noted that the bulbils were superior for pickling. Curtis has thus far provided us with an exquisite picture of a variety not now in circulation (and perhaps extinct) and an unsatisfactory genealogy. The origin of the cultivated tree onion is presently unknown and may be unknowable because the plant is a hybrid, a cross, a backyard creation. It has many wild counterparts in Central Asia, none exactly like it, but it does not exist in its present form in some untamed primitive location.

American gardeners have resorted to a wide roster of names for this onion because they have been thoroughly confused by seedsmen. Therefore we may call it tree onion, Egyptian onion, top onion, walking onion, and Catawissa onion in the same breath. Only in the case of the Catawissa connection may we be dealing with true varieties or subvarieties. The only reason for this distinction is that a Catawissa, Pennsylvania, nurseryman by the name of F. F. Merceron (little is known about this individual) engaged in improving the tree onion for commercial purposes. His strains are somewhat different from the others because they send up topsets from topsets, creating the image of plants growing out of plants. These hybrids are strong growers, often attaining 4 or 5 feet in height, and always in need of staking as a precaution against heavy summer rains.

Mary Larkin Thomas, whom I mentioned in my introduction, knew the whereabouts of one of Merceron's old fields in the vicinity of Roaring Creek Friends Meeting House near Catawissa. We went there in the early 1970s and found an entire field of Merceron's red strain, long abandoned but still thick with onions in a naturalized state. I brought a few of those onions into my garden and have cultivated them ever since.

Merceron was involved in a number of bold schemes to promote his onion for pickling. The pieces to his story are at present buried somewhere in an historical society archive, but this much is known. He developed three distinct strains of tree onions, a red variety (which I have), a white, and a yellow. Alexander Watson mentioned these strains in passing in his *American Home Garden* (1859, 159), noting that by then the onions were already being sent in large quantities to northern markets from Bermuda and the South.

Merceron was more directly involved in the establishment of a tree onion industry around Vevey, Indiana. Thus, his plant stock became widely disseminated in the Midwest. He also appears to have served as supplier or middleman to large seed houses for such New York dealers as R. L. Allen. Allen advertised "Top Onions or Button Onions" in the *American Agriculturist* (1858, 93). The final chapter in Merceron's story has not been written, and doubtless many of the heirloom varieties preserved today were improved by other breeders, yet he occupies an interesting niche in the history of the early American kitchen garden.

There are hundreds of variant forms of the tree onion now available among seed savers. I would recommend three: Merceron's Red Catawissa, Fleener's Topsetting Onion (an excellent white pearl onion), and Moritz Egyptian, a maroon-colored variety from Missouri. I would rather it were called Missouri Moritz, but it does not appear this way in seed lists—yet. Fleener's is depicted in color plate 58.

Topsetting onions are propagated by planting the topsets like onion sets, spacing them about 8 inches apart. The greens, among the first to appear in the spring, may be harvested like chives or spring onions. The onions bloom in the early summer and form topsets that can be harvested. The topsets make delightful flavored vinegars or can be used in pickles. The parent plants can be treated like a perennial. Topsetting onions will cross with other members of the *cepa* species.

The Potato Onion or Multiplier Onion
Allium cepa var. aggregatum

This variety of shallot is propagated by planting small bulbs in the fall or early spring. The bulbs grow into large onions that can be harvested the first year. Left in the ground, the onion will sprout and break down into a number of small bulbs within the outer skin. The small bulbs grow into clusters like shallots and can be harvested, dried, and used for replanting. The potato onion was cultivated both for its mature onion and for the spring "rare-ripes," which resemble sprouting shallots. It was grown in many parts of the country where common onions would not thrive.

The potato onion was introduced into England in the 1790s under the name Egyptian onion, a name also applied to tree onions in common parlance. *The Farmer's Encyclopedia* (Johnson 1844, 861) stated that the onion had been first introduced at Edinburgh by a certain Captain Burns, and for this reason it was sometimes called the Burns onion. There were two varieties, one that set bulbs on top like a tree onion, the other never sending up flowers. The onion appeared in American seed lists shortly after 1800 under the name English multiplier or English underground onion. Boston seedsman John B. Russell offered both the potato onion and tree onion in his 1828 seed catalog (no mention of Egypt, incidentally). A French pamphlet called *Exposition de fleurs et d'autres produits de l'horticulture* published at Lyon in 1840 not only provided an illustration of the potato onion—one of the earliest—but included detailed instructions for propagating it. A brief history of the onion in this country appeared in *The Onion Book* (1887, 32), noting that the most common variety was yellow-brown. This is the same yellow-brown variety depicted in the *Album Vilmorin* (1871, 22), and therefore may be considered the standard for the variety.

In the spring, when the mother bulb divides into many small bulbs, the bulbs turn a green color and, when just beginning to sprout, are harvested as "rare-ripes." This was once an extremely popular spring dish in early America. The rare-ripes were chopped and eaten raw with vinegar as a type of salad, sometimes accompanied by raw oysters.

I recommend the yellow potato onion for heirloom gardens. This variety is readily available from several seed firms.

Parsnips

The earliest evidence of the human consumption of parsnips has been found in Stone Age remains in Switzerland and South Germany. This has presented botanists with an anomaly, because the genetic home of the parsnip is believed to be the Italian peninsula. In any case, there is little doubt that those Stone Age plants were gathered from the wild rather than cultivated in a garden. Later archaeological remains from the Roman period are many, for the parsnip was one of the root vegetables commonly found in kitchen gardens of that era. The history of the plant is complicated by the fact that classic and medieval authors lumped together parsnips and carrots as two forms of the same thing, so it is often difficult to decipher which one they were discussing, especially since the terms *pastinaca* and *carota* were used interchangeably.

In the garden plan of the cloister of St. Gall in Switzerland, a parchment surviving from about A.D. 820, one of the raised beds is clearly labeled *pastinachus*, but this could also mean white carrots. The first clear reference to the cultivation of the parsnip appeared in France in 1393 and again in 1473. From that time on, parsnips were treated by themselves in herbals, so the murkiness eventually parts to reveal the vegetable with all of its familiar attributes.

By the middle of the nineteenth century, there were three distinct varieties cultivated in Europe: the long smooth parsnip (the *coquaine* of France), the turnip-rooted short parsnip known in France as the *noisette Lisbonaise*, and the yellow-rooted Siam parsnip. The first of these was developed in Holland, the others were French. All of these were once widely cultivated in France, Germany, and Central Europe. Today, the centers of parsnip cultivation are England and France.

The parsnip was a popular vegetable in the United States during the nineteenth century, indeed since the colonial period, but its popularity has now faded. Parsnips brought here by English settlers in the 1600s have escaped and naturalized in many parts of the country. These wild parsnips present a problem for seed savers, because they will cross with the cultivated sorts and cause them to degenerate. On the other hand, they offer ripe ground for breeding new varieties, for one of the most popular of our Victorian varieties, The Student, was created in England from a wild parsnip salvaged from a field in the Cotswolds.

Early American seed lists do not usually list many distinct varieties. The Shakers (1843, 12) offered the long white, the most common sort grown in this country and the one equivalent to the *coquaine* of France. Fearing Burr listed a number of others, but they were rarely seen in the United States. The Guernsey (*panais long* of France) was introduced into England in 1826, but never grown much in this country. The Hollow Crown, also dating from the early 1820s, became one of the varieties preferred by many American kitchen gardeners, and one that I heartily recommend. In fact, I would suggest only two heirloom varieties to the general gardener, The Student and the Hollow Crown. Since they are very similar in taste and texture when cooked, probably one or the other would suffice in a small garden. However, I would test them both to determine how they react to the soil, and let that success determine the choice.

Parsnips should be sown as early in the spring as possible because the cold ground revives the seed from deep dormancy. It was discovered long ago that the largest roots are produced by fresh seed, so if it is at all possible, plant the seed soon after it ripens on the plants. Otherwise, plant seed that is clearly dated and unquestionably new, for the viability is only one year. It is pointless to consider saving seed beyond what is necessary for immediate use.

Parsnips tops are large and need a good 1½ to 2 feet of elbow room in all directions. Spacing plants at this distance will produce huge, flavorful roots. Closer than that (seed packets usually recommend 6-inch spacing), the parsnips will develop into something akin to a rather plump carrot. Many people prefer these small parsnips over the large. I think it is important to realize that cultural technique will go far in determining the size of the crop. Unlike carrots, parsnips may be left in the ground all winter. They are often harvested late in the fall after the tops have been nipped by frost, yet many cooks firmly believe that the flavor peaks in the early spring right after the ground thaws. Freezing does not damage the roots. Covering them with straw makes them easier to dig when needed. Otherwise, dig the roots in the fall and store in damp sand in a cool place. Once the plants to begin to grow the following year, the roots turn pithy and cannot be used in cookery. As soon

Long Smooth Parsnip

as the plants bolt and begin to bloom, they should be staked so that the seed heads are not broken over by heavy rains. Seed is gathered and dried in the same manner as for carrots (pages 123–24).

A special word of caution: The leaves of parsnips exude a juice that causes severe skin rashes on many people, one reason why parsnip greens are not sold on the roots displayed in markets. When harvesting parsnips, always be sure to wear gloves and to wash the hands thoroughly before touching the face or eyes.

Hollow Crown Parsnip
Pastinaca sativa

This variety became popular in England in the 1820s. George Lindley (1831, 565) listed it among the varieties recommended for kitchen gardens, and it appeared on many American seed lists during the nineteenth century. The variety distinguishes itself by a sunken crown where the leaves are attached to the root. It was considered one of the best of the very long-rooted vari-

Hollow Crowned Parsnip

eties, but needs deep sandy soil to develop roots true to type. I grow it in a raised bed half filled with sand, and this seems to encourage well-shaped roots, yet if the root strikes a pebble or some other small obstacle in the soil, it will bend or divide into branches. For best results, trench the site deeply and screen the topsoil. The roots often reach 24 inches in length, so care must be taken when digging them not to cut off the ends with the shovel. Better yet, use a pitchfork.

Hollow Crown and another old variety called the sugar parsnip were often used to make muffins and small breads for tea during the Victorian period. The following recipe from Hannah Bouvier Peterson's *National Cook Book* (1855, 167) provides instructions on how this was accomplished. The result was called a "cake" in the parlance of the times, being a cupcake in shape, but more like an English muffin in texture.

Parsnip Cake
🍎

Boil your parsnips till perfectly soft; pass them through a colander. To one tea cupful of mashed parsnip add one quart of warm milk, with a quarter of a pound of butter dissolved in it, a little salt, and one gill of yeast, with flour enough to make a thick batter. Set it away to rise, which will require several hours. When light stir in as much flour as will make a dough, knead it well and let it rise again. Make it out in cakes about a quarter or half an inch thick, butter your tins or pans, put them on and set them to rise. As soon as they are light bake them in a very hot oven. When done wash over the tops with a little water, and send them to the table hot.

The Student Parsnip
Pastinaca sativa

The Vilmorin experiments with the wild Belgian carrot encouraged horticulturists in other countries to look for kitchen garden material in the wild. Professor Buckman of the Royal Agriculture College at Cirencester, England, gathered seed from wild parsnips in the Cotswold hills in 1847. In 1848 he selected plants with certain leaf characteristics, such as fewer hairs, the source of the rash-causing juice. The best of the roots were reserved for seedlings. He repeated this in 1849 and 1850 and continued selecting until 1859, when the variety attained the form we now know as The Student. Buckman sold rights to this new variety to Suttons, the London seed house that first distributed it and gave it its name. Since then, The Student has become a perennial favorite among kitchen gardeners because it produces consistently and of all the parsnip varieties is the least likely to deteriorate.

The salient features of this variety are its short length, never more than 15 inches, and its quickly tapering, wedge-shaped root that is better suited for heavy soils than Hollow Crown.

Peas

Peas are among the oldest of our garden vegetables. They have been under cultivation in the Near East and eastern Mediterranean since 7800 B.C. and over the centuries have evolved into many distinct varieties. In botanical terms, there are three major types: *Pisum sativum* var. *sativum*, the common garden pea; *Pisum sativum* var. *medullare*, the so-called "marrowfat" pea; and *Pisum sativum* var. *saccharatum* or *axiphium*, the sugar pea. There is also a subspecies called *Pisum sativum* var. *arvense*, which are smooth-seeded peas raised primarily as field crops, such as the *Golderbse* (page 243). All of these peas will cross with one another, so there are hundreds of varieties that fall between these larger divisions and sorting them out is no easy matter.

The English have raised the cultivation of the pea to an elaborate level of sophistication, and many of the old varieties found in early American kitchen gardens can be traced to English sources. The cool climate of England is conducive to pea culture, but unfortunately spring is short in most parts of the United States, so we do not have the luxury of a long, mild growing season. Many of the varieties that do well in England or on the Continent burn up at the onset of our hot summer weather, so our choices are often limited to new heat-tolerant varieties like the Italian bush pea *pisello nano sole di Sicilia*—a very fine pea, incidentally. On the positive side, sugar peas are also tolerant of hot weather, and we have recently discovered how well they fit into a lighter style of cooking. In fact, peas are an important source of vitamin E and therefore should not be omitted from a properly balanced diet.

Amelia Simmons, in her *American Cookery* (1796, 15), mentioned a number of peas for which there is considerable historical literature but which are seldom seen today, even among seed savers. These include the Crown Imperial, considered one of the best for our climate in the colonial period; the Crown pea; the Rouncival, also called Egg Pea or Dutch Admiral; and the Spanish Marotta. George Lindley commented in his *A Guide to Orchard and Kitchen Garden* (1831:567) that the Egg Pea and Spanish Marotta were considered poor man's peas. This was a comment on his sniffish social attitudes as well as revealing volumes about Amelia Simmons's working-class background. Most of these old varieties

were known from the late 1600s or early 1700s and were grown well into the middle half of the nineteenth century. They were gradually replaced by newer varieties developed in England, Holland, and Germany, but dates of introduction are difficult to determine prior to the appearance of nineteenth-century garden publications that reported on new varieties on a yearly basis.

Americans also began developing their own pea varieties in the nineteenth century. David Landreth of Philadelphia introduced Landreth's Early Bush Pea in 1823, one of the earliest datable American varieties. But there was also a marrow pea called Tall Carolina—an ancestor of Tall Telephone—and a more dwarf small-podded shelling pea called Eastern Shore. Seed savers in this country have tended to preserve the small garden varieties over the tall ones; thus there are quite a few important varieties missing from seed archives.

Extremely useful to the garden historian is an article in the *Gardener's Magazine* for August 1836, which outlines a large field test of peas conducted by George Gordon, a gardener for the Horticultural Society of London. Gordon not only described the many varieties of peas then being grown but also provided synonyms, the various aliases by which the peas were known. In addition, he explained how seedsmen classified peas on a commercial basis by dividing them into nine groups based on the type of dry seed or vine. These were divisions based not on taxonomy but on artificial similarities. However, they provided a basis for many of the names of common heirloom peas still grown today, and therefore they are useful to keep in mind.

1. *Common dwarf peas.* These are peas with round pods, white seeds, and vines no taller than 3 feet.
2. *Common tall peas.* Same as the common dwarf, except that the vines are long and require supports.
3. *Dwarf marrow peas.* These have broad pods and very sweet peas when the pods are young. The vines must not be taller than 4 feet.
4. *Tall marrow peas.* These are like dwarf marrow, but with long vines requiring support. Marrow peas are only used fresh as shelling peas or as canning peas. They are not used in cookery in their dry form.
5. *Sugar peas.* The pods of these peas lack the tough lining of other pea varieties and therefore can be eaten like string beans (cooked whole). The seeds are white.
6. *Imperial peas.* This group is characterized by the rampant vines of the marrow peas and the small, round pods of the Prussians.
7. *Prussian peas.* These have highly branched stems and small round pods, and ripen the latest of all the varieties.
8. *Gray sugar peas.* The pods are like sugar peas, but with purple or deep rose flowers. The seeds are spotted or speckled and can be any color but white.

9. *Gray common peas.* These plants have purple or white flowers and seeds of any color but white. Gray peas are generally used as dry peas in cookery because when they are boiled as fresh peas they tend to be bitter.

Peas can be planted early in the spring, as soon as the ground can be worked. They can be planted the same time as onions and potatoes, which for me is usually the end of March. Although it is more work, I prefer to force the peas in flats in my greenhouse and transplant them when the weather is a little warmer. The benefits are threefold: I know exactly which seeds have germinated and which have not, I can rogue out weak vines and plant more seed if necessary, and I avoid the loss of seedlings to cutworms, rabbits, and birds. Peas are extremely vulnerable when they first break through the ground because the new growth tastes good to a wide array of creatures. Once the plants are 4 to 5 inches tall, they are less vulnerable, and if they are planted beside netting, birds tend to leave them alone.

Historically, the taller sorts of peas were grown on devices called "pea sticks." The illustration from the *Gardener's Magazine* for June 1828 shows what they looked like. The stake shown is 6 feet tall and measures 3 by 1½ inches thick. Holes have been drilled through the stake at even intervals, and these have been stuck with elm or hazel limbs—these two types of trees produce small limbs that are ideal for this application. For taller sorts of peas, like the Carling, the stakes would be twice as tall. I like this old method of growing peas because it is environmentally friendly in that it uses no plastics or artificial materials and puts to use small branches that might otherwise end up in the township dump. The branches and dead pea vines can always be chipped for mulch at the end of the season, and the stakes themselves can be reused for several years.

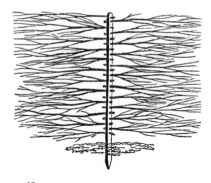

Pea sticks arranged for pea vines.

American Wonder
Pisum sativum

No matter what pea I plant in the garden, this late nineteenth-century variety is consistently the first pea to flower and usually the first to produce peas. Thus, it is well deserving of its name. The pea is a fixed hybrid of Champion of England and McLean's Little Gem, and also goes by the name Early Dwarf. It was given considerable attention by Vilmorin (1885:422) as well as many other popular writers on kitchen gardens.

American Wonder has white flowers on 10-inch, bushlike vines; anything taller than this is not American Wonder. The 2-to-2½-inch pods yield 3 to 5 shelling peas, but there are not many pods on each plant, so it is necessary to put in at least 100 vines for a worthwhile crop. I have planted forced vines from my greenhouse on April 21, only to have them in full bloom a week later, which is impressive by any stretch of the imagination. But while American Wonder may produce early, it also finishes early, so it should be planted as a first crop in conjunction with later varieties.

Peter Henderson (1904, 261) considered American Wonder one of the finest peas for kitchen gardens, and the woodcut below is reproduced from his book. It is an honest representation of the pea when the pods are ready for harvest, but there are quite a few little vines crammed together—perhaps 10—to create the effect. A similar pea, but 2 inches taller, is the old *gloire de Quimper* (SSE PEA 220), a variety developed out of the *très-nain de Bretagne* of the 1830s. It sometimes pulls ahead of American Wonder when planted at the same time and, as far as I am concerned, produces one of the finest *petit pois* of any dwarf variety.

Seed savers should note that the dry pea of American Wonder is round, smooth, and marbled with two tones of green, although some seeds also have small dimples. Do not grow it near varieties with similar seed and pod type, for there will be no way of knowing if a cross has occurred. Also, always be on the lookout for unusual peas with off colors or textures. These may be sports or crosses that could very well produce a new and distinctive variety.

Arbogast Sugar Pea
Pisum sativum

This pea was recommended to me by a member of Seed Savers Exchange who was interested in a possible connection with the Pennsylvania Dutch Arbogast family. That genealogical footnote has not yet crystallized, but there is good reason to believe that this excellent sugar pea is none other than David Landreth & Sons' once popular Tall Sugar Pea by another name. What is certain is that this pea is an old type of gray sugar pea and is therefore more closely related to the

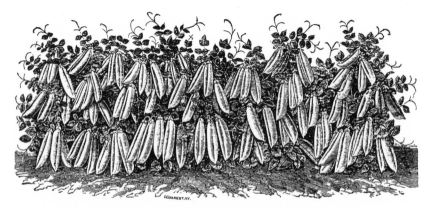

American Wonder Pea

Blue Pod Capucijner and a red pea from Brazil called *ervilha torta flor roxa* than to the common sugar peas of today. Indeed, the Arbogast pea is special in many respects, for it does not fit any of the common gray varieties known before 1850 other than the purple flowering variety sold by Landreth.

The seed is wrinkled red-brown with dark brown speckles. The seed germinates better if soaked overnight in lukewarm water the day before planting. The vines attain a height of 7 to 8 feet and require trellising or some other very sturdy support. The pods measure 3½ to 3¾ inches in length and, when fully mature, contain 7 seeds. When planted in mid-April, the vines begin producing toward the end of May, peaking during the first half of June. Cropping can be extended by continuous harvesting, especially if the vines are kept well watered. The young pods are large, flat, and crispy. They are delicious raw.

Arbogast Sugar Pea also known as Landreth's Tall Sugar Pea

Blue Pod Capucijner
Pisum sativum

The Capucijners are a Dutch category of pea equivalent to the English grays. Because they are hardy, many of the early Capucijner-type peas were sent to the Pennsylvania Dutch by Mennonites in Holland, probably as early as 1683. Folklore has assigned the development of the Capucijner pea to Capucan monks in Holland. While it may be true that a certain old type of pea now known as gray or capucan evolved in the cloister gardens of these monks during the late Middle Ages, most of the named varieties that belong to this group were created or perfected much later by Dutch seedsmen. The names have served for a long time as convenient tags for a type of pea, not necessarily denoting their origin. The Blue Pod Capucijner is a case in point, for in France it was known as *pois à crosse violette,* nothing in the name to do with monks.

Indeed, it is simply called *pisum magnum peregrinum* in the *Hortus Eystettensis* (Barker 1994, color plate 59), where it is depicted with two flowers fading to blue. This reference would date the pea to at least the 1580s. Furthermore, it may be equated with the old purple-podded gray pea of England, a gray sugar pea of robust growth reaching 6 to 7 feet tall, thus requiring substantial support. The 2½-inch pods contain 5 to 7 seeds,

Blue Pod Capucijner Pea

but it was not when the pods were full of seeds that the pea was harvested for cookery. Rather, it was when the pods were very young and underdeveloped like young scarlet runner beans (page 79). At that stage of ripeness, they were boiled or steamed until tender and eaten like string beans. The texture of the miniature pea pod is similar to that of a runner bean, slightly crinkled on the surface like the creases in leather. Dare I mention that the mature pods of the Blue Pod Capucijner are exactly *like* leather? If the peas have matured that far, let them run to dry peas. They make excellent porridge in that state. But this pea has other assets worth mentioning.

It is spectacular. The flowers are bicolored, rose pink and wine red fading to bright blue as they wilt. They are followed immediately by tiny deep maroon pods that change to inky blue as they mature. This is one of the most decorative peas I have ever raised and is always a conversation piece for visitors.

There is another Capucijner worth mentioning, the Raisin Capucijner (SSE PEA 10), a dwarf or bush type with 3-foot vines. The plants ramble over one another and produce an abundance of peas in about 60 days. The very young pods can be cooked like snow peas, but it is the dry pea that was used in historical cookery, especially in peas porridge. This is a perfect crop for restoring the soil where potatoes have been grown. After harvesting the seed, I turn under the vines as a green manure. Incidentally, the dry peas do indeed resemble raisins.

Carlin or Carling Pea

Pisum sativum

The Carling Pea (SSE PEA 163) is a tall gray pea growing on 8-to-9-foot vines and harvested strictly as a dry pea. The seeds are small and brown in 3-inch pods, somewhat resembling a horse bean (page 95). The flower is pale pink with deep rose veins. The entire plant has the appearance of great antiquity, and well it should, for this is considered one of the oldest surviving strains of peas in England, dating perhaps from the Elizabethan period. As such, it may represent a pea similar to those brought to America by English settlers in the early 1600s. The name, however, is fascinating because it alludes to an English custom of great antiquity.

The pea takes its name from Carlin or Carling Sunday, a medieval feast day still observed in northeastern England. According to John Brand in his *Observations on Popular Antiquities* (1900, 57–61), the name derives from Old English Care or Carle Sunday—in German, *Charson-tag*—the second Sunday before Easter. On this day a dole was given to the poor in the form of peas, a custom recorded in England as early as the twelfth century. The observance generally centered on March 12,

Carlin Pea dating from the Middle Ages.

which on the Celtic calendar was an important station in the lunar week. The original pagan significance of the day has been lost under layers of Christian observance, but it survives in the popular practice of serving refried peas free of charge at ale houses, or to guests at home with ham.

The general practice was to boil the peas about 20 minutes until soft, then drain and fry them in butter or lard until crisp (about 2 to 3 minutes). They were then served with salt and pepper or with sugar and vinegar as a bountiful snack, giving rise to the old English saying "Carling Sunday, farting Monday."

The vines require extensive trellising unless grown in the medieval manner, allowed to ramble over dead underbrush brought into the garden. The Carling pea ripens the same time as another heirloom field pea called *Golderbse,* a strain of a rare old pea called the Danzig Pea by Fearing Burr (1865, 519–20). The rampant vines of *Golderbse* and Carling peas can be shredded and used as a green manure. The old practice was to set fire to the dead vines on August 1, the Celtic feast of Lughnasa, thus burning up the brambles as well as providing the ground with potash and an end-of-harvest purification.

Champion of England

Pisum sativum

The original name of this pea was Fairbeard's Champion of England, introduced in England by William Fairbeard in 1843. It began as a mutation or sport of Knight's Dwarf White Marrow

Pea and quickly became one of the most widely grown peas in England and the United States. Since Knight's Dwarf White Marrow Pea was also known as Glory of England, it is not difficult to see how Fairbeard arrived at a name for his pea. Glory of England was known in the United States as the Wabash pea.

The vines of Champion of England are 5 to 6 feet tall (more generally 5), with branches beginning at about 18 inches from the ground. The plant produces 3-inch pods at each lateral joint, thus distributing peas over the plant—a good feature for avoiding top-heavy vines. The pods contain 6 or 7 peas, which become shriveled and pale olive green when ripe. This white-flowering variety is considered a late pea because it will withstand some of the hot weather we get in this country toward the middle of June. Peter Henderson (1904, 263) recommended it as "the best of all the late varieties."

Champion of England Pea

I plant the pea in early April and have peas by the middle of May. Harvesting the dry seed is thus finished by the middle of July, and space in the garden is freed for other crops. I should point out that the Champion of England pea in circulation among seed savers is only 1½ to 2 feet tall, which does not conform to the old descriptions. In all other respects, however, it appears to share similar features.

Dutch Gray
Pisum sativum

The pea that has been preserved under this name (SSE PEA 185) is not the original English Dutch gray of the past. That pea, also known as Gray Rouncival, produced 8-foot vines and broad, stumpy pods that were somewhat flat. The brown seed was flecked with yellow, had a black eye, and was considered only fit for field culture. The heirloom that is now being cultivated as Dutch gray is indeed an old gray pea as defined by Gordon, but of a dwarf type, for its vines are no taller than 36 inches, many shorter than that. The olive-tan seed is almost identical to the Arbogast sugar pea, but larger, both varieties thus resembling a medieval horse bean (page 95). The flower is yellow-ocher tinged with rose in the throat and would make a striking cut flower if it were a sweet pea.

The period of cropping is very short. If I plant these peas toward the end of April, blossoming is completely finished by early June. Harvest of the dry peas follows 2 to 3 weeks later, depending on the weather. Therefore the space can be reused for a second planting of beans or cucumbers, or such hot-weather greens as Celtuce (page 179) or Tetragonia (page 331). This pea is an excellent yielder, with 4 to 5 peas in each 3-inch pod. The dry pea may be cooked like a dry bean or ground for pea flour. Pea flour makes an excellent flat bread.

Dutch Gray Field Pea

Magnum Bonum
Pisum sativum

This is my idea of the perfect late-season pea. An English pea developed during the latter part of the nineteenth century, it is an excellent companion pea to Tall Telephone because it begins to crop almost on cue as Tall Telephone stops. Planted on the first of April, the pea does not begin to blossom until the middle of June—there is no hurrying it. And like Tall Telephone, it requires substantial trellising for support, since the peas form mostly at the top of the vines.

The vines measure about 9 to 10 feet in length, producing 3⅓-inch pods with about 6 plump peas per pod. This is a shelling pea not to be overlooked, as the peas are sweet and delicious to eat even when they are raw. The pods themselves are round and hang down straight. While they are not good eating, they can be boiled with leeks and bay leaves to create an intensely flavorful vegetable stock.

Marrowfat Pea
Pisum sativum

The marrowfats are generally treated as late or main-crop varieties since they peak toward the end of June or even July, depending on how late they are planted—later in regions with cool summers. The most esteemed of the English marrow peas were the varieties developed by Thomas Andrew Knight of Downton Castle, Herefordshire. His Knight's Gigantic or Tall Marrow Pea, introduced around 1827, remained popular for many years and was used by subsequent breeders to create a wide range of improved marrow pea varieties. New Englander Thomas Fessenden (1839, 149–50) approved heartily of Knight's peas for New England gardens.

The nineteenth-century American standard for the marrow pea was the large white marrowfat of English origin, a heavy cropper with 5-foot vines bearing long round pods, with 6 or 7 large peas in each. It was cultivated for summer crops and much favored as a soup or canning pea, although it was grown commercially as a field pea to be sold dry. The marrow pea of the seed-saving networks is a dwarf variety, with white flowers and vines ranging from 14 to 16 inches tall. It is similar in many respects to Glory of England, but half the size. Planted at the beginning of June, this pea flowers by the end of the month when only a foot tall. The peas crop in early to mid-July and must be harvested daily, or they will turn starchy and bitter.

Prince Albert Pea
Pisum sativum

Named in honor of Queen Victoria's husband, this pea was introduced in 1842 by the London seed firm of Cormack and Oliver. Fearing Burr (1865, 533) considered it indistinguishable from an old pea called Early Frame, a hothouse pea that was one of Thomas Jefferson's favorites.

In Jefferson's day, Early Frame was among the first peas planted, usually under cold frames, and a prolific bearer of high quality peas. A strain of Early Frame developed by the Baltimore seed firm of R. Sinclair Jr. & Company in 1841 and marketed under the name Cedo Nulli or Sinclair's Early is still extant in USDA seed archives.

Unfortunately, Fearing Burr was incorrect about Prince Albert; Early Frame was a bit shorter, about 4 feet tall. It exists, or existed until recently, in France under the names *Michaux de Hollande, pois Baron,* and *pois Laurent.* As far as I am concerned, if Prince Albert is like any other variety, then it is like Early Charlton, a pea that crops about 10 days later than Early Frame. The Prince Albert pea produces 6-foot vines with 2½-inch pods that are stringy when young, for this is strictly a shelling pea, though a good one. It produces pairs of snowy white flowers on long stems. I would consider this one of its salient features for easy recognition. Incidentally, Prince Albert was not alone. The Victoria pea was introduced in 1841. The royal couple can still be grown together, but not too close, mind you, or they will cavort.

Prince Albert Pea

Prussian Blue

Pisum sativum

The Prussians are a type of pea dating from the eighteenth century that were once immensely popular in England and colonial America. Thomas Fessenden (1839, 149–50) considered them a good general pea for a wide range of American kitchen gardens. Seedsman Bernard M'Mahon mentioned them as part of his standard seed stock (1806, 582). Thomas Jefferson grew them in 1809 at Monticello. The list of famous Americans who grew this pea is long. Perhaps because Prussian Blue was developed in Germany, it was already better acclimated to North American conditions, for there is no question that it will thrive in most parts of the United States, except in the Southwest. It was also popular in France for this very same reason, and was known there as the *nain vert petit, nain royal,* and *gros vert de Prusse.*

The truest strain of Prussian Blue produces vines about 3½ feet tall with white flowers. The strain in circulation among seed savers (SSE PEA 89) is only about 2 feet tall and may be descended from Groom's Superb Dwarf Blue, introduced in 1831 as an improved strain of Prussian Blue. The pods measure 2½ inches long and yield 7 or 8 peas per pod. The seed is round, smooth, and a dark blue-green verging on gray, hence the name. Since the vines are tall and narrow, three seeds are generally planted every 2 inches so that the plants can grow close together.

Prussian Blue Pea

Prussian Blue was considered an excellent summer shelling pea by most American gardeners. It was not developed to be eaten fresh, but rather originally raised as a dry pea. Fearing Burr (1865, 514) suggested planting them the first of May for pod production in July—when wilt and a host of other viral problems are most likely to strike. I move planting back to mid-April, so the peas are normally finished podding by the end of June. Crops for culinary purposes can be harvested early, once the pods wilt, and then dried artificially, but seed stock must be vine ripened.

Prussian Blue makes an excellent split pea but, like any dry pea, should never be kept for more than a year. An insightful article, "Why Peas Boil Hard," appeared in the *Gardener's Magazine* (April 1831, 249) and explained that if peas are stored for too long, they will cook "hard," never really softening no matter how long they are boiled. This observation is as true now as it was then, with one further footnote: peas stored two or three years have also lost a significant portion of their nutritional value. This is why it is important to date all stocks of dry peas and beans.

Risser Sickle Pea

Pisum sativum

I always associate early June with sickle peas bobbing on their vines in a profusion of snowy white flowers, the pleasant hum of bees, and gooseberries. Peas and gooseberries do not mix, but they come to season at the same time, and for just a fleeting period on the calendar, my garden is transported to eighteenth-century England. For indeed, the Risser sickle pea is a bona fide eighteenth-century variety. It has been preserved by the Landis Valley Heirloom Seed Project in Pennsylvania, and while the seed came most recently from the Pennsylvania German community, the sickle pea itself has been raised in Pennsylvania since colonial times by both English- and German-speaking kitchen gardeners. The pea was known in England—the probable source for the Pennsylvania seed centuries ago—and mentioned specifically by Mawe and Abercrombie (1779, 482). By the 1830s it was not even a recognized variety by most English seedsmen, nor did Fearing Burr mention it. Yet it is an excellent old-fashioned pea and freer of maladies than many of the more highly inbred varieties.

The name derives from the shape of the pod, which is 2½ to 3 inches long and curving like the blade of a sickle or crescent. The flowers are snowy white and borne on vines that can reach 8 feet in length if the soil is rich. Therefore, the plant requires sturdy support. The small pods are edible like sugar peas, or the peas may be shelled for *petit pois,* 6 to 7 peas per pod.

Tall Telephone
Pisum sativum

Named in honor of Alexander Graham Bell's invention, there are many variations of this wrinkled marrow pea, famous for its huge, fat pods: Tall Telephone Improved (SSE PEA 28), Dwarf Telephone or Carter's Daisy, and its English equivalent known as Alderman (SSE PEA 432). One of the most popular of all American heirloom peas, this is a tall pea indeed, producing 7-to-8-foot vines with hundreds of pods that hang straight down. They measure about 4 to 4½ inches in length and usually contain 8 peas, although there is also a certain percentage of empty pods. The peas are ideal for shelling, and the pods can be boiled to flavor broths and stocks. The fresh peas cook in a microwave oven in about 10 minutes on high.

The vines of Tall Telephone are top-heavy and need strong support, especially after the pods begin to form. Otherwise heavy rains or thunder-gusts will topple them, and the peas will spoil. Constant harvesting will lighten the vines and prolong the harvest, but to ensure a long supply of peas, plant Magnum Bonum for harvests later in the season.

Alderman Pea

Tom Thumb
Pisum sativum

Tom Thumb, named in honor of the famous nineteenth-century midget, was introduced by David Landreth and Sons, of Philadelphia, in the 1850s. It is a smooth-seeded pea that produces about 5 to 6 peas per pod on extremely dwarf vines no taller than 6 to 8 inches. If grown in the open in rich soil, the yield can be very high, but this pea was most often grown in cold frames for production over the winter, the reason for its small size. In the South, where its over-wintering features could be cultivated to better advantage, Tom Thumb was usually planted in the late fall in rows 10 inches apart, the seeds planted about 2 per inch. The tiny flowers are white tinged with green.

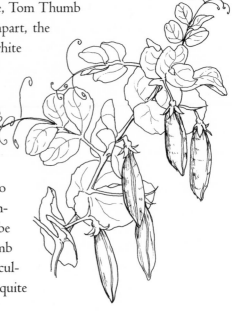

I am not as enthusiastic about Tom Thumb as many gardeners in the South, mainly because there are other varieties that overtake and outproduce it in Pennsylvania, where we do not have the benefit of consistently mild winters. Yet its resistance to freezing is impressive. One April, a cold snap of 26°F froze the ground for two days, but the peas survived unscathed. The vines were completely uncovered, a risk I took because they are said to be hardy to 20°F. However, as a cold-frame pea, Tom Thumb is probably one of the best, well adapted to polytunnel culture, and easily grown in large flats at table height. It is quite impressive to serve my own fresh peas to friends in January, and the point is well made that an efficient kitchen garden does not pause even for the winter solstice.

Tom Thumb Pea

Peppers

I must admit at the outset that I am a pepper gardener by default. I have several hundred varieties in my collection, and every year I add or create a few new ones. I fell into this because of my grandfather's pepper collection and the curious things he acquired from Horace Pippin. While there are certainly many people growing peppers today, very few of them are trying to preserve historical varieties, particularly those of culinary or ornamental merit. Even though I have been growing and sorting out crosses from my grandfather's collection for almost thirty years, there is still a great deal I do not know about peppers. But at least I am mastering the art of keeping my varieties pure, for of all the vegetables in the garden, peppers "cavort" the most.

Historically, peppers were classified by pod type, which had its own logic, since two varieties of the same pod type will cross readily. Therefore they were thought to be related. Unfortunately, it is the flower structure and other far more important genetic similarities that determine true species. In any case, it is important to know how peppers used to be classified in order to understand what writers are talking about in old garden books. Sydenham Edwards's *Complete Dictionary of Practical Gardening* (1807) broke down the pepper kingdom into four groups:

1. Annual capsicums or Guinea peppers, which included pendant, long-podded varieties, red and yellow variants, and erect sorts of a scarlet color. The Calcutta pepper illustrated in Leonhart Fuchs's *De Historia Stirpium* (1543) was assigned to this category. It is still considered a *Capsicum annuum.* The specimens that I have grown are nearly identical to Fuchs's, at least in pod shape and habit of growth. I consider it one of my oldest documented pepper heirlooms. It is extremely hot and extremely rare.

2. *Grossum,* or heart-shaped capsicums, including bell pepper, of which there were red and yellow variants, as well as the "Great Angular Pickling Kind" and the "Cherry Fruited." In this category we would expect to find the Bull Nose (page 256) and all of the peppers that today are classified as pimentos or as tomato peppers.

3. *Capsicum baccatum,* or small-fruited peppers, such as the Texas bird pepper (page 264), the Goat Horn pepper (page 259), and the cayenne called Ole Pepperpot (page 262).

4. *Capsicum frutescens* or all peppers of shrubby growth.

None of this follows modern classification, and in fact, it defies all sense of order. Yet it can be useful, for example, in understanding some of the early varieties grown in Europe.

József Csapó's discussion of Hungarian peppers in 1775 referred to a variety called *Torok-Bors,* which he equated with *poivre de Guinée* (Guinea pepper), belonging to Edwards's first group. All that is known for certain about this pepper is that it was indeed a *Capsicum annuum* (by modern classification) and that it was hot, since Csapó used the word *paprika* to describe it, one of the first references to paprika in any Hungarian work. In Hungarian, only those peppers that are used in a dried state are called paprika. Those that are eaten fresh or raw are invariably described as *zold,* as in *paradicsom alaku zold Szentesi* (Szentes tomato pepper), a popular garden pepper among American seed savers today. The word *zold* means "green" in the sense of young or unripe, as in the early American term "green corn."

Other writers, like Dr. Thomas Cooper of Philadelphia, in his additions to *The Domestic Encyclopedia* (1821, 3:190), favored a more scientific order for peppers based on Linnaeus, such as the long-podded (*Capsicum longioribus siliquis*), the heart-shaped (*Capsicum cordiforme*), and so forth, all of it reading very strangely to modern eyes. Botanist Dr. William Darlington, taking a more cautious stance, noted with intentional vagueness that "several varieties (and perhaps distinct species) with fruit of various forms are to be met with in the gardens" (1837, 139–40). Nurseryman Robert Buist, writing ten years later in the *Family Kitchen Garden* (1847, 97) remarked with a seedsman's flair for overstatement that there were twenty types of cayenne peppers being grown at the time, from the size of peas to the size of melons. Melons, no less! What this scrambled botany tells us is that a great variety of peppers existed in early American gardens, but only a handful were discussed in garden books. Documentation for many of our oldest heirloom peppers is therefore sparse.

This reality struck home further when I discovered in an old print shop a hand-colored engraving of a red beak-shaped pepper published in Philadelphia in 1838. Jean Andrews identified it as *Capsicum chinense* 'Jacquin.' Nicholas de Jacquin (1727–1817) discovered this species during a botanical expedition to the Caribbean region between 1754 and 1759. None of our old garden books even mention *chinense* peppers, let alone that some gardeners were obviously growing them in the United States, fiery hot as they were. Yet it was a *chinense* pepper that I believe to be the earliest documented *Capsicum* grown in what is now the eastern United States. This honor goes to a small orange pepper mentioned in the reports of Swedish geographer-engineer Peter Lindström, who resided on the Delaware River between 1642 and 1648 (Holm 1834, 43). It is the variety known today as the Jamaican Scotch Bonnet. After Lindström, however, history remained mum on the fate of this pepper until it was mentioned in 1768 in Philip Miller's *Gardener's and Botanist's Dictionary.*

It was not until the 1970s that botanists rethought the genus *Capsicum* and rearranged the various pepper species with the help of genetic analysis and a new understanding of the structure of their flowers. There are still a great many unsettled issues in the field of pepper studies, and for the average gardener these controversies may seem complicated or arcane. Unfortunately, this untidy botanical history has a direct bearing on heirloom peppers because we must think about them in two different ways: how horticulturists considered them years ago and how botanists treat them today. Because the understanding of species was so vague in the past, a large number of the heirloom peppers that have come down to us are often heavily crossed. Thus it might be safe to assert that pure strains of truly old pepper lines are among our very rarest heirloom vegetables.

My friend Jean Andrews has helped me immensely in untangling some of the complexities of pepper history. She is the author of a definitive study of the pepper called *Peppers: The Domesticated Capsicums* (1984), recently revised in a new edition. Jean has grown a number of my heirloom peppers in order to help me identify their proper species and to confirm their historical descriptions. I am indebted to her for this, as well as for the unusual peppers that I have acquired from her. We have had a true pepper exchange between us.

Two other books are of use in raising heirloom peppers: Dave DeWitt and Paul Bosland's *The Pepper Garden* (1993) and *Pepper Diseases: A Field Guide* (Black et al. 1991). The first work is a how-to-do-it handbook on growing most of the best-known pepper varieties now raised in the United States. The other is a booklet devoted to diseases and how to identify them. Although scientific, it is not packed with jargon and is easy to use because every problem is accompanied by a clear color photograph. The reason I recommend this book so highly is that most of the diseases affecting peppers also afflict other members of the nightshade family—tomatoes, eggplants, and potatoes in particular. Thus the information is useful for a whole range of garden vegetables. Knowing the problem is often half the battle; many dreadful-looking plant maladies have simple solutions that do not resort to chemicals.

Today, domesticated peppers are divided into five groups or species, having nothing to do with the shape or size of the pods. In fact, there is considerable agreement among botanists about doing away with the species *Capsicum chinense* and collapsing it into the species *Capsicum frutescens*. There may come a time in the near future when we can only speak of four groups of peppers, just as botanists did in the eighteenth century, but for different reasons. For the present, these are the five domesticated species generally accepted by the scientific community. There are other pepper species, but they are wild and not included in this discussion.

1. *Capsicum annuum.* This is doubtless the most diversified of all the pepper species on a worldwide basis. The scientific name means "annual," even though most peppers are actually perennials but, being tropical, are killed by frost. The chiltepin is thought to be the wild ancestor of all the peppers of this species. The Texas Bird Pepper (page 264) is representative of this ancestral type. Other members of this species represented in this book include the Bull Nose (page 256) and Fish Pepper (page 258).

    A Baccatum pepper that I developed through selection.

    The native peoples of Mexico domesticated this species about 2,500 years ago. The Aztecs had dozens of varieties. The Spanish physician Dr. Francesco Hernandez mentioned seven peppers with their Nahuatl names in his *Quatro libros de la naturaleza* (1651). It is probably fair to say that the rage for peppers that has at last conquered the American palate is the final victory of the ancient Aztecs.

2. *Capsicum baccatum.* This is an unusual family of peppers, some with exotic or strange shapes. The species originated in Peru or Bolivia about 2,500 years ago and became one of the favorite peppers of the Incas. The scientific name

means "berrylike," another misnomer, since few of these peppers look like berries. Several of the pendant varieties that I grow have shapes similar to violas or church bells. One is called *biretta vermelha* (USDA PI441551 Brazil) because it resembles a cardinal's biretta. It tastes like hops and is tolerant of light frost. Members of this species will cross sporadically with the *annuum, chinense,* and *frutescens* species, but will only produce sterile hybrids.

3. *Capsicum chinense.* The scientific name was given to it by de Jacquin because he thought the species came from China. This of course is incorrect because the species originated in the Amazon Basin of South America. Furthermore, the whole family is often called *habañero,* meaning "from Havana," although the true habañero is only found in Yucatán and in isolated areas of Cuba. Most of these peppers are extremely hot and are among the most important peppers grown in Brazil and West Africa. The Datil Pepper supposedly grown in the vicinity of Saint Augustine, Florida, for about 300 years belongs to this species, as does the Jamaican Scotch Bonnet and the Chocolate Habañero (color plate 62).

4. *Capsicum frutescens.* The name means "shrublike" or "bushy," and most of the members of this species do in fact develop into small shrubs. This species is widely distributed in India and China. Most of the wild relatives in Brazil and the Amazon are called bird peppers, the most famous of these being the *Malagueta.* In the United States, the best known member of this species is the Tabasco pepper (page 263).

5. *Capsicum pubescens.* This species originated in Bolivia about 6,000 years ago, thus making it the oldest known pepper cultivated by man. It was the most commonly used pepper of the Incas and is often found as an offering in burial sites. The scientific name means "hairy" or "fuzzy," in reference to the leaves, which are covered with soft down. There are no wild forms of this pepper, and this is the only species that will not cross with the others.

Many pepper seeds are slow to germinate, especially the wild varieties and members of the *chinense* and *frutescens* species. These should be started indoors very early in the year, preferably January, since germination may take as long as one month. The strongest plants can then be transplanted into pots and raised as pot plants until ready to plant outdoors.

Peppers prefer slightly acid soil, but more important, they like warm ground, full exposure to the sun, and a spot protected from high winds. Summer thunderstorms often do more damage to peppers than diseases or insects. It is always a good policy to stake large plants securely because the limbs are brittle and easily broken by heavy rains. Most bush varieties, like Tabasco or the Texas bird pepper, will tolerate some shade during part of the day. All peppers are self-pollinating, but cross-pollination between species is common. Cross-pollination of two varieties with the same pod type or two plants of the same species near one another is inevitable. All members of the *annuum* species will cross regardless of pod type; thus a tiny bird pepper can transform a sweet Italian frying pepper into a firebomb in one season. Worse news for the gardener is that the genes determining pungency (hotness) are dominant. Once a sweet pepper has crossed with a hot one, it is very difficult to restore the sweetness. The capsaicinoids that are responsible for making peppers hot to humans are not sensed by birds. This is why birds can feast all day on hot peppers with no ill effects. Since birds do not digest pepper seeds, they are a main distributor of seeds in the wild, and the reason I have peppers coming up like weeds all along my fences and under the trees where birds sleep at night.

The only way to ensure seed purity so that varieties grow true is to isolate them by 500 feet. If they are planted any closer than this, crossing will occur, and only caging will prevent it. Plants must be caged with screens small enough to keep out sweat bees, since they are a primary pollinator after honeybees. Another technique is to stagger blooming by forcing certain designated plants to come to fruit many weeks in advance of those near them. All flowers are pruned from nearby peppers until their turn arises. By carefully monitoring the plants, it is possible to raise a large number of varieties in a small area for seed purposes. I often pollinate plants in the ground with genetic material from potted specimens that have been selected for best traits and maintained several years as perennials. I call these my "stud" peppers.

Pepper seeds are ripe when the fruit is ripe. The seed should be removed and spread on paper towels to dry in an airy room away from direct sunlight. Let the seed dry at least two weeks, especially if the weather is humid. Damp seed will only mold in storage. When the seed is ready to put away, store it in airtight jars in a cool, dark closet. Be certain to date the seed. Viability will last approximately three years, although I have had some six-year-old seed germinate. And finally, always handle hot peppers with rubber gloves, especially when removing seed. The oils in peppers can get under the fingernails and cause severe irritation to the skin there, not to mention other parts of the body that may inadvertently come in contact with the hands.

Besler's Cherry Pepper
Capsicum annuum var. *glabrisculum*

Basilius Besler (1561–1629) did not discover this pepper, nor did he call it a cherry pepper. However, he was the earliest to illustrate it in one of his many famous botanical books, the *Celeberrimi Eystettensis Horti Icones Plantarum Autumnalium* (1613). This was a partial record of the botanical collections of Johann Conrad von Gemmingen, bishop of Eichstatt in Germany. Besler's name for it was *piper minimum siliquis rotundis*, "little round podded pepper." But over the years, almost all peppers of this pod type have been dubbed "cherry," particularly the larger-podded sorts.

The cherry pepper of Vilmorin (1885, 152) was considered more or less the standard among seedsmen, measuring one inch in diameter, much larger than any cherry I have ever seen. Besler's cherry pepper is truer to its name, ranging in size from ½ to ¾ of an inch, the same size as most wild cherries. Besler's is also different from many of the common sorts of cherry peppers because its habit is similar to a dwarf tree, about 2½ feet tall complete with woody trunk and the peculiarly arching stems of its fruit, like tails on shooting stars. This stem characteristic is quite evident in the original illustration of 1613.

Small hot peppers of this type are used throughout the Caribbean in pickles; thus I have put some beside the West India Burr Gherkins in color plate 38. Colonial American cooks grew cherry peppers of several kinds in their kitchen gardens. Many of the varieties came into the country from Jamaica or Cuba. The strain of Besler's cherry pepper that I am growing descends from seed acquired in the 1860s by the Gompf family of Lititz in Lancaster County, Pennsylvania. The Gompfs were Moravians and maintained a kitchen garden stocked with vegetables gathered from exotic places by Moravian missionaries. In this case, the peppers came from eastern Nicaragua. Jean Andrews also sent me seed, and during a comparative growout a few years ago, her plants proved to be identical to mine, which is reason to suspect that this very old pepper may exist in several places under a variety of names.

Besler's cherry pepper ripens late in the season, usually by mid-October in my garden, with brilliant red, waxy fruit. I also have several subvarieties in my collection, one with bright yellow pods, a variegated one with white fruit striped with green like the Fish Pepper, and a snowy white–podded variety that certainly outclasses all of them in terms of rarity. All of these peppers are highly ornamental and can be cultivated as perennials in pots.

Black Bird's Beak Pepper
Capsicum annuum var. *annuum*

Known throughout the French Caribbean as *piment bec d'oiseau noir* and in Spanish-speaking countries as *pico de pájaro negro*, the Black Bird's Beak Pepper is difficult to find in nineteenth-century American seed catalogs. Yet the name commonly appeared in popular literature. It was certainly considered a true variety in E. G. Storke's *The Family, Farm and Garden* (1860, 130) and by Vilmorin (1885, 154), although the latter author assigned it incorrectly to the species *Capsicum frutescens*. Dr. Jean Andrews has vetted the various bird's beak peppers in my collection, and they are all *Capsicum annuum*. This means that in

Black Bird's Beak Pepper

spite of their small size, these peppers will indeed cross readily with most common garden varieties.

In my region of Pennsylvania, several distinct types of bird's beak peppers have been preserved in gardening circles. Some of the most interesting have come out of Philadelphia's old and well-established black community. All of these African-American heirlooms share a common trait: the pods are small, pendant, tapered, and end in a hooked point very much like the upper beak of a parrot. Many are probably not true varieties but simply selections that over the years have assumed certain small variations. This would explain the variety of homey names, from crow beak peppers, hummingbird peppers, and yellow canary peppers (with orange-yellow stems and veining in the leaves), to a whole flock of beaks with appropriate colors and individualistic names that vary almost from garden to garden.

The Black Bird's Beak is undoubtedly one of the showiest of all the heirlooms of this type. It was once well known outside the Caribbean, including parts of the eastern coastal United States. Its date of introduction is not recorded, but it was grown by nineteenth-century Philadelphia black cook and caterer P. Albert Dutrieuille and passed to the de Baptiste family, also involved in catering.

Oral history has suggested that the pepper came from Haiti like the Dutrieuilles themselves. Seed came into my grandfather's collection from Horace Pippin, who was also responsible for passing along the provenance. Because the plant has blackish purple stems, black-green leaves, and fruits that ripen from purple-black to brown and finally to a deep ruby red, it is easy to understand how this pepper could be used as an eye-catching garnish in catering situations.

In the 1890s a few Philadelphia seed houses offered a related pepper called Black Nubian (there was even a Little Nubian). It was similar to black bird's beak in most respects except pod shape, which resembled a small black bell pepper. Pods of the black bird's beak measure ¾ inch in length and must be pendant, two easy features to determine whether or not the plant is growing true to variety. Furthermore, as with Black Nubian, the flowers must be purple. The plant reaches 2½ to 3 feet the first growing season, achieving a somewhat umbrella-like shape. It is perennial in frost-free areas and can be overwintered from year to year in a pot. A late-season pepper, its fruit ripens in September and October. USDA Zones 5 and colder will require pot culture exclusively.

For overwintering in pots, refer to the directions under the Texas Bird Pepper (page 264). If treated as an annual, the pepper reseeds freely—it is almost a weed in some parts of my garden. Subzero weather does not adversely affect seed vitality in fallen fruit, but for seed-saving purposes, it is best to harvest seed only from the most perfect pods and not rely on volunteers each spring.

The fruit in all its varying shades is perfect for ornamental pickles that may need a dash of heat to give them zip. But since the peppers are hot, they must be used sparingly. Because the black pods remain black when cooked, they can be used in black bean dishes. Refer to the Black Turtle Bean (page 69).

Buist's Yellow Cayenne Pepper

Capsicum annuum **var. *annuum***

Buist's Wholesale Price Current of Seeds (1891, 15) listed a long yellow cayenne that was popular among nineteenth-century gardeners. In southern New Jersey, where this pepper was grown extensively for market, it was called Buist's yellow cayenne to distinguish it from other similar long hot peppers, and should not be confused with the *piment jaune long* of Vilmorin (1885, 151). The French variety was thick and stumpy; Buist's is long and narrow.

It is not known when this pepper was introduced into the United States or under what circumstances, but it probably came in with the Demerara sugar trade in the late 1840s or early 1850s even though yellow cayenne-type peppers were known long before then. A variant form, much rarer and slightly smaller in size, has also been preserved under the name *piment jaune sucre*. It is a sweet cayenne utterly devoid of heat that is believed to have come from French Guiana. Older yet is M'Mahon's Long Orange, a pumpkin-colored variant listed in M'Mahon's catalogs as early as 1806. The orange form is very hot and was used dried and powdered in a home remedy for keeping ants out of the kitchen and beetles off cucumber vines.

The fruit on all of these variants, including Buist's Yellow, is pendant and rather close to the ground, considering that the plants range in height from 2 to

Buist's Yellow Cayenne Pepper

2½ feet. Buist's Yellow is slightly wrinkled and twisting, usually with a small claw or hook on the blossom end of the pod, and measures 4½ to 5¼ inches in length. The pods attain a maximum diameter of ¾ inches at the stem end and ripen from pale green to lemon yellow to a deep golden yellow. The plants produce all summer until frost, especially if they are harvested regularly.

For seed-saving purposes, select seed only from pods with fine color, hooked tips, and the slightly twisted appearance.

Bull Nose Pepper

Capsicum annuum **var. *annuum***

Bell peppers called Bull Nose were known to American gardeners in the eighteenth century. Thomas Jefferson grew them, and seed is available from the gardens at Monticello. What distinguishes the Bull Nose from other more recent bell pepper varieties is the crinkled "nose" on the

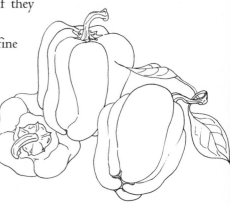

Bull Nose Pepper

blossom end of the pod. Beyond that, it resembles the common bell pepper in most other respects. However, the heirloom pepper that has been preserved as the Bull Nose is not identical to its eighteenth-century ancestor.

Philadelphia still-life painter Raphaelle Peale painted a group of Bull Nose peppers about 1814, and it is obvious that the pods in that period were much smaller than the Bull Nose of today. This would tally with early American recipes that required six peppers where today we would use three—particularly evident in recipes where the weight of six peppers was mentioned. The eighteenth-century Old Black Mango or Blue Guinea Pepper shown in the illustration below is more to the scale of the original Bull Nose, although the pod shape is elongated and pointed.

Many Americans call bell peppers "mangoes" in reference to their former use in mango pickles, a recipe that traces ultimately to India. To mango something meant to stuff and pickle it with a mixture of spices and shredded cabbage. The *Virginia House Wife* (1838:168) included a recipe for mangoing Bull Nose peppers when they were small, and it noted, "Be careful not to cut through the large veins, as the heat will instantly diffuse itself through the pod." This precautionary advice ran through most of the bell pepper recipes of the period and provides very clear evidence that the original strains of Bull Nose were also hot, or mildly so.

Old Black Mango Pepper

The bell or Bull Nose pepper described by Fearing Burr (1865, 607) was much blockier than the older sorts and contained no heat. Yet it had four small lobes on the blossom end, consistent with the peppers painted by Peale in 1814. However, during the latter part of the nineteenth century, a Victorian variety called Bull Nose or Improved Large Bell appeared in many seed catalogs. It measured 3 inches long and 2 inches in diameter and thus was boxier in shape than the old more elongated sort, with thicker flesh, and usually described as sweet. This was most likely created by crossing Bull Nose with Spanish Sweet (a Spanish variety of bell pepper) or with Burpee's Chinese Giant. In any case, it is this crossed strain of pepper that survives today under the name of Bull Nose. In all likelihood, the original Bull Nose is extinct.

Elephant's Trunk Pepper

Capsicum annuum var. *annuum*

Victorian seedsmen created a number of novelty peppers as much as marketing gimmicks as a challenge to the plant breeder's ingenuity. Today, the macho qualities of heat seem to guide the pepper industry; in the past, size and curious shape were what counted, and the Elephant's Trunk pepper has both size and shape. Popular in the 1890s and illustrated in the Maule seed catalog for 1898, this pepper was named in honor of Jumbo, a famous nineteenth-century circus elephant. It is not synonymous with a French variety of cayenne from the same period called *trompe d'elephant.* An American variety that is still a hit with children and any gardener fond of unusually sweet peppers, it is also ideal for culture in pots or tubs on a terrace.

The pods measure 10 to 12 inches in length, virtually dragging the ground, since the bushes are low, barely 1½ feet high. The general shape does indeed resemble an elephant's trunk, at most 3 to 4 inches in diameter at the top, often half that. The pods are thick and fleshy, usually divided into three long, tapering seed chambers that end in three lobes resembling the tip of an elephant's trunk. When fully ripe, the pods turn a bright scarlet red and have a slight cherry flavor.

These peppers are middle to late season, coming into peak production toward the end of August or early September. They will not do well in areas colder than USDA Zone 5 unless cultivated in pots and protected from cool nights. The plants require sturdy support, since the fruit will pull the bushes to the ground, especially during heavy rains.

Elephant's Trunk Pepper

Fish Pepper

Capsicum annuum var. annuum

The origins of the Fish Pepper are obscure. The Aztecs had a variety of pepper called White Fish Chili described in the 1569 *Florentine Codex* of Spanish friar Bernardino de Sahaguin (1963, 68). A pepper with this name existed in the early nineteenth century, but it is not certain that it was the one under discussion. All that has been ascertained thus far is that the Fish Pepper shown in color plate 65 was an African-American heirloom that began as a sport or mutation of a common serrano pepper sometime during the 1870s. Over time it became a fixed variety, but it was never sold commercially.

Seed was acquired by my grandfather from Horace Pippin, who said that the variety originated near Baltimore. By 1900, throughout the region stretching from Washington to Philadelphia, Fish Peppers were raised almost exclusively in the black community for use in oyster and crab houses, and especially for dishes using terrapin. It was one of those "secret" ingredients favored by cooks and caterers to spike a recipe with invisible heat, for the Fish Pepper was used primarily when it was white, and it could be dried to retain that color. This feature was a culinary plus in the days when cream sauces reigned supreme.

H. Franklyn Hall, chef at Boothby's Hotel in Philadelphia at the turn of this century, was a great admirer of the Fish Pepper. His *300 Ways to Cook and Serve Shell Fish, Terrapin, Green Turtle* (1901) is now considered a classic by food historians. But the pepper was not difficult to find, at least not years ago, because many fish markets carried it in conjunction with their other foods, even pickled with clams. Today, this pepper is almost forgotten, although it is available through Seed Savers Exchange.

The plant grows on sprawling bushes about 2 feet tall that are ideal for pot culture on a terrace. Since the leaves are variegated with patches of white, gray, and dark green, the pepper is a conversation piece throughout the season. As the fruit ripens, it changes from white with green stripes to orange with brown stripes, then red. Seed can be saved only from red pods.

The Fish Pepper undergoes genetic turmoil every so often, no doubt owing to its origin as a mutant. This will express itself in the form of weak, top-heavy plants, or occasional sterility. Therefore, seed should not be saved from one plant alone but from at least six different individuals. Combine this seed at the end of the season so that the genetic mix for next year's planting is as varied as possible. Furthermore, keep the plants within 15 feet, or better, plant them 3 feet apart in a square so that there is maximum cross-pollination. The fish pepper crosses readily with other common garden peppers and will spread the mutant gene that causes its distinctive coloration. For seed purity, keep it at least 500 feet from other peppers in the vicinity, and select plants from the *last* seeds to germinate.

Goat Horn Pepper
Capsicum annuum var. *annuum*

Cayenne is a city in French Guiana on the northeast coast of South America. The pepper bearing its name may have originated there at a very early date. What we know for certain is that it was not a *Capsicum annuum* and that its pods were small and cone-shaped. Fearing Burr (1865, 609) described it as too tender for American kitchen gardens, being a species akin to Tabasco. Vilmorin (1885, 151) agreed that the "true Cayenne" was too tender even for France and that it was a species apart from the long cayenne pepper, of which the Goat Horn is a selection. The difficulties in raising the true cayenne outside of the tropics gave rise to a wide range of cayenne substitutes, and that is why the history of the cayenne pepper is now so confusing.

As a matter of convenience in commerce, all long-podded hot peppers were called cayenne, simply because they could be used in making cayenne powder, the culinary condiment. Under that more generic meaning, cayenne peppers appeared in all of our eighteenth-century garden and cookery books. As early as 1805, Bernard M'Mahon offered for sale a variety of cayenne called *Capsicum siliquis longioribus,* or Long Drooping Pepper. This was more or less equated with the *piment long de Cayenne* offered for many decades by the Vilmorins of Paris and eventually illustrated in the *Album Vilmorin* (24:1873). In color and pod shape it is nearly identical to the Goat Horn.

Since it is an *annuum,* the Goat Horn will come to fruit much more readily in northerly regions than tropical species related to Tabasco. Furthermore, this long, narrow pod type comes closest in appearance to the ersatz cayennes raised in early American kitchen gardens. It is also a handsome plant, growing about 2½ to 3 feet tall. The pendant pods are black-green when unripe, an important color factor when cooking them in vinegar in the green state. Since vinegar tends to bleach some shades of green, a pepper that holds its color during processing is an asset to cooks who want their sauces visually appealing.

The pods, which eventually ripen to a bright coral red, measure about 6 inches in length and ½ inch in diameter at the stem end, tapering to a point. The pepper is an excellent representative of its type and dries well, an important feature for a pepper that is to be ground to a powder. If this heirloom pepper has a drawback, it would be its lateness in coming to fruit, ripening in early to late October. Therefore it probably would not do well in areas of the country where summers are cool and short. Shorter-podded varieties like Ole Pepperpot would be better adapted to that kind of climate.

Goat Horn Pepper

Hinkelhatz (Chicken Heart Pepper)
Capsicum annuum var. annuum

The *Hinkelhatz* is among the oldest varieties of hot pepper preserved by the Pennsylvania Dutch. It has been cultivated by this people for such a long time—well over 150 years—that it not only comes with an ethno-idiosyncratic name, it also comes in several distinct colors, the two most common being red and yellow. The Pennsylvania Dutch name means "chicken heart," which describes its shape and size, for it is not a large pepper, measuring some 1¼ inches in length and ¾ of an inch in diameter at the stem end. The pods taper to a blunt point and are covered with tiny bumps and wrinkles.

Maxatawny Hinkelhatz Pepper

I had assumed for many years that the *Hinkelhatz* was descended from the Jamaican Scotch Bonnet, but this was not the case. Charles L'Ecluse illustrated the *Hinkelhatz* pepper in his *Curae Posteriores* (1611, 99), but no place of origin was given. Presumably, it was Mexico. Jean Andrews grew this pepper for me and confirmed its taxonomy: it is not a *Capsicum chinense* but rather a *Capsicum annuum*. I remain convinced, however, that it must have a touch of habañero in its veins, because it has the same smoking heat.

David Lloyd, while discussing peppers in his *Economy of Agriculture* (1832, 83), wrote rather cryptically, "The heart-shaped kind is generally used for pickling." A Quaker living among the Pennsylvania Germans, he must have known the *Hinkelhatz*, although it is also possible that he had the heart-shaped pimento pepper in mind. In any case, the *Hinkelhatz* was rarely eaten raw. It was a pepper used almost exclusively in pickles.

The Pennsylvania Dutch cooked and pureed the *Hinkelhatz* to make pepper vinegar, a condiment similar to Tabasco sauce. Such a recipe appeared in the 1848 Pennsylvania Dutch cookbook called *Die Geschickte Hausfrau*, which I translated and published under the title *Sauerkraut Yankees* (1983, 170). Pepper vinegar was often sprinkled on sauerkraut, especially the recipes made with garlic vinegar. More recently, the *Hinkelhatz* figured in a late nineteenth-century condiment called Shirley sauce. A recipe for this pickle sauce using eight small *Hinkelhatz* peppers appeared in a Bethlehem, Pennsylvania, cookbook called *Recipes and Menus* (1921, 178).

The *Hinkelhatz* is a prolific producer but ripens late in the season, in Pennsylvania usually by mid-September. The bushes are compact, about 1½ to 2 feet tall, as can be seen in color plate 67. Both the yellow and red varieties are shown. My friend Al Lotti discovered an orange variant near Maxatawny, Pennsylvania, preserved among a small circle of Mennonite farmers. Since its shape is more toplike and its fruit much smaller in size than the typical *Hinkelhatz*, it may represent a collateral strain, or indeed a different species. The Pennsylvania Dutch who raise it consider it a *Hinkelhatz*, so I have included a drawing of it here.

For seed-saving purposes, choose only the most perfectly shaped pods. Reject any that are overly long and narrow or dimpled on the blossom end. This will insure that the distinctive shape is preserved.

Martin's Carrot Pepper
Capsicum annuum var. *annuum*

I have often been tempted to call this the Pennsylvania Dutch jalapeño, since it can be used like a jalapeño in cookery. The Pennsylvania Dutch who pickle it whole often serve it stuffed with peanut butter, which makes an interesting hors d'oeuvre, especially when eaten with salt pretzels and beer.

This rare and very old heirloom is believed to have been introduced or developed in the nineteenth century by Mennonite horticulturist Jacob B. Garber (1800–1886) of Lancaster County.

It was preserved for many years by the Martin family of Ephrata, Pennsylvania. The Old Order Mennonites who grew it in that neighborhood knew it as the *Mordipeffer* or as *Mordis Geelriewe Peffer*. A smooth-podded relative of the jalapeño, it derives its name from its distinctive shape and color: long, narrow, carrot-shaped fruit resembling the old Early Horn carrot (page 124). The pepper requires about 120 days to bear fruit, which ripen from pale green to brilliant orange, then turn a deep orange-red. Pods range in length from 3 to 3½ inches and are mildly hot to hot, depending on ripeness. Overall plant height is normally 2½ feet, although the bushes tend to sprawl close to the ground when in fruit. The fruit itself is fleshy and keeps well in cool, dry storage, in some cases for as long as 2 months. Thus it is possible, with some planning in advance, to have fresh peppers into January.

Ole Pepperpot Pepper
Capsicum annuum var. *annuum*

Perhaps it is best to begin with a soup called *mondongo*, a pepper called chiltepe, and Schell's Long Red Cayenne. Schell's pepper was essentially a selection of the large Mexican chiltepe pepper, trained to grow on a low bush for field culture. It was a variety sold to truck farmers in the 1920s by the Walter S. Schell seed company of Harrisburg, Pennsylvania, as well as by William Henry Maule in Philadelphia. This pepper was intended to supply the kitchens of the Horn and Hardart cafeteria chain with peppers for its once-famous pepperpot soup, not to mention a number of soup and scrapple companies in the region that needed fresh cayenne for seasoning. Not only is the chiltepe a pepper of great antiquity, a pod of it floating in *mondongo* (Mexican tripe soup) was considered the only proper finishing touch by Mexican cooks. Philadelphia tripe-based pepperpot is a Yankee relative of *mondongo* demanding a similar marriage of tripe and peppers. Most of the heirloom hot peppers that have survived in the Philadelphia region were connected, in one way or another, with the city's pepperpot soup culture, especially in the heyday of the nineteenth century, when this spicy soup was sold by vendors in the street.

This background history provides the explanation for the name of the cayenne pepper under discussion. Ole Pepperpot is not nearly as hot as a true chiltepe, which may explain why it was more acceptable in upper-class cookery years ago. The pepper was preserved by two families of black Philadelphia caterers, the Augustins, who were famous nationally in the 1800s, and the de Baptistes, who later married into the Augustin clan. The Augustins did not raise the pepper themselves; someone raised it for them under contract. Yet interestingly enough, Ole Pepperpot contains a "blush" of chiltepe, for it ripens like a chiltepe, with a hint of orange at its extremities while still partially green. However, the pods are much different, being twisted, sometimes even curled, about 4 inches in length and ¾ of an inch in diameter at the stem end. On the blossom end or tip of the pod there is usually a small hook that is sometimes quite pronounced. The plants are tall, often 3½ feet, and branching. The pods ripen by midsummer and produce heavily until frost.

The *Album Vilmorin* (1873, 24) illustrated an identical cayenne, but yellow in color. If Ole Pepperpot came to America with the Augustins, then it arrived about 1816 while Peter Augustin served as chef to the Spanish ambassador in Washington. Beyond this, very little else is known about the early history of this pepper, except for two interesting coincidences. The Ram's Horn pepper, preserved by the Fischer family in North Carolina since the early part of this century and now part of the Heritage Farm seed collection (SSE PEP 13), is similar in shape to Ole Pepperpot and may represent a collateral genetic line. Furthermore, the so-called Penis Pepper now so popular among pepper fanciers is a direct descendant of Ole Pepperpot. The tell-tale hook is still there, but sunken into a heavily wrinkled pod. Having crossed Ole Pepperpot with Elephant's Trunk pepper to create a little monster called Love Gun, I know how this works.

In any case, it would appear that the nineteenth century ancestors of Ole Pepperpot were widely distributed along the coast of the eastern and southern United States. Because of its close association with black cookery in this country and the fact that seed came to my grandfather from Horace Pippin, history has set this pepper apart as one of the important representative heirlooms from the African-American community.

Tabasco Pepper
Capsicum frutescens var. *tabasco*

Made internationally famous by the McIlhenny family of New Iberia, Louisiana, this is a pepper that takes its name from a sauce. Introduced without a name into Louisiana about 1848, it became the primary ingredient in a pepper vinegar originally called Extract of Tabasco Pepper, later known as Tabasco Pepper Sauce. The originators of the sauce gave the pepper its name because they believed that it had come from the state of Tabasco in Mexico. In fact, this pepper is not found in Tabasco. Nevertheless, the pepper has been cultivated by the McIlhennys for such a long period of time that it has evolved into a variety completely unlike others of its species. It is also the only member of the *frutescens* species cultivated on a commercial basis in the United States.

The pepper is well known for its heat, although it is not as hot as a habañero. Lovers of hot pepper in the nineteenth century turned to the Tabasco pepper, and for many years W. Atlee Burpee of Philadelphia offered seed that came directly from New Iberia. Unfortunately, this pepper requires a long growing season because the pods do not begin to ripen until early November. In my garden this means that I can raise enough ripe pods for seed, but most of the crop is still green or unripe when I have my first frost. Southeastern Pennsylvania is about as far north as the Tabasco pepper can be cultivated.

The gardener's rule of thumb is that the Tabasco pepper can be grown successfully anywhere that figs can be grown without winter protection. This means that the pepper is best suited to the South or Southwest. However, for culinary purposes, one or two plants are ample, and therefore, in cooler parts of the country, the pepper can be grown in pots. It makes an impressive pot plant, since it stands 3 to 4 feet tall, upwardly branching, and is covered with small 1½ inch long, slender pods. The pods are erect and ripen from pale green to yellow, orange, then red, quite showy when in full fruit.

Texas Bird Pepper
Capsicum annuum var. *glabrisculum*

The Texas bird pepper that I grow came to me from the collection of Dr. George Thomas (1808–1887), a plant collector once well known in my region for his keen interest in the rare and unusual. Thomas's original seed came from Bernard M'Mahon, and he propagated the plants as hothouse ornamentals. The reason that Thomas took such an interest in this South Texas weed was that M'Mahon obtained his seed from Thomas Jefferson. Thus, to complete the circle, I recently sent seed to Monticello for the heirloom seed program now underway there.

According to Jefferson's *Garden Book* (1944, 512–13), Samuel Brown sent Jefferson a parcel of small ovoid peppers from Natchez in May 1813. Brown had collected the peppers in the vicinity of San Antonio and reported that they grew wild throughout southern Texas. American settlers in the area referred to them as turkey peppers or bird peppers because wild fowl of all kinds found the ripe fruit irresistible.

Jefferson sent most of the pepper samples to Philadelphia seedsman Bernard M'Mahon, who in turn propagated the seed and sold it throughout the United States. The fruit of this old strain is ovoid, although there is a variant form with perfectly round berries. The ovoid fruit measures no more than ¼ to ½ inch in length and ripens from green to bright orange-red. They are ideal for drying or they can be used in pepper vinegars, hot sauces, and spicy pickles. In spite of their small size, these peppers are violently hot.

In yet another curious twist of history, John H. Rogers of San Antonio published a small report (1856, 288) recommending Texas bird peppers and predicted that in time they would become an "article of commerce." That was 140 years ago. Perhaps it is safe to say that he was right; this is one pepper that has helped to jump-start modern Tex-Mex cookery.

The Texas bird pepper is perennial in frost-free areas and annual where the ground freezes. Where it is perennial, it defoliates in the fall like a deciduous shrub. Start seed indoors in February or early March, then transplant to the garden after all danger of frost has passed. One bush will produce hundreds of tiny peppers within 120 days. If it is grown in a pot and overwintered in a greenhouse, prune the plant severely and water sparingly between December and February. Allow the plant to defoliate and go dormant. In March, fertilize and water regularly until it pushes new growth and is ready to move out of doors in warm weather.

Tomato Pepper
Capsicum annuum var. *annuum*

There are not many named varieties of tomato peppers that are documented heirlooms, even though this pod type was one of the most common in early American kitchen gardens. Judging from early botanical works and old garden books, it was also one of the earliest peppers known to Europeans. In the very same print in which Basilius Besler illustrated his cherry pepper in 1613, there is a tall pepper plant with distinctive tomato-like fruit. The pod is shaped exactly like the Early Large Red tomato (page 344) and may be considered the standard for what is meant by a tomato pepper. In fact, Robert Buist (1847, 97) confirmed this standard shape, adding that tomato peppers were also mildly hot. Hungarian pepper breeders have taken this pod type and developed innumerable variations, some red, some golden orange, resembling little pumpkins, others limy green when ripe.

Old-style Tomato Pepper

In American gardens, the red tomato-shaped pepper was one of the most common pod types, serving many cooks as their choice of "sweet" pepper, especially those varieties with thick fleshy pods. Fearing Burr (1865, 614) noted that there were several subvarieties even then. In my section of the country, the most commonly raised tomato peppers are the small varieties like the one depicted in the drawing to the left. These measure about 1½ inches in diameter and 1 inch thick. I offer this variety under the name Weaver's Mennonite Stuffing pepper through Seed Saver's Exchange. It came from my grandfather's collection and was a variety grown by his grandfather near Fertility in Lancaster County, Pennsylvania. Because of their small size, they are popular among the Pennsylvania Dutch for pickling or for stuffing with cream cheese, to be eaten as an hors

Weaver's Mennonite Stuffing Pepper

d'oeuvre. This small pod type is documented at least to the 1860s and may be considered a miniaturization of the larger-podded varieties.

The most interesting of the tomato peppers, and one of the most beautiful, is the highly ruffled one sold under the name Red Ruffled Pimento pepper by Seeds of Change. This pepper is illustrated in the *Album Vilmorin* (1865, 16) and is a classic of its type. Both this and Weaver's tomato pepper grow on small plants, at most 2½ feet tall. The small-fruited one is a very heavy producer throughout the summer. Both varieties ripen to a deep ruby red.

Willing's Barbados Pepper
Capsicum annuum var. *aviculare*

During the 1760s Philadelphia botanist John Bartram assembled a large assortment of tropical plants for botanical enthusiast Sir John St. Claire at his estate near Trenton, New Jersey. Avocados, guavas, shaddocks, blood oranges, and many other exotics were procured through Charles Willing on Barbados. This highly ornamental pepper is believed to have been part of the original St. Claire collection. It is a wild pepper (landrace) that has not submitted to the taming hand of gardeners in spite of its long cultivation in pots.

Regarding its botanical origin, Willing's Barbados pepper was probably not native to Barbados, but arrived there sometime in the seventeenth century. It is similar in some ways to the *macho* pepper of Yucatán and Central America, and was preserved for many years as a curiosity by the Cooper family of Cooper's Point, near Camden, New Jersey. From the Coopers, it passed into the collection of Mahlon Moon, a Quaker nurseryman at Morrisville, Bucks County, Pennsylvania. Both families disseminated seed through a large network of gardeners in the Philadelphia and Baltimore regions. There are a number of variant forms or strains.

In Philadelphia it was known as the Barberry or Pipperidge pepper. The diminutive 2½-to-3-foot plants produce dark, boxwood-green leaves, delicately shaped and covered with soft down. The ripe fruit resembles a barberry in size and shape, although unlike a true barberry, it is erect rather than pendant. Because it makes such a striking ornamental, the Barbados pepper was used as a houseplant during the eighteenth and nineteenth centuries. The peppers were also harvested, either green or ripe, and infused in Madeira to make pepper wine, or as some called it, "pepper sherry." This was a popular Caribbean condiment in old Philadelphia and Charleston cookery, particularly as a seasoning for soups, sauces, and fricassees. Caroline Sullivan's recipe from *The Jamaica Cookery Book* (1897, 111) is fairly easy to reproduce.

Pepper Wine

❦

Eight yellow and eight red peppers cut in small pieces or sliced and put in a glass bottle or jar. Pour half a pint of sherry on this, and put it in the sun for twelve hours. It is then fit for use. If you can get cherry peppers, the green and red mixed look very pretty together: some people prefer the tiny bird peppers which are commonly to be had. A little pepper wine is a very great addition to soups or made dishes.

For the yellow and red peppers, use Buist's Yellow cayenne and Ole Pepperpot. An accurate period cherry pepper would be Besler's cherry pepper (page 253).

Seeds of the Barbados pepper are slow to germinate and must be started early in February or March. If treated as a perennial and brought indoors in the winter, the plant will develop a woody stem and grow into a small, spreading bush. Ideal for pot culture, it can be pruned to grow in a dense, compact shape.

Potatoes

Growing heirloom potatoes presents special problems for the gardener because the old varieties are not as resistant to disease as modern ones. Furthermore, potato varieties predating the advent of the blight in the 1840s are to be found only in gene banks or in special botanical collections. Nineteenth-century varieties developed in the 1850s and 1860s from Mexican or South American stock represent the oldest sorts presently available to heirloom gardeners. The best known of these is Garnet Chile, which produced many of the leading American potato varieties of the period.

Prior to the failure of the potato crop in the 1840s, some of the most popular potatoes in my region of the country were Mercer and Foxite. New Englanders preferred Winnebagoes and Blue Jackets. In the Carolinas, it was Pink-Eye and an old variety called Brimstone (also the name of a sweet potato), the latter dating from the early eighteenth century. Each region had its favorites due to soil and climate, and this regionalization is still critical when planning an heirloom potato garden.

When potatoes are propagated through cuttings, each succeeding generation is a genetic clone of its parents, carrying down with it all of the inherited strengths and weaknesses of the variety. Diseases are also passed down, and over the years some heirloom varieties have accumulated so many viruses and other maladies that they are almost impossible to grow successfully without resorting to massive doses of sprays and fungicides. Recently, a new and highly expensive technology called tissue culture has been developed to "debug" old, ailing heirlooms in the laboratory, reducing the potatoes to marble-sized tubers. When planted, these tiny potatoes produce vines that yield potatoes of proper size and true to variety. At present, this treatment is only feasible for seed banks and similar institutional collections. However, perhaps within the next twenty years, it will allow gardeners to grow some of the pre-1850 varieties that once enjoyed great popularity.

Foremost among these would be the Mercer potato, which was sorely missed by farmers in the Middle States well into the 1860s and 1870s. This was a flat, kidney-shaped potato with a slight pinkish cast to the tapered end. It bore early and stored well. Its original name was the Neshannock, often mistakenly called the Chenango. As Charles Hovey's *Magazine of Horticulture* (1844, 310) pointed out, this variety emerged about 1809 from a seed ball in a garden on Neshannock Creek in Mercer County, Pennsylvania. Neshannock Creek is a branch of the Chenango River, and all of these geographical names have gotten muddled together in the history of this potato. The Pennsylvania German agricultural monthly *Ceres* (1839, 55) elaborated on the background of the potato's originator, one John Gilky, an immigrant from Ireland. In fact, Gilky created several subvarieties, including the Red Mercer (also known as Donaneil's Beauty, Mormon, and Olympia) and the Black Mercer, a smooth purple-skinned spring potato with white flesh. This triumvirate of Mercers was profoundly important to the development of later nineteenth-century varieties because the Mercers were viewed as models by which other varieties should be judged. Potato breeders never recreated a blight-proof Mercer, but they did manage to develop a number of varieties that effectively replaced it.

German botanist Edward Pöppig (1798–1868) traveled to Chile and Peru in 1827 in search of the "original" wild potato, which indeed he discovered. His *Reise in Chile, Peru und auf dem Amazon*, published in 1835 and 1836, not only is engaging to read even today, with its minute descriptions of the various potato preparations made by Peruvians (giving the Indian names as well), but historically Pöppig sparked a scholarly interest in native potato varieties from Mexico and South America. Garnet Chile owed its creation in part to his recognition that there was a practical side to experimenting with potatoes from their genetic homeland.

The massive failure of the potato crops in Europe and their historical repercussions of famine and human displacement are well known. The reasons for this disaster are also well understood and provide one of the strongest possible arguments for preserving genetic diversity in all living things, unheeded as this call may be. The potatoes grown in the eighteenth and early nineteenth centuries all descended from a small handful of introductions that were closely related. Through constant inbreeding, new varieties were created, yet genetically they were all nearly identical. When the blight struck, none of these old types were resistant to it, so the disease spread quickly and lethally.

The genetic aspects as we now understand them were not fully appreciated in the nineteenth century, but horticulturists did realize that the plants were inbred and therefore unable to resist disease. As the *Florist and Horticultural Journal* (1854, 163–66) editorialized on the degeneracy of the potato and the "disease of 1846," raising potatoes from tubers was unnatural because it bypassed the seed stage, thus perpetuating weaknesses and rendering them more "fixed and unchangeable." This realization brought about the Great Revival, as it was called, when old, deteriorating potato varieties were crossed with hardier wild varieties from Mexico and South America. This experimentation in the 1850s and 1860s resulted in many of the most popular heirloom potatoes of the nineteenth century. Early Rose stands out as one of the most famous and commercially important. It is still a good potato by any culinary standard, and every time I plant it, I think about its fascinating history. The other potatoes in this section were also chosen on historical merits. But the final test was in the garden. There is absolutely nothing more simple yet pleasantly satisfying than a freshly dug potato cooked to perfection. Potatoes brought out of storage cannot compare.

Potatoes are generally divided into early, midseason, and late varieties. Historically, many households planted one of each in order to keep potatoes in crop over a long period. I raise sixteen varieties of heirloom potatoes and mostly ignore their seasonality because I have more than enough potatoes for my own needs all the time. Other gardeners may create their own criteria. Much depends on questions of storage, for without proper storage it is pointless to consider raising potatoes on a regular basis.

Regardless of the variety, all potatoes are planted essentially the same way. Seed potatoes kept back from the previous year's harvest are cut into pieces, each with an "eye" as shown in the old woodcut. These eyes produce shoots that develop into plants. There is no real advantage to planting a whole potato instead of an eye. The only exception is in ground with very poor soil. In moderately rich ground, potatoes should be cut in half or quartered, otherwise cut them into eyes. I tried planting whole potatoes one year just to get rid of an overabundance of seed potatoes. With some varieties, the resulting crop produced fewer potatoes than those planted from eyes. Since seed potatoes are edible (unless they are green), find a use for the extra ones in the kitchen.

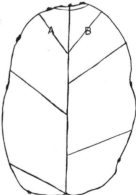

Diagram of a potato cut into "eyes" for planting.

I dig deep trenches, perhaps 14 inches deep, in rows 32 inches apart. The cuttings are planted about 13 inches apart, even for small varieties. If the variety produces many tubers, then space the cuttings 16 inches apart. Crowding only reduces harvest yields. Early varieties are planted in

March in my part of the country. Among the Pennsylvania Dutch, Saint Margaret's Day (March 17) was always considered the "official" day to begin planting potatoes, although of late, strange weather has often upset this schedule. In any case, I am usually ahead of the farmers because I plant in raised beds, which thaw and dry out sooner than open fields. The remaining varieties that I grow are normally planted by mid-April regardless of whether they are mid- or late-season varieties. They bloom at different times and crop at different times anyway.

Once the plants break surface and reach a height of about one foot, I bring in a truckload of mushroom soil (rotted horse manure in which mushrooms have been grown) and mound it at least two-thirds of the way up the stems. I usually do this twice during the growing season to ensure that the tubers are well buried. The mushroom soil creates a loose growing medium around the base of the plants that pays for itself in several ways. Potatoes form perfectly shaped tubers in it, they are not difficult to dig, and the mushroom soil helps renew the ground with humus once the potatoes are finished. I rotate regularly, as all gardeners should, because potatoes leave problems behind.

The most universal problem is scab. Scab is a barklike growth on the skin of potatoes caused by fungus. It does not poison the potatoes and can be removed from eating potatoes simply by paring it away with the skin. But it remains in the ground at least three years and will infect other root vegetables such as carrots and beets. The best method for killing it is by exposing seed potatoes to sunlight. The Pennsylvania Dutch used to spread all the seed potatoes on the floor of their barns for a few weeks so that the sunlight would turn them green. Planting later in the season also helps control scab. I eliminate any seed potatoes that show signs of scab, taking great care not to handle healthy potatoes until I have washed my hands with alcohol. Human hands will spread scab from one potato to the next.

Harvesting potatoes is backbreaking work. I know of one seed saver who digs several tons of heirloom potatoes with her bare hands so that the potatoes will not be damaged. She receives top-of-the-line prices for her picture-perfect tubers, but her hands look like driftwood. I use a pitchfork, wear gloves, and dig gently. Certain potato lovers usually show up to hover on the sidelines with words of encouragement and the keen expectation that I will accidentally impale a few treasured heirlooms, which of course I must give away for immediate cooking. The barter is a bottle of wine, so I make certain to stick a number (not too badly, of course) to keep up the deal.

Once the harvest is in and all potatoes accounted for, pick out the best for seed stock, including any green ones. Green potatoes are poisonous; do not even consider eating them, not even the ones with a small patch of green. Potatoes will store no better washed and dried than if the soil is left on. I wash and dry mine only because I want to be certain I have not missed a green spot or a patch of scab. Also, I can better determine which ones have the best skins. Beyond that, the seed potatoes go into brown paper bags, clearly labeled and dated. The bags are stored in a refrigerator set at about 40° F. The potatoes remain dormant in cool temperatures. I have never had any problems with the small varieties that tend to get soft and wrinkly for other gardeners. On the other hand, I keep the refrigerator spotlessly clean, and I check the seed potatoes from time to time to make certain that none have gone bad.

As an experiment, one year I left Conestoga in the ground until the middle of September, almost two months after it was ready to harvest. This had no effect on the quality of the potato, which happens to be a small white variety with pink eyes. But some of the tubers were attacked by nematodes, wire worms, and other boring insects. These insects only infest a piece of ground where there is food. They can be starved out of a raised bed that is planted a full season with cowpeas. For the other advantages of cowpeas, refer to page 150.

Potato Beetles

Colorado potato beetles (with distinctive black-and-yellow stripes) are another problem, but they have never been a serious one for me. On a weekly basis I spray the plants with insecticidal soap, which imparts an unsavory taste to the leaves. If the spraying is begun early enough in the season, the beetles will be contained because the spray kills the grubs; indeed, they will be the least of one's worries. The greatest threat to an organic potato patch is blight, wilt, or other viral diseases. At the slightest appearance of any of these, destroy the vines by burning them far away from the garden. These sick plants are not worth a salvage operation; while the plants are "recovering" they are also contagious and will spread the diseases to tomatoes, eggplants, groundcherries, and peppers within a matter of hours. Never touch healthy plants after handling sick ones. And kindly ask cigarette smokers not to touch members of the nightshade family. Smokers' hands carry tobacco viruses that are contagious to these plants. Smokers are as good as Typhoid Mary in an organic garden and greenhouse, and I know it irritates them to make a fuss, but after all, there are plenty of other places they can go if they want to smoke.

Finally, purchase organically raised seed potatoes only from reputable seed firms like Seeds Blüm, Ronninger's, Southern Exposure Seed Exchange, or the other seed firms listed at the back of this book. Ronninger's was particularly helpful to me in locating seed potatoes for some of the rare and unusual varieties I now cultivate. They came to my rescue when I wanted to grow out some of the varieties mentioned in the following pages. They are extremely helpful to their customers and, in fact, sent me as a gift seed potatoes for a variety called Charlotte, a small, buttery potato, enormously productive and good in storage. In fact, this is one of the varieties recommended by French chef Joël Robuchon in his *Le Meilleur et le plus simple de la pomme de terre* (1994, 44), a book that has to be the last word on potato cookery. For those tremulous readers who have never grown potatoes and feel intimidated by the idea of planting them, I would recommend growing Charlotte first to get a feel for potato culture. After that, graduate to some of the rarer, older varieties listed in the following pages.

A final question that I have often been asked: Do potatoes produce seeds? Yes. After blooming, potatoes produce seed balls that resemble tiny green eggplants. These usually turn yellow when ripe. Seed can be saved from these balls, dried, and planted in flats in the early spring like tomato seed. They will produce seedlings that can be planted out of doors after the threat of frost has passed. Potato seed does not produce plants that are true to the parent but, rather a mixture of colors, shapes, and throwbacks to ancestral types. Letting heirloom potatoes cross in the garden and planting seed from them is one enjoyable way to create new potato varieties. There are seed savers who have devoted their lives to this highly creative form of gardening. It is by no means a new art, for Amelia Simmons (1796, 11) was convinced that this was the secret to the best of the Irish potatoes. She had this to say in her famous cookbook: "I may be pardoned by observing, that the Irish have preserved a genuine mealy rich Potato, for a century, which takes rank of any known in any other kingdom; and I have heard that they renew their seed by planting and cultivating the Seed Ball, which grows on the vine." This may provide some insight into how it happened that John Gilky was so adept at creating his trilogy of Mercer potatoes.

Bliss's Triumph Potato
Solanum tuberosum

Bliss's Triumph, introduced by B. K. Bliss & Sons of New York, was originally red. It should resemble a larger version of Garnet Chile, round and somewhat apple shaped. It is a good potato for the South; indeed, it was once raised extensively in Bermuda and Florida for sale in northern markets. However, in many of those markets, red potatoes did not sell well, so through selection lighter-colored strains of Triumph were developed, including the white Bliss's Triumph. The white strain evolved simultaneously in several areas of the country and was not the product of any one particular seedsman. In the South, to differentiate it from the Triumph, the old original strain, which was identical in color to it but genetically different, was often marketed under the name Stray Beauty. The convoluted commercial history of this potato at least speaks for its enormous popularity, but it is important to keep in mind that Bliss's Triumph has come down to us as a red, a pink, and a white potato. These differences are only in the skin pigmentation. All three variants have white flowers and white flesh.

Bliss's Triumph is consistently the first potato to push shoots in my garden. In the North, this means that it should be planted late enough in the season that it will not be nipped by frost. This potato is also the most consistent cropper for me, outproducing all others, and a real pleasure to dig because the potatoes themselves are beautiful. Right from the ground, they give off a ping-like sound when rapped and snap like apples when broken open. For boiling and for potato salads, this is my favorite potato. But perfection does not come without its price. The skin of this potato is very thin and easily damaged when dug; damaged potatoes cannot be stored. In hot weather, it has a weakness for the dreaded blight. A watchful eye during hot spells and care in digging will keep both problems under control.

Champion or Vermont Champion Potato
Solanum tuberosum

Introduced in 1881 by B. K. Bliss & Sons of New York, this well-named potato is best boiled in its skin. It is a terrific as a new potato, small, round, great for salads with French dandelion (page 321), upland cress (page 318), or salad burnet (page 314). Toss in a few morels and "smother" this with chopped shallots, and you will have a potato feast made in heaven. Champion is also a first-class dumpling potato, surpassed in excellence only by the Austrian *Kipfelkrumpl*, yet the two varieties stand by themselves and should not be equated.

Early Ohio Potato
Solanum tuberosum

The *American Garden* (1889, 227) remarked that Early Ohio was "emphatically a garden potato, unreliable as a field potato." Never having grown it in a field, I cannot comment on that, but as a garden potato it is indeed perfect. The vines are not large and unwieldy, and the potatoes are a comfortable medium size that ensures good yields on small patches of ground.

Horticulturist D. B. Harrington undertook a large growout of old potato varieties in 1889 and reported on the results in the *American Garden* (1890, 122). He discovered that Early Ohio was being sold under the following aliases: Early Illinois, Prize, Royal Gem, Early New York, and Extra Early Ohio. These varieties are not extinct; they never existed except on paper.

Early Ohio Potato

Early Ohio was introduced in 1875 by the James J. H. Gregory Seed Company of Marblehead, Massachusetts. It was a seedling of Early Rose that came to crop earlier and more prolific than its parent. It is best suited for the North and comes to crop after Bliss's Triumph, almost on cue. The round, somewhat apple-shaped tubers have a parchment-colored skin, with random patches of rose. The skin is not as easily damaged during digging as that of some of the other heirloom varieties. The largest pota-toes in my garden have weighed about 12 ounces each.

Early Rose Potato
Solanum tuberosum

Beauty of Hebron was said to be better; claims against it were already readily available, yet no potato can satisfy all gardeners and all soil types. Early Rose comes close. The *American Agricul-turist* (April 1870, 123) said it very plainly: "We have seen nothing equal to Early Rose for garden culture." One of the most highly advertised potatoes of its time and one of the first in a long series of potatoes created from it, Early Rose was introduced in 1861 with considerable hyperbole by B. K. Bliss & Sons of New York. As Menno-nite seedsman John G. Kreider pointed out in the *Lancaster Farmer* (1870, 41–42), Early Rose emerged from a seed ball of Garnet Chile, the same seed ball that produced Bresee's Prolific, a dwarf variety

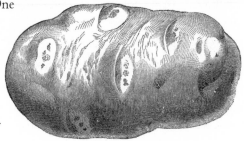

Early Rose Potato

that now appears to be extinct. Its creator was Albert Bresee, a Hubbardton, Vermont, horti-culturist who introduced a number of other highly successful varieties, among them Bresee's King of the Earlies.

Early Rose eventually replaced Pink-Eye in the South and a vast list of other highly regional-ized American varieties. The French were so taken with it that it was depicted in glowing color in the *Album Vilmorin* (1875, 26). Wilhelm Hampel, in his *Frucht-und Gemüse-Treiberei* (Berlin, 1885) declared that it was one of the best potato varieties for hothouse culture. Those were the days when wealthy European aristocrats could afford greenhouses to produce year-round what the markets failed to supply.

On this side of the Atlantic, Early Rose proved to be one of the great economic successes of the latter half of the nineteenth century. Its aliases say it all: Antwerp, Boston Market, Baker's Imperial, Chicago Market, Cayuga, Carter's Early, Clark's No. 1, Early Vermont, Early New Zealand, Early Maine, Early Dustin, Early Mohawk, Early Sunrise, Early Essex, Howard, New York Market, Pearl of Savoy, Roxanna, Sunlit Star, Summit, Spaulding, Vanguard, Waverly, and Watson's Seedling. None of these was anything other than Early Rose by another name. The flower of Early Rose is white. One of its most famous seedlings was Burbank Seedling, introduced by James J. H. Gregory in the latter part of the nineteenth century.

Garnet Chile Potato
Solanum tuberosum

There are two potatoes that may be considered American classics of the nineteenth century. One is Worcester's Seedling, developed by the Reverend Thomas Worcester of Boston and introduced commercially in 1868. The other is Garnet Chile. Regardless of its culinary merits, which are not to be dismissed, Garnet Chile shifted potato culture in this country in an entirely new direction. The Reverend Chauncy E. Goodrich of Utica, New York, introduced this variety in 1853. In response to the blight of 1846, he obtained seed stock from Chile, and from those plants he selected this small, round, pink potato that became the granddaddy of most nineteenth-century varieties we know today. Goodrich's influence was even more pervasive than his famous potato; he published an important article in the *Report of the Commissioner of Patents* (1856, 205–6) on techniques for propagating new potato varieties from seed. This article was circulated among the country's leading horticulturists, and its lessons were soon put into practice. After all, Goodrich was no novice; he had also created many other well-known potato varieties, among them Calico, Goodrich's Early, and Cuzco.

From a culinary standpoint, Garnet Chile is an excellent boiling potato, perfect for salads, and makes an attractive garnishing potato for restaurant cookery. Best of all, unlike many small potatoes, it is an excellent keeper. Oddly, it has never bloomed for me, although I understand that the flower is white.

Green Mountain Potato
Solanum tuberosum

Green Mountain has been popular ever since its introduction about 1885. Round, tan-skinned, with white flesh, it epitomizes the high-starch late-season potato that is often associated with New England cookery. It is an ideal potato for gratin or *Rösti* (grated potato pancakes), pones, or for more substantial dishes—even potato chips, or Saratoga chips as they were once called. The woodcut shows the old device that was used to make the original Saratoga chips. When boiled, Green Mountain cooks snowy white and remains firm. Like Garnet Chile, it stores well. The flower is white.

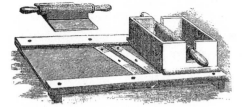

Slicer for Saratoga Chips
(original name for potato chips)

In the Sandusky, Ohio, cookbook of Eliza G. Follett called *The Young Housekeeper's Assistant* (1874, 38), there is a pone recipe for which Green Mountain is particularly well adapted. It is a species of *galette bretonne* that also can be made with white sweet potatoes. Baked in a heavy iron crepe pan, it resembles a large sweet pancake that can be eaten with stewed fruit or jam.

Potato Pone, West India Dish

🐛

Grate two pounds of potatoes, add four ounces of sugar, and the same of butter, one teaspoon of salt and one of pepper, mix well together, butter a baking dish, and bake brown.

Irish Cobbler Potato
Solanum tuberosum

A sport of Early Rose, this early-season potato reminds me of a larger version of Champion, but with a much more pronounced potato flavor and a nutty aroma to the skin. I think the similarity to Champion is in the texture and color of the cooked flesh. When tasted side by side, it is easy to confuse the two. Irish Cobbler is very fine boiled in the skins, which turn light brown when cooked but are covered with patches and irregularities that do not recommend it as the sort of elegant garnishing potato possible with Garnet Chile. This is definitely a homey potato, at its best in rustic country recipes.

Peach Blow Potato
Solanum tuberosum

This is the oldest heirloom variety on my list, dating from before 1850. It is often called Jersey Peach Blow after its state of origin. In fact, it may be the same early potato developed in Burlington, New Jersey, in 1841 alluded to in Charles Hovey's *Magazine of Horticulture* (1841, 73). That "new seedling" was circulated without name for a number of years among Jersey farmers. The vine blooms with a soft peach-pink flower, very attractive in its own right. The potatoes are small, mealy, and have a wonderful potato flavor. Thorburn's White Peach Blow was a seedling of this variety, developed in Monmouth County, New Jersey, and introduced in 1863. It should not be confused with its parent, although the tuber is very similar. A late variety called Bliss's Improved Peach Blow was created by crossing Peach Blow with Excelsior. The tuber resembles Peach Blow, but the yield is nearly double.

Peach Blow Potato

Russet Burbank Potato
Solanum tuberosum

Developed in 1876 from Early Rose, this is the archetypical Idaho potato, perfect for baking and French fries. The tubers are long and rounded on the ends, sometimes attaining very large size.

This potato is difficult to grow in the South; it requires uniform moisture throughout its growing season, and must have loose sandy soil in order to develop well-shaped tubers. I have had very little luck with it but recommend it highly for those gardeners who can meet its cultural requirements. Where it grows well, it produces abundantly, better than some of the russet varieties of more recent date.

Snowflake Potato
Solanum tuberosum

True to its name, this potato is white and flaky. It is also extremely handsome. Introduced in the spring of 1874 by B. K. Bliss & Sons of New York, Snowflake became one of the most popular of the nineteenth-century mealy potatoes. It is perfect for dumplings, potato bread, and stuffings. In D. B. Harrington's potato growout in 1889, the Michigan horticulturist discovered that Snowflake was being marketed under a large list of commercial aliases: Big Benefit, Boston Cracker, Crawford's Seedling, Centennial, Charles Downing, Mayflower, Early English, Pride of America, Early Burlingame, and Potentate. Patriotic labels do not alter the plant, but its commercial success is probably best demonstrated by the number of phony aliases used to sell it. True to its namesake, the flower is also snowy white. However, of all the potatoes I have selected for this list, Snowflake is the least productive. This may be related to my soil type and not a fault of the variety. Anecdotal evidence from other gardeners suggests that this potato may do best in sandy ground.

Snowflake Potato

Pumpkins and Other Squash

Let me begin by explaining that *pumpkin* is merely a term of convenience, for there are only squash. The common distinction that we make between the two is not based on botanical characteristics as we now understand them. On occasion I use the word in this book because "giant squash" sounds peculiar and does not evoke a clear image of shape or size in the minds of American readers. But pumpkins are really a type of squash, and that should be kept in mind at all times.

The word *squash* is derived from the Algonquin word *askutasquash*, something that is eaten green, in an unripe state. We associate this with a category of squash grown during the summer, yet even field pumpkins can be eaten young, and the eastern woodland Indians seem to have enjoyed them that way. The soft cymling or quash (*Cucurbita pepo*) of the early 1800s was a variety of miniature sugar pumpkin, somewhat apple shaped (color plate 74). It was harvested and eaten in the green state like a modern zucchini, but if allowed to ripen, it developed a hard, woody rind like a gourd.

Today botanists divide pumpkins and squash into six species, four of which include all of the common pumpkins and squash grown by American gardeners. It is important to know these botanical classifications because they serve as a useful tool in preventing unwanted crosses. It is possible to grow four types of squash in one garden, provided they are all of a different species. Of the four species, the *maxima* and the *mixta* are the most difficult to distinguish for amateur gardeners.

1. *Cucurbita maxima.* These include some of the largest of our field pumpkins, but fruit size is not a measure of this group. *Maxima* squash grow on very long vines with huge, hairy leaves. The fruit stems are soft, round, and spongy. The seeds can be white, tan, or brown, with cream-colored margins and a thin membrane coating.

2. *Cucurbita mixta.* Spreading vines with large hairy leaves also characterize this group. The seeds are coated with a thin membrane that cracks when the seeds are dry.

3. *Cucurbita moschata.* These plants produce spreading vines with hairy leaves. The stem flares out at an angle where it is attached to the fruit and is very hard. The seeds have a dark tan margin.

4. *Cucurbita pepo.* The plants of this species have prickly leaves and stems that can cause a rash on some people. The fruit stem is angular with five sides. The seeds are cream-colored with a white margin.

Recent field studies have found some indication that pollen from *Cucurbita moschata* may cross with the female flowers of *Cucurbita mixta*. This is probably a rare phenomenon, but precautions should be taken not to raise the two species near each other. In the case of most heirlooms, this finding may be moot, since very few early American squash belong to the *mixta* species. But it is important to remember that all of the squash species produce both male and female flowers on the same plant. In extremely hot, rainy weather or when the plants are subjected to environmental stress, the female flowers will abort by dropping off and thus failing to form fruit. If this happens, harvest the male flowers for stuffed squash blossoms; it is pointless to waste them.

Any list of heirloom squashes will be subjective because there are virtually hundreds of varieties to choose from. I have selected fifteen varieties that I believe represent a full range of choices for gardens with limited space, keeping mind that old fodder crops like the Tippecanoe pumpkin (introduced in 1840) and the Connecticut field pumpkin were never grown in kitchen gardens anyway. *The Farmer's Encyclopedia* (1844, 1009) listed the most popular kitchen garden squashes at that time. There were only nine, and of those I have chosen five that have survived the test of time with remarkable resiliency. In fact, the only squash from the 1844 list that has truly disappeared is Commodore Porter's Valparaiso.

According to the *Gardener's Magazine* (1827, 63), this squash was introduced about 1826. In 1827 *Le Bon Jardinier* noted that a certain Madam Adanson had published directions for cooking this squash in an unripe state in her book *Maison de campagne.* This early flurry of popularity may explain why Commodore Porter's Valparaiso was illustrated in full color in the *Album Vilmorin* (1878, 29). From a distance the squash resembled a rather large, oblong or egg-shaped coconut, the skin being brown and covered with webbing. The flesh was a rich orange, the seeds white. I have no idea how it tasted, but from an esthetic standpoint, it was downright ugly.

Also omitted from my selection are the English vegetable marrow (never popular in the United States), the *cocozelle* or Italian vegetable marrow introduced late in the nineteenth century, and the squash now known as zucchini. At one time, *cocozelle* was used in the East for all zucchinilike squash. During the 1920s and 1930s, the term *zucchini* came into general use in California, and in time the rest of the country followed suit. These are all important squash today, but they are not yet heirlooms that have passed the test of time.

Planting techniques are essentially the same for all pumpkins and squash. They should be grown on hills about 3 to 4 feet apart, depending on the leaf size—large-leafed varieties should be farther apart. For better results, start the seedlings indoors and transplant the strongest ones into large pots. Let the plants grow and become well established in the pots, then set them out on hills as soon as the weather is warm. If the plants are large and growing vigorously before the end of June when the squash beetles come into season, they will better survive the attacks of this insect.

Many of the vining squash will yield larger fruit if they are pruned and only three or four fruits are allowed to develop on each plant. The bush varieties are the most prolific and will produce all season if the fruit is harvested continuously. Squash and pumpkins are heavy feeders and should be fertilized at least three times during the season. Rotate the squash from year to year so that they are grown on the same ground only every four years.

Squash beetles are the plague of all gardens with squash, cucumbers, melons, and pumpkins. A rank-smelling relative of the bedbug, these beetles feed at night by puncturing the leaves, thus causing them to wilt within a matter of hours. If the damage is extensive, the plants will decline and eventually die, or at the very least the fruit will be small and crabbed. During the day the beetles hide on the ground under the vines and can be destroyed individually. Orange eggs are laid in patches under the leaves. If the egg sacks are crushed between the fingers on a daily basis during mating season, this will greatly reduce the beetle population and minimize damage. The hatchlings are gray and white and move in swarms. They are easy to destroy with insecticidal soap, since they do not have a hard shell at that stage. The adults hibernate over the winter and reappear in June. They hide under dead leaves or in compost heaps. If the compost heaps are near the garden, they should be turned over a few times during the winter to expose the beetles to freezing temperatures and thus kill them.

Squash varieties of the same species will cross and therefore should be separated by at least a quarter of a mile. Otherwise, hand pollination is the only method of assuring seed purity. Another method is to plant squash at three-week intervals, harvesting and destroying the plants of the same species in order to let the next planting flower and come to fruit. I have found this to be quite effective in my garden, where large production is less important than variety of crops and seed purity. Furthermore, by destroying the vines of the early plantings, space is freed for other vegetables.

To save seed, allow the fruit to ripen on the vine until the plants begin to die. Choose only the finest specimens with the best varietal characteristics for seed. Harvest the fruit and store in a cool, dry place. Further aging in storage raises seed viability. The seeds may be removed when the fruit is required for cooking. Scrape out the seeds and wash them in a colander to remove the placenta, the stringy flesh surrounding the seeds. Spread the seeds on screens or paper towels to dry. Let them dry 2 to 3 weeks, then store in dated, airtight jars in a cool, dark closet. When properly stored, squash seed will remain viable for about six years.

Autumnal Marrow Squash or Boston Marrow
Cucurbita maxima

For the kitchen garden in regions where summers are cool and short, this squash is among the very best, equal to the Hubbard (page 285). It is illustrated in the *Album Vilmorin* (1877, 28) in all its gaudy pinkness as the *courge de l'Ohio*. Oddly, Ohio has nothing to do with its origin.

Courge de l'Ohio Squash

This squash was introduced to the gardening public by John M. Ives of Salem, Massachusetts, who exhibited it at Faneuil Hall in Boston in September 1834. It soon became one of the most popular squashes of its kind, not just in the United States but in England and France as well. Ives claimed to have obtained seed from a cross brought to Buffalo, New York, by Indians from the west. On the other hand, the *Year-Book of Agriculture* (1856, 330) detected a cross created from Commodore Porter's Valparaiso squash, while Fearing Burr (1865, 203–4) remained convinced that the autumnal marrow was related to the Hubbard. What is clear is that no one gave much credit to

Ives's claim—he probably developed and stabilized the hybrid himself. When his squash was recrossed about 1853 with a pure Valparaiso, it produced a new variety called Stetson's Hybrid or Wilder. That cross was created by A. W. Stetson of Braintree, Massachusetts, and named for the Honorable Marshall P. Wilder, a well-known patron of agriculture at the time.

The autumnal marrow is a late-summer squash that fruits on vines some 14 to 16 feet long. Fruit begins to ripen in August and will continue until frost, even though this is considered a 100-day squash. It is ideal for planting under corn. The skin is eggshell-thin and easily damaged if handled roughly. But the flesh is particularly fine in texture, and if the fruit is gathered before frost and stored carefully in a cool, dry pantry, it will keep well into the following spring. The fruit is essentially top-shaped like the Hubbard, with individual fruits weighing from 8 to 9 pounds each. The skin of the European strains are smooth and bluish pink, whereas the specimens depicted in American garden books of the period show not only a pebbled roughness to the skin but also a bright orange color. It is thought that the original cross was pink but that American seedsmen selected subsequent fruit toward the (then) more desirable orange shade. In

Autumnal Marrow Squash

shape and size, at least, the squash closely resembles Marblehead, which was introduced in 1873 by the seed house of James J. H. Gregory of Marblehead, Massachusetts. Marblehead has a gray-blue skin.

When saving seed, it is important to look for signs of crossing, since this variety degenerates easily. A thickening of the skin and a green ring on the blossom end are certain evidence of impure seed. Seed from such fruit must be discarded as seed stock but may be reserved as food. French seed for the *courge de l'Ohio* consistently produces finer-fleshed fruit than its American counterparts, but unfortunately that seed is difficult to obtain.

For the lovers of pumpkin pie, this is indeed a first-class squash. The deep carrot orange of the flesh holds up well under cooking, and while not as sweet as some heirloom varieties, the flavor can be improved with a little molasses or honey. The squash that has been in storage for some length of time tends to lose moisture, which makes it better suited for pumpkin bread, pumpkin butter, and the kind of pumpkin pastes that blend so nicely with corn and bean dishes.

Banana Squash
Cucurbita maxima

Also known as Mexican Banana and Plymouth Rock, this attractive variety was introduced about 1893. Its unusual shape and very smooth, almost velvety skin make it stand out anywhere groups of squash are displayed. The original variety was bluish gray with light orange striping. In storage, this color changes to a creamy pink. After the turn of this century, Aggeler & Musser, a Los Angeles seed firm, selected out three separate colors from the original introduction: a solid bluish gray, a solid yellow, and an orange-pink with flesh-colored stripes. The yellow selection has gradually superseded the others, no doubt because its color lives up to the varietal name, which makes for easier marketing.

The banana squash is much more popular in the West and on the West Coast than in the East, although I have not met with any peculiar problems with our climate. The orange-pink selection is presently more common in the Middle States, probably because it is raised by a number of Mennonite farmers in Pennsylvania, Maryland, and Ohio. The distinctive color is very close to that of the *courge de l'Ohio*, the French version of the autumnal marrow squash (page 280).

The vines of the banana squash are 12 to 15 feet long and closely resemble those of the Hubbard, which means that they require considerable room. The fruit ripens about the same time as the Essex Hybrid, and in my garden, that means early to mid-September. The fruit measures anywhere from 18 to 20 inches long, roughly 5 to 6 inches in diameter, and weighs 10 to 12 pounds. The flesh is yellowish orange, fine textured, and dry. For culinary purposes, I think it is best steamed.

Canada Crookneck Squash
Cucurbita pepo

Although this squash has known precedents among the Indians of North America, at least in early colonial times, there are no firm references to it until the 1820s. Mary Randolph included a recipe for cooking winter crookneck squash in her *Virginia House-Wife* (1824, 135), which certainly indicates that the squash was already well known. Yet it was not introduced commercially under this name until 1834, when it was first sold by Boston seedsman Charles H. Hovey (1810–1887). It should not be confused with the large flesh-colored crookneck squash that is still available in many parts of the country today.

The fruit of this variety ranges in size from 10 to 12 inches in length and is no more than 6 inches in diameter. The skin is smooth, creamy yellow, and covered with bloom, like a plum. Handling the squash will leave fingerprints. The vines are not large and trail close to the ground, with small, dark green leaves. Thus, this is an ideal squash for small gardens.

Canada Crookneck Squash

The flesh of the fruit is reddish salmon, and of very good quality, which is one reason why this vegetable has remained perennially popular. It also stores extremely well. I have had some in my pantry that have lasted two to three years without noticeable deterioration.

Cheese Pumpkin
Cucurbita moschata

A large tan pumpkin with a distinctive *moschata* stem is depicted in a painting by Lucas Van Valkenborch (c. 1530–1597) in the Kunsthistoriches Museum at Vienna. This may be the earliest depiction of a true cheese pumpkin, although Matthias de l'Obel included a "pompion" in his *Plantarum seu Stir-pium Icones* (1591) with the correct shape. In America, the cheese pumpkin appears with definite docu-mentation in Bernard M'Ma-hon's 1815 seed catalog, although he misidentified it as a *Cucurbita pepo*. Even then, it was accepted as widespread in the Middle States well before the Revolution. Landreth

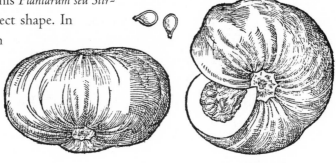

L'Obel's Cheese Pumpkin

Cheese (still available today under this name) and Mammoth Cheese are considered synonyms for this variety. The tan cheese pumpkin that I grow is also synonymous and is probably the same as the buff pie pumpkin of the nineteenth century. It resembles the tan pumpkin of Van Valkenborch.

The authors of the *Vegetables of New York: The Cucurbits* (1937, 52) suggested that the name was due to the shape of the squash and its resemblance to an old-style cheese box. Few of these vegetables resemble cheese boxes. Only one in my collection, the Appoquinnamink Cheese Pumpkin, found growing in a remote area of southern Delaware, comes close, and it is shown in the drawing. The color is bronze-gray, with blue-gray lines in the ribs. This is thought to be a seventeenth-century strain brought into the Delaware Valley from Jamaica; all of the cheese pumpkins are assumed by horticulturists to be of West Indian origin. In fact, one of the early nineteenth-century names for the cheese pumpkin was West Indian pumpkin.

More likely, the name of this variety stems from its shape, which vaguely resembles an old wheel of cheese—like the "cheeses" or seed pods of the marshmallow—coupled with the very old practice of making pumpkin cheese from squashes that do not store well, which is certainly true of this one. Pumpkin cheese, or what is now known as pumpkin butter, was a rural poverty food in the Middle Colonies. In the fall, the pumpkins were cooked down to a thick paste, often with watermelon juice, to yield a preserve that was dark brown in color and somewhat sweet, like unsugared apple butter.

All of the cheese pumpkins are characterized by deep salmon-orange flesh and trailing vines up to 18 feet in length. The leaves are blotched with grayish green; the veins are gray. The fruit is generally medium in size, no more than 14 inches in diameter, lobed, and flatter than common field pumpkins, weighing from 10 to 15 pounds. The skin color is usually dark cream or tan and very smooth. There are a number of subvarieties, most of them quite rare. The *musquée de Provence* (with a dark green rind and a truly distinctive variety) and the Cutchogue Flat Cheese are still available through seed-saving networks.

Appoquinnamink Cheese Pumpkin

Delicata Squash
Cucurbita pepo

This squash (color plate 72) has undergone a recent revival, for it is now found in many supermarkets during the early fall. Not many consumers (or gardeners for that matter) realize that this is an heirloom squash more than a hundred years old: it was introduced in 1894. It was promoted commercially for many years by Peter Henderson & Company of New York and remained popular into the 1920s. It was also known as Bohemian, Sweet Potato, and Ward's Individual, but these names have now fallen out of use.

The squash lives up to its present name because it is delicate in both shape and flavor. The fruit itself is small, usually 8 to 10 inches long, thin skinned, and waxy feeling when touched. The flesh is a deep orange-yellow, fine textured and sweet. The dark green markings on the skin turn a soft orange in storage; the cream ground color sometimes changes to a bright yellow. This color shift toward yellow is something that has developed in the past few decades, for the original variety remained a cream color throughout its storage life.

The Delicata Squash grows on 8-to-10-foot trailing vines with small silvery green leaves. The vines are prolific producers of fruit, and therefore this squash is ideal for small gardens. The vines can even be trained up wooden trellises much like cucumbers. My only complaint against this squash is that it tends to spoil quickly in storage, owing I think to its thin skin. It keeps best in a dry pantry where the temperature is maintained between 45° and 55° F.

One reason for the renewed popularity of this squash is that when it is cut in half lengthwise, it makes two single portions, and restaurants have devised many recipes for stuffing and baking this vegetable. Furthermore, the seeds are easy to remove, and the squash cooks quickly in a microwave oven, all of which contributes to its popularity with chefs.

Hubbard Squash
Cucurbita maxima

This is probably the most famous of all the American winter squashes and one of the most popular. It was introduced commercially in the late 1840s by James J. H. Gregory of Marblehead, Massachusetts. According to Gregory's own account, he obtained seed about 1842 from a Captain Knott Martin, who had grown it in Marblehead for many years. Since the vegetable was brought to Gregory's attention by a Mrs. Elizabeth Hubbard, it was named in her honor. The Gregorys claimed that the squash had been introduced into Marblehead from Boston in 1798. However, because they provided several conflicting accounts about its origin, horticulturists have always remained doubtful about their documentation and have suspected that the Gregorys had a hand in improving the squash prior to releasing it in the form we know today.

Hubbard Squash

What is known for certain about the Hubbard squash is that it originated in the West Indies or South America, for it belongs to a larger family of squashes from that region. I should also add that in a Philadelphia still life painting from the early 1820s, there is a large squash resembling a Hubbard, with warty skin that is dark green with bright yellow patches. This may represent the Hubbard squash at a stage closer to its original South American form.

The original Hubbard squash matures in 115 days on trailing vines up to 15 feet long. The leaves are lobed and somewhat large. The fruit, if it is growing true, should measure from 12 to 15 inches in length and no more than 10 inches in circumference. The maximum weight is generally between 9 and 12 pounds, but often less than that. Many markets prefer the smaller ones, since they are easier to sell. The skin of the squash is rough, wrinkled, and warty, with a prominent corky button on the blossom end. The skin color should be a dark ivy green, often with a few pale green stripes. In storage, the color normally changes to olive. The dull yellow flesh is fine, firm, moderately sweet, and excellently suited to cookery.

This old original strain has been crossed with many squash to create new varieties. Many of the specimens that come out of the fields show deterioration of seed purity, so it is not advisable to trust seed from produce stands. Two popular subvarieties have been created out of the original Hubbard: the Blue Hubbard and the Golden Hubbard.

The Blue Hubbard was introduced in 1909, originally under the name Symmes Blue Hubbard, after S. S. Symmes, a gardener from Cliftondale, Massachusetts, who worked for the James

J. H. Gregory seed company for many years. It is believed to be a cross between Middleton Blue or Marblehead and the original Hubbard.

The Golden Hubbard, which is really an orange-red, was developed by J. J. Harrison of Storr's & Harrison Company, Painsville, Ohio. It was introduced by D. M. Ferry & Company of Detroit in 1898. The Golden Hubbard should produce a dark green or olive-green patch on the blossom end, an indication that the seed is growing true to type.

Olive Squash or Courge Olive Squash
Cucurbita maxima

This may be considered the French equivalent of the Hubbard squash, and from a botanical standpoint, the two are closely related. The true origin of the Olive Squash is unknown, although Vilmorin was the first to offer it in Europe. W. Atlee Burpee of Philadelphia began offering seed in 1884, and Tuisco Greiner (1890, 257) listed it as a variety recommended for kitchen gardens. Its popularity in this country has been mixed, doubtless due to competition from so many other squashes better suited to our cookery. Perhaps it is just the dull color of the skin that Americans are not accustomed to, yet each squash yields an abundance of beautiful, thick, yellow flesh that is both sweet and flavorful. It makes excellent puddings and preserves.

The shape is similar to that of the *courge de l'Ohio*, but more slender and tapered at both ends. The French claim that the squash resembles an unripe olive (hence the name); if so, then a very young olive must be intended. None of the specimens I have grown ever looked like olives (I have even used French seed), but the skin is indeed close in color to the camouflage green used by the U.S. Army, and this might be construed as an olive shade.

Actually, the squash is quite striking in the garden because the vine leaves are very pale green, which creates a nice visual contrast. Furthermore, Greiner was correct in recommending this variety for small gardens because the vines trail close to the ground and are not long and tangled like the Hubbard. The fruit is also small in scale, measuring no more than a foot long and 6 inches in diameter. The squash can weigh anywhere from 6 to 10 pounds, but weight can suffer measurably if the growing season is dry. These squash must be kept well watered.

Pattypan or Cymling Squash
Cucurbita pepo

Like the summer crookneck, this squash originated among the native peoples of the eastern United States, for it was known from Virginia to New England by a number of local names in various Indian languages. Both the yellow and the white varieties date from pre-Columbian times, although the white has gradually supplanted the yellow over the past century and a half. In England, this squash is known as the custard marrow, in France as the *patisson panaché.*

The old name cymlin or cymling was given to this squash in the seventeenth century, owing to its similarity in size and shape to the English simnal cake, a fluted cake made during Lent. One of the oldest depictions of the pattypan squash appeared in Matthias de l'Obel's *Plantarum seu Stirpium Icones* (1591). The fruit looks very much like the pattypans of today. The fact that this East Coast squash appeared in European botanical works prior to white settlement in the region suggests intriguing precontact seed exchanges that have not been given much notice by plant historians.

L'Obel's Pattypan Squash

Aside from the yellow and white bush varieties, there was also an old warty yellow variety that grew on trailing vines. It was given the now archaic scientific designation *Cucurbita verrucosa,* and appeared under that name on Bernard M'Mahon's seed lists as early as 1806. It is believed to have been a cross between the yellow pattypan and the summer crookneck squashes, dating from the middle part of the eighteenth century. It was well known in American horticultural circles by the 1790s.

The plants are bushy, with large leaves on 30-inch stems that require plenty of space between the hills. The fruit matures in about 55 days and produces profusely until frost. Constant harvesting will promote a continuous supply of new squash. The fruit can be eaten young or when light green, or harvested when it forms a hard shell. This can be pared off with a potato peeler.

The mature fruit varies in size, some measuring 7, others as much as 9 inches across, and often weighing 7 or 8 pounds. The skin color of the white variety is dull white and some-what velvety; the yellow variety is more of a waxy lemon color. For seed-saving purposes, let a hill produce mature fruit and leave the fruit on the plants until they begin to die. It is important that the seed be allowed to mature in the squash to ensure better rates of germination. The mature squash can be stored in a cool dry pantry and will keep for several months.

The Improved Variegated Custard Marrow (color plate 75) was mentioned by Fearing Burr (1865, 202)—but not in flattering terms—and illustrated by Vilmorin (1885, 266). It appeared in the *Album Vilmorin* (1858, 7) as the *patisson jaune et panaché* and is believed to date from the early 1850s. It is a French cross between Yellow Mandan (page 294) and the white pattypan squash, a cross that I have successfully recreated in my garden several times. The fruit and plants are much smaller than other pattypans. In storage, the squash turns a rich lemon yellow. It is best harvested in the green state and prepared like zucchini.

The earliest known American recipe for pattypan squash appeared in *The Virginia House-Wife* (1824, 134). In that recipe, the squash was boiled and then pureed. The following recipe, from Mrs. Charles H. Gibson's *Maryland and Virginia Cook Book* (1894, 72–73), was also typical.

Cymlings

❦

Cut them in quarters, wash and boil them in salted water until tender. When done put them into a cullender and press out all the water. While warm add a small piece of butter, and season with a little more salt and cream. Put them in a covered dish, and before sending to table sprinkle a little black pepper. These are very nice fried like egg-plant.

Pike's Peak or Sibley Squash
Cucurbita maxima

Like the banana squash, which originated in Mexico, Pike's Peak is brown-seeded and therefore is definitely of Native American origin. However, its early history is folkloric. It was said to have

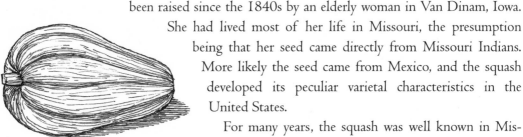

been raised since the 1840s by an elderly woman in Van Dinam, Iowa. She had lived most of her life in Missouri, the presumption being that her seed came directly from Missouri Indians. More likely the seed came from Mexico, and the squash developed its peculiar varietal characteristics in the United States.

For many years, the squash was well known in Missouri, Arkansas, and Iowa, where seed remained in circulation among truck farmers. In 1887 the squash was released commercially by Hiram Sibley & Company, a

Pike's Peak Squash

Rochester, New York, seed firm. It is considered one of the most distinctive squashes of its type and was given considerable notice in the *American Garden* (1888, 62; 1889, 181).

The vines attain a length of 12 to 15 feet and closely resemble those of the Hubbard. The squash ripens in 120 days, the same time as the Hubbard, but the fruit size is more like the Quaker pie pumpkin, about 1 foot in length and 9 inches in diameter. The fruit skin is smoother than the Blue Hubbard and Marblehead, yet almost the same color. In storage, the skin changes color to a pinkish buff, somewhat akin to the blue banana squash. The flesh is fine, moist, and pale orange in color. It is an ideal storage squash because the flesh becomes drier and richer, thus reaching its best stage for culinary uses after January 1.

Potiron rouge vif d'Etampes Squash
Cucurbita maxima

This pumpkin is known by a variety of names in American seed catalogs, perhaps the most common being Red Etampes, or more recently, Cinderella. It should not be confused with the French butter pumpkin or *potiron jaune gros*, which was introduced into England in the 1820s and the United States in the early 1850s. It was golden yellow in color. The Red Etampes is a bright brick red, as can be seen from the examples in color plate 77. On the other hand, Red Etampes was developed out of the old butter pumpkin, so the two varieties are closely related. The vines of both are nearly identical, except for leaf coloring.

W. Atlee Burpee of Philadelphia is credited with introducing this squash to American gardeners in 1883. It was cultivated in France almost fifty years prior to that, and proved extremely popular in Paris. There are two variant forms, one with smooth skin, which is considered the true type, the other with cracks and netting that is considered a partial reversion to its butter pumpkin parent. Regardless, I have grown both forms and have observed that they produce a large number of deformed fruit. Among some of my Mennonite friends who raise this squash for market, an entire field may yield only a dozen perfect specimens. The reason for this is not clear, although I suspect that seed purity has been compromised over the years, particularly in areas where the *giraumon turban* is also under cultivation.

The fruits ripen in 130 days on vigorous vines reaching 18 to 20 feet in length, without a question a true field pumpkin. The fruit often measures 18 inches in diameter, is extremely flat and somewhat sunken at the stem end, and weighs 30 to 35 pounds. The blossom scar leaves a small button of corklike material, usually surrounded by a ring of the same growth, one of the telling characteristics of this vegetable. The flesh is thick and a deep yellow color, but the flavor is lacking. The seed mass is difficult to remove. I recommend a grapefruit spoon.

This squash was popular in Paris during the nineteenth century because chefs discovered that it made an excellent base for soups, the flavor being so mild that it did not overpower other ingredients. Furthermore, it yielded a thick stock of a decidedly yellow color rather than an orange-red one, which was considered more visually pleasing. Jules Gouffé's soup recipe in *Le Livre de cuisine* (1868, 48–49) is typical for the period.

Pumpkin Soup

❦

Take 2 pounds of yellow pumpkin; take out the seeds, and pare off ½ inch of the rind; cut it in pieces 1 ½ inch square; put in a stewpan with 1 ounce of butter, 1 pinch of salt, 1 ounce of sugar, and ½ pint of water. Simmer for an hour and a half, and drain in a colander. Put back in the stewpan and add 1 ½ pint of boiled milk—otherwise, if unboiled, the milk is liable to curdle. Boil for a minute and pour in the soup tureen in which ½ ounce of bread has been sliced. Serve.

Quaker Pie Pumpkin
Cucurbita moschata

The Quaker Pie Pumpkin was introduced commercially in 1888 by W. Atlee Burpee & Company of Philadelphia. It had been growing for several years before that in the garden of a Quaker family living in Washington County, New York, hence the name. This squash never gained the widespread popularity of other fall storing varieties, and thus has always remained rather rare. Yet, unlike many squash of this type, it produces fruits with little variability, a feature that should recommend it commercially. In fact the fruit is small, no more than a foot long and perhaps 8 inches in diameter across the middle. In spite of their small size, these squashes are dense, weighing from 10 to 12 pounds, and there is not a lot of waste.

Quaker Pie Pumpkin

Perhaps part of the reason for its lack of popularity lies in its color. The skin is creamy white, overlaid with a darker cream lace pattern not often shown in old illustrations. The flesh of this squash is also white and very fine-grained. When cooked and pureed, it resembles mashed turnip in appearance. Unfortunately, in the *Vegetables of New York: The Cucurbits* (1937, 35–36), the squash is incorrectly described as having stringy, insipid flesh of a pale orange color. I can only surmise that the authors tested this squash with impure seed, for I grew the Quaker pie pumpkin many years ago from seed obtained from a family of Quakers in Iowa—Newlins by name, who owned a small seed business—and my squash grew true to the original strain. A check in several seed catalogs, including *Maule's Seed Catalogue for 1898* and *Dreer's Garden Book for 1924*, confirmed that the original introduction was white-fleshed. It also had a slight coconut flavor, like the old pineapple squash. I would think that the unusual flesh color would recommend this squash today, with so much interest now in creating an American food identity.

The squash grows on very long vines, usually 15 to 18 feet in length. This is rather large for small gardens, but since the leaves are small, the vines are not as invasive as some varieties. The leaves are also quite decorative because they are profusely marked with gray patches. More impressive are the flowers, which are extraordinarily large, some measuring 8 inches across when in full bloom. I cannot think of a more ideal source of squash blossoms for stuffing.

Summer Crookneck Squash
Cucurbita pepo

The yellow summer crookneck is one of our oldest documented varieties of squash. According to correspondence between Philadelphia Quaker Timothy Matlack and Thomas Jefferson in 1807, published by Edwin Morris Betts in *Jefferson's Garden Book* (1944, 341), the yellow crookneck squash was native to New Jersey. It was a variety preserved as an heirloom by the Cooper family of Camden, who had cultivated it for nearly a hundred years. There is no reason to discount Matlack's story because the Coopers were actively engaged in horticulture and were well known in New Jersey and Pennsylvania for their Cooper's Pale Green Asparagus, considered by many the finest variety in colonial America. The Coopers were also

Summer Crookneck Squash

responsible for preserving Willing's Barbados Pepper (page 266), which came into my collection from the late Mary Larkin Thomas. In any event, if we accept Matlack's explanation, then the summer crookneck is the only squash that can be traced directly to the Lenape peoples who once inhabited the Delaware Valley.

The summer crookneck grows on a bush rather than on a trailing vine. The leaves are large, five-lobed, and grayish green. The mature fruit measures 8 to 9 inches long and ripens from soft yellow to yellow orange. The skin surface is heavily warted. If this squash inadvertently crosses with squash in the vicinity, the warts are one of the first features to show up in subsequent seasons. The interior flesh is yellowish white, although there are now varieties that are solid yellow, but these are a later development. For culinary purposes, the squash is harvested very young, while still tender.

To yield viable seed, the squash must be allowed to ripen until the skin is pale orange and woody like a gourd. It is also advisable to let the fruit mature in this condition on the plant for two weeks so that the seed can undergo its final aging process. This precaution will ensure a larger proportion of viable seed the following season.

Tennessee Sweet Potato Squash
Cucurbita moschata

This squash is descended from the old potato pumpkin of the Upper South and Middle States. According to Thomas Jefferson (1944, 154), the variety was introduced in the late 1780s from Jamaica with the slave trade. Although eaten by whites, this squash was especially popular among the black population of the Old South. Its name is due to the fact that the taste of the flesh closely resembles that of a sweet potato; thus it served the place of sweet potatoes until they came into season. The oldest published American recipe for cooking potato pumpkin appeared in *The Virginia House-Wife* (1824, 132). The pumpkin was harvested young, when 7 or 8 inches in diameter, pared, and stuffed. It was then baked either in a pan or in a large tin mold so that it could be turned out and served like a molded pudding.

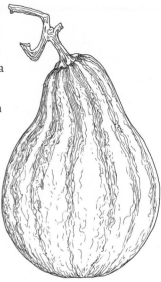

The Tennessee sweet potato squash may descend from an early variety known in the 1840s as the Green Striped Bell—indeed, that is one of its former synonyms—but thus far no firm evidence has surfaced to connect the two. W. Atlee Burpee of Philadelphia began offering the squash known today as the Tennessee sweet potato in 1883, and to date, this appears to be the first use of that name. Origins aside, this is one of the most popular heirloom varieties in the South due to its fine texture, its rich flavor, and its excellent storing qualities.

Tennessee Sweet Potato Squash

The squash ripens in 110 days on long, vigorous vines measuring 15 to 18 feet, with large, dark green leaves. I would advise planting it in an area of the kitchen garden off to itself or between teepees of pole beans, for it requires space and does not thrive if there is too much competition from other vegetables. The fruit, however, is not large, measuring 12 to 15 inches long and perhaps as much as 10 inches in diameter at it thickest point. In weight, individual fruits range from 12 to 15 pounds, similar to many Hubbards. The skin is ivory yellow with yellow-green markings that change to a mustard color in storage. The seed cavity is large, the flesh greenish white.

There are a number of lesser-known varieties worthy of note, among them the Wickersham sweet potato, the Choctaw sweet potato, and the Florida sweet potato, which are still available through Seed Savers Exchange.

Turk's Cap or Turban Squash
Cucurbita maxima

This is popularly known in France as the *giraumon turban,* and was illustrated in exquisite detail in the *Album Vilmorin* (1871, 25). The examples in color plate 76 were selected for their close approximation of the 1871 print. This variety of turk's cap squash was developed in France but was introduced into the United States early in the nineteenth century, perhaps as early as 1820. Unfortunately, it was never given much notice in American garden literature until much later, a telling sign of its original lack of popularity. Furthermore, this squash was sometimes called an acorn squash, especially in English garden books, owing to the acornlike shape of the cap. This has made it especially difficult to distinguish turbans from true acorn squash in early nineteenth-century records.

The *Bon Jardinier* for 1818 referred to this squash as a turban, and this is accepted as the source for the name. Thus it is safe to presume that the Vilmorins who published *Le Bon Jardinier* also had a hand in refining the variety as we now know it. Before 1818, there were several turban-shaped squash known to horticulturists, but most of these are now extinct because they were never considered worthy of culinary merit. Even the turk's cap is grown today more for ornament than for cookery, because its light yellow flesh is rather tasteless. On the other hand, it is an excellent keeper. When care is taken not to damage the "cap" (where rotting is most likely to occur first), the squash can be kept in storage from September to the following June without deterioration.

The reason it keeps so well is its hard, woody rind, which is very difficult to remove. The simplest way to cook this squash is to cut it in half, scrape out the seeds, and place the halves in glass bowls with about ½ cup of water. Cover the bowls with cling wrap and cook in a microwave oven on high for 15 minutes. The flesh will scoop out like mashed potatoes and can be used as a thickener for soups, especially for split-pea soups, both green and yellow.

Fearing Burr (1865, 214–15) did not consider the turban squash fit for storage. But the two varieties he discussed differed considerably from the French one treated here. The turban squash of Burr was large and fleshy, and his Improved Turban, which he considered a subvariety, was even better suited to culinary purposes, although neither one was a good keeper. Seed for both of these old American turban varieties is difficult to come by today, which is why I hesitate to devote much attention to them. However, they are excellent heirlooms well worthy of revived notice.

The turk's cap produces 8-to-10-foot vines with dark green leaves. Since the plants are small, they are excellently suited for small gardens, one reason for their continued popularity in France. The squash generally measures 7 to 8 inches thick and from 10 to 12 inches in diameter. Individual fruit may weigh anywhere from 8 to 10 pounds—most of it rind—ripening in about 115 days from planting. In short-season areas, where frost may be expected in early September, start the plants indoors in pots so that they are well advanced by the time they are set out on hills.

Yellow Mandan Squash
Cucurbita pepo

Mandan squash was introduced commercially in 1912 by the seed firm of Oscar H. Will & Company of Bismark, North Dakota. That strain was white, oblate in shape, and yielded fruit weighing 3 to 4 pounds on plants generally described as "bush," even though they sent out vines of considerable length. In any case, the squash was said to originate among the Mandan Indians of the northern Great Plains, hence the name. In fact, Mandan appears to be a variant form of several similar North American squashes of great age. No one has effectively pinpointed their true origin.

The white-skinned Mandan of Will & Company became a well-known commercial variety, more round in shape than the yellow variety that I grow (color plate 78). Its creamy skin is dappled with deep forest green between green stripes. The flesh is a pale lime-white and makes an excellent summer squash when harvested young.

The authors of *The Vegetables of New York: The Cucurbits* (1937, 201) remarked that White Mandan was similar to two old Eastern squashes: Long Island White Bush, and Green Striped Bergen, the latter introduced commercially in 1841. Because of its bell-like shape, I have always assumed that my Yellow Mandan is actually a selection of Green Striped Bergen by another name. There are several reasons to support this, nineteenth-century iconographic sources aside.

The Yellow Mandan is not a yellow White Mandan. The flesh of the yellow is either pale orange or golden yellow (depending on soil), and the skin is a creamy yellow where the white is "sea foam white," an old term for white with a tinge of green. Furthermore, the fruits of the yellow are smaller, weighing 1½ to 2 pounds, or just about half of what one would expect of a true White Mandan. The yellow is also more fragrant when ripe and stores better. It can be pared, seeded, sliced like an apple, and dried.

Varietal distinctions aside, only Mandan and Yellow Mandan are presently available through Seed Savers Exchange; the others have vanished from seed lists altogether. It is an excellent squash for small gardens. The leaves resemble large grape leaves, and they hug the ground so that the vines do not compete with taller vegetables nearby. Thus, it thrives under the protection of corn or around the base of staked tomatoes. More important, the plants produce abundantly. I am sure that I have gathered at least fifteen squash from each hill, and this during the height of a drought that in my region wiped out the Jersey pumpkin harvest.

I dry this pumpkin in order to reconstitute it as paste or puree for my ongoing recipe project in American Indian cookery. Frankly, dried pumpkin is practical, since it stores easily and does not take up much space. Otherwise, treat the mature fruit like acorn squash. Incidentally, the young fruit, when about 2 inches in diameter, may be sliced and served raw with dips or cooked like the small *ronde de Nice* zucchini.

Radishes

Radishes are now more popular in Oriental-style cooking than in mainstream American cookery. This is a vegetable that formerly played an important role in our diet, only to be relegated today to the status of a garnish, like sprigs of parsley and bits of sliced olive. Yet radishes once appeared on the early American table at every meal. I can recall many old Pennsylvania Dutch relatives who lamented the fact that people had stopped serving radishes for breakfast. A glance at seed lists from the nineteenth century would certainly support this, for there were radishes for every imaginable culinary situation, including a whole class of radishes bred exclusively to withstand the summer heat.

Radishes are grouped botanically under Brassicaceae, and are therefore part of the same vegetable clan as cabbages, turnips, watercress, rocket, and garden cress. All of these plants have very similar seed pods, so the logic for this grouping is probably more obvious to gardeners than to people who only see the vegetables in markets. Anyone who frequents American farm markets will notice immediately that the greatest variety of radishes will be found in the Asian section, even though we have a large and impressive list of our own heirloom varieties to draw on. Unfortunately, growers have not yet rediscovered them, and I think they would be quite surprised to know that the list of surviving heirlooms is huge, so choices are not limited. Best of all, since radishes are short-lived annuals, they will thrive in most parts of the country regardless of extreme winter or summer temperatures. They are also one of the easiest vegetables to grow in home gardens.

The oldest documentation of the radish takes us back to Asia in the form of literary references and archaeological remains in North China. From Asia the radish gradually moved westward, more or less following large human migrations. Ancient Greek travel writer Herodotus planted the long-held belief that the early Egyptians grew radishes, but Egyptologists have exploded this for several reasons. Herodotus could not read hieroglyphics, and if he could he would have been hard put to find one for the radish, or for *radish* used in the context of the inscription he claimed to have seen on a pyramid. The word for *radish* did not exist in Egyptian until the radish was introduced to Egypt by the Greeks. In all likelihood, the Greeks came in contact with the radish via India or with trade across the Black Sea. They were well acquainted with it long before the Egyptians and recognized many distinct varieties.

Galen of Pergamon (A.D. 129–199) wrote that radishes were eaten raw with salt and vinegar, and that the poor cooked the stems and leaves. The codex of Dioskorides, which I have mentioned many times already, contains the earliest surviving botanical picture of a radish, a long-rooted sort with fully developed seed pods. It is not surprising that physicians like Galen or Dioskorides would take note of the radish; it was considered a very important food with high medical value. It is now known that radishes are rich in vitamin C (the leaves even more so), which would explain why radishes were used to prevent scurvy or eaten as a remedy for colds. This medical theme was carried down through the Middle Ages. In the Anglo-Saxon leechdoms of England, there were over twenty references to the medical uses of the radish, including its efficacy in warding off a woman's chatter and for depression. The *superne raedic* often mentioned in that period is thought to be a large white variety something akin to the daikon radish of today, or more likely, to the white-skinned form of Long Black Spanish (page 299).

*White Skinned Long
Spanish Radish*

The small, round radishes that are now common in supermarkets are not of ancient origin. Even in the 1500s, when radish culture began to shift to newer sorts, the most common varieties were the old large-rooted ones, shaped like elongated beets. The Long Black Spanish is a survivor of this older type and is definitely of medieval origin. By the late 1500s small, round varieties began to appear in Holland and Italy. A white variety bred by the Dutch became very popular in many parts of Northern Europe as a winter radish. The Philadelphia White Box Radish (page 303) is a direct lineal descendant of this old Dutch sort. Out of Italy came the round red radishes that are associated with late spring and early fall planting.

The long, fingerlike radishes, sometimes called icicle radishes, were developed in the 1600s and first appeared in physic gardens rather than in vegetable gardens, so their dates of introduction are quite well documented in period medical archives. A long purple and a long red variety appeared in the 1670s, and by the 1680s they were being grown in Scotland and England. The Early Scarlet Short Top traces to this period and was a radish of choice among the wealthy because it could be grown in large numbers under cold frames. The long, narrow shape permitted kitchen gardeners to pack the plants close together, especially if they were grown in heavy sand.

The Abbé Rozier discussed numerous eighteenth-century radishes in his agricultural encyclopedia, dividing them out by shape, color, and place of origin. He followed the French practice of identifying radishes by the provinces or towns where they were most extensively cultivated or were presumed to have originated, with a very large division between the types of radishes grown in the Midi and those cultivated for market around Paris. There were also certain noblemen who tinkered with horticulture and who perfected radishes in their châteaux gardens. These popular French varieties carried aristocratic names that were quickly dropped during the French Revolution. All of this adds up to chaos when trying to sort out which radish was which and how they may relate to later sorts. However, when the radishes crossed the Channel and acquired English names, the work of identifying heirloom sorts becomes much easier, since the English names were also used in early America.

The lists of radishes found in our early seed catalogs are quite extensive and reveal a heavy reliance on England for seed. Pragmatically, a kitchen gardener could maintain three types, a spring, a summer, and a fall or winter radish, thus supplying the table over the course of the season. The yellow radishes (all shapes) were most generally grown for summer use because of their slowness to bolt. E. G. Storke's *Family, Farm and Gardens* (1860, 130) selected six of the many varieties of radish then available because they were considered best suited to small kitchen gardens. I have listed them below in Storke's order of preference. The comments are mine.

1. Early Scarlet Short Top, a long, narrow variety popular for its earliness.
2. Early Salmon Short Top, a pink variety recommended by Amelia Simmons in 1796.
3. Red Turnip, the round type most common today. It was preferred in this country because, true to its ultimate Italian origin, it would bear the heat better in late spring and early summer.
4. White Turnip, the round white type of Dutch origin, almost exclusively a winter radish.
5. Yellow Summer, a round yellow variety still available.
6. Black Winter or Spanish, a long-rooted, coarse radish that withstands frost.

H. L. Barnum's *Farmer's Own Book* (1836, 73) offered this practical suggestion:

They should be sown every two weeks, from April to August, to insure a succession of crops. They may be sown broad-cast, or in drills, not too thick, as the tops would run up too much, and the roots be stringy. They should stand from two and a half, to five inches apart, the seed should be covered from half an inch to an inch deep, according to the weather or season. In dry weather, water them freely—this swells the roots, and makes them crisp. To prevent worms, take equal parts of buckwheat bran, and fresh horse dung, and mix well with the ground—in forty-eight hours fermentation, and a crop of toad stools will be produced. Dig the ground over—sow the seed—they will grow rapidly and be free of insects. Leaves of radish are often used as salad; and the green pods are pickled, as substitutes for capers. Old radishes are indigestible, and render the breath bad.

It is rare to find so much useful information on radish culture condensed into such a succinct snippet, and odd as it may seem, Barnum's enthusiasm for fermenting dung to sterilize the soil is brilliant, cheap, and effective. It will work for any root vegetable, not just radishes. While radish seed can be planted broadcast on well-worked, well-raked ground and patted smooth with a shovel, the plants themselves cannot be crowded. Seedlings must be thinned to at least 4 inches apart. The beautiful radishes depicted in the photographs in color plates 79, 80, and 81 were not accidents. They were carefully spaced so that they would develop good form and color. This is especially important for market radishes. However, radishes may be sewn broadcast among onion sets with several positive results. They will not compete with the onions, so two crops can be extracted from the same piece of ground, and because of their shape, radishes will loosen the soil. Since the radishes are pulled before the onions form bulbs, the loosened soil benefits the onions just at the time when the bulbs begin swelling. Best of all, the onions discourage many of the insects that would otherwise attack the radishes.

Radishes can be harvested at any time once the roots are well formed. Europeans prefer to pull them young; Americans often wait too long, and the radishes are either pithy in the center or cracked. Heavy rains will also cause radishes to crack, so it is better to pull them before a storm than to fret over the ensuing waste. Once radishes crack innumerable insects will find the openings, and the roots will become meals for the millions. For seed saving, select out the twelve most perfect radishes, dig them up, and plant them where they are to flower. Stake the flower stalks so that they do not fall over and touch the ground, for this will ruin the seed.

It will be obvious when the radishes are in bloom because their flowers are attractive to insects, and butterflies will be everywhere. At this point the roots are no longer palatable, but the seed pods are. They were used extensively in early American cookery both raw in salads and pickled. The pickled pods make delightful garnishes. The Madras Podding Radish (page 302) was imported to this country specifically for this purpose.

While the radishes are in blossom, observe the flowers. Radish flowers produce many slight variations from one variety to the next, and these variations are important markers when looking for unwanted crosses. If one radish produces flowers with pink flecks while all the others of that variety produce white ones, there is reason to pull up the plant even if the root appears true to type. I make color transparencies of the flowers so that I remember the correct flower for each variety I grow. Do not rely on memory, since shifts can take place over the course of several years, and the results often show up when one least expects them. This precaution is especially appropriate where the purity of heirloom strains is an object. Furthermore, radishes cross readily. They are outcrossing, like all brassicas, so several plants are required for the transfer of pollen. If more than one variety is cultivated, bring them to flower at different times many weeks apart; otherwise, they must be isolated by a half mile. I have use of ground at Oaklands, an estate about a mile from me, where I grow out varieties I need to isolate from the ones at Roughwood. Similar arrangements are recommended for serious gardeners. Since radish seed remains viable for five years, it is possible to maintain as many as fifteen varieties, allowing three growouts per season.

Radish seed is ready to harvest when the pods are dry. Snip off the pods into a brown paper bag, label and date the bag, and set it away in a dry room away from heat and sunlight. In about a month, the seeds will have matured enough to remove them from the pods, a job that is a lot easier when the pods are completely dry and brittle. In order to remove the seed, the pods must be split open and the seeds picked out—they do not fall out on their own. This work can be tedious, especially since the dry pods are pointed and sharp, but there is an easy way. Put the pods in a coarse sieve or strainer and gently crush the pods between the fingers, rolling them so that the seeds come loose. If this is done over a large work bowl, the seeds will drop through the sieve and thus become separated from the debris. Sift the seed from the chaff, and winnow outdoors. Since radish seeds are heavy (unlike lettuce seeds), winnowing is quickly accomplished. Always mix the seed from the various plants to maintain genetic diversity. While a dozen of the best will supply seed enough for one garden from season to season, twenty radishes will provide a better hedge against unforeseen seed damage and at the same time increase genetic diversity in the stock. All of the radishes listed on the following pages are members of the same species regardless of root color, root shape, or intended use of pod. They will cross readily with one another.

Black Spanish Winter Radish
Raphanus sativus

The Shakers distributed seed for this radish through their vast seed network in the nineteenth century. This was one winter radish every American farmer could rely upon, and since it was well known since the seventeenth century, its merits needed no recommendation. What this radish lacked in physical beauty—it has the appearance of old rubbed tar—it far exceeded in practicality. It is so hardy that in Pennsylvania it is only necessary to throw some straw over it to protect it during the winter. Parsnips and Black Spanish radish were the first root vegetables of early spring among the eighteenth-century farmers in my part of the country.

The root is indeed long, somewhat carrot shaped but thick, ranging from 7 to 12 inches in length and 2 to 3 inches in diameter, tapering to a point. This strain, with the pointed tip, is later and more pungent tasting than the variant form with a rounded or blunt end. The pointed sort is the older of the two and was the most commonly cultivated type in this country.

There is also a small, round form called Turnip-Rooted Black Spanish in old horticultural books. It is still available and was first mentioned in 1768 by English gardener Philip Miller. The skin of the radish is charcoal black and somewhat rough, due to tiny wrinkles; the flesh is clear, crisp white. I have an old round, black variety from Turkey that is indistinguishable from this one. It may point to an eastern Mediterranean origin for this type. In any case, its small size, about 3 inches in diameter, made it popular as an inexpensive grade of winter radish, reliable for its hardiness. Philadelphia seedsman Robert Buist (1847, 107) recommended sowing seed in August and lifting the radishes in October. They can be stored in sand for use over the winter.

Since the flavor of this radish is somewhat harsh, it was common practice to shred it and marinate it in salted water. After a few hours of marination, the radish was drained, pressed dry, and served as a salad with vinegar and oil. Minced fresh herbs were sprinkled over the top.

Black Spanish Winter Radish

China Rose Radish

Raphanus sativus

China Rose is believed to have evolved directly out of the wild radish of Asia rather than out of a garden form under long cultivation. Its distinctive leaves and flowers point to its primitive origin. The radish was under cultivation in Europe many years before it was introduced into the United States. It was grown in France in the late 1840s and soon thereafter depicted in the *Album Vilmorin* (1851, 2). It was known to Fearing Burr through the Vilmorin-Andrieux *Description des plantes potagères* (1856), and by 1864 seed was being offered on a regular basis by James J. H. Gregory of Marblehead, Massachusetts. Gregory claimed to have introduced the radish to American gardeners, but this has never been verified.

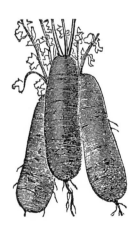

The radish is vivid rose pink, about 4 to 5 inches long, and shaped somewhat like a short, stumpy sausage. It is often more swollen on the root end than at the shoulders. A perfect specimen is shown in color plate 79. Historically, this radish was raised as a fall or winter radish, for it is best in terms of sweet flavor and snappy texture during cool fall weather. It will withstand a hard frost without damage.

China Rose Radish

There are also pure white and solid purple variants, known respectively by their French names *radis blanc d'hiver de Chine* and *radis violet d'hiver de Chine.* All three forms are ideal for raising in cold frames.

Early Purple Turnip-Shaped Radish
Raphanus sativus

This is the round or top-shaped violet version of the common red radish, and was mentioned as a good hardy sort by cookbook author Amelia Simmons (1796, 13). The advantage of the turnip-shaped varieties, as they were called, was that they overwintered well, especially when covered with straw or when raised in cold frames—a vital source of vitamin C not overlooked in colonial times. This radish was also popular due to its intense color, beautifully depicted in the *Album Vilmorin* (1863, 14). The handsomest form to my mind is the *radis ronf violet à bout blanc,* which is identical except that it is white on the root end. This color contrast seems to make the radish more visually appealing.

Due to its hardiness, the violet turnip-shaped radish was grown by market gardeners all year around and sold in radish "bouquets" of several colors, using whatever colors were then in season. The violet was always a good counterpoint to the red, white-tipped red, deep scarlet, solid white, and summer yellow variants. Such colorful radish mixtures are also quite striking when used at table.

The Purple Olive-Shaped Radish (SSE Radish 163) is the same color, but in spite of its name, it is shaped more like a small plum. I inherited this eighteenth-century variety in my grandfather's seed collection and gave seed to Seed Savers Exchange. It is only available from me or from the members of Seed Savers Exchange who now grow it. Even though Thomas Mawe mentioned the radish in *Every Man His Own Gardener* (1779, 483), it seems to be a hardy variety that dates back to the seventeenth century. It is best planted as a late fall or early spring radish. If grown in warm weather, the radish acquires a hot, mustardy taste, almost like horseradish. Touched by light frost, the radish mellows in flavor and becomes sweet. A hard frost will destroy the plant; as a winter radish it must be grown in cold frames.

Jaune hatif or Early Yellow Turnip Radish
Raphanus sativus

There are several heirloom yellow summer radishes, but the basic division falls into two categories: long or carrot-shaped and round. Alzbeta Kovacova-Pecarova (Betty to me), a seed saver in Kosice, Slovakia, has graciously shared with me some of the oldest yellow radish varieties presently in my vegetable collection, including *jaune hatif*, as it is known in France. The Abbé Rozier (1785, 534) noted that this round yellow radish was one of the most commonly raised varieties in Dauphin, Savoy, and in the vicinity of Lyon. However, documentation for yellow sorts prior to 1700 becomes murky. From a genetic standpoint, the yellows are the product of a pigment mutation in the red varieties, just as with tomatoes. Thus, the yellow radishes may be viewed as red radishes with missing genes. This natural deficiency is counter-balanced by a greater resistance to heat, allowing the yellow sorts to be planted late in the spring and enjoyed through the early summer—the reason for the *hatif* in the French name. In terms of flavor, this variety is not ranked as high as the white and red sorts.

Jaune Hatif Summer Radish

On the other hand, climate often plays the high card, and where radishes are concerned, the very reason the yellow sort was popular in the hotter sections of France also made it popular in colonial America. The round yellow variety was well known in this country as early as 1800, and it seems to have been a consistently listed type throughout the nineteenth century, not just for its ability to withstand our sultry summers but also because its color was quite striking at table, especially when mixed with white, red, violet, and even black sorts. During the latter part of the nineteenth century, a golden yellow radish became popular due to its more delicate flavor and finer texture. It is still available, but should not be confused with the earlier sort, nor grown to seed at the same time, lest unforeseen crossing occurs.

Madras Podding Radish
Raphanus sativus

This radish variety originated in India, where it has been cultivated for centuries. It was introduced into the United States from England in 1859 by one Isaac Buchanan, but the circumstances surrounding its introduction have not yet come to light. This much is certain: the radish was cultivated exclusively for its pods, since the plant does not form an edible root. Through years of careful selection, the mild-flavored pods remain crisp and tender for a long time—as much as two weeks—rather than turning tough and woody within a few days as they do for most other radishes. Furthermore, the Madras radish thrives in hot weather and therefore can be grown during July and August when most other radishes are prone to bolt. Due to its long flowering season, which only stops with the frost, this radish should be pulled up before fall radishes are allowed to flower for seed-saving purposes. The flowers of the Madras radish are distinctive: pale pink with purple tips on the petals.

The following recipe for pickling radish pods is taken from Ella E. Myers's *Home Cook Book* (1880, 71). Her expression "to turn on" means to pour over. Her suggestion to pickle the pods while still on the stems is a good one. They do look nice that way.

To Pickle Radish Pods
❦

Gather them while quite small and tender. Keep them in salt and water, till you get through collecting them—changing the water as often as once in four or five days. Then scald them with hot salt and water, let them lie in it till cool, then turn on hot vinegar spiced with peppercorns, mace and allspice. The radish tops, if pickled in small bunches, are a pretty garnish for other pickles.

Philadelphia White Box Radish
Raphanus sativus

Hovey's *Magazine of Horticulture* (1843, 98) noted the introduction of a new radish called Long-Leaved White Turnip Radish, a top-shaped fall radish that had been introduced in France in 1841. Out of this French variety, David Landreth & Sons of Philadelphia created the Earliest White Forcing Radish, which the firm introduced in the early 1880s. This strain came to be known as the Philadelphia White Box Radish among market gardeners, and this name began appearing as such in the seed catalogs of William Henry Maule during the 1890s. The popularity of the radish was nationwide, for it was considered the most delicate and quick growing of all the white winter radishes. It was even cooked as a vegetable. Perhaps the ultimate compliment to this radish came in 1909, when it was featured in the frontispiece to volume 4 of L. H. Bailey's *Cyclopedia of American Horticulture*, the book that eventually became *Hortus Third*.

Perfect specimens of the radish are shown in color plate 79. The radish is small, round, and has very small leaves. The lack of large leaves makes it ideal as a forcing radish for cold frames. While it is best and most delicate when grown under glass, this radish can be raised in the open ground as a fall radish. I have found that it performs best in light, sandy soil. Radishes harvested late in the season can be stored in cool, damp sand and used over the winter. They will retain their crisp freshness until the following spring. Since they are extremely mild, the radishes can be used in cookery like baby turnips.

Rat-Tailed Radish, Purple-Podded Radish, or Japan Radish
Raphanus sativus var. *caudatus*

The opening of Japan by the American navy in the 1850s gave American seedsmen an advantage over Europeans in getting first dibs on many rare plants and seeds. Several of our seedsmen set up factors in Yokahama to deal exclusively in horticultural material. One of the curiosities to appear on our market as a result of this trade was the rat-tailed radish, or as it was referred to in the nineteenth century, the Japan radish.

This radish was introduced commercially in this country in 1866–67 primarily by James J. H. Gregory of Marblehead, Massachusetts, although there were several other American seedsmen who carried it. The American introduction was brought directly from Japan. However, the radish had been introduced somewhat earlier in England under the name Mougri radish, after its name in Java. In Germany, the radish was called *Schlangenrettich,* or "snake" radish, in reference to the long, sinuous shape of the pod.

In spite of the exotic appearance of the seed pods that give this variety its distinctive name, the Vick seed catalog of 1872 lamented that the rat-tailed radish "may never become popular," a sentiment echoed earlier in the August 1868 issue of the *American Agriculturist.* One of the initial problems with the radish lay in its taxonomy. Botanists have consistently classified it as *Raphanus caudatus,* thus inferring that it is a species separate from the common table radish.

I do not accept this, since it crosses with every known variety of radish that I have grown. It is the true Don Juan of radishes if there ever was one, and this ability to cross and degenerate not only itself but all the radishes near it did not earn it high marks with Victorian gardeners. The only difference between this variety and the others is that it does not develop a bulbous root. Like the Madras podding radish, it was developed with other culinary features in mind.

Unlike most radishes, this variety immediately sends up flower stalks rather than developing a thick root. The flower stems may grow as high as 3 or 4 feet, and they billow with masses of sweet-smelling blossoms. The Don Juan of radishes is also crack for butterflies, which flock around the plants in the heat of summer like bees on honey. I thoroughly enjoy growing

Rat-Tailed Radish

this radish for the show alone, but since it is a great attractor of pollinators during the height of summer when many flowers go temporarily dormant, it is a very useful addition to the vegetable garden.

The curious feature of this radish is that the flowers quickly develop into long, twining purple seed pods that do indeed resemble rat tails. In their young stage, while crisp and tender, the pods are perfect for salads, chopped into stir-fries, or used in pickles. When exposed to vinegar, the purple pods turn a brilliant green that bleeds into the pickling brine. Pennsylvania Dutch housewives discovered that by using the pods in cucumber pickles and other similar green pickles, they could enhance the green color without resorting to artificial means. The pods also impart a mild horseradish flavor to pickles and therefore can be used as a substitute where horseradish is not available. Dried, the pods retain their purple hue and curious shape, and are useful in dried flower arrangements.

The seed pods tend to make the plants top-heavy, especially after a rain. It is wise to stake the plants securely so that they are not blown over in a thundergust. In temperate areas of the country, it is possible to grow three crops in one season, or even more if seed is planted in two-week intervals from early spring through September. The plant itself is not damaged by light frost, but the pods are tender and will be injured by freezing.

White Icicle Radish
Raphanus sativus

Radishes of this much-sought-after shape are difficult enough to grow in heavy soil, not to mention that most of them are no better tasting than the small, round sorts. Why do we bother? Because there are consumers who do not know enough about food to detect the difference between quality and caprice. I resist growing these sorts of radishes, but in all fairness, if long they must be, then make them white. There is good reason for this. The long, narrow, white varieties seem to be less prone to difficulties and the most consistently sweet and mild, regardless of soil. This variety is about 6 inches in length and should be cultivated in sandy soil for best results.

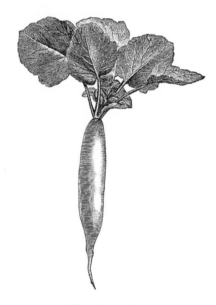

Fearing Burr (1865, 72) referred to this radish as the White Naples, White Italian, and White Transparent. All are synonyms for the same thing, and unfortunately, much to the confusion of our gardeners, there are a great many more synonyms than this. In form the radish resembles Wood's Frame, except that it is twice as long. Where the radish protrudes above the ground, the shoulders turn green. A variant form, which looks identical to this one, has shoulders that turn violet when exposed to extensive sunlight. There is no difference in taste or texture, yet the

White Icicle Radish

flowers are not quite identical. My opinion is that this purple intrusion is the result of an accidental cross, but seedsmen agitate against me because when they run out of seed for one, they substitute seed from the other, as though the two radishes are the same. Become a particular customer: only accept the green-shouldered ones as true to type.

Wood's Frame Radish
Raphanus sativus

In many ways this is the nineteenth century's answer to the bonsai vegetable. I happen to like the miniatures—the Tom Thumb lettuce, the *gloire de Quimper* pea, the Pink Pearl tomato—I guess because they are not threatening, or else because I am intrigued by their Lilliputian scale. For the diet-conscious, miniature food is not The Enemy. We eat it today because it is obviously "lite." Victorians doted on miniature vegetables for entirely different reasons. To their way of thinking, "lite" meant sickly, so Wood's Frame was seen only in the context of what it did for the food around it. In short, it was the ultimate garnish.

This is a radish with pencil-thin roots 2½ to 3 inches long and barely 1 inch in diameter at the shoulder. The skin is bright rose-red, which fades toward pink at the tip. The flesh is crisp and juicy, with a good deal of snap. Due to its small size, the radish makes an excellent addition to dainty sandwiches, one of the purposes of its development. In keeping with its small size, this radish also requires a small length of time to mature, something that takes many gardeners off guard. Twenty days, and do not forget it; 25 is too late. This is a radish

Wood's Frame Radish

that moves from perfection to flowers within a matter of days; it requires intense fussing and a commitment to cold frames. Otherwise, it is one of the easiest, one of the showiest, and one of the *cheapest* radishes to grow for profit. Imagine saving seeds every 40 days. The spring crop can pay for the fall mortgage. This is an heirloom that lays golden eggs.

Is it really an heirloom? Yes, it is a subvariety of Long Scarlet or Salmon Colored, one of the most popular red icicle-type radishes of the eighteenth century. Wood's Frame, also called New London Particular, was introduced about 1845. It became popular in this country in the 1850s and was raised almost exclusively in cold frames. In order to achieve the perfect shape, the soil in which the radish is cultivated must be deeply dug and thoroughly sifted with coarse sand. Even a small pebble will cause this radish to bend or deform. But hundreds can be grown in a small amount of space, and with experience, this is a vegetable that will heed the command of the gardener

Long Scarlet Short-Top Radish

and produce very respectable yields. For the home gardener who simply enjoys fresh produce, this radish will be a lesson in the value of heirlooms.

Saladings, Cold Weather

The convenience of supermarket vegetables the year around has led us to forget the dire shortage of green vegetables that many people suffered years ago. It has also made us forget that a well-planned kitchen garden can compensate for this seasonal ebb, for there are a great many cold-weather greens to choose from when thinking ahead toward winter. The list of greens that I have selected is admittedly short, yet I have tried to balance my choices with several overriding concerns: that the greens be easy to grow, that they not require a large amount of space in the garden, and that they provide a range of choices over the course of the season. Furthermore, my selections are compatible with all the winter lettuces in this book and can be combined creatively with fava greens, beet tops, and kales, which also serve as a source of winter greens. Lastly, none of the twelve saladings I have chosen look like one another; they are all visually distinctive, and if they are planted together, none of them will cross. For gardeners who have never dealt with winter gardening, yet who want to return to a seasonal diet, this will greatly simplify the task.

Buckshorn Plantain
Plantago cornopus

Never given much notice in American garden books, this delightful heirloom is nevertheless a garden vegetable of considerable vintage in Europe. As far as I am concerned, of all the plantains this is the most delectable, and the most beautiful. It is the *plantain corne de cerf* of Vilmorin (1885, 103) and the *Haaschhaan Selaat* (hart's horn salad) of the Pennsylvania Dutch. It is a plant that grows wild in Europe, especially in sandy areas along the coast, and when brought into cultivation, it is prolific and attains great size. But it must be kept well watered or it becomes tough, so it thrives best in the cool, damp weather of fall or early spring.

The narrow, grass-like leaves spread radially and are indented at irregular intervals in a pattern resembling the horn of a stag, hence the name. Sea plantain (*Plantago maritima*) was also called

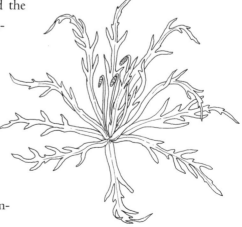

Buckshorn Plantain

buckshorn plantain in this country, and in Philadelphia, New York, and Boston it was gathered in the wild and sold in green markets prior to the Civil War. Early Americans also used tumble mustard (*Sisymbrium altissimum*) as a substitute, whose tiny radial leaves are heavily indented and a rich green. But this can be tough unless cultivated during cool weather. None of these plants would have found a place in the market had there not been a need for lavish garnishes for "standing dishes," large roasts and fancy meat dishes spread on sideboards as display pieces in nineteenth-century hotels and restaurants. The plantain is particularly attractive when tied into little bundles and used with poached ice beans (page 59) and other miniature vegetables from the period. Furthermore, it retains its color when used in aspics.

Seed can be broadcast in April and the seedlings thinned for salads, leaving the strongest plants about 4 inches apart. The leaves should always be gathered when very young, since they toughen as they mature. For fall culture, follow the directions for shepherd's purse (page 316).

Chicory
Chicorium intybus

There are three cultivated forms of chicory grown for their leaves, all *Chicorium intybus* var. *foliosum*, and one form grown exclusively for its root, *Chicorium intybus* var. *sativum*. The leafy forms include loose upright heads resembling romaine lettuce, small crimped cabbaging heads like tiny lettuces, and the tightly wrapped heads of the Witloof or Belgian endive type. The Romans raised chicory as a medical plant. There is no evidence that they had developed it into varieties similar to those known today. In fact, all of the old herbals depict chicories that resemble the wild succory of colonial America.

Years ago, when American gardeners spoke of chicory, they meant wild succory, the perennial with a long taproot now naturalized in most areas of the United States and often seen blooming with bright blue flowers along roads during August and September. This plant was introduced from Europe in the seventeenth century as a spring salad green, but mostly, its roots were used as an adulterant in coffee or as a beverage in place of coffee. For this reason, it has gained a bad reputation.

New York marketman Thomas DeVoe (1866, 329) reported that of forty-two brands of coffee tested for purity by London examiners, thirty-one had been adulterated with chicory. Chicory is still added to some coffees, and in Louisiana, where the practice is common, this is considered a local specialty and an acquired taste. German Americans also raised chicory as a source of ersatz coffee. The large rooted Braunschweig and Magdeburg varieties were developed during the 1760s specifically for this purpose.

Wild succory has another reputation which is more pertinent to the vegetable garden: it will cross with any of the cultivated forms, and therefore extreme care must be taken to ensure that it is at least half a mile from any seed-saving activity. This is further complicated by the fact that chicory is not self-fertile. Pollen from one plant must be transferred to another, and nature has endowed chicory pollen with an amazing ability to travel long distances in the wind.

The Venetian chicories that we know today as radicchio were not grown extensively in the United States until quite recently. Fearing Burr (1865, 324–25) listed several, but his material was lifted from Vilmorin seed books, not based on firsthand experience. His variegated or spotted chicory we would recognize as the *variegata di Castelfranco*, definitely an eighteenth-century variety. The red chicory called *rossa di Treviso* also dates from the eighteenth century. The latter variety has become an invasive weed in my garden. Anyone who is prepared to save chicory seed had better *like* chicory, for it will spread faster than dandelions.

This overabundance of greens would be welcome if they were not also very bitter. Bitterness is one reason the leaves are used sparingly in salads, but the plants can also be blanched by covering them with straw or soil. Most of the Venetian varieties have been bred to form tight heads, which make them easier to blanch. This is also true of Witloof endive or Belgian endive, a chicory introduced commercially about 1830.

Cooking is another method for removing bitterness. The Venetians in the Marca Trevigiana have evolved many recipes for preparing radicchio. They are served as *contorini*, light dishes following the main course, but just as appropriate

Witloof Chicory

as lunch fare. A glass of crisp pinot grigio is a good match for any of the cooked chicory dishes.

Growing chicories from seed is not difficult, but the secret to good chicory is planting it early. This means that seed should be started indoors or in cold frames so that large seedlings can be planted out as soon as the threat of severe frosts has passed. Light frosts will not damage chicory, but hot weather will certainly make it bitter. Fall plantings should be undertaken in late August.

Variegata di Castelfranco Radicchio (18th Century form)

Variegata di Castelfranco Radicchio (modern form)

Rossa di Treviso Radicchio

In areas of the country where winters are mild, chicory can even be planted in December. It overwinters in my garden, but maintains a better appearance if protected by straw.

Corn Salad
Valerianella locusta

I collect corn salad. I do not know why, but it fascinates me, and what is very surprising, I think, is the large number of varieties that are readily available. All of them are different—different leaf shapes, different habits of growth, and slightly different flavors. If I had to liken the taste of corn salad to anything, I would say it tastes like peanuts, and not surprisingly, a well-flavored peanut oil will make a delightful salad dressing because it enhances that taste. Most Americans have come to know corn salad only quite recently under its French name *mâche*, but corn salad has been in American kitchen gardens since the seventeenth century. It is very easy to find it in old garden books under its antique name, fetticus.

Corn salad is definitely antique: seeds for two species have been found in the archaeological remains of the lake dwellings in Switzerland, so it was evidently well appreciated even in the late Stone Age. Unfortunately, the archaeological and historical record remains silent after that. It appears that corn salad was not so much cultivated in gardens as it was harvested from the wild, at least until the eighteenth century. In a painting from the 1500s called *Spring*, by Lucas Van Valkenborch, an Elizabethan gentlewoman is depicted sorting through baskets of spring greens, including lovage, smallage, Persian cress (page 313), and corn salad. The leaf of Van Valkenborch's corn salad is long and narrow, a characteristic of the oldest varieties.

Our name for corn salad is equivalent to the German *Feldsalat*, meaning a green gathered from the fields—specifically, from wheatfields, for in England wheat is known as corn. The German garden writer Florianus mentioned in 1701 that in the spring corn salad should be dug up from the fields and brought into the kitchen garden. This is one of the earliest references to improving varieties through selection, but in Europe, even into the 1840s, most corn salad was gathered from the wild rather than cultivated. William Darlington (1837, 11) reported that it was growing wild in certain parts of Chester County, Pennsylvania, where I live, obviously introduced from Europe. In fact, I recently discovered a patch of a very old variety naturalized along the Schuylkill River near Norristown, Pennsylvania. It resembles the leaf type depicted by Van Valkenborch.

There are two types of corn salad, the Italian (*Valerianella eriocarpa*) and the species discussed above. The Italian species grows very tall when it blooms, as much as 16 inches, and has large, hairy leaves. It was introduced commercially in 1827 because its flavor was considered milder than the common sort, it came to perfection earlier, and it made a respectable substitute for spinach, which is often difficult to grow. Unfortunately, the Italian species is not as hardy as the *locusta,* so it has never been popular in this country. Hardiness is a key factor; it is pointless to grow corn salad as a cold-weather salading unless it can be overwintered successfully.

The variety known as Large Round Leaved was the most popular in the United States with market gardeners due to its extraordinary hardiness. It was illustrated in the *Album Vilmorin* (1869, 20) and looks very much like the strain that has naturalized in part of my garden. This variety has survived temperatures of minus 10° F without protection and any visible damage. It blooms in April and May and produces an abundance of seed. If no other variety is planted, this one will always prove itself for reliability. Fearing Burr (1865, 328) listed it among the corn salads he recommended for the garden; its reputation was well established by then, for it had been under cultivation since the 1840s. The plant is extremely rich in vitamin C and carotene, and these dietary benefits have been appreciated for a very long time. In the old days of the eighteenth century, the first appearance of corn salad was always celebrated with a plate of red herring buried beneath a heap of freshly picked corn salad. There is nothing in the chilly days of March that lifts the spirits more than this overture to summer.

For spring crops, seed should be planted in September. If seed is planted thickly, it can be thinned for salads well into December. If the plant has established itself as a "weed," it will appear toward the end of September and can be harvested, saving the strongest plants for seed the following spring. All varieties of corn salad will cross with each other, except for the Italian *eriocarpa.* I have isolated varieties by 500 feet and forced them to bloom at different times. While there is no information available on techniques for maintaining seed purity, thus far my method appears to be successful.

Endive
Chicorium endivia

The direct ancestor of the cultivated endive is *Cicorium pumilum* (also written *Cicorium endivia* L. sp. *divaricatum*), a wild plant distributed throughout the Mediterranean. At some point over two thousand years ago it was brought under cultivation, and out of this developed the garden varieties we know today. The Romans raised endives as a winter salad because the plants were hardier than lettuce. Furthermore, the Romans preferred varieties with white seed (which they felt produced more tender greens) and blanched the mature leaves by tying them up as I have suggested for Turkish rocket (page 316).

There is not much information in either historical or archaeological records linking the Roman endives of classical antiquity to those of the late Middle Ages, but it is documented that the culture of the endive moved from Italy to France, and from there to Germany. However, by the late 1400s the center of culture appears to have been the Veneto of northern Italy, especially the region around Padua, for there were many identifiable Venetian varieties early in the

1500s. It has been suggested that the breeding techniques developed for endive served Venetian horticulturists in perfecting their radicchios. Whatever the case, endive in America has been a rare bird on the vegetable market; in the days of Thomas Jefferson, it was only the gentleman farmer who could point them out in his garden.

Dr. William Darlington (1837, 440) noted that endive was cultivated in the vicinity of Philadelphia as a luxury food, which for that period made sense, given the large number of French restaurants and French caterers working in the city. I think it is fair to suggest that Americans have always associated endive with foreign cookery, and still do. Fearing Burr (1865, 335–43) devoted considerable space to endive because it was a profitable market vegetable for truck farmers near large cities, not because it was common in American kitchen gardens. His selection of varieties was lifted from the proceedings of the London Horticultural Society and thus reflected what was common in Convent Garden rather than what Americans might see in Boston, New York, or Philadelphia at the time.

New York marketman Thomas DeVoe (1866, 332) confused his chicories and endives, but at least he recognized what was then common and what was not. The curled endives were the most popular, and that is the type that I grow myself. He also mentioned the eighteenth-century variety broad-leafed Batavian (the French escarole), "principally used by the French and Germans," which was prepared in soups, stews, ragouts, and with roasts. The blanched leaves were cut for salads. This kind of cookery, whether Pennsylvania Dutch or urban "French," was always considered gourmet by American standards. Yet moss endive, as we now call it, is extremely easy to grow, and with the fecundity of Treviso chicory, it will take

Broad Leaved Batavian Endive

to the garden like a weed, if allowed to reproduce promiscuously. The most effective way to blanch moss endive is to use a cloche. Large flowerpots will also do.

Regardless of variety, all endives should be planted early. By early I mean as soon as the ground can be worked. But the seedlings should be started even earlier, so that they are already strong plants when set out. At that stage, a late frost will not hurt them, yet they should be harvested before the onset of hot weather, which not only toughens them but also causes them to bolt.

For seed-saving purposes, set aside six or eight plants and let them bolt. Tie them up to dry like shepherd's purse (page 316). Endive will not cross with common chicory, yet it will require a designated space in the garden because it takes several months to bloom and set ripe seed. Where space is crucial, this consideration is extremely important; I would plant seed stock off to the back or in a corner where it will be out of the way.

Persian Broadleaf Cress
Lepidium sativum

There are quite a number of pepper grasses grown for spring and fall salads, but this is my favorite. It is quite different from shallot cress, although both have broad leaves, and appears to be the *cresson Alenois à large feuille* of Vilmorin (1885, 207). It is an annual that reseeds freely and reappears each fall toward the early part of October. It is perfect with crisp winter lettuces, and

Persian Broadleaf Cress

years ago was stuck between the split halves of a soft pretzel to make a type of quick sandwich. It also went into "flatdog" sandwiches, made of fried sliced bologna between slices of toast. The plants are quite diminutive, even when in full bloom no more than 1½ to 2 feet tall. They begin as small clumps of radial leaves and should be harvested at that stage. The leaves resemble tiny apple leaves and make an interesting visual effect when scattered over the top of salads.

Seed saving is not complicated. The flower is white and produces a flat seed pod similar to that of shallot cress. Once the pods mature, the stems can be cut off at the base and stuck upside down into a brown paper bag. Mark the bag and date it, then set it away in a cool dry place so that the seed will dry and mature for about three months. Shake the pods so that the seed falls to the bottom of the bag. Sieve out debris, then store the seed in an airtight jar until needed. The seed will remain vital for five years, but should be renewed every two years so that there is always a supply of fresh seed on hand.

Rocket
Eruca sativa

I have several varieties of rocket in my collection, one from Turkey, another from Greece, a yellow-flowering species called meadow rocket (*Eruca selvatica*), and my favorite, an old seventeenth-century variety that came from the Villa Foscari near Venice. It is known in the Veneto as *rucola veneziana* or Venetian rocket, and has now naturalized in my garden. In the spring and fall, when it is most delicate, it has a flavor vaguely reminiscent of tuna fish. I often chop it and mix it into pasta or rice dishes, for rocket is not always eaten raw.

Rockets have become popular again in this country after a hiatus of about a hundred years. The colonial kitchen garden always had its rocket bed, not so much for culinary purposes as for medical. Thomas DeVoe, in his *Market Assistant* (1866, 364), noted that it was mostly sold among the herbs in East Coast markets, not as it is today, as a rather common vegetable tucked in among the lettuces and celeries. For some reason, quite unclear to me, American greengrocers sell rocket under the name arugula, which is southern Italian dialect. It is like calling beans *faggiul*, or snails *lumache*, or conversely, about as elegant as calling dandelion by its American dialect name, Piss-a-Bed.

Different varieties of rocket will cross easily and therefore should not be raised at the same time unless carefully caged. Otherwise, they will all blend together and degenerate into a coarse form similar to the rockets depicted in paintings from the sixteenth century. Even the Venetian rocket that I have carefully maintained for the past twenty-five years has gradually altered; now and again, it produces sports with furry leaves of a very different pattern from the rest. Close observation is the only key to success; odd-looking plants should never be allowed to go to seed.

Once the plants bloom in June and set seed, tie them up so that the pods remain off the ground. When the pods begin to turn brown, follow the same procedure as for shepherd's purse (page 316) and allow the seed to dry in bags for several months. In the late summer a different variety can be planted; thus it is possible to keep several varieties going without having them mix. All the rockets that I have grown, even the ones from the Mediterranean, remain green over the winter without protection.

Salad Burnet
Sanguisorba minor

I cannot recall when I have not grown salad burnet. I discovered it growing in a shady corner of my grandmother's garden and moved the entire patch to Devon many years ago. I have seen it growing around abandoned farmhouses in many parts of the eastern United States. It was certainly considered an important part of the Pennsylvania Dutch kitchen garden, not just as a source of flavorful salad greens but as a medical herb as well. In the spring, fresh sprigs of it were infused in wine as a tonic. It is delightful in champagne punch.

Salad burnet is a native of Europe, introduced to America during colonial times. It has small, delicate leaves that taste like cucumber. The greens are best in the early spring—one of the first greens to push new growth that time of year—and in the fall from late September to Christmas. During this time the new shoots are

Salad Burnet

pale green and very tender, and can be eaten raw. During hot weather the leaves and stems toughen, but especially so when the plant blooms. Pruning off the flower stalks will prolong salad production well into the summer. If given protection in the winter with loose straw or even dead leaves, the plant will remain green most of the winter. It will thrive in a cold frame.

In my garden, salad burnet is perennial, but it also reseeds profusely. It is easier to establish it in the garden by purchasing one or two small plants from a garden shop and then letting them reseed. I cultivate one or two large clumps for seed purposes because it is best every few years to renew the bed with younger plants. The older plants sometimes burn out during summer droughts or succumb to ice in the winter. A well-drained location is also essential because during the spring thaw too much water will kill the plants.

I have seen Pennsylvania Dutch kitchen gardens where the beds, especially saffron beds, were completely outlined with little hedges of salad burnet. This is a practical way to delineate a part of the garden that is dormant most of the year, since saffron emerges to bloom in October, its leaves remaining green over the winter, only to die back in the late spring. Salad burnet also serves as a decoy for rabbits, since rabbits prefer it to the green tops of saffron. If they eat the saffron greens, the plants will not produce flowers the following season, and in a saffron bed every flower counts.

Shallot Cress
Lepidium campestre var. *mahantongo*

Mahantongo shallot cress is a form of pepper grass that I discovered several years ago growing on the site of the old Hepler farm (now part of Christiansbrunn Cloister) near Pitman in the Mahantongo Valley of central Pennsylvania. It is an early Pennsylvania German strain brought to that area in the 1820s. With a flavor like garlic or shallots, this cress remains green over the winter and, if covered with straw, can even be harvested from under deep snows. Once used extensively in winter salads, especially with chopped cabbage or in potato salad, it is also an excellent substitute for chives while that herb is dormant during the winter months. Like chives, it can be used in stir-fries or with cooked greens.

Common pepper grass (*Lepidium compestre*) was introduced to this country from Europe in ship ballast during the eighteenth century and has become an irritating weed. However, the origin of the Mahantongo variety is obscure, and it differs in several physical respects from other common lepidiums; thus it may represent a separate but undocumented species. For one thing, its seed pods resemble those of *Thlaspi peroliatum*. Bernard M'Mahon listed a *Lepidium sativum* in 1815, which he described as a variety called "Broad-Leaved." The Mahantongo strain may be descended from this, for certainly it resembles an oversize version of an old variety of corn salad also called "Broad-Leaved."

Shown in color plate 84, the plant is a hardy biennial that blooms in the late spring with white flowers. It must be planted in the late summer if it is to be used as a garden crop over the winter. The small, compact plants produce radial leaves that quickly attain their maximum size, about 6 inches in diameter, and remain that way over the winter. Its distinct shallot flavor is improved by frost, but once the plant revives in the spring, the leaves turn bitter. Since onion greens become available by then, this tradeoff is not an inconvenience.

Shepherd's Purse
Capsella bursa-pastoris

A hardy annual or biennial that overwinters well for late spring and early summer greens, this ancient member of the mustard family was introduced in the 1600s not only as a garden green but as an important ingredient in folk medicine. The Pennsylvania Dutch call it *Bockseckel*, a name of Celtic origin meaning "ram's scrotum," doubtless in reference to the magical talisman that we know in English by its more euphemistic name. Grown in rich soil, shepherd's purse may produce leaves up to 10 inches long, which can be used as a substitute for spinach. To me, the flavor resembles that of broccoli or cauliflower, and holds up well in stir-fried vegetables. It can also be eaten raw in salads and is a rich source of vitamins and minerals.

For late spring or early summer greens, start the seeds in flats during March, then thin into individual pots or containers. In April, after the threat of frost, plant the seedlings 4 inches apart in the full sun. This crop will bolt in late June or early July and produce an abundance of seed. Start this seed in August in a cool, shady location, then thin into containers. In September, plant in the full sun. In the late fall, cover with straw to protect the plants over the winter, then remove the straw the following March. This method will produce a continuous supply of greens throughout most of the year, since the plants under the straw can be harvested during the winter. In fact, most cold-weather saladings can be maintained in full production this way.

Reserve about five or six plants for seed-saving purposes. As the seed stock ripens (the pods begin to turn from green to brown), harvest the entire stock and dry it on plain white paper or in a large bowl. The seed pods burst when ripe and will scatter over a large area of the garden unless intercepted in this manner. Shaking the stocks or touching the dry pods will also cause them to burst. If this is done over paper or a bowl, the seeds are easily collected. Since the seed is fine like sand, it is easy to separate from debris with a sieve. I have had seed remain vital for as long as six years.

Turkish Rocket
Bunias orientalis

Of all the greens in this section, Turkish rocket is one of the least known in the United States, yet it has been grown here since the eighteenth century. One of the earliest references to it appeared in the correspondence of John Bartram (1992, 520), who evidently had supplied seed to Martha Logan, a wealthy Philadelphia plant collector, for she was growing it in her garden in

1761 under the name Siberian rocket. Turkish rocket is native to that part of Asia and is therefore one of the hardiest of the salad greens in this book.

The native American sea rocket (*Calkile edentula*) was once called *Bunias edentula* and treated as a close relative, but the two plants are actually quite different. Superficially, the leaves of Turkish rocket resemble those of dame's rocket, an old-fashioned garden flower known for its sweet scent. Yet its leaves are larger, covered with fine hairs, and pale whitish green, as shown in color plate 85. The young leaves and shoots are eaten raw in salads or cooked as a potherb. The flavor is strong, resembling horseradish, although frost usually mellows the flavor and tenderizes the leaves, so it is best during the fall or spring.

Turkish rocket has naturalized in several places in the United States. In Pennsylvania, it is also known as hill mustard since it prefers to grow on bald, stony ground on slag heaps around old mining sites. Botanists have incorrectly presumed that it came to North America in ship ballast, when in fact it was imported and disseminated as a medical plant in the 1830s, especially by the Harmonites in western Pennsylvania. It is no accident that *Bunias orientalis* can still be found in areas near the old Harmonite religious communities. Its importance in homeopathic medicine lay in its application as an antiscorbutic for "lymphatic disturbances," an archaic expression for immune deficiencies. Because of this connection the plant has recently undergone a revival of interest, although its true medical properties remain unexplored.

The plant is still eaten extensively in Central Europe, where it is served chopped into sour cream with minced dill or fennel. As a cooked vegetable, it needs doctoring. Turabi Effendi noted in his *Turkish Cookery Book* (1862, 67–68) that bitter vegetables of this sort must first be scalded before they are cooked. This takes off the acrid radish taste. "If large, they are cut in pieces and placed in a stewpan, with a sufficient quantity of water, salt, and a few sliced onions previously fried a nice brown in butter or olive oil." He further explained that fresh (clear) tomato juice was often used instead of broth or water. This definitely improves the flavor.

Turkish rocket is easy to grow and will thrive in hot, dry locations where many garden vegetables fail. It can be cultivated like cardoon and blanched by tying up the leaves, or it can be raised as an ornamental like dame's rocket, since its flower is sweet-scented and attractive to butterflies. As a cut flower it will last for several days even without water. The plant is hardy and overwinters in some of the coldest sections of Pennsylvania, so for practical purposes it may be treated as a perennial, even in northern Maine.

Winter Cress, Scurvy Grass
Barbarea stricta; Barbarea verna (Barbarea praecox); Barbarea vulgaris

There are three closely related mustards that go by the common name of winter cress or herb of Saint Barbara. All three are natives of Europe that have naturalized in North America and are so similar in appearance to the casual viewer that a botanical book is necessary to point out their differences, which are mostly in the subtle shapes of the leaves. Furthermore, seedsmen often sell one for the other, so there is no telling which one is likely to appear under the name of winter cress. The only way to know for certain is to grow them side by side. However, from a culinary standpoint, these greens are all the same, since they taste like watercress and are used like watercress in cookery.

Horticulturists generally refer to *Barbarea vulgaris* as common winter cress, upland cress, or yellow rocket. *Barbarea verna* (also called *B. praecox*) is usually called early winter cress or Belle Isle cress. The plant shown in color plate 86 is *Barbarea verna* and, like the others, it has yellow flowers. Philadelphia seedsman Bernard M'Mahon devoted some attention to winter cresses (1806, 455) because they were an important market crop in colonial America. Early winter cress was also known as scurvy grass in Philadelphia and many parts of the South, because it was one of the few green vegetables available during the depths of winter as a source for vitamin C. This is one reason why I recommend it for kitchen gardens today.

Upland Cress

Culture is the same as for shepherd's purse (page 316). Once established, a patch of cresses will remain green over the winter and can be harvested even on the snowiest days of January. If covered with straw as a protection, the cresses will also retain their crisp, green appearance and take the place of watercress as a garnish. Watercress tends to turn yellow if kept too long under refrigeration; winter cress will store in the refrigerator for several weeks, especially if the entire plant is pruned to leave part of the root. But there is also another benefit: birds love the seeds.

These cresses bloom in early June, when the plants shoot up to a height of 3½ or even 4 feet if the ground is rich. They must then be staked and covered with netting or finches and grosbeaks will strip them within the course of a few hours. Cage birds such as canaries also like the seed, and at one time there was a small cottage industry devoted to growing cress seed for pets. Since the cresses produce vast quantities of seed, there is always plenty for next year's crop and the winter bird feeder. This generosity is self-serving. Encouraging birds to forage in the garden during the winter also accustoms them to foraging there during the growing season, and this greatly reduces damage from insects.

Winter Purslane
Montia perfoliata

This is an excellent native vegetable with a misleading name. It is not related to purslane (page 323) and is not even vaguely like it in taste or texture. But it is first cousin to Spring Beauty, a handsome little flower also native to North America. Named for Giuseppe Monti, a professor of botany at the University of Cologne in the eighteenth century, the plant was originally called *Claytonia perfoliata,* and is still known in England and Europe under this botanical designation. It is native to the Pacific Coast and Rocky Mountain states from Mexico northward to British Columbia, not Cuba, as Vilmorin claimed (1885, 481–82). While jogging along San Francisco Bay, I have seen it growing wild in woodsy locations, and nearly twice the size that it attains in my garden back in Pennsylvania. On the West Coast the plant develops a nodelike root that has a nutty flavor. Both the greens and the root were gathered as food by the Indians.

The plant grows anywhere from 4 to 12 inches tall in its native habitat, forming a small cluster of cup-shaped leaves that closely resemble the green flower of Bells of Ireland. It is an annual that bolts early in the summer but reseeds in damp, shady locations. The greens are usually gathered young, before the plant begins to bloom, and used in salads or cooked like spinach, which it resembles in taste. Winter purslane is grown extensively in Europe but has never been quite as popular in this country. I suspect that this has something to do with its other common name, miner's lettuce, also a misnomer.

Winter Purslane or Miner's Lettuce

The vegetable received considerable attention during the days of the California gold rush, when it served as a cheap and readily available source of greens for the miners. Unfortunately, this name carried with it the implication of a rough-and-ready emergency food, not an elegant green for proper Victorian tables. This may have helped prejudice many Americans against it in the nineteenth century, especially since it was a common "weed." Happily, it has recently undergone a revival of interest as part of a general shift toward exploring American regional ingredients.

The seed of winter purslane is very small and black. It is easiest grown by sowing broadcast where the plant is to be cultivated. Choose a moist, shady location for best results. In the spring, plant the seed after the threat of frost has passed. For a fall harvest, plant in early September or, in the South, during early November. Seed is ripe when the plants begin to turn yellow. Seed can be gathered by shaking the plants over a large bowl. It remains vital for about five years when properly stored.

Saladings, Warm Weather

There are times when I think salads have become a lost art, for no matter where I go in this country, the same insipid vegetables manage to surface on the menu. They are usually described as "fresh," which means "not dead," trucked in from a distant semidesert field harvested by underpaid Mexicans and infested with whiteflys, gray aphids, and poison. Vinegar does not hide the taste of insecticidal sprays, but chardonnay is one chic way to fool untrained palettes. A clever kitchen gardener does not need to spend one penny on dubious saladings when for just a small amount of effort in the backyard bed, extraordinary greens can be brought to perfection with little or no effort. I have chosen thirteen saladings that are for the most part insect-free, not bothered by common diseases, and will make salads of extraordinary beauty. I like salads that fall into my plate like a piñata broken open. For color and textures, my thirteen favorites will not disappoint.

Alexanders
Smyrnium olisatrum

Also known as black lovage and black potherb, this impressive tall perennial looks very much like the herb angelica but is considerably less temperamental to grow. It reaches a height of about 4 feet and prefers deep, rich soil. Today I often see it raised as a specimen plant in herb gardens rather than as a vegetable, for it is now rarely grown as a potherb. In cookery it has been replaced by celery, although the two are as different from one another as apples and pears. Furthermore, from a gardening standpoint, Alexanders is far easier to grow than celery, more resistant to frosts, and does not require the constant attention that celery demands if it is to be anything like presentable. This low-maintenance aspect is probably one reason why Alexanders was once so popular in kitchen gardens of country people.

Alexanders

Philadelphia nurseryman John Bartram distributed seed to a number of customers in the 1760s. However, there is ample evidence from New England and the South to show that Alexanders was introduced early in the 1600s and that it was popular with cooks of that period. The stems can be used like celery and the leaves like parsley, although the flavor is distinct—I would say pungent—ranging from strong celery seed to a hint of pine or rosemary. It seems to work best in recipes where we might use rosemary or sage today; thus it is excellent in stuffings, bread puddings, and most pork dishes. English diarist John Evelyn (1699, 7) recommended Alexanders as a salad green blanched under flowerpots to sweeten its flavor, or chopped and boiled in a "vernal pottage," a species of spring stew.

From the Middle Ages into the latter part of the eighteenth century, Alexanders was used extensively in "black" recipes, that is, in blood dishes like black pudding or Polish goose blood soup. The pungency of Alexanders nicely complemented the fattiness and strong taste of that type of cookery. Today, it offers an alternative flavoring for bean, potato, and lentil recipes.

The seed of Alexanders is hard and difficult to germinate because it requires a cold treatment. Plant the seed in a small flat, cover with a plastic bag, and store in the coldest part of the refrigerator for two months. Then freeze the flat for one or two days, let it thaw in the refrigerator, then uncover and move it to a cool but well-lit windowsill. The seed should germinate in a matter of two weeks. Otherwise, plant the seed in the garden during the late fall and let it overwinter in the ground to germinate the following spring.

Bliton or Horsetooth Amaranth
Amaranthus lividus (*Amaranthus viridis*)

I cannot imagine a vegetable easier to grow or more prolific of summer greens than this one. It is also one of the oldest cultivated potherbs in this book. The ancient Greeks raised it as a garden green, and people throughout the Mediterranean still grow it in kitchen gardens. In fact, my seed came from Athens, where it is grown and harvested when about a foot tall and cooked like spinach. When the plant is older, the stems toughen, so only the leaves and new shoots should be used.

During the Roman period, bliton was introduced into France and Germany, but its culture is limited to mild-climate areas. The plant grows very well in Pennsylvania. In parts of the South, it has naturalized and become a common weed. Since it is a subtropical plant, seed should be started indoors, then thinned to flats. Transplant large seedling out of doors when the ground is warm enough to plant beans. This will give the amaranth a head start against early frost, for it often sets seed only toward the end of September or early October. If it is being raised purely for greens and not also for seed, the seed can be planted broadcast where it is to grow after the danger of frost has passed. Seedlings can be thinned for salads or used like spinach.

Dandelion
Taraxacum officinale

Dandelion offers one of the richest sources of vitamins and minerals of all the garden greens. Among the Pennsylvania Dutch it was (and still is) the centerpiece of Green Thursday, the Thursday before Good Friday, when families go into the fields to gather the makings of hot salads and cooked greens. The aroma of bacon dressing and ham pervades the landscape. Many Americans still gather dandelion from the wild, but historically, there were three varieties cultivated for use in kitchen gardens.

In 1840 *Le Bon Jardinier* devoted some attention to the improvement of dandelion from the wild. By that time the three basic varieties had already evolved, each quite distinct from the other. The broad-leaved sort (*pissenlit très hautif à large feuille*), called French Broad Leaf in the United States, was the most popular in this country. It was generally cooked as a spring green or used in hot salads.

French Dandelion

The solid-hearted or cabbaging variety (*pissenlit à coeur plein*), shown in the woodcut, was considered the finest by the French. It was popular with European market gardeners because it could be blanched and sold for a high price, but was too labor intensive for most gardeners in this country. The third type, *pissenlit mousse* or moss dandelion, which resembles moss endive, was grown largely in kitchen gardens rather than as a commercial crop. It is popular in Italy, where seed is still generally available under the names *radicchiello, soffione,* or *tarassaco.* It should not be confused with Italian dandelion, the misleading commercial name used in this country for *cicoria catalogna.*

The development of dandelion as a commercial crop did not occur in this country until well after the Civil War. Peter Chase, a market gardener near Brattleboro, Vermont, who called himself "the greenest" of the green people, described dandelion farming as it was then evolving in an article for *Vick's Illustrated Monthly Magazine* (1882, 364–65). Chase recommended the French Broad Leaf variety, and that is the one I grow in my garden. Certainly, of the three types, it is the easiest to cultivate.

The leaves are large and upright, ranging from 12 to 14 inches in length, forming thick clumps rather than lying flat against the ground like the wild sort. Individual plants should be spaced two feet apart, or crowding will result in mildew damage during hot humid weather. The plants bloom about mid-April, with flower stems measuring 24 to 30 inches. The flowering is profuse and makes a perfect crop for dandelion wine. Dandelion wine well made tastes like dry sherry, and was once considered a tonic for liver complaints.

All of the cultivated dandelions will cross with wild ones, so it is extremely important to keep the garden stock well isolated. The plants of all three varieties are treated as perennials and therefore serve as a source of greens for many years. It is a good idea, however, to renew the beds every five years and to move the plants to a different part of the garden. Dandelions draw up large amounts of minerals from the soil and will exhaust the ground if raised too long on one spot. Cultivated dandelions reproduce as prolifically as their wild cousins and can become invasive unless kept in check.

Golden Purslane
Portulaca oleracea

Of all the saladings in this section, purslane is indeed the most sensitive to cold. Even weather in the range of 50° to 60° F does not agree with it. Purslane must have baking hot sun and baking hot ground, and the worse the soil the better. All of us have dry spots in our gardens where nothing seems to grow; purslane is the ideal answer.

Purslane grows wild in this country, and anyone who gardens regularly knows very well what an obnoxious weed it can be. Yet even that lowly weed is edible, a problem as simple to solve as dusting off a salad bowl. However, there are cultivated purslanes that are far superior to the wild sorts, and of these, the yellow variety is the most distinctive. It is certainly my favorite, and I have been growing it for many years.

John Evelyn mentioned golden purslane in his *Acetaria* (1699, 55–56), prepared in salads, pickled, or cooked like a potherb. Cooking reduces the leaves of all purslanes to mush, but the young stems, poached in white wine, make a delightful vegetable. They must be harvested young, for when the stems begin to turn pink or red, they will be tough and woody. John Nott provided a recipe for pickling the stems in his *Cooks and Confectioners Dictionary* (1726, 269):

To Pickle Purslain

❦

Put your Purslain into as much Wine as Water, with a little salt; then boil it, put it into a Pot, and pour as much White-wine Vinegar, as will cover it; if you please, you may add Sugar to your White-wine.

I have made this pickle, and a little sugar does not hurt, for it brings out the lemony flavor of the purslane. Actually, the flavor of purslane is neutral; it is the presence of acids in the leaves that produce the lemony sensation, which can be used to good advantage in cookery.

Golden purslane is upright rather than spreading like the wild sorts and can grow as tall as 12 inches if the situation is to its liking. The leaves are larger than the wild plants, very round, thick, and perfect for salads or as a raw garnish. Due to their brilliant yellow-green color, the young leaves are extremely decorative. As the plant matures, the yellow changes to a deeper green (color plate 88).

Purslane is raised by broadcasting the seed over the bed where it is to grow once the ground is warm enough to plant beans. The seed will not germinate if the weather is cool, so there is no point trying to plant it early. However, once summer has set in and the evenings are hot (over 70°F), purslane can be planted in two-week successions until September. It matures quickly, within 4 to 6 weeks, and goes to seed fast, so it is important to space plantings so that there is a constant supply all summer.

Golden purslane is self-pollinating, but because of insects, it will cross with the common weed as well as with the Tall Green and other cultivated varieties, even as far away as 500 feet. It is therefore best to grow only one variety at a time and vigorously exterminate the weed anywhere near the kitchen garden. Golden purslane blooms with a tiny yellow flower that is visited by small wasps and other insects early in the morning. As the seedpods form, they dry and burst open. Seed can be gathered by nipping off the seedheads with scissors and letting them dry in paper bags. The seed is black and finer than sand. A small patch of purslane in the garden 10 feet square will yield sufficient greens for family use and vast quantities of seed.

Good King Henry
Chenopodium bonus-henricus

In the Roman Open-Air Museum at Schwarzenacker near Homburg/Saar in Germany there is a large *terra sigillata* bowl ornamented with springing hares and Good King Henry. The bowl is presumed to have been buried when the town on that site burned in A.D. 275 or 276. The well-known association of Good King Henry with the fattening of geese or rabbits for feast days has survived from the religious practices of the ancient Gauls in the form of medieval folktales and customs. Good King Henry was known in England as Mercury or Allgood, which firmly places it as the herb of Lugh, the "good" god, the "clever" god of the ancient Gauls and Britons. The full meaning of the pictorial metaphors on that ancient ceremonial punch bowl cannot be precisely interpreted today, but the site near Homburg where it was found was a Gaulish market center, and therefore a *Lugdunum*, a place with a sacred grove dedicated to Lugh, for he was also the god of commerce. All of these various Lugh connections suggest a fascinating history for the vegetable with the euphemistic name Good King Henry,

Good King Henry shown with flowerhead.

and offer some explanation why the plant remained so valuable to the kitchen garden down through time.

In his Pennsylvania German herbal, the issue for 1774, Christopher Sauer described its culinary uses: "It is customary to cook this potherb, stems and tender shoots, in meat stock with butter, salt, and a few herbs, and eat it thus. It is a well-known side dish as well liked as asparagus and young hops." The tender shoots were indeed considered a delicacy, for they are among the first greens to appear in the spring—and one of the last to disappear in the fall. The plant is a hardy perennial, about a foot tall, and prefers rich soil in semishade. I have planted it in a bed five feet square, and this supplies me amply for eight months of the year. The leaves taste like spinach and can be used in any recipe where spinach or a similar green is called for.

Good King Henry has one drawback: it does not bear transplanting once established. Therefore, it must be planted when very young, or the seed must be broadcast in the fall on the spot where it is to grow. The seed requires a cold treatment like that suggested for Alexanders (page 320), and plants require a year to establish themselves before harvesting can commence. Once established, the plants can be kept cropped to about 6 inches in height. They should also be kept well watered during dry weather, or they may go into dormancy until early fall.

Goosefoot or Lamb's-Quarters
Chenopodium album

Much maligned as an invasive weed from Europe, this is one of those common annual plants that deserves better recognition. It grows 1 to 3 feet tall, but is best for culinary purposes when small, under 10 inches. The leaves are gray and taste like walnuts. They are delicious in mixed salads with hickory nuts, or with a walnut oil dressing. Furthermore, the seeds can be ground to make a flour that resembles buckwheat flour in color and taste. The seeds can also be parched, ground, and mixed with cornmeal for mush or johnny cakes. If the greens are to be cooked, they are best done in a microwave oven for about 10 minutes. A good combination is goosefoot, beet greens, and spinach; leeks of course—always add leeks.

Aside from *Chenopodium album*, there is also red goosefoot (*Chenopodium rubrum*), which has a reddish stem. It is prepared exactly like common goosefoot. Other chenopodiums worth mentioning include strawberry spinach (*Chenopodium capitatum*), which produces a red berrylike fruit—edible but seedy—and tree spinach or purple goosefoot (*Chenopodium giganteum*). All of these should be started in flats and thinned to 8 inches apart in the garden after the threat of frost has passed, or seeded broadcast in the late spring. None of the chenopodiums just mentioned will cross with one another, since they are from different species; therefore they can be grown in a bed off to themselves. It is a good idea to keep them under control; once planted, they will return year after year after year.

Indian Cress (Nasturtium)
Tropaeolum maius

There are actually two types of common garden nasturtiums, leaving out the exotic ones that produce edible tubers or the exquisitely fringed vining type known in the old days as *Tropaeolum moritzianum*, for which I will always have an eternal weakness. I am speaking simply of the small-leaved species called *Tropaeolum minus*, introduced into Europe in the 1500s, usually bush in habit, and the vining species known as *Tropaeolum maius*, introduced from Peru by Dutch botanist Hieronymus van Beverningk in 1684. While both species are sold under the rubric of nasturtium (the botanical name for watercress, to which they are not related), it is the large vining type that I recommend for the kitchen garden. Its benefits are obvious: it can be trained on a fence, and it lends a delectable backdrop that can be stripped daily for salads yet enjoyed throughout the summer season. And it comes in several colors.

Philadelphia botanist John Bartram propagated and sold it in the 1760s under the name Great Garden Cress and probably grew it much earlier. Christopher Sauer's Pennsylvania German herbal mentioned it specifically in the supplement for 1764: "The pretty orange flowers that it produces in great profusion are not only quite decorative but, above all else, they are delicious to eat as well as healthful, thus they are served in salads."

The orange-flowered cultivar was most popular in colonial America, although there were also yellow and crimson varieties. The yellow one is shown in color plate 90. The orange variety that I raise is remarkably similar to the specimen illustrated in *Curtis's Botanical Magazine*, so I suspect that it is still possible to find seed that does come close to many of the historical varieties. Botanist William Darlington noted in 1837 that the orange flowering variety was the only strain commonly cultivated at that time and this mostly for its exceptionally large seeds, which afford "a tolerable substitute for capers."

"Tolerable substitute" depends entirely on how they are prepared. I prefer to put them up with fresh bay leaves and West India Burr Gherkins (page 159), but Hannah Bouvier Peterson's recipe (1855, 119) is typical for the period: "Cut the green seeds of the nasturtiums with a piece of stem to each. Put them in a jar of cold vinegar." A piece of the stem enhances the flavor, but I would rather my readers first boil the vinegar and use sterilized jars. To 1½ cups of green nasturtium seeds, use 1½ cups of white wine vinegar, 1½ teaspoon of pickling salt, 1 clove of garlic, 6 peppercorns, and 2 fresh bay leaves. About 2 tablespoons of sugar might make this Victorian pickle more palatable to modern tastes, and there is no harm in adding three specimens of the Besler's Cherry Pepper (page 253), well crushed to release their heat. The whole plant is rich in vitamin C, which is why early Americans considered it such a healthful food, but since cooking destroys the vitamin C, nasturtiums are most nutritious when eaten raw.

I recently read in a garden book that nasturtiums should be planted in greenhouses to keep aphids off valuable specimen plants. Nasturtiums are *infested* with black aphids during much of the summer season, and I cannot imagine why anyone would want to invite that sort of trouble into a closed environment, especially since greenhouse aphids have no other enemies but us. Nasturtiums do repel white flies and squash bugs, but only in the open garden, so there is some practical purpose in planting them along fences and bordering areas to keep the predators out. The result will be fewer pests but not a clean sweep, and I say this only because there are some gardeners who attribute more to this prevention method than they should.

Vining nasturtiums should be started indoors in flats and then thinned to pots so that the roots are not disturbed when the plants are moved into the garden. This species prefers full sun but will tolerate afternoon shade. Since they grow 6 to 8 feet tall, the plants require trellising or at least draping over a fence. Otherwise, they will sprawl over the ground and entangle themselves in anything nearby. For an abundance of seed for pickling, cultivate the vines like pole beans on poor soil. All nasturtiums blossom profusely when raised on poor, sandy ground, since this closely approximates their native habitat in South America. Overfertilizing will only produce abundant leaves at the expense of the flowers.

Joseph's Coat
Amaranthus tricolor

A few showy accents of Joseph's Coat not only liven up the kitchen garden with brilliant color, the leaves make a gaudy addition to salads that is hard to resist when mixed with different colors of tomatoes and peppers. This is an old-time favorite that has been grown in American kitchen gardens since the eighteenth century, albeit mostly as an underutilized ornamental. The red, green, and yellow leaves may also carry patches of pink, bronze, even purple and brown, like the specimen in color plate 91. Visually, there are few garden plants that can compete with it.

In 1575 Leonhard Rauwolf saw Joseph's Coat growing in the gardens of Turkish officials at Aleppo and thought that it was the *Symphonium* of Pliny (Dannenfeldt 1968, 247). For this mistaken reason he called it *Papagoy Federn* or "parrot's feathers," the name by which it is still known in Pennsylvania Dutch. To my mind, the most spectacular picture of old-fashioned *Amaranthus tricolor* appeared in the *Hortus Eystettensis*, which was recently republished (1994, color plate 68). That book was engineered into existence in 1613 by Basilius Besler, who also recorded the pepper discussed on page 253. Given its early connections with kitchen gardens from Mogul India to Renaissance Europe, it is difficult for me to imagine a garden that would be complete without Joseph's Coat.

Yet, like Golden Purslane, this creature of the tropics is not happy unless the weather is hot, hot, and hot. It is also a large plant, growing anywhere from 4 to 6 feet tall. This showy stature makes it a perfect frame for gates or an impressive backdrop for large cabbages like *couve tronchuda* (page 107) or the edible tuber dahlia (page 363).

Seeds should be started indoors in March, seedlings thinned and potted, and the plants moved out of doors once the threat of frost has passed. A good rule of thumb to follow is not to plant Joseph's Coat until it is time to plant corn. Cool spring weather will only set it back and may cause the stems to rot. The black flea beetles that attack eggplant also relish Joseph's Coat. Insecticidal soap regularly applied normally keeps them under control. Spraying the plants with fish emulsion also seems to repel the beetles, I imagine because of the nasty way it tastes. Seed savers should note that the seed forms little tufts on the stalk and should be gathered in the fall when the plant begins to drop its leaves, or after the first frost.

Malabar Spinach or Land Kelp
Basella alba and *Basella rubra*

Both Fearing Burr (1865, 283–84) and Vilmorin (1885, 318–19) referred to this delightful vegetable as Malabar nightshade, although it is not a nightshade by any stretch of the imagination. Indeed, that name is quite off-putting, for it implies that the greens may be poisonous, and I am living proof that they are not. Better to call it an odd sort of spinach, because that is what it tastes like, although to my mind it is infinitely superior. Perhaps spinach with a hint of brandy and okra would be a better description of its taste; rabbit fodder it is not. Both the "white" and "red" varieties were introduced from East Asia before 1830 and were raised in Europe primarily as hothouse plants. Out of doors, they transform themselves into vigorous vines climbing to 8 feet if conditions are right and can therefore be trained over arbors or fences around the kitchen garden.

The "white" variety, shown in color plate 92, is really a bright green. It cooks beautifully in a microwave oven, which does not destroy the flavor, but it is excellent raw and quite refreshing on a hot summer day. The "red" variety differs only in that it is tinged with magenta under the leaves and on the stems. The flowers of both are insignificant but produce black berries that will stain hands and clothing a bright and unforgiving purple—a precautionary note if there are children in the garden.

The flowers are self-pollinating and produce a seed that resembles a peppercorn, although buried in stainful fruit. Plants for the garden should be started indoors and thinned to pots so that they are large (as much as 8 inches tall) by the time they are set out in the garden. Planting is best done when the ground is warm enough for beans, since cool nights will only check the growth.

The plant thrives in summer heat and is one of the most drought-resistant of all the vegetables I have ever grown. It produces all season and puts every variety of spinach to shame. In fact, where Malabar Spinach can be grown successfully, I would simply forget spinach and thus save a great deal of anguish. Best of all, no insects seem to attack Malabar Spinach, not even Japanese beetles, so I have never had to do more than water it from time to time and restrain myself from pulling too many leaves before the vines are firmly established.

The reason I suggest planting large plants is that Malabar Spinach is a perennial in the tropics and thus slow to produce seed in short summer regions. It is normally cultivated as an annual, but for seed-saving purposes it must be planted early enough so that it blooms by September. Otherwise, seed will not be ripe when the plant is cut down by frost. It is very odd, the way Malabar Spinach reacts to frost. It will keep in the refrigerator two weeks without spoiling in the slightest, yet one breath of frosty air below 33° F reduces it to green sludge. Then it really does look like kelp washed up on a beach, but not a beach that any crab would want to walk on.

For gardeners with a greenhouse or a large south-facing window, Malabar Spinach can be overwintered in large flowerpots—the plants do not have deep root systems. Seed can then be harvested the following season. The seed is ripe when the berries begin to fall off the plants. Wear rubber gloves when collecting them, to protect the hands from persistent stains. Gently mash the berries so that the seed is freed from the fruit. Put the mash in a large jar of water and let this stand until fermentation begins. Once the seed has sunk to the bottom and separated from the rotten fruit, scum off the floating material, strain out the seeds, and wash them in a strainer. Then spread them to dry on an absorbent surface. Properly stored, the seed will remain viable for five years. For those gardeners interested in dyestuffs, the juice from the berries need not be wasted; it can be fixed for dying cloth and holds up well against repeated washings.

Orach
Atriplex hortensis
Fearing Burr (1865, 288–90) listed sixteen varieties of orach, ample indication of its popularity years ago with American gardeners. Orach is truly an old kitchen garden vegetable that deserves more recognition. The plants are showy, and the leaves come in a variety of beautiful colors and textures. They make terrific salad greens and can be used like spinach, chard, or stuffed like cabbage rolls.

Bernard M'Mahon listed three varieties in his 1815 seed catalog: the Garden Orach (green), the Red-Leaved Orach (magenta), and the Purple-Leaved Orach (maroon). These correspond to three varieties still available through seed-saving networks and from small seed houses, and these are the three that I grow.

Since orach is wind pollinated and the varieties will cross, I have found it best to plant a crop of one variety in the spring and then a different variety in the latter part of the summer. Orach is day-length sensitive, thus it bolts quickly during the long days of summer, but there are plenty of other greens to take its place during that planting lull.

The plants are generally 4 feet tall when mature and therefore should be treated like corn, planted where they will not shade smaller vegetables. The best greens are harvested from young plants about 2 feet high, as shown in color plate 93. At this stage the leaves are tender and the flavor is most like chard. Orach should be planted 14 inches apart so that it develops into a bush with plenty of room to spread. Pruning the top will encourage it to branch. Leave about 6 to 8 plants for seed-saving purposes.

When the seed bracts are dry, the seed is ready to harvest. The seed is inside the bract membranes, which can be broken open. Otherwise, the bracts can be dried and simply stored in jars until seed is needed. Be certain to mix the seed from all the plants so that the next crop of plants represents a balance of seedlings from different plants.

Parà Cress or Spilanthes Cress
Spilanthes oleracea

An unusual and attractive South American vine only recently rediscovered by seed savers, Parà Cress is a salading with a flavor resembling pennyroyal. The plant sprawls on the ground in a riot of bronze and gray-green leaves with curiously shaped conical flowers that are yellow, tinged with red. The leaves produce a slight numbing sensation in the mouth, and therefore should be used only sparingly in salads. Yet the plant is so ornamental that it can be used as a handsome border plant in addition to its culinary features (color plate 95).

Most garden books suggest planting the seed broadcast where it is to grow, but I advise starting it in flats like lettuce—the seed even resembles lettuce seed. Seedlings can then be hardened off in small pots and planted out of doors once all danger of frost has passed. Parà Cress prefers a hot, dry location, but the tiny seedlings are extremely attractive to slugs. Once the plants are well established, slugs leave them alone. To discourage slugs during the initial growing stage, sprinkle diatomaceous earth around the seedlings on a regular basis. This cuts the undersides of the slugs when they crawl through it and kills them quickly. It is not poisonous and does not affect the plants. Just be certain that it is the coarse diatomaceous earth that is used, rather than the fine powdery type designed exclusively for swimming pool filters. One works against slugs, the other does not.

Seed is easily gathered in the fall from the flowers that turn brown. Roll the dead flowers between the fingers over a deep bowl. Winnow the seed by shaking the bowl and gently blowing the debris out. The gray seed is heavy and will sink to the bottom. Spread it to dry for a week on absorbent paper, then date, label, and store in an airtight container.

75. *Improved Variegated Custard Marrow (page 287) is believed to date from the early 1850s.*

77. *Potiron rouge vif d'Étampes (page 289) was developed in France as a squash for soup stock.*

76. *Turk's cap or turban squash (page 293) was first mentioned in France in 1818.*

78. *Yellow Mandan squash (page 294) changes to deep yellow-orange in storage.*

79. China Rose (page 300) and Philadelphia white box radishes (page 303). A perfectly formed China Rose should be shaped like the red radish second from the left.

80. Early Purple Turnip-Shaped radish (page 301) varies in color from magenta to deep violet depending on the type of soil.

81. Madras Podding radish (page 302) is cultivated for its crisp, crunchy pods.

82. *Large Round Leaved Corn Salad (page 310) remains green all winter if given protection.*

85. *Turkish Rocket (page 316), a native of Asia, is one of the hardiest of all winter salad greens.*

83. *Venetian Rocket (page 313) reseeds profusely.*

86. *Winter Cress (page 317) tastes like watercress and needs not protection over the winter.*

84. *Shallot Cress (page 315) is a form of pepper grass that remains green all winter.*

87. *Bliton* or *Horsetooth Amaranth* *(page 321)* is a vegetable dating from classical antiquity.

88. *Golden Purslane (page 323)* changes from yellow to yellow-green as it matures. Its delightful lemon flavor adds zest to summer salads.

89. *Goosefoot or Lamb's-Quarters (page 325)* has a flavor similar to walnuts.

90. *Indian Cress (page 326)* was a popular salad green in the eighteenth century.

91. *Joseph's Coat (page 327)* is often grown as a ornamental but it also can be eaten raw or cooked.

92. *Malabar Spinach (page 328) has thick, succulent leaves and thrives in hot weather.*

93. *Orach (page 329) is available in several colors. The maroon variety is shown here.*

94. *Two varieties of Heirloom Sweet Potatoes preserved by the Miller family of Littlestown, Pennsylvania (page 334).*

95. Parà Cress (page 330) was introduced to North America from Brazil in the 1860s.

96. Aka Shiso (page 331) from Japan makes a stunning addition to salads.

97. Tetragonia or New Zealand Spinach (page 331) is easy to cultivate and is frost tolerant.

98. An assortment of heirloom tomatoes from the garden at Roughwood. From left: Golden Queen (page 345), Redfield Beauty, Ciudad Victoria (page 342), Power's Heirloom (page 347), Chalk's Early Jewel (page 341), and Hartman's Yellow Gooseberry (page 346).

100. The long, pointed Power's Heirloom (page 347) on the far left was crossed with the Large Yellow (page 346) beside it to create Beauty of Devon (page 347), the three tomatoes on the upper right with a pink blush.

101. Lutescent (page 347) turns a honey color when ripe. Note the yellowed leaves that are characteristic of this variety.

99. Dr. Neal's or Lambert's General Grant (page 342) was first introduced in 1869.

102. Plate de Haiti (page 347) is actually an apple-shaped tomato. It is shown here with Yellow Peach (page 354).

103. Shenandoah (page 351) and Aunt Ruby's German Green (page 338). Both varieties are shown sliced.

106. Evening primrose (page 365) has a turnip-like root that can be harvested all winter.

104. Turnips, from left to right: Purple Top Milan (page 359), Orange Jelly (page 358), White Egg (page 360), and Amber Globe (page 358).

107. Skirret (page 370) must be grown in wet, sandy soil for the best results.

105. Crosnes (page 362), an Asian root vegetable, can be eaten raw or cooked.

108. Citron watermelon (page 379) has a distinctively patterned skin

Red Shiso or Black Nettle
Perilla frutescens

There are two types of perilla commonly grown among seed savers, the green and the red. The green variety is highly fragrant, the crushed leaf smells similar to lemon balm. Seed for the green sort was sent to England from Nepal in 1821 and the plants grown from it were depicted in *Curtis's Botanical Magazine* (1822, 2395). It does not seem to have been given much attention in the United States. Only the red variety, introduced from Japan in the 1850s, became popular with our Victorian gardeners.

After the Civil War, red shiso was used extensively as a bedding plant, especially as a backdrop against which blue, pink, or white flowers could create a striking contrast, precisely as recommended in Joseph Breck's *The Flower-Garden* (1858, 356–57). The plant has a great deal to offer in its favor, since it grows to a height of 18 inches, reseeds profusely, is not at all particular about soils, and thrives in either full sun or deep shade. The dried leaves even make a fragrant tea.

The Vick seed catalog for 1872 described red shiso as "very desirable for its foliage," which was characterized as a deep mulberry color, a fair assessment. Its name in Japanese is *aka shiso, aka* meaning red. The Japanese use the leaves to color pickles. The plant is entirely edible, including the flowers, hence its other old name, Japan mint. Visually, in salads the leaves resemble Purple Ruffles Basil, but of course with an entirely different flavor.

Because both the green and red shisos are used extensively in Japanese cooking, especially in vegetarian and fish dishes, there has been a recent revival of interest in their culinary possibilities, particularly among followers of macrobiotics. Perhaps the time has arrived for red shiso to become a true salad herb; it is far more prolific and much easier to grow than lettuce, albeit not quite as tender.

Seeds will germinate in a matter of days during hot weather. Either sow in flats, then thin and transplant to the garden, or sow directly in the ground where it is to grow after all danger of frost has passed. The plant flowers late in the summer, then drops its leaves well before frost. It will cross with the green variety and degenerate into a hybrid with plain leaves and little flavor. Therefore, it must be raised in isolation for seed-saving purposes. Seeds must be gathered quickly because finches are fond of them and will eat much of the seed crop unless it is protected with bird netting once flowering begins.

Tetragonia or New Zealand Spinach
Tetragonia tetragonioides (Tetragonia expansa)

I have always maintained that spinach is fickle and hard to grow, and I have had several long-time gardeners agree with me. A severe spring drought and a recent hot summer only fortified my conviction that tetragonia can overcome more adverse growing conditions than even the toughest variety of spinach, for tetragonia thrives on heat.

It does not look like spinach, but it certainly tastes like it, whether raw or cooked. The leaves are small and somewhat triangular, and the plant sprawls over the ground on stems sometimes as long as 2 feet. It is easy to cultivate, for the seed can be sown by scattering over the ground where it is to grow, and the seedlings then thinned out for salads.

Tetragonia was discovered by Sir Joseph Banks growing in Queen Charlotte's Sound, New Zealand, during the 1770 voyage of Captain James Cook. It was not until Cook's second voyage, however, that the plant's culinary qualities were fully appreciated. Yet between its initial discovery and the 1820s, tetragonia remained relatively obscure. A report in the *Annales d'Agriculture* (September 1819) on Count D'Ourches's attempts to cultivate it in France sparked considerable interest in international horticultural circles, and in 1822 *Curtis's Botanical Magazine* (50, 2362) devoted an article to it. This more or less marked the official recognition of the plant in England and the United States. However, Charles Hovey remarked in the *Magazine of Horticulture* (1841, 138) that it never quite caught on in this country: it "attracted considerable attention, was noticed in the agricultural papers, and was grown to some extent for a year or two, but as soon as it lost its novelty, is cultivation was nearly abandoned."

Nevertheless, tetragonia has had a small but consistent following in this country because it thrives in our hot summers and is generally free of pests, certainly more so than true spinach. But due to oxalic acid in the leaves, which is made more intense by certain soils, the plant seems bitter to some people, fortunately not the case in my garden. Flowers form at the base of the leaves and then develop into small green seed capsules. These can be picked and dried for next year's planting. The flowers are self-pollinating and do not cross with spinach or any of the other greens listed in this section of the book.

For best results, plant tetragonia when the ground is warm enough to plant beans. My best crops are always the ones I plant in July. The seed is very sensitive to cool weather and may rot if planted too early in the spring.

Sweet Potatoes

The sweet potato (*Ipomoea batatas*) is a morning glory that produces roots. It is a tropical plant that thrives in a warm, sunny climate and prefers loose, well-drained soil. Because it requires a long growing season, its culture is concentrated primarily in the South, where virtually hundreds of backyard varieties abound. With careful planning, however, it is possible to grow sweet potatoes in most sections of the United States. Even in Chester County, Pennsylvania, where I live, there are ample references to farmers raising sweet potatoes in the eighteenth century. Philadelphia botanist John Bartram grew both red and white varieties, which he procured from Florida, and in 1766 instructed his son on the West Indian method of planting them: cut the tubers in half

Old-style sweet potato

and plant the two pieces in the ground flat side down. That system works in the tropics, but in more northerly regions, other cultural methods prevail.

Sweet potatoes are generally classified by their leaf type, although I find this system confusing, since constant crossing between varieties has resulted in large numbers of intermediate leaf shapes that defy categorization. This is further complicated by the fact that in the South many people refer to sweet potatoes as yams, which are botanically unrelated, and categorize certain sweet potatoes with short, fat, stumpy tubers as a "yam type." Confusion is further compounded by the grocers who sell yams as sweet potatoes because the public thinks that sweet potatoes must be yellow or orange. Most are not. Sweet potatoes come in a wide variety of colors.

One of the leading books on heirloom sweet potatoes is James Fritz's *Sweet Potato Culture*, which first appeared in 1886, but was much enlarged in 1902. He lived at Keswick, Virginia, within eyesight of Thomas Jefferson's Monticello, and was a well-known cultivator of sweet potatoes. His inventory of sweet potato varieties is considered a beginner's guide for heirloom fanciers, of which there are indeed a great many.

The oldest variety of early American sweet potato thus far documented is the Spanish Potato once grown in tidewater Virginia and Maryland, as well as in colonial Pennsylvania along the Delaware River. The tuber resembled ginger root—often knobby, and sometimes even branching. It was eaten in the winter because it "fattened" in storage, that is, acquired a rich, buttery texture. This variety, which came from Cuba or Jamaica in the 1670s or perhaps even earlier, was popular among all classes of colonists, from slave to planter. In the cabins of the poor and in the kitchens of the rich, pits were dug in the floor near the area of the hearth so that the sweet potatoes could be stored in sand in a warm, dry place. This prevented the tubers from rotting, for sweet potatoes will rot quickly if stored below 50° F. A strain of the Spanish Potato is available on a limited basis through Seed Savers Exchange under the name Spanish Red. It has red skin. There is a subvariety with a more violet-tinged skin, but both produce long, sticklike tubers on trailing vines.

Two later varieties, and probably the ones raised by John Bartram in the 1760s, are the Bermuda Pink and Bermuda White, which are characterized today as "yam" types because of their stumpy shape and ability to grow plump in sandy soil. The Bermuda leaf-type also represents one of the largest groups of sweet potatoes, for many varieties have evolved out of them. The leaf is shown in the woodcut. Both varieties have creamy flesh, but they have different skin textures and colors. The pink has a rose-tinged skin covered with heavy ribs, as shown in color plate 94. The white has parchment-colored skin resembling some of the very blond varieties of potato. I raise both sorts in my garden, and their flavor is excellent. They are readily available and can be grown in many regions outside the South.

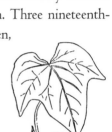

Detail of leaf of Southern Queen Sweet Potato

As a rule, northerners prefer sweet potatoes that are dry and mealy, while southerners prefer varieties that are sugary and sweet. This regional taste difference is breaking down, since sweet potato culture in the North has declined, especially in the old centers of growing in South Jersey and Delaware. Many of the nineteenth-century varieties that catered to these tastes are now extinct or extremely difficult to obtain. Three nineteenth-century varieties that are dependable and still available are Southern Queen, Nansemond, and Hayman, which I have listed in order of popularity.

Southern Queen matures in 105 days, which is about average for most of the sweet potatoes that can adapt to a wide variety of conditions. It is a vining type that produces long, narrow tubers with white skin and white flesh. The original strain was introduced from South America in 1870.

In Southside Virginia, where this variety originated, Nansemond has been a perennial favorite since 1850, made into sweet potato pies with toasted peanuts and a little peanut flour in the pie crust. There is no better way to

Detail of leaf of Nansemond Sweet Potato

pass through the Great Dismal Swamp than with this culinary treat (and maybe a bottle of Virginia Gentleman) packed into one's survival kit. Nansemond is yellow, but there is also a subvariety that is red, and an improved variety called Hanover, after the Virginia county where it was developed.

Hayman is a white-skinned white sweet potato that was developed on the Eastern Shore of Maryland. In Philadelphia, we always called it the "terrapin potato" or the "crab potato" because it was used so much in making croquettes and stews, and it is so superior to potatoes when cooked with shellfish that it is a great wonder why it is not better known. I fault the Marylanders for not sticking up for their own inventions; when cured in the sun, this sweet potato is not only highly aromatic—perfect for a crab boil—but also fragrant of cinnamon, which is not bad when it comes to making pies.

I raise a few other sweet potatoes of uncertain origin—one called Amish Pink, which does well in Pennsylvania and the Midwest, and two varieties obtained from Wayne Miller of Littlestown, Pennsylvania. These were raised without varietal names by his grandmother Bertie Missouri Miller, a formidable lady who was well known in the Gettysburg area for her sweet potatoes. All of these are vining types.

Sweet potatoes are generally started from slips created in the spring by planting sweet potatoes held back for seed in a hothouse or hotbed and letting them sprout. The suckers are pulled off and planted once the threat of frost has passed. In the South the suckers are generally planted on ridges, but this is due more to the nature of the soil there and the types of sweet potatoes grown. In the North sweet potatoes thrive better when planted on flat ground, although the ground should be worked deeply and be well manured. I use rotted horse manure—smelly maybe, but worth its weight in gold.

Sweet potato vines will sprawl across the ground and take up a great deal of space, with some vines reaching 16 feet long. It is possible to increase production by covering vines at their joints with a shovelful of soil. These joints will then root and produce tubers. In the South, the vines may blossom. If there is more than one variety in the garden, they will cross, and the seed will produce hybrids. From this seed come the numerous backyard varieties that exist today, as well as the commercial varieties created under more controlled conditions. Sweet potato vines rarely bloom in the North; in fact, I have never seen a sweet potato flower, even though I have raised sweet potatoes for quite a long time. As long as the potatoes are reproduced from the tubers, and not from seed, more than one variety can be grown in the garden at the same time, even in the same bed. It is advisable, however, not to plant varieties together that look alike, as they may become mixed together too easily during harvest.

Late in the fall, when the leaves of the plants begin to yellow—usually late in September—the potatoes are ready to harvest. They should be dug and cured in the sun for a few days to increase their sweetness, then separated, setting aside the best for seed and storing the rest for winter. Storage is a major problem for some gardeners; if conditions are too cold, the tubers will rot. Wayne Miller wraps his potatoes in old newspapers, taking care to eliminate any that are damaged or bruised, and then stores them at 65° F in a specially rigged refrigerator. This system works perfectly.

I store mine in a dry pantry and check them weekly. In reading through an agricultural report from the 1850s, I spotted a letter from an Ohio farmer who wrote that he stored his sweet potatoes in dry sand packed down in boxes in a cellar kitchen. The boxes were set up on scantling (wooden slats) so that they would not draw off dampness from the floor. This idea is very good for market gardeners who are raising sweet potatoes on a large scale, but it may not guarantee seed stock over the winter. Sweet potatoes that begin to soften or discolor can always be salvaged for cooking, but not for next year's crop.

The French were confronted with this problem in the 1830s; the king of France at that time was fond of sweet potatoes, yet the climate around Paris was not conducive to their culture.

Their solution was to grow the sweet potatoes in a hothouse and simply root shoots taken from the vines each spring. Since sweet potatoes are perennial in the tropics, this clever system works perfectly, and I use it myself. My seed potatoes are planted in Styrofoam ice chests, and from these vines I root slips for my spring plantings. By growing the mother plants as perennials, I preserve plant purity and avoid the worry of losing seed stock over the winter. Furthermore, the leaves of sweet potatoes are entirely edible and can be cooked like spinach greens. Therefore, by pruning my vines, I not only have a supply of greens over the winter, I also encourage the vines to branch and produce more rootable shoots.

Tomatoes

The 1870 catalog of Massachusetts seedsman James J. H. Gregory listed what were then the best-known tomatoes available to American gardeners. His selection is interesting for two reasons: it is more complete than any other American seedsmen's of the same period, and it represents the state of the tomato right before the vast proliferation of new varieties that followed almost annually after that time. Several of the names are familiar to tomato collectors today; many are extinct or survive only in impure seed. Here are Gregory's tomatoes: Alger, Boston Market, Cherry, Cook's Favorite, Crimson Cluster, Dwarf Scotch, Early Orangefield, Early York, Feejee, General Grant, Keyes' Early Prolific, Large Yellow, Large Smooth Red, Lester's Perfected, Mammoth Cluster, Maupay's Superior, New Mexican, Tilden, Tomato de Laye, and Strawberry or groundcherry. Gregory treated groundcherries as tomatoes, but since they are a different genus and species, I have discussed them separately on page 209.

Early Orangefield Tomato

Tomato collectors like Dr. Carolyn Male, editor of the tomato newsletter *Off the Vine*, continue to seek out old varieties such as these to grow them, reconstruct their histories, and compare them against the many thousands of tomatoes that are now part of American seed collections. Carolyn's tomato collection is one of the largest in the United States, and she has graciously dipped into it for seed to help me create the field notes that were necessary for growing out some of the varieties in this section of the book. Her advice on varieties like Greengage, which has come down heavily crossed, was invaluable. And like me, she is interested in salvaging old varieties if they have good culinary qualities.

Some heirloom tomatoes can no longer be found. Crimson Cluster, shown in the wood engraving, was introduced in 1869. It was a scarlet-red tomato, beautifully shaped and covered with golden yellow flecks. No one knows for certain what it tasted like in spite of helpful Victorian descriptions, but the striped tomatoes of England like Tigerella, or the Schimmeig Stoo of the Isle of Man, must be lineal descendants. The complexities of heirlooms extinct or heavily crossed, of seed circulated under the wrong names, of varieties that may have evolved as backyard mongrels without commercial pedigrees, make the study of American tomatoes a category of garden research unto itself. Furthermore, there are collectors whose only interest are yellow varieties, or varieties with potato-like leaves, or varieties that date from before a given period.

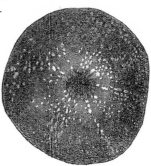

Crimson Cluster Tomato

Andrew F. Smith's *Tomato in America* (1994) traces the history of much of this from the colonial period to about the time of the Civil War. Smith's is a useful study for anyone serious about the history of the tomato, and a fascinating insight into how Americans, once suspicious of this brilliantly colored vegetable, changed their minds in the 1830s and became the most enthusiastic of tomato gardeners by the 1850s. No American kitchen garden is complete without its tomatoes. In fact, it is probably safe to say that Americans judge vegetable gardens today by the tomatoes in them rather than by the cabbages or carrots or other vegetables. Many backyard gardens contain nothing but tomatoes. Perhaps it is no exaggeration to suggest that the tomato has now become a symbol of our gardening culture.

The person most responsible for this remarkable transformation was Alexander W. Livingston (1822–1898), a seedsman from Reynoldsburg, Ohio. Livingston launched his Paragon tomato in 1870 (astutely named after a then well-known canning jar), and this in turn launched his career as the developer of thirteen major, and many lesser, commercial tomato varieties. By 1878, A. W. Livingston's Sons moved to Columbus, Ohio, and became the uncontested leader in American tomato breeding. Many of the heirloom varieties I have selected trace their ancestry to this company.

Livingston was keenly aware of the usefulness of genetic diversity, especially in wild tomatoes. For example, the wild tomato of the Galapagos Islands, *Lycopersicon cheesmanii,* is insensitive to salt water and grows within a few yards of the high-tide mark. Gardens planted with it can be irrigated with sea water. The plant therefore holds promise for developing a whole array of tomatoes that can be grown under desert conditions near the sea. Other tomatoes offer useful traits to breeders interested in extending the tomato into regions far beyond its natural frontiers such as Siberia or the far North.

Today, the divisions between yellow and red sorts, the dividing line used by gardeners in the eighteenth century, is blurred by pinks, oranges, purples, even green tomatoes. From an culinary standpoint, many of the most interesting tomatoes, those like Evergreen (green flesh, yellow skin) or Aunt Ruby's German Green (green flesh, green skin) do not date from the nineteenth century. In order to impose perimeters on my selections, I have featured varieties from before 1900. This leaves out a great many of my own favorites like Oxheart, yet I think the range of tomatoes I have chosen represents a good balance of the sorts most likely to appear in a kitchen garden, also taking into account a variety of colors and shapes. Some of them reflect shifts in regional tastes. Only purple tomatoes could be sold in Saint Louis years ago, because the residents did not like the perceived flavor of other colors. National marketing patterns have changed this, but old purple varieties like Eva Purple Ball survive to confirm that Saint Louis knew flavor in tomatoes when it *saw* it.

In reconstructing the data provided on the tomatoes profiled in this section, I have relied on three valuable field tests that described these heirlooms in minute detail. An English growout undertaken in 1867 was reported in the *American Journal of Horticulture* in 1868. It revealed that the Orangefield of one seedsman was the Large Italian Red of another, and that substitutions of similar varieties were as common then as now. New York seedsman Peter Henderson undertook a similar growout a few years later and reported his results in the *American Agriculturist.* Most useful, however, was Gordon Morrison's *Tomato Varieties,* a massive field test of most American commercial varieties at the East Lansing, Michigan, Agricultural Experiment Station in 1936. This growout might be considered the final fling of the old sorts of tomatoes on the eve of the advent of the F_1 hybrids that have taken over so much of the tomato commerce today.

Tomato growers generally try to categorize tomatoes by their seasonality: early, midseason, or late—but this type of productivity varies so much from one climate zone to the next that it is quite pointless to think in these terms for home gardens. The two basic botanical divisions are between *Lycopersicon lycopersicon,* our common garden varieties, and *Lycopersicon pimpinellifolium,* the tiny currant tomatoes. They can both come to fruit at the same time. The other way to divide tomatoes is by determinate or indeterminate, which means essentially how the vines fruit. The determinate sorts come to fruit all at once, then stop bearing. They are preferred by many commercial growers because the tomatoes can be harvested at a given time, then plowed under as green manure so that a different vegetable crop can be planted in the fields. Most Jersey tomatoes are now this type, which is why so few Jersey tomatoes come to market after August 15. The indeterminate tomatoes produce right up to a killing frost. All of the tomatoes I have profiled are this type because kitchen gardeners want as

Potato leaf of the Brandywine Tomato

many tomatoes during the course of the growing season as possible. In fact, I do not grow any determinate tomatoes.

Tomatoes are also divided by leaf type. The great variety of leaf shapes is often only evident when many varieties are planted side by side. Potato-leaf types began appearing in this country in the early 1860s, introduced here from France. Keyes' Early Prolific, developed in 1864, was one of the first commercial potato-leaf varieties. It resulted from an accidental cross of French tomatoes C. A. Keyes was growing at the time. Brandywine is an example of a potato-leaf heirloom that is still grown today. Other leaf types are "regular," a catchall term for a range of typical tomato leaves from delicate to coarsely cut profiles, and "ferny," which describes a plumelike appearance to the leaves.

Fruit types are often described as "oblate" (round but flat like a squash), "carrot-shaped" (long and pointed), or "globular" (perfectly round). There are many tomato varieties with combinations of these types or with intermediate shapes, so it is often difficult to fit them into neat schemes with fixed labels. To alleviate doubts, I have tried to provide woodcuts or drawings of all the varieties discussed, particularly where a physical feature is also a varietal distinction.

Carrot-shaped tomato typical of many of the paste types.

Hybridizing over the past few centuries has altered the structure of the tomato flower, particularly the female part of it. Thus, many older types of tomatoes are more likely to cross than newer ones. As a rule, the tomatoes most likely to cross in a given garden are those with potato leaves, those with double flowers (found on beefsteak types), and the currant tomatoes. All of these should be kept very far from other tomato varieties, at least 50 feet. Most newer types of tomatoes are self-fertile, with pollination taking place in the morning before the flower opens. However, all tomatoes should be kept at least 20 feet apart to insure seed purity. Never save seed from fruits produced by double flowers. These are the one type of tomato flower most easily pollinated by insects.

Seed should be saved from fruit most true to type, picked from several different plants over the course of the season. This seed should be mixed at the end of the season for greater genetic diversity. Tomato seed is gathered by scooping out the seed and jelly mass into jars of water and letting this ferment. Fermentation takes about three to five days. Once the mixture ferments, the scum will rise to the top and the best seed will sink to the bottom. The scum and water can be poured off and the seeds washed in a tea strainer. Spread the seed to dry on paper towels or on cookie sheets. Let the seed dry two to three weeks, then mark it carefully, date it, and store in air-tight containers away from heat and direct light. The viability of tomato seed will range from four to ten years. I have even planted seed that was fifteen years old and had half of it germinate.

Acme Tomato
Lycopersicon lycopersicon

One of the most popular nineteenth-century "apple-shaped" tomatoes, Acme was developed by Alexander Livingston and introduced by the Livingston Seed Company in 1875. It is one of a small number of classic American tomatoes mentioned by Vilmorin (1885, 571), who listed it as *tomate pomme violette*. The fruit is round, somewhat flattened on the top and bottom, and indented on the blossom end like an apple. The color is deep violet-rose. The fruit hangs in clusters of two to four, weighing 4 to 6 ounces each. The vines begin to bear midseason and continue to bear heavily until frost.

Early Melrose, Early Minnesota, Essex Hybrid, Potomac, and Tall Champion are all considered synonyms, or are so similar that they are treated as subvarieties.

Acme Tomato

Brandywine Tomato
Lycopersicon lycopersicon

This tomato is undoubtedly the most famous of all American heirloom tomatoes dating from the nineteenth century, and like the Moon and Stars watermelon (page 383), it has become a symbol of the seed-saving movement. Brandywine has a number of aliases, and there are several tomatoes called Brandywine that are not in fact related to it. This has caused some confusion among growers and consumers. Only two tomatoes are original, and the yellow one is a sport.

In spite of the mythology surrounding Brandywine and its supposed Amish origins, the tomato is a commercial variety. It was introduced in January 1889 by the Philadelphia seed firm of Johnson & Stokes. The original announcement, which also shows a picture of the tomato, is reproduced from the *Farm Journal* (1889, 5). The Johnson & Stokes advertisements describing the tomato make it clear that the pink Brandywine of today, the variety with large fruit weighing almost one pound, is the same as the original introduction. The pink Brandywine has a very thin skin, which disqualifies it as a good shipping tomato. For this reason, it is not often seen in markets far from where it was grown. However, in terms of flavor, it is ranked as the best tasting of all American table tomatoes.

The plants of this tomato are large, and the heavy fruit necessitates staking. The tomato is a potato-leaf variety, with dark green leaves. The fruit tends to be large, beefsteak-type, somewhat ribbed, oblate, and extremely meaty. In my garden, the fruit ripens at the same time as Early Large Red. A tomato of similar appearance called Sterling Old German, from the Mennonite community around Sterling, Illinois, has the texture and size of Brandywine, the potato leaf, and the same color, but none of the distinctive flavor. It is thought to be a subsequent selection of Brandywine with traces of crossing with an unknown tomato—in short, not a pure Brandywine. However, it seems better adapted to the South and may produce better fruit in humid regions, where Brandywine is known to crack or split. Sudduth's Brandywine (SSE TO-2) is a southern selection of Brandywine that retains much of the famous flavor.

Advertisement introducing the Brandywine Tomato.

Johnson & Stoke's Brandywine produced a yellow sport early in the century. The Yellow Brandywine resembles its pink parent in leaf, fruit shape, and fruit size, but is less productive and subject to blossom end rot. The Yellow Brandywine ripens the same pumpkin-gold color as Golden Queen.

Lastly, there is a red tomato called Red Brandywine that is not genetically related to the original variety. Its fruits are smaller (2½ inches in diameter), an intense, orange red, round, tough-skinned, and generally weak in the distinctive Brandywine taste. What is that famous flavor? Hard to pinpoint. Some describe it as intensely tomatoey, others as sweet and tomatoey. It is rich, that much is certain: what all tomato breeders aspire to and few have achieved. In Pennsylvania, where the variety originated, it has the lusciousness of a Burgundy wine and tastes as though minced parsley has been scattered over it. Nothing else is needed.

Chalk's Early Jewel Tomato
Lycopersicon lycopersicon
James Chalk of Norristown, Pennsylvania, developed this variety from an 1889 cross between Hubbard's Curled Leaf and Perfection. The tomato was introduced commercially in 1899. It is very similar to June Pink except for the larger-size fruit and the red color. There are 3 to 5 fruits to a cluster. Normally, I pull off fruit if there are more than 3 in a cluster so that I have better-developed fruit in each cluster.

In any case, the vines of this variety are small and cannot bear much weight. However, the small size makes the plants easy to stake and ideal for small gardens. The variety is also relatively hardy, thus I can set out plants in early May and harvest ripe tomatoes by June 30. Chalk's Early Jewel is consistently early for me, in fact, my first tomato of the season, but my garden is only six or seven miles from the spot where the tomato originated, and this proximity may have something to do with it.

When vine ripe, the fruit has a buttery texture that is enhanced by a dash of salt. The tomato is excellent when paired with steamed crab.

Ciudad Victoria Tomato
Lycopersicon pimpinellifolium

This weedy, semicultivated tomato from the region of Tamaulipas in northern Mexico is actually a species type, and as such, it will cross easily with most other heirlooms. The small leaf and fruit size are typical of the currant tomatoes, except that the fruit of this plant is larger, about ½ inch in diameter. It is also perfectly round. The fruit color is bright orange red and hangs in clusters. In size and plant type, this tomato conforms to the red cherry tomato described by Fearing Burr (1865, 648) and sold under that name by James J. H. Gregory of Marblehead, Massachusetts. There is a yellow variant of this tomato. Both the red and yellow are intensely flavored, but seedy. As heirlooms, they may be treated as the most common type of cherry tomato grown in this country between 1795 and 1865.

Dr. Neal's or Lambert's General Grant Tomato
Lycopersicon lycopersicon

This tomato was recovered from obscurity in 1985/1986 by seed saver Bill Ellis, a professor at Penn State/Hazelton Campus. Bill related some of the particulars of its discovery to me because after growing it, I recognized it as an old, long-lost heirloom. He found the tomato in a basket of tomatoes sold by a vendor whose source was a greenhouse in DuBois, Pennsylvania. On growing out the tomato the following year, Ellis discovered that the tomato improved immensely in flavor if it was allowed to ripen on the vine. If picked underripe and ripened on a windowsill, the flavor will be bland. Harvested at peak ripeness, it vies with Brandywine for flavor and texture. After I had offered seed through Seed Savers Exchange for several years, it became evident to me that many people in West Virginia and southwestern Pennsylvania recognized the tomato, but Dr. Neal, whose name it bears, remains elusive.

It later developed that "Dr. Neal" was only one of several names by which the tomato was known, and he was not the originator anyway. The creator of the tomato was a gardener by the name of Lambert in Bellefonte, Pennsylvania. Lambert, about whom little is presently known, released the tomato in 1869 under the name General Grant. The *American Horticultural Annual*

(1869, 135–36) described the tomato as oblate (usually 3 inches in diameter or more), heavy for its size, and excellent in flavor. It was thought to be a sport or a cross with an old tomato called Boston Market and was described as "a capital sort for private gardeners, and for those customers who are willing to pay a slight advance for a superior tomato," to quote the 1869 notice. However, since a tomato had already appeared under the name General Grant, the editors of the *American Horticultural Annual* suggested that Lambert find another name for his tomato. Doubtless this early confusion over names led to the development of so many aliases. The woodcut shows Lambert's tomato, which is heavily ribbed and a rich rose-pink color. It is indented on the blossom end like an apple. Most specimens like the one depicted weigh 12 to 14 ounces. It is also an early variety. When I planted it on May 4 (1995), the vines were bearing heavily by July 22.

Lambert's General Grant Tomato

The original or first General Grant tomato was developed by a garden amateur in Boston in 1862 but not introduced commercially until 1869 by Washburn & Company of Boston. Seeds had been in circulation for trial among horticulturists since 1867. That tomato was a glossy crimson red and is now considered extinct.

Earliana Tomato
Lycopersicon lycopersicon

This handsome tomato was developed by George Sparkes of Salem, New Jersey, and introduced in 1910 by the seed house of Johnson & Stokes of Philadelphia. It is now known by a huge list of synonyms and variant strains, some quite different from the original introduction. The first Earliana is believed to be a sport or derived from a sport of a tomato called Stone (introduced by Alexander Livingston in 1891), an heirloom that is still available. Gordon Morrison (1938, 28) described Earliana as scarlet red, with deeper scarlet streaks radiating from the blossom end. I have never seen this on any Earliana fruit I have grown. The fruits are medium-sized, globular, and weigh from 4 to 6 ounces. They hang in clusters of 4 to 6.

The Earliana most commonly under cultivation is orange red with deep green leaves and a different number of seed cavities (usually 2) than the scarlet-red sort, which has 8 to 12. Campbell Soup Company developed a potato-leafed variety of Earliana, and sev-

Earliana Tomato

eral agricultural stations have also created improved strains. A pink version called June Pink or Landreth, is also in circulation among seed savers. Generally, regardless of the fruit color, Earliana begins to yield crops two months after planting. Even though it is considered one of the best early varieties, one that I can always count on by the third week of July, it has never yielded ripe fruit in June in my garden, even on plants set out in May in full bloom. The fruit simply stays green until mid-July. It has always puzzled me how the tomato earned the name June Pink.

Early Large Red Tomato
Lycopersicon lycopersicon

When American tomatoes are discussed for the period 1815 to 1865, Early Large Red is most consistently mentioned, even though it was known earlier in France during the eighteenth century. It is not a true commercial variety in the same sense as Earliana just discussed, for it is very close to its wild Mexican counterpart. Yet where large red tomatoes were grown in the country before the universal acceptance of this vegetable, Early Large Red was indeed the most common. In fact, it was recommended for kitchen gardens in several early garden books, including George Lindley's *Guide to Orchard and Kitchen Garden* (1831, 555), and appeared repeatedly in horticultural works throughout the nineteenth century.

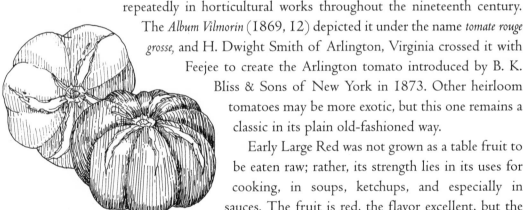

The *Album Vilmorin* (1869, 12) depicted it under the name *tomate rouge grosse*, and H. Dwight Smith of Arlington, Virginia crossed it with Feejee to create the Arlington tomato introduced by B. K. Bliss & Sons of New York in 1873. Other heirloom tomatoes may be more exotic, but this one remains a classic in its plain old-fashioned way.

Early Large Red was not grown as a table fruit to be eaten raw; rather, its strength lies in its uses for cooking, in soups, ketchups, and especially in sauces. The fruit is red, the flavor excellent, but the flesh is mealy, as one would expect in a paste-type tomato. The vines are small—no longer than 4 feet—so the tomato is well adapted to small gardens. Most

Early Large Red Tomato with shoulder cracks typical of this variety.

of the fruits are smooth, although some have light ribbing, and are about 2½ inches in diameter. The skins are tough, a feature noted by Fearing Burr in 1865. Perfect fruit will contain 9 seed chambers. In humid weather the fruit is subject to cracking, and mature fruit even in dry weather will have distinct crack scars at regular intervals on the tomato. These white lines are typical on many early prehybrid tomato sorts.

Golden Queen Tomato
Lycopersicon lycopersicon

Golden Queen was introduced in 1882 by the Livingston Seed Company and has remained one of the standards for yellow tomatoes of this type. Indeed, aside from Golden Trophy, Yellow Brandywine, and a few others, it might be appropriate to say that Golden Queen has few rivals and has never been improved upon. It has excellent color and flavor, and the vines are prolific throughout most of the season.

The vines are large, anywhere from 6 to 8 feet in length, and therefore require staking. The fruits hang in clusters of 4 to 6 and ripen from yellow to a deep persimmon gold. Both the skin and flesh are yellow-orange. Some fruits are faintly flushed with red in field tests, but I would consider this evidence of crossing. USDA seed (NSL 27357) also exhibits this. The fruit is smooth, with few creases or ribs. The blossom end is also smooth, not sunken as in the apple-shaped varieties. The fruit may measure 3½ inches in diameter and about 2½ inches thick, weighing anywhere from 6 to 8 ounces or more.

Since the flavor of this tomato is mild, almost sweet, it is improved with acid such as lemon juice or a lemon-flavored vinegar. Vinegar flavored with lemon verbena is perfect.

Greengage or Yellow Plum Tomato
Lycopersicon lycopersicon

The Vilmorin garden book (1885, 571) described this Victorian tomato under the name *tomate jaune ronde* and equated it with several other varieties (red, pink, purple) in terms of size and overall shape. The fruit is supposed to be perfectly round like a Ping-Pong ball and 2 inches in diameter. It hangs in clusters of 6 to a stem, as shown in the old woodcut. The variety was mentioned as early as 1867 under the name Yellow Plum, and at that time was sold almost exclusively in England because it was excellent for growing in tubs.

The Greengage now in circulation from USDA seed (NSL 27022) is somewhat smaller, with fruit 1½ inches in diameter and two seed chambers to a berry, and is lemon yellow in color. In fruit that is true to type, the jelly mass in slightly underripe fruit is green. This turns yellow when the fruit it ripe. The flavor of this tomato is the best of this small type.

Greengage Tomato

Hartman's Yellow Gooseberry Tomato
Lycopersicon lycopersicon

This variety entered seed-saving collections from John Hartman, an Indianapolis seedsman. It is the same small yellow tomato as Lindley's yellow cherry-shaped tomato (1831, 555), Burr's yellow cherry tomato (1865, 641), and the yellow cherry tomato sold in James Vick's *Illustrated Catalogue and Floral Guide* (1872, 113). It is also illustrated in the *Album Vilmorin* (1868, 19). The tomato appears to be the prototype yellow cherry tomato grown during much of the nineteenth century in this country.

The vines are long, rambling to 8 or 10 feet, and thus require staking. The fruit hangs in clusters of 6 to 8, and individual tomatoes are larger than a true gooseberry, and well flavored. The fruit color is lemon yellow. This variety is one of the first to come to fruit, and it remains productive until frost. The plants are somewhat frost tolerant at 28° to 32° F.

Large Yellow Tomato
Lycopersicon lycopersicon

George Lindley (1831, 555) treated this tomato as the yellow counterpart to Early Large Red. In a growout of tomatoes conducted in England in 1867, seed from the firm of Henry Veitch & Sons in Chelsea was obtained to test this variety against newer sorts. The fruits were described as yellow, large, and deeply ribbed. Lest there be any doubt that the American Large Yellow was the same, the *Album Vilmorin* (1854, 5) illustrated the tomato even to the brilliant yellow color. The yellow is in the skin, since the flesh is white, and some of the seed chambers are hollow, so there is no uniform jelly mass to enhance the pigmentation.

Of all the large yellow sorts, this was the most popular one in nineteenth-century kitchen gardens. It is only one of a handful of tomatoes that survived from my grandfather's once extensive tomato collection. It is one of the tomatoes that drew me into seed saving. My grandfather had gotten seed from William E. Hickman (his father-in-law), for it was one of the tomatoes the Hickmans raised for market in Philadelphia. My great-grandmother used the tomato to make ginger-flavored yellow tomato preserves.

Power's Heirloom Tomato

The tomato is a vigorous grower and requires staking. It is not a true varietal tomato, rather a type of species tomato that existed in Mexico from pre-Columbian times. It became popular in the United States following the war with Mexico in the 1840s. Because it is a species tomato, the sexual structure of the flower is such that the tomato will cross more easily with varieties around it, and therefore it should be isolated by 50 feet.

I used this tomato to cross with Power's Heirloom, a white paste tomato from Virginia, producing Beauty of Devon, shown in color plate 100. One of the great pleasures of growing heirloom tomatoes is breeding them to create new ones. Beauty of Devon is more delicately flavored than White Queen (page 354).

Lutescent Tomato
Lycopersicon lycopersicon

Lutescent has only recently reentered seed collections, and of all the tomatoes I have selected for this book, this variety is truly the strangest. Tomato expert Dr. Carolyn Male reintroduced this variety under the presumption that it is the same as Honor Bright, a variety originally introduced by Alexander W. Livingston in 1898. It appears to fit Livingston's descriptions.

The vines of this tomato are large, 4 to 6 feet in length, and therefore require staking. The leaves are pale, sickly yellow, appearing diseased or in need of nourishment. The upper leaves of the vines are blotched with patches of discoloration. The flowers are ivory white, a rare feature in the tomato world. The unripe fruit does not appear green like most tomatoes but is a yellowish parchment color. This gradually darkens as the fruit ripens to yellow, then orange, then red. The fruit hangs in clusters of 6 to 8 and drops from the plants when ripe. When the fruit is red, it is covered with blushes of honey-brown, giving the tomato a shellacked appearance.

The flavor is equally striking. It is pleasantly acidic and surprisingly tomatoey. The tomato plant itself is highly ornamental when in fruit, but so is the fruit when mixed with pink and white varieties. This is one of those Victorian botanical whimsies that also happens to be good eating.

Plate de Haiti or Apple of Hispaniola Tomato
Lycopersicon lycopersicon

African-American tomatoes are difficult to document, and even fewer of them are also strikingly beautiful. This is one of my favorite tomatoes, not only for its exquisite appearance but also for its flavor. It also happens to be extremely old and probably misnamed. If anything, it should be called *pomme de Haiti*, because it is not flat but somewhat apple shaped. The earliest record of this tomato is a botanical drawing in Konrad Gessner's *Historia Plantarum* (1561). Gessner's specimens were doubtless grown from seed only recently brought from the Caribbean. Whatever its true origin, the tomato has been associated since the 1550s with the island now home to Haiti and the Dominican Republic. It is known to have entered North America in 1793 with the Creole refugees who fled the slave uprising in Haiti. Beyond this, documentation of the tomato has remained elusive; little effort was made in the nineteenth century to investigate the plant varieties grown in the kitchen gardens of American blacks.

The tomato was introduced into the seed-saving network through Dr. Carolyn Male, who obtained seed from the collection of Norbert Parreira of Helliner, France. Carolyn gave me seed, I in turn donated seed to Seed Savers Exchange, and now the tomato is gaining in popularity. The plants are large, with vines reaching 6 to 8 feet. Staking is recommended. The fruit hangs in clusters of 4 to 6, each tomato about 2½ inches in diameter. As shown in color plate 102, the fruit is lobed, oftentimes with raised ridges between the lobes. The fruit is vermilion red and divided into four seed chambers, just as Gessner depicted them in 1561.

The flavor of the tomato is mild and can be enhanced with a simple dash of salt. Balsamic vinegar brings out a distinctive fruitiness that recommends this tomato for spicy salsa combinations.

Red Currant Tomato
Lycopersicon pimpinellifolium

Of all the types of tomatoes cultivated in traditional American kitchen gardens, the currant tomato is closest to the ancestral wild tomatoes of Central America and northern South America. French explorer Aédée Feuillée collected one of the earliest specimens to be depicted in a botanical work during an expedition to Peru in 1709–11. Feuillée (1713) actually found the tomato on the beach. It is difficult to know for certain what sort of plant it came from because the specimen depicted in his book (3: plate 25) is one of the most pathetic tomatoes ever shown in any botanical work, all stem, five limpish leaves, two flowers, and one berry—and he dared illustrate such a thing with the king's money. Furthermore, while he claimed the tomato was of medical value, Feuillée never really said what to do with it, so we are left guessing how the Peruvians put it to use. I have tried growing a USDA tomato called PI 143527 (Peru)—readily available through Seed Savers Exchange—and it appears to come close to the tomato of Feuillée.

Red Currant Tomato

All of the garden varieties of the currant tomato are crosses or selections of the wild forms, with improvements in fruit size or habit of growth bred into them over the years. Nonetheless, the currant tomato is a distinctive species, with small, delicate leaves, different flowers, and a more acrid odor in the leaves. The stems of the plants are small and spindly, never developing into a trunk like other garden sorts. Without support, the plants ramble over the ground and choke out any small plants growing near them. Historically, they were usually grown over fences both as a form of containment and because the fruit was most ornamental from that angle.

The tiny fruit hangs in clusters resembling red currants, hence the name. Aside from red and yellow kinds, there are also two basic berry types, one with thick skin that cracks when ripe, and one with thin skin that drops to the ground when ripe. Both fruit types are intensely flavored and can be used for juicing purposes or for sauces. Under an article called "New Receipts" in *Miss Leslie's Magazine* (1843, 103), Eliza Leslie published a recipe for pickling "button tomatoes." This is one of the old American folk names for this tomato, which was put up in pickles both while green and when ripe. The pickles were used like capers for garnishing elaborate roasts and other fancy dishes. Currant tomatoes were also sun-dried when ripe to make a type of tomato raisin.

Leaf of the Yellow Currant Tomato

Currant tomatoes are very hardy and generally withstand light frosts provided there is no strong wind. Since they reseed readily, the tomatoes can become invasive in the garden. They are also capable of crossing with other tomatoes, so they should be isolated by at least 50 feet. Two to four plants are usually sufficient for a small garden.

Red Fig Tomato
Lycopersicon lycopersicon

The fig, or pear-shaped, tomato has been raised in North American gardens at least since the eighteenth century, both as food and as an ornamental. George Lindley (1831, 555) noted both the red and yellow varieties, although the so-called red pear-shaped was the most common of the two. The *Album Vilmorin* (1857, 8) illustrated the red sort, while the red and yellow were mentioned by Fearing Burr (1865, 633–34, 642). The fruit of both the red and yellow sorts is small, generally 1 to 1½ inches in length. The vines are prolific and more bushlike in habit than many other tomatoes, so they do not require staking. Like Riesentraube, the pear-shaped tomatoes are very sensitive to frost and cold weather.

Red Fig Tomato

The name fig tomato does not denote a specific variety as much as a specific type and its culinary use. Any small, red, teardrop-shaped tomato can serve as a fig tomato, but certain strains evolved through selection with meatier flesh and fewer seeds, two traits useful in creating tomato figs. The red varieties best suited to figs were grouped together as fig tomatoes during the 1840s when the recipe came into vogue. It was considered an inexpensive way to create homemade fig substitutes. The following recipe illustrating how this was done was developed by a Mrs. Steiger of Washington, D.C., and is taken from Josiah T. Marshall's *Farmer's and the Emigrant's Complete Guide* (1854, 159).

Tomato Figs

❦

Take six pounds of sugar to one peck (or sixteen pounds) of the fruit. Scald and remove the skin of the fruit in the usual way. Cook them over a fire, their own juice being sufficient without the addition of water, until the sugar penetrates and they are clarified. They are then taken out, spread on dishes, flattened and dried in the sun. A small quantity of the syrup should be occasionally sprinkled over them while drying; after which, pack them down in boxes, treating each layer with powdered sugar. The syrup is afterward concentrated and bottled for use. They keep well from year to year, and retain surprisingly their flavor, which is nearly that of the best quality of fresh figs. The pear-shaped or single tomatoes answer the purpose best. Ordinary brown sugar may be used, a large portion of which is retained in the syrup.

Riesentraube Tomato
Lycopersicon lycopersicon

Riesentraube was reintroduced commercially in this country in 1993 by Southern Exposure Seed Exchange of Earlysville, Virginia. Seed came from Dr. Carolyn Male, but she had obtained it earlier from seed saver Curtis D. Choplin of North Augusta, South Carolina. Choplin had obtained his seed from Germany. The trail led ultimately to the seed bank at Gateisleben, where the tomato had been in storage for many years. Of all the recent success stories with saving heirloom tomatoes, Riesentraube must be considered a guidebook example, because today it is one of the most popular cherry-type heirloom tomatoes raised by home gardeners.

The exact age and origin of Riesentraube is unknown. I saw the tomato near Gyöngyös, Hungary, in 1983 and subsequently discovered an 1857 Pennsylvania German recipe for making tomato wine with it. That recipe was recently published in *Off the Vine*. The Hungarians in Gyöngyös called the tomato *kecske csöcsü* (goat tit), in reference to its peculiar shape. Only recently

(1995), a similarly shaped tomato (but of a different color) has come to light in Greece. Thus the Riesentraube is a tomato with a fascinating history that may take many years to unravel.

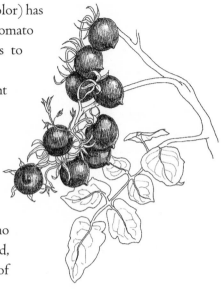

The name of the tomato is German, meaning "giant grape," but refers specifically to the Grapes of Eshcol mentioned in the Bible. Like those grapes, this tomato offers the promise of a land of plenty. To say that the tomato is productive is an understatement. The vines blossom with huge bouquets of yellow flowers, anywhere from 20 to 40 per stem. This alone makes the plant showy, even when there is no fruit. The flowers turn into large bunches of small red, heart-shaped tomatoes that hang down like clusters of grapes, as shown in the drawing. Each tomato has tiny nipple on the tip, hence the Hungarian name. The tomatoes are primarily harvested for use in sal-

Riesentraube Tomato

ads. The flavor of the fruit is good and is enhanced by sugar, which is why the tomato is so well adapted to wine making. Tomato wine made from this variety resembles dry sherry.

The plants are extremely sensitive to frost and will languish in the fall when the night temperatures drop into the low forties. It is best not to count on this tomato late in the season in areas where nights are cool even in the summer.

Shenandoah Tomato
Lycopersicon lycopersicon

James J. H. Gregory of Marblehead, Massachusetts, carried seed for a striped Mexican tomato as early as 1864 and circulated seed for it along with several other Mexican tomatoes to editors of various horticultural journals in 1872. The *Rural Carolinian* (1872, 435) took particular note of the tomatoes, but Gregory's Mammoth Chihuahua (a red variety) always solicited comments. His yellow-striped variety did not, and it became lost in the frantic shuffle for new hybrids during the market gardening boom following the Civil War. What is known for certain about it is that it came from Mexico where, according to Tracy (1918, 15), bicolored tomatoes have been documented as early as 1651. Whether Gregory's bicolor was the progenitor of the tomato featured in this sketch is another matter, probably not. A tomato called Marvel Striped, which was brought recently from Mexico, exhibits a number of features that suggest Shenandoah is the product of selective breeding.

The tomato was found among the Mennonites in the Shenandoah Valley of Virginia and has been introduced commercially under the names Old German and Mammoth German Gold. These names are quite unsatisfactory, since there are a number of other heirloom tomatoes with the same names. I have opted to call it Shenandoah to avoid all confusion about its origin, which is not German in any case. There were quite enough Mennonite missionaries in Mexico in the nineteenth century to disseminate seed among their coreligionists back home. Yet the hidden hand behind this tomato may be more botanical than religious, the product of Mennonite Jacob B. Garber (1800–1886) and his far-reaching network of horticulturists. All that can be said with certainty is that the Pennsylvania Dutch grew fond of bicolored tomatoes, and this variety is one of the best in the heap.

The vines are not large, perhaps 5 feet at their very longest, but staking is essential. The fruit is enormous, often weighing more than 16 ounces. The plants are not heavy producers, but the fruit is excellent. It is basically yellow with strongly defined lobes. Red streaks radiate from the blossom end and penetrate the tomato to the core so that when it is sliced (color plate 103), it presents a brilliant array of rich red, orange, gold, and yellow marbling. All the fruits exhibit traits of double tomatoes, which may be the result of the flower structure. Due to the large size of the fruit, there is cracking on the stem end during cool weather and on the blossom end during hot, humid weather. This is not a shipping tomato. It is best consumed when picked.

On the other hand, the plants are quite frost tolerant, virtually untouched by 28° F when Riesentraube, which I had growing not far away, was cut to the ground within an hour.

Trophy Tomato

Lycopersicon lycopersicon

Trophy is a tomato originally developed for market gardens and for canning. Historically, it was one of the first tomato varieties to revolutionize American tomato growing. The instant success of Trophy encouraged American seedsmen to take tomato breeding seriously; thus Trophy initiated a long line of nineteenth-century hybrids that have since become tomato classics.

The original strain of Trophy was created by a Dr. Hand of Baltimore, Maryland, and introduced commercially in 1870 by Colonel George E. Waring, Jr., of Newport, Rhode Island. Waring sold the seeds for $5 a packet and offered a $100 premium for the largest specimen grown by his customers. This savvy piece of marketing with a tomato variety

Advertisement for the Trophy Tomato

that also happened to be very good caused a sensation. Within a year, nearly every major American seed company was carrying Trophy and posting premiums. The *American Agriculturist* (1870, 445) stated that the tomato was "unequaled by any variety we have tested" and distributed seed to customers who renewed their subscriptions.

The woodcut from the 1870 *American Agriculturist* shows the tomato very well. It is obvious that the cross was at that time unstable, because plants were yielding both smooth fruit (note the one upturned) and heavily lobed specimens (visible in the back). The smooth tomato on the left is also badly cracked, not a high mark among growers, and a recurring problem with many of these early varieties during rainy weather. The 1871 advertisement of B. K. Bliss & Sons of New York shows a good cross section. Any tomato grown today as Trophy that does not slice like that specimen is not a true Trophy.

Trophy Tomato

The plants are dense and bright green, rather upright in growth, and in need of staking. The fruit is scarlet red and hangs in clusters of 4 to 5, each weighing from 5 to 6 ounces. The shape of the tomato is oblate, about 3½ inches in diameter and 2½ inches thick. Typical fruit is heavily ribbed, not smooth like the ones shown in the old engraving, with a distinct flower scar on the blossom end. The interior of the fruit is red, with 6 to 8 seed chambers divided like the 1871 Bliss advertisement. The flavor is good and holds up well when canned. Thus, the tomato is also excellent for cooked recipes as well as summer salads.

Trophy produced a yellow sport called Golden Trophy, which was introduced by B. K. Bliss & Sons of New York in 1875. It resembles Trophy in all respects except pigmentation, and like all yellow-fruited varieties, it is less productive than the red. However, in his 1889 growout of the leading tomato varieties, N. Hallock (1890, 294) felt that Golden Trophy was "by far the best and most solid yellow sort grown." He placed it first, even before Golden Queen.

Both the red and yellow forms of Trophy can be used in the following recipe of Cornelia Bedford, which appeared in the household magazine *Table Talk* (1897, 247).

Tomato Kromeskies

🍅

Choose tomatoes which are firm and as small as possible. Scald and peel them. Have ready some fritter batter (as for cauliflower fritters) and some grated cheese, seasoned, using for each cupful of the cheese a quarter of a teaspoonful of salt, one third of a teaspoonful of paprika, one quarter of a teaspoonful of ground mustard, a small pinch each of thyme and ground cloves. Roll each tomato in the prepared cheese until thickly coated; let stand for fifteen minutes, dip carefully in the batter and plunge into smoking hot fat. Fry golden brown, drain and serve garnished with watercress.

White Queen Tomato
Lycopersicon lycopersicon

Victorian tomato breeders developed a number of white tomatoes that were once quite popular. Among these was Shah, also known as White Mikado (a light white-yellow variety), and Ivory Ball, a small creamy white tomato also called White Apple and shown in the woodcut. But of all the white varieties, only one stands out as truly special. That tomato is White Queen.

White Apple Tomato

In *Off the Vine*, Dr. Carolyn Male has promoted White Queen as the best tasting of the heirloom whites, and I agree with her. The only problem with White Queen is that there are several tomatoes in circulation with this name; only one is the true variety. The original White Queen was released in 1882 by its creator, Alexander W. Livingston. It is a vigorous climber and a heavy producer, so the vines require sturdy stakes. The fruit has white skin and very pale, parchment-yellow flesh. There should be 8 to 9 seed cavities, and fruits should range in size from 3 to 3½ inches in diameter and about 2 inches thick.

The flavor of White Queen is different from any other I have tasted. It is fragrant, with a slight hint of rosewater. The fruit makes a delicate white tomato sauce for fish, yet it can also be served with fruits like *frais du bois*, with a splash of rosewater and sugar to enhance the fruitiness. A Gewürztraminer wine matches this tomato very well, as does cassis in champagne, diced mango, and a host of other fruit combinations.

Yellow Peach or Sorbet de Citron Tomato
Lycopersicon lycopersicon

Yellow Peach was introduced in 1862 by James J. H. Gregory of Marblehead, Massachusetts. The variety originated in France. In N. Hallock's 1890 field test of tomatoes, he remarked that the flavor was mild, sweetish, "but no peach flavor." Why should anyone expect that? "Of little value, except as a novelty," he continued. Actually, the tomato is charming, and the flavor is acid, juicy, and altogether good.

The tomato is circulated today under a variety of names, including Garden Peach, Yellow Peach, and *pêche Jaune* (its original French name), as well as the very descriptive *sorbet de citron*. As this last name would imply, the tomato does indeed look like a ball of lemon sherbet, and just to see how far I could push that resemblance, I once made a sorbet with the tomato. It was a complete surprise and happily a success.

The vines are highly productive of fruit all season. The fruit is small, round, slightly fuzzy like a peach, and pale yellow-white in color. On many fruits, the cheeks are blushed with pink, thus giving the tomato the appearance of a miniature white peach. The skin of the tomato gives it its pale yellow color, since the flesh is white or almost colorless.

In 1873 H. Beyer of New London, Iowa, advertised seed for a "new" peach tomato in the *American Agriculturist* (1873, 111). This marked the introduction from France of the Pink Peach (*pêche rosée*), which now also bears the name Tennessee Peach Fuzz. The pink variety resembles its yellow counterpart in fuzziness and in peachlike appearance, but the pink is generally hollow inside like a paste tomato. It is thought to be a

Leaf of the Yellow Peach Tomato

cross between a pink plum tomato and the older Yellow Peach. The fruit drops when ripe, and a light frost will cause all the fruit to drop regardless of ripeness.

Both the pink and yellow varieties do not bruise easily and are therefore good for shipping. They also keep long after picking and make excellent marmalades. When used directly from the garden, they are ideal salad tomatoes.

Turnips

The 1840 seed catalog of M. B. Bateham, proprietor of the Rochester Seed Store in Rochester, New York, listed several varieties of turnip popular at the time. These included Large White, Flat Norfolk, White Globe, Long Tankard, Red Top, Early White Flat Dutch, Early White Garden Stone, Rutabaga, Dale's Yellow Hybrid (a cross between White Globe and a rutabaga), Large Yellow Scotch Aberdeen, Yellow Malta, Yellow Altringham, Yellow Stone, and Early Yellow Dutch. Seed for every one of these varieties came from England. This impressive list represents the tip, in a sense, of the huge business once done in turnips. At one time, Americans were as enthusiastic about turnips as they now are about tomatoes, and it is a fascinating study in our shifting foodways to piece together the reasons why turnip consumption has gone into such a drastic decline. The most obvious explanation is that we now have many other food choices during the winter; we are not at all dependent on root-cellar vegetables. Furthermore, turnips are one of the cornerstones of soup cookery, and soup cookery has also fallen out of fashion. Yet nutritionally, these shifts are unfortunate; turnips are extremely rich in vitamin C and other nutrients not easily replaced by winter tomatoes, Iceberg lettuce, and South American grapes. Turnips were well known historically for their health benefits, and works like John Tweed's *Popular Observations on Regimen and Diet* (ca. 1815, 152) were quick to point this out.

The codex of Dioskorides (A.D. 500–511) discussed the turnip in terms of its medical properties and showed the oldest surviving botanical drawing of the plant. The turnip of the codex was round like the round varieties of today, but with very large leaves. The leaves were eaten as greens and therefore not considered a negative trait, as they are today. Since the Romans called turnips by three names, *beta, napus,* and *rapum,* there is always some confusion when consulting literary sources from that period, especially since *beta* could also refer to a beet. The rough rule was that *rapum* was used for round turnips, *napus* for long, carrot-rooted sorts, and *beta* for the varieties cultivated for their leaves. This is not a hard rule; sometimes only the context reveals what was meant.

Cow Horn Turnip

Botanists have theorized that the round-rooted culinary turnip of the type for which I have provided sketches on the following pages evolved long before the Roman era and thus has played a major role in European agricultural history. It has been proven through genetic experiments in Japan (1935) and from later verifications that sometime during pre-Roman antiquity, turnips crossed with cabbage to yield the plant now known as rape, a major source of vegetable oil. Cabbage has 18 chromosomes; the culinary turnip contains 20. Rape is a combination of both, with 38 chromosomes. Furthermore, the round white turnip mentioned by Dioskorides is also the oldest type discussed in medieval literary sources, although by the 1500s a yellow-fleshed variety was known. It too is thought to be a transspecies cross, like all the subsequent yellow varieties, with the yellow-fleshed rutabaga (*Brassica napus*).

The turnip species, if we may call it that, is a large one, including such heirloom vegetables as broccoli rabe, Chinese cabbage, and Chinese mustard. The *napus* species includes rutabaga, Siberian kale, and rape. Rapeseed oil has been used in northern Europe since the Middle Ages as a substitute for olive oil, and a processed form of it is sold as canola oil in North America. The Pennsylvania Dutch cultivated rape in the eighteenth and early nineteenth centuries for oil purposes, but this declined rapidly in the 1840s in favor of other cooking oil sources. The most popular of all the *napus* species cultivated among the Pennsylvania Dutch was the Tetlow turnip, which originated in Prussia. It was raised almost exclusively by the German-speaking community in this country, and American recipes for it are mostly found in German-American cookbooks. The turnip was described in detail in the *Transactions of the Royal Horticultural Society* (1812, 26–29) as a vegetable consumed in England only by foreigners. Of the turnips, the most favored variety among the English was Chirk Castle Black Stone, a small black-skinned variety that was perfectly suited to cottage gardens. It is still available today but I find that it turns rather tough and woody in our climate.

Tetlow Turnip

In *The American Home Garden* (1859, 185–87), Alexander Watson noted that it was common practice to sow turnips in March for a summer crop and in August for a fall and winter crop. Turnips need about eight weeks of cool, moist weather to attain their best shape and flavor. Seed is generally sown broadcast over well-prepared, well-raked ground. The best seedlings should be thinned to 4 inches apart. Turnips, more than many root vegetables, respond better to constant hoeing to keep the soil loose where they are growing. In areas of the country where spring is short and summer heat comes on quickly, grow turnips only as a fall crop. Liquid manure and frequent watering will ensure well-formed and well-textured turnips. Turnips are extremely sensitive to drought, and if they are stressed due to a lack of water, they will never fully recover and produce good roots.

For seed-saving purposes, it is important to know that turnips will cross with broccoli rabe, Chinese cabbage, and Chinese mustard, as well as with any wild turnips naturalized in the vicinity. Several forms of *Brassica rapa* have become common weeds in areas of the country settled in colonial times, so it is important to be watchful for these outside intrusions. Furthermore, rape has become naturalized in parts of the country where Pennsylvania Dutch have settled and should be destroyed if it is growing in the vicinity of the vegetable garden.

The species *rapa* is divided into two groups, even though both cross readily and should be isolated by at least 1 mile. The Rapifera group includes the root turnips discussed in the following pages. The Ruvo group includes the flowering sorts like true rape, Italian turnips, and broccoli rabe. All of these are grown as annuals, but in fact turnips are biennial and must be vernalized in order to produce flowers. In mild-winter areas turnips can be left in the open ground, but in most parts of the country, seed stock must be dug up before a hard frost and overwintered in cold storage. Damp sand or a moist environment with high humidity (90 to 95 percent) is necessary for good storage; otherwise the turnips will shrivel and eventually die. In the spring, the stored turnips are replanted and allowed to flower. Save at least twenty of the best turnips for seed. Turnips are out-pollinating, and therefore many individual plants are necessary for a good genetic balance. Pollen must be transferred from one plant to the next, not from flower to flower on the same plant.

Turnip seed is ready to harvest when the pods turn brown and brittle. The pods on the lower portions of the plants will ripen first and must be harvested first, otherwise they will burst and scatter the seed. The seed is also relished by certain birds, such as finches, so it may be necessary to cover the ripening pods with netting. Seed is harvested in succession until all the ripe pods are collected. The seed separates from the pods fairly easily once the pods are dry and brittle. As an alternative, seed pods can be stored in brown paper bags and sorted during the winter. Once it is separated, seed can be sieved of debris and stored in airtight containers. Seed viability is five years, although I have had good results with eight-year-old seed. It is better to renew seed every three years if several varieties are being maintained. I renew two varieties a year, taking advantage of isolation in a garden that is a mile from my main beds.

Amber Globe Turnip
Brassica rapa

This variety is also called Yellow Globe in old horticultural books and was depicted in the *Album Vilmorin* (1853, 3); thus color documentation is firm. It was "introduced" in England in 1840 as the Yellow Dutch turnip, but the *Gardener's Magazine* (1840, 104) was not fooled. Loudon, the editor, noted that the turnip was "nothing more than the yellow turnip, the seed of which, having formerly been chiefly procured from Holland, thus obtained the name of Dutch. It is little grown in England in gardens, but much esteemed and generally cultivated in Scotland." Americans shared the Scottish love for this yellow turnip because it was an old hardy sort dating at least from the eighteenth century that could be relied on well into the winter. In fact, this variety and a strain called Large Yellow Scotch Aberdeen could be stored through the following March and were greatly valued as a food source when other supplies were low. A fall turnip, it was generally planted about August 1.

The flesh of the turnip, shown in color plate 104, is actually yellowish or cream colored. The shoulder of the turnip usually turns green where it is exposed to sunlight. The flavor is pungent, and of all the turnips I have grown, this one is most susceptible to worm damage. For best results grow this variety on ground previously cultivated with cowpeas (page 150). This will reduce the problem with nematodes and similar pests.

Orange Jelly Turnip or Golden Ball Turnip
Brassica rapa

This handsome turnip was depicted in the *Album Vilmorin* (1870, 21), having appeared earlier in the *Album Vilmorin* (1854, 5) as Robertson's Golden Ball. Charlwood & Cummins, London seedsmen, presented seed for twenty-six turnip varieties to the United States Patent Office in 1855, among them Robertson's Golden Ball. This seed was distributed to American farmers for trial in different parts of the country. J. M. Thorburn & Company of New York continued to carry all twenty-six varieties for several years, but of these, only Robertson's is still available.

Shown in color plate 104, the turnip is not truly orange, although the color will vary greatly due to soil. The flesh is yellow and the flavor unique. It has an unexpected and pleasant aftertaste of bitter almond, very sweet and mild. It is probably one of the finest of all the culinary turnips and is excellent when paired with carrots.

Purple Top Milan Turnip
Brassica rapa

The *Gardener's Magazine* (1835, 40) reported that this turnip had just been introduced from France under the name *navet rouge plat hatif*. It appeared in the *Album Vilmorin* (1852, 3) as the Early Flat Red Top, and appeared again in the *Album Vilmorin* (1884, 35) under the name by which we now know it. For many years, while the name of this variety was not settled, it was often described as either red or purple. It is one of my favorite turnips because of its striking shape.

The turnip is shown in color plate 104. It is extremely flat, smooth skinned, and well adapted to slicing. The turnip rests above the ground like a kohlrabi, the shaded part white, the part most exposed to the sun a rich violet. It is also one of the first turnips to come to harvest. If planted early in the spring, it is ready to pull by the end of June. If the climate is hot and dry, this turnip should be planted in late summer because it can develop a strong mustard flavor if the heat is excessive. In parts of the Northwest, where the climate is cool and rainy, this variety is ideal. When grown to perfection, it is a very fine culinary turnip.

The *Table* (1898, 213), a monthly magazine issued by Marshall's School of Cookery in London, described the results of a cooking competition for turnips, with the winning recipes appended. One of the recipes, Turnips *à la Mancelle*, involved diced calf or sheep brains, velouté sauce, and an elaborate presentation *en couronne.* This approach was typical of the Victorian attempt to make over the turnip into something more in tune with elaborate silver and starched napkins. Turnips are rustic. A direct approach is always best. Mrs. Burkitt's winning recipe below was accomplished with veal or chicken stock; beef bouillon will darken the vegetables but give a richer flavor. What is not mentioned is the sugar. Normally, a tablespoon or so of sugar was added to the butter, which heightened the flavor of the turnips as they were browned.

Turnips Glazed with Gravy

🐛

Pare four or five large turnips, wash and drain them and cut into slices of uniform size, or turn them into a ball or pear shape, dissolve in a deep saucepan as much fresh butter as will cover the bottom of the pan, throw in the turnips and fry until they are lightly browned, drain the butter from them and pour over as much good stock as will cover them, let them simmer gently until they are nearly tender, remove the lid, put the saucepan over a quick fire and let the sauce boil quickly until it begins to thicken, take up, but be careful not to break them, arrange neatly on a dish and pour the gravy over. The turnips will take about twenty minutes to simmer.

Scarlet Ball or Scarlet Kashmir Turnip
Brassica rapa

Unlike the Milan turnip, this variety turns a true red or rose rather than violet. The roots are about 3 inches in diameter and somewhat flattened, not exactly ball shaped. William Henry Maule of Philadelphia carried this turnip in his catalogs in the 1890s. It was introduced from England as an improvement on a variety originating in India. The young plants make delicious greens but are subject to slug damage; I normally lose half my crop to slugs if I do not take precautions like scattering diatomaceous earth around them or setting out saucers of beer. Aside from the red color of the skin and its uniform size, this heirloom is not as flavorful as the others, but this could be the result of my soil type and not the variety. The skin of this variety may be dried and used like kohlrabi parings (page 112) for making winter soups.

White Egg Turnip
Brassica rapa

Boston seedsman John B. Russell sold seed in 1828 for a turnip called Swan's Egg, which appears to be the immediate predecessor of White Egg. In fact, based on old descriptions, the two are essentially the same. It is a fall variety that remained popular throughout the nineteenth century because of its keeping qualities. True to its name, the turnip is both egg shaped and white, generally about the size of a goose egg. The flesh is snowy white, tender, and very juicy, since there seems to be a higher water content in this turnip than in many other varieties. The flavor is somewhat sweet, and so mild that the turnip can be eaten raw, at least when fresh from the garden. In storage, the flavor intensifies. It has been said that voles destroy the

White Egg Turnip

best things first, and something about this turnip makes it extremely attractive to them. Voles will seek it out even when other turnip varieties are nearby. Their fondness for this one may be turned to the gardener's advantage, since the culls make excellent bait for vole traps.

Unusual Root Vegetables

Chufa or Earth Almond
Cyperus esculentus

This easy-to-grow perennial vegetable, with 2-to-2½-foot-long wispy, grasslike leaves, resembles several other members of the *Cyperus* genus, especially the common weed *Cyperus strigosus*, with which it should not be confused. The weed is native, but chufa was introduced from Spain in the eighteenth century in order to make a refreshing acid beverage called orgeat. The tubers were soaked for two or three days in spring water, then pounded. The liquid that ran off was strained and chilled on ice as a cooling summer drink. Chufa has since naturalized in the light sandy soils of the middle and southern states. In my part of the country it is commonly called Yellow Nut Grass, or simply Nut Grass, and at one time it was a common vegetable in our farm markets. The tubers, normally about ¼ inch in diameter, will grow much larger under cultivation if the soil conditions are right and the plants are given a healthy dose of rock phosphate each spring.

In the *Report of the Commissioner of Patents* (1856, 259), Victor Scriba, a Pennsylvania Dutch newspaper publisher in Pittsburgh, described growing chufa in 1853 and noted that it could be eaten raw like a chestnut or almond. In texture it is somewhat mealy like a chestnut, yet with a distinct almondlike flavor. It was used by country people as an

Chufa, showing leaf and tubers.

almond substitute in cookies and confectionery, and was even pounded with sugar to make a type of faux marzipan once quite popular among the Pennsylvania Germans. The Pennsylfaanisch word for it is *Aerdmandel* or "earth almond," and it is from the Pennsylvania Dutch that this alternate name derives.

The tubers should be planted 6 inches apart where they are to grow for several years. Mature clumps should be divided from time to time, and only the largest tubers replanted. This will encourage the plant to develop large tubers over a period of years. The smallness of the tuber is the only drawback at present; a concerted effort to develop a large-rooted variety would doubtless result in greater interest in this vegetable, especially since it can be eaten by people who are normally allergic to nuts.

Crosnes
Stachys affinis

Crosnes are a perennial root vegetable with small tubers that have the texture of water chestnuts. The shape of the tubers is curious and knobby, as shown in color plate 105. In France, where they are popular in the region around Lyon, crosnes are often served as an hors d'oeuvre with cardoons.

Crosnes were sent from Beijing to France in 1882 by Russian botanist Emillii Vasilevich Bretschneider (1833–1901), whose famous botanical exploits in China were later described in a fascinating account published in 1898. By 1889, the *American Garden* (10:101, 193, and 228) began reporting on the French successes with this "new vegetable." This was followed during the 1890s with a burst of interest in crosnes as part of a larger but passing fascination for Japanese vegetables and fruits. In Japan, crosnes are known as *choro-gi*. One of the leading promoters of the vegetable in this country was the seed firm of V. H. Hallock & Sons in Queens, New York, which advertised this "wonderful new food" under the unlikeliest of names: Vegetable White Bait. The firm's advertisements in the *Farm and Fireside* (March 1, 1890, 188) claimed that the tubers were a bargain at 35 cents per dozen. One plant produces many hundreds.

Since the 1890s, crosnes have been grown off and on as a curiosity, but recently there has been renewed interest in them as a winter vegetable. A few years ago I acquired plants from Phyllis Hanes, former food editor for the *Christian Science Monitor*. She had been growing crosnes in Boston for several years. The plants are extremely hardy, and their culture is simple.

The tubers are planted in the fall in rich, light soil in a sunny location. They should be set in the ground about 6 inches deep and 12 inches apart, for generous spacing encourages the development of tubers. Once the plants sprout the following spring, allow them to reach about 1 foot in height, then keep them cropped back to 6 inches. Cropping will direct growth into the roots. Plants that are allowed to flower will produce small tubers. Over the summer, keep the plants well watered, since they are sensitive to drought. In the fall, after frost kills the tops, the tubers can be harvested as needed. They can be grown in most parts of the United States and will withstand severe winters.

Due to their knobby shape, crosnes are not pared. The skin contains much of the flavor and is also rich in vitamins and minerals. To wash the tubers, place them in a large bowl of water and scrub them with a vegetable brush. A toothbrush purchased for this purpose will work beautifully, especially the brushes designed for false teeth. Once cleaned, the tubers can be eaten raw as a snack, added to casseroles, or mixed with stir-fries. They retain their crunchiness when cooked.

Earth Chestnut
Bunium bulbocastanum

Introduction of this plant from East Asia was attempted in the 1870s under the name Prescott chervil, but the venture failed. Today it is known as Earth Chestnut or Tuberous-Rooted Caraway, and to be frank, none of the names fit it very well. The leaf and plant resemble parsley, although they are rather neutral in taste. The seed is small like parsley and easy to grow. Plants should be started indoors in the spring, then planted out after the threat of frost has passed. Plants should be spaced about 10 inches apart; crowding will only result in small roots. Allow the plants to establish for at least 1 year before harvesting the tubers, which are about the size of a thumb. They can be eaten raw in salads or boiled and served as a vegetable. The taste and texture remind me of celery root. The leaves make a good mix with salad burnet, which they resemble somewhat in shape.

The earth chestnut is extremely hardy in Pennsylvania, where it is more or less evergreen during the winter; thus it makes an excellent winter salad green. In fact, the plant continues to grow even under the snow.

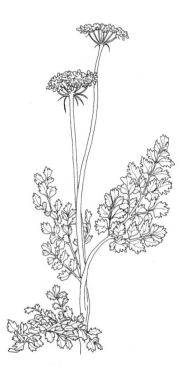

Earth Chestnut, detail of leaf and flower.

Edible Tuber Dahlia
Dahlia sp.

Perhaps it is my quirkiness, but I am always game to try new things, especially if it means introducing more cheerful color into my vegetable garden. The edible tuber dahlia recently surfaced as an untried culinary heirloom, and the adventure is worth reporting, for I have never seen dahlias listed as vegetables. In fact, Boston horticulturist Joseph Breck had this to say about dahlia tubers: "There is no danger from rats or mice or any other creature. I never knew an animal to touch them. You could not catch an old rat even to smell of them the second time" (1858, 50–51). Breck was as partial to dahlias as Victorian gardeners were to garlic. However, Roland Green, an early nineteenth-century flower specialist, noted in 1828 that the dahlia root resembled a sweet potato, and this also happens to be a fairly accurate description of its culinary merits.

The oral history concerning this attractive red double-flowering dahlia is that it was preserved among the Nanticoke Indians of Maryland for over 400 years. This pedigree is an example of how the mythology of the American Indian sometimes takes possession of an heirloom vegetable and provides it with an authenticity that is not above reproach. Simple mathematics explodes the story.

Dahlias were known in the back hills of Mexico but were not introduced to the outside world until 1787, when the flower was discovered during a French botanical expedition to Oaxaca. In 1789 seed was sent to Madrid under the name Mexican aster. This seed produced tall, gangly plants with uninteresting single flowers. It is believed that the early seed sent to Europe contained a mixture of two separate species, *Dahlia pinnata* (which grows about 6 feet tall) and *Dahlia coccinea* (which grows about 10 feet tall). All of the cultivated dahlias known today were created through hybridization or selection from these two species.

Double-flowering dahlias, like the edible one, appeared as sports in the botanic garden of Louvain in Belgium during the 1820s, and from that source the rage for double flowering and much overpriced dahlias emanated. American seedsman Thomas Bridgeman published a catalog of over 200 double varieties in his *Florist's Guide* (1836, 60–74), with a dizzying abundance of red ones. The edible dahlia of the Nanticoke Indians is probably a variety of Victorian "decorative dahlia," one of the recognized dahlia types, and with persistent research through old colored plates of dahlias, its true origin may someday be discovered. In the meantime, we shall cook it.

It is much to the credit of the Nanticokes that an observant gardener perhaps a hundred years ago, and not before that, noted certain similarities between the dahlia and the Jerusalem artichoke (page 167), for both belong to the helianthus tribe. It was a brave cook who first tried the roots for dinner, but one who must certainly have had an excellent understanding of plants—from missionary friends in Mexico with Mixteca connections. Eating a potato does not induce pangs of guilt, but eating a dahlia tuber provokes sadness for depriving the soul of an inspiring flower. To enjoy the dahlia tubers, it is important to dissociate them from thoughts of summer, and never serve them to friends who have first seen the flower, for this will only stir up endless quibbling about extraordinary waste and tastes so jaded they can only be satisfied by the sacrifice of beautiful and costly plants.

To my surprise, each plant produces four or five large, plump tubers. Thus, within the period of two or three seasons, it is possible to have an overabundance of tubers that cries out for thinning down to manageable size. Furthermore, anyone who has ever grown dahlias knows that if the tuber is accidentally broken from its stem, it will not grow. This is where cooking the culls makes absolute sense, and hunger for a gourmet treat takes hold of culinary fancy. And yes indeed, the flavor of the dahlia tuber goes perfectly well with a glass of red wine. Its approval is therefore assured.

Evening Primrose
Oenothera biennis

The evening primrose is native to eastern North America, but in colonial times its brilliant yellow flower caught the attention of European gardeners, so the wild form has undergone considerable alteration at the hands of plant breeders. The Société Royal d'Agriculture of Lyon, France, convened a small conference in 1838 to discuss the idea of cultivating the evening primrose as a root vegetable. The root is fleshy and rich in nutrients, and the plant thrives in poor soil. Such features would not only recommend it as a new type of food, similar to a turnip, but would also provide economic possibilities for farmers with poor ground.

Considerable effort was devoted to improving the evening primrose between 1838 and 1845, primarily in France and Germany, but the end result, it would appear, was only larger plants with more profuse flowers. The roots of the improved strain are indeed larger than the wild ones, but often irregular in shape. However, this improved strain came back to America, and it is the one most commonly cultivated in gardens. As an experiment, I dug some plants from the wild just to see if the differences were real, and they were.

Evening Primrose showing leaf and flower.

The boiled root is generally used in salads, mixed with cardoons or other blanched vegetables. Personally, I find the taste of the root peppery and unpleasant, like some wild mushrooms I have eaten with very sad results, or perhaps, more accurately, like biting into a spoonful of mustard seeds. Yet I have tasted roots from other gardens that are almost as sweet as carrots. This suggests to me that soil may determine the success of this vegetable more than human intervention.

The green tops overwinter like Turkish rocket (page 316), which they resemble in taste. As its botanical name would imply, evening primrose is a biennial, although some plants bloom the first year. It commonly grows to a height of 6 feet and is covered with bright yellow flowers for much of the summer. As an accent plant, it is showy in the kitchen garden, but it reseeds promiscuously. I allow volunteers to establish themselves here and there and enjoy the random spots of color, but constant weeding of seedlings is necessary to keep it under control.

Ocha, or Oca
Oxalis tuberosa

The ancestors of the Incas perfected the culture of ocha more than a thousand years ago and developed many different varieties, yet Europeans took little note of the plant until the nineteenth century. Tubers were sent from Peru to England in 1829, where they immediately caused a gardening sensation, even though the plants had been identified by Nicholas de Jacquin in the eighteenth century. James Mitchell, an English gardener who had grown ocha, wrote an article on its culinary qualities for the *Gardener's Magazine* (1833, 78–79). The vegetable was eventually trialed in the garden of the London Horticultural Society, followed shortly thereafter by a dinner in which several courses of ocha were served.

Oxalis deppei, now commonly grown under the name Good Luck plant or Lucky Clover, was introduced from Mexico in 1837 and also trialed by the London Horticultural Society. It was cooked as a root vegetable and pronounced "delicate." Fearing Burr (1865, 38) wrote that it was served like asparagus, which is not possible since no part of the plant produces a stem even suggestive of asparagus. However, if the bulbs are planted in sandy soil, they will develop by the end of the summer into a cluster of perhaps 10 or 12 and will have sent down a white carrotlike root about 3 inches long. This makes a very delicate vegetable,

Detail of the leaf of Red Ocha

but it must be allowed to mellow in the sun for several days to remove the bitterness. Furthermore, the "shamrock" leaves and the cheerful pink flowers are delightful in salads; that is the reason I cultivate it.

Oxalis Deppei or Deppe's Wood Sorrel, showing carrot-like root.

Ocha entered the United States about the same time that it appeared in England, except that our earliest stock came from Chile. It remained an exotic vegetable among our gentleman gardeners for much of the nineteenth century because interest in it was more or less shoved aside by the agricultural crisis brought on by the failure of the potato crop in the 1840s. Oddly, ocha would have made a good alternative. The only drawback is its acidity, which, if not properly dealt with, will impart a bitterness to the root, as with *Oxalis deppei*. Exposing the tubers to the sun for ten days converts this bitterness to sugars.

Fearing Burr (1865, 36–37) listed two varieties, the white-rooted (*oca blanca*) and the red-rooted (*oca colorada*). The red variety was depicted in the *Album Vilmorin* (1869, 20), as well as a yellow one. There are also "blush" and brightly speckled varieties. I grow all of them, and they are harvested the same way.

The tubers resemble miniature Jerusalem artichoke roots, except that they are waxy on the surface and brilliantly colored.

They are best started in individual pots in the late winter so that the plants are well established when they are set out after all danger of frost has passed. Loose, moist, sandy soil is their preference, and it is better to situate them in partial shade, because the blasting heat of summer may kill them. A drought certainly will, for these are plants from the High Andes that thrive in cool weather, but they also need a long growing season.

The tops or greens can be eaten as a vegetable. The stems are fleshy and slightly sour. For root culture it is important to leave the tops alone, because the plant must bloom if it is to produce a large crop of tubers, a characteristic it shares with the potato. Once it has bloomed, the tubers can be harvested. Those reserved for seed stock should be stored in a cool dry place until late winter, when the process of planting is repeated.

Oca colorada or Red Ocha

Ocha is day-length sensitive and will not form tubers until there are less than twelve hours of light a day. For most of the United States, this means that tubers will not form until November, so the plants must be covered to protect them from frost at least until Thanksgiving. In areas of the country where the ground freezes before November 1, ocha may not be an option, since this last stage is critical to the development of the crop.

Sara McCamant, a member of Seed Savers Exchange in California, not only sent me some of the most exquisite pink and white ochas I have ever seen but kindly passed along cultural advice that proved quite helpful. Sara's experience with ocha, due to its preference for cool weather, has been to plant it in a somewhat shady location, a conclusion I reached intuitively by observing its reaction to the hot sun. All members of the *Oxalis* genus thrive better in sandy soil; therefore I have created a special bed for ocha by double-digging and using cactus potting mixture as infill. This has tripled my yields.

It was interesting to see Sara's ochas, because they were quite different from mine in skin texture. Hers had skins more like that of a potato, in outward appearance anyway—ocha skin is paper-thin—whereas mine have waxy skins. There is very little written on the differences in ocha varieties, yet they go far beyond color and skin texture. There are large differences in the texture of the flesh, and some

Oca blanca (White Ocha) and Pink Ocha

varieties contain high amounts of oxalic acid, which gives them a bitter taste. This bitterness can be overcome by drying the tubers in the sun, which quickly transforms many of the starches to sugar, a technique used by the ancient Incas. Unfortunately, people who are allergic to spinach (which contains oxalic acid) are likely to experience a severe reaction and therefore should avoid ocha.

Salsify
Tragopogon porrifolius

Salsify has naturalized in my garden. I planted it a few years ago in a raised bed half filled with sand, and the salsify has taken over. It thrives on ground where it can drive its root straight and deep, and an occasional summer flood does not hurt it. My grandfather called salsify oyster plant, and I can remember it in his garden: tall wispy leaves like giant grass, and a flower some four feet high that opened in the morning a brilliant red. This was the old Pennsylvania Dutch *Hawwerwurzel* (oat root), the real heirloom salsify of colonial America. I wish today that I had that red-flowering variety, because it is now extremely rare.

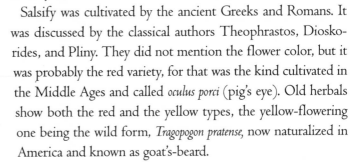

Salsify

Salsify was cultivated by the ancient Greeks and Romans. It was discussed by the classical authors Theophrastos, Dioskorides, and Pliny. They did not mention the flower color, but it was probably the red variety, for that was the kind cultivated in the Middle Ages and called *oculus porci* (pig's eye). Old herbals show both the red and the yellow types, the yellow-flowering one being the wild form, *Tragopogon pratense*, now naturalized in America and known as goat's-beard.

The red-flowering form was generally called the "common" variety in early American garden books, although as Charles Hovey pointed out in the *Magazine of Horticulture* (1842, 129–30), "to the mass of the community, it is quite a new vegetable." Aside from the that grown by Pennsylvania Dutch, who had been cultivating it since the 1700s, salsify was, in Hovey's words "scarcely seen beyond the precincts of the kitchen gardens of gentlemen in the vicinity of our large cities." Its popularity increased by the time of the Civil War, and the old red variety survived in country kitchen gardens into this century, but was eventually replaced by the blue-flowering varieties we know today.

In 1872 Rochester, New York, seedsman James Vick began offering a "new French variety" called New Blue Flowered, "said to be superior in flavor and size to the old sorts." The J. M. Thorburn seed company of New York began distributing another blue-flowering variety in the late 1880s called Mammoth Sandwich Island, which is the variety of salsify that I recommend to heirloom gardeners. The *American Garden* (1889, 99, 187) promoted it when the variety was first introduced: "We are now using this delicious vegetable . . . its yield is double that of the Common variety."

Salsify is a biennial, blooming the second year. The roots of first-year plants taste vaguely like oysters, which is why they were popular pureed into soups or cooked as a vegetable side dish with fish. Second-year plants can be woody, but the tender ones taste more like asparagus. During the early summer of the second year, they bloom with flowers resembling a dandelion. The seed-heads develop feathers that carry off the seed during gusts of wind. When the seedheads are dry, the seed can be separated and dried. Since the seed goes into deep dormancy unless planted immediately after it ripens, I think it is best to plant it then and there where it is to grow and thus keep the salsify bed in a constant state of production. Seed purchased commercially is in deep dormancy and must be planted early in the spring when the potatoes go in, mid-March if possible. This cold period will cause it to germinate. Contrary to folklore, there are no "male" and "female" seeds.

The blue-flowering salsify will only cross with other blue- and red-flowering varieties. It will not cross with goat's-beard or with scorzonera (page 370).

Both salsify and scorzonera make delightful beignets. The following recipe is from A. B. Beauvillier's *Art of Cookery* (1827, 243).

Beignets de Salsifi et de Scorsonère
🌰

Take of one of these a sufficient quantity, and cut them about three inches long; put in a stew-pan a little water and vinegar; throw them in as they are scraped; wash and cut them; put upon the fire a pot with water, salt, vinegar, and a bit of butter rubbed in flour; when they are done enough drain and marinade them in salt, pepper, and vinegar; when ready to serve, dip them into a light paste (pâté à frire); put them into a frying pan; when they are a fine colour, drain them upon a cloth.

The reason for putting the salsify in acidulated water is that exposed to the air, the pared root discolors. Vinegar will also remove the stains on the hands resulting from the sap. Normally, before cooking either scorzonera or salsify, they are first blanched in a flour-and-water *blanc* (see page 82 under Beets and Chards), which keeps them from turning black.

Scorzonera

Scorzonera hispanica

Compared to salsify, the cultivation of scorzonera is quite recent. Leonhard Rauwolf observed scorzonera at Aleppo in 1575, noting that the locals called it *corton*. Shortly after this, the plant was brought under cultivation in Italy, and by 1660 it began appearing in French kitchen gardens.

Scorzonera or Black Salsify

By the 1680s it was cultivated in Switzerland and Germany. By 1770 it had become well known throughout Europe and was already under cultivation in colonial America, particularly by the Pennsylvania Dutch. In the 1772 supplement to Christopher Sauer's *Kurtzgefasstes Kräuterbuch*, scorzonera is discussed under its old Pennsylvania Dutch name *Schlangenmord* (snake bane). It was known to other colonial Americans as viper grass, owing to its presumed medical usefulness against snake bites.

By 1865, there were four cultivated varieties, including one from Russia known as *géante noir de Russie*. This is the heirloom variety that I raise, since it is the most reliable and consistent producer for culinary purposes. The *Album Vilmorin* (1869, 12) included a handsome illustration of the Russian scorzonera in color. This appears to be the basis for the line drawing in the 1885 Vilmorin garden book.

The root of scorzonera can be prepared like salsify, but it is richer tasting and contains a large amount of vitamin E. Unlike salsify, the root of scorzonera is black and will continue to grow in the ground for several years without turning tough. If a bed of it is large enough, and well established over a period of five years, it is possible to plant new seed and harvest very large roots every season.

Furthermore, unlike salsify, the young leaves of scorzonera make a delicious salad green. If the flowering plants are pruned to the ground after they bloom in the summer, they will sprout a crop of greens for the fall. The greens are excellent in étouffées (covered steamed dishes) and cook perfectly in the microwave oven. The leaf is different from salsify in that it is very broad and not at all bitter. The culture for scorzonera is the same as for salsify, except that the scorzonera flower is yellow. The seed-saving techniques are also the same.

Skirret

Sium sisarum

Skirret is one of those vegetables that has always hovered near the periphery of the kitchen garden, a weedy-looking plant not fully tamed, yet passionately advocated by those who enjoy its roots. It fascinates me in a way because it evokes flavors from another age. When I set out a dish of skirrets on an old china plate, the light coming through the window invariably captures the mood of a Vermeer painting. It is food made for quiet contemplation.

English colonists in this country called it water parsnip due to its affinity for swampy ground and banks by streams. The Pennsylvania Dutch called it *Wassermarrich* or water marrow, in reference to the marrowlike richness of the root. Christopher Sauer noted in the 1776 supplement to his herbal, "when it is still young and crisp, it is fit for the kitchen, with pureed greens and herbs, in soups, or in salads."

The plant was introduced into Germany and Eastern Europe during the Middle Ages, yet it has been known in England only since 1548. Wherever it has been planted, it has been treated as a substitute for parsnips. Skirret was especially popular with the European peasantry because its preference for wet ground meant that it could be cultivated on boggy land or in other marginal areas where most garden vegetables do not thrive. Perennial, easy to grow, and free of pests, it offered many advantages over parsnips, especially the lack of the irritating leaves that made parsnips so unpleasant to harvest. Furthermore, with its Celtic name—*siu* means water in Celtic—the plant was thought to embody a vast array of medical benefits, one reason why there is so much space devoted to it in old herbals. In spite of this, skirret was never as popular in England as it was on the Continent.

Richard Bradley remarked in his *New Improvements of Planting and Gardening* (1718, 129–30) that "the Skirret has a very agreeable Root, altho' it is propagated but in a few Gardens; and it may be, the Rarity of it is owing to the Want of the right way of cultivating it." The right way of cultivating it is simple. Seed can be started in the early spring as easily as raising parsley. This is how I began my patch several years ago. There is much hocus-pocus about its being biennial, and needing to be dug up in regions where the ground freezes in the winter, but none of this is true. It is a hardy perennial.

The plants should be situated in the full sun about 12 inches apart, for they grow 4 to 6 feet tall, another reason why they should be planted toward the back of the kitchen garden. Once the plants begin to bloom (the white flowers look like Queen Anne's lace), they should be staked to prevent them from toppling over in a heavy rain. This also keeps the seed high and dry. Yet once a patch is established, it is not necessary to gather seed. Skirret can be propagated from rootlets.

The plant does best in sandy soil, or should I say, the root formation is better, since in loose ground they grow long and straight. The largest roots will be about the size of the small finger in diameter and perhaps a foot long. They should be pared before cooking. As the roots are harvested over the winter, save the rootlets too small for cookery for next year's crop. Either return them to the ground or store them in damp sand. I use a Styrofoam ice chest for this purpose. Plants that produce woody roots should be discarded; only plant rootlets from plants with tender roots. By this selective method it is possible over a period of a few years to develop a very tender strain of skirret.

At its best, skirret is sweeter than parsnip. As a child, I remember an old cousin in Lancaster County who made a pie of skirrets, apple schnitz, and ham. It was the perfect thing for a cold winter day.

Turnip-Rooted Chervil
Chaerophyllum bulbosum

This biennial is a native of southern Europe with hairy leaves and violet-tinted stems. It grows about 3 feet tall and produces a carrotlike root about 5 to 6 inches long, with a dark slate-colored skin and cream-yellow flesh. It is the most elegant root vegetable I grow, and one of the most difficult to grow from seed. In spite of its cultural difficulties, it gained considerable attention in the 1850s, and Fearing Burr (1865, 29–30) reported on the Vilmorin experiments with it. The idea in this country was to grow it as a luxury table vegetable, and some market gardeners began raising it around Washington, Baltimore, and Philadelphia. The plant became naturalized to some extent in all three areas after its cultivation was abandoned at the turn of this century, but recent development of old farmland into housing tracts has destroyed many of those sites.

Turnip-Rooted Chervil

I can only say that the root is worth the trouble. It is to carrots what champagne is to wine, or the true caviar of the vegetable world, yes, better even than feasting on dahlias. The plant is not much to look at. In fact, toward the end of the summer, it dies. At that point, the root can be harvested as needed. The flavor improves greatly if the roots are left in the ground, yet because they are attacked by nematodes and other boring insects, I store them in cool, damp sand. When the roots are cooked, they have an aromatic flavor similar to chervil, which pairs beautifully with fine white wines.

The plants bloom before dying and should be watched constantly so that the seed is harvested when it is ripe. The seed can be dried and planted the following spring, but it must be stratified; otherwise germination may take two years or not at all. This is because the seed goes into deep dormancy unless planted in the fall where it is to grow. I collect it immediately and plant it. It then germinates the following spring, and in this manner, crops can be kept going from year to year. If it is at all possible to purchase young potted plants from a nursery that sells specialty herbs, I would recommend starting with them. Those plants can be used to start seed in the fall rather than fussing with dormant seed that may or may not be worth the time and trouble.

Watercress

Watercress (*Nasturtium officinale*) is a hardy perennial introduced from Europe in the eighteenth century. General Peter Muhlenberg recognized it growing wild in streams at Valley Forge in 1777 and recommended it for the army then encamped there. It was a much-sought-after salading in the early spring because its vitamin-rich leaves served as an antidote to winter diets lacking green vegetables.

Historically, only one sort of watercress was grown in this country, the common green sort still found naturalized in some streams in eastern parts of the country. It had no commercial varietal name and was considered inferior to Erfurt Sweet Watercress, a German variety introduced into the United States in the early 1870s. In any case, it preferred cool, clear, running streams, and today, where it is still found, it may be used as a measure of water quality. Like trout, watercress will fail in water that is not free of pollution.

Watercress can be obtained as seed, which is scattered at the source of a gravelly stream where the water is 2 to 3 inches deep. Once established, the cress will self-propagate, but if it chokes the stream, it must be lifted and the space cleared of mud and debris. In many parts of the country, especially near large cities, farmers in the last century constructed a system of shallow paddies along streams to create beds for watercress. This effort was repaid handsomely. As Peter Henderson pointed out in *Gardening for Profit* (1886 edition: 192), "Many a farmer in the vicinity of New York realizes more profit from watercress, cut from the margin of a brook running through his farm in two or three weeks in spring, than from his whole year's hard labor in growing corn, hay or potatoes."

The development of farmland, pollution, and the diverting of streams from their natural courses has become a well-known environmental issue, but less understood is the devastating affect this has had on the culture of watercress. As a result, watercress is expensive and not always in ready supply. However, it is not necessary to be a farmer with an abundance of bottomlands to grow watercress successfully. In fact, it can be raised on a porch or under a tree, anywhere there is room for a large pot or tub.

The Victorians devised a system for raising watercress in flowerpots, a method that also produces a higher-quality cress than that grown in streams. Pot culture also keeps watercress in ready supply throughout the year and thus places it within

Old method of raising watercress in a flowerpot.

the economic reach of anyone with the patience to keep it well watered. The engraving from the *American Agriculturist* (1876, 23) shows watercress in a 15-inch pot filled with pebbles, sand, and rich soil. The pot is set inside a deep clay saucer filled with 2 inches of water. Seeds or cuttings from watercress bought at a market can be planted in the pot and maintained the year around. The water should be bottled spring water and the whole kept cool by refilling the saucer daily. Evaporation will help keep the clay pot cool; a few ice cubes during excessively hot weather in the summer will preserve the cress from heat shock, to which it is quite sensitive. Instead of a flower pot, a plastic basket designed to hold fishpond plants can be used. It should be filled with a mixture of sand and peat moss.

To harvest the cress, merely prune it with scissors or a sharp knife as needed. Cut neatly, since breaking the stems injures the plants. The cress will send out new shoots, flower, and produce seed that can be sown in a second pot or basket. The number of pots can be increased as desired, but it is best to renew the pots every two years to change the soil and clean off any moss or algae that may have established itself. The pots can be moved indoors to a sunny windowsill during the winter or stored in a cold frame. If the watercress is frozen in the pots, it will go dormant and not revive until spring.

Watermelons

Botanists have found what are believed to be the wild ancestors of the cultivated watermelon in Southwest Africa. This is an annual vine that hangs its survival on its ability to take up large amounts of water during a short rainy season and then "hibernate" over the dry season, when the vines die and the thick-rinded fruit lies scattered in the sun. Months later, the water stored in the melons provides the seedlings with a source of moisture as they burst forth from the fruit in anticipation of the oncoming rains. Curiously enough, this cycle reenacted itself in my own pantry some years ago.

It happened that one fall I had an overabundance of citron watermelons that I stored, as I normally do, in my kitchen pantry, where it is cool and dry. I still had many melons left by the following June. Within days of the summer solstice, as though on cue, the melons split open to reveal a mass of seedlings resembling green spaghetti. A few of these seedlings made their way through the cracks in the rind and would have grown across the room toward a small window had I not intervened. Such is the hardy tenaciousness of the watermelon plant.

The citron watermelon, a close relative of the melon we eat, is not very popular today, yet it is one of the oldest forms of the cultivated watermelon now found in American kitchen gardens. In Botswana, in southwestern Africa, the Bantu peoples raise a type of citron watermelon called the Tswana Melon, which is cut up, dried, then used in stews during the winter in much the same fashion that American Indians used dried pumpkin. This may be one of the most ancient uses of watermelons, aside from a ready supply of fresh water in what is otherwise one of the most arid regions of Africa south of the Sahara.

The Bantus can thus prove that Galen, the ancient Greek physician, was wrong when he wrote in his treatise *On Food and Bad Juices* that watermelons could not be dried like other fruit. On the other hand, there is some question about what is meant by "watermelon" in classical antiquity. Andrew Dalby has suggested in *Siren Feasts* (1996, 79), a study of ancient Greek foods and eating customs, that the *sikyos pepón* of the old Greek authors was indeed a watermelon. The two words literally mean a large, sweet cucumber. This may tell us something about watermelons in that distant age: oblong, white-fleshed, perhaps white-seeded as well. Or it could refer to the chate melon of the Egyptians, a melon that also fits this general description and would certainly not lend itself to drying.

In any case, by the Roman era, watermelons of several sorts were cultivated and remained under cultivation in Mediterranean countries throughout the Middle Ages. Appreciation of the watermelon was especially high among the Arabs, and even more sophisticated among the Turks, who organized their watermelon vendors into a guild in Constantinople. Trade with Alexandria brought the Venetians in contact with melon varieties from all over the Middle East, and the Moors in Spain established several sorts on the Iberian Peninsula before their departure in the 1400s. The Black Spanish watermelon brought to Philadelphia in the 1820s was a lineal descendant of those old Moorish varieties.

Watermelons reached the New World from two sources: from Spain and Portugal, and directly from Africa. The earliest references to watermelons in what is now the United States suggest a Spanish–West Indian route rather than a direct link to Africa. Watermelons are documented in Massachusetts in 1629, described as red-fleshed, with light green skin and black seeds. The Swedish geographer-engineer Peter Lindström (1925) reported seeing red-fleshed watermelons along the Delaware River in 1642, noting that they were eaten raw or pressed to make a cooling beverage, a type of watermelon cider. Additionally, watermelon juice was boiled to create a form of ersatz molasses, which it resembles in color and taste. This form of molasses was popular in the seventeenth and eighteenth centuries in early America because it was cheap and easily made. By the nineteenth century, it was considered a poverty food.

A study called "Syrup Made from Watermelons," published by the Commissioners of Agriculture of Virginia (1901, 135), tried to rehabilitate watermelon molasses as a profitable farm product. The idea did not attract many followers. Watermelon vinegar, however, was at one time well appreciated in the South and often took the place of more expensive wine vinegars. I have included an old recipe for it in the sketch dealing with the Rattlesnake watermelon because "Rattlesnake Vinegar" is what one requires for an authentic Georgia Cracker salad dressing.

Not only did the watermelon reach our shores early in the colonial period, it was quick to find its way into the gardens of the American Indians. Early travelers into the interior of the country often remarked with surprise about the variety and quality of the watermelons they encountered in out of the way places. Sweet, red-seeded varieties are known from the 1670s, and among the Indians of Illinois an oblong white-fleshed variety was recorded as late as 1822. The Curtis Showell White Flesh watermelon, available only through Seed Savers Exchange, may be a modern survivor of that old strain.

Some of the earliest commercial varieties of watermelon sold in this country appeared as early as 1802 in the seed lists of Bernard M'Mahon of Philadelphia. They included two types, the Large New Jersey Watermelon (a red-fleshed and a yellow-fleshed sort), and the Carolina Long Watermelon, which also came in red- and yellow-fleshed forms. Boston seedsman John B. Russell listed three varieties in his 1828 catalog: Carolina Long Watermelon, the Long Island Watermelon, and the Apple-Seeded Watermelon. All of these varieties date from the eighteenth century and none of them are readily available today. The Carolina Long Watermelon, shown in the old woodcut, was oblong in shape and somewhat swollen toward the blossom end. The skin was dark green, with pale green and white patterns. The flesh was deep red, the seeds black. There was a variant form with yellow flesh and white seeds, but the red-fleshed sort was the oldest and considered the "classic" American watermelon. Of all the colonial watermelon varieties, it was the one most likely to have reached this country directly from Africa. It was also the melon that was shipped to northern ports well in advance of local crops; thus its fame was almost universal from Charleston to Boston.

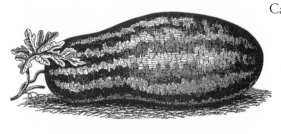

Carolina Watermelon

The Long Island Watermelon was a variety favored by market gardeners for the New York market, but it disappeared by the 1860s in favor of other sorts better adapted to the North. Only the Apple-Seeded Watermelon could be grown with success in most northern gardens, primarily because it was small and early fruiting. This sort is believed to be traceable to the earliest seventeenth-century watermelons introduced here, but its origin is unknown, since there do not seem to be any botanical surveys of apple-seeded types that might shed some light on its Old World kinships.

The most common Apple-Seeded Watermelon was red-fleshed. The fruit was round and small, with deep green skin and a very thin rind. The flavor was sweet, the seeds blackish brown and shaped like apple seeds, hence the name of the melon type. Because the plants were hardy and the fruit ripened even in short-season areas, this melon was the most widely cultivated of all the colonial American types. While Fearing Burr (1865, 182) listed only a red sort, the *Lancaster Farmer* (1870, 185) described a white-fleshed form, remarking that apple-seeded watermelons were an old type rarely seen anymore.

Alexander Watson listed six watermelon varieties in his *American Home Garden* (1859, 152). These included the Carolina Long Watermelon, the Long Island Watermelon, and the Apple-Seeded Watermelon popular earlier in the century, as well as the Black Spanish Watermelon, the Orange Watermelon (only recently introduced), and the Citron Watermelon. All of these were recommended for American kitchen gardens, although frankly, the first two were mammoth and better cultivated in fields, since there can be only one melon per vine where fruit size is a requirement.

Hawes H. Coleman, an Arkansas gardener who specialized in watermelon culture, discussed a number of southern varieties in the *Report of the Commissioner of Patents* (1856, 313–14). In particular, he noted his own variety, called the Coleman Watermelon (which he had cultivated since 1827), the Rattlesnake Watermelon—one of the most popular antebellum watermelons in the South—and a fascinating variety called the Bough Watermelon, raised only in the region between Richmond, Virginia, and Baltimore. It was a long, white-skinned watermelon with red flesh and red seeds. Only the Rattlesnake Watermelon is still available today.

Some of the colorful regional varieties like Bough were the result of breeding experiments with exotic imports. It is known from the *Gardener's Magazine* (1830, 339) that American and English diplomats stationed in Saint Petersburg, Russia, assembled a collection of watermelons from various parts of the czar's empire. Fourteen distinct varieties reached this country, one of them with green flesh, yet extremely sweet. The ultimate fate of that collection is unknown, and unfortunately nothing in it even hinted at a melon resembling the popular Moon and Stars watermelon, which some horticulturists believe may have come to this country with Mennonites from Russia.

Fearing Burr's list of watermelons in his *Field and Garden Vegetables of America* (1865) is conservative in terms of what existed and reflective of his own prejudice in favor of commercial sorts. Nonetheless, Burr included a fair selection of southern varieties, such as the Bradford Watermelon, the Clarendon Watermelon, the Ravenscroft Watermelon, and the Souter Watermelon, all of which are now unavailable to seed savers. All four of these were also developed or perfected in South Carolina in the period just prior to the Civil War. During that time South Carolina was a testing ground for many early American watermelon varieties, and its horticultural contribution in this regard deserves better recognition.

The cultivation of watermelons is simple—indeed, much less complicated than that of muskmelons, although watermelons are famously sensitive to climate. Hills should be spaced 8 feet apart in light, sandy soil with good exposure to a full day of sun. Two plants per hill is normally recommended, three if the melons are a small variety. Allow no more than three or four fruits per vine, and in order to raise truly large melons, all melons but one must be removed from each plant.

In the North it is better to start the watermelon seed indoors and thin out the best plants into pots so that they can be several weeks ahead when transplanted to the garden. In practice, watermelons should be planted when the ground is warm, essentially at the same time as beans. If the ground is too cold, the seedlings will rot, or in any case, they will not grow much. They will do much better when planted late. Furthermore, if the seedlings are weak, they are far more likely to succumb to cucumber beetles than if they are vigorous. Once established, the vines usually outgrow the beetles. Therefore, it is important to fertilize the young plants well, when it has a far more positive effect on the vines than later in the season. Fish emulsion mixed with water and applied to the hills early in the season is really all the feeding the vines will require.

For the past few years, I have had trouble with all my watermelons due to unseasonable weather. Even though watermelons are tropical, tropical weather will cause most American varieties to abort their female flowers, especially during conditions of drought or excessive humidity. Watering will lessen the stress of drought, but humidity cannot be controlled. Bearing this in mind, I would suggest overplanting so that a few fruits are guaranteed. I have had seasons when I have harvested no watermelons at all, and this is catastrophic for seed saving.

For seed-saving purposes, select only fruit that is truest to type. All varieties of watermelon and citron melon belong to the same species and will cross readily. They must be isolated by at least a half mile. Since I have many rare heirloom varieties, I isolate my melons about one mile, planting part of the crop at Oaklands, a fine old property not far from me. If isolation cannot be accomplished, resort to hand pollinating to maintain seed purity. Watermelons can be grown with cucumbers and muskmelons because they are different species and do not cross.

Watermelon seeds are mature when the melons are ripe, so seed harvesting can be turned into a picnic. A spit bucket and hungry friends are the basic tools for separating seed. After the seeds are collected, wash them thoroughly in clean water, then spread them to dry on screens. After two weeks, the seed should be dry enough to pack in airtight containers. Humidity is an important factor. If the seeds are brittle and snap when broken between the fingers, the seed harvest is ready to store. Properly stored, watermelon and citron watermelon seed will keep five years. Old-timers considered watermelon seed best for planting when it was two years old (shorter vines, better formed fruit). I have not noticed a remarkable difference, but since the weather has not been favorable for the past few years, I cannot say that I have given this a fair trial.

Black Spanish Watermelon
Citrullus lanatus

This variety was introduced to the United States from Portugal about 1829 by Henry Pratt of Lemon Hill, a famous mansion in what is now Fairmount Park in Philadelphia. Pratt was a wealthy merchant with horticultural interests whose generosity with seed ensured that this melon was soon known in most parts of the country. It was later called the Cuban Melon by many market gardeners in Philadelphia until the advent of Burpee's Cuban Queen.

The fruit is squat, slightly oblong, with distinct ribbing. The outer skin is black-green, hence its name. The rind is 1½ inches thick on well-formed specimens. The flesh is deep red, finely grained, and very sweet. The seed is dark brown, almost black. Of all the water-melons listed in this section, Black Spanish was the only variety most

Black Spanish Watermelon

consistently recommended for small kitchen gardens in nineteenth-century garden books and the only watermelon discussed by Robert Buist in his *Family Kitchen Gardener* (1847, 73–74).

Citron Watermelon (Green- and Red-Seeded)
Citrullus lanatus var. *citroides*

The citron watermelon forms an important subgroup of the watermelon species, and not many American gardeners are aware that there are several sorts. The most common are the red-seeded, generally referred to as the Colorado Preserving Melon in old American seed catalogs; the red-seeded with black speckles, a variant form of the preserving melon; and the green-seeded, often called the California Pie Melon or Texas Pie Melon. All of these were grown extensively in the nineteenth century for making "sweetmeats," candied melon rind used in fruitcakes, cookies, and puddings.

The use of the citron watermelon in preserving is extremely old and probably evolved out of similar preserves made with the colocynth melon (*Citrullus colocynthis*) known since classical antiquity. The colocynth melon preserved in honey or sugar was used exclusively as an internal medicine; in large quantities, it is poisonous. Literary evidence from the 1400s suggests that citron watermelons were initially used the same way and only later moved into the culinary realm.

The center of culture of the citron watermelon in Europe was Spain and Portugal; doubtless it was introduced there by the Moors. The Portuguese remain to this day the masters of candied fruits; the finest-quality candied citron melons are to be found in Lisbon. Early French horticulturists often refer to a Portuguese-Spanish connection when citron watermelons are mentioned, and the old French name for the melon also points to this origin: *citrouille d'Espagne à confiture.* Linguistic evidence in several languages suggests that the art of preserving these melons in sugar moved out of Spain in the mid-1500s into France and other parts of Europe. Happily, this very early variety of red-seeded citron watermelon is still available through Seed Savers Exchange.

One of the earliest depictions of the red-seeded variety appeared in the *Florilegium* of Camerarius, a manuscript dating from the 1580s, now in the library of the University of Erlangen in Germany. It shows a ripe melon with a slice removed. The Abbé Rozier, writing in 1785, described this melon under its other old French name, *pastèque à confiture*. In every case, the melon is associated with confectionery (*confiture*), not with a fresh fruit. Indeed, none of the citron watermelons make pleasant eating in the raw state, since they are rock hard and taste somewhat like an insipid cucumber. It is this lack of flavor that recommends them for sugar work; when they are cooked in sugar with lemon rind or fresh ginger, the melons absorb the taste of the flavorings. Once candied, the melon can be cut into a vast array of fanciful shapes that were once popular in the ornamentation of banquet foods.

In colonial America the citron watermelon was used as a substitute for the true citron, a tropical fruit also preserved in sugar. Since citron watermelons were easy to grow, prolific, and cheap, they offered an alternative for cooks who could not afford the imported fruit. But the citron watermelon also offered other practical applications, namely as a winter melon for pies and puddings. Both the red- and green-seeded sorts can be stored for long periods of time in dry pantries. The green-seeded variety is generally larger in size and softer-fleshed than the red-seeded sort. It is also more like an Armenian Cucumber in texture and flavor. Therefore, it can be used like a cucumber in salads or like a Chinese winter melon (*dong gwa*). Shredded, it resembles *saifun* noodles (transparent rice-starch noodles) when cooked. Diced in stir-fries, it resembles zucchini. As it ages in storage, the rind of the melon changes from marbled green to yellow, and the flesh mellows in texture. It can be sliced like apples for pies, shredded for puddings, or cooked in sugar for preserves. Most citron watermelons will last up to six months in storage, but by June they will sprout according to an internal clock, so it is pointless to keep them beyond March or April.

My great-grandmother made large quantities of citron preserves for the farmer's market in West Chester, Pennsylvania, and for sale in Philadelphia at the Reading Terminal Market. I published one of her recipes in *America Eats* (1989, 66–67), noting that cooks and kitchen gardeners appreciated the keeping qualities of the citron watermelon, since it could be held back until early winter when the major fall canning and preserving was over.

Both the green- and red-seeded varieties look alike in the garden and will cross if planted in proximity. The wood engraving on page 381 shows the appearance of the red seeded sort. The thick flesh beneath the rind is the best part for all culinary uses. The placenta (seed mass) is usually too soft for preserving, but can be utilized in pies and puddings. For seed-saving purposes,

Citron Watermelon

the melon seeds are ripe when the melon is ready to harvest. Seeds can be gathered over the course of the winter as melons are taken from storage. Seeds from melons that spoil early should be destroyed. The best seed is the seed from melons that keep the longest.

Under the heading "How to Use the Apple Pie Melon," a contributor to the *American Agriculturist* (1859, 310) who signed her name "California" provided instructions for making pies with the dark green–seeded variety of citron watermelon. Her directions show how this old melon was used but requires some explanation for the modern reader. Her tartaric acid is the same as cream of tartar, and the consistency of the cooked melon is like applesauce. This is sweetened and mixed with spices, then combined with beaten eggs (yolks and whites separated) and sour cream or milk. The batter is then poured into a prepared pie shell and baked. Her cautionary remark about copper pans relates to the use of acids in metal utensils and the poisonous substances that result from the ensuing chemical reaction. Her advice is as valid today as in 1859.

Apple Pie Melon
🐛

When ripe, which can be known by the melon turning yellow, or the seed black, remove the seed, pare and slice the flesh in small pieces, and then stew it in water just enough to have it stewed like apples; when done, add sugar, spices, and a little acid. Tartaric acid, or lemon juice, or good vinegar may be used; the latter, however, does not make as good a pie. A tablespoonful of lemon juice to four pounds of melon, I think the best proportion. The quantity of sugar must be in proportion to the acid. Without the acid the pie is tasteless. Don't put the sauce in a copper vessel.

Cuban Queen Watermelon
Citrullus lanatus

W. Atlee Burpee introduced this variety in 1881, claiming that it came from the West Indies. In fact, it appears to be related to Black Spanish, except that it is much larger (often weighing over 100 pounds) and differently marked on the skin. The melon is oblong and tapering at the stem end. The skin is striped with dark and light green. The rind is thin, but thick enough for shipping purposes. The flesh is bright red. This is a good medium-sized sort for gardens with room for rambling vines.

Cuban Queen Watermelon

Ice Cream Watermelon
Citrullus lanatus

There are a number of heirloom watermelons in circulation under the name Ice Cream, but the true Ice Cream of the nineteenth century had white seeds and white flesh. The melon was round, with pale green skin, very early to fruit, and well adapted to cool-climate areas of the country. White-seeded Ice Cream is now difficult to obtain, largely replaced by the black-seeded variety with pink flesh.

According to the *American Agriculturist* (1871, 111), Henry Dreer of Philadelphia began listing a pink-fleshed Ice Cream that year, and this has long been considered its date of introduction. Actually, the pink sort is mentioned as early as 1868 and may have existed quite a few years before that. The 1910 seed catalog of the Charles C. Navlet Company of San Jose, California, noted that the pink Ice Cream was also sold as Peerless, although I personally would categorize Peerless as a substrain, since it had a redder color than the original 1871 introduction.

Black-seeded Ice Cream was made popular as a picnic melon at the 1876 U.S. Centennial due to its sweetness and medium size, but its thin rind rendered it unsuitable for shipping. The melon is oblong in shape, with grass-green skin. There is very faint mottling on the skin that varies greatly from one melon to the next.

King and Queen Watermelon
Citrullus lanatus

This is a useful old watermelon developed for winter storage. The fruit is round, weighing about 10 pounds, with white-green skin. Dark green markings run in narrow bands from end to end. The flesh is bright red, the seeds black. If stored in a cool, dry pantry, the melon will keep through the winter and thus provide fresh fruit when watermelons are at their worst in the supermarket. The flavor of this melon is not as good as that of many summer varieties, yet if it had a high sugar

King and Queen Watermelon

content, it would not keep well. Fortunately, if the melon is harvested late in the season, yet relatively ripe, it will sweeten during storage.

I know of gardeners who have kept this melon in a refrigerator until the following April, but refrigeration not only suppresses the flavor but will hinder the fruit from ripening further. Therefore, I recommend keeping it in an unheated pantry, the drier the better.

Kleckley Sweets Watermelon
Citrullus lanatus

Also known as Monte Christo, this extremely popular watermelon was introduced in 1897 by W. Atlee Burpee of Philadelphia. Its popularity was based on its high sugar content and its lack of stringiness when fully ripe. The melon originated in Texas and took its name from the gardener from whom Burpee acquired it. The melon is oblong in shape, with dark green skin. The rind is thin, so this has never been considered a melon suitable for shipping. The fruit measures 18 to 20 inches in length and about 10 to 12 inches in diameter. This small size makes it perfect for kitchen gardens. The flesh is crisp, sugary, and bright scarlet, the seeds white. Today, there are several strains of Kleckley Sweets, many with substantial differences. None, however, compete with the good flavor of the original.

Moon and Stars Watermelon
Citrullus lanatus

No watermelon in the seed-saving movement has achieved the status of an icon more universally than this famous variety. Oddly enough, Moon and Stars was almost totally forgotten 20 years ago, only to come back and become one of the most widely grown heirloom watermelons today. Its foremost feature is the yellow patching on the dark green skin. The patches form little dots like stars in the Milky Way, interspersed here and there with large round "moons." The yellow speckling is also carried through on the leaves of the vines, a genetic pigmentation problem that is now considered a highly decorative trait. It has no effect whatsoever on the flavor or texture of the flesh. There are two basic types, one with bright pink flesh and one with yellow flesh. Recently, an orange-fleshed sort has surfaced, but as with the others, the color neither improves nor detracts from the flavor.

The story of the rediscovery of this long-lost variety appeared in the 1981 *Fall Harvest Edition* (24–25) of Seed Savers Exchange. After a television interview, Seed Savers Exchange founder Kent Whealy received a call from a gardener by the name of Merle Van Doren who had been preserving the melon in his garden. In 1982 Seed Savers Exchange began making the melon available, and it now ranks as the most heavily listed of all the watermelons in the yearbooks. The name of the originator of the Moon and Stars watermelon is not presently known, although Peter Henderson & Company of New York bought the commercial rights in the 1920s. The firm released the melon in 1926, noting that its developer called it Sun, Moon, and Stars. To quote the company's 1926 catalog: "We do not, however, offer seeds of this new melon to our friends because of its appearance, but for the reason that its 'meat' has such a delicious taste, and because this variety can be successfully grown in most parts of the United States." There is a great deal of oral history surrounding this melon, but the fact is, Moon and Stars is not very old as heirlooms go. It appears to be a variant form of Black Diamond, with better disease resistance, and of course the famous speckles and spots. Aside from flesh color, there are now two distinct shapes, one squat, the other oblong. Both types are slightly lobed, the oldest strain more like a nutmeg in shape. The seed is black. Since the melon is small like Kleckley Sweets, it is ideal for gardens with limited space.

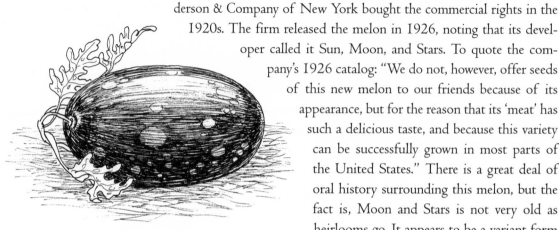

Moon and Stars Watermelon

Mountain Sweet Watermelon
Citrullus lanatus

Fearing Burr (1865, 186) noted that this melon was extremely popular in the Middle States, certainly since the 1840s. The *American Agriculturist* (1868, 103) regarded it as a melon raised almost exclusively in New Jersey for the Philadelphia and New York markets and often sold (incorrectly) as Ice Cream. It was a popular market melon because it shipped well and for some reason, its ripeness was more easily ascertained by rapping than with many other sorts. The melon is large, somewhat pear shaped, with dark green skin marbled in different shades of lighter green. The rind is about ½ inch thick, the flesh bright red or scarlet. The seeds are reddish brown. There is also a yellow-fleshed strain.

Rattlesnake Watermelon
Citrullus lanatus

Rattlesnake is one of the most famous of all watermelons grown in the South. It was developed in Georgia, presumably in the 1830s, and is often called Genuine Georgia Rattlesnake. A subvariety

Rattlesnake Watermelon

or selection known as Augusta Rattlesnake was considered the best strain in terms of flavor. Elsewhere in the country, the melon was often called Southern Rattlesnake or Gypsy Oblong.

True Rattlesnake is indeed oblong, almost cigar shaped, with light green skin. Wavy stripes of dark green running lengthwise create a striking pattern resembling the skin of a timber rattler, hence the colorful name. The flesh is scarlet pink, the seeds dark brown. Typical specimens weigh 30 to 40 pounds. Due to the shape of the melon, it could be easily stacked and for this reason was considered an ideal shipping melon, especially for northern markets. Melons that were damaged or could not be shipped because they were too ripe were often converted to watermelon vinegar. The following recipe for watermelon vinegar is taken from the *American Agriculturist* (1873, 266):

Georgia Rattlesnake Vinegar

🐛

We had a very great quantity of melons last season, and after we had cut out their crimson cores for eating, scraped the shells, from which we gained a large amount of juice. This we carefully strained, and put into jugs with small glass bottles in their mouths. We set the jugs out into the sun, and in time had a fine-flavored, clear, strong, white vinegar. The vinegar at a certain stage will be very bitter, but when perfected loses this and acquires a true vinegar taste.

Yams (Chinese)

It is pointless to grow both sweet potatoes and yams, especially in the North or where space is limited. True yams are tropical plants in any case and cannot be cultivated outside of the Deep South without the aid of a greenhouse during the winter. Thus, the only yam that I grow is the Chinese yam (*Dioscorea batatas*), which is easy to cultivate and will thrive in most parts of the continental United States, at least into USDA Zone 4. It requires a winter dormancy, so it cannot be raised successfully in frost-free areas. It is also highly ornamental, for it is known among flower fanciers as the Cinnamon Vine.

Specimens of the Chinese yam were sent to France from Shanghai by the French consul in 1848. They were received at Paris under the name *igname de la chine* with considerable fanfare, for the plant was seen as a possible solution to the failed potato crop at the time. Since the vine produces club-shaped, deep-rooted tubers, as long as 3 feet, they were considered difficult to harvest as a field crop. In fact, the tubers are brittle and must be dug by hand to ensure they are not broken or damaged. Furthermore, the tuber sends up a rampant vine that can grow as much as 20 feet in one season. Thus, the yam must be cultivated on trellising like grapevines or pole beans. This worked against its adaptation as a commercial crop, but as a small garden vegetable it is ideal.

The first gardeners in this country to cultivate the Chinese yam were the Chinese themselves who had settled on the West Coast, primarily in California during the gold rush. It may have

been this community that brought the vegetable to the full attention of American horticulturists. The 1854 *Florist and Horticultural Journal* (3:201–4) was careful to point out the great variety of Chinese names that were applied to the yam depending on its method of culinary preparation.

One of these, *chau-tchou* (as it was then written), referred to a vegetable pickle in which the shredded yam figured as a component. This word was corrupted in American English to chow-chow, a term that has lost all connection with the yam and is now used generically for any type of mixed vegetable pickle. Thus, the Chinese yam has touched American cookery in a curious, roundabout way.

While the Chinese yam failed to interest commercial growers as a substitute for the beleaguered potato, it did become a popular Victorian garden ornamental, for the bulbils were inexpensive gimmicks as premiums given away by seed houses. The promotions worked because the vine is fast growing and makes an excellent summer covering for gazebos and verandahs. Furthermore, the white cinnamon-scented flowers are powerfully fragrant, which only added to its appeal. In small gardens, the Chinese yam can double as a screen against a wall or tall fence. Because the tuber is perennial and increases in size from year to year without deterioration in quality, it can be harvested as demand requires. Harvesting is

Chinese Yam

normally undertaken in November before the ground freezes because the tubers grow most late in the season and store well for many months over the winter.

The vine itself produces hundreds of edible bulbils at the leaf axils, and these should be harvested before frost. The bulbils resemble miniaturized potatoes, and those that are not eaten can be planted to replace harvested tubers, thus ensuring a continuous supply from year to year.

While this is a true yam, it is unlike any yam American cooks are likely to find in a typical supermarket. The flavor reminds me of a blend of potato and butternuts, although physically the mature tuber resembles a long, swollen, and somewhat hairy manioc root, and is so illustrated in Vilmorin (1885, 596–97). The potato-like skin is green underneath and should be pared off when preparing the yam for cookery; otherwise, it lends itself to any recipe calling for mealy potatoes, since the white, milky flesh becomes soft and flaky once cooked. The root can also be shredded like a daikon radish and marinated in vinegar. In pickles, it should be raw packed to maintain crispness.

The bulbils make an interesting addition to rice and bean dishes, or they can be used in stuffing, like chestnuts. The rich, nutty flavor is pleasant, and I am surprised that the Chinese yam is not more readily available in our markets.

ACKNOWLEDGMENTS

This was not an easy book to write. Other books of this magnitude are usually managed by "committee." Yet, while I served in many respects as a committee of one, there was indeed a large faculty of talent that went into the making of this book, not the least being my grandfather Weaver, whose seeds planted the beginnings of my excursion into heirloom gardening many years ago. More recently and more directly, I must thank Adam Levine, my trusty garden manager, and intern Julie Houlehan for tending the massive growout of vegetables in 1995 that made the photography and illustrations possible. Dr. L. Wilbur Zimmerman's cameraman's eye for the best daylight and Signe Sundberg-Hall's extraordinary patience for drawing from life during a heat wave made me deeply grateful to have at my side four very talented coworkers who also believed in what I was trying to accomplish. Their contributions are every bit as important as mine.

Of course, there are many members of Seed Savers Exchange who were especially helpful: Louis Van Deven's seemingly endless supply of rare onion varieties; Anne Bertinuson for seeds sent me from the back reaches of Botswana in Africa; Ulrike Paradine of Kent, England, who cultivated an enthusiastic interest in some of my seed search problems; and Roland Paul of the Institute for Palatine History and Culture (Kaiserslautern, Germany) for his personal help in locating many old rare vegetable varieties. Roland has been an amazing conduit for seeds from Palatine gardens of particular relevance to my Pennsylvania Dutch background.

Dale Musselman, the general contractor who oversaw the renovation of my house, must be commended for his ability over the past few years to turn my mental pictures into actual garden fencing and cold frames resembling the sort used at Roughwood in the 1840s. His ungrumbling tolerance of my recurrent desire to build more and more raised beds is especially appreciated. Dump trucks came and went. Gradually, great mounds of soil melted into an orderly *jardin potager* that today is one of the most productive gardens in my neighborhood.

Dale also contrived the means for moving my greenhouse on rollers, ancient Egyptian style, much to the open-mouthed amazement of everyone who watched. My greenhouse is special, my little Ark where all the things that I grow change from seed to living plants. It is both my playhouse and a warm spiritual refuge in the winter, where I enjoy lemons, limes, blood oranges, guavas, and other tropical fruits, as well as a source of lettuces and other fresh saladings.

Jacob Glick made it possible. Owner of a nursery in Lancaster County and member of a committee of Mennonites whose goal is to aid the native peoples of Guatemala, Jacob possessed a disassembled greenhouse waiting for shipment to Central America. Through the intercession of a Lancaster County friend, my cramped growing plight was heard and within weeks the greenhouse was erected in my garden. I owe the Mennonite Mission heartfelt thanks for its generosity and hope that the replacement I arranged for is now standing in the rain forest of Guatemala, helping the impoverished farmers there establish a livelihood in market gardening.

Aside from the crew that helps me keep my garden under control, several individuals have helped me with the actual assembling of the book: David S. Azzolina of the University of Pennsylvania Library for ironing out several bibliographical puzzles; the staffs of the Academy of Natural Sciences and the Pennsylvania Horticultural Society for helping me in my historical research; and Karen Mullian, who came to the rescue at the last moment to guide me through a computer disaster that caused the destruction of part of my manuscript. We lost book; we lost sleep; we missed deadlines; Karen kept going. Through it all her sense of humor was the best medicine I could have had.

But above all else, there is a remarkable woman who I have come to know and admire, my editor Beth Crossman. She understood the difficulties I was going through and had the innate sensitivity to know when to leave me alone and when to nudge me gently. If it can be said that editors "midwife" books into existence, then Beth did indeed midwife this one. I especially appreciate her keen eye for gardening issues that needed sharpening. She is the best and fairest of referees, and I consider her my friend.

Last, I want to thank Blanche Schlessinger. Blanche is my literary agent, and she has believed in me and in all of my books from the very start. Most of all, she has spent many a summer afternoon in my garden, and I think what I have written in these pages will bring to life some of those pleasant memories. When German art collectors Klaus and Ingrid Stopp presented me with a copy of the *Album Vilmorin,* with its exquisite lithographic pictures of heirloom vegetables, I knew for certain that Blanche's vision would become this book.

COMMERCIAL SEED AND PLANT STOCK SOURCES

Arche Noah
Obere Straße 40
A-3553 Schloss Schiltern
Austria
Membership provides access to rare traditional vegetable varieties from Central Europe.

The Bountiful Gardens
18001 Shafer Ranch Road
Willits, CA 95490

The Cook's Garden
P.O. Box 535
Londonderry, VT 05148-0535

Deep Diversity
A Planetary Gene-Pool Resource
P.O. Box 15189
Santa Fe, NM 87506-5189

Filaree Farm
Route 2
Box 162
Okanogan, WA 98840

Fox Hole Herb and Heirloom Seed Company
P.O. Box 148
McGrann, PA 16236

Garden City Seeds
1324 Red Crow Road
Victor, MT 59875-9713

Good Seed Company
Star Route 73A
Oroville, WA 98844

Greenseeds
Underwood Gardens
4N381 Maple Avenue
Bensenville, IL 60106

Heirloom Seed Project
Landis Valley Museum
2451 Kissel Hill Road
Lancaster, PA 17601

Heirloom Seeds
P.O. Box 245
West Elizabeth, PA 15088-02451

Heritage Seed Company
Route 4, Box 187
Star City, AR 71667
Specializing in alliums

J. L. Hudson, Seedsman
Star Route 2, Box 337
La Honda, CA 94020

Le Jardin du Gourmet
P.O. Box 75
St. Johnsbury Center, VT 05863

Johnny's Selected Seeds
Foss Hill Road
Albion, ME 04910

Meadow Valley Herb Farm
20 Olde Meadow Valley Road
Lititz, PA 17543

Mellinger's Inc.
2310 West South Range Road
North Lima, OH 44452-9731

Native Seeds/SEARCH
2509 West Campbell Avenue, #325
Tuscon, AZ 85719

The Natural Gardening Company
217 San Anselmo Avenue
San Anselmo, CA 94960

Nichols Garden Nursery
1190 North Pacific Highway NE
Albany, OR 97321-4580

Oregan Exotics Rare Fruit Nursery
1065 Messinger Road
Grants Pass, OR 97527

Peace Seeds
A Planetary Gene-Pool Resource and Service
P.O. Box 190
Gila, NM 88038

P. L. Rohrer and Bro., Inc.
P.O. Box 250
Smoketown, PA 17576

Old Sturbridge Village
Gift Shop
1 Old Sturbridge Village Road
Sturbridge, MA 01566

The Redwood City Seed Company
P.O. Box 361
Redwood City, CA 94064

Ronniger's Seed Potatoes
Star Route
Moyie Springs, ID 83845

Ron's Rare Plants & Seeds
R. M. Werner, Horticulturist
415 Chappel
Calumet City, IL 60409-2122

Seed Savers Exchange
3076 North Winn Road
Decorah, IA 52101
$25 annual membership fee provides access to an international network of seed savers and selected offerings from the seed library of Heritage Farm, maintained by Seed Savers Exchange. For a free color brochure, call 319-382-5990.

Seeds Blüm
Idaho City Stage
Boise, ID 83706

Seeds of Change
P.O. Box 15700
Santa Fe, NM 87506-5700

Seeds Trust/High Altitude Gardens
P.O. Box 1048
Hailey, ID 83333

Seeds West
P.O. Box 27057
Albuquerque, NM 87125-7057

Select Seeds Antique Flowers
180 Stickney Road
Union, CT 06076-4617

Shepherd's Garden Seeds
6116 Highway 9
Felton, CA 95018

Southern Exposure Seed Exchange
P.O. Box 170
Earlysville, VA 22936

Southmeadow Fruit Gardens
10603 Cleveland Avenue
Baroda, MI 49101
Heirloom fruits and berries. Most extensive in the country.

**Thomas Jefferson Center
for Historic Plants**
Monticello
P.O. Box 316
Charlottesville, VA 22902

Tomato Grower's Supply Company
P.O. Box 2237
Ft. Meyers, FL 33902

❧ USEFUL PUBLICATIONS ❧

The Avant Gardener
Box 489
New York, NY 10028

Diversity Magazine
4905 Del Ray Avenue
Suite 401
Bethesda, MD 20814

Ecology Action Newsletter
Ecology Action/Common Ground
5798 Ridgewood Road
Willits, CA 95490-9730

The Herb Quarterly
P.O. Box 689
San Anselmo, CA 94960-9801

The Historical Gardener
1910 North 35th Place
Mt. Vernon, WA 98273-8981

HDRA News
Henry Doubleday Research Association
Ryton Organic Gardens
Ryton-on-Dunsmore
Coventry CV8 3LG
England

Network to Reduce Overconsumption, A Directory of Organizations and Leaders, 1994–1995
The New Road Map Foundation
P.O. Box 15981
Seattle, WA 98115

Off the Vine
Carolyn J. Male, ed.
21-2 Latham Village Lane
Latham, NY 12110

WORKS CITED

✑ NOTE TO THE READER ❧

Several works in this bibliography were issued over a period of years, thus making citations confusing. These sources are listed in Works Cited under the initial year of publication, such as the *Album Vilmorin* (1850) and the encyclopedia by Abbé Rozier (1781).

1591   l'Obel, Matthias de. *Plantarum seu Stirpium Icones.* Antwerp: Ex Offinus C. Plantin.

1611   du Bartas, Saluste. *Les Oeuvres de G. de Saluste, S du Bartas.* Paris: Chez Jean de Bourdeau, IX.

1611   de L'Ecluse, Charles. *Curae Posteriores.* Antwerp: Ex Officinus C. Plantin.

1613   Besler, Basilius. *Celeberrimi Eystettensis Horti Icones Plantarum Autumnalium.* Eichstätt: Norimb.

1629   Parkinson, John. *Paradisi in Sole, Paradisus Terrestris.* London: H. Lownes and R. Young.

1639   Rhagor, Daniel. *Pflantz-Gart: Darinn grundtlicher Bericht zufinden/welcher gestalten: 1. Obs-Gärten/ 2. Kraut-Gärten/ 3. Wein-Gärten.* Bern: Bey Stephan Schmid.

1669   de Bonnefons, Nicolas. *The French Gardener.* London: John Crocke.

1675   Plat, Sir Hugh. *The Garden of Eden.* London: W. & J. Leache.

1676   Evelyn, John. *Kalendarium Hortense.* London: John Martyn.

1682   Meager, Leonard. *The English Gardener.* London: T. Pierrepart.

1693   Penn, William. *Some Fruits of Solitude.* London: Thomas Northcott.

1699   Evelyn, John. *Acetaria: A Discourse of Sallets.* London: B. Tooke.

1713–25   Feuillée, Aédée François. *Journal des observations physiques, mathematiques et botaniques.* 3 vols. Paris: Chez Jean Mariette. Vol. III (1725), "Histoire des plantes medecinales," has its own pagination (section of vol. III).

1717–26   Bradley, Richard. *New Improvements of Planting and Gardening.* Parts 1 and 2 (1717), part 3 (1718), Appendix (1726). London: W. Mears.

1726   Nott, John. *The Cooks and Confectioners Dictionary.* London: Charles Rivington.

1726   Townshend, Benjamin. *The Complete Seedsman: Shewing, the Best and Earliest Method for Raising and Cultivating Every Sort of Seed Belonging to a Kitchen and Flower-Garden.* London: W. Mears.

1727   Bradley, Richard. *The Country Housewife and Lady's Director.* London: Woodman and Lyon.

1731   Switzer, Stephen. *A Compendious Method for the Raising of the Italian Brocoli, Spanish Cardoon, Celeriac, Finochi, and Other Foreign Kitchen-Vegetables.* London: Thomas Astley.

1744   *Adams' Luxury, and Eve's Cookery.* London: R. Dodsley.

1759   Verrall, William. *A Complete System of Cookery.* London: privately printed.

1768   Miller, Philip. *Gardener's and Botanist's Dictionary.* London:

1774   Vilin, Abbé. *Traité de la culture du melon.* Amiens: Chez la Veuve Godart.

1775   Csapó, Jósef. *Uj füves és virágos magyar kert.* Posonyban: Landerer Mihaly.

1779   Mawe, Thomas, and John Abercrombie. *Every Man His Own Gardener.* London: S. Crowder.

1781–1800   Rozier, Abbé. *Cours complet d'agriculture.* Paris: Rue et Hôtel Serpente. Ten volumes, plus supplements 11 and 12 (1805) by Thouin.

1787   Liger, L. *Le Jardinier fleuriste, ou la culture universelle.* Rouen: Chez la veuve de Pierre Dumesnil.

1788   Menon. *La Cuisinière bourgeoise.* Paris: P. M. Nyon Le Jeune.

1792   Carter, Susannah. *The Frugal Housewife.* New York: Rogers and Berry.

1796   Simmons, Amelia. *American Cookery.* Hartford, Conn.: Hudson & Goodwin.

[1802]   M'Mahon, Bernard. *A Catalogue of Garden, Grass, Herb, Flower, Tree & Shrub-Seeds, Flower-Roots, &. &.* Philadelphia: Bernard M'Mahon, Seedsman. Undated broadsheet.

1802   Willich, A.F.M. *The Domestic Encyclopaedia.* London: Murray and Highley.

1803   Ditrich, J. H. *Baiersches Natur- und Kunst-Gartenbuch für Gärtner.* Stadtamhof.

1806   M'Mahon, Bernard. *The American Gardener's Calendar.* Philadelphia: B. Graves.

1807   Edwards, Sydenham Teak. *A Complete Dictionary of Practical Gardening*. London: G. Keasley.

1812–48   *Transactions of the Royal Horticultural Society*. London: Royal Horticultural Society. Vols. I–7 (1812–30); 2nd series, vols. I–3 (1831–48).

1812   Maher, John. "On the Cultivation of the Crambe Maritima of Linné, or Sea Kale." *Transactions of the Royal Horticultural Society* 1:13–20.

1815   M'Mahon, Bernard. *A Catalogue of Garden, Herb, Flower, Tree, Shrub, and Grass Seeds*. Philadelphia: William Duane.

ca. 1815   Tweed, John. *Popular Observations on Regimen and Diet*. Chelmsford, England: Meggy and Chalk. This book was published without date or copyright. It is presumed to date from 1815, but this is only an educated guess.

1821   Cooper, Thomas. *A Catalogue of Useful Plants*. vol. 3 of *The Domestic Encyclopedia*. Philadelphia: Abraham Small.

1824   Randolph, Mary. *The Virginia House-Wife*. Washington, D.C.: Davis and Force.

1825   Targioni-Tozzetti, Ottavio. *Dizionario botanico Italiano*. Firenze: Presso Guglielmo Piatti.

1827   Beauvilliers, A. B. *The Art of French Cookery*. London: Longman, Rees.

1827   Tibbits, George. *A Memoir on the Expediency and Practicability of Improving or Creating Home Markets for the Sale of Agricultural Productions*. Philadelphia: J.R.A. Skerrett.

1828   Fessenden, Thomas. *The New American Gardener*. Boston: John B. Russell. Contains catalog of John B. Russell's New England Farmer Seed Store in Boston.

1828   Green, Roland. *A Treatise on the Cultivation of Ornamental Flowers*. Boston: John B. Russell.

1829   Bridgeman, Thomas. *The Young Gardener's Assistant*. Brooklyn, N.Y.: Nichols and Matthews.

1831   Hurst, W. "Why Peas Boil Hard." *Gardener's Magazine*, April 1831.

1831   Lindley, George. *A Guide to Orchard and Kitchen Garden*. London: Longman, Rees, Orme, Brown, and Green.

1832   Jacquin, M. *Monographie complète du melon*. Paris: Rousselon, Libraire-Éditeur.

1832   Lloyd, David. *Economy of Agriculture*. Germantown, Penn.: P. R. Freas & Company.

1833   Brotherton, Mary. *Vegetable Cookery*. London: Effingham Wilson.

1833   Gordon, George. "A Report on the Varieties of Peas Cultivated in the Garden of the Horticultural Society." *Gardener's Magazine*, August 1833, pp. 423–28.

1833   Mitchell, James. "On *Oxalis crenàta* Jacquin as a Culinary Vegetable." *Gardener's Magazine*, February 1833, pp. 78–79.

1834   Holm, Thomas Campanius. *Description of the Province of New Sweden.* Philadelphia: M'Carty & Davis.

1835   Fingerhuth, C. A. "Beiträge zur ökonomischen Flora des Nieder- und Mittel-rheins." *Linnaea: Ein journal für die Botanik . . . oder: Beiträge zur pflanzenkunde.* Bd 1–34: Berlin/Halle.

1835–36   Pöppig, Edward Friedrich. *Reise in Chile, Peru und auf dem Amazon.* 2 vols. Leipzig: F. Fleischer.

1836   Barnum, H. L. *The Farmer's Own Book; or, Family Receipts for the Husbandman and House-wife.* Boston: Charles J. Hendee.

1836   Bridgeman, Thomas. *The Florist's Guide.* New York: Mitchell & Turner.

1836   Bridgeman, Thomas. *The Kitchen Gardener's Instructor.* New York: Mitchell & Turner.

1836   Randolph, Mary. *The Virginia Housewife.* Baltimore: John Plaskitt.

1837–44   Bailly de Merlieux, Charles Francis. *Maison rustique du XIXe siecle.* 5 vols. Paris: Bureau du Journal d'Agriculture Pratique.

1837   Browne, Porter A. *An Essay on Indian Corn.* Philadelphia: J. Thompson.

1837   Darlington, Dr. William. *Flora Cestrica.* West Chester, Penn.: S. Siegfried.

1838   Brown, A. "Indian Corn." *Farmer's Cabinet* 2, no. 14 (March 15): 225.

1839   Bryan, Lettice. *The Kentucky Housewife.* Cincinnati: Shepard and Stearns.

1839   Adolf Bauer, ed. *Ceres, eine Zeitschrift für den Landwirth.* Lebanon, Penn.: Samuel Miller.

1839   Thomas, David. *Choice Plants for Sale.* Rochester, N.Y.: Office of the Genessee Farmer. Broadsheet distributed with the December 1839 issue of the *Genessee Farmer.*

1839   Fessenden, Thomas. *The Complete Farmer and Rural Economist.* Boston: Otis, Broaders & Company.

1840   Bateham, M. B. *Seed Catalogue of M. B. Bateham.* Rochester, N.Y.: Henry O'Reilly and John J. Reilly.

1840   Forsyth, Alexander. "On the Jerusalem Artichoke." *Gardener's Magazine* 16 (May 1840): 259.

1840   Lee, Gregory. "On the Cultivation of the Cauliflower." *New Genessee Farmer* 1 (January 1840): 9.

1840   Masters, W. "Some Remarks on the Culture of the White Carrot." *Gardener's Magazine* 16 (April 1840): 209–10.

1840   Russell, J. W. "Method of Preserving Celery Through the Winter for Family Use." *Magazine of Horticulture* 6 (1840): 94–95.

1841   Hovey, Charles. "Notices of Culinary Vegetables, New, or Recently Introduced." *Magazine of Horticulture* 7 (1841): 134–39.

1841   Russell, J. W. "On the Cultivation of the Tomato and Egg Plant." *Magazine of Horticulture* 7 (March 1841): 97–98.

1841   Seymour, James, "On the Culture of the Early Horn Carrot." *Gardener's Magazine* 17 (January 1841): 27–28.

1843   The United Society (Shaker). *The Gardener's Manual; Containing Plain Instructions for the Selection, Preparation, and Management of a Kitchen Garden.* New York: J. W. Kelly.

1844   Johnson, Cuthbert W. *The Farmer's Encyclopaedia.* Philadelphia: Carey and Hart.

1844   Landreth, David. *Descriptive Catalogue of the Garden Seeds Cultivated by David Landreth.* Philadelphia: David Landreth.

1845   *A Handbook of Foreign Cookery; Principally French, German and Danish.* London: John Murray.

1845   Walker, Samuel. *Catalogue of Vegetable Seeds.* Boston: Samuel Walker.

1846   Abel, Mrs. L. G. *The Skilful Housewife's Book.* New York: D. Newell.

1847   Buist, Robert. *The Family Kitchen Gardener.* New York: J. C. Riker.

1847   "Okra and the Science of Soups," *Horticulturist* 2: 118–21.

1848   Francatelli, Charles Elmé. *French Cookery.* Philadelphia: Lea and Blanchard.

1848   Solly, Edward. "Experiments on the Inorganic Constituents of Plants," *Transactions of the Horticultural Society of London* 3: 35–92.

1850   Soyer, Alexis. *The Modern Housewife; or Ménagère.* New York: D. Appleton & Company.

1850–84   Vilmorin-Andrieux et Cie. *Album Vilmorin / Le Jardin Potager.* Paris: Imp. Lemercier et Cie. The firm issued one plate a year for thirty-four years. Cited throughout as *Album Vilmorin* with date of plate.

1851   Leslie, Eliza. *Directions for Cookery.* Philadelphia: Henry Carey Baird.

1852   Leslie, Eliza. *New Directions for Cookery.* Philadelphia: T. B. Peterson.

1853   Hale, Sarah Josepha. *Flora's Interpreter.* Boston: Benjamin B. Mussey.

1853–55   McIntosh, Charles. *The Book of the Garden.* Vol. 1 (1853), vol. 2 (1855). Edinburgh/London: W. Blackwood & Sons.

1854   Marshall, Josiah T. *The Farmer's and the Emigrant's Complete Guide.* Cincinnati: Applegate & Company.

1855   [Peterson, Hannah Bouvier]. *The National Cook Book.* Philadelphia: Childs & Peterson.

1856   Wells, David A. *The Year-Book of Agriculture* [for 1855 and 1856]. Philadelphia: Childs & Peterson.

1856   *Report of the Commissioner of Patents for the Year 1855: Agriculture.* Washington, D.C.: Cornelius Wendell.

1856   Vilmorin-Andrieux et Cie. *Description des plantes potagères.* Paris: Vilmorin-Andrieux et Cie.

1858   "Husk Tomato," *American Agriculturist* 17: 340.

1858   Breck, Joseph. *The Flower-Garden.* New York: A. O. Moore.

1859   May, Anna. *Die kleine New Yorker Köchin.* New York: Verlag von E. Steiger.

1859   Naudin, Charles Victor. "Espèces et des variétés du genre cucumis," 11–14; "Revue des cucurbuacées cultivés au museum, en 1859," 79–164. *Annales des sciences naturelles,* vol 11, *Botanique.* Paris: Librairie Victor Masson.

1859   Watson, Alexander. *The American Home Garden.* New York: Harper & Brothers.

1860   Michener, Ezra. *Retrospect of Early Quakerism.* Philadelphia: T. Ellwood Zell.

1860   Storke, E. G. *The Family, Farm and Gardens.* Auburn, N.Y.: Auburn Publishing Company.

1865   Burr, Fearing. *Field and Garden Vegetables of America.* Boston: Crosby & Nichols. Corrected second edition; original edition 1863.

1864   Efendi, Turabi. *Turkish Cookery Book.* London: privately printed.

1865   Henderson, Peter. *Gardening for Profit.* New York: Orange Judd & Company. The edition cited throughout is the revised edition of 1904.

1866   DeVoe, Thomas F. *The Market Assistant.* New York: Orange Judd & Company.

1867   "Vegetables." *Maryland Farmer* 4 (July 1867): 197.

1868   Gouffé, Jules. *Le Livre de cuisine.* Paris: Hachette.

1868   Gregory, James J. H. *Annual List of New, Rare and Choice Vegetables.* Marblehead, Mass.: James J. H. Gregory.

1868   Gregory, James J. H. *Squashes: How to Grow Them.* New York: Orange Judd & Company.

1868   White, William N. *Gardening for the South; or, How to Grow Vegetables and Fruits.* New York: Orange Judd & Co.

1869   Peterson, Mrs. M.E.P. *Peterson's Preserving, Pickling and Canning.* Philadelphia: G. Peterson & Co.

1869   von Martens, Georg. *Die Gartenbohnen: Ihre Verbeitung, Cultur und Benützung.* 2d ed. Ravensburg: Druck und Verlag von Eugen Ulmer.

1870   Gregory, James J. H. *Annual Catalogue of Choice Garden and Flower Seeds.* Marblehead, Mass.: James J. H. Gregory.

1870   Henderson, Peter. "Asparagus Culture—The 'Colossal,'" *American Agriculturist,* January 1870, 22–23.

1870   Kreider, John G. "Description of Different Varieties of Seed Potatoes." *Lancaster Farmer* 2 (March 1870): 41–42.

1870   *Report of the Commissioner of Agriculture for the Year 1869.* Washington: Government Printing Office.

1870   Tyson, Miss. *The Queen of the Kitchen: A Collection of Old Maryland Receipts for Cooking.* Baltimore: Lucas Brothers.

1870   Wardell & Company. *Garden Seed.* West Dresden, N.Y.: Wardell & Company.

1871   Porter, Mrs. M. E. *New Southern Cookery Book.* Philadelphia: John E. Potter & Company.

1872   Michener, Ezra. *A Manual of Weeds.* Philadelphia: King & Baird.

1872   Vick, James. *Vick's Illustrated Catalogue and Floral Guide.* Rochester, N.Y.: E. R. Andrews.

1873   Ellet, Elizabeth F. *The New Cyclopaedia of Domestic Economy.* Norwich, Conn.: Henry Bill Publishing Company.

1874   Croly, Jane Cunningham. *Jennie June's American Cookery Book.* New York: American News Company.

1874   Follett, Mrs. Eliza G. *The Young Housekeeper's Assistant.* Sandusky, Ohio: Register Steam Printing.

1875   Landreth, David, & Sons. *Landreth's Land-und Garten-Kalender.* Philadelphia: M'Calla & Stapley.

1876   Bliss, B. K., & Sons. *Bliss's Illustrated Seed Catalogue and Amateur's Guide to the Flower and Kitchen Garden.* New York: B. K. Bliss & Sons.

1877   *Kettner's Book of the Table.* London: Dulan and Company.

1878   Tillinghast, Isaac. *A Manual of Vegetable Plants: Containing the Experiences of the Author in Starting All Those Kinds of Vegetables Which Are the Most Difficult for a Novice to Produce from Seeds.* Factoryville, Penn.: Tillinghast Bros.

1879   Davidis, Henrietta. *Praktisches Kochbuch für die Deutschen in Amerika.* Milwaukee: Georg Brumder's Verlag.

1880   Myers, Ella E. *The Home Cook Book: An American Cook Book.* Philadelphia: Crawford & Company.

1881   Henderson, Peter. *Henderson Handbook of Plants.* New York: Peter Henderson & Co.

1883   Tillinghast, Isaac F. *Reliable Seeds.* LaPlume, Penn.: I. F. Tillinghast.

1884   Henderson, Peter. *Garden and Farm Topics.* New York: Peter Henderson & Co.

1884   Landreth, David & Sons. *Landreth's Rural Register and Almanac: 100 Years in Business.* Philadelphia: McCalla & Stavely. Also a seed catalog with numerous illustrations.

1885 Hampel, Wilhelm. *Handbuch der Frucht-und Gemüse-Treiberei.* Berlin: Verlag von Paul Parey.

1885 Ravenel, H. W. "Goober and Pindar." *Gardener's Monthly and Horticulturalist* 27 (September): 281–82.

1885 Tennent, Mrs. E. R. *House-Keeping in the Sunny South.* Atlanta, Ga.: Jas. P. Harrison & Company.

1885 Vilmorin-Andrieux, M. M. *The Vegetable Garden.* London: Ten Speed Press. Facsimile edition.

1886 Brisse, Baron. *366 Menus and 1200 Recipes.* Mrs. Matthew Clark, trans. London: Sampson Low, Marston, Searle, & Rivington.

1887 *The Home Cook Book.* Toronto: Rose Publishing Company.

1887 *The Onion Book.* New York: Orange Judd Company.

1887 *Report of the Commissioner of Agriculture for the Year 1886.* Washington, D.C.: Government Printing Office.

1888 Parnell, Charles E. "The Okra, or Gombo." *Vick's Illustrated Monthly Magazine* 11: 144.

1889 "Tried Varieties of Vegetables," *American Garden* 10: 57.

1890 Allen, C. L. "Seeds and Seed Growing." *American Garden* 11: 143.

1890 Bull, W. H. "Some Good Varieties of Lettuce." *American Garden* 11: 291–92.

1890 Greiner, Tuisco. *How to Make the Garden Pay.* Philadelphia: William Henry Maule.

1890 Hallock, N. "Experiences with Tomatoes: Results of a Large Experiment." *American Garden* 11: 292–94.

1890 Parker, Mrs. E. R. *Mrs. Parker's Complete Housekeeper.* New York: M. T. Richardson.

1890 de Vilmorin, Henry L. "Saladings." *Journal of the Royal Horticultural Society,* July, 260–73.

1891 Buist, Robert Jr. *Buist's Wholesale Price Current of Seeds.* Philadelphia: Century Lithograph Company.

1891 Rorer, Sarah Tyson. *How to Cook Vegetables.* Philadelphia: W. Atlee Burpee & Co.

1891 Schultz, Pauline. *Schultz's Deutsch-Amerikanisches Koch-Buch.* Milwaukee: C. H. Rhode Company.

1892 Buschbauer, Hans. *Amerikanisches Garten-Buch für Stadt und Land.* Milwaukee: Druck u. Verlag von Georg Brumder.

1892 Rawson, W. W. *Success in Market Gardening.* Boston: Author.

1893 Greiner, Tuisco. *Celery for Profit.* Philadelphia: W. Atlee Burpee.

1894 Gibson, Mrs. Charles H. *Maryland and Virginia Cook Book.* Baltimore: John Murphy & Company.

1894   Lupton, J. M. *Cabbage and Cauliflower for Profit.* Philadelphia: W. Atlee Burpee & Co.

1895   Rosser, Elizabeth Winston. *Housekeepers' and Mothers' Manual.* Richmond, Va.: Everett Waddey Company.

1895   Sala, George Augustus. *The Thorough Good Cook.* London: Cassell and Company.

1897   Bedford, Cornelia C. "Summer Vegetables." *Table Talk*, July, 245–48.

1897   George, Mrs. "New Ways to Serve Corn." *Table Talk*, August, 284.

1897   Sullivan, Caroline. *The Jamaica Cookery Book.* Kingston, Jamaica: Aston W. Gardner & Company.

1898   Bretschneider, Emilii Vasilevich. *History of European Botanical Discoveries in China.* London: S. Low, Marston & Co.

1898   Maule, William Henry. *Maule's Seed Catalogue.* Philadelphia: William Henry Maule.

1899   Ross, Janet. *Leaves from Our Tuscan Kitchen; or, How to Cook Vegetables.* London: J. M. Dent and Company.

1900   Brand, John. *Observations on Popular Antiquities.* London: Chatto & Windus.

1901   "The Cow Pea the Cheapest Source of Nitrogen." *Report of the Commissioners of Agriculture of Virginia.* Richmond, Va.: J. H. O'Bannon.

1901   Hall, H. Franklyn. *300 Ways to Cook and Serve Shell Fish, Terrapin, Green Turtle, Etc.* Philadelphia: Christian Banner Print.

1901   Irish, H. C. "Garden Bean Cultivated as Esculents." *Missouri Botanical Garden: Twelfth Annual Report*, 81–165. St. Louis: Missouri Botanical Gardens.

1901   "Syrup Made from Watermelons." *Report of the Commissioners of Agriculture of Virginia*, 135. Richmond: J. H. O'Bannon.

1901   Terry, T. B. *The ABC of Potato Culture.* Medina, Ohio: A. I. Root Company.

1902   Fritz, James. *Sweet Potato Culture.* New York: Orange Judd & Company.

1902   Mills, F. B. *F. B. Mills Catalogue.* Rose Hill, N.Y.: F. B. Mills.

1905   *Glick's Seed, Plant and Poultry Guide for 1905.* Freeport, Ill.: W. H. Wagner & Sons.

ca. 1905   Bridgeman, Thomas. *Kitchen-Gardening, Containing Complete Practical Directions.* Philadelphia: Henry T. Coates.

1905   Van Ornam, F. B. *Potatoes for Profit.* Philadelphia: W. Atlee Burpee & Company.

1906   Parloa, Maria. *Preparation of Vegetables for the Table.* Farmers' Bulletin 256. Washington, D.C.: Government Printing Office.

1907   Barnes, James, and William Robinson. *Asparagus Culture.* Philadelphia: David McKay.

1910   Navlet, Charles C. *1910 Catalogue and Planters Guide.* San Jose, Calif.: Charles C. Navlet Company.

1910 Parker, Arthur C. *Iroquois Uses of Maize and Other Food Plants.* Albany: Education Department Bulletin/University of the State of New York.

1910 Wickson, Edward J. *The California Vegetables in Garden and Field.* San Francisco: Pacific Rural Press.

1912 Burpee, W. Atlee. *Burpee's Annual for 1912.* Philadelphia: W. Atlee Burpee & Company.

1914 Oehler, Gottlieb, and David Z. Smith. "Description of a Journey & Visit to the Pawnee Indians Who Live on the Platte River." New York: privately printed. Offprint from the Moravian Church Miscellany of 1851–52.

1916 Waugh, F. W. *Iroquois Foods and Food Preparation.* Ottawa: Government Printing Bureau/Canada Department of Mines.

1917 Lyman, Benjamin Smith. *Vegetarian Diet and Dishes.* Philadelphia: Ferris & Leach.

1918 Tracy, Will W. *Tomato Culture.* New York: Orange Judd & Company.

1919 Hedrick, U. P. *Sturtevant's Notes on Edible Plants.* Albany, N.Y.: J. B. Lyon Company.

1920 Ladies' Club of Herradura. *The Tropical Cook Book.* Havana, Cuba: privately printed.

1921 Corbett, L. C. *Cucumbers.* Farmers' Bulletin 254. Washington, D.C.: United States Department of Agriculture/Government Printing Office.

1921 Corbett, L. C. *Beans.* Farmers' Bulletin 289. Washington, D.C.: United States Department of Agriculture/Government Printing Office.

1921 Women's Club of Bethlehem. *Recipes and Menus: Contributed by Members.* Bethlehem, Penn.: Home Economics Committee.

1922 Schell, Walter S. *Schell's Quality Seeds: Market Gardener's Catalogue 1922.* Harrisburg, Penn.: Walter S. Schell.

1923 Morse, Lester L. *Field Notes on Lettuces.* San Francisco: C. C. Morse & Co.

1925 Farquhar, R. & J. *Farquhars's Garden Annual.* Boston: R. & J. Farquhar Company.

1925 Lindström, Peter. *Geographia Americae,* ed. Amandus Johnson. Philadelphia: Swedish Colonial Society. Originally written in 1654–55.

1926 Henderson, Peter & Company. *Henderson's Everything for the Garden.* New York: Author.

1926 Lapark Seed and Plant Company. *Lapark Seed Book and Floral Guide.* Lapark, Penn.: Lapark Seed & Plant Company.

1927 Morse, W. J. *Soy Beans: Culture and Varieties.* Farmers' Bulletin 1520. Washington, D.C.: United States Department of Agriculture/Government Printing Office.

1928 Lloyd, John William. *Muskmelon Production.* New York: Orange Judd.

1928 Mack, W. C. *Early Cabbage.* Bulletin 221. State College, Penn.: School of Agriculture and Experiment Station.

1929 J. W. Jung Seed Company. *Jung Quality Seeds.* Randolph, Wisc.: J. W. Jung Seed Company.

1930 Howard, Neale F. *The Mexican Bean Beetle in the East and Its Control.* Farmers' Bulletin 1624. Washington, D.C.: Government Printing Office.

1930 Beattie, W. R. *Lettuce Growing.* Farmers' Bulletin 1609. Washington, D.C.: Government Printing Office.

1931 Hedrick, U. P. *Beans of New York.* Vol. I, part 2 of series Vegetables of New York. Albany: J. B. Lyon Company.

1932 Maule, William Henry. *The Maule Seed Book.* Philadelphia: William Henry Maule.

1934 Bunyard, Edward Ashdown. *The Anatomy of Dessert, with a Few Notes on Wine.* New York: Dutton.

1937 Beattie, J. H., and W. R. Beattie. *Production of Spinach.* Washington, D.C.: Government Printing Office.

1937 Buyard, Edward Ashdown, and Lorna Bunyard. *The Epicure's Companion.* London: J. M. Dent and Sons.

1937 Hedrick, U. P., ed. *Vegetables of New York: The Cucurbits.* Albany: J. B. Lyon.

1938 Brunson, Arthur M., and Carl W. Bower. *Pop Corn.* Farmers' Bulletin 1679. Washington, D.C.: Government Printing Office.

1938 Morrison, Gordon. *Tomato Varieties.* Special Bulletin 290. East Lansing: Michigan State College/Agriculture Experiment Station.

1938 Pfeiffer, Ehrenfried. *Bio-Dynamic Farming and Gardening.* New York: Anthroposophic Press.

1938 Rhode, Eleanour Sinclair. *Vegetable Cultivation and Cookery.* London: Medici Society.

1940 Richard, Lena. *New Orleans Cook Book.* Boston: Houghton Mifflin.

1941 Halper, N. M. *Vittles for the Captain: Cape Cod Sea-Food Recipes.* Provincetown, Mass.: Modern Pilgrim Press.

1944 Betts, Edwin Morris. *Thomas Jefferson's Garden Book.* Philadelphia: American Philosophical Society.

1945 Stone, Huge E. *A Flora of Chester County, Pennsylvania.* Philadelphia: Academy of Natural Sciences.

1946 Rhode, Eleanour Sinclair. *Uncommon Vegetables: How to Grow and How to Cook.* London: Country Life. First published 1943.

1947 Brown, William L., and Edgar Anderson. "The Northern Flint Corns." *Annals of the Missouri Botanical Garden, St. Louis* 34: 1–29.

1948 Shewell-Cooper, W. E. *The Book of the Tomato.* London: Garden Book Club.

1953 Hunt, Rachel. *William Penn Horticulturist.* Pittsburgh: University of Pittsburgh Press.

1957 Swem, E. G. *Brother of the Spade: Correspondence of Peter Collinson of London, and of John Custis of Williamsburg, Virginia, 1734–1746.* Barre, Mass.: American Antiquarian Society.

1962 Hennebo, Dieter. *Gärten des Mittelalters.* Hamburg: Broschek Verlag.

1963 Sahagun, B. de. *The General History of the Things of New Spain: Florentine Codex.* Translated by A.J.O. Anderson and C. E. Dibble. Monograph No. 14. Santa Fe, N.M.: School of American Research.

1966 Benson, Evelyn Abraham, ed. *Penn Family Recipes.* York, Penn.: George Shumway.

1967 Harrington, H. D. *Edible Native Plants of the Rocky Mountains.* Albuquerque: University of New Mexico Press.

1967 Thomas, Lately. *Delmonico's: A Century of Splendor.* Boston: Houghton Mifflin Company.

1968 Dannenfeldt, Karl H. *Leonhard Rauwolf: Sixteenth-Century Physician, Botanist, and Traveler.* Cambridge, Mass.: Harvard University Press.

1970 Parker, Southcombe, and G. Stevens Cox. *The Giant Cabbage of the Channel Islands.* Mount Durand/St. Peter Port, C.I.: Toucan Press.

1972 Herklots, G.A.C. *Vegetables in South-East Asia.* New York: Hafner Press.

1974 Flower, Barbara, and Elizabeth Rosenbaum. *The Roman Cookery Book.* London: Harrap.

1974 Jeavons, John. *How to Grow More Vegetables Than You Ever Thought Possible.* Palo Alto, Calif.: Ecology Action of the Mid-Peninsula.

1974 Mangelsdorf, Paul C. *Corn: Its Origin, Evolution, and Improvement.* Cambridge, Mass.: Harvard University Press.

1975 von Reis, Altschul, Siri. *Drugs and Foods from Little-Known Plants.* Cambridge, Mass.: Harvard University Press.

1976 Percival, John. *The Roman Villa.* Berkeley and Los Angeles: University of California Press.

1976 Hauser, Albert. *Bauern Gärten der Schweiz.* Zürich/Munich: Artemis Verlag.

1977 Kuper, Jessica, ed. *The Anthropologists' Cookbook.* New York: Universe Books.

1978 Stoffler, Hans-Dieter. *Der Hortulus des Walahfrid Strabo aus dem Kräutergarten des Klosters Reichenau.* Sigmaringen: Jan Thorbecke Verlag.

1979 Gesner, Konrad. *Historia Plantarum.* Zürich. Facsimile of original 1561 manuscript, with notes by H. Zoller, M. Steinmann and K. Schmid.

1979 Jashemski, Wilhelmina. *The Gardens of Pompeii.* New Rochelle, N.Y.: Caratzas Brothers.

1983 Weaver, William Woys. *Sauerkraut Yankees.* Philadelphia: University of Pennsylvania Press.

1984 Andrews, Jean. *Peppers: The Domesticated Capsicums.* Austin: University of Texas Press.

1984 Jabs, Carolyn. *The Heirloom Garden.* San Francisco: Sierra Club.

1984 Mostoller, Ralph V. "Mostoller Wild Goose Bean." *The 1984 Fall Harvest Edition,* 148–150. Decorah, Iowa: Seed Savers Publications.

1985 Dremann, Craig C. *Ground Cherries, Husk Tomatoes, and Tomatillos.* Redwood City, Calif.: Redwood City Seed Company.

1986 March, Lourdes. *Hecho en casa: Conservas, Mermeladas, Licores.* Madrid: Alianza Editorial.

1986 Shapiro, Laura. *Perfection Salad.* New York: Farrar, Straus and Giroux.

1986 Whealy, Kent, and Arllys Adelmann. *Seed Savers Exchange: The First Ten Years.* Decorah, Iowa: Seed Savers Publications.

1987 Clarke, Ethne. *The Art of the Kitchen Garden.* New York: Alfred A. Knopf.

1988 Hunt, John Dixon, and Erik de Jong, eds. *The Anglo-Dutch Garden in the Age of William and Mary.* London: Taylor & Francis.

1988 Körber-Grohne, Udelgard. *Nutzpflanzen in Deutschland: Kulturgeschichte und Biologie.* Stuttgart: Konrad Theiss Verlag.

1988 Prest, John. *The Garden of Eden: The Botanic Garden and the Re-Creation of Paradise.* New Haven: Yale University Press.

1989 Rose, Peter G. *The Sensible Cook: Dutch Foodways in the Old and New World.* Syracuse, N.Y.: Syracuse University Press.

1989 Weaver, William Woys. *America Eats: Forms of Edible Folk Art.* New York: Harper & Row.

1990 Facciola, Stephen. *Cornucopia: A Source Book of Edible Plants.* Vista, Calif.: Kampong Publications.

1990 Rabinowitch, Haim D., and James L. Brewster. *Onions and Allied Crops.* Boca Raton, Fla.: CRC Press.

1990 Rountree, Helen C. *The Powhatan Indians of Virginia.* Norman: University of Oklahoma Press.

1990 Yoder, Don. *The Picture-Bible of Ludwig Denig.* New York: Hudson Hills Press.

1991 Ashworth, Suzanne. *Seed to Seed: Seed Saving Techniques for the Vegetable Gardener.* Decorah, Iowa: Seed Savers Publications.

1991 Black, Lowell L., et al. *Pepper Diseases: A Field Guide.* Taipei: Asian Vegetable Research and Development Center.

1991 de Benitez, Ana M. *Pre-Hispanic Cooking/Cocina Prehispanica.* Mexico City: Ediciones Euroamericanas.

1991 Tyler, Whittle, and Christopher Cook. *Curtis's Flower Garden Displayed.* Leicester: Magna Books.

1992 Berkeley, Edmund, and Dorothy Smith Berkeley. *The Correspondence of John Bartram, 1734–1777.* Gainesville: University Press of Florida

1992 Fussell, Betty. *The Story of Corn.* New York: Alfred A. Knopf.

1992 Punch, Walter. *Keeping Eden.* Boston: Little, Brown & Company and the Massachusetts Horticultural Society.

1992 Van Deven, Louis. *Onions and Garlic Forever.* Carrollton, Ill.: privately printed.

1993 Baumann, Helmut. *The Greek Plant World.* Portland, Ore.: Timber Press.

1993 Deppe, Carol. *Breed Your Own Vegetable Varieties.* Boston: Little, Brown, & Company.

1993 DeWitt, Dave, and Paul W. Bosland. *The Pepper Garden.* Berkeley, Calif.: Ten Speed Press.

1993 Jeavons, John, and Carol Cox. *Lazy Bed Gardening.* Berkeley, Calif.: Ten Speed Press.

1993 Michalak, Patricia S. *Rodale's Successful Organic Gardening: Vegetables.* Emmaus, Penn.: Rodale Press.

1993 Noble, Dorothy. "Grow a Variety of Potatoes." *Green Scene,* March, 25–30.

1993 Weaver, William Woys. *Pennsylvania Dutch Country Cooking.* New York: Abbeville Press.

1994 Barker, Nicholas. *Hortus Eystettensis: The Bishop's Garden and Besler's Magnificent Book.* New York: Harry N. Abrams.

1994 Becker, Robert F. "Keeney's Stringless Beans." *Historical Gardner,* Spring, 8–9.

1994 Cherfas, Jeremy. "Pea Beans." *Leaflet: The Newsletter for Seed Savers,* Autumn 7.

1994 Coe, Sophie D. *America's First Cuisines.* Austin: University of Texas Press.

1994 Detienne, Marcel. *The Gardens of Adonis: Spices in Greek Mythology.* Princeton: Princeton University Press.

1994 Ennès, Pierre, Gérard Mabille, and Philippe Thiébaut. *Histoire de la table.* Paris: Flammarion.

1994 Miller, Naomi, and Kathryn L. Gleason. *The Archaeology of Garden and Field.* Philadelphia: University of Pennsylvania Press.

1994 Noble, Dorothy. "Tantalizing Tomatoes from the Past." *American Vegetable Grower,* December, 44–47.

1994   Robuchon, Joël. *Le Meilleur & le plus simple de la pomme de terre.* Paris: Editions Robert Laffont.

1994   Smith, Andrew F. *The Tomato in America.* Columbia, S.C.: University of South Carolina Press.

1995   Noble, Dorothy. "Corn at Its Sweetest." *Green Scene,* January, 21–25.

1996   Dalby, Andrew. *Siren Feasts: A History of Food and Gastronomy in Greece.* London & New York: Routledge.

INDEX

Page numbers in *italics* indicate illustrations.

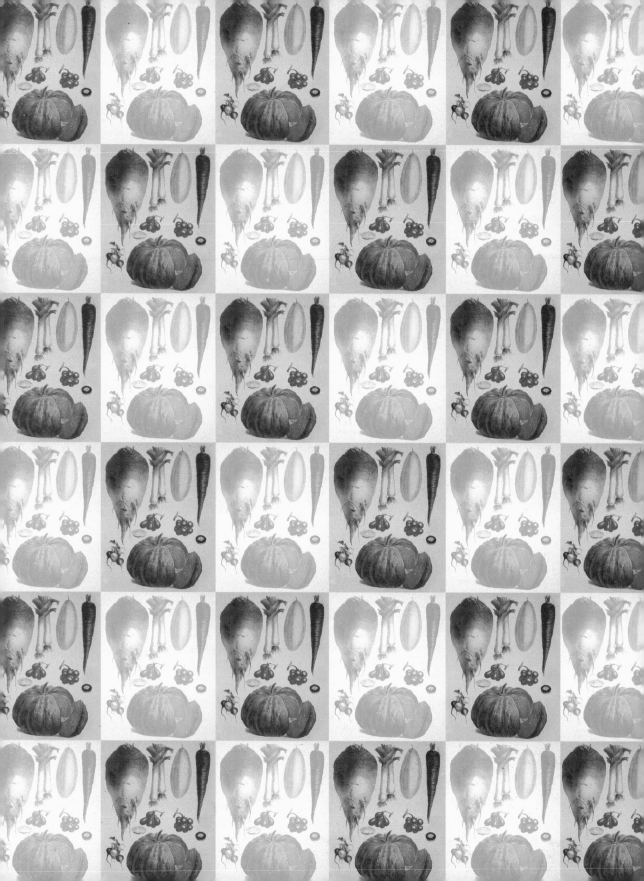